THE CONSERVATIVE FUTURIST

THE CONSERVATIVE FUTURIST

HOW TO CREATE THE SCI-FI WORLD WE WERE PROMISED

JAMES PETHOKOUKIS

Nashville • New York

Center Street
Hachette Book Group
1290 Avenue of the Americas, New York, NY 10104
centerstreet.com
twitter.com/centerstreet

First Edition: October 2023

Center Street is a division of Hachette Book Group, Inc.
The Center Street name and logo are trademarks of Hachette Book Group, Inc.
The Hachette Speakers Bureau provides a wide range of authors for speaking events. To find out more, go to hachettespeakersbureau.com or email HachetteSpeakers@hbgusa.com.

Center Street books may be purchased in bulk for business, educational, or promotional use. For information, please contact your local bookseller or the Hachette Book Group Special Markets Department at special.markets@hbgusa.com.

Library of Congress Cataloging-in-Publication Data
Names: Pethokoukis, James, author.
Title: The conservative futurist : how to create the sci-fi world we were promised / James Pethokoukis.
Description: First edition. | New York : Center Street, 2023. | Includes bibliographical references and index.
Identifiers: LCCN 2023020955 | ISBN 9781546005544 (hardcover) | ISBN 9781546006107 (ebook)
Subjects: LCSH: Economic forecasting—United States—History. | Technological forecasting—United States—History. | United States—Forecasting. | United States—Economic conditions—1945-
Classification: LCC HC103 .P468 2023 | DDC 330.973—dc23/eng/20230615
LC record available at https://lccn.loc.gov/2023020955

ISBNs: 9781546005544 (hardcover), 9781546006107 (ebook)

Printed in the United States of America

LSC-C

Printing 1, 2023

To Colette and the kiddos 7, JCAKDJC

CONTENTS

THE CONSERVATIVE FUTURIST

PREFACE

The Pale Blue Dot of Progress

As much as any economist, entrepreneur, futurist thinker, or science fiction writer, the late astronomer and author Carl Sagan played a pivotal role in my writing this book. Every day, I was deeply inspired to keep working by the image that I chose for the background wallpaper on my computer—an image Sagan was directly responsible for. It was at his request that on February 14, 1990, NASA commanded the Voyager 1 space probe to turn its camera around and take one last photograph of Earth before it departed the solar system.[1] You need to stare closely at the image to spot the single bright pixel that is Earth, an almost imperceptible speck amid the empty vastness of our solar system. But every day when I awakened my computer to start writing, my eye was immediately drawn to that pixel. Sagan later called it the "pale blue dot," which is now how that famous photo is commonly referenced. In his book of the same name, Sagan writes,

> *From this distant vantage point, the Earth might not seem of any particular interest. But for us, it's different. Consider again that dot. That's here. That's home. That's us. On it everyone you love, everyone you*

know, everyone you ever heard of, every human being who ever was, lived out their lives. The aggregate of our joy and suffering, thousands of confident religions, ideologies, and economic doctrines, every hunter and forager, every hero and coward, every creator and destroyer of civilization, every king and peasant, every young couple in love, every mother and father, hopeful child, inventor and explorer, every teacher of morals, every corrupt politician, every "superstar," every "supreme leader," every saint and sinner in the history of our species lived there—on a mote of dust suspended in a sunbeam.[2]

Consider again that image and that pale blue pixel, but in a different context. That dot? That's the roughly two-hundred-year era of modern technological progress and economic growth amid the two-hundred-thousand-year lifespan of *Homo sapiens*, millennium after millennium with little of either of those wonderful things. ("Spectacularly brief," in the words of Stanford University economist Charles I. Jones, who specializes in the study of economic growth.)[3] During these past two centuries or so have been invented almost every gadget and gizmo, almost every machine and mechanism, almost every contrivance and contraption that make our lives something more than "solitary, poor, nasty, brutish, and short," as Thomas Hobbes described our mortal existence.[4] From the Bell electrical telephone to the Apple iPhone. From the Edison Kinetoscope to the IMAX high-resolution, 3D, digital video camera. From the Wright Flyer to the reliable and reusable SpaceX Falcon 9. From the internal combustion engine to (fingers crossed) the nuclear fusion reactor. From smallpox and rabies vaccines to mRNA vaccines for COVID-19. From the Babbage difference engine to ChatGPT. During these past two centuries, we took the notion that bettering the human condition was actually possible—a concept that only goes back maybe two hundred years earlier still—and turned it into a reality. Tomorrow started becoming noticeably better than today. We lived better. We lived longer. We created the modern world. That dot? That's almost everything we think and talk about. That's here. That's home. That's us. And we made it happen.

Sagan's "pale blue dot" imagery was surely an inspiration to those worried about the current and future residents of that pixel—not to mention the future health of the pixel itself. As Sagan elaborated, "There is nowhere else, at least in the near future, to which our species could migrate. Visit, yes. Settle, not yet. Like it or not, for the moment the Earth is where we make our stand."[5] I always fixate on the "not yet" part of that quote. There's no doubt Sagan desired that humanity become, in the words of electric car and space entrepreneur Elon Musk, a "multiplanetary species."[6] Doing so would be "a step more significant than the colonization of land by our amphibian ancestors some 500 million years ago," Sagan wrote in a 1991 essay.[7] Yet in that same piece, the astronomer dismissed President George H. W. Bush's plan, announced in 1989, to land the first human on Mars in 2019. Such a journey was simply too expensive in the view of Sagan, who in a 1991 essay cited reducing homelessness, fighting the AIDS epidemic, and finding alternatives for fossil fuels among the "clear, crying national needs" that outweighed space colonization.

Earth will never be bigger than the size of a pixel, no matter how many times such a photo is taken from the outer edge of the solar system. But the pale blue dot of progress gets a bit bigger—and maybe a bit brighter—all the time, thanks to humanity's endless ingenuity. When Bush announced his plan to send Americans to the Red Planet, the *New York Times* highlighted cost estimates of $400 billion to reach both the moon and Mars.[8] But there's been a lot of progress since then, especially in the past few years. Improvements in rocket production and, more importantly, rocket reusability—in large part due to innovation at Musk's SpaceX—means launch costs are a fraction of what they were when Bush made his announcement. And those costs are headed lower still. For maybe just a sliver of the cost of that Bush plan, a Mars colony could one day be established.[9] If he were still alive, I would like to think Sagan would be among the most vocal advocates of such an endeavor, to take place ASAP.

So what about when that pixel is twice as big? What about when two centuries of progress turn into four centuries? Presenting a plan to make such a scenario as likely as possible (and accelerate it, if possible) is why I wrote this book. Thinking hard about the next two hundred years and what it could be—at least if we embrace the pro-progress actions and attitudes I will be outlining—also occupied the thinking of the optimistic postwar futurist Herman Kahn, to whom I will refer frequently in the coming chapters. Kahn saw the 1976 American bicentennial as roughly coinciding with "the turning point in what can be mankind's great transition to a world which, without being a utopia, can create both the opportunity and the foundation for an environment of relative peace and prosperity for nearly everyone, and hopefully one of relative joy and fulfillment as well."[10]

Of course, the line doesn't always go up. Progress is always uneven. And despite Kahn's optimism, the bicentennial occurred at the beginning of a long period of comparatively sluggish progress that has persisted until the present.

Still, I think that by the 2076 American tricentennial we can be firmly on the path toward the kind of outcome that Kahn imagined—something approximating the most ambitious visions of our most optimistic periods, right after World War II and right before the turn of the millennium. Again, not a world on the fast track to some impossible "utopia," Thomas More's neologism that's a pun on the Greek word meaning "nowhere." There will always be problems. It's always gonna be something, am I right? But as journalist and futurist Kevin Kelly observes, "An optimist aims for a tiny bit of progress, a world that is a tiny bit better this year than last year, even though this new world will have major new problems. So I'm optimistic because we can keep creating options for good even as we create new troubles."[11]

In other words, we need to keep moving forward. Retreat would even be riskier. In the coming pages, I hope to make clear the costs of even minor delays. Yet with each civilizational advance also comes new civilizational risk. ("It's a dangerous business, Frodo, going out your door. You step onto the road, and if you don't keep your feet, there's no knowing where you might be swept off to," to quote Bilbo Baggins in J. R. R. Tolkien's *The Fellowship of the Ring*.)[12] The Agricultural Revolution and closer human contact with animals brought new contagious diseases such as influenza and tuberculosis. The Industrial Revolution brought new weapons of war and harmful changes to our biosphere and climate. The Information and Communications

Technology Revolution brought new avenues of personal distraction and government surveillance. Perhaps an Artificial Intelligence/Machine Learning Revolution will bring a new apex intelligence to the planet, one without the best interest of its creators at heart. With each step, the risks of catastrophe, even if still highly improbable, seem to increase. The University of Chicago historian William H. McNeill called this dynamic—with every gain comes some new vulnerability—the "conservation of catastrophe," a constraint that illustrates the limits of our ability to "foresee and control economic, political, and natural events."[13] And yet humanity's historical win-loss record is firmly in the black, a record that should encourage us to take more intelligent risks for a better tomorrow and lead us, McNeill added, "to rejoice in how much we human beings can do in the way of capturing energy from the world around us and bending it to our purposes and wants."[14]

It's my strong expectation that our successes will continue to outnumber our losses, such that those 2076 Americans will have plenty to exuberantly celebrate across the country, in orbit, and perhaps so far into deep space that Earth looks like nothing more than a pale blue dot.

INTRODUCTION

America's Tomorrowland Problem

"Conservative futurism" might seem to be a comical oxymoron, much like "honest politician" or "military intelligence." But Walt Disney, one of the most famous Americans of the twentieth century, certainly qualified as a conservative futurist. Let's start with the conservative part. Walt was a capitalist and right-winger, through and through. There's no question about that. On October 24, 1947, he testified in front of the House Un-American Activities Committee—popular actor and future American president Ronald Reagan had testified the day before—about union activity at his company and employees he believed to be communists.[1] Walt was also a supporter of Republican politicians Dwight Eisenhower, Richard Nixon, and Barry Goldwater.[2] When Walt received the Presidential Medal of Freedom—the nation's highest civilian award—from President Lyndon Johnson in 1964, he wore a Goldwater button under his lapel.

Walt Disney was also perhaps the most important American futurist of the twentieth century. (Walt's futurism coexisted with a deep streak of nostalgia, a perspective expressed through his films and television shows (*Song of the South*, *Johnny Tremain*, *Davy Crockett*), as well as Disneyland itself, where the first theme land that park visitors encounter is Main Street, U.S.A., an idealized reimagining of the small-town America in which he lived briefly as a boy.) Walt's futurist reputation is based on two of his most forward-thinking ideas, although neither became what he originally envisioned. One was EPCOT, or Experimental Prototype Community of Tomorrow, Walt's plan for a futuristic model city of some twenty thousand residents that would anchor the company's 1960s expansion into Florida.[3] As Walt said in a short 1966 Disney film about this plan, "[EPCOT] will be a community of tomorrow that will never be completed but will always be introducing and testing, and demonstrating new materials and new systems."[4]

EPCOT blared 1960s-style futurism, especially the transparent dome that would cover the city's climate-controlled downtown business and entertainment district. (All cities of tomorrow in the sixties were covered with domes.) That EPCOT never happened in the way Walt envisioned says a lot about the company he built and left behind. He died just a few months after filming the concept's introduction, and the Community of Tomorrow idea died with him. So while Walt Disney World went forward in Florida, EPCOT was shelved until 1982, when it opened as a sort of permanent international exhibition, a brief monorail ride away from the Magic Kingdom.

The other pillar of Walt's futurist legacy is Tomorrowland, and its failure to fully achieve Walt's vision says something about the America he left behind. The theme land's star attraction when Disneyland opened in June 1955 was the TWA Moonliner rocket, sponsored by the Trans World Airlines of famed aviator, business mogul, and engineer Howard Hughes. The aluminum spaceship, gleaming white with red striping and the TWA logo, was the tallest structure in the park, topping even Sleeping Beauty Castle.[5] The Moonliner hosted Tomorrowland's Rocket to the Moon ride—later revamped as "Flight to the Moon" in 1967 and "Mission to Mars" in 1975—meant to simulate what a commercial lunar journey might be like in the 1980s.[6] Walt's vision can still be read today on the dedication plaque at its entrance: "Tomorrowland: A vista into a world of wondrous ideas, signifying man's achievements...a step into the future, with predictions of constructive things to come. Tomorrow offers new frontiers in science, adventure and ideals: the Atomic Age…the challenges of outer space…and the hope for a peaceful and unified world."[7]

By the mid-1960s, however, both Walt and his "imagineers" realized they had a "Tomorrowland problem." With Project Apollo in full swing and many of the innovations highlighted back in the mid-1950s—such as the microwave oven in the Monsanto House of the Future and the ubiquitous use of plastic in everyday life—beginning to make their way into the marketplace, Tomorrowland began to seem more like, in Walt's words, "Todayland" or "Yesterdayland." Technology was advancing so rapidly that Tomorrowland would always be at risk of appearing dated and dowdy without regular and expensive updates.

Then the unexpected happened—a shock not only to Disney imagineers, but also to technologists, Washington policymakers, CEOs, and the burgeoning futurist industry. In the early 1970s, the Space Age was suddenly grounded, the Atomic Age began powering down, and, most importantly, the postwar era of rapid technological progress and economic growth abruptly ended. It had been quite a run, and economists today call the period a "golden age" for good reason. American living standards, as measured by real per capita GDP, more than doubled as the economy overall grew at a rapid 4 percent annually from 1948 through 1973.

Most of that growth came from workers becoming more productive. "Productivity isn't everything," Nobel laureate economist and *New York Times* columnist Paul Krugman has famously put it, "but, in the long run, it is almost everything. A country's ability to improve its standard of living over time depends almost entirely on its ability to raise its output per worker." During those immediate postwar decades, labor productivity (output per hour in the private, nonfarm economy) grew at a blistering annual average rate of 3 percent.[8] Among the key things that make workers more productive are increases in human capital (education and training) and physical capital (the equipment, software, and buildings that business owners provide to workers so they can do their jobs).

Yet even after accounting for our workforce and machines, there's quite a bit of productivity growth left to explain, statistically speaking. And that residual portion is considered by economists to represent innovation, both technological progress and more efficient ways of deploying machines and people. Thinking different and differently—whether that means devising new technologies and applications, new techniques, or new business models—forms that missing piece of productivity growth. It's what economists call "total factor productivity." New ideas help TFP push forward the frontier of what an economy can be capable of tomorrow. That's why I refer to TFP growth as Technologically Futuristic Productivity growth. From 1948 through 1973, TFP accounted for two-thirds of overall productivity growth.[9] TFP is a key piece of the arrow of prosperity: tech progress and innovation (factories shifting to electric motors from steam, jet engines, atomic reactors, the shipping container, the microchip) → productivity growth → productivity growth drives economic growth → and economic growth drives higher incomes for everyone.

Then came what I call the Great Downshift, the fiftieth anniversary of which no one should celebrate, that statistically began in the middle of 1973. Economic growth downshifted, labor productivity downshifted, and, most importantly, TFP growth downshifted. Over the next quarter century, TFP grew at just one-fourth of the rate that it did during the previous quarter century, 0.5 percent versus 2.2 percent.[10] TFP growth then surged to 1.8 percent during the 1995–2004 tech boom before decelerating back to its sluggish post-1973 pace.[11]

This slowing of innovation and tech progress, as measured by TFP, meant Disneyland now found itself with a different sort of Tomorrowland problem. Rather than struggling to stay fifteen minutes ahead of a fast-accelerating technological present—the theme land was supposed to be grounded in reality—Tomorrowland now lacked a wildly innovative private sector and big-thinking Washington to supply it with just-around-the-corner concepts to build upon. It didn't have to be that way. If not ringing Earth with space stations and colonizing the solar system, perhaps the next big thing after Apollo could have been a massive and aspirational project devoted to advanced energy, biology (far bigger than even the War on Cancer), or transportation. But America ventured nothing anywhere near the scale of Apollo.

Instead of a moon colony, we got Skylab. Instead of nuclear fusion reactors, we got solar panels on the White House roof. Tomorrowland was neither pushed by the technological reality of today nor pulled by the technological possibilities of tomorrow.

And if Tomorrowland was failing to provide aspirational and thrilling images of tomorrow, the rest of the culture was doing even worse. During the 1960s, Hollywood provided some classic future-optimistic content, including *The Jetsons*, *Star Trek*, and *2001: A Space Odyssey*. Some of the era's most popular science fiction writers, including Isaac Asimov and Arthur C. Clarke, were also highly regarded public intellectuals on issues related to science and technology. But by the early 1970s, the era of techno-optimist television shows and films was over. It had been replaced with a far darker age where audiences were presented with numerous varieties of wrecked, dystopian futures such as *Soylent Green* (overpopulation and environmental collapse), *Westworld* (humans replaced by machines, literally), *Omega Man* (a man-made plague), *Logan's Run* (overpopulation, again, and overconsumption), and the *Planet of the Apes* films (nuclear war, intelligent but irritated simians).

Meanwhile, the optimistic forward thinkers of the previous decade were replaced as the media's and government's go-to futurist intellectuals by techno-pessimists, doomsayers who painted a grim global future that both inspired Hollywood's apocalyptic turn and gave it a coat of realism. There was just enough happening in the real world—from oil shocks to the Three Mile Island nuclear accident—to reinforce that downbeat message for the American public. Too many of us started obsessing about the environmental downsides of technological progress and economic growth, ignoring how progress and growth can also ameliorate or solve the very problems they create.

So Disneyland gave up on Tomorrowland's depicting a fantastic future that could be and instead attempted to depict one that never was. When a three-year renovation began in 1995, Disney superficially "updated" Tomorrowland with "steampunk" styling based on the late nineteenth-century books of Jules Verne that had inspired Disneyland Paris's Discoveryland.[12] More recently, Tomorrowland has opted for a mashup of concepts from Disney's Star Wars and Pixar franchises, along with the original Autopia ride from the fifties. (The conceptual amalgam is much the same at Walt Disney World's Magic Kingdom.) Maybe it should be renamed NeverNeverLand.

America's Lost Future

Disney never solved its Tomorrowland problem—its chronic inability to depict a compelling, thrilling, techno-optimist future—because America for decades has been failing to discover, create, and invent a real-world Tomorrowland future that can excite and inspire us all. This would be a future where human achievement, opportunity, and potential continue to grow; a future where America is capable of solving big problems and meeting big challenges, including some that threaten the very existence of human civilization. (Cities under climate-controlled bubbles aren't a must, however.) Here's a frustrating, even maddening, glimpse of the amazing America we really could have here in the 2020s:

- The U.S. economy could be fully powered by abundant and clean energy, whether advanced nuclear fission, nuclear fusion, superdeep geothermal, or space-based solar where satellites in near-Earth orbit capture some of the oodles of energy the sun sends to our planet every day and then transmit it back to Earth. Global warming? Never heard of it. *It's possible.*
- The COVID-19 pandemic could have been either totally prevented through immunization with a universal antivirus vaccine or maybe neutralized by nanobots swimming through our bloodstreams. *It's possible.*
- America's biggest technology companies and billion-dollar "unicorn" startups could be exploring space rather than just exploiting our attention spans. Imagine building off-world habitats, running orbital factories, or mining asteroids for precious industrial metals. *It's possible.*
- For the price of a business-class ticket, Americans could be flying—"rocketing," actually—anywhere in the world in under an hour.

So a late-morning launch from New York to London, a long business lunch, and then back home again for family dinner. *It's possible.*

- The typical American might have an income two or three times what they have today and be supremely confident that their kids and grandkids will be even better off. *It's possible.*
- And, yes, the preferred mode of daily transportation really could be autonomous electric flying cars with a maximum speed of several hundred miles per hour and capable of vertical take-off and landing. Running late for an appointment in the city? Call a SkyUber. *It's possible.*

This seemingly sci-fi America is an exciting variant that many forward-looking thinkers of fifty years ago in academia, business, and science confidently imagined for today. So did forward thinkers in the booming 1990s at the start of the Internet Era. Had they been even *mostly* correct at those pivotal periods, we might already have the economy of America's 2076 tricentennial today. If so, imagine what the America of fifty years hence might be like or the America of the quadricentennial.

Of course, many of those future-optimists of the past wouldn't have been too surprised that *some* of their forecasted wonders had failed to occur by the start of the third decade of the twenty-first century. Clarke introduces his nonfiction book *Profiles of the Future: An Inquiry into the Limits of the Possible* with this warning: "It is impossible to predict the future, and all attempts to do so in any detail appear ludicrous within a very few years."[13] True enough. But for *so many* of those marvels to have not yet happened or even come close to happening? Such a broad failure would've left those futurists shocked and appalled. Probably confused, too. Many of the 1960s techno-optimists might assume atomic war had sent civilization—what remained of it—tumbling backward toward a new dark age. And those in the 1990s might guess the millennium bug really did shut down our computer-driven society.

But America's Tomorrowland problem isn't just about a lack of fusion reactors, hypersonic passenger jets, robot servants, and colonies on the moon and Mars—feats of science, technology, and engineering sometimes called "cool shit futurism."[14] The same circumstances and factors that prevented those amazing things from happening already have *also* created a crisis of scarcity throughout 2020s America. During the pandemic, we had too few masks, too few ventilators, and not enough rapid viral tests despite the pandemic's being perhaps the most forecasted calamity in world history. But those COVID-19 shortages took place against a broader background of scarcity: too little housing, too few immigrants, too few entrepreneurs, not enough clean energy, not enough slots at top colleges, and not enough high-quality infrastructure. Also: a shortage of outrage.

Why are we not more bothered by this chronic scarcity? After all, it goes counter to the American Dream, something wonderfully described by 1930s historian James Truslow Adams as a belief that "life should be better and richer and fuller for everyone."[15] America has always been synonymous with abundance, a description that has far more to do with this being a land of almost limitless possibility than just of vast material wealth. "America is another name for opportunity" really sums up the American Dream, whether or not essayist Ralph Waldo Emerson actually said it.

As it turns out, merely avoiding obstacles such as nuclear holocaust and computer catastrophe, as well as surviving a pandemic—while necessary—is hardly sufficient to create the best possible version of America. We have our own decisions and actions to blame for that future we lost and the underwhelming present—by comparison—that we're living in. Specifically: Bursts of rapid progress in the 1960s and 1990s fooled us into greatly underestimating the difficulty of turning our visions into reality. By the early 1970s, we seemed to have squeezed out all the productivity gains from past great inventions, while at the same time big new ideas and innovations were becoming much harder to find. At almost the exact moment that inventing the future we wanted became harder, we started making some big mistakes. We stopped generously funding the science that has always supported those visions and generated new ones. We passed well-meaning laws that made it surprisingly difficult for entrepreneurs to build those visions in the real world, at least if the materials were atoms rather than bits. And then, when those future-optimist dreams failed to materialize, we simply stopped dreaming them. A brief revival—as seen in cultural attitudes and public policy as well as economic statistics—during the 1990s technology boom faded all too quickly after the popping of the internet stock bubble.

I don't want to lose the future yet again. And we just might. Recent advances in a kind of artificial intelligence called machine learning—where computers learn from various kinds of data—have reawakened concerns about mass unemployment and out-of-control, thinking machines. Just a third of Americans, versus three-fourths of Chinese, agree with the statement that products and services using AI have more benefits than drawbacks.[16] And even as autonomous driving technology continues to improve, the public fear of it is surging, to 68 percent in 2023 from 55 percent a year earlier.[17]

(A brief tech lesson: the AI advances that non-techies mostly hear about involve a kind of ML called deep learning that mimics the human brain with software to extract rules and complex patterns from data sets such as audio, video, images, and text. Netflix recommendations, Siri and Alexa, and a Tesla's vision-based, self-driving capabilities are all thanks to deep learning. Generative AI is a subset of deep learning that can create new software code, text, and images from existing content via simple natural language prompts. ChatGPT, in particular, is based on "large language models" trained on large amounts of text data, including the internet. The magic happens when an LLM takes some text as an input and predicts the next word or words in the sequence. At its core, ML is a prediction machine.)

More bad news: a brief labor productivity surge in 2020 and 2021 was, alas, more about people working at home rather than the broad economy finally enjoying the fruit of recent AI advances. Then came a productivity plunge in 2022.[18] Going forward, the Wall Street–Washington economic consensus is that the economy is only capable of consistently growing at *maybe* 2 percent or so annually versus the postwar average of 3.1 percent, due to both historically weak productivity growth and slower labor-force growth from baby boomer retirements and a declining birthrate. That outcome would make it far more likely the intolerant populism infecting our politics continues to spread. And even if the economy were to return to its postwar growth rate, such a pace might still be slower than what could be possible with better policy creating a better pro-progress ecology for science, technology, and entrepreneurship. An America where the American Dream can be more fully realized.

Turning Neither Left Nor Right But Up

This I believe: America again can enjoy the material and societal benefits of fast technological progress and rapid, innovation-driven growth. For that to happen, however, America must again become what I call an Up Wing country. *Up Wing* is my shorthand for a solution-oriented future optimism, for the notion that rapid economic growth driven by technological progress can solve big problems and create a better world of more prosperity, opportunity, and flourishing. The most crucial divide for the future of America isn't left wing versus right wing. It's Up Wing versus Down Wing. (I will use these phrases frequently to describe both policy actions and cultural attitudes.) Down Wing is about accepting limits, even yearning for them. Down Wingers are doomsters. Up Wing is about accelerating past limits—much as a rocket accelerates up through Earth's gravity well. Up Wingers are boomsters. Down Wing eschews risk, especially from innovation, unless possible threats to everyday life and the environment are well understood. The burden of proof is on the risk taker. Up Wing embraces calculated risk-taking, especially from innovation, as essential to human progress and sees the capacity for such progress as central to our humanity. The burden of proof is on the defender of stasis.

So how do you know if you're an Up Winger (regardless if you're also a Democrat, Republican, or independent)? Well, you might be an Up Winger if…

- …you think technological and economic acceleration are the keys to higher incomes, more opportunity, and healthier lives for all Americans.
- …you worry about economic inequality—not because you resent the successful and wish to tear them down but instead because so many Americans seem unable to maximize their human potential.

- …you're concerned about climate change but reject claims that dealing with it requires consigning our children to lives less full and prosperous than ours.
- …you wish Hollywood made more TV shows and films about how humanity can outthink its biggest problems as opposed to reveling in computer-generated catastrophe.

Down Wingers live in a never-ending present. They see America as a zero-sum society where only the elite would benefit from tech and economic acceleration, if even possible. Some Down Wingers think climate change is such an existential threat that rich countries must live poorer and poor countries must never become rich. Down Wingers think human-level artificial general intelligence would mean mass unemployment, disrupted communities, civil unrest, and a ruined planet—and then it would kill us. Americans exploring the solar system and perhaps beyond? Not if uberbillionaires like Jeff Bezos and Elon Musk are building the rockets. Better to tax away their fortunes so government can spend the money on more down-to-Earth challenges. You can look to the left and the right and find plenty of Down Wingers.

A humble admission: I didn't come up with the term or broad concept of Up Wing, which is derived from the right wing/left wing ideological framing that emerged from the French Revolution. "Up Wing" was coined in the 1970s by futurist writer F. M. Esfandiary. He's considered the godfather of modern transhumanism, a movement seeking to use science and technology to transcend our biological limitations.[19] Esfandiary himself went by the name FM-2030 because he hoped to live to the year 2030 when he would have turned one hundred years old. (He didn't, dying in 2000 at age sixty-nine of pancreatic cancer.) But there's always the chance for a comeback. Esfandiary's body was cryogenically frozen and stored at the Alcor Life Extension Foundation in Scottsdale, Arizona.[20] (Oh, and despite rumors, Walt Disney didn't do the same.)

In 1973—again, the moment fifty years ago when technological progress peaked and then began a long-term downshift—FM-2030 wrote the transhumanist manifesto *Up-Wingers*, in which he envisioned a future where the combination of advanced genetics and computer science would augment our intelligence to superhuman levels and make us nearly immortal.[21] And as humanity evolved, so would our politics. The key factions in this new world would be Up Wingers and Down Wingers. The former look up to the sky and dream of a posthuman civilization spreading out among the stars. The latter aren't even sure if environment-wrecking humanity should inhabit *this* planet. Of this new political paradigm, FM-2030 wrote, "To be Up you must sever all ideological ties with the Right/Left establishment. You must make a break with the traditional concept of linear historical progress. That is now too slow and limited. You must be prepared to quantum-leap forward. This means starting with a new set of premises and new visionary aims. In the coming years, you will hear much about the Up-dimension. Right and Left will become irrelevant."[22]

Forgive me for modestly reimagining the Up Wing concept for my purposes, which differ from that of FM-2030 and the transhumanist moment. I'm not waiting for the Technological Singularity when computers become self-aware and supersmart. I'm not desperate for immortality. I don't yearn for a world government to serve or an AI god to worship. Nor do I think Up Wing thinking incapable of existing within the current American political structure (while also conceding its politically disruptive potential). The broad techno-optimist, future-oriented, solutionist worldview represented by an Up Wing perspective is something intrinsic to the American experiment. The United States is the original Up Wing nation. Without an ethos of anticipating a tomorrow better than today, it never would've grown from a country of 3 million people huddled on the Atlantic coastline of North America into a technological frontier-pushing, continent-sized, space-faring superpower of more than 330 million people. Now it's our turn to continue this legacy, a task that will be neither easy nor without cost. But any sacrifices will be worth it and will deeply reflect who we are as Americans and as human beings. To quote James T. Kirk, that daring space explorer and favorite son of Iowa, "Risk is our business."

So What's Conservative Futurism Anyway?

The purpose of this book is about more than promoting a future of rapid technological progress and economic growth. It's about more than an Up Wing belief that we have the ability to make the future more prosperous, opportunity-filled, humane, and resilient. It's about more than sketching scenarios of what America could be if we confidently employ that ability. The "conservative" part of my conservative futurism informs and shapes the Up Wing futurism part. To be clear: I'm an American-style conservative, and the dual mission of this version of conservatism is, first, to be a "custodian of the classical liberal tradition," in the words of columnist George F. Will.[23] That tradition champions the freedom to choose one's pursuit of happiness, whatever the wishes of the state. In particular, American conservatism presumes the economic freedom, as Adam Smith writes in *The Wealth of Nations*, to "truck, barter, and exchange one thing for another."[24] The "propensity" to do so is rooted in human nature, Smith explains. This is why the thrust of my policy agenda involves empowering human creativity and innovation within a liberal democratic, market capitalist system that limits government to what it should morally do and can effectively do. Second, American conservatism embraces social dynamism, or the ability to change one's economic standing. It rejects the notion of a society built around class and hierarchy. America can't be an Up Wing country without the realistic possibility of upward mobility for its citizens. The mobility ethos is on full display in the musical *Hamilton*, which describes America's Up Wing patron saint of strivers, Alexander Hamilton, as the "ten-dollar founding father without a father / got a lot farther by working a lot harder."

A conservative futurist also, you know, cares about the future! Conservative statesman and theorist Edmund Burke posited in 1790 that society is a multigenerational partnership that extends back into the past and forward into the future, "a partnership not only between those who are living, but between those who are living, those who are dead, and those who are to be born."[25] That said, my conservative Up Wing futurism rejects commanding society and its resources toward fulfilling some detailed central plan created by governmental and other elites. Such blueprints would assume impossible powers of prescience. But our society and economy are complex and fluid systems created by the decisions of all of us, as well as our leaders. No lone genius or government panel of geniuses can know all or process all the information generated by our decisions nor predict all the consequences of our actions.

Humility doesn't mean all planning or consideration of various possible scenarios is useless. But as Nobel laureate physicist Niels Bohr once put it, "Prediction is very difficult, especially about the future." It's an especially relevant observation during a time of radical technological change when it's far easier to imagine things going very wrong rather than very right, easier to imagine destruction rather than creation, and easier to imagine how AI/ML might enslave humanity rather than help turn its greatest dreams into reality. From the printing press to the internal combustion engine to the computer, humanity has consistently shown an inability to imagine what might be around the corner, much less beyond the horizon, good and bad. When Johannes Gutenberg was printing his first Bible, it was impossible for him to imagine exactly how his innovation, as George Mason University economist Tyler Cowen has noted, would enable so much human flourishing (such as the Scientific and Industrial Revolutions) and so much evil (the writings of Lenin, Hitler, and Mao).[26] To paraphrase the Austrian theoretical physicist Wolfgang Pauli, not only are forecasts frequently not right, they're not even wrong.[27] Emerging generative AI models are likely to prove no different in confounding today's most respected visionaries.

Rather than forecasting the future, my conservative futurism is about determining and then establishing the best conditions for each of us to pursue the sort of future we each desire, tackling problems as they occur. This is no easy task. The Up Wing combo of technological progress and economic growth, writes Northwestern University economist Joel Mokyr, is like "a fragile and vulnerable plant, whose flourishing is not only dependent on the appropriate surroundings and climate, but whose life is almost always short. It is highly sensitive to the social and economic environment and can easily be arrested by relatively small external changes."[28] My focus here is on creating a fertile and sustainable ecology—both in policy and culture—that responds organically to the preferences of society operating through a liberal democratic government and market economy. This allows for discovery and experimentation, as well as for a society that can self-correct based on that experimentation and its changing desires. If deep geothermal turns out to be a better energy source than nuclear or if rocketing between distant cities turns out to be more efficient than supersonic flight, we can adjust. I think of the future as it relates to the "pursuit of happiness" mentioned in the Declaration of Independence. "That sort of happiness was not," writes British scholar Ritchie Robertson in *The Enlightenment: The Pursuit of Happiness, 1680–1790*, "simply a subjective state, such as might be induced by chemicals; it meant attaining the preconditions for personal happiness, including domestic affection, material sufficiency and a suitable degree of freedom."[29] Or as Neo told humanity's AI overlords at the conclusion of *The Matrix*, "You're afraid of change. I don't know the future. I didn't come here to tell you how this is going to end. I came here to tell you how it's going to begin."[30] And it begins by creating better preconditions for discovery, invention, innovation, and growth.

That said, our expectations should be informed and tempered by two things. First, trade-offs are an inevitable part of life. If as a society we decide to, say, ban nuclear power, the trade-off might be not only more expensive energy, but also dirtier energy if reactors are replaced by coal-fired plants. Second, and related, is the notion of opportunity costs. The true cost of a society abandoning nuclear power is what it gives up to get its energy from possibly more expensive and dirtier sources. Perhaps part of that true cost is that numerous downstream decisions are then driven by the need to be energy efficient rather than imagining fantastic new inventions and uses—desalination, direct air capture of carbon, space colonies—that happen to need a lot of energy.

The Story of America's Forgotten Conservative Futurist

Ultimately, it's the conservative part of conservative futurism that explains why my lodestar isn't Walt Disney. Walt didn't have some highly thought-out philosophy of conservatism. He was simply a businessman who loved capitalism and hated unions and their socialist fellow travelers, and that's about as far as it went. He guaranteed that EPCOT would "always be a showcase to the world of the ingenuity and imagination of American free enterprise."[31] But Walt also reflected his time and its widespread belief in the power of top-down planning, as demonstrated by his vision for EPCOT. Not only was this the age when Washington thought it could fine-tune economic policy and prevent big downturns, but it was also the age of the urban planner, most notably the powerful, visionary, and ruthless Robert Moses, the "master builder" and propulsive force behind numerous infrastructure projects in the New York City area—the Long Island Expressway, the Triborough and Verrazano bridges, and the United Nations complex, among many—as well as the 1964 New York World's Fair, an exhibition featuring four Disney-designed attractions.[32] Had EPCOT proceeded, Walt would've likely been its Moses, but with a big advantage: Walt could design and build his metropolis from scratch, something Moses could only dream of. Journalist Virginia Postrel sees Walt's desire for control as inherently part of his frustration with Tomorrowland: "As a system, the future is natural, out of anyone's control.... This open-ended future can't be contained in the vision of a single person or organization." Indeed, my conservative futurism embraces the unknowable dispersion of people's wants and desires, choices and decisions—as well as unexpected events that the future will undoubtedly deliver.

Rather than Walt Disney (much less FM-2030), my Up Wing conservative futurism harkens back to Herman Kahn, a true American original. A nuclear war theorist during the Cold War, Kahn provided at least partial inspiration for film director Stanley Kubrick's maniacal Dr. Strangelove in his 1964 film, *Dr. Strangelove or: How I Learned to Stop Worrying and Love the Bomb*. (The character's accent, at least, was likely based on that of German émigré and engineer Wernher von Braun, who lent his rocket expertise to Tomorrowland, as well as NASA.) Kubrick had read Kahn's 1960 treatise *On Thermonuclear War* and met with him several times when planning the 1964 black comedy.[33] That unforgettable cinematic depiction of Kahn's thinking—a nuclear conflict between the United States and USSR was far from "unthinkable," and Washington should think hard about how to win such a war—if not necessarily the man himself, helped cement Kahn's historical reputation, at least on the left, as a dangerous and megalomaniacal Cold Warrior.

Yet *On Thermonuclear War* is an oddly optimistic book, at least once you get past Kahn's morbid analysis of various war scenarios with their different estimates of casualties and destruction. Kahn in no way thought the living would envy the dead. "It would not surprise me if the overwhelming majority of the survivors devoted themselves with a somewhat fanatic intensity to the task of rebuilding what was destroyed," he writes, confident that a can-do, Yankee spirit would eventually lead to America's revival.

Given Kahn's avuncular optimism—and faith in the transformative power of market-driven techno-capitalism—it shouldn't have been a surprise that the 1970s detente between the United States and USSR helped lead to the second act of Kahn's career, that of a futurist while leading the Hudson Institute think tank. Back then, the professional forecasting industry was taking a pessimistic, anti-American, anti-capitalism turn—one fueled by environmental catastrophism. But this former strategist of Armageddon stood out as an unexpectedly sunny purveyor of pro-American, techno-capitalist optimism. In his 1976 book, *The Next Two Hundred Years*, Kahn outlined a vision of material abundance and human potential that at its edges is nearly as ambitious as what FM-2030 imagined. "New and improving technologies aided by today's fortuitous discoveries [will] further man's potential for solving current perceived problems and for creating an affluent and exciting world. Man is now entering the most creative and expansive period of history. These trends will soon allow mankind to become the master of the solar system."[34] When the U.S. government published a report in 1980 predicting the world in 2000 would be "more crowded, more polluted, less stable ecologically, and more vulnerable to disruption than the world we live in now," Kahn led the public fight to undermine the report.[35] Despite his grand vision of human potential enabled by smart choices, Kahn considered himself a "guarded optimist." When Kahn died in 1983, President Reagan described him as "a futurist who welcomed the future. He brought the lessons of science, history, and humanity to the study of the future and remained confident of mankind's potential for good."[36] Up Wing knows Up Wing.

A Step into the Future

We have yet to master the solar system as Kahn envisioned, although the prospect of someday doing so seems a lot more likely thanks to America's private sector–driven return to being a leading space power. Yet that is the sort of ambitious Up Wing ambition I'm proposing in this book: seeking a sustained advance in technological progress that amplifies our best traits—curiosity, creativity, aspiration—but doesn't ignore our inherent fallibility and imperfections in doomed pursuit of a utopia populated by posthumans. Only through an Up Wing approach focusing on technological progress and wealth-building can we create a truly resilient society, one whose strength and sustainability are derived from the messy disorder of entrepreneurial capitalism and disruptive technological changes. Although Kahn offered many trend-driven forecasts, he also knew the unexpected was inevitable. Humanity cannot exactingly design its future any more than Walt Disney could exactingly design a successful Community of Tomorrow. Kahn observes, "History is likely to write scenarios that most observers would find implausible not only prospectively but sometimes, even in retrospect....Future events may not be drawn from the restricted list of those we have learned are possible; we should expect to go on being surprised."[37]

✦ ✦ ✦

America can again become an Up Wing country. The opportunity is at hand. We're experiencing the biggest wave of emerging technologies—in computer science (AI/ML), biology (CRISPR genetic editing), energy (advanced nuclear fission/fusion and geothermal), and space (reusable rockets)—in decades. And many of our greatest challenges—fully recovering from a pandemic, mitigating the worst impacts of climate change, outcompeting a new geopolitical rival, eliminating extreme global poverty, ensuring humanity's survival against threats biological and astronomical—present an opportunity for Up Wingers currently stuck in both of today's predominantly Down Wing parties to present a vision of the future that can inspire the American people and their leaders to make it happen. Conservative futurism, in particular, recognizes that humans aren't merely passive victims of nature or fate, but active agents who can shape their own destiny and improve their condition through creative and entrepreneurial problem-solving. So let's go! The future America we used to dream about is waiting. Faster, please!

ONE

The False Start of Up Wing 1.0 (1955–1973)

Twice in the past half-century, an optimistic, future-oriented America seemed on the verge of embarking upon a journey to a wondrous tomorrow, of taking a civilizational leap forward to rival that of the Industrial Revolution, of generating a massive discontinuity with the world of the moment. At minimum a never-ending boom of technological and economic progress, but perhaps even more: a great exponential acceleration toward a future beyond imagination. (Think of exponential growth in terms of the classic metaphor of a king offering a chessboard to a servant, starting with one grain of rice on the first square and doubling the amount on each subsequent square. By square sixty-four, the servant would receive an immense amount of rice, some eighteen quintillion grains.) And each time, unfortunately, those dreams came to an abrupt and shocking end, with the ongoing Great Downshift as the long-term outcome.

The first Up Wing period of fast productivity and economic growth, can-do technological solutionism, and cultural future-optimism began soon after the conclusion of World War II—much to the surprise of the era's gloomy economists. Allied victory in 1945 left much of the profession richly deserving of its "dismal science" epithet, including those academics in the victorious and relatively unscarred United States. They worried that the abrupt transition from a centrally directed wartime economy to a more market-driven peacetime economy would sink the country back into a terrible downturn as military spending was slashed and millions of soldiers returned to civilian life, flooding the job market. A possible Second Great Depression might even be worse than the first one. Paul Samuelson, the future Nobel laureate from the Massachusetts Institute of Technology, speculated about the possibility of "the greatest period of unemployment and industrial dislocation which any economy has ever faced."[1] Harvard University's Alvin Hansen thought the best America could do going forward was a mediocre "secular stagnation" because all the great tailwinds pushing new investment had dissipated: The rate of U.S. population growth had slowed, leading to less demand for goods and services; the geographic frontier had closed now that the West was settled; and technological progress had matured. Going forward, fantastic new inventions—ones able to make companies and their workers more productive—would be lacking. America needed to lower its expectations for the future, Hansen concluded.[2]

The most well-known Up Wing thinker on either side of the Atlantic was not immune to the weary zeitgeist blowing through America and the West in the first postwar years. Here in the third decade of the twenty-first century, H. G. Wells is best known for a collection of novellas he wrote in the last half of the last decade of the nineteenth century: *The Time Machine*, *The Island of Doctor Moreau*, *The Invisible Man*, and finally *The War of the Worlds*. It's no exaggeration to credit the former science teacher and journalist—his shopkeeper parents wanted him to be a draper, to which he responded with threats of suicide—with creating the modern genre of science fiction.[3] But it's the Englishman's lesser-known works, of both fiction and nonfiction, that revealed Wells as a utopian futurist and elevated him into an important early twentieth-century public intellectual. George Orwell described his friend's philosophy as "Science can solve all the ills that humanity is heir to, but that man is at present too blind to see the possibility of his own powers."[4] In *Men Like Gods* from 1923, Wells depicts a parallel Earth some three thousand years into the future, where a telepathic, evolved race of humans lives in harmonious anarchy and prepares to explore the stars. In *The Shape of Things to Come* from 1933, Wells writes a de facto prequel to *Men Like Gods*, where he imagines a world devastated by war and plague that is saved by an enlightened NGO run by aviators from around the world. In 1901, the thirty-four-year-old Wells wrote his first substantial work of futurist nonfiction, *Anticipations of the Reaction of Mechanical and Scientific Progress upon Human Life and Thought*. His first nonfiction bestseller, *Anticipations* is an ambitious work that aims to outline "the way things will probably go in this new century."[5] Among many forecasts, Wells predicts the growth of megacities and skyscrapers, the decline of the family, mechanized warfare, and the widespread use of automobiles. (Thankfully he was eventually wrong about widespread eugenics.)

A year later, Wells built on *Anticipations* with *The Discovery of the Future*. While *Anticipations* is full of predictions about what may come, *Discovery* makes the case that such predictions are possible. The essay oozes with disdain for those "who regard the future as a perpetual source of convulsive surprises, as an impenetrable, incurable, perpetual blankness."[6] By contrast, Wells sees the truly modern thinker as one who perceives the import of the rapid change occurring around him. It is such thinkers who will lead humanity forward into a bright future. "Everything seems pointing to the belief that we are entering upon a progress that will go on, with an ever-widening and ever more confident stride, forever," Wells proclaims. "All this world is heavy with the promise of greater things, and a day will come, one day in the unending succession of days, when beings, beings who are now latent in our thoughts and hidden in our loins, shall stand upon this earth as one stands upon a footstool, and shall laugh and reach out their hands amid the stars."[7]

Yet after a lifetime depicting what could be possible with proper application of human reason, Wells retreated in his final years. He died in August 1946, living long enough to see realized his prediction of airplanes destroying cities with atomic bombs—but not long enough to see mankind avoid (so far) further atomic destruction and then take a first great leap toward the stars. Wells's *Mind at the End of Its Tether*, published in 1945, is a meditation on "the end of the world and the end of its author as paired events," writes Sarah Cole in *Inventing Tomorrow*, a literary analysis of his oeuvre.[8] It's the brief, final testament of the greatest futurist of his age whose Up Wing vision of tomorrow's vast possibilities was shattered by two global wars, global depression, and the realization that none of those catastrophes had advanced his dream of a "world state" led by enlightened men like himself. Wells places his final bit of remaining hope in the power of Darwinian evolution to create and elevate an enlightened vanguard that could lead humanity forward through their ideas and ideals. In time we all might join them in the sun and accomplish wonders. But that wasn't his most likely forecast. Wells, referring to himself: "The writer sees the world as a jaded world devoid of recuperative power. In the past he has liked to think that Man could pull out of his entanglements and start a new creative phase of human living. In the face of our universal inadequacy, that optimism has given place to a stoical cynicism.... Man must go steeply up or down and the odds seem to be all in favour of his going down and out."[9]

Four months before Wells's death, John Maynard Keynes, the other great British futurist of the first half of the twentieth century, also passed. Perhaps no other thinker had more impact on the past century as this giant of economic thought. While Wells may have created an image of the future toward which to strive, Keynes's most important contribution was to give the makers of that future in the second half of the twentieth century powerful tools that they thought would create a steadier prosperity, one without the great contractions that previously seemed as inevitable as the occasional plague. Unlike Wells, Keynes was not any sort of socialist. He was a left-liberal who sought a third way between laissez-faire capitalism and Marxist socialism. He saw the latter as an ideology of the past—an "illogical and dull" doctrine—while Wells thought it a political tool for bringing about the future. Like Wells, however, Keynes thought that wise policymakers, informed by experts, could improve upon the natural workings of economies. Keynes also offered a still-relevant analysis of where humanity seemed to be heading in a sort of non-fiction version of Wells's *The Shape of Things to Come*. Keynes's 1930 essay "Economic Possibilities for Our Grandchildren"[10] is a remarkable bit of forecasting and still widely read by economists today for its ruminations on the challenges facing a postindustrial society of such vast and widespread material abundance that work is no longer necessary. Well, not that much. While we may still need a bit of labor to order our lives, Keynes writes, "three hours a day is quite enough to satisfy the old Adam in most of us!" Published as the world was sinking into economic ruin, the essay was Keynes's attempt to create an accurate and enticing picture of the future to persuade a reeling public in the West that the pessimists—both "the revolutionaries who think that things are so bad that nothing can save us but violent change" and "the reactionaries who consider the balance of our economic and social life so precarious that we must risk no experiments"—were wrong and would be proven so over time.[11] That optimism extended to his final years, when he labored tirelessly to establish a global commercial and financial system so that the postwar world wouldn't suffer another Great Depression.

An Economic Boom Dispels Postwar Gloom

Unlike Wells, many of the purveyors of postwar economic gloom lived to see their pessimistic predictions proven wildly wrong. It didn't take long. There was no Second Great Depression, of course, or even Hansen's secular stagnation. The peacetime American economy quickly made fears of another severe downturn a distant memory. Rather than sinking, it soared, propelled by rapid Technologically Futuristic Productivity growth. The 1950s and 1960s, specifically, were the fastest-growing decades of the past century.[12] This wasn't an era of rapid growth driven merely by pent-up demand after the war. America became more innovative and productive. Workers performed existing tasks more efficiently even as the economy created new things for workers to do and new goods and services for consumers to purchase and businesses to invest in. While almost every household, on average, owned an automobile by 1950, the two-car household became common by 1970.[13] And what was optional before the war (such as automatic transmission) and even unavailable (air conditioning) became standard or at least commonly available. Television ownership rose from just one-tenth of homes in 1950 to nearly two-thirds by 1955.[14] In the kitchen, stoves with cooktops and ovens, refrigerators, and dishwashers all became increasingly common and improved in quality. "In the early postwar years, the kitchens of many American homes achieved the standard of displays at the New York 1939–40 World's Fair that seemed so futuristic at the time," observes Northwestern University economist Robert J. Gordon in his 2016 book *The Rise and Fall of American Growth*.[15]

America's extraordinary economic surge—especially coming after the deprivation of the Great Depression and rationing of the wartime economy—helped generate a period of profound Up Wing attitude and action in the postwar decades despite the risk of nuclear conflict, the Korean War, the Vietnam War, and civil unrest. Even some of the most sober observers of that era assumed America was hurtling fast and furious toward a brilliant tomorrow. We had entered both the Atomic Age and the Space Age with great hope that breakthroughs in energy and space travel would be just the first of many technological leaps, across a variety of fields, into a fantastic future that might well match or even exceed the visions of the sunniest science fiction writers and futurists of the time. By the year 2000, many thought, Americans might well look back at this golden age as the beginning of a golden century of prosperity driven by rapid and accelerating technological progress. The initial bout of pervasive postwar gloom among economists shifted to one of widespread confidence that the puzzle of maintaining rapid growth and long-lasting prosperity had been solved. The 1960s marked the apex of the belief that government economic planners had the know-how to fine-tune economic performance through taxing and spending. The 1969 Economic Report of the President triumphantly declared, "Our economy will not rest on the laurels of the 1960's. We will not relax to count or consolidate our gains. We will not retreat from the unprecedented prosperity we have achieved. This Nation will remain on the march."[16]

John Kenneth Galbraith was probably the most famous economist of Up Wing 1.0 and his work nicely encapsulates the "mission accomplished" attitude of his profession during the era. A Harvard professor, Galbraith was active in Democratic politics and served in the Roosevelt, Truman, Kennedy, and LBJ administrations. Galbraith was not only a respected academic, however. Much like Milton Friedman in the 1970s, Galbraith became a much interviewed and quoted public intellectual thanks to a series of popular books, beginning with *The Affluent Society* in 1958.[17] (The Modern Library places the book at number 46 on its list of the top 100 English-language nonfiction books of the twentieth century.)[18] In it, Galbraith explains that economics used to be a pessimistic profession, motivated by expectations of scarcity. But the booming postwar economy was generating such vast abundance that pessimism was no longer necessary. It was now time—just two decades after the Great Depression—to focus public policy on the poor. Everyone else was plenty rich enough (a theme picked up by the emerging American environmental movement), Galbraith writes, and the puzzle of maintaining those high living standards had been solved: "To furnish a barren room is one thing. To continue to crowd in furniture until the foundation buckles is quite another. To have failed to solve the problem of producing goods would have been to continue man in his oldest and most grievous misfortune. But to fail to see that we have solved it, and to fail to proceed thence to the next tasks, would be fully as tragic."[19]

✦ ✦ ✦

Although I've been mostly discussing the 1950s and '60s, the symbolic start and end of Up Wing 1.0 don't neatly align with the exact beginning of the fifties and end of the sixties. There's a powerful emotional reason to pick 1972 as the finale, especially for a space enthusiast like myself. On December 19 of that year, Apollo 17 splashed down in the Pacific Ocean after completing the program's sixth and final manned lunar landing.[20] But there's a stronger economic reason to pick 1973. The second half of that year saw the start of the deepest recession since the Great Depression and the beginning of five consecutive quarters of declining labor productivity, a downturn that most economists date as ending the postwar productivity boom. The beginning of Up Wing 1.0 is less obvious to me. I'm tempted to pick 1958. Consider: the most significant advances during Up Wing 1.0 were in the energy, transportation, and information technology sectors. And one could make a plausible case that 1958 was the most Up Wing year in American history for key technologies in those sectors. It was the year that splitting the atom was harnessed to produce a brand-new source of power, both inexhaustible and seemingly inexpensive. Just a few years after Eisenhower's December 8, 1953 "Atoms for Peace" speech at the United Nations ("The United States knows that peaceful power from atomic energy is no dream of the future. The capability, already proved, is here today."), Ike's predictions seemed to already be coming true.[21] The first commercial nuclear power plant in the United States—using technology based on the U.S. Navy's nuclear aircraft carriers—went online in May 1958 in Shippingport, Pennsylvania, with Eisenhower attending the ignition.[22]

It was also in 1958 that transatlantic air passenger travel by jet began. On October 26, Pan American World Airways began regular service from America to Europe with the Boeing 707.[23] Within a decade, the entire U.S. airline industry had converted to jets from piston engines.[24] "Until 1958, more people crossed the Atlantic Ocean aboard ships than on airplanes, and in the United States, the ten largest transportation companies that year were all railroads," writes journalist Sam Howe Verhovek in *Jet Age: The Comet, the 707, and the Race to Shrink the World*.[25] "The jet airplane changed everything, not just consigning many ships to the cruise industry and trains to the freight yards, but exponentially increasing the number of overall passengers among nations...[and changing] our perceptions of distance in relation to time."

Yet as significant as the introduction of jet air travel was, other engineers had bigger travel dreams, ones that began to be realized in 1958 with the formation of NASA and the launch of the Mercury program and its goal of putting an American in space.[26] Through Mercury, NASA learned how to launch humans into orbit and how they might live and work while up there. But these initial off-planet forays would've been impossible without a kind of analog computer: the simple slide rule. Later missions, most notably Apollo 11, benefited greatly from a historic computer breakthrough in 1958: the invention of the integrated circuit, or computer microchip.[27] It was the foundational advance—for which Intel co-founder Robert Noyce is also credited—that makes modern digital society possible. In the summer of that year, new Texas Instruments employee Jack Kilby quietly worked on a project that he finally demonstrated for coworkers in early September.[28] It may not have looked like much at first glance: a bit of germanium with wires sticking out, all glued to a small glass slide. But that DIY, jerry-rigged object would later win Kilby the 2000 Nobel Prize in Physics. When Apollo 11 launched to the moon crewed by Buzz Aldrin, Neil Armstrong, and Michael Collins, there were five microchip-powered IBM System/360 machines at NASA's Manned Spacecraft Center in Houston, including one that ran the numbers for both the lunar landing and the return trip home.[29]

These amazing technological and civilizational advances—atomic power, computers, jets, rockets—were predicted to become the building blocks of a fantastic tomorrow. Yet I'm going to date the start of Up Wing 1.0 to 1955—July, specifically. The Korean War was over, and the Cold War was entering a new phase. And for the first time, global competition between the planet's superpowers involved the sky as well as Earth. On July 29, the Eisenhower White House released a formal statement announcing that it intended to create a scientific satellite program, approving "this country for going ahead with the launching of small unmanned earth-circling satellites."[30] A few days later, the Soviet Union responded that it would also launch a satellite "in the near future" (eventually making good on the promise two years later with the launch and orbiting of the 184-pound Sputnik I on October 4, 1957).[31] The Space Race had begun. But another race ended that year, the pursuit of a safe, effective, and potent vaccine to prevent polio. The results of a field trial for the vaccine developed by Jonas Salk and a team at the University of Pittsburgh were announced on April 12, the tenth anniversary of the death of President Franklin D. Roosevelt, who contracted polio when he was thirty-nine.[32]

Along with those technological, geopolitical, and medical milestones came two big cultural ones. In April, Paramount Pictures released the ambitious *Conquest of Space*, a sci-fi film meant to depict a realistic interplanetary journey to Mars, one launched from humanity's first space station orbiting the Earth. Although the special effects were primitive by today's CGI standards, the film offered the most realistic depiction of space travel ever captured on film. As the *New York Times* reviewer opined, "There is very little doubt about who should receive a generous amount of credit and praise for 'Conquest of Space'...They are the special effects artists....In telling the fanciful tale of man's first trip to Mars, they created top-flight effects such as 'the wheel,' a self-contained station orbiting about earth, rocket flights in space and a horrendous near-collision with an asteroid. These facets of the Paramount production—and fortunately they are many and frequent—are much to marvel at."[33]

Just a few weeks before the White House satellite program announcement, there was another event that showcased America's interest in a bold future where humanity wasn't limited to this world—the July 17 opening of Disneyland and its half-finished Tomorrowland. See, Up Wing isn't just about technological advances and the economic growth they propel. Up Wing is also about a society generating and embracing aspirational images of the future. These weren't easy to find in the 1950s. Certainly Hollywood wasn't providing many of them. Perhaps the most iconic sci-fi film of the era was *The Day the Earth Stood Still* from 1951, where an emissary from an alien police force warns humanity to end the Cold War and its global nuclear stalemate: "Your choice is simple: join us and live in peace, or pursue your present course and face obliteration. We shall be waiting for your answer."[34] But thirty miles down the California coast, Walt Disney was delivering a different message. The atom wasn't just a force for destruction, nor was space merely an avenue of alien invasion. Instead, they were key aspects of a potentially awesome future.

Up Wing Visions of the Future Abound

Nuclear power, computers, rocket travel, instantaneous communication, the increasingly automated home—all things that appear in the most important piece of postwar futurism and arguably the most influential futurist work of the twentieth century: the 1962 television cartoon series *The Jetsons*. All the Up Wing era's techno-solutionism is vividly encapsulated in the program's first episode, starting with the zippy intro sequence.[35] You not only meet George Jetson, but his entire nuclear family—his wife, Jane, and the children, Judy and Elroy—as they ride in their flying "compact" saucer through Orbit City in the year 2062, replete with floating apartment buildings and offices, as well as moving sidewalks. To be clear, *The Jetsons* was a reflection of its times, not the creative catalyst. As "retrofuturist" historian and journalist Matt Novak has written, "Virtually nothing presented in the show was a new idea in 1962, but what *The Jetsons* did do successfully was condense and package those inventions into entertaining 25-minute blocks for impressionable, media-hungry kids to consume."[36] Even the show's architectural aesthetic—drawn from the geometry of atoms, boomerangs, and parabolas—and color palette was derivative. It mimicked the Googie or Populuxe style that had originated in Southern California in the 1930s and was established enough by the 1950s to influence the design of the first McDonald's restaurant and iconic Theme Building—a structure that looks like it walked out of Wells's *War of the Worlds*—that every visitor to LAX quickly notices upon arrival. *The Jetsons* suggested the outline of things to come, the beginnings of which was already surely in motion.

The same year *The Jetsons* premiered also saw a major work of Up Wing prognostication from Arthur C. Clarke, one of Wells's successors as a respected science fiction author taken equally seriously as a futurist and intellectual. Clarke—who co-wrote the *2001: A Space Odyssey* screenplay with Stanley Kubrick and whose 1951 short story *The Sentinel* loosely inspired the film—didn't depict futures wrecked by technology, even if technological problems may have provided dramatic tension and propelled plotlines, as happened with the malfunctioning HAL 9000 artificial intelligence in *2001*. Clarke remained immune from the darkening trend that afflicted much of the rest of his profession as it moved from the late 1960s through the 1970s. He envisioned an increasingly harmonious future with humanity evermore connected through space satellites and interactive digital communications. Clarke saw himself as a salesman or lobbyist for the future, his writing meant to suggest only possibilities rather than hard predictions. Tomorrow's reality, he was quite sure, would exceed the meager powers of his prophetic abilities. How could it not since, as Clarke stated in the third of what are now commonly known as his "Three Laws": "Any sufficiently advanced technology is indistinguishable from magic."[37] It's a statement that elegantly captures the importance of progress and how, over the long run, it most likely dwarfs whatever our current expectations can devise.

In his non-fiction *Profiles of the Future* from 1962, Clarke argues that at "the present rate of progress, it is impossible to imagine any technical feat that cannot be achieved, if it can be achieved at all, within the next 500 years....But the only concern is with what, not with when."[38] Yet he helpfully sketches out a possible timescale as to when major technological advances might occur. And whatever the accuracy of his timing, it does give a sense of the vast potential for human progress Clarke thought possible. The book concludes with a "Chart of the Future" that he advises shouldn't be "taken too seriously" in terms of exact timing but taken quite seriously in terms of direction.[39] By 1990, power from nuclear fusion. By 2000, human-plus artificial intelligence, colonizing planets, and mining the ocean floor. By 2020, weather control. By 2030, space mining. By 2050, antigravity and transmutation of elements. And by 2100, interstellar flight, planetary engineering, matter replicators, and immortality. Men like gods, two centuries after the Wells "scientific fantasy" with that title.

Despite Clarke's fame—as well as that of several other sci-fi authors and futurists, such as Isaac Asimov—his brand of amateur speculation was eventually eclipsed by a more scholarly futurism that first emerged after World War II. Forecasting took a serious turn with the new risk of nuclear conflict and what seemed like breakneck technological change. Futurism or "futurology" as it was termed initially—the academic and systematic thinking about the future—became a respected input for policymakers. The Manhattan Project was a persuasive proof of concept, showing Washington that gathering a bunch of great minds together could produce remarkable accomplishments. The federal government's initial foray into futurism was through the RAND Corporation, its name an acronym for "research and development." At the end of World War II, War Department officials saw a need for a private research organization to inform government policy.[40] They set up RAND via a special contract with Douglas Aircraft. Its debut research project was a study about the feasibility and operation of an orbiting space station (termed a "world-circling spaceship").[41] Among the innovations credited to RAND: the first spy satellite and packet switching, a core technology that made the internet possible.[42]

RAND was—and continues to be—a serious research organization, one that in the 1960s the Soviet newspaper *Pravda* gave the epithet "the academy of science and death and destruction" due to its close Pentagon ties.[43] In 1964, RAND published a sweeping "long-term forecasting" study based on a survey of expert opinion in six areas: scientific breakthroughs, population growth, automation, space progress, probability and prevention of war, and future weapon systems.[44] "Because of the ever more explosive rapidity with which new technological developments are apt to take hold, it becomes increasingly important to foresee the advent of such impact to prepare for their social consequences and to avert possible calamities," the report gave as its mission statement.

Among the scientific breakthroughs that the median of respondents thought would happen by 2000, as described by the study: "effective fertility control by oral contraception...automatic language translators, controlled thermonuclear power...economically useful exploitation of the ocean bottom (other than offshore drilling)...limited weather control...a central data storage facility with wide access for general or specialized information retrieval." So it's a mixed bag when comparing what they expected with what we actually got. They predicted the Pill, and maybe you can give them partial credit for the internet, though its key feature is its decentralized nature, something originally meant to ensure U.S. military command-and-control communication in event of nuclear war. But big misses on fusion, ocean mining, and weather control—though in RAND's defense, those forecasts were fairly common for the era. And beyond 2000? The following was RAND's median forecast for conceivable developments to occur no later than 2100:[45]

> *Chemical control of the aging process may have been achieved raising a persons' life expectancy to over 100 years. The growth of new limbs and organs through biochemical stimulation may be possible. Man-machine*

> *symbiosis, enabling a person to raise his intelligence, through direct electromechanical tie-in with a computer machine, is a distinct possibility. The problem with adequately providing necessities of life for all people of the earth will presumably have been solved by international agreements based on the abundance of new sources of energy and raw materials opened up in the 21st century. As for materials, it is even possible that elaborate differential mining processes will have been abandoned in favor of commercially efficient transmutation of elements. Conceivably, revolutionary developments will have become feasible as a result of control of gravity through some form of modification of the gravitational field. A permanent lunar colony may well have been established, with regularly scheduled commercial traffic between Earth and moon, a permanent base on Mars, landings on Jupiter's moons, and manned fly-bys past Pluto are likely accomplishments. Possibly even a multi generation mission to other solar systems may be on its way, aided conceivably by artificially induced long-duration coma. Two way communication with extraterrestrial intelligent beings is a definite possibility.*

Taken as a whole, this compilation of forecasts—depicting a multiplanetary civilization of abundance and longevity—from a serious think tank meant for government officials was every bit as bold as those listed in Clarke's "Chart of the Future." The biggest stumbling block was the threat of nuclear conflict. The 1960s were a perilous time for modern civilization, maybe even for the continued existence of humanity. Two rival superpowers controlled massive nuclear arsenals whose technological sophistication and explosive power outstripped either nation's ability to safely command and control. We now know there were several close calls during the 1960s that could have resulted in a devastating nuclear exchange or even an all-out nuclear war.

Yet as the threat of civilizational destruction, whether accidental or intentional, was growing, America's leading thinker about nuclear war began thinking long-term about where the combination of technological creativity and economic freedom might one day take humanity. By the mid-1960s, Herman Kahn was running the Hudson Institute, a think tank located about forty miles north of New York City, which he had helped establish in 1961 after leaving RAND.[46] While there, Kahn became a pioneer in the emerging field of futurism. In 1967, Kahn and frequent collaborator Anthony J. Wiener, a founding member of the Hudson Institute and research consultant with organizations such as NASA and Shell Oil, synthesized Hudson's scenario analysis into the book *The Year 2000: A Framework for Speculation on the Next Thirty-Three Years*. The multidisciplinary effort—confidently and systematically incorporating economics, demographics, sociology, and the physical sciences—into a sweeping work that divisively moved futurism beyond the more intuitive and literary approach taken by Wells, Aldous Huxley, and George Orwell (what Kahn called "individual visions of the future"),[47] *The Year 2000* was presented as serious scholarship, which shows just how Up Wing the 1960s was given the boldness of the book's many predictions. Kahn and Wiener described one hundred forecasts as "very likely" to happen by 2000. Some seem like pretty good calls in retrospect, even if a few were maybe a decade early: cell phones, the internet, satellite television, oil from shale, and reusable rocket boosters. Other speculations, not so much: cryogenics, space and undersea colonies, personal flying platforms, substantial increases in life expectancy, and widespread use of nuclear power. A 2002 analysis of those one hundred forecasts judged 45 percent as accurate overall, with 80 percent about computer and communications technology hitting the target.[48] The batting average of Kahn's and Wiener's "less likely but important" forecasts (100- to 150-year lifespans, commercial rocket transportation, extensive genetic editing, nuclear fusion, modification of solar system) would obviously be quite a bit lower.[49] The analysts then offer ten "far-out possibilities" about which the authors state: "We do not believe that any of them will occur by the year 2000, or perhaps ever. But some of them are discussed today; and such a list does emphasize the fact that some dramatic and radical innovation must be expected." They're pretty fun, ranging from 150-year lifespans (or maybe even immortality) to mental telepathy to interstellar travel using gravity waves.

America's leaders were willing and enthusiastic consumers of such sci-fi-tinged speculation. By the late sixties, Up Wing techno-solutionism had pervaded all sectors of elite society. In May 1968, a group called the Foreign Policy Association put together a conference of science and technology thinkers and asked them to predict the future, specifically what the world of 2018 might look like. It was an impressive group of experts, including leading academics from Harvard, MIT, and the University of Chicago, executives from leading technology companies Bell Telephone Laboratories and IBM, and various think-tankers and government consultants. The FPA later published a book based on those forecasts, *Toward the Year 2018*, a collection of mostly optimistic forecasts (overpopulation being an exception).[50] Assuming no nuclear holocaust, these experts thought America on its 242nd birthday would be a land of even greater abundance and opportunity. In their essay, Kahn and Wiener forecasted the decades to follow as ones of uninterrupted and increasing prosperity. The postwar Up Wing golden age would continue, Kahn and Wiener write, "more or less smoothly through the year 2000 and perhaps beyond, uninterrupted by world wars, world depressions, or other cataclysms."[51] Upward, then.

✦ ✦ ✦

The tumultuous 1960s, including the threat of nuclear war, initially did little to lessen such Up Wing visions of the future, including those portrayed by Hollywood. Film and television mostly presented Americans with compelling images of a tomorrow that they could see themselves happily inhabiting. The decade ended with two of the most important works of Up Wing futuristic fiction, the film version of Clarke's *2001: A Space Odyssey* and the original *Star Trek* series. While both are highly influential, they perhaps fall short of *The Jetsons* only because so little of their stories take place here on Earth. That said, both depict a future where technology has continued to rapidly progress, enabling manned exploration of deep space. In *Star Trek*, a successful struggle through wars both nuclear and genetic has brought civilization to a near-utopian state where all physical needs are met, harmony has replaced conflict, and humanity roams the extraterrestrial alien-filled Milky Way—or at least the Alpha Quadrant—on starships capable of traveling at faster-than-light speeds. *Star Trek*'s original three seasons have since turned into an extraordinarily lucrative franchise, spawning eleven television and streaming series and thirteen films (with more of both surely to come).[52] At the core of that multibillion-dollar franchise is the hopeful vision of creator Gene Roddenberry. Of *Star Trek*, Roddenberry said, "The human race is a remarkable creature, one with great potential, and I hope that *Star Trek* has helped to show us what we can be if we believe in ourselves and our abilities."[53]

Although a technological malfunction helps create dramatic tension in *2001*, the film also portrays technology as fundamentally beneficial, a value expressed visually in the famous flash-forward from a primate-tossed bone lofting slowly in the air to a majestic space station turning in stationary Earth orbit, about to dock with a commercial space plane. The scene, scored to the *Blue Danube* waltz, suggests an America utterly confident and comfortable in its technological power and superiority, even blasé about what it's achieved. Yet humanity is soon to find out it has merely taken a half step into the Cosmic Ocean when it attracts the attention of the higher intellectual powers of the universe, incomprehensible minds that will help us advance to a higher plane of existence and understanding.

The *2001* Star Child at the end of the film—representing humanity's evolution to a higher state of consciousness—may be the ultimate Up Wing construct. Sounding much like H. G. Wells, Kubrick once said in an interview: "When you think of the giant technological strides that man has made in a few millennia—less than a microsecond in the chronology of the universe—can you imagine the evolutionary development that much older life forms have taken? They may have progressed from biological species, which are fragile shells for the mind at best, into immortal machine entities—and then, over innumerable eons, they could emerge from the chrysalis of matter transformed into beings of pure energy and spirit. Their potentialities would be limitless and their intelligence ungraspable by humans."[54]

And that is where humans are headed, at least in *2001*, with a little help from our friends from space. Yet as the 1960s ended, many thought such outside assistance wouldn't be necessary given the huge—and no doubt continuing—progress being made by scientists and entrepreneurs, encouraged by Hollywood screenwriters and a new class of futurists. Depressingly, America wouldn't even make it to the midpoint of the 1970s, much less the start of the next millennium, before abandoning its Up Wing vision of what tomorrow could hold. And instead of enjoying a never-ending boom, we settled for something more akin to a momentary blip.

TWO

The False Start of Up Wing 2.0 (1995–2000)

The Great Downshift wasn't without respite. There was a fleeting half-decade of Up Wing optimism and progress halfway through the past half-century. For a moment, it looked as if America might yet fulfill some of the grandest and most futuristic aspirations of the postwar Up Wing 1.0 period. But just as the start and end of Up Wing 1.0 occurred unexpectedly, so the same with the brief blip that was Up Wing 2.0. Even America's most famous futurist next to Walt Disney was surprised by these economic and cultural advances and retreats.

Of course, Alvin Toffler didn't need to be much of a prognosticator to know his soon-to-be-released *Future Shock* was going to be a blockbuster. As the *New York Times* noted just days before the book's release in July 1970, *Future Shock* had already been chosen by three popular book clubs, as well as excerpted in *New York Magazine*.[1] *Future Shock* went on to sell more than five million copies in the United States and is still considered an influential and landmark work of futurism.[2] (A sequel, *The Third Wave*, published in 1989, was outsold in China only by the collected speeches of Deng Xiaoping.)[3] The *Times* described Toffler, a forty-one-year-old freelance writer and former editor of *Fortune* magazine, as having a self-taught expertise in what he called "the sociology of the future," which he taught at the New School for Social Research in Manhattan.[4] The Brooklyn-born son of an immigrant furrier, Toffler spent the second half of the 1960s trying to determine for himself the underlying causes and forces of the societal upheaval—something already termed "culture shock"—affecting the United States and other rich nations.[5] The result of that study was *Future Shock*, a dense and at times almost unreadable blizzard of data points, forecasts, and insights. In the *Times* review of the book, Richard R. Lingeman writes that Toffler "sends flocks of facts and speculation whirling past like birds in a tornado."[6]

Yet *Future Shock*'s premise was simple: life was changing so quickly that it risked driving us all crazy with information and progress overload. In the documentary version of *Future Shock* that was screened at the 1973 Cannes Film Festival (there was also—incredibly—a musical), narrator and on-screen presence Orson Welles described the eponymous malady as "a sickness which comes from too much change in too short a time. It's the feeling that nothing is permanent anymore."[7] The forty-minute film intends to visually provoke mental overload—or, in the psychedelic parlance of the time, a bad trip—with an opening sequence scored to early electronic music. It intersperses an ongoing scene of a silhouetted couple walking in the woods with a quick-cut series of disturbing images: a close-up of a shouting man's mouth, a line of soldiers with raised rifles, the flashing dome light of a police car, a car crash, a thermal image of a man, and several others that are less identifiable. Finally, we return to the couple on the nature walk: they're revealed as silver-faced automatons. The entire phantasmagoria is meant to suggest Toffler's big idea: rapid technological progress and disruptive economic growth had unmoored society from any sense of permanence or stability. The world's richest countries were all racing with "accelerative thrust" toward a "super-industrialism" that would provide a shocking rise in living standards and overflowing material abundance, but also mass disequilibrium. As Toffler begins the book, "In the three short decades between now and the twenty-first century, millions of ordinary, psychologically normal people will face an abrupt collision with the future. Citizens of the world's richest and most technologically advanced nations, many of them will find it increasingly painful to keep up with the incessant demand for change that characterizes our time. For them, the future will have arrived too soon."[8]

Future Shock was squarely premised on continuing and even intensifying technological acceleration. But that never happened. Instead, Americans experienced a totally unexpected *deceleration* in technological progress and economic growth starting in 1973, what I call the Great Downshift. Surprisingly soon, Up Wing 1.0 was over. The postwar Up Wing golden age didn't extend into an Up Wing golden century. The initial phase of the Great Downshift was followed by decades of productivity and economic growth far slower than what almost anyone in the 1960s had been predicting. While the 1930s Great Depression is the most famous event in modern economic history—the deep downturn plunged the world into economic and political chaos while planting the seeds for the next global war—the Great Downshift certainly rivals it in importance. As Nobel laureate economist William Nordhaus wrote in 2004, "The productivity slowdown of the 1970s does appear to be a major distinguishing feature of the last century."[9] For economist Robert Gordon, the Great Downshift signals the definitive end of his "special century" of rapid progress where Americans at the end had many multiples the material abundance of those Americans at the beginning. Although productivity and economic growth didn't come to a total stop, the substantially slower pace—both in absolute terms and compared to Up Wing 1.0 expectations—has led others to call the post-1973 period the Long Stagnation or Great Stagnation. I like how the Great Downshift parallels the Great Depression, so that is the term you will continue to see throughout this book.

Whatever descriptor you prefer, the numbers tell the story of a historic long-term slowdown. After growing 4 percent annually, in real terms, during Up Wing 1.0 and the immediate postwar decades more broadly, the American economy in 1973 began a long deceleration to 3 percent through the mid-1990s.[10] Likewise, average annual labor productivity fell by half (to 1.5 percent from 3.2 percent) and Technologically Futuristic Productivity growth by three-quarters (to 0.5 percent from 2.2 percent).[11] (GDP growth would've slowed even more if not for an expanding labor force from the postwar Baby Boom and more women working outside the home.) Then came the information and communications technology-driven productivity boom from 1995 through 2004, which looked a lot like the pre-1973 period, including rapid TFP growth. But it didn't last long. This Up Wing blip was followed by the second phase of the Great Downshift, extending through the global financial crisis and up to the COVID-19 pandemic in 2020.[12] This period has looked much like the first phase of the Great Downshift that started in 1973, especially in terms of labor productivity and TFP growth. Taken as a whole, the post Up Wing 1.0 period massively disappointed the expectations leading into it.

Why does a slowdown in seemingly obscure economic statistics like labor productivity or TFP rival the greatest economic downturn in living memory when a quarter of the country was out of work? It gets back to the notion of opportunity cost, which requires speculation about an alternate reality if things had gone differently. Again, at the heart of all those seemingly fantastical Up Wing predictions of the 1960s was the assumption of continued rapid technological progress, which in turn would drive faster productivity growth, resulting in faster economic growth. In other words, economic growth has been slower than predicted primarily because invention and innovation have been slower than predicted. It's why we have a $20 trillion American economy today rather than one of $40 trillion without the Great Downshift. It's why U.S. median household income is $70,000 today rather than the $125,000 or more we were on track to achieve before the Great Downshift. It's why future-optimistic Up Wing media is now a rarity. It's why there's no U.S. economy running on clean nuclear fusion or superdeep geothermal energy, no universal antivirus vaccine, no driverless flying electric taxis, no suborbital hypersonic flights from New York to Paris, no booming space economy. Had the postwar futurists been right, we might already have the economy of America's 2076 tricentennial today. That we don't is the true "future shock." It certainly was a shock for Toffler, who had identified the 1950s and '60s acceleration as a new and disorienting normal, not just a temporary postwar boom. "We made the mistake of believing the economists of the time," he told *Wired* magazine in 1993. "They were saying, as you may recall, we've got this problem of economic growth licked."[13]

A self-serving statement, perhaps, but Toffler was correct. The consensus of postwar experts across a variety of fields posited that the problem of generating rapid and steady growth had been solved. Toffler's fellow futurist Herman Kahn, the Cold Warrior turned techno-optimist thinker, took his best shot at generating a long-term outlook—at a time when macroeconomic forecasting was rare and rudimentary—in *The Year 2000*, written with Anthony J. Wiener in 1967. Their baseline forecast was that "the recent rates in such things as productivity growth will be equaled or increased in the future—or at least over the long run."[14] Kahn and Wiener were fully aware that they were in the middle of a period of historically high economic growth and technological progress, but they had every confidence it would continue, if not accelerate: "There is almost a general expectation that the United States ought to average [labor productivity growth of] between 2.5 and 3.5% a year or even more over the next 33 years. Indeed, some expect that as soon as automation reaches its stride, it will be 1 or 2% higher than this. Given our optimistic bias...very likely 3 or 3.5% is a good figure on which to focus."[15] (Again, productivity actually fell by half over the coming decades.)

If the Up Wing Kahn and Wiener forecast had been correct about the pace of technology-driven economic growth, the U.S. economy today would be far more technologically advanced and presumably far larger. To a great extent, it would be able to provide the capabilities and resources to create and purchase the sort of future that many imagined a half-century ago. Permanent bases on the moon and Mars? Check. A country-spanning system of high-speed rail or even hyperloops? Undersea cities? Check and check. But remember, Kahn and Wiener thought even more optimistic estimates were entirely plausible. If productivity growth had reached 5.5 percent, then overall potential economic growth—including the rapidly expanding labor force of the postwar period—could have reached 8 percent annually in the 1970s before slowing to 6 percent today.[16] At that pace, the U.S. economy of today would be $100 trillion, or five times the current level. We might be approaching a reality that looked more like exponential science fiction than linear economic extrapolation. More *Star Trek* than *2001.*

A Surprise Up Wing Turn at the Turn of the Century

America and the world entered the final decade of the past millennium with dissipating concern about mass destruction from a technology that two Manhattan Project scientists called an "evil thing": thermonuclear weapons.[17]

In 1990, the Doomsday Clock of the Bulletin of Atomic Scientists—a symbolic representation of the risk of Armageddon—displayed ten minutes to midnight. The placement suggested a world far safer than in 1984 when it was a mere three minutes from midnight thanks to the "accelerating nuclear arms race and the almost complete breakdown of communication between the superpowers…[creating] a situation of extreme and immediate danger."[18] But midnight never came. Gradually improving relations between Reagan's America and Gorbachev's Soviet Union led the Bulletin to gradually move back the clock's hands over the 1980s. Then in 1991, the hands were pushed way back to their furthest point from symbolic midnight, at 17 minutes. "The Cold War is over," the Bulletin's editors wrote. "The 40-year-long East-West nuclear arms race has ended. The world has clearly entered a new post-Cold War era."[19]

But there was little triumphalism in America. Pocketbook issues were more on the mind of most Americans than the defeat of their existential archenemy. The longest peacetime expansion had ended in July 1990 with numerous suspects to blame, including "pessimistic consumers, the debt accumulations of the 1980s, the jump in oil prices after Iraq invaded Kuwait, and a credit crunch induced by overzealous banking regulators," the San Francisco Fed concluded a couple of years later.[20] The downturn lasted through March 1991, and although the contraction in economic output was nowhere near as severe as the early-1980s recession, the recovery was anemic by historical standards. The unemployment rate kept climbing for more than a year after the economy began expanding again, likely playing a big role in President George H. W. Bush's failed reelection attempt in 1992. On Election

Day that year, only 22 percent of Americans thought the country was on the right track, according to Gallup.[21]

America's intelligentsia was in no better mood, as two seriously reviewed books from 1991 suggest. In *The True and Only Heaven: Progress and Its Critics*, historian and social critic Christopher Lasch vexingly described his fellow Americans, especially the middle class despite their current pessimism, as still too enamored with the notion of progress: "How does it happen that serious people continue to believe in progress, in the face of massive evidence that might have been expected to refute the idea of progress once and for all?"[22] That year also saw an updated version of the 1974 book *An Inquiry into the Human Prospect* by economist Robert Heilbroner.[23] In the original, Heilbroner led off with the following query: "There is a question in the air, more sensed than seen, like the invisible approach of a distant storm, a question that I would hesitate to ask aloud did I not believe it existed unvoiced in the minds of many: 'Is there hope for man?'"[24] Not much, he concluded. To grapple with the planet's growing population and increasing environmental degradation would inevitably require an authoritarian turn by governments everywhere and a severe diminution of human freedom. Two decades of tumult, including the fall of the Soviet Empire and a resurgent America, had done little to brighten Heilbroner's mood. He simply didn't think humanity cared enough about future generations to do much to help them with actions today.

Meanwhile, the severe early 1990s recession and weak recovery played into the existing notion that the 1980s economic upturn had failed to break America out of the Great Downshift. While the stock market crash on Black Monday, October 19, 1987, didn't lead to a recession, it seemed to raise an alarm. Perhaps Wall Street was sending Main Street a message that the booming U.S. economy was built on a weak foundation of unsustainable trade and budget deficits, along with continued lackluster productivity growth. "Back in 1990, the most important question about where the world was going was whether the U.S. economy was going down the drain," writes McKinsey partner William W. Lewis in his 2004 book *The Power of Productivity*.[25]

By January 1996, only 24 percent of Americans were satisfied with the country's direction—nearly five years after the end of the recession.[26] It synced with America's pessimistic outlook that the *New York Times* in March 1996 scolded the two major presidential candidates, President Bill Clinton and Senator Robert Dole, for their fanciful economic aspirations and promises. In "Trickle Down; It's a Slow-Growth Economy, Stupid," economics reporter Louis Uchitelle writes:

> *As the chief rivals for the Presidency, they are engaging in a rather traditional campaign debate—one that assumes the American economy can go back to the high growth of another era. That is what goes unsaid. The candidates challenge each other with conflicting nostrums for generating growth. Push the right policy buttons, they say, and presto, the economy will boom. What they don't debate is whether strong growth—the sort that would raise living standards and make layoffs less frequent—is in fact possible. Such growth is not possible, according to the great majority of American economists.*[27]

Uchitelle correctly identified the core economic problem as weak labor productivity growth, still moribund since the early 1970s. The decades-long IT revolution didn't appear to be having much benefit. Computers had not yielded the rapid growth in production that came from investments in railroads, autos, highways, electric power, and aircraft—all huge outlays, involving government as well as the private sector, that changed the way Americans lived and worked, he added. A familiar-sounding diagnosis? It was economist Alvin Hansen and his theory of "secular stagnation" all over again. Just as Hansen dismissed the possibility of fast productivity gains and economic growth during a time of what turned out to be rapid acceleration, so did the *New York Times* and the economic analysts Uchitelle interviewed or quoted, including Federal Reserve chairman Alan Greenspan. Surprise! When that gloomy piece was published, the great 1990s economic boom and Up Wing 2.0 had already begun. Real GDP growth averaged 4.3 percent from 1996 through 2000, 50 percent faster than its postwar average up to that point.[28] Labor productivity growth doubled to more than 3 percent annually through 2004, while TFP growth more than tripled.[29] What some economists call the Third Industrial Revolution—the combined impact of greater computing power driven by Moore's Law on the density of computer chips, personal computers, the web, and search engines—had finally arrived in a way that substantively mattered for productivity and economic growth. Moore's Law is a prediction made by Intel-co-founder Gordon Moore in 1965 that the number of transistors on a microchip would double every year, later modified to every two years, leading to an exponential increase in computing speed and data-processing capability, storage, and a decrease in the cost of delivering those functions. This observation has largely held true with a single transistor costing $150 in the early 1960s, whereas a typical Intel chip in 2019 contained 5 billion of them at a cost of a penny per 100,000 transistors.[30]

The second half of the 1990s is certainly the most Up Wing period within the living memory of most Americans. Maybe date the beginning of that techno-optimist stretch to 1995. A decade later, in a retrospective of 1990s Silicon Valley and the tech sector more broadly, *Fast Company* magazine called 1995 "The Year That Changed Everything."[31] Not much of an exaggeration. Yes, it was the year the computer revolution finally started having a big impact on the U.S. economy, driving a surprise productivity boom that lasted a decade. But a lot more than that happened. It was the year Amazon went online, Craigslist was founded, Yahoo incorporated, Microsoft released Windows 95, and browser pioneer Netscape went public.[32] Another encouraging Up Wing sign: television got another *Star Trek* show, *Voyager.* (Indeed, the decade had three *Star Trek* shows at one time or another, a handy measure of the decade's overall Up Wing attitude.)[33]

By the following year, the impact of the digital transformation was obvious. When President Bill Clinton promised at the 1996 Democratic National Convention that his administration would build America a "bridge to the future," it seemed more substantial than typical political rhetoric.[34] America was progressing economically at a pace not seen since the go-go 1960s. And America's exuberance—as expressed by voters and investors—was utterly rational thanks to technology-driven economic growth, even if Federal Reserve chairman Alan Greenspan initially thought otherwise. America was again in full Up Wing mode, at least for a while. By January 2000—with wage growth rapid, unemployment low, and stock prices soaring—69 percent of Americans thought the country was headed in the right direction.[35] Bring on the Second American Century! Indeed, the belief that the country was in a New Economy may itself have been a powerful propulsive force. In the 2020 paper "Stock Market Boom and the Productivity Gains of the 1990s," economists Urban Jermann and Vincenzo Quadrini suggested that "the mere prospect of high future productivity growth can generate a stock market boom, a financing boom for new firms, an economic expansion as well as sizable gains in current productivity of labor."[36] Up Wing belief creating Up Wing reality. At least for a bit.

A New Wave of Futurists for a New Economy

As in the 1960s, this surprise age of fast technological progress and growth created a new generation of futurists telling Americans that the good times really were here for good and the best was assuredly yet to come. They were every bit as optimistic as their predecessors a generation earlier. Rather than their enthusiasm being tempered by those failed forecasts of the past, they promised the fulfillment of them. And when they speculated, they found no more friendly or enthusiastic forum than *Wired* magazine, which spent the decade not just documenting the rise of Silicon Valley as America's economic and cultural hub—its people, companies, and products—but also promoting the Up Wing future that the technologists promised. *Wired* was a futurist publication, which opened its inaugural issue in early 1993 this way: "The Digital Revolution is whipping through our lives like a Bengali typhoon" unleashing "social changes so profound their only parallel is probably the discovery of fire." That *Wired* was "rooting for these changes was never in doubt," the magazine conceded in a 2018 retrospective on its first twenty-five years.[37]

Wired's pro-progress editorial rooting was loudest in the late 1990s. In July 1997, professional futurist Peter Schwartz and entrepreneur Peter Leyden wrote "The Long Boom: A History of the Future, 1980–2020" for the magazine. They saw the improving U.S. economy as just the start of a twenty-five-year economic boom fueled by rapid innovation and an increasingly open global economy.[38] They expected that alternative energy, biotechnology, nanotechnology, and telecommunications would build upon the productivity gains generated by the IT revolution. This speedy rate of innovation would bring mobile video chat to rural villagers in developing countries and widespread grocery teleshopping to Americans by 2005. It would also bring about electronic voting from home by 2008, gene therapies to cure cancer by 2012, quantum computing by 2015, and the replacement of the internal combustion engine with hydrogen-powered hybrid cars by 2020. Moreover, by 2020, humans would've arrived on Mars, and humanity as a whole would see itself as one global society—one free of the artificial division of race, class, gender, or nationality.

Schwartz and Leyden were no utopians, however. Like any good futurists, they offered possible scenarios rather than definite predictions for the future. They readily asserted that "a hell of a lot of things could go wrong" that might prevent their vision from coming to fruition: "A global transformation over the next quarter century inevitably will bring a tremendous amount of trauma." In particular, the Long Boom was contingent on open economic policy and strong political leadership. Schwartz and Leyden hoped for the society-wide embrace of immigrants as valuable contributors to the economy, an "All American Free Trade Agreement" that eliminated tariffs throughout the western hemisphere, and a renaissance in America's K–12 education system in which public schools competed with relentlessly innovative private schools. But whatever the challenges, Schwartz and Leyden were confident America was up to the task. "Americans don't understand limits," they concluded. "They have boundless confidence in their ability to solve problems. And they have an amazing capacity to think they really can change the world."

Then there was futurist Ray Kurzweil, a serious technologist before he got into the forecasting business. He spent the 1970s and 1980s inventing cool new technologies—primarily in the fields of image scanning, speech recognition, and music synthesizers—and starting valuable new companies.

In 1999, Kurzweil received the National Medal of Technology and Innovation, the United States' highest honor in technology, from President Clinton in a White House ceremony.[39] That same year, he published *The Age of Spiritual Machines*, a book brimming with Up Wing confidence and confident predictions of the approaching technological Singularity. Kurzweil writes, "The twenty-first century will be different. The human species, along with the computational technology it created, will be able to solve age-old problems of need, if not desire, and will be in a position to change the nature of mortality in a post-biological future....The result will be far greater transformations in the first two decades of the twenty-first century than we saw in the entire twentieth century."[40]

In its review of *Spiritual Machines*, *Wired* magazine saw little reason to doubt the inevitability of that glorious future created by exponential growth: "Kurzweil makes the convincing case that technological development will proceed at such a breakneck pace over the next 30, 50, and 100 years that by the end of the next century our species should, for all intents and purposes, be merged with its technology."[41] None of this seemed at all crazy at the time. As the tech boom kept accelerating—expressed both in economic numbers and the skyrocketing stock market, particularly internet-related stocks—many Silicon Valley techies started talking about the Singularity as something that might well happen sooner rather than later. Maybe the exploding stock market was anticipating an upcoming burst of exponential innovation and economic growth?

Another optimist was Vernor Vinge, a professor of mathematics and computer science at San Diego State University, widely regarded as the popularizer of the Technological Singularity concept through a series of award-winning sci-fi novels, including *A Fire Upon the Deep* (1992) and *A Deepness in the Sky* (1999). In 1993, he told a NASA-sponsored symposium, "Within thirty years, we will have the technological means to create superhuman intelligence. Shortly after, the human era will be ended."[42] In a 1995 interview with *Wired*, editor Kevin Kelly asked Vinge about what he wanted from life: Vinge replied: "Oh, to be a whole lot smarter and live forever."[43]

Kelly himself was a popular purveyor of Up Wing optimism. In his September 1999 essay, "The Roaring Zeroes," Kelly led off with this promise: "The good news is, you'll be a millionaire soon. The bad news is, so will everybody else."[44] Clearly, Kelly was not showing much concern about any sort of stock bubble caused by unrealistic investor expectations regarding the future profitability of fledgling but richly priced internet stocks. Rather, he imagined a permanent, unpoppable bubble, inflated by both tech progress and globalization. "What if the digital bubble is made of Kevlar?" he writes. "What if the Dow doesn't fall to 3,000, but zooms to 30,000 in four years? What if we are just at the beginning of the beginning of a long wave of ultra-prosperity?" By 2020, Kelly saw an America of full employment, where the average household has an income of $150,000, a flush government is engaging in all manner of large-scale public works, but also there's "a scandal over whose corporate logos appear on the space suits of the first manned mission to Mars."

Another Surprise: The Boom Unexpectedly Ends

Hollywood rarely makes Up Wing content. This was even true in the techno-optimist 1990s when the approach of the year 2000 provided a hook for apocalyptic visions (much as happened when the year 1000 was nigh). But *Armageddon*, the highest-grossing film in 1998 that was not *Titanic* (even though the latter was released in 1997), is a marvelous Up Wing film.[45] This moment in particular: as a gigantic asteroid heads toward a collision with Earth and NASA readies a team that will land on the rock and explode it, the American president speaks to the world in an almost perfect distillation of Up Wing sentiment:

> *The Bible calls this day "Armageddon"—the end of all things. And yet, for the first time in the history of the planet, a species has the technology to prevent its own extinction. All of you praying with us need to know that everything that can be done to prevent this disaster is being called into service. The human thirst for excellence, knowledge, every step up*

the ladder of science, every adventurous reach into space, all of our combined modern technologies and imaginations, even the wars that we've fought have provided us the tools to wage this terrible battle. Through all the chaos that is our history, through all of the wrong and the discord, through all of the pain and suffering, through all of our times, there is one thing that has nourished our souls and elevated our species above its origins, and that is our courage.[46]

A Tumultuous Start to the Third Millennium

And an end date to the temporary thaw of Up Wing 2.0? Well, that's easy enough. Although Up Wing America made it past the Y2K "millennium bug" threat without the dystopian consequences some had feared—all the power didn't go off at midnight on January 1—the year 2000 marked a turn away from 1990s Up Wing optimism and future orientation. The Nasdaq peaked in March and then fell into a deep and lengthy bear market.[47] The economy weakened in the second half of 2000, falling into recession in early 2001.[48] In the 1999 film *The Matrix*, humanity is trapped in a computer simulation based on what the master program considers the zenith of human civilization: life in the late 1990s. More than two decades later—after 9/11, the Iraq War, the global financial crisis, the Great Recession, the not-so-great recovery, and the Great Pandemic—a lot of us in this reality might agree.

But if you really want to hone in on an exact date for the Down Wing turn, you might pick April 1, 2000. That's when *Wired* published one of its most famous articles, "Why the Future Doesn't Need Us." It's a thoroughly Down Wing take from Bill Joy, a co-founder of Sun Microsystems, about the existential danger of twenty-first-century technologies, especially super-smart robots, genetics, and nanotechnology, where tiny, self-replicating robots could run amok in a *Sorcerer's Apprentice* scenario and cover the world in a "gray goo" of themselves. As Joy writes, "The 21st-century technologies are so powerful that they can spawn whole new classes of accidents and abuses.... I think it is no exaggeration to say we are on the cusp of the further perfection of extreme evil, an evil whose possibility spreads well beyond that which weapons of mass destruction bequeathed to the nation-states, on to a surprising and terrible empowerment of extreme individuals."[49]

Still, at the turn of the century, East Coast elites in Manhattan and Washington were almost as optimistic as most of Silicon Valley. The 2000 Economic Report of the President didn't hold back: "The 20th century ended on a note of great achievement for America, but the century just beginning promises to be brighter still, provided we undertake prudent policies and make strategic investments for the future."[50] Likewise, Fed Chair Greenspan spoke to the public in buoyant language rare for a central banker. In January 2000, he told the Economic Club of New York, "When we look back at the 1990s, from the perspective of say 2010, the nature of the forces currently in train will have presumably become clearer. We may conceivably conclude from that vantage point that, at the turn of the millennium, the American economy was experiencing a once-in-a-century acceleration of innovation, which propelled forward productivity, output, corporate profits, and stock prices at a pace not seen in generations, if ever."[51]

Wall Street banks are reluctant pessimists when speaking to the public, even in the worst of times. They're usually the last folks, for instance, to predict or concede a recession. During an economic boom with the stock market continually making record highs? You won't find a more fervent group of optimists anywhere. In late 1999, investment bank Lehman Brothers published a thick research report titled *Beyond 2000*, which brimmed with confidence about the decade ahead. Founded in 1847, Lehman was originally a cotton trader and broker.[52] But by the turn of the century, the firm was bringing private companies to market, including such eventual corporate American mainstays as Sears Roebuck, F. W. Woolworth, Studebaker, and B. F. Goodrich. And at the turn of the next century, Lehman felt confident it was in the middle of another Industrial Revolution, perhaps even more powerful than the first. In *Beyond 2000*, Lehman didn't just predict the good times would keep on rolling; it forecast acceleration into another postwar Up Wing golden age. The firm predicted the technology boom would continue indefinitely and the "New Economy" would grow *even faster* on a sustained basis—all the while generating no financial imbalances that might lead to a crisis. From that report: "The last decade witnessed major structural changes in the economy: the coming decade will see a maturation of those changes: the technology boom will continue, with the Internet increasingly taking the lead….There is no reason to expect this process to end anytime soon. In many ways, the current incoming decades mimic the 1950s and 60s."[53]

✦ ✦ ✦

Even committed Up Wingers who believed that the 1990s upturn represented a long-term shift in the American economy might have, in their hearts, worried that it was too good to last. Recall Greenspan's January 2000 speech in which he spoke of looking back at the 1990s from a decade hence and seeing it as a "once-in-a-century acceleration of innovation." But Greenspan also kept open the possibility that the boom was merely a blip. "Alternatively, that 2010 retrospective might well conclude that a good deal of what we're currently experiencing was just one of the many euphoric speculative bubbles that have dotted human history," Greenspan hedged.[54]

For a few years after, however, Greenspan's more bullish scenario seemed to be the clear winner. The 1990s productivity boom skipped past the internet stock bust and went right on booming through 2004 as businesses continued to learn and employ internet-connected technology. So why then do I not classify the early 2000s as part of an Up Wing era? The collapse of the internet stock bubble is a big part of it. The Nasdaq—the financial home of the U.S. technology sector and where many IPOs are launched—fell 78 percent from 2000 to 2002 and then stayed down, only recovering to its old high in 2015.[55] But the damage went far beyond share prices and portfolios. That financial bust wreaked havoc on Silicon Valley. The number of venture capital funds fell by a third, and the amount of VC funding fell by nearly half.[56] The end of the two-decade bull market in March 2000 was then followed by a brief recession the following year and a slow recovery amid the 9/11 terrorist attacks, Iraq War, and corporate accounting scandals.[57] In February 2003, the space shuttle *Columbia* disintegrated after reentering the atmosphere. The cancellation of the shuttle program was announced a year later. By 2004, the percentage of Americans saying America was on the right track fell to below 40 percent from a high of 71 percent in early 1999.[58] Strong productivity numbers, while important, were just about the only thing in the early 2000s that seemed Up Wing.

And then the economy took a Down Wing turn. It wasn't the 2007–2009 global financial crisis that ended the productivity boom. But as that crisis began to emerge, it seemed clear the boom was over. In March 2007, *Wall Street Journal* economics reporter Greg Ip wrote that the "U.S. productivity boom that began in the mid-1990s is showing signs of running out of steam. If it proves more than a temporary lull, slower growth in productivity—that is, output per hour worked—could lead to slower growth in living standards, more difficulty paying for the baby boomers' retirements and a greater risk of inflation."[59] (By the way: no mea culpas from Lehman, since the firm would not make it even another decade after that *Beyond 2000* report; it filed for bankruptcy during the global financial crisis and was essentially liquidated by the end of September 2008.)

Between 2010 and 2019, U.S. productivity grew more slowly than in any other decade of the post–World War II era, just 1.1 percent per year.[60] That this period of slow productivity growth coincided with the introduction of the smartphone—a supercomputer on a shard of glass that you could fit in a pocket or purse—and a startup boom in Silicon Valley only further suggested something was very wrong, or at least very weird, with the American economy. It sure seemed that way to Silicon Valley. "We wanted flying cars, instead we got 140 characters" is the pithy and tweetable way the Founders Fund, a San Francisco–based venture capital firm, summed up both the disappointment about what the American tech sector was doing and the disconnect of the "productivity paradox" where apparent tech advances weren't causing the economy to boom.[61]

Yet by decade's end, some signs of life, some green shoots emerged. Although TFP stayed tepid, the 2017–2019 period saw overall higher productivity—1.5 percent versus 0.9 percent in the seven years—as business investment rose. Maybe the next stage of the Information and Communications

Technology Revolution was kicking in. Then came the coronavirus. A productivity surge in 2020 and 2021 was followed by a sharp productivity slowdown. More of us working from home wasn't going to change the overall trajectory of growth, nor would nervous workers putting their shoulders to the grindstone. "The U.S. economy came into the pandemic on a slow-growth path. Despite the dislocations and discontinuities of the past few years, it seems likely to leave on a similar slow-growth path," concluded economists John Fernald and Huiyu Li in a study for the Kansas City Fed as 2022 came to an end.[62] In other words, no sign of Up Wing 3.0 on the horizon.

THREE

The Mystery of the Great Downshift: What Happened to Us

An Up Wing vision of tomorrow was on glorious display at the 1964 World's Fair in New York City. The only attraction to rival the Vatican Pavilion (which featured Michelangelo's *Pietà*) in popularity was the Futurama exhibit.[1] It was the sequel to the original Futurama at the 1939 New York World's Fair, sponsored by automaker General Motors and created by industrial designer Norman Bel Geddes, who popularized "streamlining" as a 1930s aesthetic.[2] Part carnival ride, part GM advertisement, the Depression-era Futurama presented an America twenty years into the future, one tied together by sleek automobiles and superhighways set against various American landscapes. And although it was set two decades hence, Geddes thought that timeline to be unambitious. "But it could be built today," he writes in his 1940 book *Magic Motorways*. "It is not too large a job for a generation which has replaced the plodding horse and buggy with the swift-moving automobile, which has grown wings and spanned the world with them, which has built skyscrapers a thousand feet high. Modern engineering is capable of magnificent accomplishments."[3]

The 1964 update was far more ambitious. This Futurama took visitors on a fifteen-minute tour through a possible America of tomorrow. This vision was depicted via miniature models, from lunar bases to underwater mining stations to futuristic cityscapes right out of *The Jetsons*. It was a holistic imagining of the possible shape of things to come, one presented as vaguely happening in the near future, certainly within the lifetime of the moms and dads zipping through Futurama. When the ride ended, its narration left visitors with the sort of hopeful message that typified the era: "Technology can point the way to a future of limitless promise, but man must chart his own course into tomorrow. A course that frees the mind and the spirit as it improves the well-being of mankind!"[4] Then it was on to a GM automobile showroom. Sorry, Soviet Union—America's Space Race competitor had its own grand vision of tomorrow, of course—this was a capitalist future, through and through.

There hasn't been a World's Fair in the United States since the 1984 exhibition in New Orleans, but the events used to be a pretty big deal here. The 1964 fair attracted some 51 million visitors.[5] The *New York Times* even commissioned an essay from Isaac Asimov, in which the science fiction author imagined visiting a fair in 2014.[6] Keep in mind that Asimov wasn't considered *just* an imaginative writer of the speculative. This wasn't quite the same thing as if the *Times* editors commissioned an essay from a popular sci-fi writer of today such as James S. A. Corey (the pen name used by *The Expanse* collaborators Daniel Abraham and Ty Franck) or Liu Cixin (*The Three-Body Problem*). Asimov was a frequent news commentator on where science and technology might be headed. He was also formerly a tenured professor of biochemistry at Boston University. So hiring Asimov was more like bringing in astrophysicist Neil deGrasse Tyson to give his serious and scientifically sound thoughts on what the future might hold—well, if Tyson were also a popular sci-fi writer.

Asimov gave *Times* readers a flavor of optimistic futurism that was typical of the times, including flying cars, moon colonies, and underwater cities.

(The essay also showed signs that overpopulation concerns were starting to infect the futurist community. Asimov thought that an Earth with a population of 6.5 billion in 2014, versus 7.2 billion actually, would force "increasing penetration of desert and polar areas" as well as plenty of underwater housing.) Asimov also saw a world where nuclear power was deeply embedded in everyday life. "The appliances of 2014 will have no electric cords, of course, for they will be powered by long-lived batteries running on radioisotopes," Asimov writes. "The isotopes will not be expensive for they will be by-products of the fission-power plants which, by 2014, will be supplying well over half the power needs of humanity." Asimov's future fair would also highlight the experimental nuclear fusion power plants already in successful operation.

Some sober *New York Times* readers might have seen Asimov's predictions as wildly speculative, perhaps not fit for the country's newspaper of record to print. Yet many early 1960s futurists would've seen such predictions as entirely reasonable, if not overly cautious. Forget flying cars. Where's your flying hover home? Arthur C. Clark writes in *Profiles of the Future* that many of us might eventually choose to live in nuclear-powered hover homes, "free to move across land and Sea, from continent to continent....Man might become a wanderer over the face of the earth—a gypsy driving a nuclear power caravan from oasis to oasis, across the deserts of the sky."[7]

A Series of Unfortunate Events

Yet America had not even left the 1960s much less entered the twenty-first century before cracks were showing in Asimov's vision. As I mentioned earlier, I date the end of the Up Wing 1.0 era to 1973, a year that saw a nasty recession and a big decline in labor productivity growth. But remember, as important as labor productivity growth is, a purer expression of raw innovation is Technologically Futuristic Productivity growth. And by the late 1960s, there were clear signs TFP was starting to slow. Now that we're more than a half-century on from the earliest possible dating of the Great Downshift, you might expect economics students are taught a simple and elegant consensus on what went wrong. After all, it took only thirty-five years for a consensus to solidify around Federal Reserve policy mistakes as causing the Great Depression, as famously explained in the book *A Monetary History of the United States* by Milton Friedman and Anna Schwartz.[8] (At an event celebrating Friedman's ninetieth birthday in 2002, Fed chair Ben Bernanke concluded his speech by saying, "Regarding the Great Depression. You're right, we did it. We're very sorry. But thanks to you, we won't do it again.")[9]

But there's no simple and elegant theory about the Great Downshift, no $E = mc^2$. In the 2022 book *Slouching towards Utopia*, a sweeping summary and analysis of global economic history informed by all the latest research, University of California, Berkeley, economist Brad DeLong concludes the slowdown "remains a mystery even today."[10] Researchers still haven't reached consensus on a comprehensive explanation for the slowdown.

Not that there aren't plenty of theories, with more being offered and explored all the time, especially as the Great Downshift continues to linger. Still, economists mostly do agree that theories possessing the most powerful explanatory power ideally should describe why the Great Downshift happened in a big and sustained way across advanced economies. It also shouldn't inherently exclude the impact of some other theories that are more country specific. In the end, the best explanation is almost certainly not a singular one, not a grand universal theory that gives the answer to life, the universe, and everything when it comes to the Great Downshift.

The best theories are also ones that move beyond intuition and can be fortified with data and well-tested economic concepts. Just "sounding plausible" isn't nearly enough. Nor is sounding kind of cool. One of my favorite theories floating out there is that the 1970 Controlled Substances Act played a role by limiting access to imagination-expanding drugs such as LSD. It's of a kind with the notion that the Enlightenment and the Industrial Revolution got a big kick when people started drinking less alcohol—families would often start the day getting buzzed—and consuming more caffeine delivered by coffee, as well as spending time in coffee houses.[11] Isaac Newton and Voltaire were total java junkies. Proponents of the drug crackdown theory point out, for instance, that Apple co-founder Steve Jobs took LSD in the early 1970s.[12] And he was hardly the only baby boomer tech entrepreneur to do so. Then there's the case of American biochemist Kary Mullis, recipient of the 1993 Nobel Prize in Chemistry for his role in the invention of the polymerase chain reaction technique, or PCR. In a 1998 profile, the *New York Times* called Mullis's breakthrough "highly original and significant, virtually dividing biology into the two epochs of before PCR and after PCR."[13] It's a foundational technique of molecular biology and its many beneficial applications—genetic testing, cancer diagnosis, gene-based drug development, paternity tests, criminal forensics. (Daytime reality television, with its many dramatic paternity reveals, owes a tremendous debt of gratitude to Mullis.) Although the *Times* piece makes only a single reference to the scientist's "keen interest" in psychedelic drugs, they were hardly just a diversion for Mullis. "Would I have invented PCR if I hadn't taken LSD? I seriously doubt it," Mullis once said. "I could sit on a DNA molecule and watch the polymers go by. I learnt that partly on psychedelic drugs."[14]

To be clear, I'm not blaming the Great Downshift on the Great Comedown (although the notion that tiny doses of LSD boost creativity and productivity is hardly uncommon in Silicon Valley). I only mention it to show that theorizing about the cause of the deceleration continues. Much like analysis of the causes of the Industrial Revolution, the Great Downshift continues to be an orange of economic history with plenty of juice left to squeeze. That said, here are a half dozen important theories that would likely play a part in any serious multicausal explanation:

World War II. The unnamed American president in *Armageddon* had a point: war can accelerate progress in some ways. Having nuclear weapons available could come in handy in case of alien invasion. But war also kills and destroys, and not all that devastation is immediately visible. War not only redirects technological invention and innovation away from peacetime uses; it also disrupts them. It can become more difficult for scientists to pursue their research and exchange ideas, even if not in a war zone, due to limitations on the delivery of academic journals and travel. War is bad for collaboration. In World War I, scientists in Germany (who received 40 percent of the prewar Nobel Prizes in physics and chemistry) were cut off from their counterparts in Allied countries, including the United Kingdom (20 percent of Nobel prizes) and France (15 percent of Nobel prizes).[15] And again, in World War II, perhaps the world's most scientifically fruitful region was in the middle of the conflict. Explains economist Tyler Cowen: "I think one neglected factor behind [the Great Downshift] slowdown is just the destruction of the German-language speaking and central European scientific world, which starts in the 1930s and culminates in World War II. On top of that, you have the Holocaust...You can't understand 20th century science without thinking very hard and long about that event."[16]

Indeed, an intriguing work of alt-history is the 2017 novel *Kingdom of the Wicked*, which examines the issue of how war can disrupt scientific advance. Author Helen Dale imagines a first-century Roman Empire of cable news and airplanes. How did Dale's Roman Empire industrialize? Rather than die at the Siege of Syracuse in 212 BCE, the brilliant Greek polymath Archimedes is captured by Roman forces and becomes the equivalent of the Nazi German rocket scientists (including chief rocketeer Wernher von Braun, who later advised Walt Disney on all things rocket-related) scooped up by the American military after World War II in "Operation Paperclip."[17] He invents calculus some fifteen centuries before Isaac Newton—something he almost accomplished in our reality—and brought all manner of technical know-how to the Roman military, eventually triggering a wider technological revolution. One wonders how many wonders that war has delayed and prevented. And that includes World War II. Despite its reputation as a fertile time of tech progress due to both funding and focus, Santa Clara University economic historian Alexander J. Field observes, "Much of what occurred during the war represented the exploitation of a preexisting knowledge base" and dismisses the notion of the conflict driving a "productivity bonanaza."[18] Field makes a good point. The atom bomb, radar, and computer were made possible by "a web of theoretical and technical developments," explains science policy analyst Tony Mills, that long predated the war.[19] Field also speculates as to why the narrative persists despite the evidence, writing, "In *Looking for the Good War*, Elizabeth Samet wrote that 'we search for a redemptive ending to every tragedy.'...A human predisposition to surrender to faith in embracing the benefits of the war for long-run economic growth is one manifestation of this dynamic."

The 1970s oil shocks. It's easy to see how economists and futurists alike were tempted to write off the 1973 labor productivity slowdown as a temporary hiccup related to easily identifiable economic events and policies. All they had to do was pick up a newspaper or turn on the evening news. An obvious culprit for the slowdown was the Arab oil embargo that began in October of that year and lasted about five months. During this period, crude oil prices quadrupled to a plateau that held until the Iranian revolution brought a second energy crisis in 1979 and a further doubling in price.[20] Weak productivity growth? Just blame OPEC. And economists did. The Congressional Budget Office later noted that it was "the widespread view that the decline [in productivity growth] stemmed from the dramatic rise in energy prices after 1973 [which] fails to account for the lack of a similarly strong slowdown in other countries or for the failure of TFP growth to recover after energy prices declined in the 1980s."[21]

But over the decade, economists began to realize that the productivity slowdown was no ephemeral event. The 1977 Economic Report of the President described the falloff in productivity growth as "striking," while also admitting the causes "are not fully understood at this time."[22] In the 2004 paper "Retrospective on the 1970s Productivity Slowdown," Nobel laureate William Nordhaus identifies that initial deceleration as primarily centered in the most energy-intensive sectors. "In a sense, the energy shocks were the earthquake, and the industries with the largest slowdown [pipelines, oil extraction, electric and other utilities, motor vehicles, and air transportation] were near the epicenter of the tectonic shifts in the economy," he writes. We shouldn't have kept blaming those oil shocks, however. Nordhaus cites the eventual productivity surge in the late 1990s and early 2000s as evidence that "the economy made the transition from the oil age to the electronic age."[23] That said, the energy lessons of the 1970s are being relearned by countries suffering the energy shocks emanating from Russia's invasion of Ukraine.

Up Wing 1.0 was not *quite* as wildly innovative as the statistics suggest. The booming postwar economy was not built fundamentally by atomic power, space-age rocketry, or clever Washington central planning. To an extent not fully appreciated by futurist forecasters and Washington policymakers of the era, the fast economic and productivity growth of the 1950s and 1960s was built on advances from decades earlier. And those pessimistic economists at the end of World War II had no idea of this reality, either. What many of the smartest economists at Ivy League universities, Wall Street banks, and Washington agencies failed to realize back then—in great part due to the relative immaturity of their field, especially macroeconomic data collection—was that the seeds of a prosperous period of rapid technological progress and economic growth had been planted years earlier, taken root, and been slowly growing all that time. These seeds were only waiting for the 1930s banking system to heal and the 1940s global war to finish before sprouting. What perhaps almost no one understood in the 1930s and 1940s was that the Great Depression masked a productivity boom that prepared and primed the postwar decades for Up Wing prosperity. In the influential 2011 book *A Great Leap Forward: 1930s Depression and U.S. Economic Growth*, economist Field presents the counterintuitive finding that despite the economic shock of the 1930s, it was a time of robust productivity gains. As Field writes, "Because of the Depression's place in both the popular and academic imagination…it will seem startling to propose the following hypothesis: the years 1929–1941 were, in the aggregate, the most technologically progressive of any comparable period in U.S. economic history.…It was not principally the war that laid the foundation for postwar prosperity. It was technological progress across a broad frontier of the American economy during the 1930s."[24]

What were the sources of these advances in productivity growth during those long depression years that helped create a booming 1950s and 1960s? Starting in the 1920s, Field explains, manufacturing productivity belatedly began benefitting from a revolution in factory design to better take advantage of the gradual shift from steam engines to electric generators. And in the 1930s, government invested significantly in streets and highways to create a paved road network to support the huge increase in automobile and truck production during the 1920s. It became a whole lot easier to move goods around America by both road and rail.[25]

The Up Wing postwar golden age was blessed with another massive advantage: not only was America a victor in World War II, but its domestic industry was left completely intact. The economies of all its competitors were in shambles, ready to be rebuilt by the American industrial base—at least, that was the case for a while. A National Bureau of Economic Research study describes the situation this way: "At the end of World War II, the United States was the dominant industrial producer in the world. With industrial capacity destroyed in Europe—except for Scandinavia—and in Japan and crippled in the United Kingdom, the United States produced approximately 60 percent of the world output of manufactures in 1950, and its GNP was 61 percent of the total of the countries presently part of the [Organisation for Economic Co-operation and Development]. This was obviously a transitory situation."[26]

A big downside from America's postwar dominance, however, is that although minimal foreign competition helped keep profits and worker wages high, it also meant the American economy lacked an "invisible foot" of global competition where firms faced an always-present threat from new rivals—and failure if they didn't innovate in significant ways. For many years, American businesses didn't have to think or work hard to lead the world. Postwar America's stability was the U.S. economy's eventual undoing. Even though 1960s Washington fretted that other nations were catching up through faster growth, the real concern should have been about what the United States wasn't doing to stay ahead. Too much of American industry became complacent, unproductive, and "collapsed at the first sniff of competition," note former Fed chairman Alan Greenspan and journalist Adrian Wooldridge in their 2018 book, *Capitalism in America*.[27] "The 1970s was the decade when America finally had to grapple with the fact that it was losing its leadership in an ever-widening range of industries. Corporate America lacked the constant, reinvigorating churn from the 'creative destruction,' as termed by Austrian economist Joseph Schumpeter, that forces companies to innovate or stagnate—or die."[28]

The special century ended. In late October 2012, a storm surge from Hurricane Sandy knocked out power in New York City for several days, deluged the subway system and most of the road tunnels leading into Manhattan, and disrupted voice and data communication as flooding damaged a key switching facility in lower Manhattan. For a brief stretch, the financial capital of the world wasn't New York City, as the New York Stock Exchange had to close for two consecutive days. As Robert Gordon writes in *The Rise and Fall of American Growth*:

> *Sandy pushed many of its victims back to the nineteenth century. Residents of New York City below Thirty-Fourth Street learned what it was like to lose the elevators that routinely had carried them to and from their apartments.... Anyone who had no power also lost such modern inventions as electric lighting, air-conditioning and fans to ventilate dwelling spaces, and refrigerators and freezers to keep food from spoiling. Many residents had no heat, no hot food, and even no running water. Those living in New Jersey were often unable to find gasoline needed for commuting because gas station pumps could not function without electricity. Moreover, communication was shut off after batteries were drained on laptops and mobile phones.*[29]

For a brief time, New Yorkers didn't have access to the great inventions that made what Gordon has termed the special century of rapid economic and productivity growth from the 1870s to early 1970s. Three of the most important emerged within three months in 1879: the electric light bulb, the internal combustion engine, and radio, Gordon points out.[30] These were fundamental "general purpose technologies" (GPTs) that spun off scores of inventions that made the modern world New Yorkers currently enjoy. ("What great births you have witnessed," wrote Mark Twain to Walt Whitman on the latter's seventieth birthday, referring to those and other mechanical marvels of the age.)[31] And, crucially, of all those Sandy-created deprivations, the one probably most tolerable was the dodgy wireless service. While we all love the ability to stay in touch with everyone and everything at all times, it still probably places well behind the lack of hot food, water, a heated home, and mobility (well, for most of us who aren't Twitter addicts, at least).

This difference between losing the marvels of the latter part of the Industrial Revolution (or Second Industrial Revolution) and losing those of the Information Technology and Communications Revolution (or Third Industrial Revolution) helps illustrate the nature of the slowdown that began with the Great Downshift. Those special century inventions changed life in such a profound and unrepeatable way and across so many dimensions of our lives, Gordon argues, that it's hard to imagine living without them. And while these inventions had a massive impact on American life, their effect on productivity had been exhausted by the early 1970s. And the one-off nature of them means they can't be repeated. Only once can you bring indoor plumbing to a country or cover it in concrete highways or move from an economy powered by horses to one driven by horsepower. Progress after 1970 certainly continued, but it was focused more narrowly on entertainment, communication, and information technology—important advances, but none that created a second Up Wing golden age of the sort imagined during the 1960s. At least not yet. They were significant enough to create a productivity blip in the late 1990s and early 2000s that has since faded. "[The] invention of the Internet, web browsers, search engines, and e-commerce created a fundamental change in business practices and procedures that was reflected in a...temporary, rather than a permanent, upswing in the pace of progress," Gordon writes.[32] His skepticism about the IT Revolution is the empirical conclusion that is referenced by the "We wanted flying cars, instead we got 140 characters" meme.

Productivity-boosting ideas got harder to find. The end of Gordon's special century of fast economic and productivity growth coincided with another longer-term trend undermining American progress: big game-changing ideas seem to be getting harder and more expensive to find. It really does seem as if all the easy-to-grab, low-hanging fruit of technological progress has been picked. Oh, there are probably still plenty of big winners on that tree of knowledge, but getting to them requires ever-more money and manpower. (Remember, the United States operates on the frontier of technological progress. It gets richer by pushing that frontier forward.) Nicholas Bloom, Charles I. Jones, John Van Reenen, and Michael Webb show that the number of researchers needed to achieve Moore's Law—the regular doubling of computer chip density—is more than eighteen times larger than the number required in the early 1970s.[33] It's a finding that leads to this conclusion: "Just to sustain constant growth in GDP per person, the United States must double the amount of research effort every 13 years to offset the increased difficulty of finding new ideas." And as Bloom told me: "Real R&D expenditures have gone up about tenfold, and productivity growth rates are falling. And the only way to square the circle is it's simply harder to come up with new ideas. And when I talk to my colleagues—I'm at Stanford, so you can imagine I'm in the center of Silicon Valley and all the science and technology—they tell you the same story: it's just becoming more and more expensive and difficult to push the frontier out because we've already made such good, strong progress."[34]

Instead of climbing a tree of knowledge, the researchers suggest we think about searching for ideas much like geologists explore for oil.[35] Just as newer oil sources are increasingly costly and more difficult to extract, coming up with new ideas is getting more expensive. However, it is harder to understand *why* exactly ideas are getting harder to find. At one level, his work suggests research is like any other input—there are likely to be diminishing returns. These days, pushing the frontier of knowledge out requires mastering an ever-larger body of knowledge, meaning that students have to stay longer in college and researchers increasingly work in larger teams whose members are more specialized. This all pushes up costs.

Returning to the oil metaphor, we're digging deeper into a trickier part of the rock. Of course, the techno-pessimists could be wrong, and humanity may just have been chipping away at a particularly hard point in the rock formation that will soon give way, creating decades of cheap ideas. Or perhaps we will begin to employ powerful new tools for digging. "This is the hope of those who emphasize the revolutionary power of artificial intelligence and the 'singularity'—an accumulation of technology that triggers runaway growth at some point in the future," Bloom explained.

The need for new science tools shouldn't be underestimated. In the 2023 paper "Papers and Patents Are Becoming Less Disruptive over Time," Michael Park, Erin Leahey, and Russell J. Funk find "that papers and patents are increasingly less likely to break with the past in ways that push science and technology in new directions."[36] The researchers, for instance, looked at 45 million papers over six decades to see if subsequent research was more likely to cite the original paper than the paper's references. The less likely the citation of references, the more the study itself was considered novel and disruptive. The researchers also found that 1950s-era papers tended to use verbs such as "produce" or "determine" while those in the 2010s used terms suggestive of more incremental findings such as "improve" or "enhance." Overall, they conclude, "our results suggest that slowing rates of disruption may reflect a fundamental shift in the nature of science and technology." One possible explanation here: there's a lot of science you have to understand before having a "Eureka!" moment.

The beginning of the end of Moore's Law. The Information Technology and Communications Revolution doesn't seem to (yet) have generated the overall productivity impact of electrification or the internal combustion engine. But this doesn't mean it hasn't been extraordinarily important. For six decades, Moore's Law has regularly and exponentially increased computer power and decreased cost—an electronic miniaturization that has enabled pretty much, well, *everything*, we talk about today. If cars showed a similar pace of improvements as computers, Gordon Moore once wrote, "they would get 100,000 miles to the gallon and it would be cheaper to buy a Rolls-Royce than park it. (Cars would also be a half an inch long.)"[37] The ICT Revolution accounts for perhaps a fifth of productivity growth from 1960 to 2019 with this effect highest during the 1990s and early 2000s, calculates economist Pablo D. Azar of the New York Federal Reserve.[38] Others credit Moore's Law with a third of U.S. productivity growth during the multi-decade Great Downshift.[39]

It probably isn't a total coincidence that the end of the productivity surge that began in the mid-1990s and ended in the mid-2000s coincided with a chip-making conundrum. Moore's Law, meet Shrek's Law.[40] Continual and seemingly automatic improvements in how fast a microprocessor could perform a computation, or "clock speed," helped enable the ever-more realistic depiction of Shrek, the curmudgeonly green ogre from the successful, four-film DreamWorks franchise in the 2000s (2001, 2004, 2007, 2010).[41] Over that period, all aspects of the Shrek-verse—cloth, fur, water, how illumination played off various surfaces—progressively improved. It wasn't until the third film, for instance, that Shrek could make his horn-shaped ears vibrate when trumpeting them without each ear having to be individually animated.[42]

But in 2004, Shrek's Law hit a roadblock when Intel, the world's largest chipmaker, announced it was canceling the next version of its flagship Pentium 4 chip and shifting away from boosting performance through faster clock speed. Instead, the company would focus on producing "multicore" computer chips—chips with at least two processors on a single chip. To take full advantage of multiple processors, a software program must be able to split up work among them, or be "parallelized." This shift forced a big change by the Shrek animators in 2008, according to Neil Thompson, director of the FutureTech Research Project at MIT. After benefitting from years of greater processor speed and the performance improvements it enables, Thompson explained, "Dreamworks made the expensive decision to re-write large parts of their animation code to work with the multicore chips. This allowed them to split up the work that the software was doing amongst the multiple processors on their multicore chips, which their previous unparallelized code had been largely unable to do." This pricey switch was a success, according to Thompson, providing a 70 percent overall improvement, with particular gains in areas like fluid modeling.[43] (Fluid modeling is what provides realism to water, smoke, and moving fur and hair.)

But that clever workaround shouldn't distract from the problem that making computer processors less general purpose and more specialized means computers become less of a general-purpose technology. What's more, he added in a conversation with me, this switch to specialization will worsen the economics of chip manufacturing, leading to slower improvements: "[Moore's Law] was really about the number of transistors you could fit on a chip [which] translated to this incredible speed up in the capacity of our chips and how fast we could run them. And in 2004–2005, we lost that. Chips at that point were about 3 gigahertz. The chips in your computer today are about 3 gigahertz. And so we've really plateaued, whereas before that we were improving it exponentially." And now what? "People talk about artificial intelligence…[and] quantum computing.…It's not at all clear that any of them will be able to sort of take up that mantle in the way that Moore's Law has done, particularly over so many decades."[44] Indeed, despite all the excitement about generative AI models such as Bard, ChatGPT, and DALL-E, some technologists are concerned that further progress is "beginning to be largely restricted by the computing power currently available," notes Citigroup in a 2023 analysis.[45]

The pandemic. The impact of COVID-19 on productivity growth has become its own little Great Downshift mystery. At first, the pandemic seemed to have a silver lining. Despite all the economic chaos and uncertainty, labor productivity boomed. In 2020 and 2021 labor productivity averaged roughly 3 percent annually versus just over 1 percent during the post–global financial crisis period of 2010 through 2019.[46] Among the explanations offered at the time were e-commerce, companies digitizing their workplace (such as working from home), and the "creative destruction" of low-productivity businesses going out of business. Maybe we were even seeing the emerging AI revolution finally making a big impact. Then the first half of 2022 saw a big reversal from that surprise stretch of higher labor productivity, with annualized declines of more than 6 percent in the first quarter and nearly 4 percent in the second quarter leading to a year-long decline of nearly 2 percent (and 1 percent for TFP).[47] "The abysmal productivity readings in the first half of 2022 have cast doubt on whether the pandemic generated efficiency gains in the first place," the Goldman Sachs economics team told the bank's clients. "At face value, this year's GDP and employment numbers imply a full reversal of the pandemic productivity spurt."[48]

The various explanations for the mini-boom were quickly followed by various explanations for the subsequent bust. One of the most plausible was put forward by Robert Gordon and economist Hassan Sayed of Princeton

University. First, the bad news about the initial productivity revival: it was a mirage, nothing at all like the productivity boom during another period of economic tumult, the Great Depression. "This apparent productivity growth revival has been interpreted as caused by automation, artificial intelligence, and a massive investment by households in the equipment and software needed to conduct work from home," the economists write in their 2022 paper.[49] What happened during that initial boom was an extreme version of what often happens during downturns, they explained. Productivity surges as higher-productivity workers keep their jobs with lower-productivity ones hitting the bricks. Perhaps more importantly, retained workers boost their game and work harder. This time, the conditions were so unusual—the worst pandemic in more than a century and the government basically ordering the shutdown of the economy—that businesses freaked out and slashed payrolls like crazy. (Something similar happened with the global financial crisis.) The rapid pace of productivity in 2020 can be explained by excess layoffs. And with the eventual rehiring came a drop in productivity since businesses have actually not become wildly more efficient or innovative—except perhaps for those whose workers could work from home.

So ultimately it's an Occam's razor explanation. Productivity growth just returned to normal, or its longer-term Great Downshift baseline, after a temporary upshift. Nothing to see here, unfortunately. Well, maybe something to see. There's good reason to worry about the long-term effect of disrupted education from at-home and hybrid schooling during 2020 and 2021. One of the strongest and most persistent findings of modern economics is that schooling does something important to help kids become high-functioning adults, including as workers in an advanced, globalized economy. So it should've been no surprise that by late 2022, national testing scores were showing that kids across America in almost all demographic groups had experienced troubling setbacks in both math and reading. In math, the results represented the steepest declines ever recorded since the National Assessment of Educational Progress was instituted in the early 1990s.[50]

✦ ✦ ✦

What all the above explanations have in common is that they're not directly the result of our actions. Eventually, we fully exploit the potential of even the most marvelous inventions. Eventually, the low-hanging fruits of innovation get picked. Occasionally, an unexpected event—war, energy shock, pandemic—happens and disrupts our best-laid plans. But we're not merely the victims of geopolitical, macroeconomic, and biological circumstances. Our own actions played a huge role in the Great Downshift and its half-century continuation, which I'll discuss in the next chapter.

FOUR

The Mystery of the Great Downshift: What We Did to Ourselves

Only the 1986 Chernobyl reactor explosion and core meltdown in the then Soviet Republic of Ukraine released more radiation than the meltdown at the Fukushima Daiichi nuclear power plant on March 11, 2011.[1] Both are the only nuclear accidents to merit the most severe rating on the International Nuclear Event Scale. After the meltdown, both Japan and Germany—two nations that pride themselves on taking climate change seriously—said goodbye to generating carbon-free energy through the controlled splitting of atoms.[2] Within fourteen months of the accident, Japan halted all of its nuclear power production. Germany responded even faster, immediately shutting down almost half of its nuclear power plants and promising to mothball all the remaining ones by the end of 2022.[3] (The promise was made good in 2023.)[4] Neither nation was willing to risk future nuclear accidents, the release of radiation, and casualties among the public.

Yet no fatalities have ever been found to be directly attributable to nuclear radiation exposure from the Fukushima meltdown, though there are projections of a cumulative 130 future deaths from the radiation release, as well as an estimated 1,232 deaths that occurred as a result of the evacuation after the accident.[5] (Similarly, maybe as few as thirty people died as an immediate result of Chernobyl, a figure sure to shock viewers of the recent HBO miniseries in which characters speculated about the risk of millions of fatalities. Even longer-term estimates of four thousand or more fatalities might seem surprisingly low. Also, a 2021 study looking at the adult children conceived from radiation-exposed Chernobyl parents found no genetic impact.)[6]

But those estimated deaths aren't the end of the cost-benefit calculation. The actions by Japan and Germany generated three unintended consequences. First, Japan's substitution of low-cost nuclear power with pricier power generated by imported coal and oil led to a 40 percent increase in energy prices in some regions. The price shocks then led to less wintertime energy consumption and higher mortality rates during periods of extremely cold weather, with an estimated resulting death toll of nearly five thousand through 2014.[7] Second, Japan's nuclear shutdown initially led to a nationwide electricity shortage, and so the government began a large-scale energy-saving campaign to reduce electricity consumption, especially air conditioning on hot days. Nearly eight thousand people may have died prematurely every year through 2015 as a result, with most fatalities among the elderly.[8] Third, researchers looking at the German nuclear phaseout estimate 1,100 excess deaths per year due to increased pollution from replacing nuclear power with coal-fired production in that country.[9] Keeping score here, it's almost certain that Japan's and Germany's sudden rejection of nuclear power has caused many thousands of additional deaths a year and thus many multiples of the worst-case estimate of total deaths directly from the Fukushima plant meltdown, even including the evacuation.[10]

What explains the extreme actions of the Japanese and German governments? It's not as if national leaders didn't understand the energy mix that powered their economies or the reality of their cold winters and hot summers. The economists who wrote that first Fukushima paper speculate that the perceived risk from nuclear energy is "often based more on emotions and instincts than on reason and rationality."[11] Deaths from radiation exposure after a nuclear meltdown are more visible and dramatic than those resulting from higher energy prices. In the former case, specific deaths can easily be attributed, while in the latter case fatalities are a big-picture, aggregate number generated by a statistical model. Yet, the researchers note, deaths from either cause are "equivalent from a cost-benefit perspective, and should be treated accordingly. The precautionary principle emphasizes salient events—the worst case scenario—and in doing so ignores the alternative, thereby encouraging inefficient policy-making."[12]

The "precautionary principle" mentioned above is the notion that significant activities should not proceed until threats of damage are fully understood. Shorter version: "guilty until proven innocent" or "better safe than sorry." While that may sound sensible, in practice following such an approach distracts us from considering trade-offs. We overly focus on the issue at hand. In his 1988 book, *Searching for Safety*, political scientist Aaron Wildavsky criticized that sort of hyper-cautious thinking as leading to "trial without error...If you can do nothing without knowing first how it will turn out, you cannot do anything at all."[13] Without accepting some risk, there can be no innovation.

The End of America's Atomic Age

America suffered its own Fukushima and experienced its own obsession with the precautionary principle in 1979 when there was a partial meltdown of the Three Mile Island Unit 2 reactor core near Harrisburg, Pennsylvania. Well, kind of. TMI is rated a level 5, or "accident with wider consequences," on the International Nuclear and Radiological Event Scale versus a level 7, or "major accident" for Fukushima and Chernobyl, the worst possible rating.[14] And what were the "wider consequences" of the TMI accident? There were no immediate fatalities—either from the minor radiation release or evacuation—and most studies have found no observable long-term effects, either.[15] So when it comes to "wider consequences" from the accident, the only significant detectable one was our harmful reaction and response to the accident, similar to Fukushima three decades later. Following TMI, the U.S. Nuclear Regulatory Commission ramped up inspections.[16] This led to the shutdown of two large Tennessee Valley Authority nuclear plants, shifting power generation to coal-fired plants. Then the unintended consequences kicked in. Increased particle pollution in the counties where those coal plants were located may have harmed infant health by reducing average birth weight, which can lower IQ and lead to cardiovascular problems and earlier adult mortality, writes Carnegie Mellon University economist Edson Severnini in a 2017 analysis.[17] He concludes: "Environmental regulations focused on one node of an extensive network of energy production…may trigger unanticipated chain reactions that go against the ultimate goal of protecting public health."[18]

Now spread that "unanticipated" impact over the entire past half century, and across all of America where we've burned dirty fossil fuels when we could already be getting most of our energy production from nuclear rather than just a fifth, which has been the case since TMI. (An MIT analysis finds that shutting down all U.S. reactors today would cause 5,200 pollution deaths a year.)[19] Not only is nuclear energy also clean energy as far as air pollution that harms infant health, but it's also energy that doesn't increase the carbon content of our atmosphere. Instead, today we're scrambling to generate enough carbon-free energy to mitigate climate change but also meet increased energy consumption in the future. Three Mile Island was a critical event for the American nuclear power industry, no pun intended. The company that designed and built the TMI reactors never sold another one.[20] And of the 129 nuclear plants approved for construction by the NRC at that time, fewer than half were completed.[21]

But the problems didn't start there. By the early 1970s, Atomic Age dreams of ubiquitous nuclear power were evaporating as fast as those Space Age fantasies of humanity soon spreading out into the solar system. The data show a clear break in nuclear reactor construction in 1971 and 1972, which suggests the decline in reactor construction is likely attributable to a confluence of regulatory events, perhaps creating uncertainty about the future cost of safety regulations.[22] Two of the most important events: the 1970 creation of the Environmental Protection Agency and the 1971 *Calvert Cliffs* decision, in which the DC Circuit Court ordered federal regulators to comply with the National Environmental Policy Act of 1970, widely considered the "Magna Carta" of federal environmental laws, and temporarily paused all nuclear power plant licensing. Basically, NEPA and related executive orders require federal agencies to investigate and assess the potential environmental costs, if any, of its projects and regulations.[23] (At least twenty states and localities have their own such statutes, known as "little NEPAs.")[24] The following passage from the *Calvert* decision suggests the era's Down Wing attitude: "These cases are only the beginning of what promises to become a flood of new litigation... seeking judicial assistance in protecting our natural environment. Several recently enacted statutes attest to the commitment of the Government to control, at long last, the destructive engine of material 'progress.'"

Then came Three Mile Island. Reactors that received their operating licenses before the accident had indeed experienced modest cost escalation starting in the late 1960s. But for reactors that were under construction during Three Mile Island and eventually completed afterward, median costs exploded higher and were nearly three times pre-TMI costs. The data suggest that the TMI accident in 1979 did "uniquely affect the nuclear industry" in terms of construction costs, according to researchers Jessica R. Lovering, Arthur Yip, and Ted Lovering.[25] Quite telling about America's regulatory stance toward nuclear is the anti-nuclear track record of the Nuclear Regulatory Commission. The NRC was established in 1974, replacing the Atomic Energy Commission, which was formed right after World War II by Congress to direct the development and use of nuclear energy toward "improving the public welfare, increasing the standard of living, strengthening free competition in private enterprise, and promoting world peace."[26] But in its nearly half-century of existence, there wasn't a single new nuclear power plant approved for construction by the NRC since it became operational and then subsequently built, until early in 2023 when the first of two new reactors at the Vogtle nuclear plant 150 miles west of Atlanta—both NRC approved back in 2009—finally started generating electricity and connected to the grid.[27] The United States continues "to regulate based on the risk of disaster from the 1970s" rather than today, notes a 2017 analysis from the American Action Forum.[28]

Why does France get 70 percent of its energy generation from nuclear versus a fifth for the United States? Politicians over there had to deal with (sometimes violent) anti-nuclear activists in the 1970s just like the ones over here. But Paris was devoted to nuclear unlike Washington. And those French activists had to face an unfriendly legal system. As Spencer R. Weart writes in *The Rise of Nuclear Fear*, "Unlike the American and German systems for licensing reactors—mazes of hearings in which a determined group of opponents could raise endless obstructions against a builder—French licensing was a straightforward matter of working things out among government experts."[29]

Although ninety-three nuclear reactors are still operating at fifty-five plants in twenty-eight states, a low-key pessimism continues to afflict nuclear advocates.[30] That, despite the growing realization in many countries that nuclear is needed to create a net-zero carbon economy not mired by shortages and to ensure a reliable source of energy safe from the vagaries of geopolitics. There are also technical and regulatory challenges given the likelihood that the future of nuclear fission will involve the deployment of a new generation of smaller advanced reactors. Some advocates are so desperate they're suggesting a new name: "elemental energy!" Then again, if not for America's anti-nuclear turn in the 1970s, the country might already be dotted by very safe, very small, and very easy- and cheap-to-construct advanced fission reactors—well, that's assuming decades of research (that never happened in reality) had not long ago produced the sorts of nuclear fusion breakthroughs we're seeing today. In that case, we might well have the fusion-powered economy imagined during Up Wing 1.0.

✦ ✦ ✦

America's shift away from its once-planned expansion of nuclear power—especially more regulation and increased risk aversion—helps illustrate in microcosm some of the key forces arguably contributing to the Great Downshift, and how scientific discovery, technological innovation, and economic growth failed to live up to those postwar Up Wing dreams. It wasn't just that famous promise about how "too cheap to meter" nuclear energy would supply abundant and inexpensive power to American homeowners. Eventually, the American economy would become nuclear-powered in all facets, as Isaac Asimov writes in that speculative 1964 essay for the *New York Times*. Its factories powered by on-site reactors. Its goods transported overseas by nuclear-powered cargo ships (and maybe, eventually, ocean-going hovercraft). Its people traveling in nuclear-powered airplanes. Its astronauts exploring deep space in nuclear-powered rockets. Nuclear-powered everything and anything.

Up Wing America Gets Strangled by the Regulatory State

At the same time that Up Wing growth seems to have become harder for various big-picture macroeconomic reasons, we started taking some Down Wing actions we shouldn't have and stopped some Up Wing actions we should've kept doing. Our decisions made it harder than necessary to find and commercialize big new ideas. And while there might have been nothing we could've done, for instance, about having fully exploited the great inventions of the past, we also made it harder than necessary to exploit the pretty darn good inventions of the present. Or, as the folks in Silicon Valley like to put it, we made it easier to innovate in cyberspace with bits than in the physical world with atoms. We made it hard to build everything from nuclear reactors to high-speed rail to supersonic aircraft to more housing in high-productivity cities.

One of Silicon Valley uberbillionaire Elon Musk's wilder ideas—far wilder than autonomous electric cars and reusable rocket ships, and maybe almost as wild as putting a million people on Mars by 2050—is building twin two-hundred-mile "hyperloop" tunnels connecting New York City to Washington, DC, allowing travel between the two cities in under thirty minutes.[31] These would be sealed underground vacuum tubes through which humans in pods would travel at nearly 800 miles per hour. Musk calls the concept a "cross between a Concorde, a railgun and an air hockey table."[32] Step 1 of Musk's plan announced in 2017 would be tunneling a thirty-five-mile underground connection between Baltimore and Washington. Well, that's not quite right. Step 1 would actually be meeting NEPA requirements, which demand an environmental review of federal actions that affect the human environment.[33] Sounds fairly straightforward, and you might think there would be plenty of limits and constraints built into the law to prevent it from expanding into a ginormous, expensive, time-wasting regulatory boondoggle. But you would be wrong.

The earliest environmental impact statements were often less than ten typewritten pages. But then they got steadily bigger and more time consuming after years of activist lawsuits and judicial decisions expanding what is expected from a NEPA analysis. Regulatory scholar Eli Dourado notes that of the 136 statements finalized in 2020, average preparation time was nearly five years.[34] Statements finalized between 2013 and 2017 averaged 586 pages, and 1,037 pages for EIS appendices. What's more, no project can begin until the NEPA analysis is done. And whatever the plain reading of the statute, all federal actions must take NEPA requirements into account. The entire environment counts as the human environment (maybe space, too), and federal actions include any agency decision, Dourado points out, everything from building a power plant on federal land (better ask the Bureau of Land Management) to testing a supersonic airplane at Edwards Air Force Base (better ask the FAA) to implementing congestion pricing on Manhattan roads that are technically part of the National Highway System (better ask the FHA). Really, what chance does Musk's hyperloop have, whatever the technological hurdles? A million humans on Mars sounds more likely to happen sooner. Indeed, Musk's Boring tunneling company no longer lists the DC-Baltimore tunnel on its website as of 2021.[35]

One of the earliest NEPA controversies was the 1973 discovery of the snail darter, an endangered species, during construction of the Tellico Dam on the Little Tennessee River.[36] Construction had begun in 1967, before NEPA became law. But due to NEPA delays, the dam was not completed until 1979. The absurdist nature of the dispute—a big dam being held up by this little creature—made it big news at the time. NEPA also led to big delays in building the 1970s Trans-Alaska Pipeline, which led Herman Kahn to complain that "it is difficult to find any proposed project related to the important area of new energy supplies that has not been so affected, [including] nuclear power, thermal electric power, transmission lines, pipelines, refineries, petroleum and natural gas, and even geothermal power."[37] True then and just as true today, as supporters of the Biden administration's industrial policy efforts, such as expanding the domestic chip industry and building lots of clean energy infrastructure, are finding out.[38] A terrible sign for these efforts: Nearly two decades of permitting delays since 2001 and an 800-page NEPA environmental review helped kill Cape Wind, a proposed large-scale wind project off the coast of Nantucket island, notes Aidan Mackenzie of the Institute for Progress.[39] This sort of thing is not an isolated example. Between 2008 and 2021, 53 major solar and geothermal projects were delayed or blocked, with a third facing permitting challenges.[40]

But it's not just NEPA that's the problem. Regulation researchers Leah Brooks and Zachary Liscow document how all sorts of environmental legislation from the late 1960s onward significantly expanded the scope for considering citizen concerns—including the environmental movement and the rise of homeowners as organized lobbyists—in infrastructure project design.[41] (There was plenty of that Not In My Backyard activity in the failure of Cape Wind.) In addition to NEPA, laws such as the National Historic Preservation Act of 1966 (prevents development on national historic sites), the 1973 Endangered Species Act (limits development near protected habitat), and the Clean Water Act (protects wetlands) were among a variety of federal laws that made it more difficult to develop on public lands.

All this seemed like a good idea at first. After all, regular people had information about the real-world costs of these projects that government might not have. But too often "citizen voice" became a stalling tactic by a vocal minority that impeded progress for everybody else. While Brooks and Liscow cannot establish that the rise of citizen voice in government decision-making caused, for instance, the more than threefold increase in interstate highway construction costs—with the inflection point of increase in the early 1970s—citizen voice concerns mandated by federal regulatory legislation seem to offer the strongest relationship.[42] It's an analysis that's now generally accepted by other infrastructure scholars who analyze why America can't seem to build big things anymore. Examples are legion of community input delaying completion, raising costs, or causing inefficient alterations to all manner of projects, from creating new housing to building clean energy projects (such as solar farms and windmills) to mass transit.

How Regulation Ruined America's Super Cities

If we all suddenly vanished, what would happen to all our magnificently built cities—our economic engines, our Up Wing nodes of capital, ideas, talent, and technology? Well, they wouldn't be magnificent for too long. Take New York City, for instance. With no New Yorkers to maintain the Big Apple, writes journalist Alan Weisman in the 2007 book *The World without Us*, the place would quickly fall apart.[43] Within just twenty years or so, streets would collapse into subway tunnels and burned-out skyscrapers might start to buckle. Weisman never explains humanity's disappearance. But given how quickly some experts were ready to declare "cities are over" during the pandemic—despite COVID-19 being far from the first plague to sweep through urban areas—maybe a superbug would lead to their abandonment. Of course, people fleeing cities would mark the end of some five thousand years of people moving to cities. There aren't many economic trends more persistent than urbanization. The attractive power of cities as places of commerce and opportunity meant they have always bounced back. Yet there's a lot of room between vibrant growing metropolises and "cities are over." New York City and Detroit are still here, but both have gone through down periods during the past half-century. The former rebounded. The latter? Not yet.

An Up Wing future depends on getting the most possible out of our cities. It always has. Urban economist Edward Glaeser has explained that these "dense agglomerations that dot the globe have been engines of innovation since Plato and Socrates bickered in an Athenian marketplace."[44] And to study them "is to study nothing less than human progress." In America, the ten largest metro areas account for a third of the country's total GDP, with 80 percent of the nation's five thousand fastest-growing businesses located in large urban areas.[45] And in recent decades, more and more high-paying jobs, especially in innovation sectors, have been concentrated in a few cities—Silicon Valley and the Bay Area, but also Austin, Boston, New York, and Seattle.[46]

But zoning and other land-use regulations, many of which started to be implemented in the 1970s, make living in these places more expensive than it needs to be. Economists Joseph Gyourko and Jacob Krimmel point to the "zoning tax" that regulations impose on land used for single-family housing.[47] Within fifteen miles of some metro urban cores, the zoning tax is simply massive, ranging from between $150,000–$200,000 in Los Angeles, New York City, and Seattle to $400,000 in San Francisco. Even worse, the zoning taxes are from 1 to 4 times the relatively high typical household incomes in these markets, "so the likely impact on housing affordability is meaningful," the economists conclude. And the harm goes beyond making these places more expensive for high-skilled workers to move to. The rise in housing costs versus wages, according to economist Daniel Shoag, has made it disproportionately difficult for low-skilled workers to live and work in America's productive and high-wage regions.[48] He also notes that the slow growth in housing supply in such places generates other types of inequality, with restrictive zoning rules linked to increased racial segregation, while also concentrating more wealth in a smaller share of the population.

Still doubt that America has a housing and geographic mobility problem? Research from economists Ran Abramitzky and Leah Boustan find that "children of immigrants from nearly every country in the world are more upwardly mobile than the children of U.S.-born residents who were raised in families with a similar income level."[49] But why would that be? Do their parents hand down a superior work ethic and go-getter attitude? Maybe. But what's certainly part of the story is that, as Abramitzky and Boustan write, "immigrants tend to move to locations in the United States that offer the best opportunities for upward mobility for their kids, whereas the U.S.-born are more rooted in place."[50]

Counting Up the Costs of Making It Hard to Build in America

The notion that starting around 1970 America experienced a regulatory explosion that continues to reverberate is hardly a revelation, nor is the suspicion that the explosion may have played a role in the Great Downshift, or productivity slowdown. A 1981 Congressional Budget Office report identified a flurry of environmental regulation in the 1970s as a possible cause of the productivity growth slowdown from the immediate postwar decades: "The 1969–1972 period was one of intense regulatory proliferation in the United States, with new legislation concerning air emissions, discharges into waterways, noise pollution, and occupational safety."[51]

What is new are the attempts to quantify the damage. Some sense of the overall growth opportunity from better regulation can be found in a 2013 study from economists John Dawson of Appalachian State University and John Seater of North Carolina State University, who created a model that assumes regulation affects the size of the American economy and then conducted a massively enlightening thought experiment: what would be the size of the economy today without any new regulation during the postwar era?[52] The economists find that making that one simple—albeit massive—change leads to a much, much bigger American economy, as well as faster Technologically Futuristic Productivity growth. "One channel through which regulation has reduced output is TFP. We find that federal regulation can explain much of the famous and famously puzzling productivity slowdown of the 1970s," they conclude.

Specifically, Dawson and Seater estimate that the past decades of federal regulations have reduced real GDP by roughly two percentage points a year, every year. Instead of the U.S. economy growing by 3 percent a year in aggregate real terms since World War II, it would've grown by 5 percent a year. To put it another way: if regulation had remained at its 1949 level, GDP today would be more like $75 trillion instead of a quarter of that. Imagine a U.S. economy nearly four times as big as the one today. Basically, we would have the U.S. economy of 2076 right now. Imagine median household pay of nearly $300,000 a year versus $70,000 currently.

No economist would say regulations provide no value, such as those reducing air pollution. Rather, what Dawson and Seater are doing is making clear that "the cost of regulation is substantial and must be taken seriously in any evaluation of regulation's net social benefit." But not all regulation is the same. As economists Ryan Murphy of Southern Methodist University and Colin O'Reilly of Creighton University explained it in a 2022 essay, regulation to most people means things like the minimum wage, rules for business from the Occupational Safety and Health Administration, pointless "red tape" when trying to start a new firm.[53] Then there's what they call "anti-growth safetyism" kinds of regulations. These are rules that simply stop "innovation in its place by erecting barriers in the name of safety (for people or the environment) that are basically impossible to overcome, such that many of our technologies are stuck in the 1970s," they write. Nuclear power would seem to qualify. One related analysis, they cite, suggests the effect of "safetyism" kinds of regulations is especially harmful to economies on the frontiers of technological progress and economic growth. As such, the American economy might be able to get an additional percentage point per year of growth through deregulation. So using that Dawson-Seater model, instead of median U.S. household income of $70,000 today, Murphy and O'Reilly calculate, it would be almost $120,000. Not bad at all.[54]

The End of America's Space Age

If high school students a century or millennium hence know much of anything about President Richard Nixon, I don't think it will be for the Watergate scandal. Rather, it will concern what the thirty-seventh U.S. president was doing on July 20, 1969. From the Oval Office, Nixon spoke via telephone-radio transmission to Apollo 11 crew members Neil Armstrong and Edwin "Buzz" Aldrin.[55] He congratulated them on their successful moon landing and being the first humans to set foot on a different world. Photographs and video of that historic moment show that to the left of the president, hanging on the wall, is a color photograph of Earth—a beautiful blue-and-white planetary oasis against the stark, empty black of space—taken less than a year earlier by astronaut William Anders as Apollo 8 orbited the moon.[56]

Earthrise has since become one of the most reproduced images of all time. But the photo—an artifact from a key moment in U.S. space exploration and a captured moment of wonder by an American astronaut—came down off the Oval Office wall sometime in 1970. And *Earthrise* wasn't removed because Nixon replaced it with a photo of Apollo 11 astronaut Neil Armstrong stepping onto the lunar surface. Why would he? The successful lunar landing marked the end of the Space Race, followed by the downsizing of America's off-planet ambitions. Apollo historian John M. Logsdon observes, "Nixon apparently did not want to be reminded of what remarkable things human explorers could accomplish as he made the decisions that would keep humans in low Earth orbit for the next half-century."[57] By December 1969, just a half year after the lunar landing, Nixon was already telling others in the White House that he didn't see the need to go to the moon six more times, as was planned.[58] In March 1970, Nixon put forward his "space doctrine," which included a 10 percent budget cut to space operations.[59] From now on, NASA would be just another public program competing for taxpayer dollars. Even the *New York Times*, a longtime critic of Apollo spending, bashed the decision as one of "budgetary myopia" and "an inglorious letdown for an effort whose brilliant outcome was and is one of the proudest fruits of human ingenuity and courage."[60] After the Apollo 17 splashdown at the end of 1972, Nixon issued a prescient statement: "This may be the last time in this century that men will walk on the Moon."[61] This sorry state of affairs, of course, remains ongoing, although NASA is finally again making a serious effort with its Artemis program to return to the Moon within the next few years.

One Giant Leap and Then Retreat

Ideally, Apollo 17 would've been followed by Apollo missions 18, 19, and 20, which NASA was prepared to launch. Those missions would've further analyzed the moon's radiation and surface dust in preparation for a semi-permanent scientific base.[62] And after that? A year-long crewed flyby of Mars in the mid-1970s using Apollo technology, followed by a Mars landing in the 1980s. Yet even if you knew nothing about the politics of the era or the abandoned NASA missions, the direction of the American space program would be obvious by looking at the change in what Washington was spending on R&D. As I mentioned earlier, the starting gun of the American-Soviet Space Race wasn't Sputnik. It was the 1955 Eisenhower administration announcement that it intended to launch a science satellite by the end of 1958. From that point until the mid-1960s, federal R&D spending more than tripled to a peak of nearly $88 billion in 1966 from $27 billion in 1955, all inflation adjusted.[63] Then America won the Space Race, and R&D spending gradually decreased over the next decade. This is not the pattern one would expect if America back then was serious about becoming a multiplanetary civilization. Since then, federal R&D has ebbed and flowed, standing at $141 billion heading into the pandemic—nearly double what it was during Apollo. But as a share of the economy, R&D investment is way down, from around 2 percent in the mid-1960s to 0.65 percent in 2019. Why is this a problem? America sits on the bleeding edge of global innovation. We can't grow faster only through the better and wider use of existing technology. We need to push forward the frontier through discovery, invention, and innovation. Yet, concludes economist John Van Reenen, "Both theory and empirical evidence suggest that the United States is not investing enough in innovation."[64] In other words, *moar*! Instead, we have been doing *less*! American actions haven't contributed to the Great Downshift just by regulating too much and too poorly, we've also researched too little, too cautiously, and too inefficiently.

Granted, business does a lot more R&D than it used to. So much so that it is now the primary source of overall research spending, comprising nearly three-fourths of investment today compared to a third of that in 1965. The problem is that not all research is the same. Most federal R&D funding, some 70 percent, is used to conduct basic research (scientific discovery and the overall advancement of knowledge) and applied research (solving specific technological problems). In contrast, R&D spending in the private sector tends to focus on the development of specific products and processes to enable the commercialization of an innovation.[65] Another way to think of basic research is as "curiosity research," the technological ripples of which are unknowable. Both government and business have a role to play, and government has been neglecting its role for decades.

But what if Washington had done better? Let's assume the Nixon space policy decisions stood and were supported by subsequent administrations. Was there some other big, aspirational national project to which the United States could have devoted considerable effort and resources? Actually, there was such a project, but eventually we abandoned that one, too. While the United States and Soviet Union were running their Space Race, they were also participating in a more low-key competition with Europe. Addressing the U.S. Air Force Academy's graduating class in June 1963, President Kennedy said his administration "should immediately commence a new program in partnership with private industry to develop at the earliest practical date the prototype of a commercially successful supersonic transport superior to that being built in any other country of the world."[66]

Britain and France thought much the same thing, having in November 1962 announced a partnership to jointly build their own SST, named Concorde.[67] Building the Concorde would be Europe's Apollo program. The Supersonic Race was on, with the Soviet Union soon joining to make it a three-team contest. The FAA in 1966 selected Seattle-based Boeing to design and build a prototype SST and anticipated some five hundred supersonic aircraft would be flying by 1990.[68] At the time, it probably seemed a pretty safe bet to name the new Seattle-based NBA team "Supersonics." This was 1960s Up Wing America, after all. What America wanted to do, it did. Unsurprisingly, the lead SST customer with fifteen provisional orders was Pan American World Airways.[69] The airline was at its peak during the 1960s and widely known as a top innovator. It led the U.S. airline industry into the jet age with the first purchase of the Boeing 707.[70] (The space plane arriving at the spinning space station at the beginning of *2001: A Space Odyssey*—right after that epic flash-forward from an ancestral ape tossing a bone into the air—sports the iconic blue ball on its fuselage. For audiences of the day, the branding made a lot of sense: of course it would be a Pan Am vehicle taking passengers to orbit.)

The Boeing contract, however, marked the high point of America's SST effort. Once America landed on the moon, spending more taxpayer money on the less ambitious SST project became less enticing. The iffy economics of supersonic transport were made even worse by the early 1970s oil shocks. Meanwhile, environmental opposition was growing, in part due to worries about sonic booms. Naming budgetary and environmental concerns, the House and Senate both voted to cancel funding for the SST program in May 1971.[71] In 1973, just four years after the British-French Concorde started flying, the FAA banned supersonic flight over the continental United States.[72]

And that was it. For nearly fifty years, there's been no supersonic airline industry here. We've wasted decades when we could have been researching and improving that technology—making it faster, safer, more affordable—while also competing with international rivals. Recently, several startups have announced plans to produce supersonic passenger jets, garnering some airline interest. "When I look several decades out, what I want is to be able to be anywhere in the world in four hours for 100 bucks," Boom CEO Blake Scholl told the *60 Minutes* news program in July 2022.[73] But there's been so much lost time, both for the technology and passengers. If we hadn't shut down the industry and if it had been constantly researching and innovating all this time, we could perhaps have large airliners far faster than the now-defunct Concorde and capable of carrying far more passengers, getting you from New York to LA in about thirty minutes.

To be fair, we did try one other major Up Wing effort at faster air transportation. On February 4, 1986, President Ronald Reagan gave his State of the Union address. It had been originally scheduled for a week earlier, on January 28, but earlier that day, the space shuttle *Challenger* exploded just after launch, killing all aboard. Reagan started the speech with a tribute to the "brave seven" and then promised, "We shall go forward." Later in the speech, after quoting the "Where we're going, we don't need roads" line from *Back to the Future*, Reagan offered some details on that commitment: "This nation remains fully committed to America's space program. We're going forward with our shuttle flights. We're going forward to build our space station." Oh, and one other thing: "We are going forward with research on a new Orient Express that could, by the end of the next decade, take off from Dulles Airport, accelerate up to 25 times the speed of sound, attaining low Earth orbit or flying to Tokyo within 2 hours." There was one small problem: no one in government was then working on developing a hypersonic passenger plane. What the Defense Advanced Research Projects Agency *was* doing was developing a hypersonic space plane that was intended to succeed the SR-71 Blackbird, a spy plane that could travel at more than three times the speed of sound. But after Reagan's speech, the experimental and secretive military project became the massive National Aero-Space Plane project. But the evolution from spy plane to passenger airliner meant costs ballooned.[74] The program was eventually canceled by President Bill Clinton in 1993 after spending almost $2 billion to develop a prototype. But what if it hadn't been canceled? What if the research had continued? A couple of billion bucks wasn't that significant of a federal expenditure, even thirty years ago. In *The Imagineers of War*, Sharon Weinberger quotes one engineer from the original military program who thinks Copper Canyon would've eventually allowed payloads to reached orbit for far less than what SpaceX reusable rockets can do today. If the National Aero-Space Plane project had gone forward, maybe today's space boom happens decades ago.

An even more intriguing counterfactual involves energy. Nuclear fusion has been a longtime dream of environmental worriers—at least those who aren't against greater prosperity—and sci-fi writers. Nuclear fusion would generate an inexhaustible supply of zero-carbon energy in much the same way as the sun: smooshing atoms together rather than splitting them as happens with nuclear fission. And no long-lived, radioactive nuclear waste. "[B]eyond fission lies fusion—the welding together of light atoms such as hydrogen and lithium," Arthur C. Clarke writes in *Profiles of the Future*.[75] This is the reaction that drives the stars themselves; we have reproduced it on earth, but have not tamed it. When we have done so, our power problems will have been solved forever."

Clarke thought the 1990s were a good target date for nuclear fusion when he made that prediction in the 1960s. Of course, the joke about fusion is that it's thirty years away and always will be. But recent advances in material science, artificial intelligence, and nuclear science itself have led to a crop of fusion startups funded by billions in venture capital. The consensus of those entrepreneurs is that commercial fusion power is possible by the 2030s. And in December 2022, Lawrence Livermore National Laboratory announced it created a fusion reaction—firing 192 giant lasers at a fuel pellet the size of a pencil eraser—that produced more energy than it consumed, or "net energy gain." In a press conference, U.S. secretary of energy Jennifer Granholm called the accomplishment "one of the most impressive scientific feats of the 21st century."[76]

But imagine if generating a fusion reaction had been one of the most impressive feats of the late twentieth century, as Clarke predicted. Maybe that would've happened had the technology for decades been as big a federal research priority as Project Apollo was in the 1960s with years of massive government investment. Fusion might already be a big part of America's power portfolio. But nuclear fusion wasn't the new Apollo. Nothing was. That's why it's still a trope of political campaign ads to highlight the moon landing of a half century ago as the prime example of American greatness. As Arthur Turrell, a plasma physicist whose book *The Star Builders: Nuclear Fusion and the Race to Power the Planet* documents the effort to achieve nuclear fusion, told me soon after the breakthrough, "How fast technological progress goes depends on how much we, as a society, want it. Societal will and investment can speed up technology—just look at the development and deployment of vaccines during the [coronavirus pandemic]. Given that achieving fusion is perhaps the greatest technological challenge we've ever taken on as a species, funding for fusion to date has not been equal to the task. Progress could have been much faster."[77]

When Science Stops Taking Risks

While some bold ideas are underfunded, some are ignored despite massive potential. There are wondrous possibilities that have yet to happen because we never really tried. In 1989, two University of Utah chemists claimed a small tabletop experiment had generated a nuclear fusion reaction—no lasers involved![78] Their "cold fusion" breakthrough, if replicated, would profoundly change how humanity generated energy. Unfortunately, those results couldn't be replicated. The "science" of cold fusion fell into disrepute—right along with phrenology and alchemy—and all government funding stopped.[79] In 2019, Google announced that it has spent the previous four years running a secret $10 million experiment in cold fusion. Although the tech titan failed to make it work, the company said "finding breakthroughs requires risk-taking, and we contend that revisiting cold fusion is a risk worth taking."[80] It's a risk Washington has little interest in.

Another intriguing area where the lack of federal research funding has meant the loss of a potentially massive opportunity is nanotechnology. The (so far) fictional version of nanotech has become a staple of modern science fiction where the idea of gazillions of tiny molecular machines—all acting together en masse to do or create just about anything—works whenever a writer wants to put a scientific gloss on something that in earlier times might have been attributed to magic. In the Marvel Cinematic Universe, super-tiny nanomachines or "nanites"—*nano* is a Greek prefix meaning "dwarf," and a nanometer is a billionth of a meter—are what give the Black Panther's supersuit and Iron Man's super-armor many of their amazing abilities and properties. As described by engineer Eric Drexler in his 1986 book *Engines of Creation: The Coming Era of Nanotechnology*, these tiny, controllable, self-assembling machines would allow humanity to "build almost anything that the laws of nature allow to exist."[81] Molecular manufacturing could build a rocket engine from the atomic level up and also give it the ability to repair itself. Nanomachines inside the body could not only hunt down cancerous tumors but also repair human tissue and organs. With this sort of nanotech, every home could have a *Star Trek*–like food replicator, or something like the home "matter compiler" in Neal Stephenson's *The Diamond Age*, a kind of 3D printer that can turn inexpensive feedstock, rearranging the substance atom by atom, into a variety of goods. Drexlerian nanotech would be almost indistinguishable from magic.

But the version of nanotech funded by government is far less ambitious, merely a branch of material science. Human-made nanoparticles—they're also naturally occurring—can be found in a variety of commercial products, including waterproof fabrics, scratch-resistant coatings on camera lenses, and engine lubricants. There are nanoparticles in sunscreens, while carbon nanotubes make bikes stronger and lighter. Smartphones and superfast 5G wireless technology have also benefited from nanotech advances. Still, as *Wall Street Journal* columnist Christopher Mims has pointed out, "It's all still a far cry from the more outlandish past predictions about nanotech's future."[82] Many of those real-world examples, by the way, come from the government's National Nanotechnology Initiative, started in 2000 under President Clinton, with expanded funding under President George W. Bush in 2002.[83] And while the NNI was originally hyped as pursuing something like Drexlerian nanotech, it never did.[84] The decision not to was perhaps influenced by a desire to avoid criticism that it was researching a dangerous technology that could overwhelm the world in just the sort of "gray goo" scenario outlined by Bill Joy in his "Why the World Doesn't Need Us" essay for *Wired* magazine.

✦✦✦

Think of all the big scientific and technological advances and breakthroughs of recent years, among them CRISPR genetic editing, nuclear fusion, reusable rockets, and machine learning that can both predict the structure of proteins and create intelligent essays and breathtaking images from brief prompts. Now imagine all of those occurring two or three decades ago. Then there are advances and breakthroughs that might never happen because no effort is being made, such as with cold fusion and nanotechnology. But neither the various macroeconomic headwinds nor our policy mistakes provide a complete explanation of our current predicament. Yes, progress was harder than almost anyone imagined. But when progress failed to happen as expected, decade after decade—especially when it became clear our interventions weren't working as well as hoped—why didn't we work harder and smarter to make those Up Wing dreams come true anyway? Why did we let ourselves lose the future?

FIVE

Eco-Pessimism, Techno-Pessimism, and a Down Wing America

To fully understand why the postwar Up Wing era ended fifty years ago—and only briefly revived in the 1990s before slipping back into hibernation as the century turned—also means understanding *why* we let that Down Wing turn happen. Why didn't we do more to achieve all those marvelous dreams of what the future could be? To begin answering that question means looking back at 1970, the approximate end of economist Robert Gordon's special century and just a few years before the end of Up Wing 1.0 as I've defined the immediate postwar period. Gordon is hardly the only economist to fixate on that year. Yale University economist Ray Fair has noted an interesting historical coincidence. First, U.S. infrastructure spending as a percent of GDP began a steady decline around 1970, a pattern seen in no other rich country. "The United States appears to be a special case in this regard," Fair writes.[1] And at roughly the same time as America started ignoring its roads and bridges—not to mention advances such as high-speed rail and supersonic air transport—Washington started running big budget deficits. It has continued to do so ever since, except for a few years at the end of the twentieth century.

Fair argues the two trends provide evidence of a sustained change in national attitude: "The overall results suggest that the United States became less future-oriented beginning around 1970. This change has persisted." The reasoning here is straightforward enough: repairing your roof while the sun is shining and trimming spending before the bill collector calls require some foresight and the ability to place your current self in the shoes of your future self. And why did America seem to become less future-oriented in actions and attitudes—I would go further: becoming less likely to anticipate an optimistic future—around that time? Fair is "doubtful" the sustained shift can really be explained, not that he doesn't float some possible explanations:

> *The years 1968, 1969, and 1970 had many noticeable events: the early baby boomers moving into their 20s; the assassinations of Martin Luther King Jr. and Robert Kennedy; the beginning of the women's movement; the draft, the bombing of Cambodia, and unrest on college campuses; Woodstock; Stonewall. Did any of these increase the impatience of the country in a permanent way? There are likely stories that could be woven, undoubtedly more than one, but it is unclear whether anything could be tested. The question is probably too big, but the fact is interesting.*[2]

✦ ✦ ✦

Explaining the deep reasons for America's Down Wing shift reminds me of the various economic explanations for the Industrial Revolution: why it started when it did (the late eighteenth century) and where it did (England). There are lots of them, and they're not all mutually exclusive. Perhaps it was because England had the highest wages in the world and the cheapest energy thanks to abundant and easily accessible coal.[3] Industrialists had good reason, then, to replace labor with capital: the steam engine, the coke-fueled blast furnace, and various textile machines such as the spinning jenny, water frame, and power wheel. Perhaps it was the dissolution of the English monasteries, which created a market for lands that could then be more effectively commercialized.[4] Perhaps it was the discovery of the New World, particularly the accumulation of overseas slave wealth that could eventually provide financing for investment in marvelous new machines.[5]

Coal, monasteries, slaves. All factors supported to some degree by economic research. Now let me add another factor: belief about the future. Having positive yet broadly realistic images of the future seems essential to any society's health and progress. Just as an individual's future behavior is to some extent governed by his self-image of the kind of person he hopes to be and his dreams of what he hopes to accomplish, so too a society's. "The rise and fall of images of the future precedes or accompanies the rise and fall of cultures," writes Dutch futurist Frederik Polak in *The Image of the Future*, his 1961 treatise exploring how various ancient cultures envisioned the future.[6] "Any culture which finds itself in the condition of our present culture, turning aside from its own heritage of positive visions of the future, or actively at work in changing these positive visions into negative ones, has no future."[7] When he wrote those words, Polak was greatly concerned that postwar Europe lacked such a vision, having experienced the failures of liberal democracy and capitalism, as well as the brutal collectivism of communism and fascism. "Our time is the first in the memory of man which has produced no images of the future, or only negative ones."[8]

For most of humanity's existence, however, we envisioned neither utopia nor dystopia. The story we told ourselves about the future of this world was no story at all. Why would we even try? One day, one decade, one century was much like the one before and the one after. It was a universe of cycles—seasons came and went, empires rose and fell—but life for most people didn't change a whole lot. To outline a vision of the future that was different and worth taking action to create risked accusation of disrespecting the past and previous generations. American historian Carl Becker notes in his 1936 book *Progress and Power* that "a Philosopher could not grasp the modern idea of progress...until he was willing to abandon ancestor worship, until he analyzed away his inferiority complex toward the past, and realized that his own generation was superior to any yet known."[9] The ancient Greeks, for instance, conceived of the future in a fundamentally different way than the modern West. My Hellenic ancestors didn't "face the future" to see what was coming. They instead metaphorically had their backs turned to the future and faced the past, viewing what had already happened as a guide to what might happen next. (In his *History of the Peloponnesian War*, Thucydides writes, "The absence of romance in my history will, I fear, detract somewhat from its interest; but if it be judged useful by those inquirers who desire an exact knowledge of the past as an aid to the interpretation of the future, which in the course of human things must resemble if it does not reflect it, I shall be content.")[10] It was only by remembering what had come before and understanding the wisdom of those that lived through those ages that one could make sense of one's life and live it well. The classical thinkers would've thought it entirely sensible that their wisdom on astronomy, medicine, physics, and other sciences was still considered valid scholarship a millennium later.

But in the two centuries between Columbus sailing to the New World and the death of Isaac Newton in 1727, doubts arose about the wisdom of the ancients. If the natural philosophers of the past didn't know about the vast continent and peoples across the Atlantic or about gravity, what else might they not have known or gotten wrong? As Northwestern University economic historian Joel Mokyr has explained, "In the 16th and 17th centuries, there was a growing movement that said, 'You know what? These classical writers were wrong about lots of things.'...Even [with] the writings of Aristotle—whose work really was the gospel of physics for centuries—slowly people started criticizing Aristotle saying that 'Aristotle was wrong about this, and he was wrong about that.' People started saying 'These old people were very smart, but we are smarter.' And that takes a huge leap of faith to make that transition."[11] This newfound skepticism helped power the Scientific Revolution, the Enlightenment, and the rise of an Up Wing culture among the literate elite of Europe—astronomers, chemists, clergymen, doctors, engineers, mathematicians. A transnational "Republic of Letters"—they connected through letters delivered by trusted intermediaries such as friends, diplomats, and merchants—among the learned of fractured Europe saw the free exchange of novel notions about the natural world. At the core of this informal collective was the belief that observing, studying, and testing the world—what we would today call research in science and technology—could give humanity the power to radically improve the human condition. As Mokyr elaborates in *A Culture of Growth*, this belief was "the cultural breakthrough that made what came after possible."[12]

And what came after was the Industrial Revolution and the Great Acceleration in human welfare. On Independence Day, 1776, the total output of the thirteen American colonies was below $2,500 per person, adjusted for inflation.[13] Nearly a quarter millennium later, per person GDP for the United States has increased by nearly thirty times to $70,000.[14] In other words, output per person in one year back then was equal to the average American's output in just two weeks today. What's more, that simple calculation hardly captures the extent of change in our everyday lives. Even if you were among the richest people in early America—say, George Washington—you couldn't have purchased at any price a host of today's modern marvels, including air conditioning, an airline flight to London (or anywhere), antibiotics, proper dental care(!), internet, television, or a smartphone. What's more, U.S. life expectancy was half of what it is today.

Humanity's realization that it could contemplate a better future and employ its God-given agency to work toward that future led us to stop looking backward and start facing tomorrow with new optimism and confidence. All of which suggests the question driving this chapter: Did America—a nation built on Up Wing future optimism—come to the opposite realization in the early 1970s about its ability to create a wondrous future worth living in and thus worth inventing, innovating, and building? And if so, why?

America the Rich versus America the Beautiful

It's unremarkable that an increasingly affluent postwar America grew increasingly concerned about the natural environment. At a certain level of affluence, economists and political scientists find, people start assigning a greater value to clearer skies and cleaner water. They become more willing to accept the possible trade-offs, such as costlier energy or pricier consumer products, that come with government making pollution reduction a greater priority. Supporting this well-known preference are some psychological traits—also called "cognitive illusions"—about how we evaluate risk. One relevant illusion or bias is that of loss aversion, where the more you have, the more you fear losing what you have, and you tend to feel losses more strongly than gains. As a species, we place a huge value on safety and certainty. We easily panic when safety is threatened. And once a society reaches a certain level of affluence, finds research from Stanford University economist Charles I. Jones, safety even becomes a luxury good much like jewelry, automobiles, and home appliances.[15] The combo of wanting a cleaner environment and loss aversion creates what policy analyst Brink Lindsey has neatly termed the "anti-Promethean backlash," referencing the Greek god who was punished for stealing fire—which can be viewed as knowledge and technology—from his fellow divine beings and giving it to humanity.[16]

So there was always going to be an American environmental movement. It's also not surprising that Washington policymakers attempted to satisfy that increasingly revealed preference for a cleaner environment. In addition to the various factors mentioned by Yale economist Ray Fair as reflecting a changing attitude about the future, let me add this one: on New Year's Day 1970, Nixon signed the National Environmental Policy Act, mentioned in the previous chapter for its impact especially on building infrastructure in modern America, either quickly or inexpensively. Now the point of NEPA was not to shutter nuclear reactors, ground supersonic aviation, or derail construction of a nationwide high-speed train system. Many in Congress saw the bill merely as a toothless statement of congressional concern, and not much more. "For many legislators, undoubtedly, a vote for NEPA was symbolic—akin to a vote for motherhood and apple pie," writes Richard Liroff in *A National Policy for the Environment: NEPA and Its Aftermath*.[17]

And maybe in an alt-history America, that's exactly what NEPA would've been. One could imagine an environmental movement that fully embraced economic growth and technological progress to give us the resources and tools to create a cleaner and more prosperous planet. I'm thinking about something more akin to today's growing "eco-modernist movement" which advocates "humans use their growing social, economic, and technological powers to make life better for people, stabilize the climate, and protect the natural world."[18] (These folks love nuclear energy.) Eco-modernists view humanity as both the cause of and solution to our environmental problems. It sees climate change, for instance, fundamentally as a clean energy problem, not a problem of dirty consumerism ruining the planet through carbon pollution.

But that's not the Up Wing environmental movement America got. Rather what emerged in the 1970s was a thoroughly Down Wing movement that saw further human economic progress, driven by rapacious techno-capitalism, as undermining the long-term viability of Spaceship Earth, destructively taxing its "carrying capacity." Earth was a place of scarce resources growing ever scarcer. Faster economic growth and technological progress would only accelerate humanity's rush toward creating an unlivable planet with a dying biosphere and chaotic climate. Even today, plenty of environmentalists, whether actual activists or just concerned citizens, think Greta Thunberg shows wisdom beyond her years when she scolds, "You have stolen my dreams and my childhood with your empty words...People are suffering. People are dying. Entire ecosystems are collapsing. We are in the beginning of a mass extinction, and all you can talk about is money and fairy tales of eternal economic growth. How dare you!"[19] While an environmental movement was inevitable, this Down Wing version was not. Why we didn't get Up Wing environmentalism is an interesting question—and an important one given the impact of the Down Wing version we *did* get in the second half of the twentieth century and that largely continues through the first decades of the twenty-first.

None of this is to say a cleaner environment is unimportant. Let me highlight a particular Up Wing impulse to want a cleaner environment given the focus of this book: economic growth, something which has a strong positive correlation to national average IQ. High IQ individuals tend to be more patient, more cooperative, more skillful, and more likely to support pro-market, pro-trade policies (pro-prosperity policies).[20] Given that correlation, it's good we no longer burn leaded gasoline in cars. A 2022 study found

American children lost an average of 2.6 IQ points before 1996 due to lead in the environment, mostly due to inhaling the exhaust from cars using leaded gas.[21] Keep in mind, however, that the driving force behind banning lead was to protect humans, not to protect the environment as an intrinsic good apart from humans. (Indeed, the 1970 Clean Air Act is one environmental law that seems to have generated obvious pro-growth benefits.)[22] We primarily need a clean environment so humans can live longer, live healthier, and prosper in an Up Wing world of abundant and diverse plant and animal life.

The Environmental Fallout from the Atomic Age

So why did we get a Down Wing environmental movement? One culprit was atomic weapons, but not mostly due to the World War II bombings of the Japanese cities of Hiroshima and Nagasaki. In March 1954, an American nuclear weapons test at Bikini Atoll, part of the Marshall Islands, produced a blast that was three times bigger than U.S. atomic scientists expected. About ninety minutes after the test, code-named Castle Bravo, Japanese tuna fishing boat *Lucky Dragon 5* was contaminated with radioactive fallout from the massive explosion.[23] The crew members suffered from radiation sickness, burns, and other health problems as a result of their exposure, with eventually one death. This was a huge global news story, as was emerging research about birth defects suffered by the children of Hiroshima and Nagasaki survivors, who had been exposed in utero. Still, public concern about radiation and nuclear fallout from testing or war didn't immediately lead to a rejection of nuclear power. But the seeds of deep nuclear doubt were planted. Moreover, rising nuclear fears helped kick off a broader question about the benefits of technological progress and economic growth. Remember, the Atomic Age was technologically foundational to postwar expectations of growing prosperity. But the "increasing awareness of the destructiveness of atom bombs and the threat that their proliferation posed for the future of civilization greatly stimulated among the public a counterreaction to technology," writes historian Thomas P. Hughes in *American Genesis: A Century of Invention and Technological Enthusiasm, 1870–1970*.[24]

It wasn't just radiation, whether from nuclear testing or a military conflict, that worried the first wave of postwar environmentalists. It was much bigger than that. They feared where the vast technological systems that enabled nuclear weapons and nuclear energy, as well as the new space program—what President Eisenhower described as the military-industrial (and university) complex—were taking America. "The Manhattan Project, with its systematic linking of military funding, management, and contract letting, industrial, university, and government research laboratories, and numerous manufacturers, became the model for these massive technological systems," Hughes writes.[25] They feared the United States was turning into one giant Manhattan Project, one that would eventually extend into the solar system.

The War That Led to the War on Progress

As "what if" kinds of scenarios go, the following is a favorite of military historians and alt-history writers alike: what if the Vietnam War had never happened, had ended with a clear American victory, or had at least ended in the early 1960s rather than 1970s? One could reasonably speculate about at least a few key differences between what *did* happen versus what *might have* happened. For example, war or no war, there almost certainly would've been a powerful new "youth culture" or counterculture given the demographic influx of baby boomers. But this energetic societal force might have been less rebellious without the military draft and the risk of dying in a distant, unpopular conflict. Likewise, a war that ended early with American withdrawal—just sixteen thousand troops fighting when President John F. Kennedy was assassinated versus more than a half million at the peak in 1969—might have initially avoided domestic political upheaval, but it also might have proven true the famous "domino theory" as Vietnam's quick victory could have created momentum for communist revolution throughout Southeast Asia.

One of the more interesting sci-fi counterfactuals about this premise can be found in the 2019 HBO limited series *Watchmen*, a sequel to the 1986 comic book series of the same name. In that universe, President Richard M.

Nixon deploys the seemingly all-powerful (and all-blue) superhero Doctor Manhattan to Vietnam in March 1971. By the end of June, North Vietnam offers its unconditional surrender. Nixon's popularity soars. He easily wins a second term, then several more after the Twenty-Second Amendment is abolished. (Among the many Democratic rivals he defeats is Robert Redford.) In October 1985, the Vietnam Admission Act takes effect, making Vietnam the fifty-first state. In the comic, a Captain America homage, the Comedian, tells Doctor Manhattan, "I mean, if we'd lost this war…I dunno. I think it might have driven us a little crazy, y'know? As a country. But thanks to you, we didn't, right?"[26]

Unfortunately, we did lose in Vietnam, and it could be argued that the defeat did drive us crazy. It certainly helped lead to decades of political polarization that could be seen as the start of the multi-decade "culture war" that continues to plague America. *The other side isn't just wrong; they are evil and must be defeated or America will collapse!* It's also plausible the Vietnam War played a key role in creating an environmental movement that contributed to America's Down Wing shift both in attitudes and actions. With that conflict in Southeast Asia, the first generation of postwar environmentalists seemingly saw their fears realized. It turned out that America's massive and sophisticated technological system of systems, what technology philosopher Lewis Mumford termed the "Megamachine," didn't need atomic weapons to unleash devastation.[27] According to Hughes:

> *The use by the U.S. military…of technological systems to lay waste Vietnam only heightened the public's anger toward, and anxieties about, technology.…Thoughtful Americans could no longer glibly associate technology with incandescent lamps, Model T's, and "better things for better living."…[Activists and intellectuals] began to see modern technology, especially large technological systems, as the common cause of the cultural and social maladies about which they were protesting. Chemical corporations producing the napalm and destructive herbicides used in Vietnam also made, for example, the pesticides, herbicides, and pollutants fouling the environment at home. Corporation heads presiding*

over large systems of production shuttled back and forth to the Department of Defense, where they managed systems of destruction. Talk of efficiency, order, centralization, and systematization was common to the military and to industry.[28]

Many of Mumford's themes on the militarization of science are on full display in the 1971 film *The Andromeda Strain*, based on the 1969 novel of the same name by Michael Crichton. What begins as a thrilling scientific procedural—a team of scientists at a secret government laboratory investigate a deadly microorganism returned from space by a crashed satellite—turns into a cynical commentary on the Megamachine.[29] The scientists eventually realize the Apollo-era space mission was really a Pentagon military project to find new biological weapons and their lab—full of tech first developed for astronauts—built for germ warfare research. "Another giant leap for mankind?" one scientist sarcastically asks.

But you didn't need to be a countercultural activist or Ivy League intellectual to find something compelling in the Megamachine thesis. Americaland wasn't exactly turning into Disneyland's Tomorrowland. Economic growth and technological progress had downsides the Disney imagineers never presented. Two weeks before Thanksgiving in 1959, the government set off the Great Cranberry Scare with a warning that the popular holiday fruit might be contaminated with cancer-causing weed killer.[30] It received huge media coverage, leading to supermarket chains taking cranberries off their shelves, restaurants removing them from menus, and states banning their sale. A pair of events at the end of the 1960s are also worth noting. Both reinforced the notion that we were bad caretakers of the planet. In January 1969, an explosion at a Union Oil rig off the coast of Santa Barbara, California, caused 3 million gallons of crude oil to spill into the ocean.[31] Then in June, a section of the Cuyahoga River near Cleveland caught fire.[32] Those incidents created a receptive audience for quasi-scientific tales of economic doom, starting with Rachel Carson's 1962 bestseller *Silent Spring* about the dangers to the biosphere from synthetic pesticides. The book was a key catalyst in the rapid emergence of eco-pessimism during the 1960s. On its fiftieth anniversary, the *New York Times* wrote that Carson influenced the environmental movement as no one had since the nineteenth century's most celebrated hermit, Henry David Thoreau, wrote about Walden Pond: "We still see the effects of unfettered human intervention through Carson's eyes."[33]

The combination of increasing public concern about radiation and chemicals was catalyzed into the Megamachine thesis by Vietnam. And guess, what? The Soviet Union was also ruled by its own Megamachine. The Megamachine was bigger than the Cold War. Hughes, commenting on the views of technology philosopher Jacques Ellul, writes, "All-embracing technological systems had swallowed up the capitalistic and socialistic economies, and were, for Ellul, a far greater threat to our freedom of action than authoritarian politics. Denying the primacy of politics, Ellul argued that the state is no longer as influential a factor in shaping lives and history as technological systems. For him, political activity is unreality; technology is reality."[34] The flavor of this view of the global Megamachine was perhaps best captured in a monologue written by Paddy Chayefsky for the 1976 dark comedy film *Network*:

> *There is no America. There is no democracy. There is only IBM, and ITT, and AT&T, and DuPont, Dow, Union Carbide, and Exxon. Those are the nations of the world today. What do you think the Russians talk about in their councils of state, Karl Marx? They get out their linear programming charts, statistical decision theories, minimax solutions, and compute the price-cost probabilities of their transactions and investments, just like we do. We no longer live in a world of nations and ideologies, Mr. Beale. The world is a college of corporations, inexorably determined by the immutable bylaws of business. The world is a business, Mr. Beale. It has been since man crawled out of the slime. And our children will live, Mr. Beale, to see that perfect world in which there's no war or famine, oppression or brutality. One vast and ecumenical holding company, for whom all men will work to serve a common profit, in which all men will hold a share of stock. All necessities provided, all anxieties tranquilized, all boredom amused.*[35]

To the environmental megamachinists, the big and the complex and the connected were the enemies of humanity; the small and the simple and self-sufficient our allies. The future would be a human-sized one where humanity lived in harmony with nature. (That, even though humanity has been altering nature since the Agricultural Revolution.) "Wisdom demands a new orientation of science and technology toward the organic, the gentle, the elegant and beautiful," writes economist E. F. Schumacher in what became a key text for the Down Wing environmentalists, the 1973 book *Small Is Beautiful: Economics as if People Mattered*.[36] Schumacher's writings and philosophy are an obvious influence on the 1975 futurist novel *Ecotopia* by Ernest Callenbach, which imagines a new countercultural country formed by the secession of Northern California, Oregon, and Washington from the rest of the materialistic United States.[37] Really, it's a giant Portland where everyone wears natural fibers and eats organic, locally grown food.

Back then, the whimsical and countercultural grooviness of Callenbach and Schumacher seemed to be supported by hard science. Whatever wisdom demanded, as the latter put it, it seemed to the environmental megamachinists that Earth itself was demanding much the same thing. *The Limits to Growth* was published in 1972. Although *Limits* was commissioned by the Club of Rome (an international group of technocrats and businesspeople), it was generated at MIT using computer simulations to outline the long-term impact of global resource constraints amid continuing economic and population growth. *Limits* tells a story of shocking future scarcity, of a world running out of everything and then civilization running down. Down Wing forever. With reserves of key industrial minerals exhausted by the early twenty-first century and with poverty and malnutrition expanding, the "most probable" result of current trends "will be a rather sudden and uncontrollable decline in both population and industrial capacity."[38]

The original *Limits* was translated into at least thirty languages and sold millions of copies. Not only was *Limits* well timed—it was published during a period of rising pollution concerns and right before the 1973 oil crisis—but its frightening forecasts were given plausibility by their origin in early-days computer modeling at MIT. Some experts were unimpressed. "It is hardly surprising that dead rabbits are pulled out of the hat when nothing but dead bunnies have been put in" is how Nobel laureate economist William Nordhaus once described the primitive modeling of *Limits*.[39] But *Limits* offered a prescription as well as a diagnosis. Averting catastrophe required a global economic equilibrium, a state of non-growth. The book longed for "a totally new form of human society—one that would be built to last for generations." What was needed was "a realistic, long-term goal [to]...guide mankind to the equilibrium society"—and the powers of government and personal transformation to get there. But to be clear, this new society would be a poorer one. Referring to *Limits II*, the twenty-year update released in 1992, Nordhaus points out that the report's "proposals would limit our material aspirations to attaining the living standards of Somalia or Chad."[40]

Our Image of the Future Turns Dark

The impact of the emergence of Down Wing eco-pessimism goes far beyond how it influences public policy to this day, including the persistent rejection of nuclear energy and regulation driven by the "better safe than sorry" precautionary principle, which itself is driven by the cognitive bias of loss aversion. Also important, but less well understood, has been the impact of the Down Wing shift in futurist thinking, another result of the emergence of the eco-pessimist environmental movement. In the 1960s, futurists such as Isaac Asimov, Arthur C. Clarke, Alvin Toffler, and Herman Kahn were celebrities and an important source of Up Wing optimism and ideas for policymakers. But the environmental movement put the profession in full Down Wing mode. To be a futurist by the late 1970s was to be more like the prophets of ancient times, exhorting repentance for the sin of reckless overconsumption—or else doom would follow. We must learn to live more poorly, as *Limits* demanded, and if we also avoided nuclear war and stopped having so many babies, maybe a rump of humanity might survive. (Understood within that claim, given the environmental movement's deep roots in the early twentieth-century eugenics movement, was the notion that "right" people must be the ones to survive.) "The battle to feed all of humanity is over," declared the famous opening line of *The Population Bomb*, the 1968 bestseller by Paul Ehrlich, an entomologist at Stanford University.[41] It predicted worldwide famine in the 1970s and 1980s due to overpopulation. He promised "hundreds of millions of people are going to starve to death" and that "nothing can prevent a substantial increase in the world death rate." It says something about the zeitgeist of the era that from 1968 through 1981, Ehrlich appeared twenty times on *The Tonight Show Starring Johnny Carson* versus just twice for that group of Up Wing futurists, one each for Asimov and Toffler.[42]

The decline of Up Wing futurism since the 1960s, other than the brief 1990s revival, has deprived us of a source of optimistic images of the future and left Hollywood as the leading source of futurism, at least until the rise of Silicon Valley in the 1990s—which didn't have to be a bad thing. Often when science fiction is praised, especially in film or on television, it's because some technological breakthrough or future setting is used to warn about the dangers of an emerging technology (AI run amok) or to highlight some worrisome, ripped-from-the-headlines social trends (inequality, hostility toward immigrants) from a different perspective and perhaps where it might lead. But while those things can be valuable, "political" science fiction might not be the genre's highest calling. As technology analyst Dan Wang puts it, science fiction "is most useful when it can be used to spur hard work to build the future. Science fiction has the capacity to inspire by setting the vision of a radically better future, and by making it clear that the future won't happen unless we put in the work."[43]

All this assumes art is of civilizational importance even in times of economic, geopolitical, and technological tumult. But of course it is. Always has been. "Great nations," posited nineteenth-century English art critic John Ruskin, "write their autobiographies in three manuscripts, the book of their deeds, the book of their words, and the book of their art. Not one of these books can be understood unless we read the two others, but of the three the only trustworthy one is the last."[44] (Art historian Kenneth Clark adds his own twist on Ruskin in the magisterial 1969 documentary series *Civilisation*: "If I had to say which was telling the truth about Society, a speech by a minister of housing or the actual buildings put up in his time, I should believe the buildings.")[45]

America's vision of the future as told through its popular art and culture certainly shows an interest in the future, but too rarely is it a future in which anyone would choose to live. The techno-optimism of the 1960s seen in the books of Isaac Asimov and Arthur C. Clarke, television shows such as *The Jetsons* and *Star Trek*, and the film *2001: A Space Odyssey* was by decade's end being joined and eventually overwhelmed by cynical and dystopian competitors. George Jetson meet George Taylor, an astronaut stranded in a future where it's abundantly clear that intelligent primates really should not be part of any techno-optimist vision. Portrayed by Charlton Heston, Taylor will go down in cinematic history for his famous film-ending wail in 1968's *Planet of the Apes*, "You blew it up! Ah, damn you! God damn you all to hell!"[46] While Taylor was referencing the end of human civilization from nuclear holocaust, he might have well been talking about America as a country whose future orientation was expressed in its culture. The 1970s was a series of techno-pessimist films—Heston was in several—showing failed futures riven by overpopulation, environmental degradation, plague, atomic holocaust, robots gone wild, and intelligent apes bearing a grudge. Sure, the biggest hit of the era was pretty upbeat, but it took place a long time ago, in a galaxy far, far away. The result: a sort of self-reinforcing doom loop or "idea trap" in which bad ideas and bad stories lead to bad policy, bad policy leads to bad growth, and bad growth cements bad ideas and encourages more bad stories.

When a more Down Wing image of the future began emerging from the Up Wing 1960s, it was mostly about one specific type of existential threat: nuclear war. In addition to *Planet of the Apes*, nuclear war was a recurring theme in *The Twilight Zone* television anthology series. And there were two films about atomic holocausts in 1964 that had themes and a character inspired by Herman Kahn: *Doctor Strangelove* and *Fail Safe*. But fear of a radioactive future eventually started feeding into the broader concerns of the emerging environmental movement and helped create a more general Down Wing perspective on the future. The problem was not merely the existence of doomsday devices created by an innately violent and aggressive humanity, but rather the existence of humanity itself. The more of us there were, the worse the world would be. It's a view clearly seen in *Soylent Green*, starring Heston and Edward G. Robinson. Watching the 1973 film is like opening a cinematic time capsule filled with the era's post–*Silent Spring* anxieties. It's all there: overpopulation, hunger, global warming and oppressive humidity, stark inequality, depleted natural resources, widespread euthanasia—not to mention a solid performance by Heston as our laconic guide through this hellscape of sticky squalor. No sign of much technological progress in that world, much less technology run amok. Just stagnation along with a growing population that science never quite figured out how to feed. An intentional return to Malthus by Hollywood. In the 2018 essay "Malthus at the Movies: Science, Cinema, and Activism around Z.P.G. and Soylent Green," Jesse Olszynko-Gryn and Patrick Ellis write that Heston was concerned about overpopulation and used his influence with MGM to get *Soylent Green* produced.[47] (The script was loosely based on *Make Room! Make Room!*, a 1966 science fiction novel by Harry Harrison):

> *Heston was particularly concerned with overpopulation, a then bipartisan issue supported not only by leftwing environmentalists, but also by Republican conservationists and conservative anti-immigration activists. According to his biographer, Soylent Green was "the only film that Heston made with the express purpose of advancing a political message.... Heston was able to push Harrison's novel through the studio system, but only after the commercial success of Skyjacked, in which he starred."*

✦ ✦ ✦

A shift toward dystopianism and techno-pessimism became a dominant mass media theme that has continued through the present. To be sure, the optimist strain never fully disappeared. *Star Trek* is arguably the most successful entertainment franchise ever. But mostly what Hollywood brings us are portrayals of devastation from climate change, killer AI, or zombie plagues. That dark turn of American science fiction—and continued journey deeper into the gloom—speaks to concerns about today and anxieties about tomorrow, as well as a lack of confidence in our ability and desire to fashion a brighter future. Or even to simply imagine one. As sci-fi author William Gibson told the *New York Times* in 2020, "In my childhood, the 21st century was constantly referenced. You'd see it once every day, and it often had an exclamation point. We don't seem to have, culturally, a sense of futurism that way anymore. It sort of evaporated."[48]

We only seem consistently capable of creating images of wrecked futures, so much so that our failure has become cliche. The popular TV Tropes website is an encyclopedic compilation of common storytelling motifs and themes, including many categories about television programs—as well as films, books, comics, and video games—that depict life in a failed fictional future. Among them: "Dystopia," "Techno Dystopia," "Dystopia Justifies the Means," "Dark World," "Future is Shocking," "Future Scares Me," "Ominous Message from the Future," "False Utopia," and "Zombie Apocalypse." Even in the era of "premium television," where bigger budgets permit cinematic-level special effects, much of science fiction falls into the broad category of "20 Minutes into the Future," which doesn't take place in the present but also not so far into the future that it's not immediately obvious that the story takes place in "the future." As TV Tropes describes: "This genre is perfect for exploring unsettling realities and extrapolating just a bit on current trends such as inequality, intolerance, and creeping authoritarianism.... typically a linear extrapolation of national malaise or existing crises."[49] Examples include *The Handmaid's Tale*, *Westworld*, and, perhaps most on point, *Black Mirror*, a British anthology devoted to creating near-future dystopias. "The dearth of optimistic visions of the future, at least in the United States, is central to the psychic atmosphere of this bleak era," writes *New York Times* opinion writer Michelle Goldberg in an early 2020 piece, "The Darkness Where the Future Should Be."[50] Perhaps the creators of all this dystopian art justify their pessimism by persuading themselves that their pessimistic visions are warning society about existential dangers. I think film critic Tasha

Robinson is closer to the truth when she writes that these filmmakers and writers actually "encourage passive fatalism and 'It has to get worse before it gets better' thinking."

✦ ✦ ✦

Underlying the rapid advance of human progress over the past quarter millennium has been a powerful optimism about tomorrow combined with what the sociologist Elise Boulding has described as a "utopian sense of human empowerment."[51] We really used to believe we could invent the future. Now, not so much. According to Boulding: "In eras when pessimism combines with a sense of cosmic helplessness, the quality of human intentionality declines and, with it, the quality of imagery of the not-yet. Societies in that condition live bounded by the present, with no social dynamic for change available to them." Thanks to the emerging environmental movement, America's vision of the future changed for the worse. Too many Americans began to believe and act as if growth were only possible with environmental degradation. Technological progress was more dangerous than we could have imagined. The pursuit of Up Wing abundance, a capitalist consumerist suicide pact for all of humanity.

SIX

Today's Down Wing Enemies of Up Wing Progress

In 1900, sponge divers off the coast of the Greek island of Antikythera came across a two-thousand-year-old sunken Roman cargo ship.[1] The wreckage was filled with art objects such as bronze and marble statues. Among the less obviously interesting items retrieved was an unremarkable lump of corroded bronze. Not long after, however, a closer examination found the greenish lump contained bronze plates to which were adhered clock-like gears and a protractor-like ring seemingly divided into degrees. A few deciphered words on what came to be called the Antikythera mechanism, probably built between 200 and 60 BCE, suggested it was some sort of astronomical instrument.[2] Modern imaging systems have discovered enough intriguing details over the past two decades that the mechanism is commonly classified as the first computer. It was able to predict solar eclipses and organize the calendar into the four-year cycles of the Olympiad, forerunner of the modern Olympic Games.[3] The mechanism was more sophisticated than any known device for at least a millennium afterward. And it was almost certainly not the only one in existence. "We believe that this mechanism cannot have been the first such device since it is so sophisticated and complex," the *New York Times* quoted one expert as saying in 2008.[4] "And we don't understand why this extraordinary technology apparently disappeared, [only] later to emerge in the great astronomical clocks of the 14th century onwards." Yale University science historian Derek de Solla Price, who co-wrote a major analysis of the Antikythera mechanism in 1974, urged historians to "completely rethink our attitudes toward ancient Greek technology. Men who could have built this could have built almost any mechanical device they wanted to."[5]

✦ ✦ ✦

Those ambitious Up Wing forecasts of the 1960s and '90s weren't crazy. They could have happened—or, if not those *exactly* (I've always doubted the infatuation with supersmart apes in Up Wing 1.0), at least many equally amazing advances could have happened. We just needed the rapid pace of technological progress and productivity growth of those decades to have continued. Not easy, but also not impossible. But let's take the idea further: what if we had been living in an Up Wing world for, say, the past millennium or maybe even two? We might be looking at a civilization so different as to challenge the imagination of even the most visionary science fiction writers. (*Star Trek*, after all, is supposed to take place only a few hundred years from now.) In that scenario, we might've already met and solved some of the biggest challenges we currently face: chronic diseases such as cancer and dementia, global poverty, climate change, and existential risk from both plague and space objects. Humanity might be well along its dispersion throughout the solar system and beyond.

The website Future Timeline was started in 2008 by London writer and futurist William James Fox.[6] The imaginative thinkers there see humanity in the year 3000 as far along toward becoming a type 2 civilization on the Kardashev scale, which measures technological advancement by the amount of energy a civilization can employ.[7] Humanity today, by contrast, is only nearing level 1. That designation means we could use and store all the energy located on this planet. (So still a ways to go.) A level 2 civilization, by contrast, can channel and employ all the radiated energy of a star. It might do this, perhaps, via a vast mega-megaproject such as constructing a "Dyson sphere" shell (named for mathematician and physicist Freeman Dyson, who first theorized the idea in 1959) or a swarm of artificial structures around the Sun to collect its energy.[8] "Imagine the energy crisis of a really advanced planetary civilization," astronomer Carl Sagan says. "They've used up all their fuels, they depend on solar power...An enormous amount of energy is generated by the local star, but most of the star's light doesn't fall on their planet. So perhaps, they would build a shell, to surround their star, and harvest every photon of sunlight. Such beings, such civilizations, would bear little resemblance to anything we know."[9] See what could be accomplished without NEPA!

Why Didn't the Ancient Greek Land on the Moon or Invent the iPhone?

Of course, these are only speculations, perhaps bordering on or even exceeding the fanciful—even if the physics works in theory. My point in highlighting them is to give some sense of the scope of what humanity might have already accomplished in 2023 had the Industrial Revolution not begun 250 years ago in northern Europe but a thousand or two thousand years earlier, perhaps somewhere else on the globe. Why not an Industrial Revolution in ancient Greece, for instance, as the historian de Solla Price suggested wasn't impossible? Economic historians offer several possibilities as to why ancient societies—not just Greece, but also especially Rome and China—failed to take off, as later happened in eighteenth-century England and Western Europe. Some suggest slavery undercut the incentive to pursue labor-saving innovation. Preindustrial society also had too much respect for the wisdom of their ancestors, as I noted earlier. More fundamentally, these early false starts also were stymied by a lack of basic scientific knowledge. China, Greece, and Rome just didn't know enough to sustain their brief bouts of progress. According to economic historian Joel Mokyr: "The huge amount of economic growth that we have experienced in the last 200 years is first and foremost the result of the fact that we know so much more than people did in 1500....We understand physics better, we understand chemistry better, we understand biology better, and we manipulate this knowledge and harness it to our needs."[10]

Advanced economies today don't have slavery, while they do have vast scientific establishments devoted to discovery, even if it's getting harder to do. One common element that connects the past to today is that some people oppose growth and the necessary disruption it generates. Progress has always had its enemies. "One reason economic growth was stagnant for millennia is that the world was caught in a technology trap, in which labor-replacing technology was consistently and vigorously resisted for fear of its destabilizing force," writes economist Carl Benedikt Frey.[11] Emperor Tiberius executed rather than rewarded a man who had invented unbreakable glass, "fearing the possibility of angry workmen rebelling."[12] In 1397, the city of Cologne banned machines that pressed pinheads after tailors complained. Queen Elizabeth I declined to grant a patent to the inventor of the stocking-frame knitting machine, worrying that the invention would bring her subjects to "ruin by depriving them of employment, thus making them beggars."[13] And as Frey explained to me, "Craft skills were a source of political clout. They didn't have any interest in technologies that threatened their jobs and incomes. And, fearing social unrest, monarchs of governments typically sided with the guilds rather than pioneers of industry, fearing that they might challenge the political status quo."[14] The Down Wingers of old, such as the textile machinery–wrecking Luddites in early nineteenth-century England, only started to fail politically when governments started to fear losing wars to richer technologically superior rivals and thus started siding with innovators and disruptors.

✦ ✦ ✦

The monarchs and guilds are long gone, and rich economies compete intensely across a range of industries. So who are today's enemies of progress and growth? There are many things I, as a conservative, think are Down Wing about center-left Democrats, especially when it comes to taxes and regulation broadly. That said, President Joe Biden's infrastructure bill and 2022 science investment bill could meet approval from Up Wingers on the left and right. The administration has also been supportive of nuclear power. Energy secretary Jennifer Granholm has repeatedly praised nuclear as "clean energy" and vital to creating good-paying jobs, supporting our energy transition, and "saving our planet." The Inflation Reduction Act, signed in August 2022, includes clean energy tax credits that apply to advanced nuclear energy, as well as tax credits for clean hydrogen production that includes hydrogen produced using nuclear energy.[15] But other actions have been taken to appease environmentalists still in 1970s Down Wing mode. Not only does the Biden administration's trade policy continue that of its predecessor, but it reversed decent Trump administration reforms to the National Environmental Protection Act.[16] Those reforms had exempted many projects from review, shortened the time frames for conducting those reviews, and instructed federal agencies to ignore "indirect" environmental impacts, such as those affecting the climate. But to earn the label "Down Wing enemy of Up Wing progress," you need to be far more extreme.

The Down Wing Right Wing. Here's another fascinating alt-history scenario, perhaps almost as intriguing as America winning the Vietnam War. What if former House Speaker Newt Gingrich had won the 2012 Republican presidential nomination and then defeated incumbent President Barack Obama to become the 45th president? Whatever Gingrich might have done about taxes or Social Security reform, restoring America as a spacefaring nation might well have been a top priority. During the real-world GOP primaries, he promised to build a permanent American base and mining site on the moon by the end of his second term as president. Someday, he added, Luna might even be the fifty-first state. (Sorry, Puerto Rico.)[17] It was a bold campaign promise, but then again Gingrich was a longtime devotee of futurism, particularly of futurist Alvin Toffler.[18] His rivals, however, mocked the idea as unserious, while some in the media treated it as a weird gaffe. Mitt Romney, the eventual nominee that year, remarked, "The idea that corporate America wants to go off to the moon and build a colony there, it may be a big idea, but it's not a good idea."[19]

It's a good thing Elon Musk was probably too busy building SpaceX to watch that debate. (I also think he was more of a liberal back then, though still an Up Winger.) That said, Romney's skepticism shouldn't have been surprising. Part of traditional conservatism is a healthy respect for, well, *tradition* and the slow trial-and-error process of societal experimentation that created the modern world and its institutions. With this respect comes a disdain for those who would sweep away tradition when in the thrall of a new philosophy, plan, or, yes, technology. William F. Buckley Jr., in his 1955 mission statement for *National Review* magazine, designates opposition to "energetic social innovators, plugging their grand designs" as a key reason for the publication's launch.[20] Around the same time, conservative theorist Russell Kirk wrote an essay calling the automobile a "mechanical Jacobin…[that from] courting customs to public architecture…tears the old order apart."[21] Similarly, some on the right today are skeptical of self-driving cars for reasons that have nothing to do with their safety or long-haul truckers losing their jobs. In a 2017 essay, *National Review* editor Charles Cooke wrote of a driverless future in Orwellian terms: "The car, far from serving as a liberator, would become a telescreen on wheels—an FBI-approved bug, to be slipped beneath the chassis in plain sight of the surveilled. At a stroke, my autonomy would be gone."[22]

So maybe Ronald Reagan was a genetic error in the DNA code of American conservatism, much as Mikhail Gorbachev was in Soviet Communism. Not only did Reagan have an expansive view of human potential—he loved a Thomas Paine quote that many conservatives hate: "We have it within our power to begin the world over again"—but he also embraced a techno-solutionist ethos.[23] It was technology that Reagan saw as the means to end the threat of nuclear annihilation through the Strategic Defense Initiative. It was technology that made mockery of the Malthusian predictions of the limits to growth and predictions of global famine. "We're breaking through the material conditions of existence to a world where man creates his own destiny," Reagan told the students at Moscow State University back in 1988.[24]

So what happened to the Up Wing, Reagan variant of conservatism? The first-order answer is pretty straightforward. Conservatives in the 2000s began to see the American technology sector as just another left-wing interest group. The key moment here was the 2008 presidential campaign, when the emergence of social media made techies key players in politics as never before—especially in Barack Obama's insurgent campaign. And as president, according to the *New York Times*, Obama "stoked deep and meaningful connections with scores of entrepreneurs in Silicon Valley: Steve Jobs, Bill Gates, Mark Zuckerberg."[25] Republican concern about Silicon Valley intensified after the 2016 election of Donald Trump. Not only were Big Tech bosses almost uniformly anti-Trump, but it seemed to the right that content moderation on social media was directed at suppressing conservative speech. Moreover, tech progress and economic growth will always involve disruption and dislocation. So there's a natural tension between many Up Wing policies and the GOP's new working-class voters who often see themselves as victims of change—as with global trade—rather than beneficiaries. "A country is more than an economy," said populist activist and Trump supporter Steve Bannon.[26] It's not hard to see this new national populist GOP opposing job-disrupting tech just as it now does trade. It also provides another reason to oppose immigration (beyond race) given the importance of newcomers to the American innovation engine.

But there's perhaps a deeper reason at play than the changing nature of the GOP electorate, though a complementary one. Advances in biotechnology, including a working-draft sequencing of the human genome in 2000, created a semi-plausible *Brave New World* future that would be repellent to many religious conservatives. It could be a future, as conservative bioethicist Leon Kass wrote in a 2001 essay during the national debate over federal funding of embryonic stem cell research, "peopled by creatures of human shape but stunted humanity."[27] President George W. Bush's decision that August—research would only be permitted on existing stem cell lines—was a victory for bio-conservatives. In *Rapture: How Biotech Became the New Religion*, Brian Alexander opts for the less charitable "bio-Luddites" and writes how "many people were convinced that monsters were coming, that the biotechnological agenda placed people at risk of dehumanizing themselves."[28] These fears are no less evident today, especially given CRISPR and other biotech advances. "We are moving very quickly into the post-human future," writes conservative Christian thinker Rod Dreher in a 2017 essay titled "We Shall Be As Gods."[29] For those bio-conservatives, Silicon Valley is a transhumanist fifth column pushing America and the world to a posthuman future where bugs are a dinnertime staple and we all live packed tightly together in impossibly high super-skyscrapers, one outlined regularly to rank-and-file conservatives on right-wing websites. One can anticipate future battles like the 2001 clash over stem cells involving human enhancement. But whether it's fear of job loss or loss of humanity, Down Wing populism appeals to our innate aversion to risk and uncertainty. In *Things to Come*, the 1938 film version of H. G. Wells's *The Shape of Things to Come*, one character expresses his revulsion at the nonstop scientific and technological progress of his future, near-utopian society in words that surely resonate with anti-growth populists of today:

> *How can we...[let you go through with your plans] when your science and inventions are perpetually changing life for us—when you are everlastingly rebuilding and contriving strange things about us? When you make what we think great, seem small. When you make what we think strong, seem feeble. We don't want you in the same world with us. We don't want this expedition. We don't want mankind to go out to the moon and the planets. We shall hate you more if you succeed than if you fail. Is there never to be rest in this world?*[30]

The climate and anti-capitalism Left. Move beyond the broad center left of the Democratic Party and you will start to run into the eco-socialist or "degrowth" left that thinks dealing with climate change will require far more than some tax subsidies here and a bit more regulation there as carrots and sticks for consumers and business. These Down Wingers don't imagine an America that is more or less like this one, but powered by solar and wind. Nope, everything must change. Degrowth must replace growth. The whole world in permanent recession. The Great Downshift, but forever and everywhere. We must accept and encourage an extreme transformation of our way of life. Public policy and public attitudes must constrain consumption and move beyond capitalism as a prerequisite to saving the planet, as Greta Thunberg exhorts. And here is Brazilian degrowth activist Felipe Milanez speaking to CNN in 2022: The "love of growth" is "extremely violent and racist, and it's just been reproducing local forms of colonialism."[31]

So back to *The Limits to Growth*, more or less. And what is the degrowther image of the future since it rejects one where, say, a nuclear fusion–powered humanity spreads across the solar system? I noted earlier that Nobel laureate economist William Nordhaus once pointed out that *Limits*' proposals "would limit our material aspirations to attaining the living standards of Somalia or Chad."[32] Obviously, this is not the degrowth message fed to the public. Advocates of a "steady-state" global economy assure us that a degrowth future is not one of deprivation, pain, and sacrifice. Rather we would be rich in our simplicity.[33] Making and mending our own clothes, DIY everything, recycling everything. Homes made of clay, sand, and straw. One big problem with this pre-industrial vision of a tedious tomorrow: There's a strong association between economic growth and per person GDP to all sorts of measures of well-being, including happiness, health, life expectancy, and leisure time. Nor have degrowthers noticed that over the past decade, thirty-three countries, home to more than a billion people, have managed to increase their GDP while reducing their carbon emissions thanks to economies that have become more service oriented and powered by more clean—or at least cleaner—energy.[34]

But not all degrowthers are the same. Even the glowering, hectoring, Thunbergian types are far more benign than extremists who find inspiration in the writings of perhaps the most famous degrowth activist until Thunberg. Mathematician and mad bomber Ted Kaczynski offers an infamous anti-technology critique that sounds broadly similar to Lewis Mumford's attacks on the Megamachine. Kaczynski rails, for instance, against the "techno-industrial system" that he sees as a disaster for humanity.[35] There are also degrowthers, however, who advocate a cheerier, eco-socialist version called "solarpunk," a response to dreary 1980s cyberpunk futurism of the sort seen in the 1982 film *Blade Runner*.[36] Its roots, however, extend back to the 1970s and the desire to replace the Megamachine with a cozier, organic, and more humane world *not* built around the sort of technology that needs massive societal systems to build and maintain it. A search of online images quickly reveals the solarpunk vision. Solar panels and windmills, not nuclear reactors and carbon capture vacuums. Buildings are made of wood and adobe brick, and seem to merge into the landscape. Also, typically, not many people. "Somewhere in this world there are cities and lithium mines, factories and sewage treatment plants," writes Ted Nordhaus of the Breakthrough Institute.[37] "But they're literally not in the picture." It's a future for people who disdain "late capitalism" but never let their iPhone charge fall below 50 percent.

But how would we get from here to there, from resource-depleting today to a sustainable solarpunk tomorrow? The plan seems to be something like the one outlined by Drew Pendergrass, a doctoral student in environmental engineering at Harvard University, and Troy Vettese, an environmental historian at the European University Institute, in the recent book, *Half-Earth Socialism: A Plan to Save the Future from Extinction, Climate Change, and Pandemics*. Pendergrass and Vettese imagine a socialist world where "scientists calculate how to provide for everyone's basic needs without trashing the planet." Their thought experiment has a democratically elected world government setting aside half the Earth for "rewilding," rationing energy use, encouraging a vegan diet, and abolishing private car ownership. And then the vision gets really solarpunkish:

> *While [the central planning agency] liquidates the suburban real estate market early on, millions of construction workers and tradespeople find work retrofitting buildings to conserve energy and adapting private mansions and corporate headquarters to communal use.... Private lawns and golf courses are likewise either rewilded or turned into community gardens.... Large swathes of manufacturing become rationalized when "planned obsolescence" itself is made obsolete. Resources are redirected toward building solar panels, wind turbines, super-efficient insulation and railways.*[38]

So an entire world becomes a sort of homeowners association from hell. Hard pass. By the way, the planning agency doing all that resource directing is called Gosplant, its name inspired by the Soviet Union's central planning board, Gosplan. That is not a joke, unfortunately. Solarpunkers and socialism go together. And even though few policymakers and regular people would likely ever subscribe to this extreme vision, a version of it still makes its way into our thinking, such as the popular notion that everyone in China, India, and Africa cannot live as well as we do in advanced economies without destroying the planet. Even environmental groups that probably seem utterly mainstream and uncontroversial have subscribed to the notion that too much economic growth is a bad thing. Take the Sierra Club, which in the past has criticized nuclear power as contributing to "unnecessary economic growth."[39]

Job worriers. History strongly suggests that AI isn't going to take all the jobs. Mechanical switching technology, for example, eliminated most telephone operator jobs, one of the most common jobs for young women in the first decades of the past century. But those positions were replaced by clerical and other office jobs.[40] And the introduction of automatic teller machines in the 1990s was actually followed by an increase in the number of bank teller jobs as it became cheaper to open more bank branches.[41] Since the start of the Industrial Revolution, machines have always been eliminating jobs—while also creating lots of new ones. Farm workers became factory workers and then office workers—all the while their education and skills kept improving. Tomorrow, they might be metaverse workers.

Even in the tech-optimistic Up Wing 1960s, there were worries about automation due to the obviously rapid pace of tech progress. *Time* magazine explored the issue in a February 24, 1961, article titled "The Automation Jobless."[42] As the jobless rate declined over that decade, concerns about job loss remained, however. In 1964, President Lyndon Johnson signed into law a National Commission on Technology, Automation, and Economic Progress. Its report reflected prevailing economic orthodoxy that it was Washington's job to make sure there was adequate business and consumer demand in the economy through fiscal and monetary policy."[43] Others wanted a more directed and vigorous response. An array of social activists warned in an open letter to LBJ, "The Triple Revolution," that a "cybernation revolution has been brought about by the combination of the computer and the automated self-regulating machine. This results in a system of almost unlimited productive capacity which requires progressively less human labor."[44] To avoid mass technological unemployment, America must institute "large-scale public works, low-cost housing, public transit, electrical power development, income redistribution, union representation for the unemployed, and government restraint on technology deployment." Martin Luther King Jr. mentioned the "The Triple Revolution" and the threat of automation in his final Sunday sermon, just six days before his assassination on April 4, 1968.[45]

Leading into the pandemic, business news was warning that AI and robots were on the verge of causing mass unemployment among carbon-based lifeforms. That, even though unemployment was at a fifty-year low, wages were rising (especially at the lower end), and measured productivity was uninspiring.[46] (Those statistics were exactly the opposite of what you might expect to see if robots were starting to take all the jobs.) Yet there was a popular notion that a robopocalypse in the labor market was nigh. Advances in AI—many hyped by Silicon Valley for their automation potential, such as autonomous driving—led to numerous academic studies and news stories about the "future of work" and the risk of widespread technological unemployment. There were also books with titles such as *Rise of the Robots: Technology and the Threat of a Jobless Future* and *Competing in the AI Age*. (Recall Andrew Yang warning of the forthcoming trucker riots during the 2020 Democratic presidential race.)[47] The common message was that this new software and these new machines were far more powerful than those of the past, and thus the threat to human work considerably higher. Even Microsoft co-founder Bill Gates, hardly a neo-Luddite, one would think, got into the act, suggesting a "robot tax" to slow down the pace of technological adoption.[48]

Although the pandemic disrupted all aspects of the economy, those pre-pan fears never really went away and are starting to make a comeback. Even before generative AI exploded into public consciousness, scary headlines about automation such as "No really, robots are about to take A LOT of jobs" reemerged. And the new AI chatbots and image generators have only heightened these concerns, especially among educated, white-collar workers with the sorts of jobs that could be affected, including accountants, customer-service agents, graphic artists, interpreters, journalists, paralegals, software coders, and teachers.

But it's important to think about automation the way economists often do. A "job" is a bundle of different tasks. And any new technology will affect various tasks differently. Maybe it can do the task itself or help workers do the task. It might even create brand new tasks for workers. The exact mix is hard to predict as technology evolves and spreads throughout the economy. It's natural that many will be concerned that entire occupations will be wiped out, and that carbon-based lifeforms who worked those occupations might be out in the street. But AI should lead to big gains in income for the economy as a whole. That would increase the demand for consumer goods and services and fuel innovation for new goods and services—which in turn would create new tasks and entirely new occupations for workers. And keep in mind how AI can make humans better at what they do in all sorts of ways. Professional Go players have become much better by playing against AI-powered Go programs. "Our findings suggest that the development of superhuman AI programs may have prompted human players to break away from traditional strategies and induced them to explore novel moves, which in turn may have improved their decision-making," according to the paper "Superhuman Artificial Intelligence Can Improve Human Decision Making."[49]

What are the best current guesses for AI's impact? Goldman Sachs, a bank, finds a third of tasks that make up nearly a thousand U.S. occupations are exposed to the current state of AI automation.[50] That translates to some two-thirds of all occupations. But that doesn't mean two-thirds of all jobs are going away. Some occupations are more exposed than others. GS economists see a high level of exposure in administrative and legal jobs, low exposure in "physically intensive" jobs such as construction and maintenance. Overall, the bank's assumptions would mean 7 percent of current U.S. employment being substituted by AI, 63 percent being complemented, and 30 percent being unaffected. But not even a megabank knows for sure.

Of course, AI will only become more capable. Maybe the reassuring story that history tells us about automation (machines destroy jobs but, eventually, create more new ones) will be a poor guide going forward. But that's not my baseline case. In his 2022 paper "The Labor Market Impacts of Technological Change: From Unbridled Enthusiasm to Qualified Optimism to Vast Uncertainty," MIT economist David Autor offers a cautiously optimistic prediction on continued human employment (although he includes a caveat that tech progress faster than what current experts predict could make his forecasts too rosy).[51] Even if AI ends up replacing far more of what humans do than augmenting what they do best—making those tasks more valuable—or creating new things to do, the economy's increased productivity could be such that average wages would rise. Workers would get less of the economic pie, but the pie would be bigger.

Without the emergence of human-like artificial general intelligence, Autor sees an upper limit to the automation process. He thinks humans will continue to have a "comparative advantage" in a number of areas: creativity, judgment, hypothesis formation, contextual thinking, causal analysis, communication, emotional intelligence—"the importance of which we likely do not fully appreciate and the difficulty of which we surely vastly underestimate." Autor is also confident that the most skilled workers "will likely continue to be complemented by advances in computing and AI—such as workers who invent, design, research, lead, entertain, and educate."

The next obvious question is what humans will do for work if AGI is reached, which some experts are predicting could happen by 2040, if not earlier. Again, history should be the baseline here. We always overstate the impact of technology on jobs. Who would guess that just one of the 270 jobs in the 1950 U.S. census has been eliminated by automation?[52] And who would guess further that job is elevator operator? Beyond looking at history, it's hard to say what comes next for workers. And that's OK. "The limits of both our collective knowledge and our individual imaginations constrain well-intentioned efforts to plan for the workforce of the future," Adam Thierer, a policy analyst, observes.[53] It's always been easier to recognize which current jobs can be automated than to envision the jobs and industries that don't exist yet but will be created by new technologies. When ChatGPT was first unveiled, I don't recall anyone predicting the emergence of prompt engineers, or "AI whisperers," some of whom are paid more than $300,000 to nudge better results from GenAI systems.[54] (Good news, humanities majors, college degrees in English, history, and philosophy look to be great backgrounds for these jobs.) Some image-generation prompts can run to hundreds of words requiring a deep knowledge of art history and techniques, as well as photography.

What's the bigger risk, that history no longer proves to be an accurate guide or that preemptive efforts to delay or ban technological progress deprive us of the wondrous possibilities created by that progress? For the moment and years to come, as I see it, the big economic problem is too little progress, not too much.

Inequality alarmists and the *Blade Runner* Fallacy. Imagine living in a world where you have access to unlimited energy, resources, and opportunities: a world where you can travel to the stars or stay on Earth and enjoy its beauty. Sounds like a kind of paradise, right? This should be the world of *Blade Runner*, a world of human-level AI, genetically engineered androids, space colonies, and flying cars. All these staggering technological developments should have created a world of almost unimaginable prosperity where humanity has new capabilities to solve big problems. Rather, *Blade Runner* is a film classic known for its visually impressive, dystopian world-building. Like the lesser *Elysium*, the Ridley Scott–directed film contends all the fruits of future tech progress and faster economic growth go to a tiny elite. In *Blade Runner*, most of those humans not fortunate enough to emigrate to off-world colonies are stuck in a wet and dreary existence beneath towering corporate skyscrapers in 2019 Los Angeles on a climate-shattered planet. It's this image of the future that seems to drive many analyses of the film as a neo-Marxist cautionary tale of late capitalism.

I call this the *Blade Runner* Fallacy. Economic history has shown repeatedly that in a dynamic, progressing economy the consumption habits of the rich—automobiles, air travel, computers, giant TVs, smartphones—eventually become the consumption habits of everyone else. It's not like Musk has access to a better COVID-19 vaccine than I do. Indeed, what Musk is doing at SpaceX is a good example of this phenomenon. Its innovations are dramatically reducing the cost of space launches such that a realistic path now exists for regular people eventually going to and living in space, not just the super-rich.

Now there is one way in which the economics of these films make a bit more sense, though I doubt the filmmakers were thinking about it. During the first phase of the Industrial Revolution, there was a period that economists now call "Engels' pause"—after Friedrich Engels, who co-authored *The Communist Manifesto* with fellow German philosopher Karl Marx in 1848—when productivity and output were expanding but real wages were stagnant.[55] As AEI economist Michael Strain has described this period, "Real wages fell dramatically for some occupations. Many who held those occupations couldn't be retrained to compete in the new economy. Lives were shattered. Some families suffered across generations. People flocked from the countryside to dirty, disease-infested cities. For decades there was deep social unrest. British society was shaken to its core."[56] Even so, why aren't things much better in the sequel, *Blade Runner 2049*? At some point between the two films, the United States is struck by a massive electromagnetic pulse, an attack likely carried out by replicants.[57] Perhaps that disaster extended a neo-Engels' pause into the twenty-first century. More likely, of course, director Denis Villeneuve simply wanted to further the original's themes about capitalism, inequality, and the environment—no matter how illogical and contrary to economic history and data. Yes, the most recent numbers from the Congressional Budget Office find the size of the income gap between higher- and lower-income households—also known as the "Gini coefficient"—has risen by 7 percent from 1990 through 2019, the year the original *Blade Runner* was set. But as economist Strain points out, "All the increase occurred between 1990 and 2007, before the explosion of political and media interest in inequality. Since 2007, inequality has fallen by 5 percent."[58] Maybe the politicians and Hollywood will notice, eventually.

SEVEN

Seven Down Wing Myths about Economic Growth

Even as Stanford's Paul Ehrlich was predicting global mass starvation in 1968, others could see a path to victory.[1] The same year Ehrlich's book was published, William Gaud, director of the U.S. Agency for International Development, coined the term "Green Revolution," referring to the creation of high-yielding crop varieties, especially rice and wheat, and more productive agronomic techniques.[2] In 1970, when Ehrlich was spreading his starvation message on talk shows, scientist Norman Borlaug, the central figure of the Green Revolution, was awarded the Nobel Peace Prize. From the Nobel committee's presentation speech: "The world has been oscillating between fears of two catastrophes—the population explosion and the atom bomb. Both pose a mortal threat. In this intolerable situation, with the menace of doomsday hanging over us, Dr. Borlaug comes onto the stage and cuts the Gordian knot. He has given us a well-founded hope, an alternative of peace and of life—the green revolution."[3] It was an award well earned. The Green Revolution has prevented maybe a billion starvation deaths since the

1960s. We also live in a wealthier world because of it. Researchers find that just a ten-year delay of the Green Revolution would in 2010 have generated a cumulative GDP loss of $83 trillion, or about one year of current global GDP.[4] From the 2018 paper "Two Blades of Grass: The Impact of the Green Revolution": "Indeed, our results suggest that the investments in the development of [high-yielding varieties of] crops by far have been the most successful form of foreign aid to developing countries in the past half-century."

The Down Wing enemies of technological progress and economic growth argue that both are overrated, that their benefits only go to a thin slice of the population. Another common Down Wing opinion: not only is market capitalism inherently exploitative and immoral, but it doesn't even deliver the economic goods to the vast majority of us—at least not since the end of the postwar golden age. That's when America fell under the sway of "neoliberalism" and its calls for more limited government interventions in the economy, as well as economies more open to immigration and trade. Now we're supposedly in the age of late capitalism, where capitalism hasn't helped workers on just about any basis you could imagine. Instead of a long stagnation, they argue what we've actually been experiencing is a long decline. Time for some Up Wing myth-busting of Down Wing myths about innovation-driven, entrepreneurial market capitalism and the economic growth it generates.

Myth #1: Worker wages have gone nowhere for decades. For years, left-wing politicians have hammered home the supposed fact that worker wages have been flat since leisure suits were in style and disco music was all the rage. Now, too, the populist right wing echoes this criticism as a way of arguing that decades of American-led globalization have badly harmed domestic workers. To be fair, there's a seed of truth to the claim. Average wages for regular workers, not the bosses, are up about 5 percent since the Nixon administration, adjusted for inflation.[5] Not flat exactly, but pretty darn close. But using that 5 percent number as shorthand to explain some five decades of American economic history is terribly misleading. The postwar Up Wing boom where rapid wage growth matched rapid labor productivity growth was followed by a period—from the mid-1970s through the mid-1990s of stagnant or even declining wage growth. Weak income growth now matched the Great Downshift in productivity growth. With Up Wing 2.0, wages accelerated again before a roller-coaster period during the first two decades of this century as incomes were buffeted by another productivity deceleration and the global financial crisis.

Keep two things in mind: First, workers today are mostly not the same workers as in the 1970s and didn't suffer that mid-1970s through mid-1990s part of the Great Downshift in both productivity and wage growth. Second, the influx of new and improved products over the decades makes adjusting wages for inflation a particularly thorny economic problem—one that tends to cause an overstatement of inflation and thus an understatement of real wage growth. Since the 1990 business cycle peak, wages are up 40 percent in real terms, according to work by American Enterprise Institute economist Michael Strain.[6] So, you know, not stagnation—but also not as good as they could have been with strong labor productivity growth and stronger Technologically Futuristic Productivity growth.

Myth #2: Workers don't benefit from faster productivity and economic growth. Again, I would like those wage gains I just mentioned to have been way stronger. And they would've been if productivity growth had been faster over the past half-century. But another Down Wing claim is that making workers more productive doesn't result in higher wages paid to them. It used to, maybe, but no longer. This supposed severance or delinkage is what some call the "productivity-pay gap." But the reality is that productivity and pay remained tightly linked. Economists Anna M. Stansbury and Lawrence Summers find "substantial evidence" of linkage between productivity and compensation.[7] From 1973 to 2016, they find that 1 percentage point higher productivity growth has been associated with 0.7 to 1 percentage point higher median compensation growth. Their conclusion: "[productivity] growth still matters substantially for middle-income Americans." Or consider the 1990s boom, when wage growth accelerated after the dismal 1970s and 1980s. Labor productivity growth back then rose at a spectacular 3 percent annually versus just 0.7 percent annually more recently. A telling example, according to top Obama White House economist Jason Furman, that "greater productivity growth holds the potential of being the most powerful source of sustained wage growth across the income spectrum."[8]

What if the early 1970s Great Downshift in labor productivity growth hadn't happened? Stansbury and Summers calculate that if productivity growth overall had been as fast over the 1973–2016 period as it was over the 1949–1973 period—twice as fast, basically—"median and mean compensation would have been around 41 percent higher in 2015, holding other factors constant," such as inequality. Another analysis finds that if we had grown the TFP part of productivity growth at 2 percent per year during the Great Downshift—again, the pace during Up Wing 1.0—median household income would be twice what it is today, all else equal, around $150,000 instead of today's $70,000.[9] Likewise, as the Bureau of Labor Statistics recently noted, the downshift in productivity growth from the boomy mid-1990s to the mid-2000s translates into a loss of $95,000 in output per worker (as well as an overall loss of $11 trillion in economic output).[10] What one should take from all these estimates is just how much income growth we're leaving on the table by not focusing more on productivity growth.

Myth #3: Upward mobility has up and gone. The notion that you will live a better life—greater income, health, opportunity, and choice—is central to the notion of Up Wing progress and the American Dream. The aspect of rising living standards that economists mostly focus on is growth in personal incomes. But likewise, the notion of economic mobility—or, rather, its supposed steep decline—is also central to the Down Wing case that American capitalism isn't working anymore (assuming it ever did). One kind of economic mobility is "relative mobility," which measures how a child's ranking in a society's income distribution compares to that of their parents. If you're in the 60 to 80 percent quintile—the second fifth—while your parents were in the quintile below—the third fifth—then you've experienced upward relative mobility. Of course, one could imagine a scenario in which it became easier to move from bottom to top even as the bottom became poorer in absolute terms. So rather than income rank, "absolute mobility" looks at whether your income is higher or lower than that of your parents at the same age. Strain calculates that around three-quarters of Americans have higher (inflation-adjusted) family incomes than their parents, and nearly 90 percent of Americans raised in the bottom 20 percent—today's forty-somethings—have higher family incomes than their parents.[11] And what about the working class Americans who are often seen as the core of populist movements? About three-quarters have higher incomes than their parents. The American Dream abides.

Myth #4: Money isn't everything. Faster growth isn't just about the ability to buy more stuff. The faster TFP growth that began at the start of Robert Gordon's special century and continued through Up Wing 1.0, notes the Congressional Budget Office, "was paralleled by a similar, contemporaneous wave of improvement in life expectancy at birth."[12] A child born in 2010 could expect to live nearly thirty-five years longer than a child born in 1870. Again, the CBO: "That improvement suggests that the conditions that made the wave in measured productivity possible involved sweeping advances that contributed to progress across many different types of economic activity."[13] And the connection remains true today. Recent advances in genetic editing could end chronic scourges such as Alzheimer's and cancer. Let's focus on the former for a moment. By 2050, the number of Alzheimer's cases is expected to almost triple to 14 million.[14] As it is, the United States spends close to half a trillion dollars annually on care related to Alzheimer's, including both treatment and caregiving costs. "There are other diseases with high prevalence, from diabetes to HIV to cancer, but none match the medical and care needs of AD," note researchers in the 2021 paper "What Can Economics Say about Alzheimer's Disease?" Now imagine Alzheimer's cured.

Or how about vaccines? In their first two years of availability, COVID-19 vaccines may have prevented nearly 20 million U.S. hospitalizations, more than 3 million deaths, and saved the country $1.15 trillion.[15] Even the simple measles vaccine—no fancy genetic tinkering necessary—continues to have a huge impact. Vassar College economist Alicia Atwood finds that a vaccinated adult is "less likely to live in poverty, and is more likely to be employed than an adult who did not have the opportunity to be vaccinated." The vaccinated also earn more. Atwood calculates that almost a half percent of annual U.S. personal income, $76 billion a year, is due to the benefits of measles vaccination.[16]

But we shouldn't undervalue the benefits of cash. Higher incomes are linked with higher life satisfaction. And higher incomes can bring more happiness, even among wealthier people. A 2023 analysis from a team of economists, including Nobel laureate Daniel Kahneman, finds that happy people get steadily happier as their incomes rise.[17] The study examines some 33,000 American adults who were surveyed via an app at random moments throughout the day on their subjective well-being. The researchers did detect an income plateau, but only when incomes hit six figures and only when people were really unhappy, or the unhappiest 20 percent. On the other hand, the happiest 30 percent find an increased rate of happiness that accelerates as incomes surpass $100,000.

But who's really shocked by such findings, other than degrowth types? Our desire for new things and experiences is unlimited. And those desires, what we eventually think of as needs, economist Branko Milanović has explained, are socially determined rather than psychological. More economic growth generates new needs that require more growth to satisfy them, probably without end. "We did not have a need for mobile phones before they existed," he has written. "But we have that need now. We do not have a need to fly to Mars for a weekend outing right now (even if Elon Musk might feel that way). It seems slightly bizarre to us today to have such a 'need.' But in several generations, it will not be so bizarre. It will be like our 'need' to go on vacation to Mexico or Italy."[18]

Myth #5: Capitalism-fueled growth doesn't reduce global poverty. It might even cause it. It isn't complicated: raising incomes broadly is the most effective way to reduce poverty. "Growth is enough and growth alone does eliminate extreme poverty," declares Lant Pritchett, a developmental economist at Oxford University.[19] Faster global economic growth—especially export growth by and incoming foreign investment in China and India—has already moved more than a billion humans out of extreme poverty over the past quarter century, according to the World Bank.[20]

Yet much remains to be done. Nearly every tenth person still lives on less than $2.15 a day.[21] Even with tremendous economic gains, some 3 billion people cannot afford a healthy diet. About the same number have no access to clean water and have never used the internet. Over 80 percent of the world has never taken an airline flight.[22] The ultimate goal of poverty warriors everywhere should be that every country in the world should be considered an "advanced economy." Denmark, for instance, has a per capita GDP of $68,000.[23] Just 14 percent of Danes live under a poverty line of $30 a day. It's a nation that scores highly on happiness levels, and leftists often praise its social democracy. What would it take to lift the 85 percent of the world that live on less than $30 per day to a living standard comparable to the poorest seventh of Danes? The folks at Our World in Data calculates that the minimum necessary growth to reduce global poverty to the level of poverty in Denmark is 410 percent—or a fivefold increase in the global economy. Those Down Wing degrowthers arguing that humanity would be fine if global incomes were back at 1990 levels, for instance, are gravely mistaken. Degrowthers should also think about the energy needs of the world's poorest people. A fifth of humanity lives in Africa and will need to use a lot more energy if it's to become a continent of advanced economies.

Myth #6: We're running out of Earth. A classic Down Wing argument that goes back to the 1972 *Limits to Growth* report: we can have economic growth for a while or a bountiful natural environment, but not both, and eventually, resource depletion will cause growth to collapse. But the Down Wing eco-pessimists were wrong. As you may have noticed, the global economy didn't collapse as we didn't run out of the natural resources necessary for modern industrial capitalism. Commodity prices fell for decades rather than rose, indicating abundance rather than scarcity. Copper, chromium, nickel, tin, and tungsten were nearly a quarter cheaper in 2015 compared to 1980.[24] These commodities were the subject of a famous 1980 bet between Paul Ehrlich and economist Julian Simon over resource depletion. Simon thought humanity could innovate its way out of potential shortages, but Ehrlich disagreed. Simon won. Or to look at it another way, Cato Institute research finds the inflation-adjusted price of fifty key global commodities fell by 36 percent between 1980 and 2017.[25] (Of those fifty commodities, forty-three declined in price, two remained equally valuable, and five increased in price.) And taking into account that between 1980 and 2017, inflation-adjusted global hourly income per person also grew by 80 percent, those commodities became 65 percent cheaper.

In the excellent *More from Less*, Andrew McAfee highlights research finding a "dematerialization" of the American economy since the early 1970s. With the mass substitutions of bits for atoms has come a decline in the absolute consumption of key commodities such as steel, copper, fertilizer, timber, and paper. McAfee writes, "We invented the computer, the Internet, and a suite of other digital technologies that let us dematerialize our consumption: over time they allowed us to consume more and more while taking less and less from the planet."[26] How many devices on a pre-smartphone desk—calendar, clock, newspaper and magazines, reference books, landline phone—have been effectively replaced by the now ubiquitous device? Climate change eventually usurped the resource scarcity argument as a driving force of modern Down Wing environmentalism. Same with the notion that humanity remains on the verge of mass starvation. Ehrlich still believes, for instance, "There are too many super-consumers on the planet," combining fears of overpopulation with capitalist overconsumption.[27] (The World Counts organization runs a countdown clock showing that we're just a generation away before humanity runs out of food.)[28] Meanwhile, a new Green Revolution is emerging. Chinese scientists report that by giving "a Chinese rice variety a second copy of one of its own genes, researchers have boosted its yield by up to 40 percent," according to *Science*.[29] Researchers at the Innovative Genomics Institute estimate that CRISPR gene-editing technology could improve plant photosynthesis between 25 percent and 50 percent.[30] No doubt the starvation countdown clocks will continue counting down no matter what other green shoots of agricultural progress emerge.

Myth #7: Economic growth is only about consumerism and materialism. Is an Up Wing, future-oriented society also one that's more tolerant, more compassionate, and more democratic? Does it encourage us to be an open, "drawbridge down" country rather than an inward-looking "drawbridge up" country? There's some evidence it does. In the 2005 book *The Moral Consequences of Economic Growth*, Harvard University economist Benjamin M. Friedman tells a compelling story about how economic growth boosts social justice, while economic hardship promotes retreat from such values as tolerance for racial and ethnic differences, concern for the poor and disadvantaged, and a respect for civil liberties. Friedman writes:

> *The experience of many countries suggests that when a society experiences rising standards of living, broadly distributed across the population at large, it is also likely to make progress along a variety of dimensions that are the very essence of what a free, open, democratic society is all about... Conversely, experience also suggests that when a society is stagnating economically—worse yet, if it is suffering a pervasive decline in living standards—it is not only likely to make little if any progress in these social, political, and (in the eighteenth-century sense) moral dimensions; all too often, it will undergo a period of rigidification and retrenchment, sometimes with catastrophic consequences.*[31]

It's an appealing intuition that Friedman supports through a political and economic analysis of American and Western European history.[32] In the United States, the Civil Rights Act of 1875 emerged from the post–Civil War industrial boom, just as the Up Wing post–World War II decades ended with the Civil Rights Act of 1964, the Hart-Celler Immigration and Nationality Act of 1965, and Great Society programs such as Medicaid and Medicare. (I would also note that the United States ran a successful Space Race even as it also expanded civil rights and the welfare state, something left-wing critics of the current U.S. space effort seem to have forgotten.) On the other hand, economic downturns and volatility led to retrenchments, such as the reversal of minority voting rights that followed the panic of 1893 and the decline in support for affirmative action, welfare, and immigration after the stagflationary 1970s. The rise of anti-immigration, white ethnic nationalism in the aftermath of the 2007–2009 global financial crisis and slow economic recovery would further seem to support Friedman. Imagine what America looks like after another decade of slow economic growth of the sort economists on Wall Street and in Washington are forecasting. It's easy to think even more national populism and economic nostalgia would be in store, making even that slower pace of economic growth difficult to achieve. Ban immigration, for sure. But maybe also ban machines over fears of job displacement. It's possible. "The hideous architecture reflects the hideous philosophy" was the reaction on Twitter last year by the culture editor of The Federalist, a popular Trumpy news site, to an automated McDonald's concept store in Texas.[33]

No small benefit: Economic growth is supportive of democracy. A 2022 analysis by MIT economist Daron Acemoğlu and a team of researchers establish that an association between exposure to democracy and support for democracy is driven almost entirely by people's experience with successful democracy.[34] In particular, it's exposure to democratic regimes that deliver economic growth, peace, political stability, and public services that make people more willing to support democracy. In contrast, greater exposure to democracies that are hampered by stagnant economies, mired in political instability, or unable to provide public services doesn't appear to increase support for democracy. To be clear, economic growth isn't the only thing that matters. It's part of a package of achievements that make people support democratic governance. And those achievements can create the societal readiness and trust needed to attempt the next moonshot project—or even build a new bridge or subway tunnel. "In a country where people don't trust the government to be honest, or businesses to be ethical, or members of the opposite party to respect the rule of law, it is hard to build anything quickly and effectively—or, for that matter, anything that lasts," argues Derek Thompson, staff writer at *The Atlantic*.[35]

But some people seem to have an instinctual aversion to market capitalism, no matter the bounty it provides. They seemingly see the world of business as fundamentally grubby, one where greedy corporate executives crush workers, mislead consumers, cheat suppliers, and devastate communities in pursuit of maximizing the company's share price. American political philosopher and market-capitalism critic Michael Sandel argues that humans must be treated as persons "worthy of dignity and respect," rather than as "instruments of gain and objects of use."[36] To Sandel—and to Karl Marx, for that matter—market capitalism is inherently dehumanizing. Any heroes in this dystopian reality? Maybe mom-and-pop retailers in small towns and bodega owners in big cities. And Patagonia, the upscale outdoor clothing designer and retailer. But it's a misguided view. For example, *Fortune* magazine annually compiles a list of the "Best Companies to Work For" that takes into account worker and customer satisfaction. And guess what? The market performance of these companies shows no conflict between the interest of labor and capital. A 2021 study analyzed a portfolio consisting of the companies on the *Fortune* list and found it has outperformed the broader market by two to three percentage points a year since 1984.[37] As hedge fund manager Cliff Asness argues, "If the stock price is indeed the long-term value of the company, then things like treating customers well, compensating employees fairly, etc., are likely vital parts of maximizing the stock price."[38] An unsurprising result if you start from the premise that a business-loving society is chock full of virtue. Economist Deirdre McCloskey has written beautifully of such virtues:

> *[T]he* ***Prudence*** *to buy low and sell high...to trade rather than to invade, to calculate the consequences, to pursue the good with competence...the* ***Temperance*** *to save and accumulate, of course. But it is also the temperance to educate oneself in business and in life, to listen to the customer, to resist the temptations to cheat, to ask quietly whether there might be a compromise here...the* ***Justice*** *to insist on private property honestly acquired. But it is also the justice to pay willingly for good work, to honor labor, to break down privilege, to value people for what they can do rather than for who they are, to view success without envy... the* ***Courage*** *to venture on new ways of business. But it is also the courage to overcome the fear of change, to bear defeat unto bankruptcy, to be courteous to new ideas, to wake up next morning and face fresh work with cheer...the* ***Love*** *to take care of one's own, yes. But it is also a bourgeois love to care for employees and partners and colleagues and customers and fellow citizens, to wish all of humankind well, to seek God, finding human and transcendent connection in the marketplace...the* ***Faith*** *to honor one's community of business. But it is also the faith to build monuments to the glorious past, to sustain traditions of commerce, of learning, of religion, finding identity in Amsterdam and Chicago and*

> *Osaka...the **Hope** to imagine a better machine. But it is also the hope to see the future as something other than stagnation or eternal recurrence, to infuse the day's work with a purpose, seeing one's labor as a glorious calling.*[39]

Lovely words, but also ones supported by hard evidence, not just philosophical preference. In the 2022 paper "The Moral Costs of Markets: Testing the Deterioration Hypothesis," researchers Justin Callais of the University of Louisiana and Colin Harris and Ben Borchard of St. Olaf College examine the notion put forward by capitalism critics that markets push aside and undermine existing moral values, resulting in moral deterioration.[40] Do we lose our souls in pursuit of higher living standards? Callais, Harris, and Borchard compare countries' trends toward or away from market capitalism over time, as measured by the Fraser Institute's Economic Freedom of the World index, against their responses to various values issues—trust, discrimination, ethics—in the World Values Survey, administered every three to five years. From the paper: "We find that becoming a more market-oriented society does not cause a significant reduction in a society's moral values." Growth is good, for our body, minds, and souls.

EIGHT

The Most Important Reason to Embrace Up Wing Growth

The benefits of economic growth, driven by technological progress, are myriad. Growth raises living standards, makes us healthier, and creates a more interesting world of greater fairness, tolerance, and opportunity. Even during the ongoing Great Downshift, Americans are better off than they used to be across all those metrics, as I highlighted in the previous chapter. And globally, the decline in extreme poverty has been nothing short of miraculous thanks to faster growth enabled by tech progress—including global communication and the standardized shipping container—especially in Asia. Yet as important as all those things are, and as important as future advances might be, we shouldn't ignore the most important benefit of all: an Up Wing society is one capable of solving big problems, even if those problems are unforeseen or poorly prepared for. An Up Wing society is a more resilient society.

The COVID-19 pandemic has provided ample proof of this. Who can forget all the criticism of our preparedness in the country during 2020? Not enough high-quality masks and other personal protective equipment, too few ventilators, too few respiratory specialists, a shortage of disinfectant wipes. In a June 2020 piece, "We Are Living in a Failed State" for *The Atlantic*, journalist George Packer wrote, "Every morning in the endless month of March, Americans woke up to find themselves citizens of a failed state.... When test kits, masks, gowns, and ventilators were found to be in desperately short supply, governors pleaded for them from the White House, which stalled, then called on private enterprise, which couldn't deliver. States and cities were forced into bidding wars that left them prey to price gouging and corporate profiteering. Civilians took out their sewing machines to try to keep ill-equipped hospital workers healthy and their patients alive. Russia, Taiwan, and the United Nations sent humanitarian aid to the world's richest power—a beggar nation in utter chaos."[1]

America's apparent lack of preparedness was even more striking given how predictable the pandemic was. The twenty-first century had already experienced several dangerous global outbreaks: SARS in 2004, H1N1 in 2009, and the Ebola outbreak in 2015. (When the coronavirus hit, my family was lucky to still have several boxes of N95 masks left over from the 2009 avian flu episode.) And after each of these events, global health experts warned of worse to come. The world was long overdue for a far more serious pandemic, something more like the influenza pandemic of 1918. Global health organizations and think tanks prepared numerous studies in the years leading up to COVID-19, warning about a systemic lack of preparedness. Then there's the reality that those previous outbreaks led twenty-first-century American popular culture to obsess about the idea of a mysterious, apocalyptic virus—although it may turn you into a zombie after killing you. And still, we weren't ready.

While U.S. preparedness may have fallen far short of our expectations and may have been inadequate on some absolute level, it actually wasn't so bad compared to other nations. In 2019, the Johns Hopkins Center for Health Security helped develop a measure of pandemic preparation, the Global Health Security Index, which measured and ranked 195 countries across dozens of indicators such as "Does the country have a national law requiring prescriptions for antibiotics?" and "How many hospital beds per capita does the country have?"[2] The country that ranked highest for pandemic preparedness? The United States. The lowest? Equatorial Guinea. Still, as George Mason University economists Robert Tucker Omberg and Alex Tabarrok observe in their 2022 analysis "Is It Possible to Prepare for a Pandemic?," the United States has a far higher COVID-19 death rate per capita than Equatorial Guinea.[3] Their overall finding is that "almost no form of pandemic preparedness helped to ameliorate or shorten the pandemic. Compared to other countries, the United States did not perform poorly because of cultural values such as individualism, collectivism, selfishness, or lack of trust.…A final lesson may be that a pandemic is simply one example of a low-probability but very bad event. Other examples which may have even greater expected cost are super-volcanoes, asteroid strikes, nuclear wars, and solar storms. Preparing for X, Y, or Z may be less valuable than building resilience for a wide variety of potential events."

So when you consider the idea of "building resilience for a wide variety of potential events" and, as the researchers also conclude that "vaccination was by far the best weapon against the virus," it's hard to avoid concluding that what really matters is a country's wealth and technological capability. It was the United States that both developed mRNA vaccines and created a $20 billion public-private partnership, Operation Warp Speed, to accelerate their development and manufacture, saving an estimated 140,000 American lives between December 2020 and May 2021, plus nearly $2 trillion in economic benefits.[4]

Rich, technologically advanced nations have options. Assuming decent governance, they can deploy vast resources and know-how to solve problems as they happen. They don't need perfect foresight and planning, which is impossible anyway. We don't know all the existential challenges ahead. Nor do we understand the exact nature of the challenges we're already facing. And even when our understanding seems sound, human flaws impede our response. We're bad at properly assessing and addressing catastrophic risks, especially ones that are extremely rare (nuclear accidents), are likely not to happen for a long time (the worst impacts of climate change), and are outside our personal experience (nuclear, climate change, asteroid strike). We sometimes even fail at dealing with risk when the possible event meets none of those criteria (rare, distant, strange) such as the pandemic.

✦✦✦

In the previous chapter, I wrote about alternate history: what if the Industrial Revolution had occurred two thousand rather than two hundred years ago—and why it didn't. In a similar vein, here are four other thought experiments of more recent vintage, which suggest the power and benefits of technology-driven economic growth:

Global warming 1900. "Three things exercise a constant influence over the minds of men," the philosopher Voltaire observed in 1704. "Climate, government and religion."[5] Some 150 years late, humanity gained a key insight into the first item on that list. Swedish chemist Svante Arrhenius, eventually that nation's first Nobel laureate, was the first scientist to roughly calculate the impact of rising levels of atmospheric carbon dioxide on Earth's surface temperature. But as significant as that advance was in 1896, it was not until the postwar decades that scientists understood two key facts: First, humanity was increasing the amount of heat-trapping greenhouse gases in the atmosphere.[6] Second, Earth's climate can change significantly within the span of a human life, not just over thousands of years. But what if that information had been known a century earlier? And what if the sort of scary impacts from climate change, such as rising sea levels and deadly drought, forecasted to occur over the next century had actually started to happen a century ago? What could we have done in a world that had only recently invented the combustion engine, discovered radioactivity, and begun the long process of electrification? Even building sea walls to protect miles of low-lying coastal areas would've been out of reach of all but the wealthiest nations. Physicist David Deutsch has observed: "All relevant machines were underpowered, unreliable, expensive, and impossible to produce in large numbers. An enormous effort to construct a Panama Canal had just failed with the loss of thousands of lives and vast amounts of money, due to inadequate technology and scientific knowledge."[7] The one bit of good news here is that the first modern air conditioner was invented in 1902 by engineer Willis Haviland Carrier. So maybe a warming planet would've prompted greater research and resources into the technology so that it became widespread in the 1930s and 1940s rather than the 1960s and 1970s. Today, however, not only do we have A/C and a growing number of clean energy options, there's also the growing possibility of climate engineering, such as spraying tiny particles in the stratosphere to reflect sunlight away from Earth and cool the planet or removing carbon from the atmosphere through direct air capture. (DAC, by the way, might use more energy than is now used to power all current homes, which makes environmentalist opposition to nuclear power even more short sighted.)[8]

Energy collapse 2008. In the late 2000s, there was widespread and growing concern, prompted by sharply rising oil prices, that global oil and gas production was maxing out and would soon roll over into permanent decline. After the 1970s energy shock, crude oil prices headed steadily lower, bottoming at $20 a barrel in 2001. Then they started rising again, tripling by 2006 and then rocketing even higher to a record $147 a barrel in July 2008. Middle East tensions and demand from China's booming economy were among the causal factors cited at the time—but also fears about declining oil production. Those years of rising prices revived Down Wing thinking about the threat of resource depletion that had dominated the 1970s. "The global surge in commodity prices is reviving a question we haven't heard much since the 1970s: Will limited supplies of natural resources pose an obstacle to future world economic growth?" asked columnist Paul Krugman in 2008.[9] The same year saw the premier of the new James Bond film *Quantum of Solace*, which took the idea that the world was running out of oil as a given and used it as a core plot point.

Many gloomsayers glommed onto the analysis of journalist James Howard Kunstler as laid out in his 2005 book *The Long Emergency: Surviving the End of Oil, Climate Change, and Other Converging Catastrophes of the Twenty-First Century.* That title alone gives the flavor of Kunstler's analysis. In one interview, he warned that due to a growing oil shortage, "the complex systems that we rely on for daily life are going to start destabilizing and wobbling. They will mutually amplify their instabilities and many will reach a state of dysfunction."[10] The vast, suburban, consumerist American middle class—one relying on global supply chains for their cheap Walmart shopping habit—would return en masse to an agricultural, self-sustaining way of life more typical of 1900 America. As Kunstler later put it, "[Suburbia] has three probable destinies: slums, salvage operations, and ruins, perhaps in that order."[11] Also: only the rich could afford to drive. Also: many of us will probably die.

Well, the suburbs are still here. Crude oil fell back to nearly $30 by the end of 2008 as the world became gripped by the global financial crisis and economy after economy fell into recession, reducing global energy demand. But economic recovery didn't send oil prices back to stratospheric levels of peak oil because peak oil theory was flawed. What the energy pessimists didn't anticipate was the powerful combination of government scientific research and private-sector entrepreneurship and innovation. The result of that combo—something I would argue is second only to the internet as the key technological advance of the past four decades—allowed drillers to access and extract oil and gas from shale rock in areas such as the Permian Basin, stretching from Texas to New Mexico. Overall, the shale revolution boosted U.S. oil and gas production by 60 percent before the economic shocks of the coronavirus pandemic.[12] What's more, the shale revolution reduced energy-related greenhouse gas emissions by substituting cleaner natural gas for coal. Even better, the technical advances of the shale revolution are now being used by the emerging advanced geothermal energy sector, which holds out the promise of clean, abundant energy at any time, anywhere on the planet.

Coronavirus 2010. When news of a "mystery virus" outbreak in Wuhan, China—a city of 11 million that few Americans had ever heard of—began penetrating our collective consciousness in January 2020, many of us (my family included) turned to Netflix and watched the 2011 film *Contagion*. Whatever exactly was happening in Wuhan and those suspicious wet markets, most of us were confident it would never turn into the sort of pandemic depicted in the movie. So, at least at first, *Contagion* seemed like mere escapism. By the end of March, however, it started to seem prophetic as schools closed, people began hoarding supplies, governments began instituting lockdowns, and conspiracy theories ran wild. And we kept watching *Contagion*, making the decade-old film consistently one of the most popular on streaming services.[13] But what if COVID-19 had struck in 2010, the year before *Contagion* was released? Moderna was formed only that year after Stanford researcher Derrick Rossi pitched a Boston-based venture capital firm on his idea for using a genetic molecule called messenger RNA as a virus-fighting catalyst for the body's immune system. If this virus had hit in 2010, only the older and slower method of vaccine development as seen in *Contagion*—stimulating the body's immune system by injecting inactive or weakened viruses—would've been pursued.

This is pretty incredible: analysis from the Center for Global Development finds that with previous vaccines for which there's data, the average period between microbe isolation and vaccine development was forty-eight years, with a record of about four years (the mumps in the 1960s).[14] What's more, the average time between vaccine development and 40 percent population coverage was forty-two years, with a record of fourteen years for rotavirus. For COVID-19, the period between microbe isolation and a vaccine was less than a year, according to the report. And it was just eleven months between vaccine development and 40 percent coverage. Warp speed progress, indeed.

Deep impact 2023. Humanity is living on borrowed time. How much time, exactly, no one knows. But eventually another very big hunk of rock or chunk of ice will slam into the third planet from the sun. Earth is immersed in a swarm of such objects. And we have pondered the possibility of catastrophic impact since at least the Great Comet of 1680. It was the first comet discovered by a telescope and was studied by both Edmond Halley and Isaac Newton. Newton was later persuaded by his friend William Whiston, a mathematician, that the comet's close passage to Earth four thousand years earlier had caused the Great Flood mentioned in the Holy Bible.[15] For centuries after, humanity was no more able to deflect a dangerous space object than they were in Newton's time. Consider: if the comet that on June

30, 1908, vaporized over Tunguska, Siberia—releasing one thousand times more energy than the Hiroshima atomic bomb—had entered the atmosphere four hours earlier, it would've exploded over London, which lies on the same latitude. And for decades after the Tunguska blast—despite all the advances in astronomy and space flight—we're no better able to deflect a dangerous space object even if given several years of warning. More than eight decades later, on March 23, 1989, a football field–sized asteroid, called Asclepius after the Greek demigod of medicine, passed within 425,000 miles of Earth.[16] Although outside of the moon's orbit, it was considered a close call—at least once astronomers figured out what happened nine days after Asclepius's closest approach to Earth. By one estimate, a rock that size could generate an energy release equal to a theoretical six-hundred-megaton atomic bomb, ten times the impact of the biggest hydrogen bomb exploded, the Soviet Union's Tsar Bomba in 1961, and sixty times that of the nickel-iron meteorite that fifty thousand years ago blasted a crater some four thousand feet in diameter and nearly six hundred feet deep in the desert of what is now northern Arizona. Had Asclepius slammed into the planet, it would've excavated a crater 10 miles wide and a mile deep.

What's more, we may be in greater danger than we've previously assumed because Earth's large impact craters are bigger than previously thought, according to a recent NASA analysis.[17] The larger size suggests the impacts were far more violent events than scientists had calculated. Given that reality, how sophisticated are our current asteroid deflection capabilities? In September 2022, NASA crashed a 1,300-pound probe into Dimorphos, a space rock just five hundred feet wide, that was orbiting a larger asteroid called Didymos, altering the small rock's orbit. "This mission shows that NASA is trying to be ready for whatever the universe throws at us," said NASA administrator Bill Nelson at the time. "NASA has proven we are serious as a defender of the planet.[18] This is a watershed moment for planetary defense and all of humanity." The phrase "trying to be ready" is key here. Earth remains as deeply vulnerable to stray asteroids and comets as it was in 1908 or ever.

✦ ✦ ✦

The Bowthorpe Oak near Lincolnshire, a county in England's East Midlands, running along the North Sea, is thought to be the country's oldest oak. It's more than a thousand years old. Locals were enjoying its shade when Vikings were still raiding the island's coast. The tree sits by itself now, but trees do better together. When you see a thriving, healthy forest of oaks, it means that it consists of a population of trees well suited to that particular environment—at least if that environment remains stable. But what if that environment suffers a sudden shock, like a powerful storm? Trees can maintain their stability under high winds, especially when standing together, but if they break, that's it. The damage is irreversible. Once the storm passes, a shattered forest remains. Now consider the humble blade of grass. It's less stable day-to-day than the mighty oak as it sways with every breeze, bending this way and that, to and fro, without breaking. Even hurricanes can do their worst, but the blade abides. A blade's lack of stability is the very thing that gives it resilience. Stability can be destabilizing, to paraphrase economist Hyman Minsky, who specialized in examining the nature of financial crises.

It's much the same with a wealthy, technologically progressive society. Although the dynamism generated by the advanced economies of such societies can be disruptive—jobs come and go, industries and cities rise and fall—instability and churn also produce long-term resilience through the generation of wealth and technology. Such societies have the resources to adapt and thrive in the face of challenges both predictable and unpredictable. Political scientist Aaron Wildavsky was pro-grass rather than pro-tree as a societal model. In *Searching for Safety*, he outlined two strategies for dealing with risk.[19] One is anticipation: developing models, plans, and policy agendas so a society can predict and prevent potential dangers. The other is resilience: building the capacity to effectively and flexibly respond to dangers, either unanticipated or ones that play out in unanticipated ways, after they emerge and learning to bounce back. Anticipation is about avoidance. Resilience is about response. Of the two strategies, anticipation might seem the obviously preferable approach. If one can accurately forecast future dangers and avoid some damaging result, why not do so?

But that is the tree model of thinking! There are a lot of potential challenges and dangers out there. Which are most likely to occur and which will be the most harmful? In the 2020 book *The Precipice: Existential Risk and the Future of Humanity*, "longtermist" philosopher Toby Ord explores numerous natural and human-made threats either to modern civilization or humanity's existence. And there's an uncomfortably large number of them: asteroids and comets, supervolcanic eruptions, stellar explosions such as supernovas and gamma-ray bursts near our solar system, nuclear war, climate change, pandemics natural and engineered, hostile AI, a totalitarian surveillance state, and extraterrestrial contact. When he adds up his best guesstimates of all those existential risks, he figures there's a one-in-six chance of an existential catastrophe over the next hundred years.[20] Some of those risks worry Ord more than others. An all-out nuclear war may seem like it would end humanity, but Ord thinks that while billions would die, there's a 99 percent chance humanity would endure.[21] Although climate change is often talked about as an existential risk, he thinks it difficult to come up with plausible scenarios that scientists think would cause the unrecoverable collapse of civilization or the extinction of humanity, dire though some of the outcomes could be. He's far more worried about engineered pandemics and about unaligned artificial intelligence—two things that aren't going to kill us this year or next year but over the next few decades could become serious threats.

So what to do? Perhaps bold action on all fronts to either extinguish the potential threat (outlaw genetic editing, ban further AI advances, shutter SETI). Or perhaps prepare society for it (subsidize existing and well-understood technologies, build a network of deep bunkers for millions so civilization could carry on). Of course, there are trade-offs to these actions. Resources are limited and might be wasted on false leads. Some measures will have pitfalls. Banning emerging technologies would also mean losing their benefits. Ord himself is no Luddite. I asked him about banning or suppressing technologies such as AI or genetic editing because they're just too risky. But he rejected that approach. "If there was a fundamental kind of renunciation of technological progress," he said, "I think that itself would destroy our future potential—we would achieve only a tiny fraction of what we could have done if we were to do that."[22] (Hopefully, I have been at least somewhat successful in outlining how grand that potential might be.) Again, stability and preserving the status quo may seem like the safest path. Back to trees: always quickly extinguishing a forest fire may, counterintuitively, be the riskiest long-term move if the result is a build-up of leaves and fallen branches on the forest, which are fuel for a truly devastating and massive blaze. Likewise, quashing tech progress might set the stage for a truly devastating crisis where we lack the tools to tackle it. Some environmentalists, for example, are deeply against solar radiation management, a type of geoengineering where particles of some sort would be sprayed into the atmosphere and then reflect sunlight back into space. A bit less sunlight hitting the planet would help offset global warming from carbon emissions. Of course, maybe there would be unforeseen consequences, especially if a rogue nation or individual decides to go it alone. Then again, it would be a nice option to have in our toolbox if the climate should become more chaotic than climate models currently suggest.

Adding to the complexity of our choices is that each course of action also interacts with existing patterns of life and creates new developments that we do not yet understand but that may turn out to be harmful. All actions, including those that are intended to increase safety, are potential hazards. Should we always reduce risk in advance, or is it sometimes better to enable people to cope in a resilient fashion with dangers when, as, and if they manifest themselves, Wildavsky writes, "doing as much as we can, ruling out only high probability dangers that we can effectively prevent and relying otherwise on our ability to deal with harms as they arise?"[23] When you boil it down, proponents of an overweighting of anticipation and the precautionary principle, with their emphasis on avoiding risk, are creating a recipe for stagnation and stasis. According to Wildavsky: "If you can do nothing without knowing first how it will turn out, you cannot do anything at all. An indirect implication of trial without error is that if trying new things is made more costly, there will be fewer departures from past practice; this very lack of change may itself be dangerous in forgoing chances to reduce existing hazards."[24]

Avoiding innovation and progress for their potential risk may be the riskiest strategy of all. That notion is really at the heart of the proactionary principle, the counterpart of the precautionary principle, which seeks to minimize harm by avoiding policies whose worst outcomes are uncertain. The proactionary principle embraces uncertainty and risk as opportunities for enhancing human welfare and giving us the tools to meet big challenges and problems. The proactionary principle doesn't deny or dismiss the potential problems that science and innovation can cause. Rather, it encourages us to face them head-on and find solutions that can benefit everyone. It also empowers us to use our God-given creativity and intelligence to shape our own future, rather than letting others decide for us or leaving things to chance. It's a way of making the most of our potential as human beings, rather than settling for less or fearing for worse. Captain Kirk has it right again: "You know the greatest danger facing us is ourselves, an irrational fear of the unknown. But there's no such thing as the unknown—only things temporarily hidden, temporarily not understood."[25]

Which approach seems to better approximate the reality in which human society exists? Anticipation strategies seek to maximize stability. The less fluctuation the better. Resilience attempts to accommodate variability in the environment. Which approach seems to better approximate the reality in which human society exists? Whichever answer a society sees as more logical, humanity sees as more compelling, is pretty important given the stakes. "The future is vast," writes economist Max Roser of Our World in Data, a claim backed up, not surprisingly, with data and math.[26] Consider: the lifespan of the typical mammalian species is about a million years. With 200,000 years already in the books, the kind of mammal running this planet has about 800,000 years still ahead. If the global population of human mammals stabilizes at around 11 billion as predicted by the UN with, say, a fifteen-year rise in the global life expectancy to eighty-eight, that means the next 800,000 years will see another 100 trillion people coming online. But what if we really get our act together and learn how to prevent space rocks from smashing into us? Maybe then that million-year lifespan turns into a billion-year lifespan. There will be lots of changes, including continents shifting and mountain ranges rising and falling. But humanity will keep on keepin' on in this future where 125 quadrillion children will be born. And if we can make it as long as the sun burns, we're talking about 625 quadrillion children. According to Roser: "If the current world population was represented by a tiny beach of one square meter, then 625 quadrillion people would make up a beach that is 17 meters wide and 4600 kilometers long. A beach that stretches all across the USA, from the Atlantic to the Pacific coast."[27] And that could be just the start if we leave this planet. The stars are our destination. Our future is vast. The risks are vast. The opportunities are vast. Let's make good choices for ourselves and our kids!

NINE

Why Up Wing Progress Is Possible

The computer, especially when it combined with the internet in the 1990s, is the general purpose technology (GPT)—again, the kind of invention that has a broad and significant impact on an economy and our everyday lives—that drove the Information and Communications Technology Revolution.[1] And while its measurable impact on productivity and economic growth may underwhelm as compared to some previous GPTs, such as electrification and the internal combustion engine, at least it's given Hollywood a seemingly can't-miss cinematic villain: the evil (or at least terribly misguided) supersmart networked computer. Artificial intelligence that has broken bad and broken out. The breakthrough AI cinematic performance was arguably HAL (Heuristically programmed ALgorithmic computer) 9000 in *2001: A Space Odyssey*. And '80s kids will surely remember the military supercomputer WOPR (War Operation Plan Response, pronounced "whopper") that almost launched a nuclear war in 1983's *WarGames*. The following year came a movie that firmly established malevolent machines as movie money-makers. In *Terminator*, the first entry in the film, television, and video game franchise, we find out that the Pentagon's fictitious Global

Digital Defense Network computer system, also known as Skynet, accomplished what WOPR didn't. And once the Cold War ended—taking the Soviets off the table as dangerous baddies with world-dominating ambitions—the Technological Singularity became a frequent go-to villain. Lots of us now believe that should computers ever wake up and become sentient, these brilliant machines will be super-intelligent sociopaths. Job one: exterminating their only rivals, as in the world of *Terminator*, or enslaving us, as in the world of *The Matrix*. The Singularity would mark the end of history, at least for humans. Recent advances in AI guarantee that apocalyptic AI doomerism will continue to be a popular Down Wing theme in our popular culture, though the COVID-19 pandemic will no doubt give new life to zombie and other disease-outbreak media. *The Last of Us* will hardly be the last.

But AI, whether equal to or even exceeding human intelligence, doesn't have to be villainous despite what Hollywood suggests. Such technology could be a powerful tool to help humanity create a more prosperous and opportunity-filled world and then solar system. There's some sci-fi speculation about this more Up Wing scenario, mostly in books rather than films and television, but not much overall. Here's the problem: with the Singularity, writes sci-fi writer Vernor Vinge in his classic essay on the subject, comes "a throwing-away of all the human rules, perhaps in the blink of an eye—an exponential runaway beyond any hope of control."[2] To describe a post-Singularity world is a tough task for any author, sort of like describing heaven. (Indeed, the concept and the notion of the Singularity and post-humanity both have religious overtones.) That's why even the most imaginative writers tend to stick to the events leading up to the Singularity or the moment of awareness rather than spending much time in a post-Singularity world—at least one that isn't apocalyptic.

The chances of a world with human or superhuman-level AI probably aren't zero, however. While Bill Gates doesn't think the recent generative AI breakthroughs "have moved us substantially closer to strong AI,"[3] researchers at the company he co-founded are less skeptical. "Given the breadth and depth of GPT-4's capabilities, we believe that it could reasonably be viewed as an early (yet still incomplete) version of an artificial general intelligence

(AGI) system," concluded a group of scientists at Microsoft Research in early 2023.[4] AGI is the ultimate mission of ChatGPT creator OpenAI. The company's CEO, Sam Altman, has repeatedly said AGI is achievable, even inevitable, whatever the concerns of some worried critics: "Technology happens because it is possible."[5]

For now, AGI is still science-fictional, but some serious economists have found the notion of such a technological leap igniting insanely fast economic growth to be a subject worthy of scholarly consideration. Economist Robin Hanson of George Mason University has envisioned a bio-digital breakthrough that would enable the human brain to be infinitely copied into a computer-based emulation. Now it's not quite the Singularity. Those computer brains, in his scenario, would be only as smart as human ones. But they would run faster and there would be lots of them, so the economy could grow much faster with all of them researching and solving our most challenging problems. Hanson speculates that such an advance would lead to global economic output doubling every two weeks.[6] With that kind of growth, economic statistics would be obsolete. The whole world would be constantly changing almost in the blink of an eye. The idea of smart machines totally replacing workers also features in "The Future of U.S. Economic Growth," by economists John Fernald of the San Francisco Fed and Charles I. Jones of Stanford University. They consider a scenario where "artificial intelligence and machine learning could allow computers and robots to increasingly replace labor in the production function for goods...[And] if capital can replace labor entirely, growth rates could explode, with incomes becoming infinite in finite time."[7]

But we don't need the Singularity or even something just short of it to create a fantastic future. We only need the sort of economic and tech-driven productivity growth that has already happened in the real world—although that happening again with the American economy would stun many forecasters given current expectations. The consensus of economists on Wall Street and in Washington is that U.S. economic growth will hover a touch below 2 percent annually, adjusted for inflation, over the long term. A reasonable goal would be to try to double that pace through faster labor productivity and faster Technologically Futuristic Productivity growth. That pace is about what the American economy did in the Up Wing 1960s and 1990s.[8] The difference between an economy growing at 2 percent for the next fifty years and growing at 4 percent over that span is massive—a $60 trillion economy in 2076 versus $160 trillion. In the former case, there would be economic progress, but it would be so slow that it might seem like stagnation to most people. In the latter Up Wing scenario, however, it might well seem like America was on the fast track toward a *Star Trek*–esque world.

Big Gains from Small Improvements

We need big ideas, of course, but even smaller ones can play an important part. During the pandemic, chipmaker Intel used machine-learning models to help identify alternative supply chain routes to avoid disruptions at factories in China.[9] At megabank JPMorgan, machine-learning systems have allowed for the approval of 1 million "good" customers who might otherwise have been declined, while an equal number of fraudulent applications were turned down.[10] Big Oil is looking to artificial intelligence to help predict equipment problems and increase oil and gas output. Mercedes is converting "dumb" robots on its production line into human-operated, AI-assisted "cobots." This enables a high level of customization such that "no two cars coming off the production line are the same," according to a report in *Harvard Business Review*.[11] New generative AI tools may or may not be the next step toward human-level AI. But even myriad minor impacts such as helping real estate agents quickly write online house listings[12] or reducing the cost of creating professional-quality computer images will add up.[13]

The many possible applications of AI/ML are what give it the potential to be a GPT that extends and accelerates the ICT Revolution. They either make existing things work better or make things possible that weren't possible before. And that often takes a lot of time. "It was clear that electricity would be a transformative technology by the end of the 1870s," explains AI expert and data scientist Avi Goldfarb at the University of Toronto's Rotman School of Management.[14] "It didn't hit half of US factories until the 1920s."

But as electric power slowly diffused throughout the economy, its impact as a GPT became obvious. Goldfarb continues, "Electric power led to innovation in power generating and transmission, but also to innovation in electric light, home appliances, and machine tools." But none of that was obvious at first. It never is with GPTs. That said, Goldfarb is optimistic that AI/ML will be an important GPT.

How important? How much more productivity growth? There are plenty of guesstimates. Maybe AI/ML's impact will be like that of robots, which one study found may have added 0.4 percentage points of annual GDP growth between 1993 and 2007 on average for seventeen advanced economies.[15] Tamay Besiroglu, an economist and researcher at MIT's Computer Science & Artificial Intelligence Laboratory, sees perhaps a 25 percent chance that AI will boost TFP growth—say, reverting to the 2.0 percent to 2.5 percent rate observed before the productivity slowdown that occurred in the early 2000s—by the end of the 2020s.[16] And that's not nothing. Such an acceleration would equate to a $10 trillion increase in U.S. GDP between now and 2030, or about $15,000 per household.[17] But Besirgolu is more hopeful for the years beyond that. "Over longer timescales—say, 15 or 30 years—I think there are good reasons to expect that conservative extensions of current deep learning techniques will be generally useful and reliable enough to automate a range of tasks in sectors beyond IT; notably in manufacturing, energy and science and engineering. Concretely, I think it is more likely than not that over such a time frame AI productivity effects will dominate the productivity effects that computers had in the late 20th century."

But no one knows for sure. As economists John Fernald and Charles Jones conclude in their 2014 paper, AI introduces "a fundamental uncertainty into the future of growth."[18] GenAI, just one kind of AI and machine learning, provides ample evidence of that "fundamental uncertainty." In March 2022, Metaculus, a platform that crowdsources, aggregates, and scores a community of forecasters, had a consensus forecast that AGI would be "devised, tested, and publicly announced" by July 2057. Just twelve months later, that date had been pulled forward to February 2032.[19] The catalyst for the twenty-five-year change in expectations was the emergence and rapid improvement in GenAI models, starting with OpenAI's announcement of ChatGPT in November 2022.

Yet even if that new AGI forecast turns out to be overly ambitious, GenAI might already be consequential enough to end the Great Downshift. "Despite significant uncertainty around the potential of generative AI, its ability to generate content that is indistinguishable from human-created output and to break down communication barriers between humans and machines reflects a major advancement with potentially large macroeconomic effects," concluded the Goldman Sachs economics team in a March 2023 analysis.[20] Specifically, GS thinks GenAI could boost annual U.S. labor productivity growth by just under 1½ percentage points over a decade following widespread business adoption. In other words, GenAI alone—excluding any other pro-productivity impact from other variants of AI/ML or robotics—could return productivity growth to the 3 percent or higher pace seen during previous Up Wing periods. Or even better. Depending on GenAI's capability to automate and complement tasks and how deeply it penetrates the economy, GS thinks 3 points of faster productivity growth is possible. Such a gain would put overall economic growth back to where it was in the 1960s, around 4.5 percent. Remember, current long-term growth forecasts are less than 2 percent. That pace of economic acceleration would finally return the American economy to the growth path assumed by the optimists of Up Wing 1.0 and 2.0.

Some people are quite certain of what the future holds, however. A frequently cited analysis by Down Wing techno-pessimists is a 2005 paper by physicist Jonathan Huebner, of the Pentagon's Naval Air Warfare Center. In it, Huebner presents two big claims. The first: "The rate of innovation peaked in the year 1873 and is now rapidly declining."[21] (He arrives at this claim by comparing major innovations and scientific advances to that of world population.) The second: "This decline is most likely due to an economic limit of technology or a limit of the human brain that we are approaching. We are now approximately 85 percent of the way to this limit, and the pace of technological development will diminish with each passing year." Huebner summed up his views in an interview with *New Scientist*:

"My feeling is we've discovered most of the major branches on the tree of technology."[22]

All of which reminds me of an apocryphal quote from the commissioner of the U.S. patent office in 1899: "Everything that can be invented has been invented."[23] That wasn't true then, and it's no closer to being true today even after more than another century of discovery, invention, and innovation. As economist Paul Romer writes, "Every generation has perceived the limits to growth that finite resources and undesirable side effects would pose if no new recipes or ideas were discovered. And every generation has underestimated the potential for finding new recipes and ideas. We consistently fail to grasp how many ideas remain to be discovered."[24]

Romer famously compares innovation to numerous recipes combining and recombining elements from the periodic table. The number of possible recipes for mixing elements grows very fast as you add more elements, a "combinatorial explosion." Romer: "Once you get to 10 elements, there are more recipes than seconds since the big bang created the universe. As you keep going, it becomes obvious that there have been too few people on earth and too little time since we showed up, for us to have tried more than a minuscule fraction of all the possibilities."[25]

Infinite Combinations and Economic Acceleration

The way we can combine and recombine elements, objects, and past innovations is only limited by our imagination and the laws of nature as we currently understand them. Even better, our imagination might be enhanced through AI/ML. This goes directly to Huebner's point about tree branches, as well as the notion that the low-hanging fruit of big ideas has all been picked. There's an awful lot of knowledge out there. And a lot of technological progress comes from hybrid inventions—putting together two things and making some new third one. Romer's right about the power of combinatorial innovation. Searching that stock of knowledge is a very fruitful way of making advances. Rather than thinking of that stock of knowledge as an impossibly tall single tree, instead think of an orchard. As knowledge continually increases, the number of trees in the orchard increases. There are so many that you can't scan all their branches effectively, even the low-hanging ones. (Or as sci-fi author Octavia Butler once said, "There's nothing new under the sun—but there are new suns.")[26] We need some help. The help could come with AI. "That would be the big potential change, the big potential advantage," Warwick University economist Nicholas Crafts explained to me. "That really goes to the way quite a lot of economic historians think about the idea of an industrial revolution: It's the nature of invention that changes. And we've seen that several times in the past."[27]

Crafts explains that the First Industrial Revolution—the part from the late eighteenth century through the first half of the nineteenth that was centered around weaving, iron, and steam—was full of invention and innovation. But perhaps the greatest was a significant change in the method of invention, one based on empiricism and experimentation to see what worked and then making that knowledge accessible. Starting in the late 1600s, there arose many of what Crafts calls "knowledge access institutions,"[28] or KAIs, whose objectives were to produce and disseminate scientific and technological knowledge. Among the most famous are the Royal Society established in 1660 and the Lunar Society in 1765. These were clubs of learned people who met regularly to exchange the latest news about scientific discoveries and inventions. Isaac Newton was a president of the Royal Society, while the Lunar Society included some of the key inventors of the First Industrial Revolution as its members, including James Watt. The total number of such KAIs was only three in 1761 but had risen to 1,014 by 1851, according to Crafts.

The Second Industrial Revolution, say, 1870 to 1914—the beginning of Gordon's special century of great inventions such as antibiotics, the chemical industry, the electrical grid, the internal combustion engine, and the telephone—saw the rise of the industrial research and development laboratory, a development epitomized by Thomas Edison's establishing his first laboratory in Menlo Park in 1876. By 1918, 665 R&D labs had been established across American manufacturing, and by 1930 about half of all patents granted in the United States went to firms and half to the sort of independent inventors and tinkerers that dominated the early decades of the Industrial

Revolution.[29] (The latter had accounted for about 95 percent of patents in 1880.) The innovation of industrial labs as a new method of invention was a critical element of economic acceleration. "The lab and the corporation are what allowed the likes of Thomas Edison and Nikola Tesla to become inventors," writes economist Brad DeLong in *Slouching towards Utopia*.[30] "They did not have to fulfill the ten other roles that their predecessors had had to fill, from impresario to human resource manager. That work was left to the corporation."

The Third Industrial Revolution typically refers to the period from the 1960s to the 2000s when computer science came of age: the rapid development of computer hardware and software. The mainframe, the PC, and the internet provided more inventions for invention. Crafts thinks AI and, in particular, deep learning may be the basis for a Fourth Industrial Revolution as a GPT that provides the invention of a new method of invention, and this may ultimately be its biggest contribution to productivity growth. This is perhaps its most intriguing potential promise: how it can have a permanent impact on how humans discover knowledge and solve problems across all fields of science research and technological development, he explains. It can take data analysis to a new level and become the world's most effective research assistant.

Recall Romer's recipe of ideas. Innovation can be characterized as a search for combinations over a vast range of possibilities.[31] And AI can accelerate that search. "Given the importance of technological progress for driving economic growth among frontier economies, I pay particular attention to the use of AI tools for automating key tasks in science and engineering, such as drug discovery, software engineering, the designing of chips, and so on," says Besiroglu.[32] "The widespread augmentation of R&D with AI could enable us to improve the productivity of scientists and engineers." This is important: AI/ML won't just be "automating key tasks" but suggesting entire new directors for future research much as GO programs play in ways humans had never considered.

It's already happening and will only accelerate from here. In 2020, for instance, MIT researchers announced the discovery of a new antibiotic, halicin, through AI-driven drug discovery.[33] (The drug is named after *2001* computer HAL.)[34] They trained an ML algorithm to search through a collection of over 6,000 molecules. A molecule with a novel chemical structure and strong antibacterial activity was identified by the model. Another machine-learning model then indicated that this molecule would probably have low toxicity to human cells. In 2022, Google's DeepMind announced that its AlphaFold deep-learning AI solved one of biology's greatest challenges, predicting the 3D shape of the proteins that underpin the process of all life. DeepMind CEO Demis Hassabis said the AI had "provided structural biologists with this powerful new tool now, where you can look up a 3D structure of a protein almost as easily as doing a keyword Google search," with potentially huge potential for drug discovery and other health benefits.[35] Earlier this year, Professor David Baker, a biochemist and computational biologist at the University of Washington, told the *Wall Street Journal* that DeepMind's work has inspired his research team "to use deep learning to accelerate the design of new protein." He estimates, as the *WSJ* describes it, "that the pace of innovation in his field has increased by a factor of 10 during the past 18 months."[36] Complementing the DeepMind breakthrough are more such AI tools that could quicken the development of new and more effective vaccines and accelerate research for the cure to cancer.[37] Already, several biotechnology firms have progressed to clinical trials with drugs—including treatments for Alzheimer's disease and various cancers—discovered or developed using AI.

As exciting as those AI-driven, biological breakthroughs: the potential in materials science. In late 2022, nanoengineers at the University of California San Diego's Jacobs School of Engineering announced they had developed a deep learning algorithm that predicts the structure and properties of any material—whether existing or new—almost instantaneously.[38] For instance, the researchers say they can now predict how particular material can affect how quickly a lithium-ion battery can charge. Also expect to see more announcements, for instance, of "supermaterials" that are both super light and super strong.[39] Yes, making Iron Man–like armor might well be possible. And maybe much more. The ability to find patterns in mountains of data could be especially powerful in discovering new fundamental laws of nature. As physicist Stephen Hawking once quipped about the impact of growing computer power applied to his field, "The end might not be in sight for theoretical physics. But it might be in sight for theoretical physicists."[40] The way AI is helping push forward nuclear fusion is a good example of the combinatorial effect where technological advances feed off each other. A DeepMind AI system is being used to help an experimental Swiss reactor adjust its magnetic coils thousands of times per second so as to best confine its extremely hot plasma and achieve a fusion reaction.[41]

✦✦✦

Erik Brynjolfsson of Stanford University and Robert Gordon of Northwestern University are probably the leading well-known techno-optimist and techno-skeptic economists, respectively. Their views about the future of productivity growth are often contrasted with each other. To raise the stakes just a bit, the two have engaged in a "long bet" with each other through the Long Now Foundation. The wager itself: "Private Nonfarm business productivity growth will average over 1.8 percent per year from the first quarter (Q1) of 2020 to the last quarter of 2029 (Q4)."[42] Recall that labor productivity growth averaged just 1.1 percent a year in the decade before the pandemic. So a decade of almost 2 percent productivity growth would represent a significant acceleration, with faster TFP growth likely playing a significant part. That said, it would be no Singularity.

Gordon thinks recent advances in AI and robotics are unlikely to prove as consequential as the great inventions of the past, particularly electricity and the internal combustion engine: "AI is nothing new, and for more than a decade has replaced human customer service representatives by annoying voice-recognition systems without reviving growth. Much economic activity, from home construction to slicing deli meats at the local supermarket, remains immune from a radical AI transformation." Brynjolfsson, on the other hand, argues that AI is both a general purpose technology and the invention of a new method of invention that can accelerate the pace of discovery. "Recent breakthroughs in machine learning will boost productivity in areas as diverse as biotech and medicine, energy technologies, retailing, finance, manufacturing, and professional services," he explains.

Besiroglu, who works on AI and economics, thinks it's possible that by the middle of this century, the widespread augmentation of R&D with AI "could increase productivity growth rates by 5-fold or more."[43] That would be amazing. But can we do even better, a lot better? Well, when you think about how the modern world is the result of economic growth accelerating from nothing to almost nothing to something, just about anything seems plausible. "It took thousands of years for growth to increase from 0.03 percent to 0.3 percent, but only a few hundred years for it to increase from 0.3 percent to 3 percent," notes researcher Tom Davidson in a report for Open Philanthropy called "Could Advanced AI Drive Explosive Economic Growth?"[44] Davidson continues: "If you naively extrapolate this trend, you predict that growth will increase again from 3 percent to 30 percent within a few decades." But for me, the more intriguing aspect is what Davidson calls the "ideas feedback loop." It comes from the notion that people generating ideas is the core of innovation-driven growth. As economist Charles I. Jones writes in a different paper, "The Past and Future of Economic Growth: A Semi-Endogenous Perspective":

> *Where do ideas come from? The history of innovation is very clear on this point: new ideas are discovered through the hard work and serendipity of people. Just as more autoworkers will produce more cars, more researchers and innovators will produce more new ideas.... People produce ideas and, because of nonrivalry... more colloquially, infinitely usable... those ideas raise everyone's income. This means that income per person depends on the number of researchers. But then the growth rate of income per person depends on the growth rate of researchers, which is in turn ultimately equal to the growth rate of the population.*[45]

So what if people were replaced or joined in that model by AI? Again, Davidson argues that after the demographic transition—where rich countries shifted from higher to lower birth rates—in about 1880, more output did not lead to more people as economic growth increased. Instead people had fewer children as output increased. This disrupted the ideas feedback loop Jones describes where more brains equals more discovery, invention, and innovation. But, Davidson observes, "suppose we develop AI systems that can substitute very effectively for human labor in producing output and in R&D. The following ideas feedback loop could occur: more ideas → more output → more AI systems → more ideas....Before 1880, the ideas feedback loop led to super-exponential growth. So our default expectation should be that this new idea's feedback loop will again lead to super-exponential growth."[46]

Maybe. But achieving economic growth isn't just about plugging some numbers into a model. Benjamin Jones of Northwestern University responds to Davidson by arguing that at 30 percent annual growth, not only would living standards double every 2.5 years, but after 25 years we would be a thousand times richer. And that would mean "creat[ing] and deploy[ing] some set of advances that raise standards of living by 10 times more than all the things we have ever figured out and deployed through all of history."[47] So much "creative destruction"—including rapid turnover and obsolescence in technology and worker skills—that societal pushback would be inevitable. Jones: "Governments face large challenges with the churn of creative destruction at ordinary growth rates, where displaced workers or business owners seek protection. It's a little hard to imagine the political implications of rates of change and churn beyond all historical precedent." For his part, economist Dietrich Vollrath essentially follows up Jones's point about the unintended real-world consequences of 30 percent growth: if people's incomes are rising so fast, wouldn't some of them dial down their effort and hours and live off their skyrocketing investment portfolios or "work the 15-hour weeks that Keynes speculated about, or do things like retire early or take extended time off"?[48] The point here is that crazy-fast tech progress and growth might not have the impact on output growth that you might expect.

Then again, as I have been explaining, we don't need warp-speed, sci-fi growth to get the sci-fi future we've been promised. We just need to create a more Up Wing environment for discovery, invention, innovation, and commercialization by not doing the obvious bad things, and starting to do more of the obvious good things.

TEN

Five Technologies for an Up Wing Future

I hope I've already successfully made the case for why faster technological progress and economic growth are necessary for maximizing future human potential, prosperity, and flourishing—and, you know, are actually possible. But I've also explained why generating fast growth has been so hard in the past and might remain difficult going forward. What makes me so confident, then, that a New Roaring Twenties—followed by a Thrilling Thirties, Fantastic Forties, Fabulous Fifties, et cetera—can really happen?

Think again about the Up Wing fifties and sixties and all those failed futurist forecasts I mentioned earlier in the book. While I concede that being early is a lot like being wrong, it's starting to look like many of those predictions really were just early (with our own bad decisions playing a huge role in the delay). And in a few cases, they might even turn out to be right on schedule, finally. It has to be a harbinger of good Up Wing things, for instance, that flying cars are happening. In a way, this brings us back to nuclear power. Like many other Up Wing forecasts, visions of flying cars often depended on continuing advances in nuclear power to supply a powerful energy source. They probably also never assumed a regulatory environment so different than the one they knew. But set aside the classic, cinematic version of flying cars seen in *The Jetsons*, *Blade Runner*, and *Back to the Future*. Not only did these vehicles run on futuristic power sources, but their actual levitation or antigravity technology was also something more akin to magic than science.

The real-world version is something a lot less like *The Jetsons* and more like the air taxi being developed by German startup Lilium. In 2020, working with a Spanish infrastructure company, Lilium struck a deal to build a network of at least ten "vertiports" across Florida to service its five-person "all-electric vertical takeoff" and landing vehicle with a nearly two-hundred-mile range that the company claims will be "five times faster than a car, and produce less noise than a motorbike."[1] A number of commercial airlines are interested in the technology to speed up the trip to the airport. In October 2022, Delta Air Lines invested $60 million in Joby Aviation, a company developing eVTOL aircraft as air taxis.[2]

Longer term—probably not many eVTOLs dotting the skies this decade—this could be a $1.5 trillion business, according to Wall Street firm Morgan Stanley.[3] The bank thinks that autonomous aircraft could be common by 2040, once key hurdles are cleared, including technical limitations related to batteries and propulsion. However, the bank doesn't believe technology ultimately will be the limiting factor. Instead "the regulatory and societal concerns surrounding the technology will need to catch up to the tech itself. As expected, addressing safety will be at the top of regulators' lists."[4] But don't hand-wave away the tech hurdles. Roboticist Rodney Brooks cautions that "all radically new products, and air taxi eVTOLs certainly count as radically new, require the convergence of many different capabilities and technologies. Often one or more technology will be lagging and it may take decades for them all to come together in the right place at the right time."[5]

Still, if "they" are finally making good on their promise of flying cars rather than just giving us Twitter, many of the most exciting technological advances happening right now are potentially far more consequential. Let's see how we're progressing toward the most ambitious visions of the future as outlined by that 1964 RAND study, the Arthur C. Clarke *Profiles of the Future* chart, and what sci-fi was predicting during Up Wing 1.0. Let's mainly focus on what I see as five of the most exciting areas of technological progress that were also identified back then: artificial intelligence, biotechnology, energy, robotics, and space.

1. Artificial intelligence. Information and communication technology was certainly a sector of widespread optimism back then. The consensus view of the RAND expert survey was an internet—or "central data storage facility with wide access for general or specialized information retrieval" by 1980. Clarke's ballpark estimate was a "translation machine" in the 1970s, artificial intelligence in the 1990s, and a "global library" in the 2000s.[6] Well, we at least beat Clarke when it comes to the internet. Of course, the most famous depiction of a thinking machine for that era—or maybe ever—was the sentient HAL 9000, the fictional artificial intelligence from Clarke's *2001: A Space Odyssey.* The timeline of Clarke's fictional AI syncs with his *Profiles* forecast. HAL became operational on January 12, 1992, at the University of Illinois's Coordinated Science Laboratory in Urbana, Illinois.

Obviously, we're not there yet, even if the stunning recent advances in generative AI seem at times to have created new intelligences possessing the spark of true creativity and imagination. But, again, the optimistic forecasts in this book don't depend on human-level artificial general intelligence, much less a superintelligence, to have significant economic importance. What is needed is for AI/machine learning to be a general purpose technology. Stanford University economist Erik Brynjolfsson points out that large language models are "incredibly effective at stringing together statistically plausible chunks of text in response to prompts. But to claim they are sentient is the modern equivalent of the dog who heard a voice from a gramophone and thought his master was inside."[7] That said, their potential adaptability to many different fields—law, biomedicine, healthcare, education—shows their powerful GPT potential.

At some point, breakthrough scientific discoveries and technological inventions need to translate into valuable commercial innovations and greater worker productivity. And for that to happen, there need to be years of complementary investments before the productivity benefits of GPT innovation typically show up in the official statistics. As Brynjolfsson has found, productivity growth may even be initially *suppressed* by important innovations as companies invest time and effort creating "intangible assets"—new business processes, new skills, new goods and new services—to take advantage of the advance. Later, these investments are harvested, boosting productivity.[8] For example, there was plenty of excitement about e-commerce in the 1990s. But it took nearly two decades, until 2019, for online business models to approach 10 percent of total retail sales. "The sector as a whole required the build-out of an entire distribution infrastructure," Brynjolfsson explains. "Customers had to be 'retrained' to buy online. Organizational inertia held back innovation in business processes, supply chains, and product selection....Self-driving cars, medical applications of machine learning, and many other AI breakthroughs will likely follow a similar trajectory."[9]

The good news: We're seeing those complementary investments happen. In the latest data from the AI Index Report, published annually by the Stanford Human-Centered AI, everything you would want to be up is up: the AI hiring rate, private AI investment, new AI startup funding, demand for AI skills, AI skill training, and increased computer science graduates and postgraduates.[10] These stats are likely a big reason that Brynjolfsson takes the Up Wing side in his bet with economist Robert Gordon. And already what we're seeing in GenAI shows immense productivity promise. Early research finds that ChatGPT helps people who write as part of their jobs (such a grant writers and human resources professionals) produce emails, press releases, and brief reports nearly 40 percent faster with better quality.[11] Even more impressive: Software developers using Copilot, a GenAI tool that allows them to present a problem in natural language and then have the solution presented as code, complete a task twice as fast as developers not using Copilot as part of an experiment.[12] That sort of advance starts to look like the "automation of automation," writes policy analyst Robert Tracinski. "We're on the cusp of technology that will allow us simply to decide what new thing we want to do, and as with Copilot, the AI will figure out how to do it."[13] Early days but exciting days.

But what about human-level AI, or AGI? What's a realistic timeline? Depends on what experts you ask, of course. A 2022 survey of hundreds of machine-learning researchers asked when "high-level machine intelligence"—defined as "unaided machines [that] can accomplish every task better and more cheaply than human workers"—would be feasible.[14] The consensus estimate was a 50 percent chance of HLMI by 2059. Of course, this survey was taken before the various generative AI models were introduced to the public. That same survey taken today might show a more aggressive forecast. In June 2022, the Metaculus forecasting platform gave the question "Human/Machine Intelligence Parity by 2040" a 59 percent chance of happening. ChatGPT and DALL-E pushed the odds to 80 percent by early 2023.[15] (Metaculus also forecast superintelligence just 10 months after AGI is achieved.) That sort of expectation is no doubt strengthened by GPU-maker Nvidia's prediction of AI models one million times more powerful than ChatGPT within 10 years.[16] So far it sure might seem like AI is on the fast track to changing, well, everything. Still, the same need for complementary investments to turn AGI into a productivity-enhancing GPT certainly still apply. That's likely why Sam Altman, CEO of OpenAI, the research lab behind ChatGPT, predicts AGI "gets built sooner than most people think, and takes much longer to 'change everything' than most people imagine."

Yet even machine-learning AI that's well short of human-level cognition can provide virtual helpers to us as workers and business owners. "What would you build with a million such 'interns' in the cloud, available on demand, 24/7, and at close to zero marginal cost?" imagines Matt Clifford, chair of ARIA, the UK's Advanced Research and Invention Agency. "In 2023, we can expect thousands of entrepreneurs to show us."[17] But AGI could do a whole lot more, of course. What if your virtual team member was as smart as Elon Musk or creative as Steven Spielberg? "You could say, 'I want to make a movie or a comic book or something like that, give me the team that I need to go do that,' and then run it on the cloud—that's kind of my vision for it," explains virtual-reality technologist John Carmack, who sees a 60 percent chance of AGI by 2030.[18]

2. Biotechnology. Among the health breakthroughs predicted by the 1964 RAND expert survey were universal immunization, control of some hereditary defects through gene modification, and chemical control of the aging process. The consensus about the first two saw their arrival before 2000 and life extension within the first decade of the twenty-first century. Clarke's *Profiles of the Future* forecasts were more cautious, seeing "control of heredity" by the 2020s and "bioengineering" by the 2030s. Interestingly, this is one area that *Star Trek* is notoriously squeamish about. It's franchise canon that the Federation frowns upon genetic modification due to the late twentieth-century Eugenics Wars, where genetically engineered supermen attempted to take over the world in the *Trek*-verse.

Although I'm a space nerd, it's hard to argue that the greatest innovation of the past few years—albeit one built upon decades of research—was the rapid development of the Moderna and BioNTech/Pfizer vaccines. Millions of people are alive today because mRNA vaccines can instruct our cells to make a protein that will trigger an immune response. This ability to program cellular protein production has raised hopes that we might also be able to produce universal vaccines for both the coronavirus and influenza as well as preventing HIV infection and malaria. Maybe cancer, too. And the hopes are already proving to be justified. Researchers from the University of Pennsylvania reported in late 2022 that they have developed a new mRNA vaccine that could protect against all existing flu strains with one injection.[19] And in early 2023, Moderna and Merck's mRNA vaccine for skin cancer received breakthrough therapy designation from the FDA.[20] This means that the drug can be developed and reviewed faster for treating serious diseases.

But let's not forget about CRISPR. Future generations and historians may look back at the first part of the twenty-first century as the emerging Age of AI or Age of Atomic Fusion—but also maybe the Age of Gene Editing, thanks to the revolutionary molecular scissors of CRISPR. Humanity can now go into its cells and insert a gene sequence to create new therapies to fight all manner of ailments—and perhaps end many hereditary diseases in humans (cystic fibrosis, muscular dystrophy, and Huntington's disease), as well as design disease-resistant crops. The pace of progress with CRISPR has been breathtaking. In 2022, just a decade after eventual Nobel Prize winners Jennifer Doudna and Emmanuelle Charpentier proved that part of the bacterial immune system could be used to alter DNA, treatments for a variety of genetic ailments—blood cancers, spinal muscular atrophy, hemophilia, sickle-cell disease—started to go before regulators and perhaps soon into our bloodstreams. Perhaps you've heard about "personalized medicine" where treatments could be tailored to each person's individualized genetic makeup. In late 2022, a team of UCLA researchers showed CRISPR could "alter immune cells so that they will recognize mutated proteins specific to a person's tumors," *Nature* reported. "Those cells can then be safely set loose in the body to find and destroy their target." As 2022 ended, news broke that CRISPR was used to create a therapy that attacked a thirteen-year-old's stubborn leukemia. "This is a very impressive technological feat, with the best possible clinical outcome so far in the one patient treated so far," Bruce Levine, a professor specializing in cancer gene therapy at the Perelman School of Medicine at the University of Pennsylvania, told Bloomberg.[21]

Earlier this year, San Diego–based startup Rejuvenate Bio and a Harvard University research team both announced that they had, separately, used a similar gene therapy approach to reverse the signs of aging in mice. Soon after, David Sinclair, the leader of the Harvard team, said his findings show "it's possible to reset the age of the body up to as much as 50 percent. And, when you can reverse aging and not just slow it down, then all bets are off."[22] Indeed, a slowdown in aging that increases life expectancy by a single year—we're not talking about immortality here—would be worth $38 trillion, according to a 2021 analysis from Sinclair and colleagues.[23] From that report: "The economic value of gains from targeting aging are large because delaying aging produces complementarities between health and longevity [and affects] a large number of diseases due to the rising prevalence of age-related comorbidities." And while we're waiting for those therapies to progress, AI/ML can help diagnose age-related conditions. For example, researchers at Massachusetts General Hospital in Boston have trained a model than can analyze brain scans to detect Alzheimer's disease risk with more than 90 percent accuracy.[24]

But even as CRISPR techniques continue to improve, its uses have also extended beyond human biology. Pioneer Doudna observes various ways the technology can help reduce the impact of agriculture on climate change. Among them: editing or altering microbes that emit greenhouse gases from soil or animals; enhancing the capacity of plants and microbes to capture and store carbon in soil; reducing the need for fertilizers and pesticides that have high carbon footprints and environmental risks; and making plants more resilient to drought and heat stress as Earth's climate continues to warm.[25]

3. Energy. One of the most important energy advances over the past decades, right with the Shale Revolution, has been the massive decline in the cost of renewable energy, with the cost of electricity from utility-scale solar photovoltaics falling by 85 percent, concentrated solar power 68 percent, onshore wind 56 percent, and offshore wind 48 percent.[26] And the impacts of those cost declines have only just started. In the United States, the share of electricity production coming from renewable sources, aided in part by subsidies contained in the 2022 Inflation Reduction Act, is expected to climb to 37 percent in 2032 from 17 percent in 2022.[27]

But solar and wind aren't the energy sources that jazzed those 1960s futurists. They were confident the Age of Atomic Fission would soon lead to the Age of Atomic Fusion. The RAND report saw "controlled thermo fusion" by the 1980s, a prediction that no doubt underlay many others that would seem to require cheap, abundant energy—from desalination plants to undersea mining and habitats to colonizing the Solar System. (As energy researcher Charles Scarlott writes in the 1968 anthology *Toward the Year 2018*, "It is not too much to suggest that success [in developing nuclear fusion] would assure mankind an ample source of energy for thousands of years.")[28] Clarke also expected a pre-millennium fusion breakthrough. These advances were all seen as eventually leading by the end of the twenty-first century to novel forms of energy somewhat akin to the warp drives on *Star Trek*.

Better late than never. Although some skeptics continue to joke that fusion is just a few decades away and always will be, surely fewer of us are chuckling these days. No, the historic fusion breakthrough announced on December 13, 2022, probably won't directly lead to commercial fusion reactors feeding into the grid tomorrow or the day after tomorrow. But by generating the first artificial fusion reaction that produced more energy than it directly consumed, the scientists at Lawrence Livermore National Laboratory in California did move us "one significant step closer" to having zero-carbon fusion energy "powering our society," as Energy secretary Jennifer Granholm excitedly told a news conference in Washington that day.[29]

More milestones need to be achieved before fusion-generated energy starts powering our smartphones—and those critical next steps won't be taken solely by government. Fusion research has long been thought to be the sort of scientific megaproject that needed big business and big government to succeed. But the recent improvements in the superconducting magnets needed to contain the superhot plasma inside a reactor and new reactor designs have pointed to a path for commercial viability and startup success. Take the case of Commonwealth Fusion Systems, a spin-off from MIT's Plasma Science and Fusion Center that was founded in 2018 by MIT postdoctoral researcher Robert Mumgaard. Since then, it's generated some of the most encouraging news about nuclear fusion in the technology's frustrating history. A fusion reactor, such as the ones being planned by Commonwealth Fusion Systems, could be built on the site of current plants and then plugged into the grid, which could be totally powered by three thousand reactors at a cost of some $1 trillion.[30] (Some estimates put the potential value of the technology at nearly $40 trillion to $50 trillion.)

And even if the news, once again, turns discouraging, there are still plenty of advances happening in nuclear fission to help make the case—beyond concerns about climate change and energy shortages—for reembracing that technology. The future could be a smaller, cheaper, quicker-build version. Small modular reactors are about a fifth of the size of a standard light-water reactor. One big SMR selling point is that these reactors can be mass-produced to reduce costs, unlike large reactors, which typically end up as bespoke megaprojects. SMRs no bigger than a small warehouse—able to power small towns or large city neighborhoods—could be built in factories and then shipped in sections for rapid on-site assembly. These are important features, especially standardization so nuclear reactors are more cookie-cutter projects than bespoke. A 2020 MIT analysis notes that the nuclear industry's history of high construction costs has been "associated with delays caused by the need to make last-minute design changes," due to changing safety regulations and local conditions at construction sites.[31] An example of this dynamic is what happened in the late 1960s and early 1970s with the Sequoyah Nuclear Plant near Chattanooga, Tennessee.[32] The plant began construction in 1968 with a projected cost of $336 million. And already by 1974, the cost estimate had risen to $675 million with the Tennessee Valley Authority projecting additional costs of $317 million due to "design and engineering changes, higher interest on borrowed money than anticipated, and schedule delays." The GAO noted that "TVA officials informed us of 23 cases at the Sequoyah project where a structure or component had to be torn out and rebuilt, or added because of required changes."

Despite its depressing history as an obstacle to nuclear power in the U.S., the Nuclear Regulatory Commission has certified the design of NuScale's small modular reactor design, saying it "meets the agency's applicable safety requirements."[33] The company intends to have a full powerplant with multiple reactors on-site at the Department of Energy's Idaho National Laboratory site by 2030.[34] But there are more regulatory steps to be taken and skepticism about the NRC is warranted. It would be helpful if Congress made it clear to the NRC that a modernized and streamlined system is needed for both fission and fusion.

And while some entrepreneurs and technologists are trying to recreate star power, others are trying to harness the sun beneath our feet. That description of geothermal energy is no exaggeration. The Earth's molten core is roughly as hot as the surface of the sun, nearly 11,000°F. Also like the sun, Earth's core will generate heat for billions of years in the future as naturally occurring radioactive elements continually decay. The continuous energy flow is roughly thirty terawatts, almost double all current human energy consumption. And that's just the core. Extracting "just 0.1 percent of the heat content of Earth could supply humanity's total energy needs for 2 million years," according to the U.S. government's Advanced Research Projects Agency–Energy.[35] We could even tap the power of a supervolcano, such as the one simmering beneath Yellowstone Park, without worry about disastrous consequences. Yellowstone could theoretically power the entire country, but it's been off limits to developers since the 1970 Geothermal Steam Act to preserve its pristine environment—not because anyone fears somehow setting it off. How would that even work? One idea would be to insert a hundred, five-mile-long, engineered copper cylinders deep into the Yellowstone Caldera magma chamber. Those cylinders would then connect to ten steam turbines linked to a nationwide energy grid. At an estimated cost of $3.5 trillion, the "Yellowstone Caldera Volcanic Power Generation Facility" would definitely qualify as an infrastructure megaproject.[36] We better start the permitting process now.

But Up Wing excitement over geothermal has little to do with potentially tapping supervolcanoes. Advances in drilling technology due to the Shale Revolution have enabled the sector to move beyond merely taking advantage of what nature gives us: those areas, such as in Iceland and California, where heat, water, and porous rock come together to create natural hydrothermal reservoirs near Earth's surface. Entrepreneurs, such as those at Fervo Energy, want to use a modified form of hydraulic fracturing to extract geothermal energy by creating artificial underground reservoirs by drilling several miles deep, injecting water into hot rock, and then pushing it back to generate steam and electricity. Further in the future, we may not even need to fracture the rock, but instead use horizontal drilling and pipes to run fluid through closed-loop systems that simply circulate fluid from the surface deep into the Earth and back through a pipe system. Quaise Energy is trying to combine conventional rotary drilling with rock-evaporating, millimeter-wave beam technology—first developed for nuclear fusion research—to drill down more than twelve miles where temperatures approach 1,000°F. That approach would enable geothermal anywhere and at a scale that could satisfy energy consumption for, well, forever.

Isaac Asimov's 1941 short story "Reason" is about a space station that supplies solar energy from space via microwave beams to Earth. And as is typical with his stories, there's plenty of science fact embedded with the fiction. There are no theoretical obstacles to placing tech in low-Earth orbit that would convert some of the 173,000 terawatts (trillions of watts) of solar energy continuously striking Earth, an amount ten thousand times total global energy consumption. The U.S. Department of Energy envisions small self-assembling satellites being launched into space, along with reflectors and a microwave or laser power transmitter.[37] Reflectors or inflatable mirrors would then spread over a vast swath of space and direct solar radiation onto solar panels. These panels then convert that solar radiation into microwaves and beam it down to Earth-based collectors—giant wire nets measuring up to four miles across that could be installed across deserts or farmland or even over lakes. From there, the electricity would flow to the grid and finally into your smartphone. This "solar swarm" approach is very different than the megaproject some imagined back in the 1970s. "The cost estimates suggested at that time that it might be as much as a trillion dollars to get to the first kilowatt-hour because of the way the designs worked. Essentially a single satellite, a platform, an integrated, monolithic platform about the size of Manhattan," physicist and advocate John Mankins told CNBC in 2019.[38]

For decades, a key technological limitation has been the cost of putting satellites and other objects into orbit. But the rapid and deep decline in launch costs has gone a long way toward removing that barrier. It could cost anywhere from $200 million to $2.5 billion to transport a four-gigawatt power station into orbit.[39] And with that decline in costs has come increased interest in the possibility of space solar. In April 2021, Pentagon-funded scientists successfully tested a prototype solar panel, about the size of a pizza box. "Some visions have space solar matching or exceeding the largest power plants today—multiple gigawatts—so enough for a city," the project's leader told CNN.[40] "The unique advantage the solar power satellites have over any other source of power is this global transmissibility. You can send power to Chicago and a fraction of a second later, if you needed, send it instead to London or Brasilia."

Private investors are also interested. Caltech's Space Solar Power Project was funded by entrepreneur Donald Bren after reading about the technology in *Popular Science* magazine back in 2011.[41] China, too, has a huge interest. The solar power station plans being contemplated by China include the launch of small to medium-sized solar power projects in the stratosphere to generate electricity by 2025, followed by a space-based solar power station that can generate at least a megawatt of electricity in 2030, and a commercial-scale solar power plant in space by 2050.[42] The UK is also active in this sector. Its Space Energy Initiative, a partnership between government, industry, and academia, is seeking to build a space-based solar fleet to connect to the country's power grid in the 2040s. When might a U.S. effort start beaming power from the heavens? In 2022, Ali Hajimiri, co-director of the Caltech effort, told me a demonstration project was probably possible by the end of the 2020s. He added: "But if you want to have a substantial amount of power transferred…that takes another decade or two to get to that point—if this pathway turns out to be the right pathway to go down."[43]

4. Robotics. We've long dreamed about the existence of mechanical beings who could do our bidding. In ancient Greek mythology, Hephaestus, the maker-god, built an automaton named Talos—a project commissioned by Zeus—to defend King Minos's kingdom of Crete. As described in *Gods and Robots: Myths, Machines, and Ancient Dreams of Technology* by Adrienne Mayor, Talos was super fast (he marched around the island three times a day), super smart (he was programmed to recognize approaching strange ships), and super strong (he would pick up boulders and throw these at the invaders).[44] In close combat, Talos could heat his metal body red hot and then crush Minos's enemies to his chest to roast them alive. Robots have also been a key element of science fiction since the birth of the genre, from the female Futura in Fritz Lang's *Metropolis* to Rosey the housemaid in *The Jetsons*, the automaton perhaps most relevant to speculation in Up Wing 1.0.

The Up Wing futurists of the 1960s, however, were far less focused on such smart machines than Hollywood. They also seemed immune to the automation concerns of politicians and activists. In 1964, the same year that President Lyndon Johnson created his national automation commission, Isaac Asimov wrote his speculative essay about a World's Fair of 2014—and was utterly dismissive about humanoid robots, saying such machines "will neither be common nor very good in 2014, but they will be in existence.…

[The] IBM building at the 2014 World's Fair may have, as one of its prime exhibits, a robot housemaid—large, clumsy, slow-moving but capable of general picking-up, arranging, cleaning and manipulation of various appliances. It will undoubtedly amuse the fairgoers to scatter debris over the floor in order to see the robot lumberingly remove it."[45]

Many futurists seemed far more interested in turning apes into smart workers than machines. That RAND survey, for instance, predicted that by 2020 we would be breeding super-intelligent apes to do manual labor, including chauffeuring us around. Clarke also featured such an advance in his forecast, but saw it happening in the 2040s. No wonder, then, that the 1968 film *Planet of the Apes* struck a chord with moviegoers. Experts were telling them such a future wasn't purely a work of science fiction. If the bombs and missiles didn't get them, maybe our upgraded simian relatives would!

Such enthusiasm for animal upgrades has not weathered well the passage of time, but their skepticism about sophisticated robots has. Set aside humanoid robots, for a moment. The robots you're most likely to find in American business are those performing repetitive tasks such as welding on the assembly lines in automotive plants. But that's changing. Automakers and manufacturers of auto components accounted for 42 percent of robot orders in 2021, down from 71 percent in 2016.[46] Meanwhile, notes the *Wall Street Journal*, "robots made inroads into other sectors including food production, consumer products, and pharmaceuticals. Executives said improved capabilities are allowing robots to be programmed for more-complex tasks requiring a mixture of strength and nimbleness."[47] Amazon, for instance, is intent on installing its new Sparrow robot arm, which can pick up and sort millions of individual unpackaged products, across its warehouses.[48] (The retailer says its employees can now focus on less repetitive tasks in the company's warehouses and has created seven hundred new job "categories" related to robotics.) Increasing the number of industrial robots is especially a priority in China, where the working-age population might have already peaked, with UN projections showing a sharp decline after 2030.[49] In 2021, China installed almost as many industrial robots as the rest of the world combined.[50]

But even nations with a stronger demographic outlook than China—one with higher fertility rates and a younger population, as well as more potential to attract immigrants—will find it useful to increase their number of robots to boost productivity, plug their own widening labor market gap, and keep production costs down. So much so, that one Wall Street bank thinks the potential of Hollywood-style humanoid robots might be worthy of being mentioned in the same breath as the smartphone and electric vehicles as hugely profitable Next Big Thing innovations of the twenty-first century. In a 2022 report, Goldman Sachs offered a "blue sky" scenario where the humanoid robot sector would be a $150 billion market by 2035—assuming the "hurdles of product design, use case, technology, affordability, and wide public acceptance be completely overcome"—which would be a market close to that of the global electric vehicles and one-third of global smartphone sales.[51] This would be a world where "labor shortage issues such as for manufacturing and elderly care can be solved to a large extent." One reason for optimism is that a humanoid robot—such as the one being developed by Elon Musk and Tesla—would largely be based on existing applications, such as industrial robots, autonomous vehicles, and those automatons doing parkour in viral videos. As much as technical issues, the bank is as concerned with softer challenges such as concerns about job loss and safety.

5. Space. The RAND experts survey predicted a permanent lunar base ("10 men, indefinite stay") right around 1980 with a Mars landing about a decade later and a permanent Mars base in the early decades of the twenty-first century. Clarke offered much the same outlook, so it's not surprising that the initial action in *2001: A Space Odyssey* takes place at a lunar research station. (Recall that he co-wrote the screenplay with director Stanley Kubrick, using his 1951 novella, *The Sentinel*, as inspiration.) These forecasts ended up syncing with one of the options for the future of manned space exploration that NASA presented to President Richard Nixon in 1970.[52] "Option 1" of the post-Apollo scenarios saw a lunar base established no later than 1985, serviced by an Earth-orbiting space station capable of launching reusable nuclear shuttles. There were big dreams for the Red Planet, too, with a nuclear rocket taking the first American there for a 1982 landing.[53]

NASA's timeline reflected a fundamental economic misunderstanding, however. Building rockets and launching missions using the Apollo model simply cost too much *without* the justification of geopolitical competition with the Soviet Union and *with* an economy that downshifted in the early 1970s. A 2022 Citigroup analysis notes that average launch costs "remained relatively stable" in the four decades after Apollo.[54] Former NASA deputy administrator Lori Garver, a key player in the eventual commercialization of U.S. space flight, points out that NASA has sent roughly 350 astronauts (some more than once) into space since Apollo at a cost of around $350 billion—an unsustainable billion bucks per person. For forty years, there was little innovation either in launch technology or in how development was funded with a few large government contractors—often employing former NASA officials and astronauts—operating with cost-plus contracts. "A self-licking ice cream cone" is how Garver terms this cozy space-industrial complex.[55]

Then came Elon Musk and SpaceX, which pioneered a massive drop in launch costs to $2,500 per kilogram with the Falcon 9 rocket in 2010 and $1,500 per kilogram with the Falcon Heavy in 2018.[56] As Citi notes, these costs are "30× lower than the launch cost of NASA's Space Shuttle in 1981 and 11× lower than the average launch costs from 1970 to 2010."[57] Next up: the SpaceX Starship which holds the promise of being both the largest and most powerful rocket ever built, but also fully reusable with an ambitious goal of achieving a launch cost of $10 per kilogram or less than $2 million per launch versus $60 million for a Falcon 9.[58] If successful, Starship's initial purpose will be satellite delivery. Beyond that, Starship will be able to lift large amounts of cargo into space setting the stage for lunar and Mars outputs. It's no exaggeration to call Starship, if successful, the most important step forward since Project Apollo in humanity becoming a true spacefaring and multiplanetary civilization.

Dramatically lower costs are also being promised by Jeff Bezos–owned Blue Origin and the Ariane Group for the European Space Agency. Citi also forecasts that launch costs will fall another 95 percent to $100 per kilogram by 2040 "driven by reusability, scale, lower input costs, and cost-efficient production methods" with a drop to a mere $30 per kilogram also possible.

This continuing decline in launch costs is the key factor enabling the emerging space economy, the value of which is expected to triple to more than $1 trillion by 2040. The dominant revenue generator is expected to be the satellite industry, which Musk has said is key to funding his larger space ambitions. But perhaps more exciting are new space applications that could be worth $100 billion within a couple of decades, including commercial space stations, space-based solar power, space exploration, moon/asteroid mining, space logistics, space tourism, and microgravity R&D. Take that last item: chemical compounds can behave differently in a zero-gravity environment. Los Angeles-based startup Varda Space Industries hopes to take advantage of low-Earth orbit through an automated drug lab that's small enough to fit in a space capsule. The company thinks it can successfully pursue new treatments for cancer, chronic pain, and diabetes. "We have built a unique way to manipulate chemical systems," Will Bruey, Varda's co-founder and chief executive officer, told Bloomberg in early 2023. "And the most expensive chemical systems on Earth are drugs. We knew that making them in space was the killer app of microgravity."[59]

By the end of this decade, NASA will have likely returned to the moon—it's already awarded a contract to build lunar infrastructure on the moon such as landing pads, habitats, and roads—whether on its own Space Launch Systems rocket or Elon Musk's bigger, more powerful, and far cheaper to launch Starship, which would be the first fully reusable rocket with both its first and second stages able to land and be used again. NASA also envisions a series of robotic missions to Mars every two-year launch window starting as soon as 2030.[60] But will there already be humans there to greet those little fellows? Musk has recently suggested a crewed mission to Mars is possible in 2029.[61]

⁂

So taken all together, we might well start the 2030s having finally met or exceeded a host of technological predictions from Up Wing 1.0. And that's the direction we're headed. But America needs to do far more to make sure it hits that goal and then far surpasses it.

ELEVEN

Eleven Ways to Build an Up Wing Economy

Imagine if Elon Musk eventually achieves the goal on which some part of his vast personal wealth is based: developing and manufacturing a fully self-driving electric automobile that can operate anywhere, at any time, in any weather. (Already autonomous taxis are zipping around Phoenix and San Francisco with service to more U.S. cities on the way.) Punch in your destination and take a long nap. Such a supersafe car would be one of the most sophisticated machines ever devised, right up there with the latest reusable rocket from Musk's SpaceX. And let's further imagine that the first vehicles off the line were targeted at well-off—also adventurous—consumers. Maybe the first model of an autonomous Tesla goes for, say, $100,000. A nice round number.

Now imagine something goes wrong. Even this marvelous machine could blow a tire or suffer some mechanical problem. Or a non-autonomous car could smash into it. But whatever the cause of the accident, let's say this self-driving Tesla is utterly totaled. A complete loss. In a flash, it's become the world's most sophisticated hunk of junk. But the pre-crash, self-driving Tesla and the post-crash Tesla have one important thing in common: they both contain the same number of atoms. The amount of matter in one is the same as the other. The only real difference between the two vehicles is how that matter and those atoms are arranged. And the difference in that arrangement means that even though the weight of the Tesla is the same, its value has disappeared.

The physical arrangement of atoms is what some academics mean by the term *information*, which is obviously not how the rest of us use the term. But if you think of information in this weird, special way (as the physical order of atoms), then when that order is changed—such as when a self-driving electric car crashes or a bit of sand is turned into a microchip—there's been a change in information. In the first case, the change has led to a less complex and ordered arrangement, in the second case far more. And economic value is often embedded in complexity. All the value in the pre-crash autonomous Tesla was stored in the complex arrangement of its atoms, not in the atoms themselves.

That sort of car example is a favorite of statistical physicist César Hidalgo.[1] He describes the information concept this way: "If you take a deck of cards and you shuffle it, you don't change the mass, you don't change the energy, but you change the information that it contains. And the creativity of our universe and our economy depends on our ability to create information, to change how things are ordered."[2] If you're interested in progress and growth, you definitely want a TMI, or too much information, economy. From this economic perspective, one that merges with physics, information is one of three key factors in economic growth, along with matter and energy. In traditional economics, the key elements are labor, capital, and ideas. Both are correct but offer a different analytical framing when thinking about economic policy. Processing information, using energy and ideas to change physical order in a way that gives meaning or value, is what economies do. The greater such computational capacity, the greater capability an economy has to make information grow and the greater the possible complexity of economic activities such as making an iPhone, a Tesla, or ChatGPT. Countries with less computational capacity might only be able to produce basic commodities or simple products such as clothing. They're less able to create the physical objects that embody and accumulate complex information, what Hidalgo elegantly calls "crystals of imagination,"[3] adding that some economies "are able to produce packets of information that embody concepts begotten by science fiction. Others are not quite there."[4]

And what separates national economies that possess high computational capacity from the ones that don't? It comes down to the size and density of their networks, which come in many forms. So think of the American economy as a $21 trillion living supercomputer, a wondrous, wealth-generating, techno-organism constructed from a lattice of human-powered networks—companies, cities, regional governments, and universities—all connected to each other. This economic supercomputer has one primary purpose: to process information (to reorder matter). In other words, the complex structure needed to create a modern techno-capitalist society that Lewis Mumford ominously called the Megamachine and others simply referred to as "the system" is the entity that creates prosperity and opportunity to build the future we want.

Pro-complexity, pro-network, pro-connection economics is pro-progress Up Wing economics. It is critical public policy to make sure each node of the networks that form the high-energy, American economic supercomputer works as creatively and productively as possible. Policy must help produce lots of educated, trained, healthy humans who can effectively generate and easily acquire knowledge and connect with each other through networks of various sorts to produce complex, information-dense crystals of imagination.

Throughout this book I write about the need for America to embrace a smart, risk-taking ethos. But to assume that even the most promising of emerging technologies of today can neither be helped nor hindered by public policy would be an unwise risk to take. Here are eleven pro-progress policy ideas to help America build a dynamic and high-productivity Up Wing economy:

1. Colonize the Moon. In *The Expanse*, much of the drama stems from tense relations among the United Nations of Earth and the moon (or Luna), the Red Planet's Martian Congressional Republic, and the Outer

Planets Alliance, a burgeoning separatist movement in the asteroid belt and on the moons of Jupiter and Saturn. It's too bad *The Expanse*, especially the television version, doesn't seriously grapple with the economics of a future when humanity has become a multiplanetary civilization. The following passage from the book, however, does give a tantalizing hint of the impact from extreme resource abundance: "Platinum, iron, and titanium from the Belt. Water from Saturn, vegetables and beef from the big mirror-fed greenhouses on Ganymede and Europa, organics from Earth and Mars. Power cells from Io, Helium-3 from the refineries on Rhea and Iapetus. A river of wealth and power unrivaled in human history came through [the dwarf planet of] Ceres."[5]

But first things first. Yes, Musk talks a lot more about Mars than the moon. One of the few Up Wing things Donald Trump may ever have said—tweeted, actually—was this: "For all of the money we are spending, NASA should NOT be talking about going to the Moon—We did that 50 years ago. They should be focused on the much bigger things we are doing, including Mars (of which the Moon is a part), Defense and Science!"[6] But again, first things first. While there may be a new Space Race happening—and it isn't just America versus China, and not just governments competing—the goal this time is as much about geoeconomics as geopolitics. Which space superpower will have greatest access to the innovation, jobs, and resources that will eventually flow to and from this final frontier? "The moon is absolutely central to that incorporation of the inner solar system into the Earth's economic sphere because it's close, because it has low gravity, because it is resource-rich," said defense and space consultant Peter Garretson in 2022.[7] "And of course, if a foreign power can limit your access to resources, like on Earth you can see Russia limiting access to natural gas for Europe, you lose national security in that exchange."

What does the moon have that we would want? Three potential resources are key: water (to sustain a permanent outpost and create rocket fuel), helium-3 (a rare helium isotope that could be used for innovations in the energy sector—namely nuclear fusion), and various rare earth metals vital in emerging technologies such as smartphones, computers, medical equipment, and car batteries. Moon mining these resources would be persuasive proof of concept for asteroid mining, something with potentially far more value. Kevin Cannon, an assistant professor in geology and space resources at the Colorado School of Mines, points out "there are much richer sources of helium-3 in the outer Solar System, and we can use lunar He-3 which is more abundant than previously thought to work out the learning curve before transitioning to these more plentiful supplies. In this view, the overall amount of He-3 on the Moon isn't all that important, as long as it's enough to figure out how to use it as a [nuclear fusion] fuel."[8] Earlier this year came news that improves the viability of a long-term and expanding human presence on the moon. Blue Origin, the rocket company backed by Amazon founder Jeff Bezos, announced it has manufactured both solar cells and electricity transmission wires from simulated lunar soil, or "regolith," containing silicon, iron, and magnesium, among other important elements.[9] Space engineers have noodled the concept since Apollo, and now we know it's possible.

And why might space resources be valuable, wherever we find them? Cannon highlights two examples: First, the economics of space-based solar, the energy technology mentioned in the previous chapter, look more viable if such structures are made from space resources.[10] Second, one way to potentially deal with global warming is to block out a tiny fraction of solar radiation through a "planetary sun shade." As Cannon explains, "You put up a structure in space at the Lagrangian point between the sun and the Earth, and that structure blocks out, say, 1 to 2 percent of the sunlight and cools the planet and helps as a mitigation effort. That structure is so large that we could not possibly launch that into the space. We would have to build that out of materials that we find."[11]

We might also discover some new and useful resources up there, such as meteorites containing strange but useful compounds, such as the alloy recently discovered in some meteorites that struck Earth. Called tetrataenite, it's a combination of nickel and iron that has since been replicated in the lab. Researchers think tetrataenite could be used in sophisticated magnets across a range of industries.[12] And, of course, a moon colony would be proof-of-concept for a Mars settlement. Success on the moon, like Project Apollo, might also politically enable more federal R&D spending on space, dollars that could help create the manufacturing and logistics systems necessary for a multitrillion-dollar space economy. The base might eventually turn into a colony and then America's fifty-first state (as Newt Gingrich suggested back in that 2012 debate), while also becoming the gateway to the rest of the solar system and all its riches, both mineral and scientific.

2. Don't regulate AI to death. One of the greatest conservative-futurist policy victories happened in 1997 when President Bill Clinton endorsed the idea of a hands-off approach to regulating internet commerce. The internet "should be a place where government makes every effort…not to stand in the way, to do no harm," Clinton said.[13] Looking back at how the digital economy has changed, both in content and how we access it, the futility of attempting to heavily regulate an evolving, embryonic technology is obvious. Back then, Amazon was still strictly a book retailer, a search engine was merely a list of interesting websites, and smartphones were still a decade away.

That 1990s lesson should strongly inform how government regulates artificial intelligence/machine learning, including generative AI, given the tremendous potential benefits to humanity. It's deeply concerning that there have already been efforts to pause their development to give their creators time to figure out new safety protocols. There have even been calls for a government moratorium. (Quips University of Washington computer scientist Pedro Domingos, "In the 70s, the big scare was overpopulation, but even Paul Ehrlich never proposed a six-month moratorium on sex.")[14]

Set aside the difficulty of enforcing a voluntary delay (hello to secret "dark labs" everywhere run by the worst actors) across numerous companies and countries (especially China) or the ability and authority of Washington to legislate such a stoppage when many lawmakers are still trying to figure out how Facebook works. I fear such rash efforts—including the stunning suggestion to look to the National Environmental Protection Act for regulatory inspiration[15]—would deeply enmesh the "mother may I," better-safe-than-sorry Precautionary Principle into AI governance and regulation, with some Down Wing activists eventually pushing for a permanent pause over concerns economic (so long to white-collar jobs), environmental (we must avoid economic acceleration), and existential (say "hello" to our new AI overlords). They've certainly been successful in the past in stymieing new technologies, from nuclear energy to supersonic flight to genetically modified foods. (Anti-GMO activists have also demanded pauses, which may be inspiring similar calls regarding AI.) Let's not go down that road again with a technology that could be as important, as AI "godfather" Geoffrey Hinton observes, as "the Industrial Revolution, or electricity…or maybe the wheel."[16] Let's neither lock in the technological status quo nor hold AI to a standard of error-free perfection. GenAI will almost certainly move faster than private actors or government attempting a burst of regulatory activity. New rules and institutions will take time and plenty of trial and error (with the issue being a worthy subject of government research funding). Until then, the Proactionary Principle should apply. Let's do no harm nor needlessly delay the benefits from what appears to be a fundamental technological breakthrough as government, academia, and business (the big AI players, by all accounts, take safety quite seriously) continue to research various AI risks. And if time is of the essence, a federally funded moonshot on AI safety would be worth consideration. Meanwhile, it's best to muddle through and learn on the fly as we see how the technology evolves.

3. Double all forms of R&D in the American economy. At the height of the 1960s Space Race, the United States spent nearly 3 percent of its economy on scientific and technological research and development.[17] Of that total, about 2 percent was government funding and 1 percent business funding. Today, the United States spends just over 3 percent on scientific and technological R&D with a bit more than 2 percent conducted by business and about 0.75 percent by government. (All the various spending bills passed during the first half of the Biden administration—the Bipartisan Infrastructure Act, the CHIPS and Science Act, the Inflation Reduction Act—didn't change federal R&D investment that much.) So especially on the government side, there's still plenty of room to dramatically ramp up spending without approaching those Apollo-era levels. Now there's no such thing as a free lunch or a money tree. But America's science and technological innovation system is about as close to having a tasty free lunch beneath a blooming money tree as you're likely to find. Or think of it this way: imagine having a miracle machine where we can put in $1 and get back $5 in the form of higher standards of living, health, and worker productivity, as some economists calculate.[18]

Of course, the exact product of this machine is hard to predict. Think of the daisy chain of science research and commercial innovation that created Uber. It started with Albert Einstein's special theory of relativity, without which we wouldn't have the Global Positioning System.[19] For GPS to work, it needs to compare extremely accurate time signals from atomic clocks on satellites. But since those satellites are moving at a high velocity compared to Earth-bound Uber app users and experience time differently, they need to be adjusted according to Einstein's equation. And if no GPS, no Uber with its smartphone-based business model.

Northwestern University economist Benjamin F. Jones calculates that doubling both business and government R&D spending in the U.S. economy could raise U.S. productivity and real per capita income growth rates by 0.5 percentage points per year over the long term.[20] According to Jones, "This would lead to enormous increases in standards of living over time. It would greatly advance the competitiveness of U.S. businesses and workers and the overall position of the U.S. economy in the world. And this economic orientation leaves out the health gains of longer and healthier lives, which are among the most valuable deliverables from the science and innovation system." So let's do that, both through increased spending from Washington to return federal spending to Apollo levels, but also by making the corporate tax code more research-friendly, such as by permanently allowing R&D expenses to be fully and immediately expensed, rather than forcing business to deduct, say, a $100 million investment over five years as is currently the law.[21] And if we want government to take more risks, here's an encouraging sign that Washington, in part due to climate concerns, is becoming more open-minded about radical energy technologies, even if they border on the fanciful. Last year, the U.S. Department of Energy announced as much as $10 million in funding to figure just how researchers could determine if cold fusion, or "low-energy nuclear reactions" might be the basis for "a potentially transformative carbon-free energy source.…If LENR can be irrefutably demonstrated and scaled, it could potentially become a disruptive technology with myriad energy, defense, transportation, and space applications, all with strong implications for U.S. technological leadership."[22]

4. Spend smarter on R&D. Up Wing economic policy would be a lot simpler if it were only about spending more money on science and technology research. But proponents of increased government spending need to think hard about extracting more bang for the taxpayer buck—and not just for budgetary reasons. There's good reason to think R&D isn't as productive or as bold as it could be. In addition to the challenge of processing the sheer volume of scientific knowledge, the incentives and structures of federally funded research may also play a role. We need to create a less bureaucratic and more efficient government review and funding process. For example, writing grant proposals takes up to half of the time of leading medical scientists.[23] It also looks as if many good but novel ideas get suffocated in peer review committees. One possible way to boost researcher efficiency and combat reviewer bias would be to fund projects via lottery once proposals have cleared some basic level of scientific plausibility. National Science Foundation boss Sethuraman Panchanathan wants to give truly bold and transformative ideas more of a chance through a Willy Wonka–inspired funding mechanism called the "Golden Ticket," which would allow a single reviewer to support a project even if their peers do not agree.[24] Venture capital firms use a similar approach because they prioritize the potential upside of long-shot investments rather than seeking to minimize risk.

A Silicon Valley–esque model is also credited for the success of the Defense Advanced Projects Research Agency (DARPA). Among the successes that the agency can claim at least partial credit for are Moderna's COVID-19 vaccine, weather satellites, drones, stealth aircraft technology, and the internet. Rather than basic research, DARPA tries to build things to solve problems. It's a bureaucracy-light agency with projects run by some one hundred managers on fixed short-term contracts. They're the ones who put together the outside networks to work on problems. Wherever a DARPA model can be employed with DARPA 1.0 characteristics, it should be. One possibility: a fully funded Agricultural Advanced Research Development Agency to help the U.S. detect new agricultural diseases, improve crop productivity significantly, and develop new food production technologies.[25]

We should also think creatively about how to build upon our Operation Warp Speed experience during the pandemic. Operation Warp Speed was so successful at accelerating vaccine development and manufacture that it has become the go-to reference among policymakers for an effective public-private partnership. America was the first nation to roll out a vaccine. And it did so rapidly, getting the COVID-19 vaccine to the American people in less than ten months. And it wasn't just a single vaccine. Operation Warp Speed delivered three in record time. What's more, there's something in its success for everybody. It was an acknowledgment that drug companies had lost money during previous public health emergencies, such as the 2014 Ebola outbreaks, when treatments they developed turned out to be unnecessary.[26] But now we needed those companies to make numerous big and bold—and risky—bets. So Operation Warp Speed placed orders for vaccines and therapies while still undergoing clinical trials, regardless of the outcomes. This encouraged pharmaceutical companies to expand manufacturing capacity so vaccines and therapies were ready to be distributed once they had the FDA's green light. There you had it: the private sector innovating with the public sector providing a safety net. The success of Operation Warp Speed also showed the overall strength of the American Innovation System. The spike protein used in the most successful vaccines was first designed by researchers at the University of Texas and National Institutes of Health, while the key discoveries enabling mRNA vaccines were made at the University of Wisconsin and the University of Pennsylvania. Operation Warp Speed was a big win for the twenty-first-century Megamachine.

While funding science is considered a "push" approach, the Operation Warp Speed purchase agreements represented a "pull" approach that works by increasing market predictability if a product is successfully developed, explains Rachel Silverman of the Center for Global Development.[27] She suggests, for example, "an advance commitment for rapid tuberculosis diagnostics, and a moonshot prize plus manufacturing support to develop and scale next-generation whole genome sequencing for global genomic surveillance" to help tackle the next emerging pandemic. Alec Stapp of the Institute for

Progress would do the same for medical countermeasures, such as a universal coronavirus vaccine, as well as carbon removal from the atmosphere, among other big-think ideas.[28] Most importantly, perhaps, policymakers should make increased federal R&D funding entirely contingent on further research into boosting science productivity, as well as implementation of funding reforms.

5. Say goodbye to the 1970s. Washington needs to send a powerful substantive and symbolic message that the growth-suffocating seventies are finally, mercifully over. That the half-century crusade against building anything is over. That the Precautionary Principle is out and the Proactionary Principle is in. Let's start with the National Environmental Protection Act. Forget about building hyperloops; whether you want to build high-speed rail, clean energy infrastructure (both power plants and transmission lines), new launch facilities for the space economy, or even structures in space, NEPA is a barrier of permission-slip paperwork raised by government that does little to no good. So let's raze that bureaucratic barrier. No more delays from a law with delay at its core. Of course, many environmental groups would go absolutely bonkers at the prospect of repealing NEPA. If repeal proves to be a bridge too far, sensible reform would be better than the status quo. It makes a lot of sense, for instance, to give geothermal energy the same regulatory treatment oil and gas already get when drilling on federal lands (a permitting exclusion that helped enable the Shale Revolution). A geothermal energy project may trigger as many as six NEPA reviews and take ten years before the project can start.[29] Among the "back to basics" reforms suggested by regulatory policy analyst Eli Dourado are having Congress end public involvement in the NEPA review process, make it harder for courts to vacate agency NEPA decisions and stall projects over quibbles with environmental reviews, and create authority for the president to "designate certain projects or decisions to be overwhelmingly in the national interest and exempt from the requirements of NEPA."[30] Dourado explains the exemption would cover both emergencies and "actions that are urgently necessary for global strategic purposes, such as the development of semiconductor fabrication facilities."

Oh, and while Congress is wishing the 1970s a not-so-fond farewell, it can reverse a singularly bad Down Wing decision from that decade by rescinding the

1973 FAA ban on overland supersonic flight.[31] Indeed, a pro-build, pro-innovate bias should become the new default among both lawmakers and regulators. An important idea is not immediately an important innovation. Economist Martin Weitzman explained in 1998 that "the ultimate limits to growth lie not so much in our ability to generate new ideas as in our ability to process an abundance of potentially new ideas into usable form." For example, Alexander Fleming discovered penicillin in 1928, but it then took two decades of development by pharmaceutical firms before becoming available to the U.S. public in 1945. What economist Kevin R. James, Akshay Kotak, and Dimitrios P. Tsomocos term "innovativity" requires both ideas and the ability to process those ideas into new products and/or techniques."[32] Examining U.S. innovativity over the past 120 years, they find it plausible that idea processing capability is "now and has been the binding constraint on U.S. TFP growth." All good reasons to think hard about the downsides to a rush to regulate AI/ML.

6. Upgrade infrastructure. Better infrastructure makes it easier to connect all those network nodes—nations, cities, universities, companies, individuals—to each other. Even in the age of the Zoom meeting, personal connection—including the chance meeting where ideas are exchanged, especially among people doing different things—remains important to scientific discovery and technological innovation. Sometimes upgrading infrastructure means building new roads and bridges. Those are the kind of shiny new things that politicians love to tout with fancy ribbon-cutting ceremonies. But the bigger infrastructure priority isn't nearly as exciting, which is one reason it's a bigger problem than adding new assets to America's vast infrastructure portfolio. Even with $550 billion in new money being funneled into transportation, broadband, and utilities by the 2021 Bipartisan Infrastructure law, there's still a massive backlog of deferred maintenance for existing infrastructure. Repairs and modernization upgrades to the nation's aging infrastructure could cost over $1 trillion at the federal and (mostly) state level, or 5 percent of the country's gross domestic product, according to the 2019 Volcker Alliance report.[33] Other studies report comparable findings.

But we need new infrastructure as well. This is a subject where China envy plays a role. Over the past two decades, that nation has built nearly twenty-five thousand miles of high-speed railway and now accounts for two-thirds of the global total. So what would a practical American version look like? One of the best plans has been put forward by Alon Levy.[34] It takes into account that America is as dense as Europe and already has a well-developed air transportation system for transcontinental travel. So keeping in mind potential ridership levels, Levy imagines multiple regions with high-speed rail, with many of these connected to each other, but not all. So you could board a train in Boston and travel to Chicago or Miami, but not Dallas or Los Angeles. And government funding, especially from Washington, might well play a key role. A lot of infrastructure will be done by the private sector, such as vertiports for air taxis or satellite internet such as the Starlink system. In some cases, this can be done with a public-private partnership or simply through vouchers, as with Starlink. It should, at this point, go without saying that NEPA reform, broadly, plays a key role here.

7. Make our cities denser and more affordable. And maybe make more of them. Does housing explain it all? Well, it might just explain a lot of the Down Wing condition of modern America. There's a plausible case that our inability and unwillingness to build more housing where people want to live drives myriad challenges, including slow economic growth, weak productivity growth, economic inequality, falling fertility, and more. Let's just focus on one of those problems: productivity growth. America's cities are the economy's high-productivity engines. They're also where wages are highest. But zoning rules and other land-use regulations have impeded homebuilding for decades, making housing in many such cities unnecessarily expensive and disrupting the historical economic process where people raise their living standards by moving to where the good jobs are. They also become more productive as workers. America's most productive cities should be a lot bigger. "An economy like that of San Francisco should be able to support a city the size of Shenzhen, with 23 million people," Hidalgo told me.[35] "But the Bay Area today is barely able to house 7 to 8 million people."

Economists Chang-Tai Hsieh and Enrico Moretti find that the "creeping web of these regulations has smothered wage and gross domestic product growth in American cities by a stunning 50 percent over the past 50 years."[36]

Let's say just three high-productivity cities—New York, San Jose, and San Francisco—changed their housing rules to the level of restrictiveness of the median U.S. city. The net effect of this increased density would be a 4 percent increase in U.S. GDP and an additional $4,000 in average earnings for all American workers.[37] Regulation costs in home building are 11 percent higher today than five years ago, accounting for $94,000 of the final price of the average new single-family home.[38] Over the past decade, regulation costs have increased by 44 percent. And if there's any sector that could probably use a technological boost to productivity—such as robotics and 3D printed homes—it's housing. In the 2023 paper "The Strange and Awful Path of Productivity in the U.S. Construction Sector," economists Austan Goolsbee and Chad Syverson find not slow productivity but rather *declining* productivity. "A lot less productive: value added per worker in the sector was about 40 percent lower in 2020 than it was in 1970," they write.[39]

Americans need to get moving again. Washington can encourage people to move to more productive job-rich regions by creating a relocation benefit as an add-on to the traditional unemployment system. To combat the NIMBY problem, state legislatures need to override local zoning rules and force local governments to apply cost-benefit analysis to new ones. They can create local mandates, enforced by linking local government funding to population growth, suggests economist Daniel Shoag. And Washington can help by restricting infrastructure dollars to cities and regions that don't comply. Link federal funding for affordable housing to progress on land-use restrictions.

An Up Wing attitude toward urban policy wouldn't just make them more populous by making it easier to build a larger supply of affordable housing. Some might get geographically bigger. Jason M. Barr, a Rutgers University–Newark economist, has proposed reshaping the southern part of the Manhattan shoreline by extending the island into New York Harbor by 1,760 acres. "New Mannahatta" would create new housing and help protect against storm surges.[40] And not just larger cities, maybe even some brand-new cities. City planner M. Nolan Gray notes an odd metropolis-free stretch between Los Angeles and San Francisco when "there should really be two, maybe three million-plus cities on this stretch of coast. Instead, it's a NIMBY paradise anchored by a city whose tallest building is a parking garage."[41] With housing deregulation, some groups may want to intentionally build new cities. Musk wants to build his on a thousand acres near Austin, Texas, for his employees that work at SpaceX, Tesla, and Boring, his tunneling company. Another possibility is Praxis, a startup effort to build a futuristic city-state in the Silicon Valley worthy of being described as Florentine. As the *Financial Times* reports, the founders "hope to gather together a new society of founders, engineers, artists and other pioneers who want to help create the world's first city-cryptostate."[42] It would be more like a Chinese "special economic zone," with its own taxes and regulatory rules, than Saudi Arabia's Neom effort to build its own futuristic mega-city off the coast of the Red Sea, but perhaps an inkling of the shape of things to come.

8. Open the economy further for immigration and trade. An Up Wing economy is an open economy. Drawbridge down, not up—which makes sense given that connectivity is at the core of Up Wing economics, both within America and between America and the rest of the world. So naturally one key aspect of an open Up Wing economy is immigration. No single pro-innovation policy is supported by stronger evidence and has such clear benefit as immigration, especially skilled immigration. Immigrants have been key to the creation of America's world-leading digital economy. No immigrants, no Silicon Valley as we know it. Half of Silicon Valley's billion-dollar "unicorn" startups have at least one foreign-born founder, including two-thirds of the "most promising" AI startups, as ranked by *Forbes* magazine.[43] Immigrants also account for nearly half of the U.S. workforce with a science or engineering doctorate, as well as 60 percent of doctorates in computer and mathematical sciences.[44] But it's not just the cognitive firepower and skills immigrants bring that benefit the economy at the high end or their inexpensive labor that helps it at the lower end. (One way immigration boosts labor supply is by increasing female labor force participation by reducing childcare costs.) Immigrants are also more likely to start businesses than native-born Americans, whether high-impact startups or small family-owned stores.[45]

Immigrants, whatever their skill levels, also help the American economy just by being different than native-born Americans. They see things differently, allowing them to challenge preexisting business thinking and further driving productivity benefits. Immigrants "help to globally connect capital, talent, and ideas because they bring international linkages and are more willing to explore globally, spotting new opportunities and potential innovations," explains a 2018 analysis from Citigroup and the University of Oxford.[46]

An Up Wing America is also a more populous America. (Don't worry: with half of U.S. counties losing population, we have plenty of room.)[47] A much bigger country, say a doubling in population over the rest of the century, would create a bigger domestic economic market and also offset the demographic decline from lower birthrates. Also: more big ideas. "Other things equal, a larger population means more researchers which in turn leads to more new ideas and higher living standards," explains Stanford University economist Charles Jones in his 2020 paper "The End of Economic Growth? Unintended Consequences of a Declining Population."[48] And as a policy matter, boosting immigration is far easier than boosting birthrates. At a minimum, we should encourage as many high-skilled immigrants as possible to come here and stay. (It certainly would make China surly if more of its artificial intelligence experts decided never to go back home. Of the thirty-two Chinese contributors to OpenAI's GPT-4, nearly 80 percent completed their graduate studies in the United States and ended up staying.)[49]

A foreign student who gets an advanced degree in a STEM field should be granted permanent residency. Congress should also raise the caps that are holding back employment-based green cards from highly qualified and promising talent. Some modeling suggests, for example, that if the U.S. doubled the H-1B visa cap from 85,000 to 170,000, it would raise the economic growth rate by 9 percent, or 0.12 percentage points.[50] Every bit helps. Also helpful: more funding for U.S. Citizenship and Immigration Services to process visas efficiently and bring their system into the digital age. And perhaps also creating a new section within the USCIS or the State Department, as outlined by Caleb Watney of the Institute for Progress, that would "identify talented scientists, engineers, academics, and supply chain managers from abroad, then proactively recruit them to the United States with an offer of permanent residency or even citizenship."[51] "The Department of Promigration," Watney calls it. Indeed, our Down Wing immigration system is so broken, such as the lack of work visas, that it's forcing domestic U.S. companies to outsource and relocate foreign employees overseas.[52]

America needs all the smart people it can get. On that economists seem unanimous. A 2016 survey found zero percent disagreeing with the idea that allowing "many more immigrants with advanced degrees in science and engineering" would make America richer over time.[53] If the Biden administration wants more high-end semiconductor manufacturing to be located in the U.S., it's going to require lots of very smart workers. The U.S. has a limited number of such workers because only a small fraction of the population has a very high IQ, observes economist Alex Tabarrok.[54] "The US might be able to place only say 100,000 high-IQ workers in high-IQ professions, if we are lucky. It's very difficult to run a high-IQ civilization of 330 million on just 100,000 high-IQ workers—the pyramid of ability extends only so far.... [We] also need to draw on high-IQ workers throughout the world—which explains why some of the linchpins of our civilization end up in places like Eindhoven or Taiwan."

The other critical part of an open economy is trade. Again, think drawbridge down, not up. The connections between free trade and growth have been at the heart of economic analysis since Adam Smith. Econ 101 has it right. Trade allows countries to specialize in the goods and services they're relatively efficient at producing. Trade gives access to larger markets, and economies of scale occur when firms spread fixed costs by producing for a larger market. Trade encourages technological spillovers by accelerating the diffusion of technology throughout the world. Finally, import competition reduces the monopoly power of domestic firms and forces them to compete and innovate. The power of trade for developing nations can be seen in the dramatic upturn in economic growth and reduction in poverty since the 1970s. But what about a rich, advanced economy like America's? Freer trade is important for us, too. Even after the Trump-era turn toward protectionism, average U.S. tariff rates remain pretty low, about 2 percent on industrial goods.[55] And half of all industrial goods imports enter the United States duty-free.[56] Much of the increase reflects tariffs on Chinese goods, which average 19.3 percent, more than six times higher than before the U.S.-China trade war began in 2018, according to the Peterson Institute for International Economics.[57] According to a Peterson Institute analysis, removing all remaining trade barriers would increase U.S. production by approximately $450 billion to $600 billion annually. Gains in this range would increase U.S. per capita income between $1,500 and $2,000 annually and U.S. household income between $4,000 and $5,300 annually.[58]

9. Invest in Up Wing education. The most important nodes in the almost impossibly complex and dense network that is the American economy are you and me. Like Soylent Green, economic growth is, fundamentally, made from people. Recall the notion that long-run economic growth is linked to long-run population growth because people create ideas, which can then be copied and used by everyone. Also important: the innovativeness of the environment in which people grow up. The latest economic research suggests a potential Up Wing zoom loop: if more kids were raised in high-innovation areas—which would happen if our high-productivity areas were bigger because they were more affordable—there's some reason to believe more of them would become researchers and thus contribute to faster growth.

London School of Economics economist John Van Reenen notes a correlation between areas with strong science-based universities and private-sector innovation—regions such as Silicon Valley in California, Route 128 in Massachusetts, and the Research Triangle in North Carolina—with individuals more likely to become inventors in specialties of the regions, such as software in the Valley and medical devices in Massachusetts.[59] Moreover, "kids who move to high-innovation areas at an earlier age are more likely to become inventors than kids who move at a later age." The results suggest the largest long-run effects on growth could come from using STEM classes to target "high ability but disadvantaged potential inventors at an early age." (This research also shows the value of making housing more affordable in high-productivity regions.)

But will America's young inventors and STEM smarties have the opportunity to attend an elite university such as Harvard, MIT, Northwestern, and

Stanford? (My assumption here is that America's top private schools provide something of real educational value, something beyond networking opportunities and signaling.) But as demand for these schools has risen, the supply of slots hasn't. In the 2021 paper "Why Don't Elite Colleges Expand Supply?" economists Peter Q. Blair of Harvard and Kent Smetters of Wharton note that the incoming class of Yale College freshmen in 2015 was 1,360, just 14 more students than in 1979.[60] At the same time, however, the number of applications had surged from 9,331 to 30,932. Harvard, Princeton, Stanford, and Yale have increased their enrollment by just 7 percent since 1990 versus 61 percent for colleges in the bottom 25 percent of SAT selectivity. Blair and Smetters think the problem is something they term "prestige," or how elite schools compete on reducing admission rates and appearing ever-more selective. One possible fix: legal collusion to end the race to the selectivity depths: "the top 200 U.S. colleges could agree to minimum enrollments by college that increase over time, much like maximum carbon caps by country found in the multinational Paris climate accord that decrease over time for some nations," the economists suggest.

✦ ✦ ✦

Few statistical observations have stuck with me like this one from a 2010 McKinsey report on education: Top-performing nations—such as Singapore, Finland, and South Korea—recruit all their teachers from the top third of college students versus just 23 percent in the United States.[61] Having dropped those numbers into more than one conversation about the state of American education, I know they cause an aha moment in the thinking of many people. People naturally assume students benefit from having high-achieving teachers.

And there's more good reason to think that intuition a correct one. In the 2018 study "The Value of Smarter Teachers: International Evidence on Teacher Cognitive Skills and Student Performance," a research team led by Stanford University economist Eric Hanushek finds "substantial differences in teacher cognitive skills across countries that are strongly related to student performance."[62] Now, it's not as if you want all your smartest people to become teachers. We still need plenty of computer scientists, biotechnologists, physicists, and engineers. Economists, too. But we also don't want the U.S. education system drawing from the bottom half or worse of all college grads. There's no doubt teacher quality matters. A study released earlier this year from Hanushek and several colleagues documents how the Dallas Independent School District offered salary supplements of as much as $10,000 a year to high-performing teachers who were willing to work in the most educationally disadvantaged schools. The researchers find the progam led to "dramatic" improvements, "bringing average achievement in the previously lowest performing schools close to the district average."[63]

Not every teacher needs to be brilliant. Changes at the margin matter a lot. Replacing just the bottom 5 to 10 percent of teachers with merely average teachers could boost the U.S. international education rank to mid-single digits from mid-teens. What's more, such an increase suggests, Hanushek adds, "that future economic growth would be noticeably higher, like eight-tenths of a percent per year higher of annual growth."[64] Or to put it another way, the lifetime value of having American kids scoring as well as Canadian or Finnish kids would amount to an increase in total U.S. economic output of $112 trillion in present value.[65]

But it's not all about STEM and teacher quality. One criticism of English curriculum standards in the United States has been that they devalue "great literature." But books that inspire have every bit as much economic value—as well as contributing to personal growth—as ones meant to get you hired. "[What] a modern economy needs more than personnel with expository skills is people eager to exercise their creativity and venturesome spirit in ever-new and challenging environments," writes Nobel laureate Edmund Phelps in *Mass Flourishing*.[66] Schools should get back to assigning classic authors such as Jack London, Jules Verne, Laura Ingalls Wilder, Arthur Conan Doyle, and H. P. Lovecraft, Phelps suggests, to which I would add newer Up Wing works of adventure and imagination such as J. K. Rowling's Harry Potter series and Andy Weir's *The Martian*.

Getting this piece of the education puzzle right might be more important than you think. A 2020 analysis by Peter Cauwels and Didier Sornette at ETH Zurich documenting significant inventions over the past two centuries finds a clear decline in "bold, high-risk, explorative discovery" versus "low-risk incremental innovation." Too little of the former, too much of the latter.[67] Here's how the researchers attempt to explain their findings: "It is a sign that our affluent society has become extremely risk averse; we refer to this as the zero-risk society. When wealth and age in society increases, people become ever more risk averse, focus on going concern, protection of existing wealth and rent seeking." So how can we offset our zero-sum tendencies? In addition to funding more high-risk research, Cauwels and Sornette think our kids need different role models. From their paper: "Why not promote the risk-taker, the explorer, the creative inventor as a new type of social influencer acclaimed like a Hollywood or sports star? Only by such a deep cultural change, by bringing back the frontier spirit and making risk-taking great again will we be able to escape from the illusionary and paralyzing zero-risk society and deal with the massive lurking risks that it produces."

By the way, Herman Kahn had some thoughts about education, too. One of his final projects before his death was promoting an Up Wing education program that would, in Kahn's words, address "the imbalance of unrelenting negativism" about the future of the world being taught in public schools with "'more accurate and therefore more optimistic data' about energy, pollution, resources, population, food supplies, economics, and technology."[68] Obviously that's an effort that would still be incredibly relevant today. Maybe it's also time for an Advanced Placement class, AP Progress I've named it, that examines the influence of technological progress—from the compass and printing press to the steam engine and railroad to microchips and the internet—on economic history.[69]

10. Create a labor market "imaginarium." An Up Wing society needs more than the desire to pursue the adventure that is discovery and innovation; it also needs the capacity. It needs a free space where dreams and ideas can be pursued with as little friction as possible from rules or regulations, whether they come from business or government. Phelps writes that the core of the innovative economy is a "vast imaginarium—a space for imagining new products and methods, imagining how they might be made, imagining how they might be used."[70] There are numerous ways that government can foul that imaginarium and prevent the pursuit of discovery and happiness by allowing friction to happen.

A 2020 paper by Morris M. Kleiner and Ming Xu finds that over one-fifth of all U.S. workers are employed in licensed occupations, jobs that require a government license.[71] This number was only 5 percent in the 1950s. For workers who are trying to enter or change a profession, "increased licensing may also result in barriers such as restricted geographical and occupational worker mobility; decreased worker welfare; increased consumer prices; and ultimately, impaired economic growth." One example: the average cosmetologist spends 372 days in training to receive an occupational license from the government versus just thirty-three days for the average emergency medical technician.[72] Not only should every state review their licensing system, but if someone has a license in another state, every state should recognize that license.

It's not just government disrupting that imaginarium. Workers are also stymied by noncompete agreements, in which workers agree not to join or start a rival company for a certain period after leaving their current employer. Many economists give at least some credit for the continued vibrancy of Silicon Valley to California's decision to nix noncompetes. Massachusetts, like most other states, enforces noncompetes. And while Boston's Route 128 tech corridor once rivaled Silicon Valley in the 1950s and 1960s, it started lagging badly in the 1990s—a slowdown some economists blame on noncompetes.[73] Overall, a fifth of American workers, including lower-income workers, are covered by the agreement that suppresses wage growth by limiting the need for businesses to compete for their services.[74] The Federal Trade Commission estimates a total ban on noncompetes would increase worker earnings by $250 billion to $300 billion per year.[75] And although a case can be reasonably made that not all workers should be treated the same—some knowledge workers might legitimately have information that would create a new competitor or unfairly aid an existing rival—it's hard to see why fast-food workers should have their job mobility restricted.

11. Create a safety net for new dynamic Up Wing economy. It's recently become easier to envision a world of AGI and advanced humanoid robots, of a near future where software and machines can do everything humans can do. The end of the Age of Labor would be a leap forward to rival that of the

Agricultural Revolution, when humanity shifted from forager to farmer, and of the Industrial Revolution, when farmers became factory workers. Likewise, observes University of Virginia economist Anton Korinek, "We hope that our society will also be able to adapt to the end of the Age of Labor if and when it occurs, enabling humans to enjoy their lives freed from the drudgery of having to work."[76] Korinek explains that a successful adaptation would require new institutions such as how the shift from foraging to farming required the creation of property rights. He argues that governments should prepare now for a world where they provide a basic income for all their citizens. "Ultimately, with the right economic institutions to distribute the abundant output in a world in which labor is made economically redundant by autonomous machines, we may be able to implement the dream of Arthur C. Clarke that 'the goal of the future is full unemployment, so we can play,'" Korinek concludes.

But, again, we should not underestimate the difficulty of achieving AGI and a subsequent Infinite Age of Play. So let's take a step back and imagine brilliant machines that merely take *a lot* of jobs and substantially reduce the rate at which adults participate in the workforce. (But don't forget that when superhuman intelligence arrived in Go, it made players better.) In that case, exclusively focusing on the broad distribution of AI-driven income gains probably isn't the right answer. Rather, argues economist Michael Strain, government would need to make work as financially attractive as possible and help people build skills so they can use AI and other technology as tools to boost their own productivity. "This could require a radical rethinking of public policy," Strain says.[77] Government may need to provide large earnings subsidies such that working Americans with relatively few skills receive the majority of the financial returns from their labor via a check from Washington and not from their employer. "But I'd rather live in that world than in a world where they weren't making any contributions and instead were just receiving checks financed by the productivity of the machines," Strain adds.

✦ ✦ ✦

The endgame here is to create an America that would be the premier global destination and hub for highly educated, entrepreneurial people who want to live in a country where government encourages innovation and success rather than throwing up roadblocks. My vision is partly inspired by the New Canaan Holdfast in the *Brilliance* book series by Marcus Sakey.[78] In Sakey's alternate America, one percent of the U.S. population is born with superhuman smarts. Many of these "brilliants" decide to live in a huge section of Wyoming purchased by a brilliant uberbillionaire to both escape growing persecution and live in a place that encourages their talents. The X-Men meet Silicon Valley. In the NCH, brilliant scientists greatly advance all manner of technology. Eventually those marvels will create a more prosperous America and world. We need to find the brilliance in everyone and put it to work.

TWELVE

How to Nurture an Up Wing Culture

Black Mirror, the techno-dystopian television series, has been described as a show asking the question "What happens when the technology that it is claimed improves our lives creates intractable problems and nightmarish consequences?"[1] Among the most popular or well-critiqued episodes is one in which humans are chased by murderous robot dogs, a ghoulish spin on those viral videos from robotics company Boston Dynamics of automatons running, jumping, and tumbling—doing parkour, basically. While *Black Mirror* is often compared to *The Twilight Zone* from the 1960s, the latter was not premised on a dark future. Perhaps Hollywood doesn't believe an Up Wing *White Mirror* show would be possible or popular. A typical episode of such a show, physicist and author David Deutsch has said, might imagine some technology that's plausibly on the horizon—and then that technology turns out much *better* than imagined.[2] In the typical *Black Mirror* episode, by contrast, the imagined tech improvement happens—and then "Everything goes horribly wrong."[3] Synthetic pets become canine murderbots rather than lifetime companions and caretakers. *Jurassic Park* author Michael Crichton, who specialized in the terror potential of emerging technology, once said, "If you imagine a future that's wonderful, you don't have a story."[4] That's obviously wrong. Despite our cultural gloom, we do get the occasional glimpse of what an Up Wing, techno-solutionist culture might look like through art that optimistically imagines what direction artificial intelligence, genetic editing, and a burgeoning new age of space flight might take humanity. There's more out there than just *Star Trek*, though not as much as there could and should be. But what is available should teach some valuable Up Wing creative lessons:

- **The value of innovation.** In the book and later film *The Martian*, astronaut Mark Watney is stranded alone on the Red Planet.[5] Although NASA eventually figures out he's alive and mounts a rescue mission, Watney still needs to survive for 549 Martian solar days (Earth days are just a smidgen longer) until that spacecraft arrives. He also has to figure out a way to get himself into orbit as the ship zooms by. He needs to innovate—or, as he famously puts it, "science the shit" out of his problem. He uses his brain and his tools in ways NASA never anticipated. To use Apple's old advertising tagline, *The Martian* is a story about someone needing to "think different" to survive. Watney is also a botanist, and he figures out how to grow potatoes in Martian soil, including extracting water from rocket fuel. Innovation. To power and heat a land rover for long treks, he repurposes some solar panels and a radioactive plutonium battery. Innovation. He devises a special code to speed up communication with NASA. Innovation. Even after Watney launches himself into space, he has to manage one final innovation (in the movie, at least): piercing his spacesuit so he can use the escaping air as propulsion to rendezvous with the rescue ship. Innovation.
- **Too little progress can be a big problem.** A year before the premier of the original *Star Trek*, the same network, CBS, launched another hour-long sci-fi show, *Lost in Space*. Just like *Star Trek*, it lasted for three seasons (but shot four more episodes), yet with hardly the long-term cultural impact. Its budgets were low, and its plotlines more geared toward kids. It wasn't a show of great ambition.

The 2018 Netflix reimaging kept the core elements. The Robinson family—parents John and Maureen, kids Judy, Penny, and Will—is still lost in deep space, as is the villainous Doctor Smith (now gender swapped). Up Wing thinking is built into the very premise. The Robinsons are part of a colonization mission to another planet. Earth's climate was destabilized by an asteroid strike, not carbon emissions. In other words, a lack of technological expertise is the problem here, not too much technology. Most of the drama comes from tough circumstances, not bad guys. As in *The Martian*, the Robinson family has to solve technical problem after problem to survive. (To quote Mark Watney from *The Martian*: "You solve one problem…and you solve the next one…and then the next. And if you solve enough problems, you get to come home.")[6] There's a deep "maker" ethos embedded in the show's DNA. Since the show is set only a quarter century from now, problems are solved through understandable ingenuity and (mostly) realistic tech, not theoretical or impossible superscience.

- **Rejecting progress creates existential risk.** Director Christopher Nolan's 2014 *Interstellar* may seem at first like another Down Wing film. A mysterious global blight is killing the planet's vegetation—a plague that will eventually render Earth uninhabitable if science can't stop it. But whatever the plague's origin, our ability to cure it is hampered by an America that's turned its back on science, progress, and reason. No more NASA or MRI machines. It's a scenario lamentably easy to imagine given the current denial of manmade climate change, anti-vaccine sentiment, and belief that the COVID-19 pandemic was a hoax concocted by evil global elites. In *Interstellar*, Cooper, played by Matthew McConaughey, is an astronaut turned farmer when America abandoned space exploration. "We used to look up in the sky and wonder at our place in the stars. Now we just look down and worry about our place in the dirt," he laments early in the film. But Cooper hasn't abandoned that image of the future. He still sees space as our salvation: "Mankind was born on Earth. It was never meant to die here."[7]

- **Today's reality is hardly the best we can do.** The 1960s Space Race never ended in the alt-history series *For All Mankind*, which premiered on Apple TV+ in 2019. The show begins with a bummer: the Soviet Union lands on the moon first, with America following soon after with a crash landing. (The key point of divergence is that Sergei Korolev, the father of the Soviet space program, doesn't die under mysterious circumstances in 1966 in the *FAM*-verse as he did in ours.) Both nations get a deep and invigorating sense of national mission from that start and duel peacefully (mostly) in the heavens for decades after. For America, there's no Great Downshift, as it continues to pour money into federal R&D. Those ambitious NASA plans that never happened in our reality come to fruition in *FAM*: a permanent lunar base, Jamestown, is established in 1973; the space shuttle begins resupplying the lunar base in 1982; NASA's Sojourner mission lands on Mars in 1995. But the advances aren't just about space. All that government investment means Americans are using cell phones and driving electric cars by the early 1980s. In 1987, a private company wins a NASA contract to mine lunar deposits of helium-3, helping spark a nuclear fusion revolution. In 1988, NASA's James Hansen testifies to Congress that global warming has slowed thanks to widespread use of nuclear fusion. (In our universe, he sounded the alarm about climate change.)[8]
- **Even global disaster won't doom humanity if we keep an Up Wing attitude.** Although science fiction writer Neal Stephenson has repeatedly expressed his concern about pessimistic sci-fi, he's also created just about the most Down Wing scenario imaginable, but one with an incredibly Up Wing finish. In *Seveneves* from 2015, the moon shatters "without warning and for no apparent reason"—maybe aliens, maybe a tiny black hole—with the pieces eventually raining down to Earth in a fiery cleansing of all life.[9] But before that Hard Rain happens, humanity creates a refuge in orbit, a cluster of connected habitats. Flash forward five thousand years. Three billion genetically modified humans live above the slowly healing planet in a complex

> network of rings made out of what was left of the shattered moon. We climbed our way back through our wits, perseverance, and unbreakable confidence that a bright future was still possible—even though we had to invent it as we went along. There was no master blueprint. Microsoft co-founder Bill Gates gave *Seveneves* a glowing review, writing how he loved its emphasis on scientific accuracy and adhering to physical laws, but also "the way the book pushes you to think big and long-term."[10] Or, to put it another way, how to think Up Wing.

All those films and shows have Up Wing attitude at their core. But even future-oriented media that *don't* might be more Up Wing than first appears. Given the deep pessimism of so many visions about the future, depicting *any* future at all seems sort of optimistic. While William Gibson's 1984 book *Neuromancer* created or solidified various cyberpunk tropes—ruthless megacorporations, massive inequality, AI with its own agenda—Gibson himself doesn't see his book as obviously dystopian: "It seemed to me when I wrote *Neuromancer* that it was an act of optimism because so many intelligent, well-informed adults around me at that time thought that our fate was going to be mutually-assured destruction. And in *Neuromancer* that hasn't happened.…So it did seem optimistic to me then."[11] Or take a more recent work of Gibson's, *The Peripheral*, in which 80 percent of the global population is wiped by a series of unfortunate events, from severe climate change to numerous mini-pandemics. Yet even as civilization is collapsing, "science started popping"—huge breakthroughs in AI, energy, nanotechnology, and robotics. Whatever Gibson intended, I view *The Peripheral* as a warning against technological delay. And had that message been made explicit, it would suddenly be an Up Wing work while not losing any of its drama or characterization. Sorry, Crichton.

Our Beliefs about the Future Matter, So Let's Act Like It

When Herman Kahn wrote on how to transition to a world of mass abundance and opportunity, he argued that perhaps "the single most important thing that could be done would be to substitute reasonably accurate positive images of the future for the depressing images that now prevail, especially in the Advanced Capitalist nations."[12] Ideally, such an image would be vivid enough that we could picture a version of it in our minds. Researchers Andrew M. Carton and Brian J. Lucas find evidence that organizational leaders can inspire employees by communicating "a vision of the future with image-based rhetoric—words and phrases that are readily envisioned in the mind's eye."[13] They point out that Bill Gates envisioned a "computer on every desk and in every home," and President John F. Kennedy challenged NASA to land "a man on the moon."

So how do we create vivid Up Wing images and stories, especially if rapid economic acceleration isn't currently providing the technological sneak preview or inspirational support that it did in previous Up Wing periods? It might seem unlikely. Not only is Hollywood deeply enmeshed in Down Wing eco-catastrophism, but creating a nuanced fictional reality that's better in many ways but also maybe worse in some others requires ambitious worldbuilding. Much easier to go full-on dark, ramp up the CGI destruction porn, and maybe tack on a perfunctory and unearned feel-good ending. All the more reason, then, for Up Wingers with resources to directly finance Up Wing cultural efforts.

It's hardly a crazy idea. Take *The Expanse* on Amazon Prime Video. The show is set in the year 2350 when the average lifespan on Earth is 123 years, Mars has three billion inhabitants, and humanity mines deep-space asteroids that it quickly travels to via fusion propulsion technology. Not dystopia, but also not a utopia, given the brewing geopolitical conflict between Earth (where unemployment is high but people also receive a universal basic income), Mars, and those mining colonies. Also, no zombies, no incinerated Earth, and no collapsed civilization. Humanity has survived and expanded. The first three seasons of *The Expanse* aired on Syfy, and although the show received considerable critical acclaim, audience numbers fell sharply during the second and third seasons. Some one hundred thousand fans signed an online petition lobbying Amazon Studios and Netflix to pick up the expensive series.[14] They even created a crowdfunding campaign that paid for an airplane to fly a "#SaveTheExpanse" banner over Amazon Studios in Santa

Monica, California. But it's unlikely that any of those efforts would've worked if Amazon founder Jeff Bezos wasn't one of the show's big fans. "It's his favorite TV show," Andrew Kosove of Alcon TV, which produces the program, told the *Los Angeles Times*.[15] "I believe [the 2018 move to Amazon] was because of Jeff Bezos: 'I like watching the show, so let's make it work.'"

✦ ✦ ✦

But we don't have to count on uberbillionaires cutting big checks to create Up Wing visions, as helpful as that would be. Back in 2011, Arizona State University president Michael Crow heard a conference talk given by Stephenson, during which the author bemoaned America's retreat from space and other big-think ideas.[16] Crow then challenged Stephenson to create a sci-fi response to the problem. In Stephenson's *Wired* essay on that gathering, he offers complementary theories about how sci-fi was relevant to our decline in national ambition. First, "inspiration theory": Sci-fi is important because it inspires people to choose science and engineering as careers, as happened with Elon Musk and many other technologists. Second, "hieroglyph theory." Stephenson writes, "Good [science fiction] supplies a plausible, fully thought-out picture of an alternate reality in which some sort of compelling innovation has taken place." In other words, "good" sci-fi supplies an image of the future that nudges society toward action rather than mere fantasizing and speculation.

This led to the creation of ASU's Center for Science and the Imagination at Arizona State University, which brings together scientists, engineers, creative writers, storytellers, and artists to come up with technically grounded, optimistic visions of the future. One big project was *Hieroglyph*, a collection of short stories that, as Stephenson described them, would all be throwbacks "to 1950's-style SF, in that they would depict futures in which Big Stuff Got Done. We would avoid hackers, hyperspace, and holocausts. The ideal subject matter would be an innovation that a young, modern-day engineer could make substantial progress on during his or her career."[17] In "Periapsis" by James L. Cambias, young adults compete in a series of challenges to win citizenship on Deimos, the prosperous near-zero-gravity moon of Mars.[18] In

"The Man Who Sold the Stars" by Gregory Benford, an entrepreneur uses the profits from asteroid mining to fund research to find Earth-like planets.[19] In Stephenson's piece, "Atmosphæra Incognita," an ambitious tech entrepreneur constructs a twenty-kilometer-tall tower that jump-starts the moribund U.S. steel industry and reveals novel methods for generating renewable energy.[20] As the book's introduction puts it, "This is a sketchbook for the future, with ideas we hope will leap off the page and into real life."

✦✦✦

The *most effective* thing government can do to create an Up Wing culture is to inspire one through public policy that helps create a better ecology for scientific and technological progress, business innovation, and high-impact entrepreneurship. But lots more Up Wing economic policy isn't *all* government can do.

Consider: The near-miraculous achievements of the Industrial Revolution were not forgotten by Oscar-winning director Danny Boyle when he organized the opening of the 2012 Summer Olympic Games in London. The ceremonies begin with a "Green and Pleasant Land" segment depicting idyllic rural life—England as Hobbiton in Tolkien's Middle Earth—before suddenly shifting to "Pandemonium" with its propulsive drums and now iconic visuals of seven coal-smoke belching chimney stacks rising from green fields.[21] Then arrive the top-hatted capitalists (led by actor Kenneth Branagh) to oversee the steam-powered factories, tended by grimy workers performing rhythmically as if machines themselves. William Blake's dark Satanic mills, as designed by Sauron, basically. But the story doesn't end there. Those sooty workers have been casting iron rings, the famous five Olympic rings, which are raised above the performers as they rain down silver and gold sparks. It's that image of the glowing rings, ignited as much by the spirit of the age as molten iron, that appeared on the front pages of newspapers around the world. Here's how Boyle thought about that second segment: "We call it Pandemonium, which is Milton's invented word for the capital of hell in *Paradise Lost*, and you know all the stories about Victorian Britain, but it also unleashed tremendous potential, and the growth of cities and the growth of a working base was extraordinary really, and it has changed all our lives. It has certainly allowed me to be here."[22] At the end of the segment, a BBC television presenter said the scene was more like "paradise found."

Those opening ceremonies showed the power of spectacle on a global scale to both inform and inspire. The mid-twentieth-century equivalent for displays of Up Wing oomph were World's Fairs, especially those in the United States. Although several fairs figure prominently in the story of the American Century—especially the 1933 "Century of Progress" exposition in Chicago, the final pre–World War II fair in New York City in 1939, Seattle's 1962 Century 21 Exposition, and the 1964 New York World's Fair (not approved by the governing Bureau of International Expositions, by the way)—they probably seem to many Americans like bits of nostalgia that gave us a few interesting landmarks (and favorite Hollywood film locations) such as the Space Needle and Unisphere. Unfortunately, the United States hasn't hosted a World's Fair for almost four decades, and Washington got out of the business of providing any funding in 2001, even leaving the international governing body. Our final two efforts were the energy-focused 1982 Knoxville World's Fair (later mocked in an episode of *The Simpsons*) and a full-scale World's Fair two years later in New Orleans.[23] Both were plagued with attendance problems, and the latter had to declare bankruptcy during its run.

But outside of North America—the last one here was Vancouver in 1986—World's Fairs are going strong. Just as they were showcases for rising American power in the first half of the twentieth century and then postwar U.S. geopolitical dominance in the middle, they're now major events for a rising Asia to raise its global profile. Although the BIE is headquartered in Paris, the World Expo Museum is located in Shanghai, a city that saw the largest-ever World's Fair in 2010, with more than 190 countries and around fifty international organizations, along with 73 million total visitors, taking part.[24] One could make a geopolitical argument for the United States returning to hosting World's Fairs and devoting taxpayer resources to them. Such reasoning might be why the Trump administration in 2017 decided to rejoin the BIE.[25] But having the United States return as a frequent World's Fair host and enthusiastic participant would be far more important than as just a mere expression of American soft power. America can again leverage World's Fairs to create a more Up Wing culture that both supports and promotes technological progress and economic growth. "World's Fairs, especially American World's Fairs, gave us the future...and tried to sell people on the future," according to Charles Pappas, author of *Flying Cars, Zombie Dogs, and Robot Overlords: How World's Fairs and Trade Expos Changed the World.*[26] "Lately a lot of the vibe of the world fairs is ecological, kind of canary-in-the-coal-mine experience. I think we've lost the idea of optimism. I think we've lost the idea of what we can do [with the fairs]."

At their Up Wing best, World's Fairs have the ability to present a holistic view of what a better tomorrow might look like. TEDx event organizer Cameron Wiese has been promoting a twenty-first-century update to the exhibitions through his World's Fair Co. startup as a means of creating aspirational images of the future. As he told me, "If done right, the World's Fair can be the catalyst for us to translate the hopeful stories we tell about the future into the real world. For that to happen, people need to leave the Fair with renewed hope; they need a vision of where we're going, paths to get there, and the belief that they have a role to play."[27] And what might a reimagined World's Fair look like? Wiese offers this example:

> *In this world, you explore the depths of our oceans, take a mission to Mars, and travel back in time to the 1893 Chicago World's Fair recreated in VR. You tour the geothermal plant powering the Fair, see the 3D-printed homes of tomorrow, and watch synthetic organisms decompose the plastic polluting our oceans. You meet the bright minds of tomorrow at the World's Science Competition, watch de-extinct wooly mammoths play, and cheer researchers as they debut the cure for aging. You grab dinner made from ingredients grown at the Fair's cellular meat lab and vertical garden. You sit down at a table with other guests from around the world to laugh, share stories, and talk about the future—your words translated to each other in real-time.*[28]

And, of course, you take a driverless taxi, maybe even a flying electric one, home at the end of your Up Wing evening at the fair.

Inspiring Humanity with Elevators, Radio, and Clocks

Apollo brought America a lot more than just geopolitical prestige and Tang. Economically, it played a critical role in the emerging Information Technology and Communication Revolution. NASA was the largest purchaser of microchips in the 1960s, eventually scooping up 60 percent of all that were manufactured during that decade for its Apollo guidance computer and other systems.[29] But Apollo didn't just provide a financial catalyst for the Digital Revolution. It also launched a cultural acceptance and embrace of technology that helped make America a gadget-obsessed nation of first adopters. Apollo provided an Up Wing counterargument to postwar Megamachine fears about the destructive power of technology. It presented the computer as something that enabled mankind to launch itself into perhaps its greatest adventure, not just calculate ICBM trajectories. It created science heroes in the astronauts, but also heroes of the more everyday sort in the technicians back on Earth. "[Apollo] helped give Americans a sense of excitement and anticipation about the Digital Age, a sense of excitement that had been completely missing when the 1960s began," writes journalist Charles Fishman in *One Giant Leap: The Impossible Mission That Flew Us to the Moon*.[30] "Going to the Moon inspired a whole generation—maybe two generations—of young people to become scientists, engineers, and computer programmers."

Perhaps no witness to Apollo 11 back in July 1969 ever described its wonder and deep meaning better than philosopher and novelist Ayn Rand, who visited Cape Canaveral during the days leading up to the historic launch. Her words should again prove relevant as America begins a new era of journeys into deep space:

> *The next four days were torn out of the world's usual context, like a breathing spell with a sweep of clean air piercing mankind's lethargic*

> *suffocation. For thirty years or longer, the newspapers had featured nothing but disasters, catastrophes, betrayals, the shrinking stature of man, the sordid mess of a collapsing civilization; their voice had become a long, sustained whine, the megaphone a failure, like the sound of the Oriental bazaar where leprous beggars, of spirit or matter, compete for attention by displaying their source. Now, for once, the newspapers were announcing a human achievement, were reporting on a human triumph, were reminding us that man still exists and functions as a man. Those four days conveyed the sense that we were watching a magnificent work of art—a play dramatizing a single theme: the efficacy of man's mind.*[31]

Time for more adventures, both out there and down here. To that end, I humbly present two aspirational and inspirational megaprojects for humanity. And while these projects may well have huge economic benefits, I list them here for their potential to create a more aspirational and adventurous Up Wing culture, both in America and globally.

Climbing into space. Humanity has long dreamed of building towers to God in His heaven. And in 1895, Russian scientist Konstantin Tsiolkovsky presented an idea for doing so: Build another Eiffel Tower and then, you know, keep on building.[32] And inside that (almost) impossibly tall tower, an electric elevator could transport cargo and people to an orbiting "celestial castle." The next iteration of the tall tower idea had no tower at all. Rather than a structure that extended into orbit, a cable would be lowered from a counterweight—maybe a space station, maybe a captured asteroid—in geostationary orbit, some 36,000 kilometers above the surface of Earth. The centrifugal force of the counterweight would hold the cable in tension, allowing mechanical "climbers" to scoot up and down. Spinning in sync with Earth, the counterweight could be used as a deep-space launch platform, slingshotting cargo to the moon and beyond—at a fraction of current rocket-launching costs. SpaceX has already lowered the cost to $1,500 per kilogram, but space elevator researchers say they could get the delivery price down below $100 per kilogram or even less.[33]

Although space elevators have only rarely been depicted on screen—most notably in the television series *Foundation* on Apple TV+, based on the Isaac Asimov book series—they've long been a feature of sci-fi literature. Space elevators first appeared in two 1979 novels, Arthur C. Clarke's *The Fountains of Paradise* and *The Web between Two Worlds* by Charles Sheffield.[34] More recently, a space elevator constructed on the Red Planet is a key element of Kim Stanley Robinson's Mars series. As Robinson describes his version:

> *The construction took 11 years, circa 2047–2058. The cable was 35,000 km long and 10 meters thick, weighing 6 billion tons. The space station Clarke, named after the author, was built on the remainder of the asteroid at the end of the cable. The cable was attached to the Martian surface at Pavonis Mons caldera, which was suitably situated at the equator, and in which the city of Sheffield had grown. The attachment point was the Socket. 400 cars went up and down the cable at 300 km/h; the journey took five days. The elevator greatly improved Mars's exporting capability. Martian minerals were massively exported to Terra and Terran immigrants flooded Mars.*[35]

One thing those three authors have in common is that they wrote within the genre of hard science fiction—stories grounded in scientific accuracy, logic, and the realm of possibility. Space elevators are theoretically possible, though as with the Apollo program, innovations would be needed to solve many formidable engineering challenges, such as creating carbon nanotube–based composites or some other material—perhaps many multiples stronger than any that currently exist—for the tether. For his cable, Clarke created "hyperfilament," constructed from "continuous pseudo-one-dimensional diamond crystal."[36] Although he needed fictional superscience to make his elevator work, Clarke was confident that real-world tech would eventually do the trick. He joked that an elevator would be built "about 50 years after everyone stops laughing," bringing that number down to ten years, just before his death in 2008.[37] Is it time to start that ten-year clock ticking? Some countries think so, including China and Japan, thanks to advances in material science, such as the ability to manufacture super-strong sheets of one-atom-thick carbon graphene.[38]

In a 2022 essay for *Scientific American*, Stephen Cohen, a physicist at Montreal's Vanier College, writes that while "the synthesis of potentially suitable materials has progressed in recent years, we are still at least 10 years away from a material solution (one having adequate properties, and that can be manufactured reasonably quickly at a reasonable cost)."[39] That said, he believes space elevators could exist within "two or three decades." What could a space elevator do—if one could be built, it might cost far less than NASA's current budget of $30 billion—that would merit government support? (Of course, a massively wealthy entrepreneur could always bankroll the project...such as space elevator fan Elon Musk.[40]) It would be a powerful tool to enable an orbital, lunar, and deep space economy in a way far more cheaply and safely than rockets and without polluting the atmosphere. As Cohen writes, "A space elevator becomes a bridge to the entire solar system. Release a payload in the lower portion, and you orbit Earth, but do so in the upper portion, and you orbit the sun; all without fuel."[41] Ironically given Musk's apparent interest in space elevators, the biggest threat to such a project might be SpaceX. First, all the satellites it's launching could create space junk that could pose a danger to an elevator. (Of course, this isn't just a SpaceX issue.) Also, the reusable rockets of SpaceX or some other company could reduce the cost of getting stuff to orbit as price competitive with a theoretical elevator, about $100 per kilogram, if not less.

Building a mega-telescope on the moon. If we're to ever discover the existence of extraterrestrial life—much less intelligent life and alien civilizations—it most likely won't come from interviewing naval aviators about what they saw whizzing around their aircraft off the coast of San Diego. And whether it's searching for ETs or learning more about the wonders of the universe, astronomers see the moon as the perfect location for a massive radio telescope. By picking up electromagnetic waves emitted from distant celestial objects, Earth's radio telescopes have enabled astronomers to make discoveries that couldn't be observed with optical telescopes, such as relic radiation from the origins of the universe. But the moon has some big advantages over the Earth in detecting those waves. The moon has no atmosphere, and its far side is protected from light and radio waves coming from Earth. Such a telescope could also observe the so far largely unexplored wavelengths reflected by the Earth's ionosphere.

NASA is considering two projects to make a moon telescope reality. The Lunar Crater Radio Telescope project calls for crawling robots to transform a half-mile-wide crater into an observatory by attaching a wire mesh along the crater walls.[42] NASA has already approved $500,000 for further study of the LCRT idea. The other project is the Farside Array for Radio Science Investigations of the Dark ages and Exoplanets, or FARSIDE. Robotic rovers would deploy 128 special antennas over an area 10 kilometers in diameter to study the universe's history before stellar ignition and the formation of the first stars and galaxies as well as planets outside the solar system.[43] Most intriguingly, FARSIDE would allow us to better study the magnetic fields of those exoplanets, giving us a clearer idea of just how many planets are capable of supporting life. (Planets without magnetic fields can't maintain atmospheres.) Discovering an improbable cluster of such planets would suggest an alien civilization was terraforming these bodies by giving them a magnetosphere.

Imagine if we detected such an advanced civilization. Their indisputable presence and technological advancement—even if we never saw them up close or were able to examine their technology—would show humanity that we're nowhere close to our potential. Good ideas might be getting harder to find, but we're nowhere close to finding all of them. Maybe there's a warp engine out there somewhere, waiting for us. There would be renewed interest in science of all sorts, in discovery, in maximizing human potential—especially when we could see such vivid evidence that advanced civilizations won't ultimately destroy themselves through war or planetary negligence. Given the upside here, another option is for government to fully fund a full-scale version of the Breakthrough Starshot initiative, a private R&D program trying to build tiny, proof-of-concept spacecraft—it would use laser-pushed lightsails to reach 20 percent of the speed of light—for a twenty-year journey to Alpha Centauri.[44] It's the next solar system over and home of possible Earth-like planets.

Counting the Minutes and Seconds to a Sci-Fi Future

As of the writing of this book, the famous Doomsday Clock of the Bulletin of the Atomic Scientists is at mere one hundred seconds to midnight, "the most dangerous situation that humanity has ever faced."[45] This analysis, while taking into account the nuclear issues that led to the clock's creation, also factors in myriad other risks such as climate change and "disruptive" technologies like AI, cyberattacks, and genetic editing. Interestingly, the clock has been stuck at the time since 2020 when it was moved closer from two minutes to midnight. That, even with Russia's invasion of Ukraine and loose suggestions from the former about using nuclear weapons. But with the clock already just shy of midnight, perhaps the Bulletin is hesitant to move it any closer. Then again, let's not overthink things here. Although the clock is a powerfully evocative symbol, it doesn't really tell us much of substance. During the 1960s, for example, the clock suggested that the decade became existentially safer with the hands moving from two minutes to midnight at the start to ten minutes at the end.[46] The Bulletin made those adjustments based mostly on the signing of various international nuclear weapons treaties. Yet we now know the decade was filled with nuclear close calls, including during the Cuban Missile Crisis, when a Soviet patrol submarine almost launched a nuclear-armed torpedo.[47]

But the Doomsday Clock isn't the only conceptual chronometer here. There's also the Clock of the Long Now, an actual mechanical clock meant to run for ten thousand years—if it ever gets built and installed on the top of Mount Washington in Nevada. While the Doomsday Clock is meant to warn of approaching disaster, the Long Now Clock would offer perspective. "Such a clock, if sufficiently impressive and well-engineered, would embody deep time for people," explains Stewart Brand, a founding board member of the Long Now Foundation.[48] "It should be charismatic to visit, interesting to think about, and famous enough to become iconic in the public discourse.

Ideally, it would do for thinking about time what the photographs of Earth from space have done for thinking about the environment. Such icons reframe the way people think."

Let me suggest a new clock, one that would be an evocative symbol like the Doomsday Clock, but also offer perspective more like the Long Now Clock. I call it the Genesis Clock. The name is inspired by the Genesis Device from 1982's *Star Trek: The Wrath of Khan.*[49] (Yes, more *Trek.*) When initiated on an uninhabited planet, the device would begin a process of rapid terraforming, preparing the planet for human colonization. As one character in the film puts it, "What exactly is Genesis? Well, put simply, Genesis is life from lifelessness." The Genesis Clock would attempt to tell humanity how close or distant it might be to a period so different from modern life that it would qualify as a new beginning for our civilization, a new human epoch. "New life," one might even say. As I explained above, the Doomsday Clock is pretty subjective in how it determines how close we're to destroying ourselves. Might the Genesis Clock suffer the same problem as it suggests how close we were to the dawn of a new age rather than the midnight of our existence? To some degree, but the factors driving the time setting would be more objective. Among the possible factors that would determine how close we are to dawn:

- How close are we to achieving artificial general intelligence?
- How close are we to extending the average human lifespan to 120?
- Do we have a cancer vaccine and a cure for Alzheimer's?
- Can we deflect a larger asteroid or comet headed toward Earth?
- Is carbon in the atmosphere declining?
- Is less than 1 percent of the world's population undernourished with a caloric intake below minimum energy requirements?
- Are we bringing back extinct species?
- Is even the poorest nation no poorer than the average economy in 2000?
- Is even the least free nation as free as the average nation in 2000?
- Is average Technologically Futuristic Productivity growth among rich nations at least 50 percent higher than its postwar average?

- Do we have sustainable off-planet human outputs that could continue with no help from Earth? Are we a true multiplanetary civilization?

How close are we to dawn? Probably a lot closer than many people think, especially those who believe we're running out of resources on Earth, headed toward overpopulation, and must abandon our "fantasies of infinite economic growth." When the Doomsday Clock was started, it was set at seven minutes to midnight. Given recent technological advances and the growing awareness of the need for more progress—not to mention the existence of this book!—I would also start the Genesis Clock at seven minutes to dawn.

THIRTEEN

Why an Up Wing Future Can Happen—and Why It Might Not

In 2016, there emerged a strange kind of mutant voter who seemed to defy the laws of political reality: the Bernie Sanders–Donald Trump voter. How could such a strange creature exist? Sanders, who challenged Hillary Clinton for the Democratic presidential nomination that year and then Joe Biden four years later, was a self-described democratic socialist who constantly railed against "millionaires and billionaires." Trump was a self-described billionaire who used "socialist" and "communist" interchangeably when attacking Democrats. And yet the hardcore Bernie "bros" and MAGA Trumpers had a lot in common. Both groups seemed angry at "Wall Street, stagnating middle-class wages, international trade agreements, the influence of rich donors in political campaigns and, most of all, American political elites," noted the *Washington Post* back then.[1] When the November election came around, more than one in ten of those who voted in the primaries for the progressive Sanders ended up voting for the populist Trump rather than for the Democratic candidate, Clinton.[2]

Some Up Wing enthusiasts see the 2016 election as evidence that major political realignment is possible, with the pandemic increasing the odds. The outbreak has already led to the pre-pan, anti-vaccine crowd on the Left Coast finding common cause with Red Staters who refused to accept their "Fauci ouchie" jabs, what *New York Times* columnist Ross Douthat called "the New Age–QAnon overlap, the Covid-era migration of formerly left-wing skeptics of Big Pharma onto right-wing shows and platforms."[3] Maybe the seeds have been sown for an Up Wing versus Down Wing political future without donkeys and elephants. Steve Fuller, a social philosopher at Warwick University, has offered perhaps the most fleshed-out theory of how such a radical realignment would happen. Conveniently enough, Fuller also borrows the terminology of Up Wing and Down Wing from FM-2030. He explains how the progressives of the Democratic Party and the traditionalists of the Republican Party could form a "down-winging Green pole" in politics, while the Democratic technocrats and the Republican libertarians could comprise an "up-winging Black pole"—black referring to the inky black of space, where human destiny lies, for Up Wingers and green for Down Wingers given their preoccupation with preserving this planet. "These will be the new right and left—or, rather, down and up," Fuller wrote in 2012. "One group will be grounded in the earth, while the other looks toward the heavens."[4]

Imagine the possible U.S. politics of 2032 or 2036. On one side, the Progress and Prosperity Party (symbol: a spritely unicorn). It mostly consists of the center right and center left of the old Democratic and Republican parties—people who voted for early 2000s politicians such as Barack Obama, Hillary Clinton, George W. Bush, and Mitt Romney. The P&P takes historical inspiration from Founding Fathers such as Benjamin Franklin (a scientist and inventor who fully believed in man's capability to adapt the world around himself for the better) and the upward-striving Alexander Hamilton. It's a drawbridge-down party that broadly favors economic openness—liberal trade and immigration policies, for instance—and the proactionary principle of governing: public policy should encourage innovation even if all the consequences aren't well understood and it causes economic disruption. Pedal to the metal on advancing artificial intelligence. Human-level AI can't come too soon. P&P supporters are typically better educated and found in denser suburbs and cities, as well as on Wall Street and in Silicon Valley.

On the other side: the Progressive Populist Party (symbol: a dour two-headed eagle—one side looking left, the other right). It mostly consists of the further left and further right voters who in the past supported democratic socialist Bernie Sanders and nationalist populist Donald Trump. Rather than a Founding Father, they see the proto-ProPop politician as President Andrew Jackson, who famously killed the Second Bank of the United States. Makes sense since the ProPops are skeptical of, well, everything: big business, Silicon Valley, Wall Street, U.S. military intervention, the Federal Reserve (naturally), and vaccinations. They eschew the disruption from open trade and the impact of immigration on native worker wages. (Not all are thrilled with the color of those immigrants, either.) They push for taxes on AI and robots to stem job loss, or even a ban on research that could lead to artificial general intelligence. AGI winter is coming. Their policy ideas are infused with the precautionary principle: better safe than sorry, whether it comes to technological innovation or economic disruption. Its voters tend to be less well educated and from less dense areas such as rural counties and the exurbs, as well as higher-income ProPop enclaves in Marin County, California, and Vermont.

✦ ✦ ✦

Is any of the above possible? Consider: the U.S. economy isn't the only part of American society affected by a kind of Schumpeterian creative destruction. There's churn in our politics, too. It wasn't so long ago that a Democratic president told the country that the "era of big government is over" and a Republican president was signing trade agreements and arguing that promoting global democracy was part of our sacred national mission.[5] It wasn't so long ago that white voters without college degrees were the cornerstone of the Democratic electoral coalition. And if you're GenX or older, you might remember when the GOP was thought to have an unbreakable electoral lock on California. In politics, the trend is your friend until it isn't. And sometimes the change happens quickly. Ronald Reagan's presidential victory in 1980, Bill Clinton's in 1992, and Donald Trump's in 2016 seemed to rapidly change the nature of their political parties.

Still, it's hard to imagine the culture warriors on both sides coexisting in a new party, given their differing views of the political implications of sex, gender, class, and religion. Their joint skepticism on vaccines and urban density probably isn't enough to get them together. Far more likely is that macro circumstances will make more obvious and viable the sort of agenda I have outlined throughout this book, giving strength to the remaining Up Wing bits and instincts of both parties. These groups would then work when possible together on curing Alzheimer's and cancer, advancing nuclear fusion and deep geothermal, boosting productivity and economic growth to raise incomes at the bottom, and promoting greater urban density and affordability. It could be a loose Up Wing coalition in favor of abundance. And yet given how polarized and distrustful American politics is, it's easy to see how none of that happens. Staying in Down Wing mode might seem the more likely path. Then again, when Washington has passed big, forward-looking legislation such as land grant colleges or the GI Bill, there was often some sense of emergency or national defense need that was helping spur Washington to action. Operation Warp Speed is a great example still fresh in the minds of the American public. Maybe putting this country in Up Wing mode doesn't require, at least in the short term, a more future-optimistic attitude or image about what tomorrow could be. We currently have multiple catalysts that could nudge America in a conservative futurist, Up Wing direction.

Three Tailwinds That Could Accelerate an Up Wing Future

Nuclear renaissance. If you were to ask someone if they were pro-progress (who but you, gentle reader, knows what "Up Wing" is?), they would probably answer yes. Most people probably think of themselves as broadly pro-progress. Most of us don't want to live without the internet, modern medicine, or indoor plumbing. America is also a first-adopter culture. So perhaps another way of raising that question about progress is to ask if someone is for or against nuclear power. The answer would say something useful about how they view all sorts of issues. It would serve as a clue to their opinions about supposed overpopulation and how to balance environmental protection and economic growth, as well as personal attributes such as risk tolerance and confidence in science. The answer might even say something about their belief in human agency and our ability to use technology as a powerful problem-solving tool.

Good news then: both in the U.S. and around the world concerns about generating clean energy and energy security due to Russia's invasion of Ukraine have pushed national leaders to reembrace nuclear power, a great sign for global Up Wing thinking. Japan's nuclear restart, for example, aims to maximize the use of nuclear reactors, including tripling the share of power the country gets from nuclear energy to 20 percent by 2030.[6] If Japan, a nation that has been attacked by atomic weapons and experienced a serious nuclear meltdown, is willing to give nuclear energy another try, it just might be possible anywhere. And that's exactly what seems to be happening. All across Europe, commitments to phase out nuclear energy have been reversed and plans to build new nuclear reactors announced. Even activist Greta Thunberg is saying good things about nuclear, arguing against Germany's taking its remaining nuclear power plants offline. "I personally think it's a very bad idea to focus on coal when [nuclear power] is already in place."[7]

Then there's the United States. President Joe Biden has set a goal of 100 percent carbon pollution–free electricity by 2035 and is relying on U.S. nuclear power plants, the nation's largest supplier of clean energy, to help achieve it. The 2022 Inflation Reduction Act contained funding for advanced nuclear reactor R&D, as well as numerous tax credits and loan guarantees that would apply to existing and advanced nuclear plants.[8] In California, the state's last remaining power plant—Diablo Canyon, situated on the Pacific Coast between San Francisco and Los Angeles—long scheduled to be scrapped, will remain open at least for a while. It's a remarkable turnaround in a state where anti-nuclear activists and progressive Democratic lawmakers have fought with great success to rid the state of nuclear power. Again, when faced with actual scarcity, such as in the form of power shortages, people choose abundance.

If political leaders on both sides become loudly pro-nuclear—and it's looking more and more like that might be the case—with political support strengthened by continuing technological advances, this nuclear revival might stick. If so, more and more folks might begin to realize that the environmental movement led America and other rich countries into making a massive mistake back in the 1970s—one without which we would be generating ample clean energy with no one talking about climate change. The result of that realization could be a considerable drop in the perceived authority of and support for the traditional environmentalist movement and a swing in favor of something more like the eco-modernist movement that sees technological progress as the best way of tackling climate change while also keeping the global economy growing. A new public perception of nuclear energy and technological risk would make many of the regulatory changes I've proposed far easier and new bad ones less likely to happen. More broadly, we might start thinking hard about what a world of clean energy abundance—from solar and wind, nuclear fission, nuclear fusion, and advanced geothermal—might mean: the production of clean hydrogen fuel, seawater desalination, pulling carbon from the skies, and human habitation, including in polar regions and maybe on and under the oceans as dreamed of during Up Wing 1.0. I would love to see what else entrepreneurs and technologists here and around the world might think up.

The rise of the Up Wing "abundance" left. When Biden was elected president, there was talk of a "transformational" presidency. The core of his domestic agenda was suggested by its campaign name: Build Back Better. The Biden administration would both repair the pandemic-broken economy and prepare it to dominate this century as it had the past one—in a carbon-free manner, of course. He vowed to cut U.S. greenhouse gas emissions in half (from 2005 levels) by 2030 and to net zero by 2050.[9] Doing this would require spending some $2 trillion to electrify the transportation sector with numerous car-charging stations, upgrade the energy grid, deploy utility-scale battery storage across the country, and install numerous large-scale wind farms and solar panel installations. Also toss in carbon-free hydrogen fuel and advanced nuclear reactors.

Then Biden's supporters realized two things about this ambitious climate agenda. First, Democrats in Congress didn't have the votes to pass anything so sweeping. Second, America had a building problem. As left-wing *New York Times* columnist Ezra Klein wrote in 2020, "If the Biden administration gave every American a check to transition to renewables, the policy would fail because we haven't built that much renewable capacity, to say nothing of the supply chain needed to deploy and maintain it."[10] And good luck getting the permits. Just one of many stunning examples of the phenomenon: In November 2007, TransWest Express Transmission Project asked the Bureau of Land Management for permission to build a 732-mile electric transmission line to connect a wind farm in southern Wyoming to a power grid around Las Vegas. Only in April of 2023 did the BLM finally grant permission. The delay is "a perfect illustration of the fact that the biggest obstacle to the government's renewable energy goals is often, in fact, the government itself," writes Eric Boehm in *Reason* magazine.[11]

And then once Klein and some other left-of-center policy journalists started looking around, they saw production problems everywhere, not just with clean energy. They realized government restrictions were making it hard to supply housing, education, and healthcare. Again, Klein: "There are sharp limits on supply in all of these sectors because regulators make it hard to increase supply (zoning laws make it difficult to build housing), training and hiring workers is expensive (adding classrooms means adding teachers and teacher aides, and expanding health insurance requires more doctors and nurses) or both."[12] And a similar sentiment from *The Atlantic* staff writer Derek Thompson, "Scarcity is the story of the decade. We don't have enough housing, semiconductor chips, or clean energy deployment."[13]

As I said in the introduction to this book, you can be Up Wing and techno-solutionist from the right and from the left. It's not hard to see that many of the ideas I've been advocating have some crossover with the "supply-side progressivism" of Klein and Thompson. Both are concerned with expanding the productivity capacity of the American economy. One obvious area where Up Wingers of the left and right can work together—in addition, now, to nuclear energy—is urban density and housing, as I wrote about earlier. In California, Governor Newsom is a liberal Democrat who has been pushing hard against housing regulation and getting pro-density laws passed. "NIMBYism is destroying the state."[14] This is a version of the Democratic party that center-right, pro-abundance Up Wingers can find issue-by-issue common ground. I only hope these folks are willing to buck those on the left who want to slow down further advances in artificial intelligence.

The China threat. "Why do great nations fall," asks the lecturer in front of a ginormous video screen in a 2030 Beijing college classroom with tech-noir lighting right out of Ridley Scott's *Alien* or *Blade Runner* franchises. "The Ancient Greeks, the Roman Empire, the British Empire, and the United States of America. They all make the same mistakes: turning their back on the principles that made them great." This 2010 television ad was produced by a Washington anti-debt advocacy group during the height of the Tea Party movement as an attack on the Obama administration's economic stimulus spending during the global financial crisis and passage of the Affordable Care Act. But as journalist James Fallows noted at the time, although "the ad is clearly meant to make Americans shudder at the idea of a Chinese-dominated future, at no point does it say that the canny foreigners did anything wrong. It uses them as a spur for us to do better."[15]

Specifically, the ad is trying to spur Americans to embrace fiscal probity—which the country actually did for a while. The federal budget deficit fell from $1.4 trillion in the year the ad was made to $440 billion in 2015 before rising again.[16] In any event, there's nothing new about politicians pointing to geopolitical and geoeconomic competition as a reason for domestic action. Vice President Richard M. Nixon ran a presidential campaign ad in 1960 justifying civil rights for Black Americans by pointing to the Cold War. Nixon said "we cannot compete successfully with communism if we fail to utilize completely the minds and energies of all of our citizens. [Also] the whole world is watching us. When we fail to grant equality to all, that makes news—bad news for America all over the world."[17] From civil rights to the space program to education, politicians back then pointed to competition with the Soviet Union as reasons for action beyond military spending and preparedness.

And now it's happening with China. The 2022 CHIPS and Science Act was passed on a bipartisan basis because both Democrats and Republicans thought it necessary to successfully compete with China from semiconductor manufacturing to R&D. President Biden made the stakes clear in a speech selling the package: "Folks, to compete for the jobs of the future, we also need to level the playing field with China and other competitors. That's why it's so important to pass the Bipartisan Innovation Act sitting in Congress that will make record investments in emerging technologies and American manufacturing. We used to invest 2 percent of our G.D.P. in research and development. We don't now. China is."[18] It's not hard to see how the China threat could be used, to use inside-the-Beltway phraseology, as an "action-forcing mechanism" for much of my Up Wing agenda, from science investment to immigration to space. To update LBJ's famous statement about Project Apollo, I don't believe that this generation of Americans is willing to resign itself to going to bed each night by the light of a moon colonized by the Chinese Communist Party. But America continuing to lead at the technological frontier is about more than national prestige. We don't want a Sputnik moment with an AGI breakthrough, warns former Google CEO Erich Schmidt, that "could usher in an era of predominance not unlike the short period of nuclear superiority the United States enjoyed in the late 1940s."[19]

Three Headwinds That Could Undermine an Up Wing Future

And what might go wrong? What could prevent a Roaring Twenties, Thrilling Thirties, or Fantastic Forties? An obvious answer: Maybe the technologies mentioned in this book simply turn out to be less significant than now appears, justifying the skepticism of economist Robert Gordon. Or maybe it takes longer for them to diffuse throughout the economy and generate important commercial applications than we now think. As economist Erik Brynjolfsson said, regarding his "long bet" with Gordon: "If I end up being wrong about productivity in 2029 it would probably be because I made the same mistake as I made about productivity in the last decade. The technology has progressed as fast or faster than I expected in most areas, but our organizations and skills have consistently been slower to adapt....Great technology is important, but it is a catalyst for the real changes needed to boost productivity: updating business processes and the skills of the workforce."[20] I agree, but let me take it further: the biggest causes for concern are that worst Down Wing impulses of the past again dominate our actions and attitudes as a society.

The social limits to growth. The flipside of more affluent nations valuing the environment more: they value economic growth relatively less—or at least have less tolerance for the disruption from creative destruction that's inherent in a growing, dynamic economy. Schumpeter himself was aware of this. He famously thought highly productive capitalism would one day be replaced by socialism due to its success, unlike Marx, who predicted the same outcome because of its inevitable failure. A highly productive economy affords a larger intellectual class of academics, journalists, and bureaucrats who would be so removed from the entrepreneurial and productive mechanism of the economy that they would attack and undermine it. (Silicon Valley heartily agrees with this framing.) The success of entrepreneurial capitalism thus plants the seeds of its own destruction by the uncreative, at least in an economic sense. As Schumpeter writes in his 1943 book *Capitalism, Socialism, and Democracy*, "Unlike any other type of society, capitalism inevitably and by virtue of the very logic of its civilization creates, educates and subsidizes a vested interest in social unrest."[21]

This phenomenon of a society taking its own success for granted was very much also at the heart of Herman Kahn's thinking. In his final book, 1982's *The Coming Boom*, he writes, "New generations of more affluent children take affluence and welfare for granted, and as a result tend to be less motivated than their parents in acquiring material goods. They are also less willing to accept...the notion that rapid economic growth often destroys the old (from historic buildings to biological species to traditional ways of life) when introducing the new. Opposition to creative destruction has become a very important social limit to growth."[22] Now four decades later, it's a diagnosis of risk intolerance that continues to be unfortunately relevant. And it's not just NEPA. Economist Tyler Cowen notes in his 2017 book *The*

Complacent Class that Americans move to other states less frequently than they used to, they start businesses less frequently than they used to, and they let their kids play outside unsupervised less frequently than they used to. "What I see is a country that has so deeply built itself into lower levels of risk-taking, self-protection, not letting other people move in, safeguarding your community, your children, that there actually isn't a way out of that box anymore," Cowen observes.[23] Again, richer nations are more worried about the downsides from AI, while poorer nations anticipate opportunity.[24] Sixty percent of Americans in April 2023 favored a pause on "some kinds of AI development" versus 20 percent opposed.[25]

I've not spent much time exploring how emerging technologies might make life worse. There are already plenty of news stories, think-tank reports, and books about the topic: AI doing things we don't want it to, genetic editing creating superplagues, and so forth. My concern is that our Down Wing instincts will push us to be overly cautious and we'll retreat from developing anything that could theoretically create existential risk, such as AGI or new genetic technologies. It's just so easy to focus on potential downsides. Economist Robin Hanson points out how people didn't think about television very much ahead of time. If back in the early postwar years, we could've imagined that in twenty years people were going to spend many hours day watching TV, "people would've freaked out," he argues.[26] Likewise, if people at the start of the twentieth century could've envisioned the future of cars—"automobile accidents, individual people controlling a thing going down the street at 80 miles an hour"—they might have rejected the horseless carriage. As such, Hanson worries a focus on tech dangers will enable both our natural caution and Down Wing activists. The economist isn't saying it's optimal for potential risks from AI or existential threats from asteroids to be downplayed… "[But] it might be in fact true that the world today is broken so much that if ordinary people and policymakers don't know about a future risk, the world's better off, because at least they won't mess it up by trying to limit it and control it too early and too crudely," Hanson explains.

A nuclear accident. Should fighting in Ukraine result in a radiation release from any of the sixteen Ukrainian reactors at four power plants, it would undoubtedly be a setback. For that matter, an accident anywhere would be a setback if handled by the media like similar accidents, with wild speculation about potential injuries and deaths. "We need to avoid a major accident in Ukraine," Rafael Mariano Grossi, director general of the International Atomic Energy Agency, a UN nuclear watchdog, said in 2022.[27] "If we have a major accident in Ukraine, the societal license we need to do whatever we may be wanting to do will—and rightly so—be even more difficult to get."

Societal license, or societal consent, is something the sector lost in the 1970s. In a democracy, nuclear energy needs it as much as it needs to meet regulatory standards and economic viability. How high is the risk of nuclear losing the societal consent that it seems to be slowly regaining? History suggests the risk is hardly insignificant, but the sector is likely more resilient than in the past, thanks to the shock of soaring prices for oil and gas, as well as the growing realization that to reduce carbon emissions, we need the sort of flexible and abundant power supply that solar and wind can't give us. Activists are also likely to overplay their hands with statements like this one from Steven Cohen, the former executive director of Columbia University's Earth Institute: "I do not underestimate the threat of climate change, but if I had to choose between a radioactive planet and a warm planet, I'd go with the warmth."[28] Such hyperbole is more likely to undermine the anti-nuclear case than promote it.

But I don't think the risk of an accident only applies to nuclear. I think a lot about how President Nixon was shaken by the almost disaster of Apollo 13, as well as the effect of the two space shuttle disasters. How resilient would we be today to a catastrophic Artemis moon mission or, even worse, with a SpaceX rocket given the number of critics eager for Elon Musk to fail? As Musk himself has said about the current opportunity in space (comments that could also apply to AGI):

> *There's a window that could be opened for a long time or a short time where we have an opportunity to establish a self-sustaining base on Mars before something happens to drive the technology level on Earth below where it's possible.... I don't think we can discount the possibility of a*

> *third World War. You know, in 1912, they were proclaiming a new age of peace and prosperity, saying that it was a golden age, war was over. And then you had World War I followed by World War II followed by the Cold War....Let's say nuclear weapons are used. I mean, there could be a very powerful social movement that's anti-technology.*[29]

Learning the wrong lessons from China's success. Too much of Washington has failed to notice that Chinese state capitalism, or "socialism with Chinese characteristics," isn't working so well lately. China's retreat from economic liberalization—and the growth it helped spur for decades—could be seen even before President Xi Jinping's "common prosperity" program meant to accelerate China's shift away from Western-style market capitalism and economic openness. The World Bank calculates that China's Technologically Futuristic Productivity has grown by just over 1 percent annually since 2008, less than a third the rate of the previous three "rising China" decades.[30] Over this period, China had steadily veered off the pro-market path and showed little interest in returning. According to the World Bank, "Earlier reforms led to state-owned enterprises catching up to private sector productivity levels in manufacturing, but convergence stalled after 2007."[31] The Chinese Communist Party is also spreading its tentacles further and deeper into the private sector. As the *Harvard Business Review* notes: "All companies with more than 50 employees must have a Communist Party representative on-site. This muddies decision-making, skews rewards, and bureaucratizes the innovation process."[32]

Increased emphasis on top-down control of the economy is a bet that the state can effectively encourage innovation through government investment in promising sectors. Easier said (and spent) than done. China has plowed billions of dollars in trying to catch up to the world's most advanced semiconductor companies and still isn't close. In the 2020 paper "Picking Winners? Government Subsidies and Firm Productivity in China," economists Lee G. Branstetter, Guangwei Li, and Mengjia Ren find little evidence that the Chinese government successfully picks winners.[33] If anything, "direct subsidies tend to flow to less productive firms rather than more productive firms." They conclude: "In the longer run, this approach is unlikely to promote the kind of significant productivity improvements the Chinese economy will need to maintain growth in the face of an aging population, a declining workforce, and mounting evidence of diminishing returns to capital investment."

Still, I'm concerned that some American policymakers, on the left and right, are too impressed with China's rapid economic rise and thus think Chinese-style "capitalism" with American characteristics has much merit. The alarm, with a dollop of envy, about China's economic and technological advance goes back to 2015 when Beijing published its "Made in China 2025" blueprint that aimed to make the country globally competitive, if not dominant, in ten key technology sectors.[34] Those happen to be many of the same sectors—including artificial intelligence and machine learning, advanced manufacturing and advanced materials, and quantum information science—that will receive applied research funding (research meant to solve a specific problem identified by the federal government) in the Biden administration's 2022 CHIPS and Science Act.[35] But targeted research spending, as well as the occasional moonshot and Operation Warp Speed–type initiatives, should not be seen as a substitute for spending on basic research or R&D spending by the private sector, not to mention the risk-taking of entrepreneurs—something America does better than any other country. It's our Deep Magic.

I'm concerned about this bipartisan shift toward industrial policy, which also seems to have traction among the embryonic supply-side progressive movement mentioned above. Government action meant to solve certain well-defined technological problems (as DARPA does) and support certain technologies important to national security (including less reliance on Taiwan for chip making) or urgent national need (like a pandemic or climate change) is one thing, but the core idea behind "industrial policy" as economists typically use the term concerns supporting domestic manufacturing jobs or reviving a specific industry. (This impulse can also be seen in "Buy American" policies that restrict federal funds to goods and services made domestically, almost certainly making federal infrastructure projects more expensive, including delays). The examples of successful industrial policy, broadly defined, mentioned in this book, such as how Project Apollo boosted the nascent chip industry and Operation Warp Speed, shouldn't be ignored. But examples of failure are legion—especially as powerful interest groups distort Washington policymaker actions—and economists typically advocate a narrow approach. China's troubles with industrial policy, especially as it tries to shift from catch-up mode to pushing forward the technological frontier, are hardly surprising.

✦ ✦ ✦

The benefits of warp-speed tech progress and economic growth are so obvious and powerful that merely reminding people of them should be enough to spur society to action. And on the margin, I think nonfiction books like this one, along with all manner of Up Wing fiction and art, can help prime us for action. But conservative futurists and Up Wingers everywhere must aggressively and continuously make the pro-progress case whenever and wherever possible. (This should be twice as true for conservative futurists, given their supposed recognition of a deep obligation to future generations.) We currently stand at a moment when great progress is possible thanks to a host of emerging technologies and exogenous factors such as the pandemic and war in Europe. Future generations will render harsh judgment if we again miss our opportunity to take a giant leap forward.

CONCLUSION

2076, the American Tricentennial

In the summer of the bicentennial year of 1976, Atlantic Richfield, a Los Angeles–based oil and gas company, ran an advertisement across American media. It was featured in newspapers and magazines, as well as on television. The ad invited readers and viewers to write letters to their future fellow Americans in the tricentennial year of 2076. Some great future-optimistic, Up Wing thinking was built right into the premise. First, the project assumed there would still be a United States. Second, the project assumed the U.S. would be a nation-state still organized enough to keep a collection of these letters available for public access and display. (Certainly there were some Down Wing thinkers back then skeptical of both assumptions.) If you ever have a chance, read *The Tricentennial Report: Letters from America*, an eighty-page selection of the some sixty thousand responses.[1] Published as a book in 1977—I snagged my copy on eBay—it will quickly become clear that Atlantic Richfield's outlook made it far more upbeat about the future than many of the folks who took time to write in. The letters contain plenty of dystopian speculation and fiction—not all of it with a strong scientific foundation—about America and the world of one hundred years hence. Bruce of Pleasantville, New Jersey, writes about a young man named Nemo Outis reflecting on the state of our shattered country:

> *Crises, Nemo thought sourly, as if there had ever been a time without one. He remembered when he had been young, only five or so, and when the UPC (United Plains Confederacy) had been formed out of the smoldering wreckage of the United States and the British Commonwealth State of Canada. There were the "terrible years of hardship" alluded to by UPC historians which had followed the Ecology War of 1977, the last of the so-called "world wars" of the 20th century. There was a crisis, he reflected, spawned of overpopulation and the pollution of the oceans that supplied life to many parts of the Earth.... The net result was the near total destruction of mainland Asia, large parts of Europe, the Middle East, Africa, and of course the United States.*[2]

The vignette hits many of the themes common to the more catastrophic letters: overpopulation, environmental degradation, and America's inevitable dissolution. One calamity not mentioned was a severe shortage of energy, though many other writers—themselves living through the decade's oil shocks—assumed fossil fuels would supply little if any of our power beyond the twentieth century. Solar was a popular alternative to oil and gas, as was nuclear—though the latter was often criticized for the possibility of dangerous accidents and the difficult disposal of nuclear waste. (Remember, this was before Three Mile Island, additional proof that the accident more signaled the finale of the Atomic Age than the beginning of the end.) Many of the Down Wing letters were highly detailed like the one above, suggesting the writers were familiar with the dystopian science fiction of the day. Ralph of Cambridge, Massachusetts, tells a tale worthy of treatment from 1970s Hollywood:

> *New towns will have sprung up in the 1980s as a result of increasing middle-class flight from the decaying cities. At first, inhabitants of the new towns will commute, but rising food prices and deteriorating*

commuter service will drive them to become farmers and artisans living in self-sufficient communities. Before the obsolescence of the automobile, armed gangs from the cities will often raid the new towns, which would respond to the threat by building walls and fortification. As the car disappears and the threat from the cities lessens, rivalries and wars with nearby towns will erupt, and the walls will stay. The face of 21st-century America, then, will resemble that of medieval Europe... On a lighter note, since most of the population will barely be subsisting on the results of their agriculture, almost everyone will be thin.[3]

By contrast, many of the more Up Wing–leaning letters had a looser, dreamier quality—albeit one infused with the classic "clean, green" imagery that makes it seem more like a sci-fi Utopia than a real place. This from Jane of Brooklyn:

I see a world of peace and beauty. The air is clear and invigorating. The tall, clean, stainless and blue tinted glass business/living complexes seem to blend with the greenery that abounds everywhere.... There is no anxiety, no loneliness. There is happy activity and tranquility.... Man has controlled disease, population growth and his hostilities.[4]

The Tricentennial Report also includes interviews with "five distinguished Americans" who served as an advisory board to the project. Poet Nikki Giovanni hopes space exploration will help us "overcome our nationalistic nearsightedness. We can actually see the whole earth from space and, in a very simple way, will help us all to understand the concept of Spaceship Earth—that we are all interdependent and have to cooperate."[5] Famed anthropologist Margaret Mead says her optimism is "based on human nature" and her pessimism "on the fact that there are nuclear bombs all around the world, enough to blow up the world seven times."[6] Urban scientist Harvey Perloff worries that cities are on a permanent, postindustrial downward spiral, although perhaps they could focus more on services, tourism, R&D, and being corporate headquarters.[7] William Ruckelshaus, the first administrator of the Environmental Protection Agency, thinks the "paramount problem" facing the world is overpopulation, which requires collective global cooperation.[8] (Republicans were a lot different back then.)

Then there was futurist Herman Kahn, who touches on some of his favorite themes, the most important being that we have it within our power to create a world of abundance. What we decide and what we do matter a whole lot.

> ***Question: You seem to have a very optimistic image of the future. For example, you strongly disagree with the idea of limits on economic growth as put forth by the Club of Rome. Is that correct?***
> *Herman Kahn: Absolutely given only two caveats: we don't have disastrously bad luck and that we don't do things that are incredibly dumb. It takes a moderate but not extraordinarily good level of decision-making to overcome the problems we can imagine in the future.*
>
> ***Question: In your writings about the future, you place a lot of hope for solving our problems on the development of new technology. Which areas do you think that changes in technology will be most dramatic or will have the most effect on how we live our lives?***
> *Kahn: The first area is more of the same—improved energy sources and increased productivity. Space and the oceans will be among the new industrial frontiers. Space satellites may well be used not only for greatly improved weather forecasting and communication links, but also for specialized industrial purposes and for energy production. New communications and computer technologies allow everyone access to enormous amounts of information and may allow us to do away with traditional work patterns. Agriculture may become automated, involving methods that are unthought of today and a whole new food processing industry is a very definite possibility.*
>
> ***Question: If technology is not a problem for ensuring future energy supplies, what types of problems do you see us facing?***
> *Kahn: A lot of problems will stem from mismanagement. Many people seem unable to accept the fact that we will have to make some sacri-*

> *fices and accept certain trade-offs. Today, there's no absolutely safe, clean, cheap form of energy production, and it will be a long time until there is, if ever. No one wants to live next-door to an energy facility, but everyone wants energy. We can't have it both ways—or at least not for very long.*[9]

✦ ✦ ✦

We're now roughly halfway between the bicentennial and tricentennial. And if judged by the expectations of many of the more Down Wing "Letters to America," we're doing OK. Not only are fossil fuels still plentiful, but the only thing preventing a future of abundant, cheap, clean energy is our actions and attitudes. The typical American is a lot richer than in 1976, and so are the planet's poorest of the poor. Our environment is less polluted, and the world a lot freer. And rather than a failed state, the U.S. showed during the pandemic years what it can still do when its people put their minds and efforts to work, whether rapidly creating a vaccine or returning to space.

What does the next half century hold in store? As I explained at the beginning of this book, my sort of conservative futurism is based on creating the capabilities and resources for America to organically, bottom-up "decide" what the future will look like through the billions of choices we all make every day. As economist Friedrich Hayek said in his 1974 Nobel Prize lecture, "To act on the belief that we possess the knowledge and the power which enable us to shape the processes of society entirely to our liking, knowledge which in fact we do not possess, is likely to make us do much harm."[10] Government's role mostly is doing its proper part: investing in its citizens and regulating wisely. Rather than fashioning all sorts of long-term plans and projections, especially ones that attempt to predict what's next for science and technology and their economic and societal impacts—although I eagerly consume such content—my futuristic focus is on creating the best possible conditions for discovery, invention, innovation, and growth. As such, I haven't spent much time in this book with detailed scenarios and forecasts of what is *likely* to be, only a rough sketch of what *could* be so as to give a sense of grand possibility. But certainly others have done plenty of that kind of imaginative forecasting, and to the extent it helps us conceive a future worth suffering and striving for, it can be a useful effort.

Here's a great example from Prime Movers Lab, a venture capital firm that focuses on breakthrough scientific startups with a focus on "reinventing energy, transportation, infrastructure, manufacturing, human augmentation, and agriculture." It's put together a road map of sorts about how the next three decades might play given the advances the firm is currently seeing among young companies.[11] By the end of the 2020s: next-generation geothermal power, commercially competitive low-carbon cement, return of commercial supersonic jets, sale of cell-growth meat, longevity drugs to treat age-related diseases, powered exo-skeletons. By the end of the 2030s: the first commercial nuclear fusion power plant, cheap and effective desalination, commercial hypersonic aviation, robots automate construction, brain repair and reversal of neurodegenerative diseases, bio-factories produce chemicals currently derived from fossil fuels. By the end of the 2040s: direct air capture of CO_2 below \$100/ton, domestic robots become commonplace, lab-grown organs replace organ donation, higher yields from next-generation crops, genetic technologies restore lost species and ecosystems, battery energy density five times that of today, lunar helium-3 mining for fusion energy.

That's one investment firm's opinion about tomorrow based on what startup tech firms are attempting today. The forecasters at Metaculus also offer a host of intriguing predictions. Some of their consensus vision of the future: a universal flu vaccine by September 2032,[12] first human on Mars by August 2039,[13] first tourist on Mars by January 2050,[14] revival of woolly mammoth by March 2054,[15] nuclear fusion supplies more than 10 percent of global energy by March 2058,[16] U.S. labor force participation rate below 10 percent by September 2134,[17] and Mars GDP exceeds that of Earth by the end of the year 3000.[18]

Again, just informed guesses. No guarantees. But what I like about both sets of forecasts is that even though some experts might consider them overly optimistic—others perhaps not optimistic enough—the predictions are based on a reality where scientific breakthroughs and new technologies don't change everything everywhere all at once. It takes time for an economy and society to learn how to fully accept and efficiently use innovations before they can generate Technologically Futuristic Productivity growth. Understanding that reality is a key element of conservative futurism. Such was the timeline with electrification and computers, and it will likely be that way with artificial intelligence, including generative AI and other forms of machine learning. As the process plays out, our actions and attitudes will have a critical role to play in creating Up Wing public policy and culture that encourage the continued advance of tech progress and our adaption to it, as well as countering and overcoming Down Wing resistance. Aside from that, as Kahn put it, we should be OK as long as "we don't have disastrously bad luck and that we don't do things that are incredibly dumb." That's about as conservative futurist as one can get.

✦ ✦ ✦

On July 4 in the bicentennial year of 1976, I was a bookish nine-year-old eager to attend that night's big fireworks display at the huge city park a couple blocks from my house. But for much of that day, my thoughts were fixed on what was right in front of me: a piece of paper on which I was writing a letter to the America of 2076. Now I can't recall if I saw the Atlantic Richfield ad in a newspaper or on television. Nor do I recall the content of my letter—or if it was ever even mailed, to be honest, given my unorganized family life—although considering my sci-fi interests, the letter probably included a prediction of domed cities on Earth and space colonies across the solar system. Probably flying cars, too. (I was well aware of *The Jetsons*, of course.) Time for another try. This is my letter to the America of fifty-three years from now:

> *My fellow Americans of 2076: Hope all is well. I'm just going to assume this book was a monster bestseller, one that not only allowed me to build a Malibu mansion in the style of Tony Stark's from the successful Iron Man trilogy (did they ever recast Robert Downey Jr., or just deepfake him?), but—more importantly, I assure you—also played a pivotal role in providing a path forward to the Up Wing future that is your present. Humbly, you're welcome. Likewise, I'm going to assume that you, like*

your parents and grandparents, are living through another amazing American Century where the USA remains the indispensable nation and leader of the free world, pushing forward the frontiers of both technology and human freedom. The latest version of Tomorrowland at Disneyland Luna is probably pretty awesome. I'm also assuming that American know-how played a critical role in developing AI as a valued helper to humanity, sources of abundant clean energy, technology to remove excess carbon from the air, a thriving orbital economy, and all manner of universal vaccines for disease and treatments for chronic conditions. Existential risks from killer comets to viruses now seem more manageable, I'm guessing. And even if this planetary home were under lethal threat, humanity is now able to permanently live elsewhere—a place, perhaps, where kids might attend Nikola Tesla Academy, the most prestigious school in Musk City, located in Valles Marineris on the Red Planet. But I'm sure lots of bad things have happened, too, as will always be the case. Perhaps another Engels' pause as economies adjusted to greater automation. Maybe another accident with a new energy source or a space mission. I would like to think depressions, pandemics, and wars were obsolete, but in a world with flawed humans that is probably hoping for too much. I pray you are living in a future worthy of the risks taken to create it, one that also makes you confident to take more risks to create an even better tomorrow. And I hope to deliver this letter to you in person.

THE END FOR NOW

ACKNOWLEDGMENTS

This book almost certainly would still be just a very long file in Google Docs without the direct efforts of Melissa Pranger, book publicist at my employer, the American Enterprise Institute. First, Melissa saw the book's potential, which is exactly what I needed to hear at the time. Second, she reached out to Hachette and persuaded her contact there of the book's value and that it was worth taking a Zoom call with me to discuss. That contact was Hachette–Center Street editor Kathryn Riggs. As important as Kathryn's confidence in my little pandemic-era project (and excellent edits and suggestions): her enthusiasm. After the intense solitude of writing most of this book during the pandemic, Kathryn's positive feedback was tremendously energizing as I raced to the finish line. It's amazing that two people I didn't even know before the autumn of 2022 became so important in my life. I'm so thankful for them both.

Early on in 2020, about the only person who knew I was writing a book was my eventual literary agent, Jay Mandel of William Morris Endeavor. Jay was the Lennon to my McCartney, providing great practical advice, not only about how to make the book more marketable, but also how to create the best possible incarnation of my vision. Also a big thanks to my AEI colleague, the great Jonah Goldberg, who connected me with Jay.

Once AEI became broadly aware of the book, the response was super positive, from AEI president Robert Doar on down. Michael Strain, director of Economic Policy Studies, was especially supportive and gave me numerous helpful suggestions and ongoing feedback, both on economics and popular science fiction. And I wouldn't even be at AEI if not for former president Arthur Brooks and former executive vice president David Gerson. Certainly this entire project benefited tremendously from the hard work of Josiah Johnson and John Konicki, my brilliant research assistants who were as involved with this project as anyone. I would still be writing it if not for them both.

There are few opportunities to publicly thank the most important and influential people in your career. But a book allows that opportunity. My first job in journalism was at *Investor's Business Daily* in Los Angeles, and later Washington, DC, where I was hired by Wesley Mann and edited by Donald Gold, Mike Woods, and John Merline. My first step into a larger world. From there, I went to *USA Today* in Washington. My time there was brief, but I learned a lot about working at a major news organization from Money section editor Jim Henderson. Far longer was my time at *U.S. News and World Report.* So many great professionals there helped take my writing and reporting to a higher level: James Bock, Warren Cohen, Avery Comarow, Damon Darlin, James Fallows, Brian Kelly, and Tim Smart. It's harder to write short than long, and I became way better at the former during my time at Reuters Breakingviews thanks to my colleagues Rob Cox, Hugo Dixon, Jonathan Ford, and Martin Tripp.

It was while I was at *U.S. News* that I first started appearing on CNBC, eventually becoming an official contributor. None of that would've happened without my professional godfather, sensei, mentor, and dear friend, Lawrence Kudlow. (Never forget the Kudlow Creed: "Free market capitalism is the best path to prosperity!") I'm so grateful to so many of the folks—anchors, books, reporters, producers—at the Washington bureau and New Jersey mothership over the years: Jesse Bergman, Krista Braun (also an excellent actress), Erin Burnett, Donna Burton, Sandy Cannold, Jennet Chin, Dan Colarusso, Matthew Cuddy, Mary Duffy, Joanne Denyeau, Jason Driscoll, Nick Dunn, Kelly Evans, Even Falk, Kevin Flynn, Kerima Greene, John Harwood, Dan Holland, Adam Idleberg, Eamon Javers, Toby Josephs, Joe Kernan, Torrey Kleinman, Lori Ann LaRocco, Crystal Lau, Prashant Patel, Meghan Powers,

Carl Quintanilla, Megan Rogers, Sameepa Shetty, Gino Siniscalchi, Linda Sittenfeld, Brian Sullivan, Toby Taylor, Ben Thompson, A.J. Vielma, and Lisa Villalobos.

Finally, there are those who provided plenty of Up Wing ideation and influence into my thinking: Marc Andreessen, Erik Brynjolfsson, Jason Crawford, Tyler Cowen, Eli Dourado, Jason Furman, Kevin Kelly, Scott Lincicome, Andrew McAfee, Joel Mokyr, Virginia Postrel, Will Rinehart, Alec Stapp, Adam Thierer, Caleb Watney. May they live in a future of vast abundance, and sooner rather than later. Faster, please!

NOTES

Preface: The Pale Blue Dot of Progress

1. "Voyager 1's Pale Blue Dot," NASA, February 5, 2019, https://solarsystem.nasa.gov/resources/536/voyager-1s-pale-blue-dot.

2. Carl Sagan, *Pale Blue Dot: A Vision of the Human Future in Space* (New York: Random House, 1994), 5–6, Kindle.

3. Charles I. Jones, "The Facts of Economic Growth," National Bureau of Economic Research Working Paper no. 21142 (May 2015), https://www.nber.org/papers/w21142.

4. Thomas Hobbes, *Leviathan* (Scotts Valley, CA: CreateSpace Independent Publishing Platform, 2011), 77.

5. Sagan, *Pale Blue Dot*, 7.

6. Christian Davenport, "Elon Musk Offers Glimpse of Plans to Deliver Humans to Mars," *Washington Post*, September 27, 2016, https://www.washingtonpost.com/news/the-switch/wp/2016/09/27/elon-musk-to-discuss-his-vision-for-how-he-plans-to-colonize-mars.

7. Carl Sagan, "Why Send Humans to Mars?" *Issues in Science and Technology* 7, no. 3 (Spring 1991): 80–85.

8. Bernard Weinraub, "President Calls for Mars Mission and a Moon Base," *New York Times*, July 21, 1989, https://www.nytimes.com/1989/07/21/us/president-calls-for-mars-mission-and-a-moon-base.html.

9. Mike Brown, "SpaceX Mars City," *Inverse*, April 11, 2022, https://www.inverse.com/innovation/spacex-mars-city-codex.

10. Herman Kahn, William Brown, and Leon Martel, *The Next 200 Years: A Scenario for America and the World* (New York: William Morrow, 1976), 8.

11. My conversation with Kevin Kelly: "What to Do about 'Climate Anxiety,' America's New Dystopian Disease," *Faster, Please!* (newsletter), February 7, 2022, https://fasterplease.substack.com/p/-eco-anxiety-americas-new-dystopian.

12. J. R. R. Tolkien, *Lord of the Rings: The Fellowship of the Ring*, paperback ed. (Boston: Mariner Books, 1994), 72.

13. William H. McNeill, "The Conservation of Catastrophe," *New York Review*, December 20, 2001, https://www.nybooks.com/articles/2001/12/20/the-conservation-of-catastrophe.

14. Ibid.

Introduction: America's Tomorrowland Problem

1. U.S. Congress, House of Representatives, Committee on Un-American Activities, *Hearings Regarding the Communist Infiltration of the Motion Picture Industry. Public law 601 (section 121, Subsection Q (2))*, 80th Cong., 1st sess., 1947.

2. A discussion of Walt Disney's political views can be found in Neal Gabler, *Walt Disney: The Triumph of the American Imagination* (New York: Alfred A. Knopf, 2006), 612, Kindle.

3. Ibid., 609.

4. The Original EPCOT, "Walt Disney's E.P.C.O.T. film (1966)," YouTube video, September 23, 2013, 1:12, https://www.youtube.com/watch?v=sLCHg9mUBag.

5. "TWA Moonliner," Airline History Museum, https://www.airlinehistory.org/twa-moonliner.

6. "Rocket to the Moon: Presented by TWA," Yesterland, last modified June 9, 2020, https://www.yesterland.com/moonrocket.html.

7 "Tomorrowland: Walt's Vision for Today," Walt Disney Family Museum, https://www.waltdisney.org/exhibitions/tomorrowland-walts-vision-today.

8. Cited in Robert J. Gordon and Hassan Sayed, "A New Interpretation of Productivity Growth Dynamics in the Pre-Pandemic and Pandemic Era U.S. Economy, 1950–2022," National Bureau of Economic Research Working Paper no. 30267 (July 2022), https://www.nber.org/papers/w30267.

9. Ibid.

10. Ibid.

11. Ibid.

12. Chris Woodyard, "A Spin on the Future: Disney's Eisner Plans Major Renovation for Tomorrowland," *Los Angeles Times*, February 28, 1995, https://www.latimes.com/archives/la-xpm-1995-02-28-fi-37054-story.html.

13. Arthur C. Clarke, *Profiles of the Future: An Inquiry into the Limits of the Possible*, rev. ed. (New York: Harper & Row, 1973), xiii.

14. José Luis Ricón Fernández de la Puente, "Cozy Futurism," *Nintil* (blog), March 29, 2021, https://nintil.com/cozy-futurism.

15. Cited in Jonas Clark, "In Search of the American Dream," *The Atlantic*, June 2007, https://www.theatlantic.com/magazine/archive/2007/06in-search-of-the-american-dream/305921.

16. "Artificial Index Report 2023," Stanford HAI, April 2023, 324, https://aiindex.stanford.edu/report/.

17. Matt Novak, "68% of Americans Afraid of Self-Driving Cars, Up from 55% in 2022," *Forbes*, March 2, 2023, https://www.forbes.com/sites/mattnovak/2023/03/02/68-of-americans-afraid-of-self-driving-cars-up-from-55-in-2022/.

18. Nonfarm business productivity numbers accessed at the U.S. Bureau of Labor Statistics, https://www.bls.gov/productivity.

19. Brian Alexander, *Rapture: How Biotech Became the New Religion* (New York: Basic Books, 2003), 53–55.

20. Douglas Martin, "Futurist Known as FM-2030 Is Dead at 69," *New York Times*, July 11, 2000, https://www.nytimes.com/2000/07/11/us/futurist-known-as-fm-2030-is-dead-at-69.html.

21. F. M. Esfandiary, *Up-Wingers: A Futurist Manifesto* (New York: John Day, 1973), PDF version accessed at https://slowlorisblog.files.wordpress.com/2015/05/esfandiary-up-wingers-a-futurist-manifesto.pdf.

22. Ibid.

23. George F. Will, *The Conservative Sensibility* (New York: Hachette Books, 2019), introduction, Kindle.

24. Adam Smith, *An Inquiry into the Nature and Causes of the Wealth of Nations* (London: W. Strahan and T. Cadell, 1776), 18, https://eet.pixel-online.org/files/etranslation/original/The%20Wealth%20of%20Nations.pdf.

25. Edmund Burke, *Reflections on the Revolution in France* (London: James Dodsley, 1790), Kindle.

26. Tyler Cowen, "Existential Risk, AI, and the Inevitable Turn in Human History," *Marginal Revolution* (blog), March 27, 2023, https://marginalrevolution.com/marginalrevolution/2023/03/existential-risk-and-the-turn-in-human-history.html.

27. "Not Even Wrong," *Wikipedia*, https://en.wikipedia.org/wiki/Not_even_wrong.

28. Joel Mokyr, *The Lever of Riches: Technological Creativity and Economic Progress*, paperback ed. (Oxford, U.K.: Oxford University Press, 1992), 16.

29. Ritchie Robertson, *The Enlightenment: The Pursuit of Happiness, 1680–1790* (New York: Harper, 2021), 3.

30. "The Matrix," IMDb, https://www.imdb.com/title/tt0133093/charactersnm0000206.

31. The Original EPCOT, "Walt Disney's E.P.C.O.T. film."

32. Judith Schiff, "Robert Moses and the World's Fair," *Yale Alumni Magazine*, March–April 2014, https://yalealumnimagazine.org/articles/3850-robert-moses-and-the-worlds-fair; Erin Glover, "The 1964 New York World's Fair—A New Disney Technology Is Born," *Disney Parks Blog*, April 21, 2011, https://disneyparks.disney.go.com/blog/2011/04/the-1964-new-york-worlds-fair-a-new-disney-technology-is-born.

33. Louis Menand, "Fat Man," *New Yorker*, June 19, 2005, https://www.newyorker.com/magazine/2005/06/27/fat-man.

34. Paul Dragos Aligica and Kenneth R. Weinstein, eds, *The Essential Herman Kahn: In Defense of Thinking* (Lanham, MD: Lexington Books, 2009), 106, Kindle.

35. Cited in Gerald O. Barney, *The Global 2000 Report to the President: Entering the Twenty-First Century* (Arlington, VA: Seven Locks Press: 1988), PDF accessed at https://www.cartercenter.org/resources/pdfs/pdf-archive/global2000reporttothepresident--enteringthe21stcentury-01011991.pdf.

36. Ronald Reagan, "Statement on the Death of Herman Kahn," Ronald Reagan Presidential Library and Museum, July 8, 1983, https://www.reaganlibrary.gov/archives/speech/statement-death-herman-kahn.

37. Herman Kahn and Anthony J. Wiener, "The Use of Scenarios," Hudson Institute, January 1, 1967, https://www.hudson.org/technology/the-use-of-scenarios.

One: The False Start of Up Wing 1.0 (1955–1973)

1. Cited in David Henderson, "Paul Samuelson's Prediction for Post World War II," *EconLog* (blog), June 21, 2010, https://www.econlib.org/archives/2010/07/paul_samuelsons.html.

2. Alvin H. Hanson, "Economic Progress and Declining Population Growth," *American Economic Review* 24, no. 1 (March 1939): 1–15, http://digamo.free.fr/hansen39.pdf.

3. Norman Mackenzie and Jeanne Mackenzie, *H.G. Wells* (New York: Simon and Schuster, 1973), 46.

4. George Orwell, "The Rediscovery of Europe" in *The Collected Essays, Journalism and Letters of George Orwell*, vol. 2, *My Country Right or Left, 1940-1943,* ed. Sonia Orwell and Ian Angus (New York: Harvest Books), 201.

5. H. G. Wells, *Anticipations of the Reaction of Mechanical and Scientific Progress upon Human Life and Thought* (London: Chapman & Hall, 1902), 1.

6. H. G. Wells, *The Discovery of the Future* (New York: B. W. Hubesch, 1913), 22.

7. Ibid., 60–61.

8. Sarah Cole, *Inventing Tomorrow: H. G. Wells and the Twentieth Century* (New York: Columbia University Press, 2019), 62, Kindle.

9. H. G. Wells, *Mind at the End of Its Tether* (London: William Heinmann, 1945), 30, accessed at Internet Archive, https://archive.org/details/in.ernet.dli.2015.33876.

10. John Maynard Keynes, "Economic Possibilities for Our Grandchildren," in John Maynard Keynes, *Essays in Persuasion* (New York: Harcourt Brace, 1932), 358–373, https://www.aspeninstitute.org/wp-content/uploads/files/content/upload/Intro_and_Section_I.pdf.

11. Ibid.

12. Author's calculations from economic data found at Measuring Worth, https://www.measuringworth.com.

13. The quantity and quality of American automobile ownership is discussed in Robert Gordon, *The Rise and Fall of American Growth* (Princeton, NJ: Princeton University Press, 2016), 376–389, Kindle.

14. Ibid., 415, Kindle.

15. Ibid., 356, Kindle.

16. "Economic Report of the President," Council of Economic Advisers, January 1969, 23, https://www.presidency.ucsb.edu/sites/default/files/books/presidential-documents-archive-guidebook/the-economic-report-of-the-president-truman-1947-obama-2017/1969.pdf.

17. John Kenneth Galbraith, *The Affluent Society* (New York: Houghton Mifflin, 1978).

18. "100 Best Nonfiction," Modern Library, https://www.modernlibrary.com/top-100/100-best-nonfiction.

19. Galbraith, *The Affluent Society*, 275.

20. "Apollo 17," NASA, https://www.nasa.gov/mission_pages/apollo/missions/apollo17.html.

21. "Atoms for Peace Speech," International Atomic Energy Commission, https://www.iaea.org/about/history/atoms-for-peace-speech.

22. "#47 Shippingport Nuclear Power Station," American Society of Mechanical Engineers, https://www.asme.org/about-asme/engineering-history/landmarks/47-shippingport-nuclear-power-station.

23. Michael Lombardi, "Seventh Heaven: 50 Years Ago, Boeing and Pan Am Revolutionized Travel with the 707," *Frontiers* VII, no. III (July 2008): 8–9, https://www.boeing.com/news/frontiers/archive/2008/july/july08frontiers.pdf.

24. Gordon, *The Rise and Fall of American Growth*, 525, Kindle.

25. Sam Howe Verhovek, *Jet Age: The Comet, the 707, and the Race to Shrink the World* (New York: Avery, 2010), preface, Kindle.

26. NASA, "The Birth of NASA," March 28, 2008, https://www.nasa.gov/exploration/whyweexplore/Why_We_29.html.

27. Charles Fishman, "How NASA Gave Birth to Modern Computing—and Gets No Credit for It," June 3, 2019, *Fast Company*, https://www.fastcompany.com/90362753/how-nasa-gave-birth-to-modern-computing-and-gets-no-credit-for-it.

28. Patricia Sullivan, "Engineer's Tiny Chip Changed the World," *Washington Post*, June 22, 2005, https://www.washingtonpost.com/archive/politics/2005/06/22/engineers-tiny-chip-changed-the-world/7e17ba53-c1ea-4c48-878a-83b79d7574e9/.

29. "The Apollo Missions," IBM, https://www.ibm.com/ibm/history/ibm100/us/en/icons/apollo/breakthroughs.

30. Eisenhower Presidential Library, accessed at https://www.eisenhowerlibrary.gov/sites/default/files/research/online-documents/igy/1955-7-29-press-release.pdf.

31. "Sputnik and the Dawn of the Space Age," NASA, https://history.nasa.gov/sputnik.html.

32. "Just 25 Years Ago Today in Warm Springs...," *New York Times*, April 13, 1970, https://www.nytimes.com/1970/04/12/archives/just-25-years-ago-today-in-warm-springs-.html.

33. Oscar A. Godbout, "Special Effects Show 'Conquest of Space,'" *New York Times*, May 28, 1955, https://www.nytimes.com/1955/05/28/archives/special-effects-show-conquest-of-space.html.

34. "The Day the Earth Stood Still (1951 Film)," Wikipedia, last edited on July 22, 2021, at 14:09, https://en.wikiquote.org/wiki/The_Day_the_Earth_Stood_Still_(1951_film).

35. Levisk1212, "The Jetsons Intro," YouTube video, August 14, 2008, 1:01, https://www.youtube.com/watch?v=FyinD6ZDqeg.

36. Matt Novak, "50 Years of the Jetsons," *Smithsonian Magazine*, September 19, 2012, https://www.smithsonianmag.com/history/50-years-of-the-jetsons-why-the-show-still-matters-43459669.

37. Gerald Jonas, "Arthur C. Clarke, Author Who Saw Science Fiction Become Real, Dies at 90," *New York Times*, March 19, 2008, https://www.nytimes.com/2008/03/19/books/19clarke.html.

38. Arthur C. Clarke, *Profiles of the Future: An Inquiry into the Limits of the Possible*, rev. ed. (New York: Harper & Row, 1973), xvi.

39 Ibid., 237.

40. "A Brief History of RAND," RAND Corporation, https://www.rand.org/about/history.html.

41. "Preliminary Design of an Experimental World-Circling Spaceship," RAND Corporation, https://www.rand.org/pubs/special_memoranda/SM11827.html.

42. Virginia Campbell, "How RAND Invented the Postwar World: Satellites, Systems Analysis, Computing, the Internet—Almost All the Defining Features of the Information Age Were Shaped in Part at the RAND Corporation," *Invention & Technology*, summer 2004, https://www.rand.org/content/dam/rand/pubs/reprints/2009/RAND_RP1396.pdf.

43. "The Rand Corporation: The Think Tank That Controls America," *Mental Floss*, June 30, 2009, https://www.mentalfloss.com/article/22120/rand-corporation-think-tank-controls-america.

44. "Report on a Long-Range Forecasting Study," T. J. Gordon and Olaf Helmer, RAND Corporation, September 1964, https://www.rand.org/content/dam/rand/pubs/papers/2005/P2982.pdf.

45. Ibid.

46. Joseph B. Treaster, "Herman Kahn Dies; Futurist and Thinker on Nuclear Strategy," *New York Times*, July 8, 1983, https://www.nytimes.com/1983/07/08/obituaries/herman-kahn-dies-futurist-and-thinker-on-nuclear-strategy.html.

47. Herman Kahn and Anthony J. Wiener, *The Year 2000: A Framework for Speculation on the Next Thirty-Three Years* (New York: Macmillan, 1967), 4.

48. Richard E. Albright, "What Can Past Technology Forecasts Tell Us about the Future?" *Technological Forecasting and Social Change* 69, no. 5 (June 2002): 443–464, https://doi.org/10.1016/S0040-1625(02)00186-5.

49. Kahn and Wiener, *The Year 2000*, 53–55

50 Foreign Policy Association ed., *Toward the Year 2018* (New York: Cowles Education Corp., 1968), back cover.

51. Kahn and Wiener, *The Year 2000*, 149.

52. "Shows & Movies," Star Trek, CBS Studios Inc., accessed January 30, 2023, https://www.startrek.com/shows.

53. Cited in Alex Kurtzman, "Welcome to the New StarTrek.com," Star Trek, September 8, 2019, https://www.startrek.com/news/watch-welcome-to-the-new-startrekcom.

54. Cited in Jason Hellerman, "What Does the Ending of '2001: A Space Odyssey' Mean?" *No Film School*, May 16, 2019, https://nofilmschool.comthe-ending-of-2001-a-space-odyssey-explained.

Two: The False Start of Up Wing 2.0 (1995–2000)

1. Henry Raymont, "'Future Shock': The Stress of Great, Rapid Change," *New York Times*, July 24, 1970, https://www.nytimes.com/1970/07/24/archives/future-shock-the-stress-of-great-rapid-change.html.

2. Steve Marble, "She Saw the World to Come: 'Future Shock' Co-Author Heidi Toffler Dies at 89," *Los Angeles Times*, February 13, 2019, https://www.latimes.com/local/obituaries/la-me-heidi-toffler-20190211-story.html.

3. Keith Schneider, "Alvin Toffler, Author of 'Future Shock,' Dies at 87," *New York Times*, June 29, 2016, https://www.nytimes.com/2016/06/30/books/alvin-toffler-author-of-future-shock-dies-at-87.html.

4. Raymont, "'Future Shock.'"

5. Schneider, "Alvin Toffler, Author of 'Future Shock.'"

6. Quoted in ibid.

7. An image of the musical version's advertisement at Patrick McCray (@LeapingRobot), "It's 1977 and a Musical Version," Twitter, August 19, 2021, 3:57 p.m., https://twitter.com/LeapingRobot/status/1428445998720765955; *Future Shock*, directed by Alexander Grasshoff (Metromedia Producers Corporation, 1972), 43 minutes.

8. Alvin Toffler, *Future Shock* (New York: Random House, 1970), 11, Kindle.

9. William Nordhaus, "Retrospective on the 1970s Productivity Slowdown," National Bureau of Economic Research Working Paper no. 10950 (December 2004), https://www.nber.org/papers/w10950.

10. Author's calculations from economic data found at Measuring Worth, https://www.measuringworth.com.

11. Robert J. Gordon and Hassan Sayed, "A New Interpretation of Productivity Growth Dynamics in the Pre-Pandemic and Pandemic Era U.S. Economy, 1950–2022," National

Bureau of Economic Research Working Paper no. 30267 (July 2022), https://www.nber.org/papers/w30267.

12. Shawn Sprague, "The U.S. Productivity Slowdown: An Economy-Wide and Industry-Level Analysis," Monthly Labor Review (Washington, DC: U.S. Bureau of Labor Statistics, 2021), https://doi.org/10.21916/mlr.2021.4.

13. Quoted in Hillel Italie, "Alvin Toffler, Author of Influential 'Future Shock,' Dead at 87," *USA Today*, June 30, 2016, https://www.usatoday.com/story/life/books/2016/06/30/alvin-toffler-author-of-future-shock-dead-at-87/86570846/.

14. Herman Kahn and Anthony J. Wiener, *The Year 2000: A Framework for Speculation on the Next Thirty-Three Years* (New York: Macmillan, 1967), 118.

15. Ibid., 124.

16. My thought experiment assumes labor force growth remained the same, averaging about 1.5 percent in the postwar period, including a high of 2.7 percent in the 1970s, as cited in Mary C. Daly, "Raising the Speed Limit on Future Growth," Federal Reserve Bank of San Francisco Economic Letter, April 2, 2018, https://www.frbsf.org/economic-research/publications/economic-letter/2018/april/raising-speed-limit-on-future-growth.

17. Annie Jacobsen, *The Pentagon's Brain: An Uncensored History of DARPA, America's Top-Secret Military Research Agency* (New York: Little, Brown and Company, 2016), 11, Kindle.

18. "Three Minutes to Midnight," Bulletin of the Atomic Scientists 40, no. 1 (1984): 2, https://doi.org/10.1080/00963402.1984.11459153.

19. "A New Era," Bulletin of the Atomic Scientists 47, no. 10 (1991): 3, https://doi.org/10.1080/00963402.1991.11460045.

20. Carl E. Walsh, "What Caused the 1990–1991 Recession?" *Federal Reserve Bank of San Francisco Economic Review*, no. 2 (1993): 33–48, https://www.frbsf.org/economic-research/wp-content/uploads/sites/4/93-2_34-48.pdf.

21. Jeffrey M. Jones, "U.S. Satisfaction Rises to Match Historical Norm," Gallup, November 8, 2016, https://news.gallup.com/poll/197300/satisfaction-rises-match-historical-norm.aspx.

22. Christopher Lasch, *The True and Only Heaven: Progress and Its Critics* (New York: W. W. Norton & Company, 1991), 13.

23. Robert L. Heilbroner, *An Inquiry into the Human Prospect: Looked at Again for the 1990s* (New York: W. W. Norton & Company, 1991).

24. Ibid., 11.

25. William. W. Lewis, *The Power of Productivity* (Chicago: University of Chicago Press, 2004), xiii.

26. Jeffery M. Jones, "National Satisfaction Lowest in More Than a Decade, Just 29% Satisfied with Direction of Nation," *Gallup*, March 20, 2006, https://news.gallup.com/poll/21982/national-satisfaction-lowest-more-than-decade.aspx.

27. Louis Uchitelle, "Trickle Down; It's a Slow-Growth Economy, Stupid," *New York Times*, March 17, 1996, https://www.nytimes.com/1996/03/17/weekinreview/trickle-down-it-s-a-slow-growth-economy-stupid.html.

28. All inflation-adjusted GDP data from Measuring Worth, accessed at https://www.measuringworth.com/aboutus.php.

29. Gordon and Sayed, "A New Interpretation of Productivity Growth Dynamics in the Pre-Pandemic and Pandemic Era U.S. Economy, 1950–2022."

30. Asa Fitch and Don Clark, "Gordon Moore, Intel Co-Founder and Author of Moore's Law, Dies at 94, *Wall Street Journal*, March 24, 2023, https://www.wsj.com/articles/gordon-moore-intel-co-founder-and-author-of-moores-law-dies-at-94-f3a6fcf6.

31. Harry McCracken, "The Year That Changed Everything," *Fast Company*, December 30, 2015, https://www.fastcompany.com/3053055/1995-the-year-everything-changed.

32. Ibid.

33 "Star Trek: Voyager, 28 Years Later," Star Trek, January 16, 2023, https://www.startrek.com/gallery/star-trek-voyager-25-years-later.

34. Bill Clinton, "Remarks Accepting the Presidential Nomination at the Democratic National Convention in Chicago," American Presidency Project, August 29, 1996, https://www.presidency.ucsb.edu/documents/remarks-accepting-the-presidential-nomination-the-democratic-national-convention-chicago.

35. Jones, "National Satisfaction Lowest in More Than a Decade."

36. Urban Jermann and Vincenzo Quadrini, "Stock Market Boom and the Productivity Gains of the 1990s," National Bureau of Economic Research Working Paper no. 9034 (July 2002), https://www.nber.org/papers/w9034.

37. Quoted in Neil Selkirk, "The Original WIRED Manifesto," *Wired*, September 18, 2018, https://www.wired.com/story/original-wired-manifesto.

38. Peter Schwartz and Peter Leyden, "The Long Boom: A History of the Future, 1980–2020," *Wired*, July 1, 1997, https://www.wired.com/1997/07/longboom; Deanne Cheuck, "25 Years of WIRED Predictions: Why the Future Never Arrives," *Wired*, September 18, 2018, https://www.wired.com/story/wired25-david-karpf-issues-tech-predictions/.

39. Lauren Clason, "Ray Kurzweil: 1999 National Medal of Technology and Innovation Communications," National Science and Technology Medals Foundation, https://nationalmedals.org/laureate/ray-kurzweil.

40. Ray Kurzweil, *The Age of Spiritual Machines* (New York: Penguin Publishing Group, 1999), prologue, Kindle.

41. Paul Bennett, "From Gear to Eternity," *Wired*, February 1, 1999, https://www.wired.com/1999/02/from-gear-to-eternity.

42. Vernor Vinge, "The Coming Technological Singularity: How to Survive in the Post-Human Era," *New York Times*, March 30–31, 1993, https://archive.nytimes.com/www.nytimes.com/library/cyber/surf/1120surf-vinge.html.

43. Kevin Kelly, "Singular Visionary," *Wired*, June 1, 1995, https://www.wired.com/1995/06/vinge.

44. Kevin Kelly, "The Roaring Zeros," *Wired*, September 1, 1999, https://www.wired.com/1999/09/zeros.

45. "Domestic Box Office for 1998," Box Office Mojo, https://www.boxofficemojo.com/year/1998.

46. "Quotes / Emergency Presidential Address," TVTropes, https://tvtropes.org/pmwiki/pmwiki.php/Quotes/EmergencyPresidentialAddress.

47. Dominic Rushe, "Nasdaq Reaches New Record High, 15 Years after Dotcom Tech Surge," *The Guardian*, April 13, 2015, https://www.theguardian.com/business/2015/apr/23/nasdaq-new-record-high-dotcom-bubble.

48. "U.S. Business Cycle Expansions and Contractions," NBER, July 18, 2021, https://www.nber.org/research/data/us-business-cycle-expansions-and-contractions.

49. Bill Joy, "Why the Future Doesn't Need Us," *Wired*, April 1, 2000, https://www.wired.com/2000/04/joy-2.

50. "Economic Report of the President," Council of Economic Advisers, February 2000, 283, https://fraser.stlouisfed.org/title/45/item/8099.

51. Alan Greenspan, "Remarks by Chairman Alan Greenspan before the Economic Club of New York," Federal Reserve Board, January 13, 2000, https://www.federalreserve.gov/boarddocs/speeches/2000/200001132.htm.

52. "Lehman Brothers: 1850–2008," Harvard Business School, Baker Library Bloomberg Center (website), accessed January 30, 2023, https://www.library.hbs.edu/hc/lehman.

53. Lehman Brothers, "Beyond 2000," December 1999.

54. Greenspan, "Remarks by Chairman Alan Greenspan."

55. Mark Hulbert, "Lessons from the Dot-Com Bust," *Wall Street Journal*, March 8, 2020, https://www.wsj.com/articles/lessons-from-the-dot-com-bust-11583192099.

56. Michael Brown, "What Will Happen to Venture Capital When the Recession Hits?" Bowery Capital, November 1, 2019, https://bowerycap.com/blog/insights what-will-happen-to-venture-capital-when-the-recession-hits.

57. "U.S. Business Cycle Expansions and Contractions," NBER, https://www.nber.org/research/data/us-business-cycle-expansions-and-contractions.

58. Jones, "National Satisfaction Lowest in More Than a Decade."

59. Greg Ip, "Productivity Lull Might Signal Growth Is Easing," *Wall Street Journal*, March 31, 2007, https://www.wsj.com/articles/SB117530287229455363.

60. Gordon and Sayed, "A New Interpretation of Productivity Growth Dynamics in the Pre-Pandemic and Pandemic Era U.S. Economy, 1950–2022."

61. Pascal-Emmanuel Gobry, "Facebook Investor Wants Flying Cars, Not 140 Characters," *Business Insider*, July 30, 2011, https://www.businessinsider.com/founders-fund-the-future-2011-7.

62. John Fernald and Huiyu Li, "The Impact of COVID on Productivity and Potential Output," Federal Reserve Bank of Kansas City, September 15, 2022, https://www.kansascityfed.org/Jackson%20Hole/documents/9112/output_post_covid.2022.09.15.b.pdf.

Three: The Mystery of the Great Downshift: What Happened to Us

1. Aileen Jacobson, "Back to the Futurama and the Ferris Wheel," *New York Times*, April 1, 2011, https://www.nytimes.com/2011/04/03/nyregion/03artsli.html.

2. Roland Marchand, "The Designers Go to the Fair II: Norman Bel Geddes, the General Motors 'Futurama,' and the Visit to the Factory Transformed," *Design Issues* 8, no. 2 (1992): 22–40, https://doi.org/10.2307/1511638.

3. Norman Bel Geddes, *Magic Motorways* (New York: Random House, 1940), 10.

4. Jen Carlson, "Experience the Futurama Ride at the 1964 World's Fair," *Gothamist*, March 11, 2013, https://gothamist.com/arts-entertainment/experience-the-futurama-ride-at-the-1964-world8217s-fair.

5. "1964 New York World's Fair," Wikipedia, https://en.wikipedia.org/wiki/1964_New_York_World%27s_Fair.

6. Isaac Asimov, "Visit to the World's Fair of 2014," *New York Times*, August 16, 1964, https://archive.nytimes.com/www.nytimes.com/books/97/03/23/lifetimes/asi-v-fair.html.

7. Arthur C. Clarke, *Profiles of the Future: An Inquiry into the Limits of the Possible*, rev. ed. (New York: Harper & Row, 1973), 60.

8. Milton Friedman and Anna Schwartz, *A Monetary History of the United States, 1867–1960* (Princeton, NJ: Princeton University Press, 1963).

9. Ben S. Bernanke, "On Milton Friedman's Ninetieth Birthday," Federal Reserve Board, November 8, 2002, https://www.federalreserve.gov/boarddocs/speeches/2002/20021108.

10. J. Bradford DeLong, *Slouching towards Utopia: An Economic History of the 20th Century* (New York: Basic Books, 2022), 431, Kindle.

11. Michael Pollan, "How Caffeine Fueled the Enlightenment, Industrial Revolution, and the Modern World," *Open Culture*, August 24, 2021, https://www.openculture.com/2021/08/how-caffeine-fueled-the-enlightenment-industrial-revolution-the-modern-world.html.

12. "Higher Than the Shoulders of Giants; Or, a Scientist's History of Drugs," *Slime Mold Time Mold*, August, 19, 2021, https://slimemoldtimemold.com/2021/04/19/higher-than-the-shoulders-of-giants-or-a-scientists-history-of-drugs; Cullen Browder, "'Microdosing' Growing in Popularity among Tech Workers, but Is It Safe?" Associated Press, August 10, 2018, https://apnews.com/article/steve-jobs-19667206b7418099ef6a9a09f8cc575f.

13. Nicholas Wade, "Scientist at Work/Kary Mullis; After the 'Eureka,' a Nobelist Drops Out," *New York Times*, September 15, 1988, https://www.nytimes.com/1998/09/15/science/scientist-at-work-kary-mullis-after-the-eureka-a-nobelist-drops-out.html.

14. Quoted in Will Burns, "The Beckley Foundation Intends to Study Links Between Microdosing LSD and Creativity," *Forbes*, February 26, 2018, https://www.forbes.com/sites/willburns/2018/02/26/the-beckley-foundation-intends-to-study-links-between-microdosing-lsd-and-creativity/.

15. Alessandro Iaria, Carlo Schwarz, and Fabian Waldinger, "Frontier Knowledge and Scientific Production: Evidence from the Collapse of International Science," *Quarterly Journal of Economics* 133, no. 2 (May 2018): 927–991, https://doi.org/10.1093/qje/qjx046.

16. My conversation with Tyler Cowen: "5 Quick Questions for... Tyler Cowen on the State of the Great Stagnation, Pro-Progress Policy, Metascience, and More!" *Faster, Please!* (newsletter), February 10, 2023, https://fasterplease.substack.com/p/tyler-cowen-on-the-state-of-the-great.

17. Helen Dale, *Kingdom of the Wicked Book One: Rules* (Balmain, New South Wales: Ligature, 2017), 450.

18. Alexander J. Field, "The Decline of US Manufacturing Productivity Between 1941 and 1948," *Economic History Review*, January 16, 2023, https://doi.org/10.1111/ehr.13239.

19. M. Anthony Mills and Mark P. Mills, "The Science Before the War: How the Technological Feats of World War II Grew Out of Curiosity-Driven Research," *New Atlantis*, Winter 2020, https://www.thenewatlantis.com/publications/the-science-before-the-war.

20. Scott L. Montgomery, "Oil Price Shocks Have a Long History, but Today's Situation May Be the Most Complex Ever," *Conversation*, March 11, 2022, https://theconversation.com/oil-price-shocks-have-a-long-history-but-todays-situation-may-be-the-most-complex-ever-178861.

21. Robert Shackleton, "Total Factor Productivity Growth in Historical Perspective," Congressional Budget Office Working Paper, March 18, 2013, https://www.cbo.gov/publication/44002.

22. White House thinking about the downshift in labor productivity growth is discussed in "Economic Report of the President," Council of Economic Advisers, January 1977, 45–51,

https://www.presidency.ucsb.edu/sites/default/files/books/presidential-documents-archive-guidebook/the-economic-report-of-the-president-truman-1947-obama-2017/1977.pdf.

23. Quoted in Carlos Lozada, "The Productivity Slowdown of the 1970s," *The Digest*, National Bureau of Economic Research, no. 6 (June 2005), https://www.nber.org/digest/jun05/productivity-slowdown-1970s.

24. Alexander J. Field, *A Great Leap Forward: 1930s Depression and U.S. Economic Growth* (New Haven, CT: Yale University Press, 2011), chap. 1, Kindle.

25. Ibid., chap. 2.

26. William H. Branson, Herbert Giersch, and Peter G. Peterson, "Trends in United States International Trade and Investment since World War II," in *The American Economy in Transition*, ed. Martin Feldstein (Chicago: University of Chicago Press, 1980), 183–274, http://www.nber.org/books/feld80-1.

27. Alan Greenspan and Adrian Wooldridge, *Capitalism in America* (New York: Penguin Publishing Group, 2019), 311, Kindle.

28. Joseph A. Schumpeter, *Capitalism, Socialism and Democracy* (London: Taylor & Francis, 2003), chap. 8, Kindle.

29. Robert Gordon, *The Rise and Fall of American Growth* (Princeton, NJ: Princeton University Press, 2016), 6, Kindle.

30. Ibid., 61.

31. "What Great Births You Have Witnessed!" *Letters of Note* (blog), April 12, 2011, https://lettersofnote.com/2011/04/12/what-great-births-you-have-witnessed.

32. Gordon, *The Rise and Fall of American Growth*, 529.

33. Nicholas Bloom, Charles I. Jones, John Van Reenen, and Michael Webb, "Are Ideas Getting Harder to Find?" National Bureau of Economic Research Working Paper no. 23782 (September 2017), https://www.nber.org/papers/w23782.

34. My conversation with Nicholas Bloom: "What Happens When Ideas Become Harder and Harder to Find? A Long-Read Q&A with Nicholas Bloom," *AEIdeas* (blog), September 14, 2018, https://www.aei.org/economics/what-happens-when-ideas-become-harder-and-harder-to-find.

35. Michael Webb, Chad Jones, John Van Reenen, and Nicholas Bloom, "Ideas Aren't Running Out, but They Are Getting More Expensive to Find," VoxEU, September 20, 2017, https://cepr.org/voxeu/columns/ideas-arent-running-out-they-are-getting-more-expensive-find.

36. Michael Park, Erin Leahy, and Russell J. Funk, "Papers and Patents Are Becoming Less Disruptive over Time," *Nature* 613 (January 4, 2023): 138–144, https://www.nature.com/articles/s41586-022-05543-x.

37. Quoted in Holcomb B. Noble and Katie Hafner, "Gordon E. Moore, Intel Co-Founder Behind Moore's Law, Dies at 94," *New York Times*, March 24, 2023, https://www.nytimes.com/2023/03/24/technology/gordon-moore-dead.html.

38. Pablo D. Azar, "Moore's Law and Economic Growth," Federal Reserve Bank of New York, no. 970 (October 2022), https://www.newyorkfed.org/research/staff_reports/sr970.

39. David Rotman, "We're Not Prepared for the End of Moore's Law," *MIT Technology Review*, February 4, 2020, https://www.technologyreview.com/2020/02/24/905789/were-not-prepared-for-the-end-of-moores-law; James Titcomb, "The Chips Are Down: How Tech's Innovation Crisis Threatens Global Economy," *Telegraph*, December 20, 2021, https://www.telegraph.co.uk/technology/2021/12/20/techs-innovation-crisis-poses-threat-global-economy.

40. The detailed story of how Intel canceling the next version of its flagship Pentium 4 chip in 2004 affected the *Shrek* film franchise is told in Neil Thompson, "The Economic Impact of Moore's Law: Evidence from When It Faltered," SSRN, January 18, 2017, https://dx.doi.org/10.2139/ssrn.2899115.

41. "Shrek," Wikipedia, last edited December 30, 2022, at 22:26, https://en.wikipedia.org/wiki/Shrek.

42. Bill Desowitz, "A Decade of 'Shrek' Tech," *Animation World Network*, May 20, 2010, https://www.awn.com/vfxworld/decade-shrek-tech.

43. Thompson, "The Economic Impact of Moore's Law."

44. My conversation with Neil Thompson: "The End of Moore's Law and the Future of Computers: My Long-Read Q&A with Neil Thompson," *AEIdeas* (blog), July 6, 2022, https://www.aei.org/economics/the-end-of-moores-law-and-the-future-of-computers-my-long-read-qa-with-neil-thompson.

45. "Generative AI: ChatGPT and Search," Citi GPS: Global Perspectives and Solutions, February 16, 2023, https://icg.citi.com/icghome/what-we-think/citigps/insights/generative-ai.

46. Nonfarm business productivity numbers accessed at the U.S. Bureau of Labor Statistics, https://www.bls.gov/productivity.

47. Ibid.

48. Spencer Hill and Manuel Abecasis, *The Productivity Pullback: Signal vs. Noise*, Goldman Sachs, September 5, 2022.

49. Robert J. Gordon and Hassan Sayed, "A New Interpretation of Productivity Growth Dynamics in the Pre-Pandemic and Pandemic Era U.S. Economy, 1950–2022," National Bureau of Economic Research Working Paper no. 30267 (July 2022), https://www.nber.org/papers/w30267.

50. Sarah Mervosh and Ashley Wu, "Math Scores Fell in Nearly Every State, and Reading Dipped on National Exam," *New York Times*, October 24, 2022, https://www.nytimes.com/2022/10/24/us/math-reading-scores-pandemic.html.

Four: The Mystery of the Great Downshift: What We Did to Ourselves

1. "Comparing Fukushima and Chernobyl," Nuclear Energy Institute, October 2019, https://www.nei.org/resources/fact-sheets/comparing-fukushima-and-chernobyl.

2. The details of the Japanese response to the Fukushima nuclear meltdown are discussed in Matthew J. Neidell, Shinsuke Uchida, and Marcella Veronesi, "The Unintended Effects from Halting Nuclear Power Production: Evidence from Fukushima Daiichi Accident," National Bureau of Economic Research Working Paper no. 26395 (December 2022), https://www.nber.orgpapersw26395.

3. The details of the German response to the meltdown can be found in Christoph Steitz, Vera Eckert, and Tom Käckenhoff, "Factbox: How Fukushima Helped to Transform Germany's Power Sector," Reuters, March 10, 2021, https://www.reuters.com/business/energy/how-fukushima-helped-transform-germanys-power-sector-2021-03-10.

4. Alex Lawson, "Germany's Last Three Nuclear Power Stations to Shut This Weekend," *Guardian*, April 15, 2023, https://www.theguardian.com/environment/2023/apr/15/germany-last-three-nuclear-power-stations-to-shut-this-weekend.

5. Neidell, Uchida, and Veronesi, "The Unintended Effects from Halting Nuclear Power Production."

6. The various estimates of Chernobyl fatalities are discussed in Hannah Ritchie, "What Was the Death Toll from Chernobyl and Fukushima?" Our World in Data, July 24, 2017, https://

ourworldindata.org/what-was-the-death-toll-from-chernobyl-and-fukushima; Meredith Yeager et al., "Lack of Transgenerational Effects of Ionizing Radiation Exposure from the Chernobyl Accident, *Science* 372, no. 6543 (April 22, 2021): 725–729, https://doi.org/10.1126/science.abg2365.

7. Neidell, Uchida, and Veronesi, "The Unintended Effects from Halting Nuclear Power Production."

8. Guojun He and Takanao Tanaka, "Energy Saving May Kill: Evidence from the Fukushima Nuclear Accident," SSRN, September 23, 2019, https://dx.doi.org/10.2139/ssrn.3451021.

9. Stephen Jarvis, Olivier Deschenes, and Akshaya Jha, "The Private and External Costs of Germany's Nuclear Phase-Out," National Bureau of Economic Research Working Paper no. 26598 (December 2019), https://www.nber.org/papers/w26598.

10. Ibid.

11. Matthew Neidell, Shinsuke Uchida, and Marcella Veronesi, "Be Cautious with the Precautionary Principle: Evidence from Fukushima Daiichi Nuclear Accident," IZA Institute of Labor Economics Working Paper no. 12687 (October 2019), https://docs.iza.org/dp12687.pdf.

12. Ibid.

13. Aaron Wildavsky, *Searching for Safety* (London: Taylor and Francis, 1988), 41, Kindle.

14. "International Nuclear Event Scale," Wikipedia, https://en.wikipedia.org/wiki/International_Nuclear_Event_Scale.

15. "5 Facts to Know about Three Mile Island," U.S. Department of Energy, May 4, 2022, https://www.energy.gov/ne/articles/5-facts-know-about-three-mile-island.

16 The federal regulatory reaction to Three Mile Island and resulting health effects are discussed in Edson Severnini, "Impacts of Nuclear Plant Shutdown on Coal-Fired Power Generation and Infant Health in the Tennessee Valley in the 1980s," *Nature* 2, no. 4 (April 2017) https://www.nature.com/articles/nenergy201751.

17. Ibid.

18. Edson R. Severnini, "Nuclear Shutdown, Coal Power Generation, and Infant Health: Evidence from the Tennessee Valley Authority (TVA) in the 1980s" (paper presented at Institute for Labor Economics Workshop: Labor Market Effects of Environmental Policies, Berlin, August 28, 2015).

19. Lyssa M. Freese et al., "Nuclear Power Generation Phase-Outs Redistribute Us Air Quality and Climate-Related Mortality Risk," *Nature Energy* (April 10, 2023), https://doi.org/10.1038/s41560-023-01241-8.

20. James Mahaffey, *Atomic Awakening* (New York: Pegasus Books, 2010), 317, Kindle.

21. Ibid.

22. Jessica R. Lovering, Arthur Yip, and Ted Nordhaus, "Historical Construction Costs of Global Nuclear Power Reactors," *Energy Policy* 91 (April 2016): 371–382, https://doi.org/10.1016/j.enpol.2016.01.011.

23. Calvert Cliffs' Coordinating Committee, Inc. v. U.S. Atomic Energy Commission, 449 F.2d 1109 (D.C. Cir. 1971).

24. U.S. Department of Energy, "States and Local Jurisdictions with NEPA-Like Environmental Planning Requirements," Council on Environmental Quality, https://ceq.doe.gov/laws-regulations/states.html.

25. Lovering, Yip, and Nordhaus, "Historical Construction Costs of Global Nuclear Power Reactors."

26. "Atomic Energy Act of 1946," Atomic Archive, https://www.atomicarchive.com/resources/documents/deterrence/atomic-energy-act.html.

27. "Combined License Applications for New Reactors," United States Nuclear Regulatory Commission, updated September 28, 2022, https://www.nrc.gov/reactors/new-reactors/large-lwr/col.html.; Drew Kann, "First New Vogtle Reactor Begins Generating Electricity," *Atlanta Journal-Constitution*, April 1, 2023, https://www.ajc.com/news/georgia-power-says-plant-vogtle-unit-3-has-started-generating-electricity/LOT2MRURKFBSHLAPYA62GDV3BM/.

28. Sam Batkins, Philip Rossetti, and Dan Goldbeck, "Putting Nuclear Regulatory Costs in Context," American Action Forum, July 12, 2017, https://www.americanactionforum.org/research/putting-nuclear-regulatory-costs-context/.

29. Spencer R. Weart, *The Rise of Nuclear Fear* (Cambridge: Harvard University Press, 2012), 207, Kindle.

30. U.S. Energy Information Administration, "Nuclear Explained," April 18, 2022, https://www.eia.gov/energyexplained/nuclear/us-nuclear-industry.php.

31. Morgan McFall-Johnsen and Dave Mosher, "Elon Musk Says He Plans to Send 1 Million People to Mars by 2050 by Launching 3 Starship Rockets Every Day and Creating 'a Lot of Jobs' on the Red Planet," *Business Insider*, January 17, 2020, https://www.businessinsider.com/elon-musk-plans-1-million-people-to-mars-by-2050-2020-1; Tanya Snyder, "Elon Musk's D.C.-to-Baltimore 'Loop' Leaps an Early Milestone," *Politico*, April 17, 2019, https://www.politico.com/story/2019/04/17/elon-musk-dc-baltimore-loop-1279708.

32. Jay Yarrow, "Elon Musk Has Plans for a New, Magical Form of Transportation Called The 'Hyperloop,'" *Business Insider*, May 30, 2013, https://www.businessinsider.com/elon-musk-has-plans-for-faster-transportation-called-the-hyperloop-2013-5.

33. Eli Dourado, "Much More Than You Ever Wanted to Know about NEPA," Center for Growth and Opportunity at Utah State University, October 20, 2022, https://www.thecgo.org/benchmark/much-more-than-you-ever-wanted-to-know-about-nepa.

34. Ibid.

35. Ian Duncan, "Elon Musk's Boring Company Removes D.C.-Baltimore Tunnel from List of Projects on Website," *Washington Post*, April 16, 2021, https://www.washingtonpost.com/local/trafficandcommuting/elon-musk-hyperloop/2021/04/16/b340314e-9edd-11eb-9d05-ae06f4529ece_story.html.

36. Charles Strum, "Follow-Up on the News; The Snail Darter," *New York Times*, December 6, 1981, https://www.nytimes.com/1981/12/06/nyregion/follow-up-on-the-news-the-snail-darter.html.

37. Herman Kahn and Anthony J. Wiener, *The Year 2000: A Framework for Speculation on the Next Thirty-Three Years* (New York: Macmillan, 1967), 145.

38. Steven Rattner, "Red Tape Threatens U.S. Efforts to Revive Chip-Making," *Washington Post*, March 22, 2023, https://www.washingtonpost.com/opinions/2023/03/22/chips-act-tied-in-red-tape/.

39. Aidan Mackenzie (@AidanRMackenzie), "Permitting delays and wealthy NIMBYs…," Twitter, March 31, 2023, 10:48 a.m., https://twitter.com/AidanRMackenzie/status/1641814712164777986.

40. Lawrence Susskind, et al., "Sources of Opposition to Renewable Energy Projects in the United States," *Energy Policy* 165 (June 2022), https://doi.org/10.1016/j.enpol.2022.112922.

41. Leah Brooks and Zachary Liscow, "Infrastructure Costs," Brookings Institution, August 2019, https://www.brookings.edu/wp-content/uploads/2019/08/WP54_Brooks-Liscow updated.pdf.

42. Ibid.

43. Alan Weisman, *The World without Us* (New York: St. Martin's Thomas Dunne Books, 2007).

44. Edward Glaeser, *Triumph of the City: How Our Greatest Invention Makes Us Richer, Smarter, Greener, Healthier, and Happier* (New York: Penguin Press, 2011), introduction, Kindle.

45. My calculation is based on "List of U.S. Metropolitan Areas by GDP," Wikipedia, last edited April 28, 2022, at 01:39, https://en.wikipedia.org/wiki/List_of_U.S._metropolitan_areas_by_GDP; Ian Hathaway, "High-Growth Firms and Cities in the US: An Analysis of the Inc. 5000," Brookings Institution, February 5, 2018, https://www.brookings.edu/research/high-growth-firms-and-cities-in-the-us-an-analysis-of-the-inc-5000.

46 Mark Muro and Yang You, "Superstars, Rising Stars, and the Rest: Pandemic Trends and Shifts in the Geography of Tech," Brookings Institution, March 8, 2022, https://www.brookings.edu/research/superstars-rising-stars-and-the-rest-pandemic-trends-and-shifts-in-the-geography-of-tech.

47. Joseph Gyourko and Jacob Krimmel, "The Impact of Local Residential Land Use Restrictions on Land Values across and within Single Family Housing Markets," National Bureau of Economic Research Working Paper no. 28993 (July 2021), https://www.nber.org/system/files/working_papers/w28993/w28993.pdf.

48. Daniel Shoag, "Removing Barriers to Accessing High-Productivity Places," The Hamilton Project, January 31, 2019, https://www.hamiltonproject.org/papers/removing_barriers_to_accessing_high_productivity_places.

49. Ran Abramitzky and Leah Boustan, *Streets of Gold: America's Untold Story of Immigrant Success*, (New York: PublicAffairs, 2022), 11, Kindle.

50. Ibid., 98.

51. Alice M. Rivlin, "The Productivity Slowdown: Causes and Policy Responses," Congressional Budget Office, June 1, 1981, https://www.cbo.gov/sites/default/files/97th-congress-1981-1982/reports/1981_06_01_slowdown.pdf.

52. John W. Dawson and John J. Seater, "Federal Regulation and Aggregate Economic Growth," *Journal of Economic Growth* 18, no. 2 (June 2013): 137–177, https://papers.ssrn.com/sol3/papers.cfm?abstract_id=2223315.

53. Colin O'Reilly and Ryan Murphy, "Anti-Growth Safetyism," Works in Progress, October 12, 2022, https://www.worksinprogress.co/issue/anti-growth-safetyism.

54. Renard Bourlès et al., "Do Product Market Regulations in Upstream Sectors Curb Productivity Growth? Panel Data Evidence for OECD Countries," *Review of Economics and Statistics* 95, no. 5 (December 2013): 1750–1768, https://ideas.repec.org/a/tpr/restat/v95y2013i5p1750-1768.html.

55. "A Historic Phone Call," National Archives, last reviewed on August 15, 2016, https://www.archives.gov/presidential-libraries/events/centennials/nixon/exhibit/nixon-online-exhibit-calls.html.

56. Ibid.; William Anders, "Apollo 8: Earthrise," December 24, 1968, https://www.nasa.gov/image-feature/apollo-8-earthrise.

57. John M. Logsdon, "When Nixon Stopped Human Exploration," Planetary Society, October 28, 2014, https://www.planetary.org/articles/1027-when-nixon-stopped-human-exploration.

58. John M. Logsdon, *After Apollo?: Richard Nixon and the American Space Program* (New York, Palgrave MacMillan: 2015), 123.

59. Jason Callahan, "How Richard Nixon Changed NASA," Planetary Society, October 4, 2014, https://www.planetary.org/articles/20141003-how-richard-nixon-changed-nasa.

60. "Retreat from the Moon," editorial, *New York Times*, September 4, 1970, https://www.nytimes.com/1970/09/04/archives/retreat-from-the-moon.html.

61. Richard Nixon, "Statement Following Lift-Off from the Moon of the Apollo 17 Lunar Module," American Presidency Project, https://www.presidency.ucsb.edu/documents/statement-following-lift-off-from-the-moon-the-apollo-17-lunar-module.

62. Adam Hadhazy, "What If NASA's Apollo Program Had Not Been Canceled?" *Scientific American*, September 1, 2011, https://www.scientificamerican.com/article/what-if-nasas-apollo-program.

63. R&D data from "Federal R&D Budget Dashboard," American Association for the Advancement of Science, https://www.aaas.org/programs/r-d-budget-and-policy/federal-rd-budget-dashboard.

64. John Van Reenan, *Innovation Policies to Boost Productivity*, The Hamilton Project, June 2020, https://www.hamiltonproject.org/assets/files/JVR_PP_LO_6.15_FINAL.pdf.

65. "U.S. Research and Development Funding and Performance: Fact Sheet," Congressional Research Service, September 13, 2022, https://crsreports.congress.gov/product/details?prodcode=R44307.

66. John F. Kennedy, "Address to the Graduating Class of the U.S. Air Force Academy," American Rhetoric, June 5, 1963, https://www.americanrhetoric.com/speeches/jfkairforceacademycommencement.htm.

67. Stephen Dowling, "The American Concordes That Never Flew," *BBC*, March 22, 2016, https://www.bbc.com/future/article/20160321-the-american-concordes-that-never-flew.

68. "Boeing 2707," Wikipedia, last edited December 3, 2022, at 09:48, https://en.wikipedia.org/wiki/Boeing_2707; "How the SST Will Be Financed," *Time* 89, no. 21, May 26, 1967: 88–89, https://time.com/vault/issue/1967-05-26/.

69. Sam Howe Verhovek, *Jet Age: The Comet, the 707, and the Race to Shrink the World*, paperback ed. (New York: Avery, 2011), preface, Kindle.

70. Michael Lombardi, "Seventh Heaven: 50 Years Ago, Boeing and Pan Am Revolutionized Travel with the 707," *Frontiers* VII, no. III (July 2008): 8-9, https://www.boeing.com/news/frontiers/archive/2008/july/july08frontiers.pdf.

71. "Congress Ends U.S. Funding of Supersonic Aircraft," *CQ Almanac*, 1971, https://library.cqpress.com/cqalmanac/document.php?id=cqal71-1252799.

72. "Supersonic Flight," Federal Aviation Administration, November 25, 2020, https://www.faa.gov/newsroom/supersonic-flight.

73. Bill Whitaker, "Startups and NASA Working to Return Passenger Supersonic Flights to the Sky," CBS News, July 10, 2022, https://www.cbsnews.com/news/supersonic-commercial-air-travel-60-minutes-2022-07-10/.

74. Sharon Weinberger, *The Imagineers of War: The Untold Story of DARPA, the Pentagon Agency That Changed the World* (New York: Alfred A. Knopf, 2017), 273, Kindle.

75. Arthur C. Clarke, *Profiles of the Future: An Inquiry into the Limits of the Possible*, rev. ed. (New York: Harper & Row, 1973), 142.

76. Quoted in Ben Lefebvre, "U.S. Touts Fusion Breakthrough As One of 'Most Impressive Scientific Feats' This Century," *Politico*, December 13, 2022, https://www.politico.com/news/2022/12/13/fusion-breakthrough-doe-energy-sustainability-00073666.

77. My conversation with Arthur Turrell: "Is This Really America's Age of 'Anti-Ambition' and Decadence?," *Faster, Please!* (newsletter), February 28, 2022, https://fasterplease.substack.com/p/-is-this-really-americas-age-of-anti?s=w.

78. "University of Utah N-Fusion Press Release," *New Energy Times*, https://newenergytimes.com/v2/reports/UniversityOfUtahPressRelease.shtml.

79. Tim Fitzpatrick, "Energy from Nuclear Fusion? Utah Has Been There, Not Done That," *Salt Lake Tribune*, December 13, 2022, https://www.sltrib.com/news/2022/12/13/energy-nuclear-fusion-utah-has.

80. Curtis P. Berlinguette, et al., "Revisiting the Cold Case of Cold Fusion," *Nature* 570 (June 2019), https://www.nature.com/articles/s41586-019-1256-6.

81. Eric Drexler, *Engines of Creation: The Coming Era of Nanotechnology* (New York: Anchor, 1987), 14.

82. Christopher Mims, "The Nanotechnology Revolution Is Here—We Just Haven't Noticed Yet," *Wall Street Journal*, January 22, 2022, https://www.wsj.com/articles/the-nanotechnology-revolution-is-herewe-just-havent-noticed-yet-11642827640.

83. "Applications of Nanotechnology," U.S Department of Energy, https://www.nano.gov/about-nanotechnology/applications-nanotechnology.

84. Cited in Nicholas Varchaver, "Is Nanotech Ready for Its Close-Up?" *CNN Money*, May 17, 2004, https://money.cnncom/magazines/fortune/fortune_archive/2004/05/17/369606/index.htm.

Five: Eco-Pessimism, Techno-Pessimism, and a Down Wing America

1. Ray C. Fair, "U.S. Infrastructure: 1929–2019," Working Paper, September 2021, https://fairmodel.econ.yale.edu/rayfair/pdf/2019D.PDF.

2. Ibid.

3. Robert C. Allen, *The British Industrial Revolution in Global Perspective* (New York: Cambridge University Press, 2009).

4. Leander Heldring, James A. Robinson, and Sebastian Vollmer, "The Long-Run Impact of the Dissolution of the English Monasteries," *Quarterly Journal of Economics* 136, no.4 (November 2021): 2093–2145, https://doi.org/10.1093/qje/qjab030.

5. Stephan Heblich, Stephen J. Redding, and Hans-Joachim Voth, "Slavery and the British Industrial Revolution," National Bureau of Economic Research Working Paper no. 30451 (September 2022), https://www.nber.org/papers/w30451.

6. Fred Polak, *The Image of the Future*, translated by Elise Boulding (Amsterdam: Elsevier Scientific Publishing Company, 1973), 19.

7. Ibid., 300.

8. Fred L. Polak, *The Image of the Future: Enlightening the Past, Orienting the Present, Forecasting the Future, Vol. 2, Iconoclasm of the Images of the Future, Demolition of Culture* (New York: Oceana, 1961), 89.

9. Quoted in Joel Mokyr, "Progress Isn't Natural," *The Atlantic*, November 17, 2016, https://www.theatlantic.com/business/archive/2016/11/progress-isnt-natural-mokyr/507740.

10. Thucydides, *The History of the Peloponnesian War*, translated by Richard Crawley (Project Gutenberg, updated September 7, 2021), https://www.gutenberg.org/cache/epub/7142/pg7142-images.html.

11. My conversation with Joel Mokyr: "'A Culture of Growth': A Long Read Q&A with Economic Historian Joel Mokyr, *AEIdeas* (blog), September 15, 2017, https://www.aei.org/economics/a-culture-of-growth-a-long-read-qa-with-economic-historian-joel-mokyr.

12. Joel Mokyr, *A Culture of Growth: The Origins of the Modern Economy* (Princeton, NJ: Princeton University Press, 2017), xiii.

13. Max Roser, "Economic Growth," Our World in Data, https://ourworldindata.org/economic-growth.

14. My calculations using data from the World Bank, https://data.worldbank.org/indicator/NY.GDP.PCAP.CD.

15. Charles I. Jones, "Life and Growth," *Journal of Political Economy* 124, no. 2 (2016), https://doi.org/10.1086/684750.

16. Brink Lindsey, "The Anti-Promethean Backlash," *The Permanent Problem* (newsletter), November 15, 2022, https://brinklindsey.substack.com/p/the-anti-promethean-backlash.

17. Richard Liroff, *A National Policy for the Environment: NEPA and Its Aftermath* (Bloomington: Indiana University Press, 1976), 5.

18. "An Ecomodernist Manifesto," http://www.ecomodernism.org/manifesto-english.

19. Greta Thunberg, speech at the United Nations Climate Action Summit,September 23, 2019, accessed at https://www.npr.org/2019/09/23/763452863/transcript-greta-thunbergs-speech-at-the-u-n-climate-action-summit.

20. Garett Jones, "National IQ and National Productivity: The Hive Mind Across Asia," *Asian Development Review* 28, no. 1 (June 2011): 51-71, https://ssrn.com/abstract=1869472.

21. Elizabeth Chuck, "Lead from Gasoline Blunted the IQ of about Half the U.S. Population, Study Says," *NBC News*, March 7, 2022, https://www.nbcnews.com/health/health-news/lead-gasoline-blunted-iq-half-us-population-study-rcna19028.

22. Nicholas Z. Muller, "Long-Run Environmental Accounting in the U.S. Economy," National Bureau of Economic Research Working Paper no. 25910 (May 2019), https://www.nber.org/papers/w25910.

23. Ariana Rowberry, "Castle Bravo: The Largest U.S. Nuclear Explosion," *Up Front* (blog), Brookings Institution, https://www.brookings.edu/blog/up-front/2014/02/27/castle-bravo-the-largest-u-s-nuclear-explosion/; Spencer R. Weart, *The Rise of Nuclear Fear* (Cambridge: Harvard University Press, 2012), 98.

24. Thomas P. Hughes, *American Genesis* (Chicago: University of Chicago Press, 1989), 444, Kindle.

25. Ibid., 442.

26. Alan Moore and Dave Gibbons, "Watchmen," trade paperback ed. (New York: DC Comics, 1986), chapter 2.

27. Ibid., 446.

28. Ibid., 453.

29. Robert Wise, dir., *The Andromeda Strain* (1971; Universal City, CA: Universal Pictures); Michael Crichton, *The Andromeda Strain* (New York: Alfred A. Knopf, 1969).

30. Adrian Ma and Stacey Vanek Smith, "The Great Cranberry Scare of 1959," November 12, 2019, in *The Indicator from Planet Money*, produced by Leena Sanzgiri, podcast, MP3 audio, https://www.npr.org/2019/11/12/778606901/the-great-cranberry-scare-of-1959.

31. Jon Hamilton, "How California's Worst Oil Spill Turned Beaches Black and the Nation Green," *NPR*, January 28, 2019, https://www.npr.org/2019/01/28/688219307/how-californias-worst-oil-spill-turned-beaches-black-and-the-nation-green.

32. Elijah Olomoniyi, "The Cuyahoga River: Once on Fire, Now a Recreation Destination," National Park Service, updated March 2, 2022, https://www.nps.gov/articles/000/the-cuyahoga-river-once-on-fire-now-a-recreation-destination.htm.

33. Eliza Griswold, "How 'Silent Spring' Ignited the Environmental Movement," *New York Times*, September 21, 2012, https://www.nytimes.com/2012/09/23/magazine/how-silent-spring-ignited-the-environmental-movement.html.

34. Hughes, *American Genesis*, 450.

35. "American Rhetoric: Movie Speech: 'Network' (1976)," American Rhetoric, https://www.americanrhetoric.com/MovieSpeeches/moviespeechnetwork4.html.

36. E. F. Schumacher, *Small Is Beautiful: Economics as if People Mattered* (New York: Harper & Row, 1973), 29.

37. Ernest Callenbach, *Ecotopia: The Notebooks and Reports of William Weston* (Berkeley: Banan Tree Books, 1975).

38. Donella Meadows et al., *The Limits to Growth* (New York: Universe Books, 1972), 24.

39. William D. Nordhaus, "Lethal Model 2: The Limits to Growth Revisited," Brookings Institution, July 1992, https://www.brookings.edu/wp-content/uploads/1992/06/1992b_bpea_nordhaus_stavins_weitzman.pdf.

40. Ibid.

41. Paul R. Ehrlich, *The Population Bomb* (New York: Ballantine Books, 1968), prologue.

42. My count from "List of *The Tonight Show Starring Johnny Carson* Episodes," Wikipedia, last edited March 11, 2022, at 16:07, https://en.wikipedia.org/wiki/List_of_The_Tonight_Show_Starring_Johnny_Carson_episodes.

43. Dan Wang, "2019 Letter," January 1, 2020, personal blog, https://danwang.co/2019-letter.

44. John Ruskin, *Bartleby*, https://www.bartleby.com/73/1236.html.

45. Quoted in Kenneth Clark, *Civilisation: A Personal View* (London: John Murray and BBC Book, 1969), 1.

46. *Planet of the Apes*, directed by Franklin J. Schaffner, 20th Century Fox, 1968.

47. Jesse Olszynko-Gryn and Patrick Ellis, "Malthus at the Movies: Science, Cinema, and Activism around Z.P.G. and Soylent Green," *Journal of Cinema and Media Studies* 58, no. 1 (Fall 2018): 47–69, https://www.jstor.org/stable/26608643.

48. Quoted in Michelle Goldberg, "The Darkness Where the Future Should Be," *New York Times*, January 24, 2020, https://www.nytimes.com/2020/01/24/opinion/sunday/william-gibson-agency.html.

49. "20 Minutes into the FutureTV," TVTropes, https://tvtropes.org/pmwiki/pmwiki.php/Main/TwentyMinutesIntoTheFuture.

50. Goldberg, "The Darkness Where the Future Should Be."

51. Elise Boulding, "Why Imagine the Future?" Human Dignity and Humiliation Studies, https://www.humiliationstudies.org/documents/BouldingWhyImaginetheFuture.pdf.

Six: Today's Down Wing Enemies of Up Wing Progress

1. Jo Merchant, "Decoding the Antikythera Mechanism, the First Computer," *Smithsonian Magazine*, February 2015, https://www.smithsonianmag.com/history/decoding-antikythera-mechanism-first-computer-180953979.

2. Jennifer Ouelette, "Researchers Home in on Possible 'Day Zero' for Antikythera Mechanism," *Ars Technica*, December 23, 2022, https://arstechnica.com/science/2022/04/researchers-home-in-on-possible-day-zero-for-antikythera-mechanism.

3. J. R. Minkel, "Ancient Greek Eclipse Calculator Marked Olympics," *Scientific American*, July 30, 2008, https://www.scientificamerican.com/article/antikythera-mechanism-eclipse-olympics.

4. John Noble Wilford, "Research Links Ancient 'Analog Computer' to Archimedes," *New York Times*, July 31, 2008, https://www.nytimes.com/2008/07/31/technology/31iht-computer.4.14921721.html.

5. Quoted in Carl Benedikt Frey, *The Technology Trap: Capital, Labor, and Power in the Age of Automation* (Princeton, NJ: Princeton University Press, 2020), 39.

6. "About Us," Future Timeline, https://www.futuretimeline.net/about-us.htm.

7. Jolene Creighton, "The Kardashev Scale—Type I, II, III, IV & V Civilization," *Futurism*, July 19, 2014, https://futurism.com/the-kardashev-scale-type-i-ii-iii-iv-v-civilization.

8. Adam Hadhazy, "Could We Build a Dyson Sphere?," *Popular Mechanics*, June 9, 2022, https://www.popularmechanics.com/space/deep-space/a11098/dyson-sphere/.

9. "Encyclopaedia Galactica," *Cosmos: A Personal Voyage*, PBS, 53:48, December 14, 1980.

10. My conversation with Joel Mokyr: "'A Culture of Growth:' A Long Read Q&A with Economic Historian Joel Mokyr," *AEIdeas* (blog), September 15, 2017, https://www.aei.org/economics/a-culture-of-growth-a-long-read-qa-with-economic-historian-joel-mokyr.

11. Carl Benedikt Frey, *The Technology Trap: Capital, Labor and Power in the Age of Automation* (Princeton, NJ: Princeton University Press, 2019), preface, Kindle.

12. Ibid., 40.

13. Ibid., 54.

14. My conversation with Carl Benedikt Frey: "The Future of Employment in an Age of Automation: A Long-Read Q&A with Carl Benedikt Frey," November 11, 2019, https://www.aei.org/pethokoukis/carl-benedikt-frey-on-the-technology-trap.

15. Darrell Proctor, "Biden Signs Bill to Transform U.S. Energy, Combat Climate Change," *Power*, August 16, 2022, https://www.powermag.com/biden-signs-bill-to-transform-us-energy-combat-climate-change.

16. Dino Grandoni and Anna Phillips, "Biden Restores Climate Safeguards in Key Environmental Law, Reversing Trump," *Washington Post*, April 19, 2022, https://www.washingtonpost.com/climate-environment/2022/04/19/biden-nepa-climate-trump.

17. Robin Bravender, "Moon Eclipses Debate," *Politico*, January 27, 2012, https://www.politico.com/story/2012/01/moon-base-takes-center-stage-072067.

18. Newt Gingrich, "Remembering Alvin Toffler: 1928-2016," *Politico Magazine*, December 31, 2016, https://www.politico.com/magazine/story/2016/12/alvin-toffler-obituary-future-shock-214561.

19. Stephanie Condon, "Romney Tells Gingrich: I'd Fire You for Your Moon Proposal," CBS News, January 27, 2012, https://www.cbsnews.com/news/romney-tells-gingrich-id-fire-you-for-your-moon-proposal.

20. William F. Buckley Jr., "Our Mission Statement," *National Review*, November 19, 1955, https://www.nationalreview.com/1955/11/our-mission-statement-william-f-buckley-jr.

21. From a November 28, 1962, General Features Corp. newspaper column, Russell Kirk, "The Mechanical Jacobin," Russell Kirk Center, November 10, 2017, https://kirkcenter.org/environment-nature-conservation/the-mechanical-jacobin.

22. Charles C. W. Cooke, "The War on Driving to Come," *National Review*, December 18, 2017, https://www.nationalreview.com/2017/12/autonomous-vehicles-will-spark-government-efforts-ban-driving.

23. Ronald Reagan, remarks at the Annual Convention of the National Association of Evangelicals, Orlando, Florida, March 8, 1983, https://www.americanrhetoric.com/speeches/ronaldreaganevilempire.htm.

24. Ronald Reagan, "Moscow State University Address," Moscow, Russia, May 31, 1988, https://www.americanrhetoric.com/speeches/ronaldreaganmoscowstateuniversity.htm.

25. Jenna Wortham, "Obama Brought Silicon Valley to Washington," *New York Times*, October 25, 2016, https://www.nytimes.com/2016/10/30/magazine/barack-obama-brought-silicon-valley-to-washington-is-that-a-good-thing.html.

26. Quoted in Philip Bump, "Steve Bannon Once Complained That 20 Percent of the Country is Made Up of Immigrants. It Isn't," *Washington Post*, February 1, 2017, https://www.washingtonpost.com/news/politics/wp/2017/02/01/steve-bannon-once-complained-that-20-percent-of-the-country-is-made-up-of-immigrants-it-isnt.

27. Leon Kass, "Preventing a *Brave New World*," June 21, 2001, https://essaydocs.org/preventing-a-brave-new-world-by-leon-kass.html.

28. Brian Alexander, *Rapture: How Biotech Became the New Religion* (New York: Basic Books, 2003), 157.

29. Rod Dreher, "We Shall Be As Gods," *American Conservative*, July 26, 2017.

30. *Things to Come*, directed by William Cameron Menzies (London Films Productions), https://en.wikipedia.org/wiki/Things_to_Come.

31. Julia Horowitz, "Degrowth: A Dangerous Idea or the Answer to the World's Biggest Crisis?" CNN Business, November 15, 2022, https://www.cnn.com/2022/11/13/economy/degrowth-climate-cop27/index.html.

32. Nordhaus, "Lethal Model 2."

33. Samuel Alexander, "Life in a 'Degrowth' Economy, and Why You Might Actually Enjoy It," Local Futures, April 18, 2017, https://www.localfutures.org/life-in-a-degrowth-economy/.

34. "Economic Growth No Longer Requires Rising Emissions," *Economist*, November 10, 2022, https://www.economist.com/leaders/2022/11/10/economic-growth-no-longer-requires-rising-emissions.

35. Ted Kaczynski, "Hit Where It Hurts," 2002, https://theanarchistlibrary.org/library/ted-kaczynski-hit-where-it-hurts.

36. Solar Punk, TV Tropes, https://tvtropes.org/pmwiki/pmwiki.php/Main/SolarPunk.

37. Ted Nordhaus, "Twilight of Environmental Idols," Breakthrough Institute, September 26, 2022, https://thebreakthrough.org/issues/energy/twilight-environmental-idols-what-comes-after-environmentalism.

38. Troy Vettese and Drew Pendergrass, *Half-Earth Socialism: A Plan to Save the Future from Extinction, Climate Change, and Pandemics* (London: Verso, 2022), 111.

39. Paul P. Craig, "Environmental Values and Risk: A Review of Sierra Club Policies," Paper presented at Values in Decisions on Risk Symposium: Stockholm (June 1999), accessed at https://inis.iaea.org/collection/NCLCollectionStore/_Public/31/016/31016484.pdf.

40. James Feigenbaum and Daniel P. Gross, "Answering the Call of Automation: How the Labor Market Adjusted to the Mechanization of Telephone Operation," National Bureau of Economic Research Working Paper no. 28061 (April 2022), https://www.nber.org/papers/w28061.

41. James Bessen, "How Computer Automation Affects Occupations: Technology, Jobs, and Skills," Boston University School of Law, Law & Economics Working Paper no. 15-49 (November 13, 2015), https://www.bu.edu/law/files/2015/11/NewTech-2.pdf.

42. "The Automation Jobless," *Time*, Feb. 24, 1961, https://content.time.com/time/subscriber/article/0,33009,828815,00.html.

43. Quoted in "Automation and Job Loss: The Fears of 1964," *The Conversable Economist* (blog), December 1, 2014, https://conversableeconomist.blogspot.com/2014/12/automation-and-job-loss-fears-of-1964.html.

44. "The Triple Revolution," *International Socialist Review* 24, no. 3 (Summer 1964), https://www.marxists.org/history/etol/newspape/isr/vol25/no03/adhoc.html.

45. "Transcript: The Last Sunday Sermon of MLK (March 31, 1968)," *Sinju Post*, August 31, 2022, https://singjupost.com/transcript-the-last-sunday-sermon-of-mlk-march-31-1968.

46. Unemployment data accessed at "Employment Situation," U.S. Bureau of Labor Statistics, https://www.bls.gov/news.release/empsit.toc.htm. See also James Pethokoukis, "Wages Rising: The US Economy Is Now Working Best for Lower-Wage Workers," *AEIdeas* (blog), March 13, 2019, https://www.aei.org/economics/wages-rising-the-trump-economy-is-now-working-best-for-lower-wage-workers. Productivity numbers accessed at "Productivity," U.S. Bureau of Labor Statistics, https://www.bls.gov/productivity.

47. Peter Hasson, "'Mass Riots': Democratic 2020 Candidate Warns Driverless Trucks Will Lead to 'Outbreak of Violence,'" *Daily Caller News Foundation*, February 16, 2019, https://dailycaller.com/2019/02/16/andrew-yang-joe-rogan-driverless-trucks.

48. Sally French, "Bill Gates Says Robots Should Pay Taxes If They Take Your Job," *MarketWatch*, February 20, 2017, https://www.marketwatch.com/story/bill-gates-says-robots-should-pay-taxes-if-they-take-your-job-2017-02-17.

49. Minkyu Shin, et al., "Superhuman Artificial Intelligence Can Improve Human Decision Making by Increasing Novelty," *arXiv* (March 13, 2023), https://arxiv.org/abs/2303.07462.

50. "The Potentially Large Effects of Artificial Intelligence on Economic Growth," Goldman Sachs, March 23, 2023.

51. David Autor, "The Labor Market Impacts of Technological Change: From Unbridled Enthusiasm to Qualified Optimism to Vast Uncertainty," National Bureau of Economic Research Working Paper no. 3007 (July 2022), https://www.nber.org/papers/w30074.

52. James Bessen, "How Computer Automation Affects Occupations: Technology, Jobs, and Skills," VoxEU, March 22, 2016, https://cepr.org/voxeu/columns/how-computer-automation-affects-occupations-technology-jobs-and-skills.

53 Adam Thierer, "Why Isn't Everyone Already Unemployed Due to Automation?" *Technology Liberation Front*, March 11, 2023, https://techliberation.com/2023/03/11/why-isnt-everyone-already-unemployed-due-to-automation/.

54. Conrad Quilty-Harper, "$335,000 Pay for 'AI Whisperer' Jobs Appears in Red-Hot Market," *Bloomberg*, March 29, 2023, https://www.bloomberg.com/news/articles/2023-03-29/ai-chatgpt-related-prompt-engineer-jobs-pay-up-to-335-000.

55. Robert C. Allen, "Engels' Pause: Technical Change, Capital Accumulation, and Inequality in the British Industrial Revolution," *Explorations in Economic History* 46, no. 4 (October 2009): 418–435, https://www.sciencedirect.com/science/article/abs/pii/S0014498309000199.

56. Michael Strain, "Robot Workers Could Tear America's Social Fabric," *Washington Post*, May 28, 2014, https://www.washingtonpost.com/posteverything/wp/2014/05/27/robot-workers-could-tear-americas-social-fabric.

57. Phil Hornshaw, "'Blade Runner 2049': What Exactly Is 'the Blackout'?" *The Wrap*, October 7, 2017, https://www.thewrap.com/blade-runner-2049-exactly-blackout.

58. Michael Strain, "The Myth of Income Stagnation," *Project Syndicate*, December 15, 2022, https://www.project-syndicate.org/commentary/myth-of-us-income-stagnation-by-michael-r-strain-2022-12.

Seven: Seven Down Wing Myths about Economic Growth

1. Paul R. Ehrlich, *The Population Bomb* (New York: Ballantine Books, 1968), prologue.

2. William S. Gaud, "The Green Revolution: Accomplishments and Apprehensions," AgBioWorld, http://www.agbioworld.org/biotech-info/topics/borlaug/borlaug-green.html.

3. Mrs. Aase Lionaes, "Award Ceremony Speech," Nobel Prize, December 10, 1970, https://www.nobelprize.org/prizes/peace/1970/ceremony-speech.

4. Douglas Gollin, Casper Worm Hansen, and Asger Wingender, "Two Blades of Grass: The Impact of the Green Revolution," *Journal of Political Economy* 129, no. 8 (2021): 2344–84, https://doi.org/10.1086/714444.

5. Michael R. Strain, *The American Dream Is Not Dead (But Populism Could Kill It)* (West Conshohocken, PA: Templeton Press, 2020), 45.

6. Wage calculations obtained directly from Michael Strain.

7. Anna M. Stansbury and Lawrence H. Summers, "Productivity and Pay: Is the Link Broken?" National Bureau of Economic Research Working Paper no. 24165 (December 2017), https://www.nber.org/papers/w24165.

8. Jason Furman, "The Real Reason You're Not Getting a Pay Raise," *Vox*, August 11, 2018, https://www.vox.com/the-big-idea/2018/7/31/17632348/wages-lagging-inequality-income-recovery-recession-wage-puzzle-economics.

9. Will Rinehart, "The Abundance Agenda," *The Exformation Newsletter*, October 15, 2022, https://exformation.substack.com/p/the-abundance-agenda.

10. "The U.S. Productivity Slowdown: An Economy-Wide and Industry-Level Analysis," U.S. Bureau of Labor Statistics, April 2021, https://www.bls.gov/opub/mlr/2021/article/the-us-productivity-slowdown-the-economy-wide-and-industry-level-analysis.htm.

11. Strain, *The American Dream Is Not Dead*, 77.

12. Shackleton, "Total Factor Productivity Growth."

13. Ibid.

14. All statistics about the disease come from Amitabh Chandra, Courtney Coile, and Corina Mommaerts, "What Can Economics Say about Alzheimer's Disease?" National Bureau of Economic Research Working Paper no. 27760 (July 2021), https://www.nber.org/papers/w27760.

15. Meagan C. Fitzpatrick et al., "Two Years of U.S. COVID-19 Vaccines Have Prevented Millions of Hospitalizations and Deaths," Commonwealth Fund, December13, 2022, https://www.commonwealthfund.orgblog/2022/two-years-covid-vaccines-prevented-millions-deaths-hospitalizations.

16. Alicia Atwood, "The Long-Term Effects of Measles Vaccination on Earnings and Employment," *American Economic Journal: Economic Policy* 14, no. 2 (2022): 34–60, https://doi.org/10.1257/pol.20190509.

17. Conrad Quilty-Harper, "It Turns Out Money Does Buy Happiness, At Least Up to $500,000," *Bloomberg*, March 7, 2023, https://www.bloomberg.com/news/articles/2023-03-07/money-does-buy-happiness-at-least-up-to-500-000.

18. My conversation with Branco Milanović: "5 Quick Questions for…Economist Branko Milanovic on the Russian Economy, Global Capitalism, and More," *Faster, Please!* (newsletter), July 26, 2022, https://fasterplease.substack.com/p/-5-quick-questions-for-economist.

19. Lant Pritchett and Addison Lewis, "Basically, Economic Growth Is Enough, and Only Economic Growth Is Enough for the Basics" (Working Paper), March 18, 2022, https://lantpritchett.org/wp-content/uploads/2022/03/Basics-legatum-paper_first_final.pdf.

20. "Poverty and Shared Prosperity 2022: Correcting Course," World Bank, 2022, https://www.worldbank.org/en/publication/poverty-and-shared-prosperity.

21. Joe Hassell, "From $1.90 to $2.15 a Day: The Updated International Poverty Line," *Our World in Data*, October 26, 2022, https://ourworldindata.org/from-1-90-to-2-15-a-day-the-updated-international-poverty-line.

22. Lizzy Gurdus, "Boeing CEO: Over 80% of the World Has Never Taken a Flight. We're Leveraging That for Growth," *CNBC*, December 7, 2017, https://www.cnbc.com/2017/12/07/boeing-ceo-80-percent-of-people-never-flown-for-us-that-means-growth.html.

23. The amount of economic growth needed to eradicate global poverty is calculated in Max Roser, "How Much Economic Growth Is Necessary to Reduce Global Poverty Substantially?" Our World in Data, March 15, 2021, https://ourworldindata.org/poverty-minimum-growth-needed.

24. Michael Cox and Richard Alm, "Onward and Upward! Bet on Capitalism—It Works," *2015-16 Annual Report of the William J. O'Neil Center for Global Markets and Freedom*, Southern Methodist University Cox School of Business, https://www.smu.edu/-/media/Site/Cox/CentersAndInstitutes/ONeilCenter/Research/AnnualReports/2016_annual_report_full.ashx?la=en.

25. Gale L. Pooley and Marian L. Tupy, "The Simon Abundance Index: A New Way to Measure Availability of Resources," CATO Institute, https://www.cato.org/policy-analysis/simon-abundance-index-new-way-measure-availability-resources.

26. Andrew McAfee, *More from Less: The Surprising Story of How We Learned to Prosper Using Fewer Resources—and What Happens Next* (New York: Scribner, 2019), 3.

27. Richard Webb, "Paul Ehrlich: There Are Too Many Super-Consumers on the Planet," *New Scientist*, November 11, 2020, https://www.newscientist.com/article/2232011-paul-ehrlich-there-are-too-many-super-consumers-on-the-planet.

28. The World Counts, https://www.theworldcounts.com.

29. Erik Stokstad, "Supercharged Biotech Rice Yields 40% More Grain," *Science*, July 22, 2024, https://www.science.org/content/article/supercharged-biotech-rice-yields-40-more-grain.

30. Claire Benjamin, "Scientists Boost Crop Production by 47 Percent by Speeding Up Photorespiration," RIPE Project, May 31, 2018, https://ripe.illinois.edu/press/press-releases/scientists-boost-crop-production-47-percent-speeding-photorespiration.

31. Benjamin M. Friedman: "Economic Growth and the Moral Society," Institute for Jewish Ideas and Ideals, https://www.jewishideas.org/articleeconomic-growth-and-moral-society-dr-benjamin-m-friedman.

32. Benjamin M. Friedman: *The Moral Consequences of Economic Growth* (New York: Vintage, 2006).

33. Emily Jashinsky (@emilyjashinsky), "The hideous architecture reflects the hideous philosophy," Twitter, December 22, 2022, 10:14 p.m., https://twitter.com/emilyjashinsky/status/1606125972926988291; Aimee Picchi, "McDonald's Unveiled an Automated Store. SomeConsumers Aren't Loving It," *CBS News*, December 23, 2022, https://www.cbsnews.com/news/mcdonalds-automated-restaurant-robots-drive-thru-conveyer-belt.

34. Carlos Molina et al., "(Successful) Democracies Breed Their Own Support," VoxEU, September 15, 2021, https://cepr.org/voxeu/columns-successful-democracies-breed-their-own-support.

35. Derek Thompson, "Why the Age of American Progress Ended," *The Atlantic*, December 12, 2022, https://www.theatlantic.com/magazine archive/2023/01/science-technology-vaccine-invention-history/672227/.

36. Michael Sandel, "What Isn't for Sale?" *The Atlantic*, April 2012, https://www.theatlantic.com/magazine/archive/2012/04/what-isnt-for-sale/308902.

37. Cited in Sabrina Escobar, "The 100 Best Companies to Work for Are Great Stocks to Buy in a Crisis," *Fortune*, July 6, 2022, https://www.barrons.com/articles/100-best-companies-to-work-for-stocks-51657127674.

38. Cliff Asness, "Shareholder Value Is Undervalued," AQR Capital Management, January 6, 2015, https://www.aqr.com/-/media/AQR/Documents/Insights/Perspectives/Shareholder-Value-Is-Undervalued.pdf.

39. Deirdre N. McCloskey, *The Bourgeois Virtues: Ethics for an Age of Commerce* (Chicago: University of Chicago Press, 2006), 507–508, Kindle.

40. Justin Callais, Colin Harris, and Ben Borchard, "The Moral Costs of Markets: Testing the Deterioration Hypothesis," *Journal of Economic Behavior and Organization* 204 (December 2022): 200–220, https://doi.org/10.1016/j.jebo.2022.10.007.

Eight: The Most Important Reason to Embrace Up Wing Growth

1. George Packer, "We Are Living in a Failed State," *The Atlantic*, June 2020, https://www.theatlantic.com/magazine/archive/2020/06/underlying-conditions/610261.

2. Cited in Robert Tucker Omberg and Alex Tabarrok, "Is It Possible to Prepare for a Pandemic?" *Oxford Review of Economic Policy* 38, no. 4 (Winter 2022): 851–875, https://doi.org/10.1093oxrep/grac035.

3. Ibid.

4. Stephanie Baker and Cynthia Koons, "Inside Operation Warp Speed's $18 Billion Sprint for a Vaccine," *Bloomberg*, October 29, 2020, https://www.bloomberg.com/news/features/2020-10-29/inside-operation-warp-speed-s-18-billion-sprint-for-a-vaccine.; Arielle

D'Souza, "How To Reuse the Operation Warp Speed Model," *Institute for Progress*, February 7, 2023, https://progress.institute/how-to-reuse-the-operation-warp-speed-model/.

5. Randall J. Stephens, "When Climate Catastrophes Spark Religious Turmoil," *Washington Post*, June 18, 2021, https://www.washingtonpost.com/outlook/when-climate-catastrophes-spark-religious-turmoil/2021/06/17/1012b992-af72-11eb-b476-c3b287e52a01_story.html.

6. Spencer Weart, "The Discovery of Global Warming [Excerpt]," *Scientific American*, August 17, 2012, https://www.scientificamerican.com/article/discovery-of-global-warming/.

7. David Deutsch, *The Beginning of Infinity Explanations that Transform the World* (New York: Viking Penguin, 2011), 438.

8. Will Mathis, "Carbon-Sucking Tech Could Need More Energy Than All Homes Use," *Bloomberg*, March 21, 2023, https://www.bloomberg.com/news/articles/2023-03-21/carbon-sucking-tech-could-need-more-energy-than-all-homes-use.

9. Paul Krugman, "Running Out of Planet to Exploit," *New York Times*, April 21, 2008, https://www.nytimes.com/2008/04/21/opinion/21krugman.html.

10. Amanda Little, "An Interview with Doomsaying Author James Howard Kunstler," *Grist*, May 25, 2005, https://grist.org/article/little-kunstler.

11. James Howard Kunstler, "Why America's Urban Dreams Went Wrong," *American Conservative*, January 24, 2020, https://www.theamericanconservative.com/why-americas-urban-dreams-went-wrong.

12. David Wethe, "The Shale Revolution," *Bloomberg Business QuickTake*, December 27, 2019, https://www.bloomberg.com/quicktake/fracking.

13. Alissa Wilkinson, "The 2011 Film Contagion Is Even More Relevant in 2020, and Not Just because of Coronavirus," *Vox*, February 4, 2020, https://www.vox.com/2020/2/4/21120178/contagion-movie-coronavirus-itunes-fake-news.

14. Amanda Glassman, Charles Kenny, and George Yang, "The COVID-19 Vaccine Rollout Was the Fastest in Global History, but Low-Income Countries Were Left Behind," Center for Global Development, February 9, 2022, https://www.cgdev.org/blog/covid-19-vaccine-rollout-was-fastest-global-history-low-income-countries-were-left-behind.

15. Mark Strauss, "Why Newton Believed a Comet Caused Noah's Flood," *National Geographic*, December 30, 2016, https://www.nationalgeographic.com/science/article/comet-new-years-eve-newton-flood-bible-gravity-science.

16. Rebecca Boyle, "A (Small) Pre-Emptive Strike against the Doomsday Asteroid," *Smithsonian Magazine*, June 2021, https://www.smithsonianmag.com/air-space-magazine/doomsday-mission-180977800.

17. Paul Voosen, "Earth at Higher Risk of Big Asteroid Strike, Satellite Data Suggest," *Science*, March, 20, 2023, https://www.science.org/content/article/earth-higher-risk-big-asteroid-strike-satellite-data-suggest.

18 "NASA Confirms DART Mission Impact Changed Asteroid's Motion in Space," NASA, October 11, 2022, https://www.nasa.gov/press-release/nasa-confirms-dart-mission-impact-changed-asteroid-s-motion-in-space.

19. Aaron Wildavsky, *Searching for Safety* (New York: Routledge, 1988).

20. Toby Ord, *The Precipice: Existential Risk and the Future of Humanity* (New York: Hachette, 2020), 39.

21. My conversation with Toby Ord: "Is Humanity Prepared to Handle Catastrophic Threats? My Long-Read Q&A with Toby Ord," *AEIdeas* (blog), July 6, 2020, https://www.aei.org/economics/is-humanity-prepared-to-handle-catastrophic-threats-my-long-read-qa-with-toby-ord.

22. Ibid.

23. Aaron Wildavsky, *Searching for Safety* (New York: Routledge, 1988), 86, Kindle.

24. Ibid., 41.

25. Quoted in Alex Knapp, "Five Leadership Lessons From James T. Kirk," *Forbes*, March 5, 2012, https://www.forbes.com/sites/alexknapp/2012/03/05/five-leadership-lessons-from-james-t-kirk/.

26. Max Roser, "Longtermism: The Future Is Vast—What Does This Mean for Our Own Life?" *Our World in Data*, March 15, 2022, https://ourworldindata.org/longtermism.

27. Ibid.

Nine: Why Up Wing Progress Is Possible

1. Boyan Jovanovic and Peter L. Rousseau, "General Purpose Technologies," National Bureau of Economic Research Working Paper no. 11093 (January 2005), https://www.nber.org/papers/w11093.

2. Vernor Vinge, "Technological Singularity," *Whole Earth Review*, no. 88 (January 1993): 88–95, https://frc.ri.cmu.edu/~hpm/book98/com.ch1/vinge.singularity.html.

3. Bill Gates, "The Age of AI has Begun," *GatesNotes* (blog), March 21, 2023, https://www.gatesnotes.com/The-Age-of-AI-Has-Begun.

4. Sebastien Bubeck et al., "Sparks of Artificial General Intelligence: Early experiments with GPT-4," arXiv (March 22, 2023), https://arxiv.org/abs/2303.12712.

5. Cade Metz, "The ChatGPT King Isn't Worried, but He Knows You Might Be," *New York Times*, March 31, 2023, https://www.nytimes.com/2023/03/31/technology/sam-altman-open-ai-chatgpt.html.

6. Robin Hanson, "Singularity, Part 2," Foresight Institute, February 12, 2009, https://foresight.org/singularity-part-2.

7. John G. Fernald and Charles I. Jones, "The Future of U.S. Economic Growth," National Bureau of Economic Research Working Paper no. 19830 (January 2014), https://www.nber.org/papers/w19830.

8. Author's calculations using data from Measuring Worth, https://www.measuringworth.com.

9. Sara Castellanos, "Intel CIO Says AI Playing a Growing Role in Chipmaker's Operations," *Wall Street Journal*, September 1, 2020, https://www.wsj.com/articles/intel-cio-says-ai-playing-a-growing-role-in-chipmakers-operations-11598996924.

10. Lucy Colback, "The Impact of AI on Business and Society," *Financial Times*, October 15, 2020, https://www.ft.com/content/e082b01d-fbd6-4ea5-a0d2-05bc5ad7176c.

11. Quoted in ibid.

12. Samantha Murphy Kelly, "Real Estate Agents Say They Can't Imagine Working without ChatGPT Now," CNN Business, January 28, 2023, https://www.cnn.com/2023/01/28/tech/chatgpt-real-estate/index.html.

13. "Big Ideas 2023," Ark Investment Research, January 31, 2023, https://research.ark-invest.com/hubfs/1_Download_Files_ARK-Invest/Big_Ideas/ARK%20Invest_013123_Presentation_Big%20Ideas%202023_Final.pdf.

14. My conversation with Avi Goldfarb: "Progress Is Hard. And a New Study Suggests It Might Be Even Harder Than We Think," *Faster, Please!* (newsletter), April 25, 2022, https://fasterplease.substack.com/p/-progress-is-hard-and-a-new-study.

15. Cited in Jason Furman and Robert Seamans, "AI and the Economy," *Innovation Policy and the Economy* 19, no. 1 (2019), https://doi.org/10.1086/699936.

16. My conversation with Tamay Besiroglu: "5 Quick Questions for…MIT Research Scientist Tamay Besiroglu on the Huge Economic Potential of AI," *Faster, Please!* (newsletter), August 2, 2022, https://fasterplease.substack.com/p/-5-quick-questions-for-mit-research; Tamay Besiroglu, Nicholas Emery-Xu, and Neil Thompson, "Economic Impacts of AI-Augmented R&D," arXiv (January 2, 2023), https://arxiv.org/abs/2212.08198.

17. Charles Atkins, et al., "Rekindling US Productivity for a New Era," McKinsey Global Institute Report, February 16, 2023, https://www.mckinsey.com/mgi/our-research/rekindling-us-productivity-for-a-new-era.

18. Fernald and Jones, "The Future of U.S. Economic Growth."

19. "Date Weakly General AI is Publicly Known," Metaculus, https://www.metaculus.com/questions/3479/date-weakly-general-ai-is-publicly-known.

20. Joseph Briggs and Devesh Kodnani, "The Potentially Large Effects of Artificial Intelligence on Economic Growth," Goldman Sachs Research, March 26, 2023.

21. Jonathan Huebner, "A Possible Declining Trend for Worldwide Innovation," *Technological Forecasting and Social Change* 72, no. 8 (October 2005): 980–986, https://doi.org/10.1016/j.techfore.2005.01.003.

22. Quoted in Robert Adler, "Entering a Dark Age of Innovation," *New Scientist*, July 2, 2005, https://www.newscientist.com/article/dn7616-entering-a-dark-age-of-innovation.

23. Joel Mokyr, "The Next Age of Invention," *City Journal*, Winter 2014, https://www.city-journal.org/html/next-age-invention-13618.html.

24. Paul Romer, "The Deep Structure of Economic Growth," PaulRomer.net, April 13, 2016, https://paulromer.net/economic-growth.

25. Ibid.

26. Cited in Gerry Canavan, "'There's Nothing New / Under the Sun, / But There Are New Suns': Recovering Octavia E. Butler's Lost Parables," Los Angeles Review of Books, June 9, 2014, https://lareviewofbooks.org/article/theres-nothing-new-sun-new-suns-recovering-octavia-e-butlers-lost-parables.

27. My conversation with Nicholas Crafts: "Can Artificial Intelligence Reverse the Productivity Slowdown? My Long-Read Q&A with Nicholas Crafts," *AEIdeas* (blog), July 17, 2020, https://www.aei.org/economics/can-artificial-intelligence-reverse-the-productivity-slowdown-my-long-read-qa-with-nicholas-crafts.

28. Nicholas Crafts, "Artificial Intelligence as a General-Purpose Technology: An Historical Perspective," *Oxford Review of Economic Policy* 37, no. 3 (Autumn 2021): 521–536, https://doi.org/10.1093/oxrep/grab012.

29. Ibid.

30. J. Bradford DeLong, *Slouching toward Utopia: An Economic History of the Twentieth Century* (New York: Basic Books, 2022), 35.

31. Ajay Agrawal, John McHale, and Alexander Oettl, "Superhuman Science: How Artificial Intelligence May Impact Innovation," Brookings Working Paper, April 2022, https://www.brookings.edu/research/superhuman-science-how-artificial-intelligence-may-impact-innovation.

32. James Pethokoukis, "5 Quick Questions for...MIT Research Scientist Tamay Besiroglu."

33. Anne Trafton, "Artificial Intelligence Yields New Antibiotic," *MIT News*, February 20, 2022, https://news.mit.edu/2020/artificial-intelligence-identifies-new-antibiotic-0220.

34. Jo Marchant, "Powerful Antibiotics Discovered Using AI," *Nature News*, February 20, 2022, https://www.nature.com/articles/d41586-020-00018-3.

35. Quoted in Madhumita Murgia, "DeepMind Research Cracks Structure of Almost Every Known Protein," *Financial Times*, July 28, 2022, https://www.ft.com/content/6a088953-66d7-48db-b61c-79005a0a351a.

36. Steven Rosenbush, "Biologists Say Deep Learning Is Revolutionizing Pace of Innovation," *Wall Street Journal*, March 22, 2023, https://www.wsj.com/articles/biologists-say-deep-learning-is-revolutionizing-pace-of-innovation-eeb79c1b.

37. Oracle, "Computational Chemistry and AI Create a Quantum Leap in Drug Discovery," *FastCompany*, November 11, 2022, https://www.fastcompany.com/90810071/computational-chemistry-and-ai-create-a-quantum-leap-in-drug-discovery; Edward O. Pyzer-Knapp, Jed W. Pitera, Peter W. J. Staar, et al., "Accelerating Materials Discovery Using Artificial Intelligence, High Performance Computing, and Robotics," IBM Research, April 25, 2022, https://research.ibm.com/publications/accelerating-materials-discovery-using-artificial-intelligence-high-performance-computing-and-robotics.

38. "Nanoengineers Develop a Predictive Database for Materials," *ScienceDaily*, November 28, 2022, www.sciencedaily.com/releases/2022/11/221128112928.htm.

39. Steven Gislam, "New Super-Material Is Light as Plastic & Twice as Strong as Steel," Industry Europe, February 7, 2023, https://industryeurope.com/sectors/construction-engineering/new-super-material-is-light-as-plastic-twice-as-strong-as-st.

40. Quoted in Thomas Lewton, "Will Artificial Intelligence Ever Discover New Laws of Physics?" *New Scientist*, November 21, 2022, https://www.newscientist.com/article/mg25634141-200-will-artificial-intelligence-ever-discover-new-laws-of-physics.

41. Nathan Benaich and Ian Hogarth, "State of AI Report 2022," https://www.stateof.ai.

42. Erik Brynjolfsson and Robert J. Gordon, "Bet 868," Long Bets, https://longbets.org/868.

43. James Pethokoukis, "5 Quick Questions for...MIT Research Scientist Tamay Besiroglu."

44. Tom Davidson, "Could Advanced AI Drive Explosive Economic Growth?," Open Philanthropy, June 25, 2021, https://www.openphilanthropy.org/research/could-advanced-ai-drive-explosive-economic-growth.

45. Charles I. Jones, "The Past and Future of Economic Growth: A Semi-Endogenous Perspective," National Bureau of Economic Research Working Paper no. 29126 (August 2021), https://www.nber.org/papers/w29126.

46. Davidson, "Could Advanced AI Drive Explosive Economic Growth?"

47. Comment by Benjamin F. Jones on ibid., https://docs.google.com/document/d/1jP9Bb6J6BXH5v6EshsPF2NE1GiWatPxUUrK9wDEpTqA/edit#heading=h.sx1v2jfwct7w.

48. Comment by Dietrich Vollrath on Davidson, "Could Advanced AI Drive Explosive Economic Growth?," https://docs.google.com/doument/d/1NScJzPLzLjYRkKJOjwlrPFO8PJ1xXUX81ksP7GwtCEU/edit.

Ten: Five Technologies for an Up Wing Future

1. Ryan Browne, "German Start-Up Lilium Snags Orlando Deal to Launch U.S. Hub for Flying Taxis," *CNBC*, November 11, 2020, https://www.cnbc.com/2020/11/11/lilium-to

-launch-us-hub-for-flying-taxis-in-orlando-florida.html; Christopher Jasper, "Jet-Powered Flying Taxi Unveiled following First Flight," *Bloomberg*, May 16, 2019, https://www.bloomberg.com/news/articles/2019-05-16/jet-powered-flying-taxi-unveiled-following-first-flight.

2. Mikaela Cohen, "How Electric Air Taxis Could Shake Up the Airline Industry in the Next Decade," *CNBC*, December 2, 2022, https://www.cnbc.com/2022/12/03/how-electric-air-taxis-could-shake-up-the-airline-industry.html.

3. "Are Flying Cars Preparing for Takeoff?" Morgan Stanley, January 23, 2019, https://www.morganstanley.com/ideas/autonomous-aircraft.

4. Ibid.

5. Rodney Brooks, "Where Are the Crewed eVTOL Videos?" November 5, 2022, https://rodneybrooks.com/where-are-the-crewed-evtol-videos/.

6. T. J. Gordon and Olaf Helmer, "Report on a Long-Range Forecasting Study," RAND Corporation, September 1964, https://www.rand.org/content/dam/rand/pubs/papers/2005/P2982.pdf.

7. Erik Brynjolfsson (@erikbryn), "Foundation models are incredibly effective at stringing...," Twitter, June 12, 2022, 12:05 p.m., https://twitter.com/erikbryn/status/1536016934868725760.

8. Erik Brynjolfsson, Daniel Rock, and Chad Syverson, "Artificial Intelligence and the Modern Productivity Paradox: A Clash of Expectations and Statistics," National Bureau of Economic Research Working Paper no. 24001 (November 2017), https://www.nber.org/papersw24001.

9. Erik Brynjolfsson, Daniel Rock, and Chad Syverson, "Unpacking the AI-Productivity Paradox," *MIT Sloan Management Review*, January 16, 2018, https://sloanreview.mit.edu/article/unpacking-the-ai-productivity-paradox.

10. "Artificial Index Report 2023," Stanford HAI, April 2023, https://aiindex.stanford.edu/report/.

11. Shakked Noy and Whitney Zhang, "Experimental Evidence on the Productivity Effects of Generative Artificial Intelligence," MIT Working Paper (March 2, 2023), https://economics.mit.edu/sites/default/files/inline-files/Noy_Zhang_1.pdf.

12. "Artificial Index Report 2023," Stanford HAI.

13. Robert Tracinski, "The Spectacular Promise of Artificial Intelligence," *Discourse*, January 10, 2023, https://www.discoursemagazine.com/ideas/2023/01/10/the-spectacular-promise-of-artificial-intelligence/.

14. "2022 Expert Survey on Progress in AI," Machine Research Institute, August 3, 2022, https://aiimpacts.org/2022-expert-survey-on-progress-in-ai.

15. "Human/Machine Intelligence Parity by 2040," Metaculus, https://www.metaculus.com/questions/384/humanmachine-intelligence-parity-by-2040.

16. Jeremy Laird, "Nvidia Predicts AI Models One Million Times More Powerful than ChatGPT Within 10 Years," *PC Gamer*, February 23, 2023, https://www.pcgamer.com/nvidia-predicts-ai-models-one-million-times-more-powerful-than-chatgpt-within-10-years/.

17. Matt Clifford, "Infinite AI Interns for Everybody," *Wired*, January 18, 2023, https://www.wired.com/story/artificial-intelligence-labor.

18. Quoted in Glenn Hunter, "Exclusive Q&A: John Carmack's 'Different Path' to Artificial General Intelligence," Dallas Innovates, February 2, 2023, https://dallasinnovates.com/exclusive-qa-john-carmacks-different-path-to-artificial-general-intelligence.

19. Adam Miller, "New mRNA Vaccine Targeting All Known Flu Strains Shows Early Promise," *CBC News*, November 24, 2022, https://www.cbc.ca/news/health/mrna-flu-vaccine-study-influenza-pandemic-universal-flu-shot-1.6662809.

20. "Investigational Personalized mRNA Cancer Vaccine Gains Breakthrough Therapy Designation from FDA," *PharmTech*, February 28, 2023, https://www.pharmtech.com/view/investigational-personalized-mrna-cancer-vaccine-gains-breakthrough-therapy-designation-from-fda.

21. Quoted in Lisa Jarvis, "Another Crispr First: New Treatment Wipes Out Teen's Cancer," *Bloomberg Opinion*, December 13, 2022, https://www.bloomberg.com/opinion/articles/2022-12-13/crispr-gene-editing-breakthrough-brings-cancer-cures-closer.

22. Alvin Powell, "Has First Person to Live to Be 150 been born?" *Harvard Gazette*, January 30, 2023, https://news.harvard.edu/gazette/story/2023/01/has-first-person-to-live-to-be-150-been-born.

23. Andrew J. Scott, Martin Ellison, and David A. Sinclair, "The Economic Value of Targeting Aging," *Nature Aging* 1 (July 23, 2021): 616–623, https://doi.org/10.1038s43587-021-00080-0.

24. Mallika Marshall, "Artificial Intelligence Used at Mass General to Identify Patients at Risk for Alzheimer's," *CBS News Boston*, March 6, 2023, https://www.cbsnews.com/boston/news/artificial-intelligence-mass-general-hospital/.

25. Jennifer Doudna, "Crispr Wants to Feed the World," *Wired*, January 27, 2023, https://www.wired.com/story/crispr-gene-editing-climate/.

26. "Renewable Power Generation Costs in 2020," International Renewable Energy Agency data, 2021, foreword, https://www.irena.org/-/media/Files/IRENA/Agency/Publication/2021/Jun/IRENA_Power_Generation_Costs_2020.pdf.

27. Brian Singer et al., "US Decarbonization: How the IRA Accelerates Emissions Declines, What's Still Needed, and Stocks to Own," Goldman Sachs Research, January 25, 2023.

28. Charles Scarlott, "Energy" in *Toward the Year 2018* (New York: Cowles Education Corporation, 1968), 121.

29. U.S. Department of Energy, "Press Conference: Secretary Granholm and DOE Leaders Announced Fusion Breakthrough by DOE National Lab," YouTube video, 33:32, https://www.youtube.com/watch?v=K2ktAL4rGuY.

30. John Thornhill, "It Is Time to Bet Big on Fusion Energy," *Financial Times*, November 18, 2021, https://www.ft.com/content/af4a3478-cca3-4610-9325-615716f95a71.

31. David L. Chandler, "Study Identifies Reasons for Soaring Nuclear Plant Cost Overruns in the U.S.," *MIT News*, November 18, 2020, https://news.mit.edu/2020/reasons-nuclear-overruns-1118.

32. "Sequoyah Nuclear Plant," U.S. General Accounting Office Staff Study no. 097098 (March 1975), https://www.gao.gov/products/097098.

33. "NRC to Issue Rule Certifying NuScale Small Modular Reactor," *NRC News*, July 29, 2022, https://www.nrc.gov/reading-rm/doc-collections/news/2022/22-029.pdf; Eric Wesoff, "Will the Feds Approve Any of the New Small Modular Nuclear Reactors?" *Canary Media*, March 3, 2023, https://www.canarymedia.com/articles/nuclear/will-the-feds-approve-any-of-the-new-small-modular-nuclear-reactors; Jeremy Harrell, "America—and the World—Needs More Nuclear Power," *POWER*, March 1, 2023, https://www.powermag.com/america-and-the-world-needs-more-nuclear-power/.; Jeff Luse, "Lessons From Poland's Nuclear Energy Renaissance," *RealClear Energy*, March 6, 2023, https://www.realclearenergy.org/articles/2023/03/06/lessons_from_polands_nuclear_energy_renaissance_885615.html.

34. Casey Crownhart, "We Were Promised Smaller Nuclear Reactors. Where Are They?" *MIT Technology Review*, February 8, 2023, https://www.technologyreview.com/2023/02|/08/1067992/smaller-nuclear-reactors/.

35. Advanced Research Projects Agency Energy, "Millimeter-Wave Technology Demonstration for Geothermal Direct Energy Drilling," U.S. Department of Energy, https://arpa-e.energy.gov/technologies/projects/millimeter-wave-technology-demonstration-geothermal-direct-energy-drilling.

36. Thomas F. Arciuolo and Miad Faezipour, "Yellowstone Caldera Volcanic Power Generation Facility: A New Engineering Approach for Harvesting Emission-Free Green Volcanic Energy on a National Scale," *Renewable Energy*, no. 198 (October 2022): 415–425, https://doi.org/10.1016/j.renene.2022.08.063.

37. Daniel Wood, "Space-Based Solar Power," Energy.gov, March 6, 2014, https://www.energy.gov/articles/space-based-solar-power.

38. Quoted in Scott Snowden, "Solar Power Stations in Space Could Supply the World with Limitless Energy," *Forbes*, March 12, 2019, https://www.forbes.com/sites/scottsnowden/2019/03/12/solar-power-stations-in-space-could-supply-the-world-with-limitless-energy/?sh=2e4dc31a4386.

39. "Space: The Dawn of a New Age," Citi GPS: Global Perspectives and Solutions, May 11, 2022, https://icg.citi.com/icghome/what-we-think/citigps/insights/space_20220509.

40. Quoted in Nick Paton Walsh, "A Solar Panel in Space Is Collecting Energy That Could One Day Be Beamed to Anywhere on Earth," CNN, February 23, 2021, https://www.cnn.com/2021/02/23/americas/space-solar-energy-pentagon-science-scn-intl/index.html.

41. Kathy Svitil, "Caltech Announces Breakthrough $100 Million Gift to Fund Space-Based Solar Power Project," *Caltech News*, August 3, 2021, https://www.caltech.edu/about/news/caltech-announces-breakthrough-100-million-gift-to-fund-space-based-solar-power-project.

42. Kirsty Needham, "Plans for First Chinese Solar Power Station in Space Revealed," *Sydney Morning Herald*, February 15, 2019, https://www.smh.com.au/world/asia/plans-for-first-chinese-solar-power-station-in-space-revealed-20190214-p50xtg.html.

43. My conversation with Ali Hajimiri: "Faster, Please—The Podcast #1," *Faster, Please!* (newsletter), July 7, 2022, https://fasterplease.substack.com/p/-faster-please-the-podcast-1.

44. Adrienne Mayor, *Gods and Robots: Myths, Machines, and Ancient Dreams of Technology* (Princeton, NJ: Princeton University Press, 2018).

45. Isaac Asimov, "Visit to the World's Fair of 2014," *New York Times*, August 16, 1964, https://archive.nytimes.com/www.nytimes.com/books/97/03/23/lifetimes/asi-v-fair.html.

46. Bob Tita, "Robots Pick Up More Work at Busy Factories," *Wall Street Journal*, May 29, 2022, https://www.wsj.com/articles/robots-pick-up-more-work-at-busy-factories-11653822002.

47. Ibid.

48. Dave Lee, "Amazon Debuts New Warehouse Robot That Can Do Human Jobs," *Financial Times*, November 10, 2022, https://www.ft.com/content/c8933d73-74a4-43ff-8060-7ff9402eccf1.

49. Jason Douglas, "China's Factories Accelerate Robotics Push as Workforce Shrinks," *Wall Street Journal*, September 18, 2022, https://www.wsj.com/articles/chinas-factories-accelerate-robotics-push-as-workforce-shrinks-11663493405.

50. Ibid.

51. Jacqueline Du et al., "Global Automation: The Investment Case for Humanoid Robots," Goldman Sachs Research, November 2, 2022.

52. David S. F. Portree, "Five Options for NASA's (Lunar) Future (1970)," *Wired*, September 5, 2012, https://www.wired.com/2012/09/five-options-for-nasas-future-1970.

53. Mark R. Whittington, "NASA's Forgotten Plan to Land People on Mars in the 1980s," *The Hill*, July 26, 2019, https://thehill.com/opiniontechnology/454795-nasas-forgotten-plan-to-land-people-on-mars-in-the-1980s.

54. "Space," Citi GPS.

55. My conversation with Lori Garver: "Faster, Please!—The Podcast #5," *Faster, Please!* (newsletter), August 11, 2022, https://fasterplease.substack.com/p/-faster-please-the-podcast-5.

56. "Space," Citi GPS.

57. Ibid.

58. Joey Roulette, "What Is Starship? SpaceX Builds Its Next-Generation Rocket," *New York Times*, February 11, 2022, https://www.nytimes.com/article/elon-musk-starship.html.

59. Ashlee Vance, "Drugs in Orbit: One Startup's Big Idea for Microgravity," *Bloomberg*, March 15, 2023, https://www.bloomberg.com/news/articles/2023-03-15/satellite-startup-varda-eyes-drug-development-process.

60. Paul Voosen, "NASA Lays Out Vision for Robotic Mars Exploration," *Science*, March 29, 2023, https://www.science.org/content/article/nasa-lays-out-vision-robotic-mars-exploration.

61. Rina Torchinsky, "Elon Musk Hints at a Crewed Mission to Mars in 2029," *NPR*, March 17, 2022, https://www.npr.org/2022/03/17/1087167893/elon-musk-mars-2029.

Eleven: Eleven Ways to Build an Up Wing Economy

1. Cesar Hidalgo, *Why Information Grows: The Evolution of Order, from Atoms to Economies* (New York: Basic Books, 2015), 11–26, Kindle.

2. My conversation with Cesar Hidalgo: "A Long-Read Q&A with Cesar Hidalgo, Author of *Why Information Grows*," *AEIdeas* (blog), July 31, 2018, https://www.aei.org/economics/a-long-read-qa-with-cesar-hidalgo-author-of-why-information-grows.

3. Hidalgo, *Why Information Grows*, 45.

4. Hidalgo, *Why Information Grows*, introduction.

5. James S. A. Corey, *Leviathan Wakes (The Expanse Book 1)* (London: Orbit, 2011), 19, Kindle.

6. Donald J. Trump (@realDonaldTrump), "For all of the money we are spending," Twitter, June 7, 2019, 1:38 p.m., https://twitter.com/realDonaldTrump/status/1137051097955102720.

7. Quoted in Kimberly Adams and Sasha Fernandez, "Among the Goals of Artemis I: Launching the Lunar Economy," *MarketPlace*, September 1, 2022, https://www.marketplace.org/shows/marketplace-tech/among-the-goals-of-artemis-i-launching-the-lunar-economy.

8. Kevin Cannon, "Steelmanning Helium-3," *Planetary Intelligence* (newsletter), December 6, 2022, https://planetaryintel.substack.com/p/steelmanning-helium-3.

9. Eric Berger, "Blue Origin Makes a Big Lunar Announcement without Any Fanfare," *Ars Technica*, February 13, 2023, https://arstechnica.com/science/2023/02/blue-origin-makes-a-big-lunar-announcement-without-any-fanfare/.

10. My conversation with Kevin Cannon: "Faster, Please!—The Podcast #19," *Faster, Please!* (newsletter), January 26, 2023, https://fasterplease.substack.com/faster-please-the-podcast-19.

11. Ibid.

12. Paddy Hirsch, "They Made a Material That Doesn't Exist on Earth. That's Only the Start of the Story," *Planet Money*, NPR, November 8, 2022, https://www.npr.org/sections/money/2022/11/08/1134461777/they-made-a-material-that-doesnt-exist-on-earth-thats-only-the-start-of-the-stor.

13. Sandra Sobieraj, "Clinton Issues 'Hands Off' Policy on Internet Commerce," *New York Times*, July 2, 1997, https://archive.nytimes.com/www.nytimes.com/library/cyber/week/070297commerce.html.

14. Pedro Domingos (@pmddomingos), "In the 70s the big scare was overpopulation…," Twitter, March 30, 2023, 8:55 p.m., https://twitter.com/pmddomingos/status/1641605059808219138.

15. Adam Thierer, "Getting AI Innovation Culture Right," R Street Policy Study no. 281 (March 2023), https://www.rstreet.org/research/getting-ai-innovation-culture-right/.

16. "'Godfather of Artificial Intelligence' Weighs in on the Past and Potential of AI," *CBS Mornings*, March 25, 2023, https://www.cbsnews.com/news/godfather-of-artificial-intelligence-weighs-in-on-the-past-and-potential-of-artificial-intelligence/.

17. American Association for the Advancement of Science, "Federal R&D Budget Dashboard."

18. Benjamin F. Jones, "Science and Innovation: The Under-Fueled Engine of Prosperity," Aspen Institute, July 14, 2021, https://www.kellogg.northwestern.edu/faculty/jones-ben/htm/Science%20and%20Innovation%20_%20Underfueled%20Engine%20of%20Prosperity.pdf.

19. For a discussion of the roots of GPS, see ibid.

20. Jones, "Science and Innovation: The Under-Fueled Engine of Prosperity."

21. Erica York et al., "10 Tax Reforms for Growth and Opportunity," February 22, 2022, Tax Foundation, https://taxfoundation.org/economic-growth-opportunity-tax-reforms.

22. U.S. Department of Energy, "U.S. Department of Energy Announces Up to $10 Million to Study Low-Energy Nuclear Reactions," *New Energy Times*, September 13, 2022, https://news.newenergytimes.net/2022/09/15/u-s-department-of-energy-announces-up-to-10-million-to-study-low-energy-nuclear-reactions.

23. Kelsey Piper, "Science Funding Is a Mess. Could Grant Lotteries Make It Better?," *Vox*, January 18, 2019, https://www.vox.com/future-perfect/2019/1/18/18183939/science-funding-grant-lotteries-research.

24. "How to Escape Scientific Stagnation," *Economist*, October 26, 2022, https://www.economist.com/finance-and-economics/2022/10/26/how-to-escape-scientific-stagnation.

25. Adin Richards, "The Case for AgARDA," Institute for Progress, February 28, 2023, https://progress.institute/the-case-for-agarda/.

26. Helen Branswell, "'Against All Odds': The Inside Story of How Scientists across Three Continents Produced an Ebola Vaccine," *STAT*, January 7, 2020, https://www.statnews.com/2020/01/07/inside-story-scientists-produced-world-first-ebola-vaccine.

27. Rachel Silverman, "A Rallying Cry for More US Health Innovation at 'Warp Speed,'" Center for Global Development, November 28, 2022, https://www.cgdev.org/blog/rallying-cry-more-us-health-innovation-warp-speed.

28. My conversation with Alec Stapp: "5 Quick Questions for…Alec Stapp on Accelerating Progress through Public Policy," *Faster, Please!* (newsletter), April 4, 2022, https://fasterplease.substack.com/i/51584516/quick-questions-for-alec-stapp-on-accelerating-progress-through-public-policy.

29. Brian Potter, Arnab Datta, and Alec Stapp, "How to Stop Environmental Review from Harming the Environment," Institute for Progress, September 13, 2022, https://progress.institute/environmental-review.

30. Eli Dourado, "Bringing NEPA Back to Basics," Center for Growth and Opportunity, March 2023, https://www.thecgo.org/wp-content/uploads/2023/03/Bringing-NEPA-Back-to-Basics-v1.pdf.

31. Eli Dourado, "Congress Should Legalize Supersonic Flight," Center for Growth and Opportunity at Utah State University, January 18, 2023, https://www.thecgo.org/benchmark/congress-should-legalize-supersonic-flight/.

32. Kevin R. James, Akshay Kotak, and Dimitrios P. Tsomocos, "Ideas, Idea Processing, and TFP Growth in the US: 1899 to 2019," SSRN (July 13, 2022), https://ssrn.com/abstract=4161964.

33. Jerry Zhirong Zhao, Camila Fonseca-Sarmiento, and Jie Tan, "America's Trillion-Dollar Repair Bill: Capital Budgeting and the Disclosure of State Infrastructure Needs," Volcker Alliance, November 2019, https://www.volckeralliance.org/sites/default/files/attachments/Americas%20Trillion-Dollar%20Repair%20Bill%20-%20Capital%20Budgeting%20and%20the%20Disclosure%20of%20State%20Infrastructure%20Needs.pdf.

34. Alon Levy, "High-Speed Rail Followup," *Pedestrian Observations*, March 22, 2021, https://pedestrianobservations.com/2021/03/22/high-speed-rail-followup.

35. My conversation with César Hidalgo: "5 Quick Questions for…Physicist César Hidalgo on Economic Complexity," *Faster, Please!* (newsletter), August 30, 2022, https://fasterplease.substack.com/p/5-quick-questions-for-physicist-cesar.

36. Chang-Tai Hsieh and Enrico Moretti, "How Local Housing Regulations Smother the U.S. Economy," *New York Times*, September 6, 2017, https://www.nytimes.com/2017/09/06/opinion/housing-regulations-us-economy.html.

37. Chang-Tai Hsieh and Enrico Moretti, "Housing Constraints and Spatial Misallocation," *American Economic Journal: Macroeconomics* 11, no. 2 (2019): 1–39, https://doi.org/10.1257/mac.20170388.

38. Paul Emrath, "Government Regulation in the Price of a New Home: 2021," National Association of Home Builders, May 5, 2021, https://www.nahb.org/-/media/NAHB/news-and-economics/docs/housing-economics-plus/special-studies/2021/special-study-government-regulation-in-the-price-of-a-new-home-may-2021.pdf.

39. Austan Goolsbee and Chad Syverson, "The Strange and Awful Path of Productivity in the U.S. Construction Sector," National Bureau of Economic Research Working Paper no. 30845 (February 2023), 10.3386/w30845.

40. Jason M. Barr, "1,760 Acres. That's How Much More of Manhattan We Need," *New York Times*, January 14, 2022, https://www.nytimes.com/2022/01/14/opinion/eric-adams-manhattan-expand.html.

41. M. Nolan Gray (@mnolangray), "There should really be two, maybe three…," Twitter, April 3, 2022, 5:42 p.m., https://twitter.com/mnolangray/status/1510734607724937217.

42. Elaine Moore, "Dreams and Reality Collide in Praxis's Vision of a Utopian Crypto City," *Financial Times*, April 11, 2022, https://www.ft.com/content/f5844f5c-5961-478a-90d0-1dbea11ddf3d.

43. Tina Huang, Zachary Arnold, and Remco Zwetsloot, "Most of America's 'Most Promising' AI Startups Have Immigrant Founders," Center for Security and Emerging Technology Data Brief (October 2020), https://doi.org/10.51593/20200065.

44. "Science and Engineering Labor Force," National Center for Science and Engineering Statistics, https://ncses.nsf.gov/pubs/nsb20198/immigration-and-the-s-e-workforce.

45. Pierre Azoulay, et al., "Immigration and Entrepreneurship in the United States," National Bureau of Economic Research Working Paper no. 27778 (September 2020), https://www.nber.org/papers/w27778.

46. "Migration and the Economy," Citi GPS: Global Perspectives & Solutions, Citigroup and University of Oxford, September 2018.

47. Matthew Yglesias, "Too Much of America Is Emptying Out. More Immigration Can Help," *Bloomberg*, April 2, 2023, https://www.bloomberg.com/opinion/articles/2023-04-02/too-much-of-america-is-emptying-out-more-immigration-can-help.

48. Charles I. Jones, "The End of Economic Growth? Unintended Consequences of a DecliningPopulation," *American Economic Review* 112, no. 11 (November 2022), https://doi.org/10.1257/aer.20201605.

49. AJ Cortese, "The Chinese Talent Behind Your Favorite Generative AI Product," *Macro Polo*, April 4, 2023, https://macropolo.org/chinese-talent-generative-ai/.

50. Martina Prato, "The Global Race for Talent: Brain Drain, Knowledge Transfer, and Growth," Yale University, November 27, 2022, https://drive.google.com/file/d/1AdHMVfhKBpf2_gTxIRYBKlTBy8x6XvgH/view.; https://doi.org/10.1287/mnsc.2019.3388nes.

51. Caleb Watney, "The Egghead Gap," *New Atlantis*, Winter 2021, https://www.thenewatlantis.com/publications/the-egghead-gap.

52. "2023 Immigration Trends Report," Envoy Global, March 6, 2023, https://resources.envoyglobal.com/reports/2023-immigration-trends-report.

53. Chelsea Vail, "What Economists Think about Admitting Highly Skilled Immigrants," *Chicago Booth Review*, September 20, 2016, https://www.chicagobooth.edu/review/what-economists-think-about-admitting-highly-skilled-immigrants.

54. Alex Tabarrok, "The Extreme Shortage of High IQ Workers," *Marginal Revolution* (blog), January 9, 2023, https://marginalrevolution.com/marginalrevolution/2023/01/the-extreme-shortage-of-high-iq-workers.html.

55. "Industrial Tariffs," Office of the U.S. Trade Representative, https://ustr.gov/issue-areas/industry-manufacturing/industrial-tariffs.

56. Ibid.

57. Chad P. Bown, "US-China Trade War Tariffs: An Up-to-Date Chart," Peterson Institute for International Economics, April 22, 2022, https://www.piie.com/research/piie-charts/us-china-trade-war-tariffs-date-chart.

58. Scott C. Bradford, Paul L. E. Grieco, and Gary Clyde Hufbauer, "The Payoff to America from Global Integration," Peterson Institute for International Economics, January 1, 2005, https://www.piie.com/commentary/speeches-papers/payoff-america-global-integration.

59. John Van Reenen, "Innovation and Human Capital Policy," National Bureau of Economic Research Working Paper no. 28713 (April 2021), https://www.nber.org/papers/w28713.

60. Peter Q. Blair and Kent Smetters, "Why Don't Elite Colleges Expand Supply?" National Bureau of Economic Research Working Paper no. 29309 (September 2021), https://www.nber.org/papers/w29309.

61. Byron Auguste, Paul Kihn, and Matt Miller, "Closing the Talent Gap: Attracting and Retaining Top-Third Graduates to Careers in Teaching," McKinsey & Co., September 2010, https://www.mckinsey.com/~/media/mckinsey/industriespublic%20and%20social%20sector

/our%20insights/closing%20the%20teaching%20talent%20gap/closing-the-teaching-talent-gap.pdf.

62. Eric A. Hanushek, Marc Piopiunik, and Simon Wiederhold, "The Value of Smarter Teachers: International Evidence on Teacher Cognitive Skills and Student Performance," National Bureau of Economic Research Working Paper no. 2072 (March 2018), https://www.nber.org/papers/w20727.

63. Andrew J. Morgan, et al., "Attracting and Retaining Highly Effective Educators in Hard-to-Staff Schools," National Bureau of Economic Research Working Paper no. 31051 (March 2023), https://www.nber.org/papers/w31051.

64. My conversation with Eric Hanushek: "What's Wrong with American Education? A Long-Read Q&A with Eric Hanushek," *AEIdeas* (blog), May 11, 2018, https://www.aei.org/economics/whats-wrong-with-american-education-a-long-read-qa-with-eric-hanushek.

65. Eric A. Hanushek, "Valuing Teachers: How Much Is a Good Teacher Worth?," *Education Next* 11, no. 3 (Summer 2011): 40–45, http://hanushek.stanford.edu/publications/valuing-teachers-how-much-good-teacher-worth.

66. Edmund S. Phelps, *Mass Flourishing* (Princeton, NJ: Princeton University Press), 324, Kindle.

67. Peter Cauwels and Dider Sornette, "Are 'Flow of Ideas' and 'Research Productivity' in Secular Decline?," Swiss Finance Institute Research Paper (October 22, 2020), http://dx.doi.org/10.2139/ssrn.3716939.

68. William E. Geist, "Pondering the Year 2000 with Kahn, Haig & Co.," *New York Times*, October 2, 1982, https://www.nytimes.com/1982/10/02/nyregion/pondering-the-year-2000-with-kahn-haig-co.html.

69. James Pethokoukis, "Let's Add AP Progress to the High School Curriculum," *Faster, Please!* (newsletter), February 1, 2023, https://fasterplease.substack.com/p/lets-add-ap-progress-to-the-high.

70. Phelps, *Mass Flourishing*, 27.

71. Morris M. Kleiner and Ming Xu, "Occupational Licensing and Labor Market Fluidity," National Bureau of Economic Research Working Paper no. 27568 (July 2020), https://www.nber.org/papers/w27568.

72. Editorial, "Why Is It So Hard to Become a Cosmetologist in America?" *Bloomberg*, September 16, 2012, https://www.bloomberg.com/opinion/articles/2012-09-16/why-is-it-so-hard-to-become-a-cosmetologist-in-america-.

73. Timothy B. Lee, "Massachusetts Just Stole an Important Page from Silicon Valley's Playbook," *Vox*, July 1, 2016, https://www.vox.com/2016/4/12/11349248/noncompetes-silicon-valley-route-128.

74. Chris Marr, "FTC's Noncompete Ban Mirrors State Proposals before Scaling Back," Bloomberg Law, January 9, 2023, https://news.bloomberglaw.com/daily-labor-report/ftcs-noncompete-ban-mirrors-state-proposals-before-scaling-back.

75. "FTC Proposes Rule to Ban Noncompete Clauses, Which Hurt Workers and Harm Competition," Federal Trade Commission, January 5, 2023, https://www.ftc.gov/system/files/ftc_gov/pdf/noncompete_nprm_fact_sheet.pdf.

76. Anton Korinek and Megan Juelfs, "Preparing for the (Non-Existent?) Future of Work," National Bureau of Economic Research Working Paper no. 30172 (June 2022), https://www.nber.org/papers/w30172.

77. Interview with Michael Strain, April 2023.

78. Marcus Sakey, *Brilliance* (New York: Thomas & Mercer, 2013).

Twelve: How to Nurture an Up Wing Culture

1. New Scientist (@NewScientist), "Netflix's *Black Mirror* asks what happens when the technology…," Twitter, June 5, 2019, 3:09 p.m., https://twitter.com/newscientist/status/1136349369379229696.

2. David Deutsch (@DavidDeutschOxf), "Why isn't there a *White Mirror* show that guesses…," Twitter, October 23, 2022, 6:32 a.m., https://twitter.com/DavidDeutschOxf/status/1584130525106966528.

3. David Deutsch (@DavidDeutschOxf), "In a typical *Black Mirror* episode…," Twitter, October 25, 2022, 5:22 a.m., https://twitter.coDavidDeutschOxf/status/1584837868216020992.

4. Cited in Pessimists Archive (@PessimistsArc), "'Futuristic science fiction tends to be pessimistic…,'" Twitter, July 1, 2022, 3:29 p.m., https://twitter.com/PessimistsArc/status/1542953504716857344.

5. Andy Weir, *The Martian* (New York: Random House, 2014).

6. MovieQuotes, "*The Martian*—If you solve enough problems, you get to come home," YouTube video, December 31, 2021, 0:12, https://www.youtube.com/watch?v=xomL-V4gjCw.

7. "*Interstellar* (film)," Wikiquote, https://en.wikiquote.org/wiki/Interstellar_(film).

8. Philip Shabecoff, "Global Warming Has Begun, Expert Tells Senate," *New York Times*, June 24, 1988, https://www.nytimes.com/1988/06/24/us/global-warming-has-begun-expert-tells-senathtml.

9. Neal Stephenson, *Seveneves* (New York: William Morrow, 2015), 3, Kindle.

10. Bill Gates, "The Day the Moon Blew Up," *GatesNotes* (blog), May 17, 2016, https://www.gatesnotes.com/Books/Seveneves.

11. William Gibson, interview with David Naimon, *Between the Covers* (podcast), MP3 audio, November, 2014, 24:15, https://tinhouse.com/podcast/william-gibson-the-peripheral/.

12. Herman Kahn, "Current Western Cultural Trends," in *The Essential Herman Kahn: In Defense of Thinking*, ed. Paul Dragos Aligica and Kenneth R. Weinstein (Lanham MD: Lexington Books, 2009), chap. 22, Kindle.

13. Andrew M. Carton and Brian J. Lucas, "How Can Leaders Overcome the Blurry Vision Bias? Identifying an Antidote to the Paradox of Vision Communication," *Academy of Management Journal* 61, no. 6 (2018): 2106–2129, https://doi.org/10.5465/amj.2015.0375.

14. Lewis Beale, "Jeff Bezos' 'Favorite TV Show' Is Coming to Amazon. The Creators Say It's a Perfect Fit," *Los Angeles Times*, December 10, 2019, https://www.latimes.com/entertainment-arts/tv/story/2019-12-10/the-expanse-syfy-amazon-jeff-bezos.

15. Ibid.

16. The story of Neal Stephenson and Arizona State University is related in Neal Stephenson, "Neal Stephenson: Innovation Starvation," *Wired*, October 27, 2011, https://www.wired.com/2011/10/stephenson-innovation-starvation.

17. Quoted in Logan Booker, "Project Hieroglyph Could Be the Best Thing to Happen to Science Fiction in over 50 Years," *Gizmodo*, April 15, 2012, https://www.gizmodo.com.au/2012/04/project-hieroglyph-could-be-the-best-thing-to-happen-to-science-fiction-in-over-50-years/.

18. James L. Cambias, "Periapsis," in Finn and Cramer, eds., *Hieroglyph*, 283–305.

19. Gregory Benford, "The Man Who Sold the Stars," in Finn and Cramer, eds., *Hieroglyph*, 307–351.

20. Neal Stephenson, "Atmosphæra Incognita," in Finn and Cramer, eds., *Hieroglyph*, 1–37.

21. Olympics, "The Complete London 2012 Opening Ceremony | London 2012 Olympic Games," YouTube video, streamed live on Jul 27, 2012, 3:59:49, https://www.youtube.com/watch?v=4As0e4de-rI.

22. "Danny Boyle Explains His Vision of a 'Green and Gracious' Land," *Yorkshire Post*, July 28, 2012, https://www.yorkshirepost.co.uk/news/danny-boyle-explains-his-vision-green-and-gracious-land-1894657.

23. William E. Schmidt, "The Desolate Legacy of Knoxville's World's Fair," *New York Times*, May 18, 1984, https://www.nytimes.com/1984/05/18/us/the-desolate-legacy-of-knoxville-s-world-s-fair.html; Wayne King, "Failed Fair Gives New Orleans a Painful Hangover," *New York Times*, November 12, 1984, https://www.nytimes.com/1984/11/12/us/failed-fair-gives-new-orleans-a-painful-hangover.html; "Bart on the Road," *The Simpsons*, season 7, episode 20, directed by Swinton O. Scott III, written by Richard Appel, aired March 31, 1996.

24. Georgi Kantchev, "World Expositions Can Benefit or Haunt Host Cities," *New York Times*, August 25, 2013, https://www.nytimes.com/2013/08/26/technology/getting-a-seat-at-the-global-table-for-a-price.html.

25. Jennifer Hansler, "These Are the Bills Trump Signed into Law in his First Year as President," CNN, January 20, 2018, https://www.cnn.com/2017/06/29/politics/president-trump-legislation/index.html.

26. U.S. Department of State, "How World's Fairs and Trade Expos Brought You the Future," YouTube video, October 4, 2018, 56:45, https://www.youtube.com/watch?v=sfwECS-HjbI; Charles Pappas, *Flying Cars, Zombie Dogs, and Robot Overlords: How World's Fairs and Trade Expos Changed the World* (Guilford, CT: Lyons Press, 2017), Kindle.

27. My email conversation with Cameron Wiese, "5 Quick Questions for…Cameron Wiese, Advocate for a New World's Fair," *Faster, Please!* (newsletter), May 9, 2022, https://fasterplease.substack.com/i/54064635/quick-questions-for-cameron-wiese-advocate-for-a-new-worldsfair.

28. Cameron Wiese, "It's Time to Build: A New World's Fair," personal blog, https://www.cameronwiese.com/blog/worlds-fair.

29. The role of the U.S. space program is discussed at Charles Fishman, *One Giant Leap: The Impossible Mission That Flew Us to the Moon* (New York: Simon & Schuster, 2019), 301–305, Kindle.

30. Fishman, "How NASA Gave Birth to Modern Computing."

31. Ayn Rand, *The Voice of Reason: Essays in Objectivist Thought by Ayn Rand* (New York: New American Library, 1990), chap. 17.

32. "Audacious & Outrageous: Space Elevators," NASA, September 7, 2000, https://science.nasa.gov/science-news/science-at-nasa/2000/ast07sep_1.

33. Morgan McFall-Johnsen, "A Giant Elevator Could Connect Earth to Space Using Current Technology, Experts Say—Here's How That Might Work," *Business Insider*, October 6, 2019, https://www.businessinsider.com/space-elevator-on-earth-moon-2019-9.

34. "Space Elevator," *KimStanleyRobinson.info*, https://www.kimstanleyrobinson.info/content/space-elevator.

35. Ibid.

36. Arthur C. Clarke, *The Fountains of Paradise* (New York: Ballantine Books, 1979), 54.

37. "The Space Elevator Will Be Built about 50 Years after Everyone Stops Laughing," *Quote Investigator*, June 9, 2017, https://quoteinvestigator.com/2017/06/09/elevator.

38. Scott Snowden, "A Colossal Elevator to Space Could Be Going Up Sooner Than You Ever Imagined," *NBC News*, October 2, 2018, https://www.nbcnews.com/mach/science/colossal-elevator-space-could-be-going-sooner-you-ever-imagined-ncna915421.

39. Stephen Cohen, "Space Elevators Are Less Sci-Fi Than You Think," *Scientific American*, November 25, 2022, https://www.scientificamerican.com/article/space-elevators-are-less-sci-fi-than-you-think.

40. Eric Berger (@SciGuySpace), "Funny story on this. Robert Rose…," Twitter, March 17, 2023, 2:34 p.m., https://twitter.com/SciGuySpace/status/1636798209346371602.

41. Cohen, "Space Elevators Are Less Sci-Fi Than You Think."

42. "Lunar Crater Radio Telescope: Illuminating the Cosmic Dark Ages," Jet Propulsion Laboratory, May 5, 2021, https://www.jpl.nasa.gov/news/lunar-crater-radio-telescope-illuminating-the-cosmic-dark-ages.

43. Nancy Atkinson, "Just Four Robots Could Deploy a Huge Radio Telescope on the Far Side of the Moon," *Universe Today*, November 2, 2022, https://www.universetoday.com/158409/just-four-robots-could-deploy-a-huge-radio-telescope-on-the-far-side-of-the-moon.

44. Breakthrough Starshot, https://breakthroughinitiatives.org/initiative/3.

45. John Mecklin, ed., "At Doom's Doorstep: It Is 100 Seconds to Midnight," Bulletin of the Atomic Scientists, January 20, 2022, https://thebulletin.org/doomsday-clock/current-time.

46. "The Doomsday Clock: A Timeline of Conflict, Culture, and Change," Bulletin of the Atomic Scientists, https://thebulletin.org/doomsday-clock/timeline.

47. Elizabeth Kolbert, "The Day Nuclear War Almost Broke Out," *New Yorker*, October 5, 2020, https://www.newyorker.com/magazine/2020/10/12/the-day-nuclear-war-almost-broke-out.

48. Quoted at Brian Eno, "The Big Here and Long Now," Long Now Foundation, January 15, 1995, https://longnow.org/essays/big-here-and-long-now.

49. "Project Genesis," *Memory Alpha*, https://memory-alpha.fandom.com/wiki/Project_Genesis.

Thirteen: Why an Up Wing Future Can Happen—and Why It Might Not

1. Jim Tankersley and Scott Clement, "The Crazy Logic behind an Alliance of Trump-Sanders Supporters," *Washington Post*, March 30, 2016, https://www.washingtonpost.com/news/wonk/wp/2016/03/30/the-crazy-logic-behind-an-alliance-of-trump-sanders-supporters.

2. Danielle Kurtzleben, "Here's How Many Bernie Sanders Supporters Ultimately Voted For Trump," *NPR*, August 24, 2017, https://www.npr.org/2017/08/24/545812242/1-in-10-sanders-primary-voters-ended-up-supporting-trump-survey-finds.

3. Ross Douthat, "How the Right Became the Left and the Left Became the Right," *New York Times*, November 2, 2022, https://www.nytimes.com/2022/11/02/opinion/left-right-reversal.html.

4. Steve Fuller, "The Future of Ideological Conflict," *Project Syndicate*, May 7, 2012, https://www.project-syndicate.org/commentary/the-future-of-ideological-conflict-2012-05.

5. William Clinton, State of the Union Address (speech), Washington, DC, January 23, 1996, https://clintonwhitehouse4.archives.gov/WH/New/other/sotu.html.

6. Mari Yamaguchi, "Japan Adopts Plan to Maximize Nuclear Energy," *AP News*, December 22, 2022, https://apnews.com/article/russia-ukraine-business-japan-climate-and-environment-02d0b9dfecc8cdc197d217b3029c5898.

7. Quoted in Michael Lee, "Greta Thunberg Reverses Course on Nuclear Power, Argues Germany Is Making a Mistake by Taking Plants Offline," *Fox News*, October 12, 2022, https://www.foxnews.com/world/greta-thunberg-reverses-course-nuclear-power-argues-germany-making-mistake-taking-plants-offline.

8. Quoted in Catherine Clifford, "Why Silicon Valley Is So Hot on Nuclear Energy and What It Means for the Industry," *CNBC*, December 2, 2022, https://www.cnbc.com/2022/12/02/why-silicon-valley-is-so-hot-on-nuclear-energy.html.

9. Ari Natter, Jennifer A. Dlouhy, and Will Wade, "Biden to Vow Cutting U.S. Climate-Warming Emissions in Half," *Bloomberg*, April 20, 2021, https://www.bloomberg.com/news/articles/2021-04-20/white-house-to-pledge-cutting-global-warming-emissions-in-half.

10. Ezra Klein, "The Economic Mistake the Left Is Finally Confronting," *New York Times*, September 19, 2021, https://www.nytimes.com/2021/09/19/opinion/supply-side-progressivism.html.

11. Eric Boehm, "It Took 15 Years for the Feds to Approve a 700-Mile Electric Line," *Reason*, April 17, 2023, https://reason.com/2023/04/17/it-took-15-years-for-the-feds-to-approve-a-700-mile-electric-line/.

12. Klein, "The Economic Mistake the Left Is Finally Confronting."

13. My conversation with Derek Thompson: "Doomsday Economics: What If Someone Explodes a Nuclear Bomb?" *Faster, Please!* (newsletter), January 21, 2022, https://fasterplease.substack.com/p/-doomsday-economics-what-if-someone.

14. Quoted in Sophia Bollag, "'NIMBYism Is Destroying the State.' Gavin Newsom Ups Pressure on Cities to Build More Housing," *San Francisco Chronicle*, May 22, 2022, https://www.sfchronicle.com/politics/article/newsom-housing-17188515.php.

15. James Fallows, "The Phenomenal 'Chinese Professor' Ad," *The Atlantic*, October 21, 2010, https://www.theatlantic.com/politics/archive/2010/10/the-phenomenal-chinese-professor-ad/64982.

16. "Fiscal Data," U.S. Treasury Department, https://fiscaldata.treasury.gov/americas-finance-guide/national-deficit/#us-deficit-by-year.

17. PoliticalHistory, "1960—Nixon on Civil Rights," YouTube video, June 29, 2008, 0:58, https://www.youtube.com/watch?v=dAlZHfaksQM&t=3s.

18. Joe Biden, "Remarks by President Biden in State of the Union Address," March 1, 2022, https://www.whitehouse.gov/briefing-room/speeches-remarks/2022/03/02/remarks-by-president-biden-in-state-of-the-union-address.

19. Eric Schmidt, "Innovation Power," *Foreign Affairs*, February 28, 2023, https://www.foreignaffairs.com/united-states/eric-schmidt-innovation-power-technology-geopolitics.

20. My conversation with Erik Brynjolfsson: "Is AI finally ready to supercharge the US economy?," *Faster, Please!* (newsletter), March 17, 2022, https://fasterplease.substack.com/p/-is-ai-finally-ready-to-supercharge?s=w.

21. Joseph A. Schumpeter, *Capitalism, Socialism, and Democracy* (London: Taylor & Francis, 2003), 146, Kindle.

22. Herman Kahn, *The Coming Boom* (New York: Simon & Schuster, 1983), 31.

23. My conversation with Tyler Cowen: "America's Complacency Problem: A Brief Q&A with Tyler Cowen," *AEIdeas* (blog), April 10, 2017, https://www.aei.org/economics/americas-complacency-problem-a-brief-qa-with-tyler-cowen.

24. "Artificial Index Report 2023," Stanford HAI, April 2023, 324, https://aiindex.stanford.edu/report/.

25. Carl Bialik and Taylor Orth, "AI Doomsday Worries Many Americans. So Does Apocalypse from Climate Change, Nukes, War, and More," *YouGovAmerica*, April 14, 2023, https://docs.cdn.yougov.com/bfoyxp7p28/results_AI%20and%20the%20End%20of%20Humanity.pdf.

26. My conversation with Robin Hanson: "Faster, Please—The Podcast #6," *Faster, Please!* (newsletter), August 18, 2022, https://fasterplease.substack.com/p/-faster-please-the-podcast-6.

27. Quoted in Jeremy Beaman, "Future of Nuclear Power at Risk with War Near Ukrainian Plants, UN Official Warns," *Washington Examiner*, October 25, 2022, https://www.washingtonexaminer.com/policy/energy-environment/nuclear-social-license-avoid-accident-in-ukraine-grossi-says.

28. Steve Cohen, "Ukraine Demonstrates the Problem with Nuclear Power," *State of the Planet*, March 14, 2022, https://news.climate.columbia.edu/2022/03/14/ukraine-demonstrates-the-problem-with-nuclear-power/.

29. Quoted in Chris Heath, "How Elon Musk Plans on Reinventing the World (and Mars)," *GQ*, December 12, 2015, https://www.gq.com/story/elon-musk-mars-spacex-tesla-interview.

30. Cited in "China's Future Economic Potential Hinges on Its Productivity," *The Economist*, August 14, 2021, https://www.economist.com/briefing/2021/08/14/chinas-future-economic-potential-hinges-on-its-productivity.

31. Loren Brandt et al., "China's Productivity Slowdown and Future Growth Potential," World Bank Working Paper no. 9298 (June 2020), http://hdl.handle.net/10986/33993.

32. J. Stewart Black and Allen J. Morrison, "Can China Avoid a Growth Crisis?" *Harvard Business Review*, September–October 2019, https://hbr.org/2019/09/can-china-avoid-a-growth-crisis.

33. Lee G. Branstetter, Guangwei Li, and Mengjia Ren, "Picking Winners? Government Subsidies and Firm Productivity in China," National Bureau of Economic Research Working Paper no. 30699 (December 20220), https://www.nber.org/papers/w30699.

34. Scott Kennedy, "Made in China 2025," June 1, 2015, https://www.csis.org/analysis/made-china-2025.

35. "Fact Sheet: CHIPS and Science Act Will Lower Costs, Create Jobs, Strengthen Supply Chains, and Counter China," White House, August 9, 2022, https://www.whitehouse.gov/briefing-room/statements-releases/2022/08/09/fact-sheet-chips-and-science-act-will-lower-costs-create-jobs-strengthen-supply-chains-and-counter-china.

Conclusion: 2076, the American Tricentennial

1. "The Tricentennial Report: Letters from America," Atlantic Richfield Company, 1977.
2. Ibid., 6–7.

3. Ibid., 35.
4. Ibid., 5.
5. Ibid., 65.
6. Ibid., 70.
7. Ibid., 71–73.
8. Ibid., 76.
9. Ibid., 67.
10. Friedrich von Hayek, "The Pretence of Knowledge," Lecture to the Memory of Alfred Nobel, December 11, 1974, https://www.nobelprize.org/prizes/economic-sciences/1974/hayek/lecture/.
11. "Breakthrough Science Roadmap," Prime Movers Lab, https://www.primemoverslab.com/roadmap.
12. "Development of Universal Flu Vaccine," *Metaculus*, https://www.metaculus.com/questions/4791/when-will-a-universal-flu-vaccine-be-available.
13. "Date First Human Lands on Mars," *Metaculus*, https://www.metaculus.com/questions/3515/when-will-the-first-humans-land-successfully-on-mars.
14. "Date of First Tourist Landing on Mars," *Metaculus*, https://www.metaculus.com/questions/10218/date-of-first-tourist-landing-on-mars.
15. "Date of Revival of Wooly Mammoth," *Metaculus*, https://www.metaculus.com/questions/6499/when-will-the-mammoth-be-revived.
16. "Nuclear Fusion Power > 10% of Global Energy," *Metaculus*, https://www.metaculus.com/questions/9465/nuclear-fusion-power-10-of-global-energy.
17. "US Labor Force Participation Rate below 10%," *Metaculus*, https://www.metaculus.com/questions/8480/us-labor-force-participation-rate-below-10.
18. "Mars GDP Exceeds Earth's," *Metaculus*, https://www.metaculus.com/questions/5506/mars-gdp-exceeds-earths.

INDEX

Index

ABOUT THE AUTHOR

JAMES PETHOKOUKIS is a policy analyst and the Dewitt Wallace Fellow at the American Enterprise Institute, where he also writes and edits the AEIdeas blog and writes the *Faster, Please!* newsletter. In addition, he is an official contributor to CNBC television. A graduate of Northwestern University and the Medill School of Journalism, Pethokoukis is a 2002 *Jeopardy!* champion. Before joining AEI, he was the Washington columnist for *Reuters Breakingviews,* the opinion and commentary wing of Thomson Reuters, and the business editor and economics columnist for *U.S. News & World Report.*

CW01020550

Raymond A. Dart

Skill and Poise

Raymond Arthur Dart (1893–1988) was an Australian-born South African anatomist and anthropologist. He graduated in medicine at Sydney in 1917, and became Professor of Anatomy at Witwatersrand University in Johannesburg in 1923. As Dean of the Faculty of Medicine he played a leading role in the establishment and continued development of medical training facilities.

Dart's international fame as a scientist came in 1925 with his description of the Taung skull of a fossil child which he recognized as a human ancestor. He described the discovery and interpretation of *Australopithecus africanus* in his best known work, *Adventures with the Missing Link* (1959). His theory that human evolution has not been a single progressive sequence and that bipedalism preceded brain expansion has since been well corroborated.

Dart's interest in the evolution and maintenance of bipedalism, both neurologically and physically, was further stimulated by lessons in the F. M. Alexander Technique from 1943 onwards. Several articles on the subject of skill and poise and the Alexander Technique, informed by his broad practical and anatomical knowledge, were written in 1946–47.

Dart retired in 1958 but continued to lecture, write and research. The Institute for the Study of Man in Africa was founded in his honour, conferring an honorary Doctorate of Science upon him in 1964 on the occasion of the first Raymond Dart Annual Lecture. In 1966 Dart was appointed to the United Steel Workers Chair of Anthropology at the Avery Post Graduate Institute of the Institutes for the Achievement of Human Potential, Philadelphia.

Raymond A. Dart

Skill and Poise

STAT Books

Published February 1996 by

STAT❧Books

The books division of
The Society of Teachers of the Alexander Technique
266 Fulham Road
London SW10 9EL
England

ISBN 0-9519304-5-1 Hardback

British Library Cataloguing-in-Publication Data
A catalogue record for this book is available from the British Library

The greatest care has been taken to ensure that the information presented in this book is correct. However, no responsibility can be accepted for the accuracy of the information presented. Where opinion is expressed it is that of the author and does not necessarily coincide with the editorial views of STAT Books or of the Society of Teachers of the Alexander Technique.

Line drawings by Delia Hardy
Captions by Alexander Murray and Delia Hardy
Glossary by Jean M. O. Fischer
Photoset in 12/14 Monotype Bembo
Design and layout in Adobe PageMaker 5.0 by Jean M. O. Fischer

Printed on 90 gsm Matt Coated Cartridge
and bound in Wibalin by
The Bath Press, Avon

2 4 6 8 10 9 7 5 3 1

Contents

List of illustrations

Figures

Introduction

Just over three years have passed since the publication of *Skill and Poise*, a desk-top, limited edition (100 copies) of the writings of Raymond Dart. As I explained at the time, the project had been a quarter of a century in incubation.

In the summer of 1967, my wife and I returned to London after our first term in residence at Michigan State University. During our daily visits to Walter Carrington, stimulated by an article by Frank Pierce Jones, I was discussing the rôle of the jaw in head balance, observing that the centre of gravity of the head could not be independent of the relative position of the upper and lower jaw. Walter asked if I had been reading Dart. The only writing of Dart of which I had knowledge at that time was *Adventures with the Missing Link*. Walter searched his files and produced "The Postural Aspect of Malocclusion" which so intrigued me that I copied it out by hand.

As luck would have it, Professor Dart was travelling from South Africa to Philadelphia by way of London, and we had a long telephone conversation, the upshot of which was that we returned to Michigan with a stopover in Philadelphia where we were guests of Kitty Wielopolska. We visited Dart at the Institutes for the Achievement of Human Potential where he had been appointed to the Chair of Anthropology, and we spent two stimulating days in his company.

I was astonished to hear that none of his South African colleagues had discussed his paper with him, as we had found it both fascinating and useful in a practical way. Our demonstration in which we connected his writing with what we then understood of the Alexander Technique intrigued him. He then showed us what he considered the most important stage of the developmental sequence, the fœtal, which he he had failed to describe (perhaps because it was so obvious to him).

We left the Institutes with an invitation to return early in 1968 for an Intensive Orientation Course of a week's duration. In the interim, with the help of Dart's secretary, Sara Russock, and the use of the University Library, I had begun a collection of Dart's papers. By 1970 I had accumulated a considerable number, centering around the evolution and development of skill. Dr Carl Delacato, co-founder of the Institutes, became aware of the breadth of Dart's interests and requested copies of the papers I had unearthed. He suggested that Dart should republish them. (Three of them appeared in the Journal of the Institutes.) Delacato persuaded his own publishers, Thomas of Illinois, to publish an anthology of Dart's writings. Dart was too busy to undertake such a project and asked me to do so.

With encouragement from the Head of the School of Music and a grant from Michigan State University I was able to visit Professor Dart in Johannesburg in 1971, by which time the 'procedures' had taken shape in my mind and in the sketch books of Pam Hartman, a student at Walter Carrington's training course. I returned to the University fired with enthusiasm to spread the ramifications of Alexander's discoveries as seen through the eyes of this visionary anthropologist.

When I had assembled a representative collection of papers I sent an outline to the publishers. Their reaction was negative. They expected a book on Dart's ideas and did not consider republished papers to be marketable. (This in spite of the fact that they had successfully published and marketed reprints of the papers of Temple Fay, a Philadelphia neurosurgeon on whose work the Institutes was founded.)

Initial disappointment gave way to relief, as I had begun to realise the work involved and was already wearing two hats—Professor of Music and Alexander Technique teacher.

Not long after, we returned to Europe to an appointment at the Royal Dutch Conservatory in the Hague. We had by this time integrated many of Dart's ideas into our teaching and corresponded with him on a wide range of related subjects.

In 1977 we returned to the USA where I was appointed to a Professorship at the University of Illinois and again visited the Institutes. We were intrigued to see the way in which Dart's ideas had filtered into the daily routine.

When Centerline Press began publication of Alexander Technique material in 1984, it evinced interest in publishing Dart but could not undertake the work involved in preparing the papers for the press. It nevertheless published four articles in a small booklet, entitled *Skill, Poise, and the Alexander Technique* (which soon went out of print).

In 1992, with the development of 'desk-top publishing' and due to the skills of a number of our Alexander students (we began a Teachers' Training Course in 1978) it became feasible to publish the collection ourselves. This we did to commemorate the centenary of Dart's birth (1893) and presented the book at the NASTAT Annual General Meeting in Chicago, 1992. Our limited printing was soon sold out and we were unable to undertake a second edition due to pressure of work and, of course, unavailability of time and money.

We tried to interest the Illinois University Press but the book did not fit any available category. Witwatersrand University Press was interested, thanks to Professor Tobias, Dart's student, friend and successor, but could not follow through. When Jean Fischer of STAT Books said he would like to make a shortened form available we were both pleased and relieved. His qualities as an editor will be apparent to anyone who compares our amateur production with his consummately professional one. Our only regret is that he was unable to include all the articles of the centenary collection. Perhaps these will be published at a later date.

Many years spent following the highways and byways of Raymond Dart's life and work have reinforced my initial impression of its importance to those of us who wish to consider Alexander's legacy in the broadest possible context. Both men were far ahead of their time and both applied their findings to their personal development, practising what they preached and preaching what they practised. I hope this collection will encourage others to view the Alexander Technique from Dart's global perspective.

I am happy to announce that an extended biography of Professor Dart will soon be available, thanks to the hard work of two fellow-Australians, Frances Wheelhouse and Kay Smithford.

A comparison of the diagrams in the two books will show how much we owe to the skill and understanding of Delia Hardy, particularly in the developmental diagrams which, combined with the glossary provided by Jean Fischer, should enable the reader to follow Dart's remarkable train of thought with relative ease.

In conclusion, I would like to say what a debt of gratitude we owe to the community into which we were introduced by the work of F. M. Alexander. We are especially grateful to Irene Tasker, who introduced us directly to Walter Carrington and indirectly to Professor Dart. To Dart's patience, generosity of spirit, and genius, the book you hold in your hands is due.

Professor Alexander Murray
Urbana, USA.
November 1995

Publisher's Acknowledgements

Thanks to the editors at *Transvaal Educational News* for permission to reprint 'The Significance of Skill' and 'Teacher's Act of Dedication'; to *The Leech* for permission to reprint 'The Human Monthly Cycle'; to *British Journal of Physical Medicine* for permission to reprint 'The Voluntary Musculature of the Human Body'; to *South African Medicine* for 'The Attainment of Poise'; to *Journal of the Dental Association of South Africa* for 'The Postural Aspect of Malocclusion'; to *South African Journal of Physiotherapy* for 'Weightlessness'; to Alexander Murray for permission to include 'The Dart Procedures'; to Frances Wheelhouse for permission to reproduce a photo of Raymond Dart from her book, *Raymond Arthur Dart: A Pictorial Profile.*

1

The Significance of Skill

THE place of individual and socialized skill in all human affairs is coming to be realized gradually but very surely. The subject of skill is so vast that only the barest aspects of the matter can be discussed here. But it will be adequate to consider the general question and certain of its major implications, so that we may appreciate the increasing emphasis that should be placed on skill in education.

Man owes his place in Nature to his skill of body, hand and mind. His surpassing skill is due to certain accidents (or designs, according to our point of view) of Nature. She endowed him through his arboreal life with an agile body, stereoscopic vision and grasping hands and feet. Later by means of the terrestrial environment she gave him an elastic, fleet-footed and virtually erect body surmounted by a far-seeing brain. His hands, now liberated from the tree-climbing functions of the remoter past, were adapted to the business of hurling projectiles, wielding clubs, and fashioning intentionally-designed implements under the guidance of his improved brain.

Two significant facts emerge from this brief retrospect of the evolutionary story. The first is that human skill is merely an advance upon the skill of all animals. The lightning-like quality of the shark and other finny denizens of the deep reminds us that rhythmical co-ordination of the entire body musculature was essential, even at the lowliest vertebrate or fishy stage of human evolution, for the pursuit of prey and for all those vital activities which characterize piscine economy such as swallowing, breathing and ridding the body of its waste products.

The reptilian phase of human evolution reveals another phase in the evolution of bodily skill. When the fishy ancestor came out on land, rhythmical movements were useless and were inhibited. The

---

This article was first published in *Transvaal Education News* in 1934, 10:39–41 (October), 11:13–17 (November), 12:15–17 (December).

brain became modified to restrain them to a minimum and to superimpose upon that chronic state of reptilian rest or sluggishness the disjointed movements of a four-legged but weak-kneed apparatus which could be called upon spasmodically and at a moment's notice to waddle after food or to scurry under cover. The torpedo-like body of the fish was broken up in the reptile into a head, neck, trunk and tail, each capable of movement relative to the adjacent parts. So trivial were the advantages of limbs and body divisions at this stage that some lizards, such as the snakes were derived from, discarded them almost entirely and went back to undulating eel-like body movement, in which their scaly covering served them reasonably well.

The mammalian family, however, was developed from a reptilian group that turned their scales into hair and lifted their bodies up permanently off the ground in a perpetual state of muscular tension on their straightened stilt-like limbs. To use these highly sensitive and active limbs, a more expectant and attentive type of brain was evolved and a rapidly pulsating, four-chambered heart forcibly supplied adequate blood to the alert musculature. The lithe and mobile trunk, still further broken into a true thorax and abdomen, was more capable of rapid oxygenation and removal of wastes from the blood. Life became more adventurous, because of the better brain, improved muscles, greater heat and heightened metabolic rate. Agility, enterprise, and with them increasing skill came into their own. It is because they are so much nearer to us in warmth and skill that rabbits, dogs, and horses thrill us instead of 'leaving us cold' as do the crocodile, frog and fish.

Our skill, therefore, is one with that of all animals, especially that of mammals and particularly that of primates. The second fundamental fact revealed by the evolutionary story is that every human being has inherited this fundamental mammalian mechanism of skill. We are far too prone to hunt after the paltry differences between human beings. Omitting the trees on account of the scraps of wood, we are not impressed by the overwhelming similarities between ourselves and other men. The psychological reason for this human mania is doubtless the inferiority complex we all enjoy. It demands that we ourselves should be distinctive and, if possible, superior to our fellow men; in order to make ourselves superior we search for our distinctiveness from others. We classify our fellows as brilliant or stupid, for the purpose, I suppose, of putting ourselves in the brilliant class we have so ingeniously created.

But Nature will have none of this anthropomorphism. Discarding, for the time being, consideration of those structural and mental misfits who fill our infirmaries, we were all conceived, born and suckled in the same way as mammals. We all had the same trials of learning to see, hear, taste and smell things; to kick, squirm, crawl, walk, climb, run and ultimately leap. We all found intense interest in grabbing, tearing and hurling things. Later we learned to touch, stroke and handle things with growing precision, while our restless bodies were kept under control by the subconscious exercise of restraining will-power. By dint of painful experiences we discovered how to discriminate between coarse and fine movements, between inaccurate and accurate procedures. We were able to direct more or less skilfully the movements of our hands to wash our bodies, to put on our clothes, to throw a brick, to draw figures, to thread a needle, to shove a pen, and the movements of our vocal apparatus to use words, string sentences together, and recite our alphabet.

However glibly we accept these common achievements as ordinary, in the realm of Nature they are extraordinary. Some of them are activities common to all vertebrates, but others are distinctive only of mammals, while a few others can be performed by mankind alone. Man is extraordinary in his endowments but, if this human inheritance were restricted to a chosen group and not general, education would be fruitless. Education belongs to all because we can all arrive at approximately the same height of development if we pursue the necessary training or develop the appropriate skills.

Having recognized that man's skill is simply an advance upon the skill of animals and that, for all practical purposes, the inherited mechanism for skill in the eyes of Nature is approximately identical in all human beings, we are in a position to understand and examine the universality of skill in all human pursuits. Then we will return to the mechanism itself, analyse its character, and see what bearing the lessons we have learned therefrom should have upon our educational system and the life of the future.

Skilled human activity may be loosely divided into sport and labour. Labour itself may be virtually entirely physical as in the case of the wharf-labourer, the artisan or the housewife, or both physical and mental as in the craftsman and the artist, or largely intellectual as in the scientist or professional man. Irrespective of how we classify human effort into athletics, arts, crafts, sciences, professions or studies, they all involve muscular and mental collaboration and consequently entail the exercise of skill.

Every human achievement, from the savage's making a palæolithic tool, or engraving a symbolical figure, or dancing around a campfire, or conferring on pre-arranged signals to hunt and capture a wild beast, up to the educated man's planning, building and decorating a skyscraper (or a cathedral), or writing an epic (or a scientific treatise), or producing a ballet (or an Olympic carnival), with all their pageantry and performance, or holding a congress in politics, religion, or science, is an expression of skill.

Work proceeds everywhere. It embraces the expenditure of energy by the body or the mind, on the sportsfield or in the study. The physician finds the brain, heart and lungs actively working even when his patient is unconscious in sleep or in coma. The physicist knows that work is being performed whenever force overcomes resistance, even that producing molecular change in every body cell after death and during disintegration. Hence what we choose to call 'work' is but that fraction of bodily activity we partially control with our minds in order to carry out purposive acts. We insult the name when we apply it to those acts which we ought to carry out but find distasteful. It were better to call them 'toil' or 'labour'. We scarcely do the name credit when we fail to find work in both sport and labour.

The physical (stereoscopic eye, delicate hand and erect body) and mental (co-ordinating brain) mechanism of skill is inherited in exuberant quantity by all except the mentally and bodily deficient. But inheritance of itself has never worn Olympic laurels or produced Pavlovas. The inherited mechanism must be controlled by each individual. It can only be put under mental control by tireless practice. This work, whose object is control, in the infant takes the form of learning to control eye movements, hand movements and foot movements. Day after day by ceaseless exercise it comes to control these and so painstakingly develops its body muscles to the extent of rolling about, turning over, sitting up, crawling about, standing up, climbing, walking, running, and, ultimately, leaping. Each of these separate achievements is ultimately heralded by crowing laughter and all the emotion of joy. However great the effort, grief and pain they have entailed at each stage in the cycles of human growth, joy cometh in the morning.

In terms of bodily and mental skill, many human beings never progress beyond this infantile or quasi-anthropoidal stage. To pass beyond it in sport, craftsmanship or science, is a work of art. The processes involved in achieving artistic sports, crafts or sciences are identical with those automatically followed in childhood, or even before childhood, within the womb! To cease achieving skill by well directed work during life is to die in that respect, just as surely as partial or complete death results from cessation of intra-uterine activities. Life is movement! Skilled movement connotes skilled living, *i.e.* art!

It is a curious fact that the only work which we really find laborious is that in which we are unskilled. Grief and loss accompanies the process of becoming skilled; once skill is achieved, profit and pleasure result. The history of the race and the history of the individual agree in showing that developmental advances occur through rendering procedures happily automatic, by replacing unskilled mechanisms with joyfully skilled ones. If we had not succeeded in rendering relatively more skilled and automatic the processes of circulation, digestion, excretion and the activities of hunting, feeding and sleeping, we would scarcely be farther advanced than the fish.

Work, therefore, is universal and human work is performed by a highly-evolved muscular mechanism capable of infinite skill. The measure or test of that skill is the degree of accuracy attained during the work. Yet absolute accuracy is unattainable; no two yardsticks in the world have exactly the same length; no two gold coins are absolutely identical. Accuracy represents an ideal which, like truth, our spirits eternally strive after but never quite attain. The most accurate tools designed by Man have never yet duplicated their first output with entire precision. The body and hand of Man is even more fallible than his tough metallic tools.

Thus, absolute skill seems unattainable and what we term skill is the capacity to repeat with tolerable accuracy the pictured movements of body and hand which our brain demands for its particular purposes.

Human skill is achieved largely by mimicry. For hundreds of thousands of years mankind the world over copied practically the same simple patterns of palæolithic instruments. Today the standards of skill we generally apply are those set by our colleagues and neighbours. The universal sense of inadequacy in human beings leads them to compare their work with that of others alongside. They deprecate the efforts of those who attempt, by exercising the quantum of creative energy each person possesses, to outstrip their fellows. Each school has its standards of achievement. They are set by some outstanding, but frequently deeply resented, teacher or student.

By the vision or picture of skill in action, the minds of those in the vicinity are impressed. The very admiration or resentment of the curious herd evokes the degree of interest or attention necessary to imprinting the skilled movement on their brains. The spirit of emulation or competition, or the will to outshine this temporary evidence of mental or physical leadership, prompts immediate steps to initiate and even excel the cunning of the self-constituted champion. Alternatively, it compels the jealous Achilles to retire to his tent when his self-approved skill is not accepted at his own valuation.

The primary mechanism of skill is therefore emotional and physical, the two being combined in the stimulated, interested and understanding brain. The physical apparatus whereby the brain receives its impressions are the organs of sight and the tracts leading from them to the brain. But this visual information would be useless were it not for the millions of impressions previously poured into and preserved in the same receptacle throughout life through the organs of sight, hearing, balance, touch, and muscle and joint sense. Correlated and stored in an amazing fashion in the cerebral cortex, the emulative individual thereby builds up for himself, instantaneously or by reflection, an initiative pattern of movement. This pattern he then exploits or tests out. By a process of trial and error he ultimately comes to repeat that pattern with gradually increasing success or accuracy.

Five outstanding factors in the mechanism of human skill are presented here. They are visual, auditory, balancing, tactile and muscular memory. It might be thought that defects in one or other of these factors would result in a gross lack of skill. History shows that this is not the case. The most famous painters and sculptors have suffered from defective vision—poets like Homer and Goethe, artists like Whistler and Goya. Beethoven had defective hearing. Demosthenes and Moses were stutterers. Leonardo da Vinci was left-handed. By an extraordinary quality of compensation, it has frequently happened that the defect itself has been turned by the man, who determined to overcome it, into his greatest asset.

These very compensations show the tremendous capacity for skill the human brain possesses even in the presence of defective organs; what that capacity can be, when the organs are effective, mankind has not yet begun to realize. Human beings, even when they are what we call educated, employ only a trifling fraction of their brains and other physical organs of skill. Only a few jugglers, acrobats, and ballet dancers really exercise and enjoy the human balancing mechanism. Only a few athletes and sportsmen develop a co-ordinated body musculature; only a few artists and craftsmen really experience the thrill of manual skill. Few indeed can sing, speak and play instruments publicly with real skill. We have yet to devise a system of education that is truly well balanced and actually produces skilled eyes, ears, hands, bodies and voices. Nor will we produce such an educational system until we appreciate more fully the biologically sound nature of a system reared on the concept of skill and the ambition of its enjoyment.

Insensibly and empirically, the education of mankind is gravitating in this direction. The increasing functional capacity and proper nutrition and community drill and singing are symbolical of this tendency. The idea of emancipating the child from stodgy studies of books and liberating him to handle skilfully plants, animals and implements, and to indulge happily in creative fancies with pencils or crayons on plane surfaces or with modelling materials in the round, is a further stride towards the ideal of skill. But these practices do not touch more than the fringe of the subject. It demands intense study by anatomists of the altering structure of the growing child, by physiologists of the increasing functional capacity and proper nutrition of the nascent youth, by psychologists and physicians of the mental and physical distresses from which individuals suffer, thereby failing to enjoy and employ the marvellous apparatus of human skill. By such knowledge we may come ultimately to evoke interests and grade activities appropriate in their intrinsic appeal to the bodily and mental state of the child.

This does not mean that we should idle in anticipation of this wonderful future knowledge. If we had the capacity to apply rationally what is already known, the whole educational situation could be revolutionized. The compensating mechanisms of which I spoke demonstrate that even if we did our utmost in joining with Nature to frustrate skill, we would be powerless against its emergence here and there. Not all the concentrated might of Church and State could exterminate Galileo, Copernicus and similar liberators of human thought. Frustration itself almost seems to have been essential for evoking certain valuable responses in terms of living skill in humanity.

Instead of repressing skill or awaiting its automatic emergence, we require to be capable of, and alert in, recognizing it and in encouraging its most elementary forms of expression. Acuity of vision and hearing should be noted and, as far as possible, promoted by medical assistance. Man did not become intellectually skilled until he had passed through æons of bodily and appendicular skill. If the body lacks skill, the mind is to that extent warped. As T. H. Pear said, there is an 'intellectual respectability in muscular skill'. If we fail to achieve that skill we lose correspondingly in self-respect. I am not advocating what we are pleased to term sport but a rational education in skill. All children should be especially encouraged in all exercises which educate their sense of balance such as skipping, roller-skating, dancing, swimming and the like. Thereby alone can they come to enjoy the basic achievement of Man—the erect attitude. Frequently it occurs that their lack of proficiency in all sporting exercises arises merely from lack of practice in this primary and fundamental human trait of balancing the body on one or two feet. It came first in evolution and must come first in sporting education.

It is important, too, for the teacher to know that the cultivation of all skill of the upper limb is secondary to that of trunk and feet but, as in them, it is dependent upon the capacity to memorize muscular sensations.

Such simple movements as writing or knitting, climbing or batting come into the category of skill and require the co-ordination of the entire body musculature for that one particular purpose. Every muscle which is not required in the upper limb movement has to be set at rest by force of will. Some people never succeed in keeping them at rest. While writing or reading their tongues, lips and heads are in perpetual motion even if the body is still. In the same way some never learn to swim or skate because the unwanted muscles overact and their rigidity prevents smooth execution of movement by those muscles whose particular responsibility the movement happens to be. In every game and craft, perfect relaxation of the unwanted muscles is the key to skilled performance.

The best way of securing that relaxation is by concentrating attention upon the simplest bases of movement involved. Just as in drill and dancing we divide movements into one, two and three, so in drawing and writing and printing we should concentrate the child's attention on mastering first the straight, then the curved line and only begin to combine curved and straight lines at will to produce figures after the fundamental simplicities have been mastered.

Teachers are frequently more shoddy than their pupils. They never master the bases of movement themselves and blindly attempt to lead the blind. I continually discover my own faulty techniques to lie in passing too rapidly over basic essentials and rushing ahead to performance of stardom. Like Stephen Leacock's 'retroactive personality' I find myself being constantly led further and further back to unexpected essentials and principles previously entirely neglected or overlooked.

Let me illustrate! It may disappoint you to hear that my first weeks in teaching anatomy are taken up in showing students that they can all print if they can make a straight line and a circle, persuading unbelievers that if they are capable of doing these correctly they will all draw anatomical and histological objects beautifully with practice. The year is consumed chiefly not in instructing them in anatomical facts but in the wielding of a scalpel and the holding of forceps, in protecting and giving proper attention to dissected parts and delicate apparatus, in showing them how to use dictionaries and books of synonyms and other literature to improve their writing both for examination and other written records, and in encouraging them by similar means to enlarge their vocabularies so that they may be able to vocalize words accurately and lucidly not only in *viva voce* examinations, but also to patients and before public audiences. If I had my wish all medical students would first be called upon to graduate from a school of trades, arts and crafts.

These skilful procedures all depend upon the excellence or otherwise of their memories of muscular sensations perceived during coordinated movements. This muscular type of memory is so fugitive and indescribable that it is most difficult to remember. Our language is singularly lacking in a terminology of muscle movement and its memory. The golfer refers to it as the 'feel of the movement'. Constant practice, constant repetition is essential in order that we come to 'feel it' in such detail that in any one movement we set in motion the right muscles at the right time with exactly the right balance and in precisely the right sequence. That 'feeling memory' is essential to skill!

Such memories can only be accumulated by infinitude of repetition. It is practice that makes perfect. Nor is mere repetition sufficient. The repetition must be accompanied by unmitigated attention. Such attention is the outcome only of desire or love of the work. Only love can evoke intelligent concentration on the nature of the movement involved and the will or determination to remember precisely those movements.

Anyone who has learned a swing in golf or a stroke in swimming will understand that any such complicated movement can be resolved into numerous subsidiary movements of each portion of the body—eye movements, respiratory movements, trunk movements, hip, leg, foot and arm, forearm, wrist, hand and finger movements. It is only when we analyse a sport that we can understand why its mastery is so difficult!

Kotany distinguishes two important aspects of attention. The first is *depth of attention*. This is the attention that is directed to one object or several closely associated objects simultaneously. It is not rare; its prototype is found even in children. It is the type of attention that, when developed in business, is capable of making an expert in one particular class of movement or in one field of industry, buying or selling one particular class of goods, performing rhythmically and accurately one special line of work. It is the grade of attention called for in a meat-packing factory or a Ford motor-works. It creates the one-track specialist.

The other aspect of attention is *width of attention.* This is the attention that, having analysed the details of numerous movements and mastered them by exercising depth, is directed towards the relations between them and so finally into synthesizing them into rhythms and themes. It then co-ordinates, subordinates, and architecturally builds them up into compositions of perhaps unprecedented character. Such width of attention is rare. In sport its prototype creates the good all-rounder. In industry, it is the attention demanded in the general manager who must co-ordinate departments of buying, manufacturing and selling so as to maintain a steady stream of production and distribution. Extraordinary width of attention is the mark of genius in industry, in art or in science.

Absence of attention or concentration is the mark of the nitwit. In the rabbit or canine world, attention flits longitudinally from object to object without depth or width concentration. In the primate world, considerable depth of attention can be exerted on assiduous and tireless hunting down of body-lice and other irritants, or similar occupations that demand a nicety of sight and touch. But anthropoidal attention at best is one-track. Further, it lacks depth as compared with the attention of which human beings are capable from earliest childhood. The industry of children with a pencil, a shovel or other toys, with mud-pies, building blocks or a Meccano set is wonderful and beautiful in its profundity. Unfortunately, for reasons as yet undiscovered, much of the depth of attention found instinctive in childhood is ruined by our educational mechanism. It loses in depth and it fails to gain in width. By lack of development it becomes superficial, stultified and even extinct, or it reverts to the quasi-anthropoidal condition of the one-track.

The keystone of attention and therefore of skill is that intangible factor of interest or absorption. Unless our educational methods arouse, maintain and increase enthusiasm, they are worse than useless. They destroy instead of construct. Nor will we interest children and youth until we discover work of gradually increasing length, width and depth, such as is capable of gratifying indefinitely the instinctive desires of all for probing and reasonably exercising every form of skill that their brains have prepared them to exhibit and express in bodily, manual and mental work.

I lay no claims to a considered system, but the skills which I imagine to be fundamental to citizenship are:

1. the erect skills of general body and lower limb movements, as in general sports such as deportment, walking, climbing, balancing, dancing and swimming;
2. the skills of accurate co-ordinated eye and hand movements, as in the most attractive arts and crafts such as needlework, drawing, modelling and sculpture;
3. the skills of accurate eye-work or measurement as in mathematics, especially through carpentry and metalwork, or out of school in surveying and astronomical observation;
4. the skills of accurate language by mastering the use of words in speaking and writing and so expressing thoughts; and
5. the skills of accurate music by mastering the human voice and hearing the value of time, expression and rhythm in singing.

These skills are the basis of all the public and domestic crafts, arts and sciences. The curriculum should be so arranged that the greatest possible joy and interest is evoked in the scholars so that the maximum attention will be automatically employed by them.

If, then, skill is so important, if human beings strive so assiduously and so successfully thereafter that they can turn even a defective skill-apparatus into an asset, and if its importance is rapidly emerging into the limelight of public recognition, I feel that educationalists cannot bring the matter too early or too frequently to the consciousness of their students.

It is amazing, if we pause to consider them from the point of view of skill, how many avenues are being prosecuted by individuals and by nations whose intangible goal is socialized skill. Never in the history of mankind have there been so many teachers of individual sports, or bodily exercises, arts and craft-hobbies as at the present day. Never before has there been as much interest in all branches of applied science, organized drill and community effort generally. Never before have such colossal activities in terms of skill been staged as exist today throughout the world, *e.g.* in the Boy Scout and Girl Guide movement and the German, Italian, Russian and other youth movements. In our own country we have our Special Service and Labour battalions in order to introduce the youth to individualized bodily skill and the pleasures of corporate work. These mechanisms of socialized skill based on individual skill have come to stay; they are not merely military; they are the expression of something far vaster, whose rapid emergence has been forced upon mankind by the Great War, but whose development would have taken place, war or no war!

It is an evolutionary process, deep-seated in the biological fact that Man is not only a skilled but also a social animal. Nature has seen social organization at one end of the biological scale in the symbiosis of cells that forms a sponge, in the colonial existence of hydroid polyps that forms the corals, in the corporate life of insects such as bees and ants. A looser sort of group organization is found at every stage of vertebrate evolution in shoals of fish, companies of reptiles, flocks of birds and herds of mammals. For better or worse mankind has been so prolific and so capable of community life that the race is faced with the dreadful alternatives of perfect socialization (*i.e.* organized skill) or extinction. The huge interrogative of the future is, therefore, who amongst men will survive, and how they will survive. As far as the immediate future of this and the next century is concerned, the unmistakable answer appears to be the perfectly organized group. Humanity appears to be most busily engaged in finding out what that 'perfect human organization' may be. That process of finding out during the past has been for the most part subconscious, empirical and, therefore, chaotic. Any conscious cerebration on the matter has been left, on the one hand, to the philosophers, such as Lao-Tse, who said we should leave things alone and not stir up the muddy pool, as Confucius, who found the key in family organization and reverence of ancestors, as Plato, who found it in his Utopia, as Christ, who found it in all-embracing love, as Buddha, who found it in rising above everything material to Nirvana, as Mahomet, who found it in acceptance of fate, the will of Allah.

On the other hand, independently of its dreamers, the stream of mankind, especially in the Mediterranean area and Western Europe, has rushed madly on. Submissive to the hereditary instincts of millennia, it has exhibited the whole gamut of animal and human emotion from unswerving fidelity to infamous treachery, from divine love to satanic hatred, from heavenly peace and kindliness to hellish war and unbridled hatred. These emotions have found expression in skill! Taking advantage of these biological facts, another group of men has cerebrated. The men of the moment, the pragmatists, those who did things, the Alexanders, Cæsars and Napoleons, not merely in the military world but in the arenas of public affairs, in trade, industry, finance, economics and the professions and science, have pursued their various paths with lip-service to the philosophers, but carving out the pragmatic philosophies of their own, suiting their day and generation, according to immediate needs as they discovered them. They achieved skill, they did things, but chiefly with the idea of personal aggrandizement and leaving their personal mark on human affairs.

The times have changed! As Nicholson points out in his biography of *Lord Curzon*:

> Human affairs are no longer manageable by a single individual will, nor can they be comprehended as a whole by any single human intelligence. They have outgrown the capacity of any individual brain. Statesmanship henceforward will have to be a corporate and not a one-man business.

That is where human affairs differ from the affairs of a bee colony which is only concerned with gathering and storing honey and producing new swarms of bees. There is no philosopher's stone, no one magical 'open sesame' to the discovery of human riches, unless it can come through some grand synthesis of the mental and emotional skill shown by all our philosophers, plus all that we have suffered and gleaned from its pragmatists in the more practical skills of the arts, industry and science.

The course of history has exposed the fallacy of physical or mental tyranny in human affairs. The so-called 'dictatorships' of the present era can prove stable only insofar as they are founded upon skilled human organizations and co-operation. Only a system that ensures the realization simultaneously of the seeming paradox of absolute individualism and absolute collectivism is capable of satisfying human needs.

Is such a synthesis possible? The optimists of our generation believe that it is. They see a humanity freed from individual physical slavery by means of the skilled machine. They refuse to believe that the problems of distribution cannot be solved as easily as the problems of production. Individuals, however widely dispersed over the earth's surface and whatever their colour, creed or condition, demand the full heritage of the combined skill of the human race. Unless that heritage is conferred on them in full they will destroy it, just as the Persian hillmen sacked Mesopotamia, the barbarians overran Greece and Rome, the Arabian fanatics devastated Africa and Europe, and the Bantu hordes turned prehistoric Rhodesian civilization into a howling wilderness.

Let us take a long glimpse into the future and imagine that these problems have been solved. In a world girdled by wireless, talkies (and television), automobiles and æroplanes, the logical conclusion is that nobody, however listless, can avoid being educated, even if he never goes to school. Theoretically, we could close all those schools and universities, that are merely talking-shops, and I think humanity certainly will close them in time. But what is mankind to do if he is liberated, as he most certainly will be, from taking thought concerning the morrow relative to those things which previously occupied his skill, *viz*. his food, his household, and his family? It was not to a futile purpose that Sparta aforetime and Russia today threw the responsibility of children on the state; it was not merely in order to be generous and to amuse that Imperial Rome should have given *panem et circenses* to the plebeians, that England has doled millions, and that America is facing the problem of feeding and caring for 20 million unemployed. Politicians, however indifferent, must ultimately face the problem and even politicians today, the world over, realize how insistently immediate and imperative are these solutions.

A recent survey of mechanical development, for instance, estimates that the amount of work done by 'robots' in Great Britain would demand the toil of 1,000 million hard-driven slaves; in America, of 3,000 million.

The modern world of marvels and high living standards, in fact, would not be possible without the robot to work for us. For he not only takes over human tasks and releases men from other than high-grade work, but also performs functions which men are not adroit, or quick, or sensitive enough to perform.

Assuming that these physical problems have been solved, what is mankind to do in his spare time? Some use must be found for human intelligence! Writers such as L. P. Jacks of Mill Hill School have already addressed themselves to this great question of the future, 'the occupation of human leisure', refusing to believe that the modern pursuits of raising dust in a high-powered motor car and burning the night in dancing and bioscopes represent the climax of human happiness.

Mankind is facing the greatest of its testing times and during the remainder of the century will discover whether civilization represents Dead Sea fruit! If the highest enterprises that can occupy socialized human mentality are parades of hundreds of thousands of men, women and children for the purpose of marching, drilling, bombing and killing, however skilled its performance, then humanity is certainly destitute. Nor is there any denying that we are destitute of mental capacity and vision when so much money and human effort is still being expended in these puerile performances throughout the so-called civilized world.

But indications are not lacking that these are but training grounds and that other social skills are on the increase. The greatest intellectual outcome of the war and these post-war activities is the increased recognition by humanity of the power possessed by knowledge and the pursuit of knowledge to occupy an infinitude of human attention. Some short time ago, when addressing University Students' Society on the place of organization in the future of science, I suggested that if the pursuit of a relatively inert and useless metal such as gold could employ 30,000 Europeans and 300,000 Bantu in South Africa, then the pursuit of knowledge concerning a single Bantu organ like the Bantu heart could employ 10,000 times 10,000 human beings and still leave plenty to be done during the future in South Africa—that what is true of the heart is true of every organ in their bodies, every stone underfoot, every star in the universe. Humanity need not sit down like Alexander and weep because it has no further worlds to conquer. There lie before us the infinities of the ineffably small and the incalculably large to explore. Ample employment is ready in Nature for all time, for every variety and every component in organized human skill. The world finds itself today in the childhood and teething stage of social organization. What will be the adolescence and manhood of the human race?

2

An Anatomist's Tribute to F. Matthias Alexander

Introduction

I appreciate deeply the privilege of speaking to you in person this evening. My wife and I are happy to meet here so many old friends and especially Miss Irene Tasker. To her knowledge and understanding of the Alexander Technique we and our family have been for the past 27 years, and naturally still are, most deeply indebted.

Some of what I have written I will read but you may do that, I hope, at your leisure later. I prefer to talk to you now about myself and my approach to the Technique so you may understand both better. At the outset, too, I must say how much you and I must have been helped by the information conveyed about F. M. Alexander's life in our chairman's, Mr Walter Carrington's *Centenary Memorial Lecture*. He had 20 years of personal contact with Alexander; I had little more than 35 minutes with him just 21 years ago. So I would urge all those who knew him well to place on record all that they find worthy in their recall about him. Personal experiences, however underrated by ourselves, often prove very meaningful not merely to oneself but naturally to many more others.

Mr Carrington has expressed his disagreement with my having confessed to him that I deemed my knowledge of the Technique and the teaching of it abysmal. But this is the truth. Indeed, as nearly as I can recall the words used in 1947, Dr Mungo Douglas told me in our home in Johannesburg at the time of the crucial libel action: 'If you consider yourself an exponent of the Technique, you are a pretty poor example of it!' My response then was: 'It was my consciousness

---

This F. M. Alexander Memorial Lecture delivered before The Society of Teachers of the Alexander Technique, 20 March 1970, was first published by the Sheildrake Press, London, 1970.

of the imperfections in my posture that first interested me in his technique; but I am far from regarding myself an exponent of its value.'

If I can communicate to you tonight something of what this remarkable fellow-countryman from the Antipodes of Australia was contending against in his striving to explain, here in London over 60 years ago, *i.e.* in the first decade of this century, the discoveries he had made about body misuse and its correction far, far away in Tasmania, I will have succeeded beyond my expectations.

His principal barrier, of course, was that no visual means were available to him to display his discoveries about human bodies to the public. No incontestable, no irrefragable ocular proofs could be provided then of the changes that he had wrought in the people who had learned a better use of themselves. When I was writing nearly 30 years later, many visual experimental observations had been recorded photographically by leading physiologists such as Sherrington and Magnus; some radiographic studies, too, of patients like those of the dentist Nove, could be cited. More recently, of course, the incontrovertible and irresistible stroboscopic studies of Dr Frank Pierce Jones have been published.

Alexander laboured in that materialistic, scientific environment before the psychiatric studies of Freud, Jung, and Adler had become acceptable as current knowledge. The multi-million human displacement and five-year trench warfare of 1914–18 had to be endured before mental conditions such as *shell-shock* could be recognized as realistic disease entities and the minds of individuals be treated as part and parcel of their bodies.

Our chairman in his centenary lecture referred to 'evolution' as 'quite a daunting word to many people even today'. In that first decade of the twentieth century it was at best only a 'theory' which meant 'you need not take any notice of it'! Two decades later, in 1925, when *Pithecanthropus* had been known for a generation and *Australopithecus* had been publicized, William Jennings Bryan, the silver-tongued Vice-President of the United States, had been summoned to Dayton to uphold Tennessee's law preventing school teachers like Scopes from teaching evolution. It was only during 1969—the year of Alexander's centenary—that the Supreme Court of the United States found comparable Arkansas legislation to be contrary to the teacher's liberty of thought, and evolution could be taught without let or hindrance throughout all the states.

Alexander lived until 1955; in 1954 the Piltdown forgery had been exposed; the broad path of human evolution was no longer theoretical. Viruses had revealed the continuity between animate and inanimate things; atomic bombs had rent the veil between energy and matter. With radiocarbon dating already in human hands and potassium-argon and other forms of isotopic dating only three years distant, the factual world which confronts every educated, thoughtful individual today has become utterly different from the inquisitive but nebulous and speculative world within which Alexander's active exploratory mind had functioned in his youth.

Alexander's handicaps and our assets

Born in Tasmania, Australia, in 1869, just a decade after the publication of Charles Darwin's *The Origin of Species*, F. Matthias Alexander's influence upon his generation and humanity a century after his birth is diffuse and widespread. Yet, probably few of the many profiting from his teaching today are aware of its nature or source. Edward Maisel's *The Resurrection of the Body* (1969) has celebrated the centenary of his birth by extracting the essentials of his teaching from Alexander's own publications.

The basic discovery Alexander made from 1888 onwards was the practice of deliberate conscious inhibition. He stopped doing habitual things seen reflected in a mirror and recognized by him as being wrong, such as pulling his head back when speaking emphatically. He had discovered it to be a useless action! It diminished his standing height, strained his tensing throat, and, in particular, it interfered with the ease and regularity of his breathing when speaking, reciting and acting as he wished to do publicly. As Walter Carrington said in his centenary lecture: 'He became known as the "breathing man" and people wanted to know how he did it.'

In my opinion, a natural left-handedness* assisted that realization and detailed analysis of himself, and also facilitated his teaching others

---

* All interested in this subject will enjoy *The Left-Handed Book: An investigation into the sinister history of left-handedness* by Michael Barsley (London, Souvenir Press, 1966).

to do it. (Mr Carrington corroborates the truth of that assumption here this evening.) His right-handed friends' imperfections would therefore have been more patent through their resembling more closely those he saw mirrored in his own glass. Alternatively, he had so mastered the freedom of his hands and head, lengthened and widened his torso, and liberated his throat and diaphragm in breathing—whatever postures or limb movements his recitals demanded—that he had become both as agile and ambidextrous as photographs of him in action seem to me to have displayed.

The transformation experienced in health and self-confidence based upon his improved respiratory, circulatory and physical well-being impressed not only himself but also his brother and his dramatic and medical colleagues. He communicated these discoveries to his acquaintances and students, teaching them by manipulations, self-observation and self-instruction what *not to do* to themselves. Amongst them, too, emerged increasingly those who improved in elocution and carriage and who also became bettered in health and relieved from habitual aches and pains.

The essential part of what gradually became thus known as the Alexander Technique is for the student to experience a use of his musculature other than that to which he has hitherto allowed his body to become habituate, *i.e.* to become aware of the difference between an unusual and improved use of his muscles and joints and his previous or customary wrong use of them when moving from one ordinary postural situation to another, *e.g.* from the sitting to the standing or from the lying to the sitting position.

In 1965, *i.e.* a decade after his death and three-quarters of a century after F. M. Alexander's self-analysis, an arresting neurological fact came to light through its having become recorded electronically in numerous encephalograms. Changes in electric potential take place in the nerve cells in the frontal lobes of human brains *before*, as well as during and after voluntary muscular movements. H. H. Kornhuber and L. Deecke, two German neurologists, found that while an individual is thinking about carrying out an action the action, is being *preceded by a slow negative wave* occurring in that front region of his brain.

In the same year Drs M. A. Falconer and W. G. Walter, after studying such encephalographic waves also with radiotelemetry, affirmed that negative waves of this sort 'precede and accompany *every* conscious, spontaneous, voluntary decision and action, such as deciding to talk or walk, throwing or catching a ball, starting and stopping a vehicle, as well as in response to arbitrary external signals, as in the laboratory.' They have therefore called it 'the contingent negative variation (CNV), *or expectancy wave*'; but Dr H. L. Teuber likes to think that some of these electrophysiological *antecedents of actions* are not just neural commands sent to the muscles but 'the concomitant foresetting of cerebral systems for the expected consequence of the impending action, so that the results can be compared, centrally with the intent' (my italics).

The general effect of the suprasegmental structures in our central nervous systems, whether in our fore-, mid- or hind-brains, is to produce co-ordination and control of segmental reflexes by *inhibiting* useless, isolated muscular activities and combining them in purposive movements. As Dr Purpura stated at the same conference on the 'brain mechanisms underlying speech and language' at Princeton, New Jersey: 'It is likely that many of the functional interactions between cortex, basal ganglia, and thalamus are directed toward securing a greater inhibitory control of sensorimotor activities. Many of these events operate at the microtime but also at the macrotime level.' To him, Dr Purpura, the long latencies recorded in such evoked cortico-cortical responses suggested 'multi-synaptic connections—and the more synapses, the greater possibility for interaction, convergence and integration.'

It has taken nearly a century to get such ocular electronic proof of the neuronic activity preceding each moment in our decision-making! But, plainly, the sequential timing and presetting of all our learned movements were continually being exposed to the possibility of becoming disturbed or disordered to either a minor or a major degree during every stage in that learning and also through any genetic, nutritional or environmental lack that each of us may have suffered during our infantile development or by any nocuous agent, accident or infectious disease experienced by us then or later in our lives. Obviously too, few, if any, civilized human beings could have been fortunate enough to escape the effects of all of the innumerable deleterious impacts endured by most of them from the moment of their conception to the maturity of their adulthood.

Can any of us civilized human individuals claim physical and mental perfection? On the contrary, such statistics as we possess and were cited in those of my papers to which I will refer, proclaim the virtual universality of human physical and mental imperfections, despite the hundreds of millions of years that geologists, zoologists and physicists inform us have elapsed in our long evolutionary journey from a pre-molecular state of existence to the manhood that has been deemed worthy of being called sapient.

Our physicists today can also date with C-14 the time that has elapsed since the emergence of man's civilization; they can follow our australopithecine forefathers' activities back with potassium–argon isotopic dating over the past two million years or more. In the forward march of science and compulsory education, public attitudes have changed so vastly during the past 56 years that the introductory words of John Dewey, then America's most eminent educationist, to Alexander's first book, *Man's Supreme Inheritance* (1910), has itself become a kind of museum piece to illustrate the contemporary, dominating, pre-first-world-war attitudes of fear which children, parents and grandparents then held towards their own bodies:

> Popular fear of anything sounding like materialism has put a heavy burden on humanity. Men are afraid, without even being aware of their fear, to recognize the most wonderful of all structures of the vast universe—the human body. They have been led to think that a serious notice and regard would somehow involve disloyalty to man's higher life.

Alexander's declared wish in writing that book was to show that 'every man, woman and child holds the possibility of physical perfection; it rests with each of us to attain it by personal understanding and effort.'

This was not an easy objective to advocate at the time. There was a whole panel of named colours in that Alexander–Dewey era that anyone familiar with physics could produce from any white light with the aid of a spectrum and sufficient diversity in geometrically labelled shapes and forms. So any educated person could give elaborate expression in words to the thoughts that the vast majority of hard-headed human beings were then sharing about business and concrete objects such as people could handle as well as see. There was also in current use a formidable catalogue of different sound-names that we still voice and hear, like soprano, tenor and bass, and a huge variety of named sounds characteristic of the creatures both domesticated and wild that make them. Tactile terms, too, were available in quantity about temperature, rugosity and weight to confirm those litanies of sight and sound! But apart from the internal aches and pains of their joints and muscles, the throbs of headache and the pangs of colic, words capable of describing the finer variations in their own muscle and joint feelings lay then, as they still lie, hidden, indescribable, and relatively mute within our subconscious, like our viscera and their concomitant emotions.

Even to write about such personal matters, much less to discuss any of them in mixed company in other than the most evasive or general terms, was unthinkable in materialistic Victorian England. The emotional could scarcely be separated from the metaphysical! The barriers of sex were nevertheless gradually being broken down in the first decade of the twentieth century through the writings of Strindberg in Scandinavia, of Havelock Ellis (another aberrant Australian immigrant) in England, of Freud in Vienna, and of many others less generally known, their contemporaries and followers.

Yet, despite the handicaps of that era's 'modesty' and its lack of an adequate, popular descriptive terminology of the anatomy and functions of the body—it was half a century and more before our modern best-seller salesmanship and our electronic technology with its satellitic colour television, circum-mundane and peri-lunar navigation, and trans-Venusian spatial telemetry—the demand for Alexander's first book, *Man's Supreme Inheritance*, had become so insistent by the 1920s that his second book, in 1923, ran through seven editions before the 1930s ended. In producing that second book and the others that followed, as well as in the teaching of his technique, he had had the assistance of two outstanding women—Irene Tasker and Ethel Webb.

There was another problem! Indeed, to Alexander, as to few if any other of his English-speaking contemporaries, the mental side of existence was so intimately integrated with the physical side that the two parts, *body* and *mind*, had become, to his way of thinking, inseparable—they were merely two aspects of a single entity, the *self*. One of these later books was entitled *The Use of the Self*. Human beings had merely assumed for themselves two separate names to describe those two aspects of their lives. They did not know how this dualism had arisen and had become so utterly confused in their thinking about these two names that they had come to regard their *physical bodies* as entities entirely separate from their *mental souls*. To alter that customary thinking had also become a mission to Alexander.

Mankind was unavoidably doing his most simplistic thinking when he first arrived at the stage of uttering, 50,000 or more years ago, the earliest of the name-giving words that were to produce ultimately a speech that would become articulate. Those original thoughts were naturally about themselves—my self and your self, him and her, us and them, ours and theirs, friends and enemies. So the primary business of man's naming was to separate from the chaos of all the unnamed things he saw: the othernesses, or dualities of existence—the my and your, this and that, male and female, body and thought, dead and alive. This contradistinctional or splitting-up process that naming things and their opposites gave to Man has been going on endlessly ever since it was begun. One of the handicaps of language, whether used conversationally or in public speaking, is that it became so popular; hence we still have far too many languages—between 5,000 and 10,000 of them.* Instead of drawing people more closely together, the greatest success of articulate speech, as at the Tower of Babel, has clearly been in keeping peoples and, more especially, the sexes of all peoples, apart.

Worse still, that mastery of articulate speech has been regarded as so magical a power to possess that humanity became spontaneously tricked by habit into as much wrongful, as rightful, thinking. Thus, whenever another word has been invented by somebody and adopted by a human group to name a part or aspect of the body, some of its people, innocently or otherwise, would imagine a new object had been brought into being. Mistakes were inevitable when that word referred only to an aspect, or appearance, of one and the same thing.

Once a fancy thing like talking starts, the facts or realities about things also tend to run out of control. Just put three women round three cups of tea! For some peoples, one single word for *soul* has been quite inadequate. Even Aristotle, the tutor of Alexander the Great, when writing about the soul, had to talk about *four* of them! The

---

* According to Joseph H. Greenberg: 'Language Universals: a research frontier', *Science* 166:3904:473–78, 24 October 1969.

Egyptian, Hebrew, and other Near East languages had even more names for the various aspects of the 'soul' that each of them recognized.

Our own thinking processes, also, can easily get out of hand in much the same way. The splitting apart of things that we achieve by this process of name-giving becomes confusing if we do not have alongside the splitting words other corresponding words that cause our minds to put the pieces back immediately into the wholes, or totalities, that the broken-apart things compose. Thus, even the *self* cannot exist without everything in the '*not self*', or environment that surrounds it—the world and the universe of which each individual self forms such an utterly fragmentary part.

Human beings are the only creatures so far known to us that have indulged in this gigantic and attractive, yet most deceptive, name-giving word-play that has been preoccupying human attention during the last 50,000 years, or maybe more. It has resulted in the stupefying modern environment of fragmented civilizations in which our own particular selves are living after two world wars and their aftermath. Only during this very last century, since Darwin's book on *The Origin of Species* (1859) was published, have all biologically-oriented scientists been forced to confront the probability that humanity had not been created instantaneously but had emerged laboriously from unicellular creatures during at least five hundreds of millions of years. Since the atomic bomb ended the Second World War (1945), however, every thinking, literate person has been directly confronted further by the energetic unity of the inanimate world with all living things. Unfortunately, 1,500 million persons, or half of the world's population, is still utterly illiterate and thus unaware of these basic, yet elementary, facts. So, stupendous problems face our ludicrous immaturity as a mankind that is scarcely even semi-literate when, at the same time, men have walked on the surface of the moon.

My involvement in Alexandrian and Doman–Delacato methodologies

The saga of F. M. Alexander's life and teaching was the theme of the centenary volume* this year in which a laconic preface appeared

* *The Resurrection of the Body: The writings of F. Matthias Alexander*, edited by Edward Maisel (New York, University Books, 1969).

over my name. Its terseness corresponds rather with the brevity of my personal contact with him than with the longevity of the influence his teaching has had upon my existence. I met him at 16 Ashley Place and received a single lesson only at his hands. We were in London then, on our way, my wife and myself, to New York in 1949 to demonstrate the australopithecine fossils found in South Africa during the preceding quarter of a century.

Six years previously (September 1943), in Johannesburg, I had received at the hands of Miss Irene Tasker, one of his pupils, a series of daily demonstrations of Alexander's self-analytical technique. They had revealed to me how my own malpostured habits of sitting, standing, walking and lying down could be bettered. She had manipulated my moving body concurrently with my conscious desire to sense the feelings in my muscles and joints while striving to inhibit those feelings 'wrongful, intermeddling with reflex details'. The experimental physiological works of Sir Charles Sherrington and of R. Magnus and the work of their anatomical and clinical colleagues and predecessors had already demonstrated amply by that time how reflex activities of both simple segmental and complex intersegmental and suprasegmental character underlay the postural equilibrium of mammalian and primate, as well as avian, body movements.

The most eminent comparative neurologist in the entire English-speaking world during the same period had been another immigrant Australian, Sir Grafton Elliot Smith.* His investigations into the comparative anatomy of reptilian, mammalian (proto-, meta-, and eutherian), primate, and human brains laid the foundations of our present understanding of the human brain. It had been my good fortune to learn from him and to know personally his American neurological friends and colleagues such as George L. Streeter in Baltimore and C. Judson Herrick in Chicago.

Presently in her eighty-third year and still teaching the Alexander Technique, Miss Tasker, long before I had met her, had become aware herself of the value of Alexander's work educationally to gravely handicapped children as well as to average youths and adults.

---

* The contributions he made, e.g. in his *Evolution of Man: Essays*, however novel when first discovered, have become so implicit in modern teaching that their source is rarely, if ever, acknowledged nowadays.

She had, in addition, been one of the early students to pass through Girton College, before Cambridge University in England was prepared to award degrees to women. She had also been one of, if not actually the first Englishwoman to appreciate what Dr Montessori, the first Italian woman to obtain a medical qualification, had done for education. Miss Tasker had therefore gone to Rome and learned directly from Dr Montessori the techniques that premier woman among child psychologists and infant educationalists had elaborated.

The nineteenth century had produced a good many women of this stamp, who were already awakening twentieth-century women, as well as men, to the educational, as well as to the political, potentialities of all women, and starting especially to stimulate their own sex, the mothers who are primarily responsible for all our physical and most of our mental instruction during the first post-natal year, the most impressionable period of our entire lives.

Unfortunately, Miss Tasker had to return to England shortly after our first meeting; but I continued studying the wrongful and rightful performance of muscular acts so intensively that it became to some extent habitual. In the absence of my teacher I, too, had been forced to pursue a 'do-it-yourself' technique. Within the next four years I had written three papers about what I had learned already therefrom—one for my anatomy students, one for my dental colleagues, and one for our fellow members of the medical profession. Only the latter two had been published by 1947, the intended first having been delayed in its appearance until 1950.*

In America, meanwhile, J. Goldthwait in *Body Mechanics* (Philadelphia, 1941), D. G. Hansson in the *Journal of the American Medical Association* (1945), and R. Pemberton in *Principle and Practice of Physical Therapy* (Hagerstown, Maryland, 1947) and various other medical and dental practitioners had been recognizing the evidence for an intimate relationship between body mechanics and health and in the prevention of disease. Similar views were also current amongst eminent medical authorities in Great Britain.

---

* 'The Postural Aspect of Malocclusion' 1946 (pp. 73–107), 'The Attainment of Poise', 1947 (pp. 109–51), 'Voluntary Musculature in the Human Body: The Double-Spiral Arrangement', 1950 (pp. 57–72).

Some clinicians, too, more especially in the neurological field, found evolutionary concepts inescapable. Amongst those in America, Temple Fay, neurosurgeon at Temple University in Philadelphia, was outstanding. To him, in particular, the involuntary movements of patients during seizures or epileptic fits were simply exhibiting ancestral and beneficial movement patterns reminiscent of piscine, amphibian or reptilian antiquity. He encouraged his physiotherapeutic and psychological conferences to learn from and utilize these and other basic sensory information and reflex symptoms, the procedures by whose employment one might prevent or even totally eliminate such lacks in bodily control.

His most comprehending lieutenants were Glenn Doman, a physiotherapist, and Carl Delacato, a psychologist. They were soon joined by Glenn's younger brother Robert, who had specialized in physical medicine. They became, along with Hazel Doman, a qualified nurse, and Janice Delacato, a qualified educationalist, a team who, with their assistants, soon transformed the Rehabilitation Centre at Philadelphia of 1955 into the Institutes for the Achievement of Human Potential of 1960.

In 1966 I received a laudatory citation from the International Forum of Neurological Organization stating that a statuette would be presented to me by Glenn Doman and Dr Carl Delacato in the first week of August, if convenient, on their safari through Africa from Johannesburg *via* the Kalahari to Nairobi. As I had been instrumental when Dean of the Faculty of Medicine in the University of the Witwatersrand in initiating advanced nursing, physiotherapeutic, and occupational therapeutic training in South Africa, the present Dean, Dr F. Daubenton, kindly arranged with the present librarian, Miss Mary Lucas, to have their presentation made in the Witwatersrand Medical Library, with whose foundation and early growth both my wife and I had been intimately concerned.

Subsequently, Doman and Delacato carried out their intended investigation of Bushman infants belonging to the Bechuanaland tribe studied by Dr H. Heinz, and also of Bantu infants encountered during their travels through Rhodesia, Malawi, Tanzania and Kenya. No sooner had they returned to Philadelphia than they were demanding by cable my immediate presence in Philadelphia, even if for only two days, owing to unexpected developments.

I went, and after the two days devoted to seeing and hearing about the work which had been responsible for my writing a congratulatory letter to them six years previously on the results of their breakthrough in therapeutic procedures based on Fay's teaching, they told me that the United Steelworkers of America had proffered sponsorship of an Institute of Anthropology, the chairmanship of which they now wished me to occupy as Professor. Having been retired for eight years from professorial responsibilities, I was naturally hesitant about accepting this challenge, especially as it involved resuscitating neurological interests. These, however dominant they had been during my academic and investigational past, had lain dormant since the writing of those papers some twenty years previously. In any event, however pleasing such a reversion might be to me, my wife's reactions were of primary concern, as was also the maintenance of my domicile in South Africa.

The challenge of these problems lies behind our presence here tonight; it has also caused the reprinting in *Human Potential* of those three above-mentioned papers in the sequence of their writing instead of the temporal disorder of their publication. So we trust that they also will be accessible to those of you who, I have been assured, desire to possess them. But most of all we cherish our commuting between Philadelphia and Johannesburg because it has assisted us in establishing an improved understanding between yourselves as students and teachers of Alexander's technique, who are concerned mainly with enabling average persons to become increasingly skilled in the use of themselves, and these instructors of the parents of innumerable brain-damaged children (and of all categories of professional people concerned with that vast segment of the world's population) in the means whereby each individual concerned can attain his maximal human achievement.

How stupendous the present-day challenge is that brain damage presents can perhaps best be assessed by these extracts I will read first from the Wednesday, 18 March 1970 issue of *International Herald Tribune*, p. 3:

> A scathing report of the American Public Health Association says America's medical care system is broken down, with millions of people exposed to 'health brutality' each day.

> Circumstances that can only be called 'health brutality' pervade the lives of millions of American people who live in communities that seem designed to break the human spirit.
>
> It was prepared by the current association president, Dr Paul B. Cornely, and the immediate past president, Dr Lester Breslow, after the two visited six communities across the United States last year. The association is a private organization representing 18,000 doctors and public health workers.

The report offered case studies that included:

> A 59-year-old Mexican-American grandmother in Houston, Texas, who is ineligible for welfare or Social Security, must support herself and her two-year-old grandson on $10 a week from her son. Four of her 12 children died from diarrhœa, 'a common disease in children who suffer from malnutrition'.
>
> Several hundred predominately Mexican-American farmworkers in Tulare County, California, who sicken each year after being sprayed with pesticide from crop-dusting planes.
>
> 'As public health physicians, we thought we knew pretty well the nature and extent of these conditions,' Dr Cornely and Dr Breslow said in the report titled *Health Crisis in America*, 'but frankly we were shocked and are still reeling'.
>
> While there has been considerable improvement in the quality of life for most Americans, the fact still remains that a large proportion of the 20 million blacks, five million Mexican-Americans, 500,000 American Indians, and millions of others live day in and day out in conditions we would not let animals endure.

Humanity as a whole is passing through an age gradually becoming conscious also of exploding populations, and alongside this distressing statement there was a second message of the same date dealing with President Nixon's creating a commission to evaluate American population growth, which he described as 'explosive in every way as we head into the last third of this century,' and his announcing that the commission's chairman will be John D. Rockefeller 3rd.

The President's message to Congress last 18 July called for this Commission on Population Growth and the American Future. It was estimated then that by the year 2000 the nation will have grown from 200 to 300 million people, and he said 'perhaps the most dangerous element in the present situation is the fact that so few people are examining these questions from the viewpoint of the whole society'.

If, as has also been estimated, approximately five million of the American population are handicapped mentally, it is patent that this total will increase proportionately unless the faults responsible can be eliminated through increased understanding. But a menacing thought naturally arises. Three *per cent* of the human beings in the technologically most advanced, the financially most affluent, the educationally most informed, administrationally most independent, and vocally least restrained section of the world's 3,000 million people are mentally retarded! What, then, are the overall dimensions of the physical and mental handicap problem humanity as a whole is called upon to face if the achievement of human potential by each and every living individual should become for Man an actual goal?

For that to take place the prime essential is for human beings to take a hard look at themselves not only as people and group—such as priests and laity, as humanists and scientists, as professionals and technicians, as 'snobs and slobs', or as all the other divisive categories each civilized entity has spent its past in erecting and elaborating—but also as individuals. This, too, is happening increasingly and hopefully. After Robert Ardrey's *African Genesis* and *The Territorial Imperative* had awakened the intelligent reading public to the relevance of animal behaviour for our understanding of our own human behaviour, further books such as Desmond Morris's *The Naked Ape* and Philip Wylie's *The Magic Animal* also became essential information for the individual desirous of understanding himself.

T. P. Hipkens, President, Appalachian Regional Hospitals, in delivering the Donald Dabelstein Memorial Lecture (1969) entitled 'Rehabilitation has outlived its Usefulness' at the National Rehabilitation Association's Annual Conference in New York (see *Journal of Rehabilitation* 36, 2:12–16, March–April 1970) said:

> Currently the population of the US is in excess of 200 million. A recent Public Health Service survey revealed more than 23 million persons with chronic activity-limiting conditions. . . A somewhat similar survey by the Social Security Adminis-

> tration (covering only adults aged 18–64) listed 17 million with work-limiting conditions. In both cases the surveys did not cover people who reside in institutions.
>
> *Who are these people?* They are children, older people, poor people, black people; more than 50% of them are over 65 years of age. In the 18–64 group, over six million are disabled by reason of impairments of the musculo-skeletal and/or nervous system. . . .
>
> *What are we doing about it?* In 1968, over 200,000 persons were 'rehabilitated' by the state–federal programs; but as former Commissioner Hunt has stated, 'This is less than the number of new disabled accruing during the same year alone', to say nothing of the backlog as indicated by the statistics mentioned above.

This outspoken address, based on about 25 years of service, then proceeded to discuss the various obstacles of a financial and medical, vocational, and manpower nature to be confronted and surmounted so that rehabilitation could become 'more than the buzzing of a gnat around the elephant-sized problems of the handicapped'.

The most remarkable example of this type of national self-examination process up to the present time however, was the *Progress Report of the National Commission on the Causes and Prevention of Violence* to President Lyndon B. Johnson, issued on 9 January 1969, released to radio and television on 30 January at 6:30 p.m. and in newspapers, 31 January 1969, and sold by the Superintendent of Documents, US Government Printing Office, Washington DC.

In his 'simple and direct' but demanding charge to this Commission under the chairmanship of Dr Milton S. Eisenhower, the President asked them 'to undertake a penetrating search for the causes and prevention of violence—a search into our national life, our past as well as our present, our traditions as well as our institutions, our culture, our customs, and our laws'.

Needless to say, the Commission's labour was then 'far from finished'. Set up after the people of America had 'seen a President struck down by an assassin's bullet and then seen the assassin himself slain while in police custody', its members witnessed plenty of violence thereafter, but its research proceeded by setting up seven task forces whose personnel and central staff numbered approximately 70, and caused more than 140 research projects and special analyses to be undertaken by outside experts and scholars. An eighth task force consisting of study teams meantime investigated recent violent events of which no other factual record had as yet been made.

The Commission itself met almost weekly, studied reports and articles, and held hearings and conferences with over 150 public officials, scholars, experts, religious leaders and private citizens. Its final report, *To establish Justice, to ensure Domestic Tranquillity*, was published in December 1969. I mention these facts so that we, as students of individual awareness, can be as fully informed as many amongst us are bound to desire about the most candid national survey hitherto made of modern human group behaviour. As Saul Pett wrote in his masterly article 'Whatever happened to the Quality of Life—an American Survey' in *Today's World*, Section 7 of *The Philadelphia Inquirer*, Sunday 15 February 1970: 'It was, after all, an official commission appointed by a President of the United States which said this is a racist nation and another Presidential Commission which documented the full extent of its violence. A majesty clings to a system which says these things about itself'.

The problems of brain damage, deficiency of medical care, and violence amidst an exploding population are formidable enough, but a factor contributory to them all is doubtless the fact disclosed by James E. Allen, Jr., US Commissioner of Education, in the April 1970 issue of *Reader's Digest* on 'We can end Juvenile Illiteracy', that about 25%, *i.e.* eleven million out of today's 45 million United States school children 'suffer from significant reading problems'; of these children, three in five, or 6 million 'have problems so severe that they cannot be corrected in today's ordinary classroom'.

Having indicated the immensity of the national problems that not only the United States, but the whole of the world's 3,000 million human beings in less favoured communities confront today, it will be a relief to turn, as Alexander did, to a consideration of what each literate human individual should know about himself.

Basic facts about cranial phylogeny and body movements

Alexander's terminology of 'primary control' and 'head–neck relationship' on the one side, and the work of Sherrington and Magnus on segmental and suprasegmental reflexes on the other side, had riveted my attention while writing the aforesaid three papers on several anatomical and neurological facts about the segmental structure of the head and body and the means whereby they inter-articulate, that now assumed a novel and self-evident, yet hitherto unrecognized significance from the phylogenetic point of view. Mr Maisel referred in the introduction to his book to 'the lack of any coherent theory as to how and when Man went awry in the use of himself'. So it seemed potentially helpful to those investigating their individual awareness to discuss here some of the basic developmental, anatomical and neurological facts about the human head, as well as practical matters about simple head and body movements that we perform.

All mammals, including human beings, have seven neck vertebræ but eight neck nerves. In all of them, the first two vertebræ (atlas and axis) are built so as to allow nodding (*i.e.* fore and aft) or flexion and extension movements of the skull on the atlas; and rotational (*i.e.* left and right swinging) movements of the skull and atlas upon the axis, in which the rest of the neck vertebræ participate to a lesser extent.

Ancestrally there are only two sorts of striped muscular response. Flexion or extension are the only alternative movements that any muscle can perform. So all our muscles were and still are either *extensors* (those behind) or *flexors* (those in front of the transverse processes) of our vertebræ. Rotational movement is *a resultant of interaction* between them.

Twisting can only occur ordinarily by differential action between flexor and extensor action in several body segments adjacent to one another. Rotation of the intermediate segments occurs spontaneously in any segmented creature—from caterpillar to human being—when one or several segments flex a part of the body while another one or several segments extend another part at a shorter or greater distance away. The segments in between simply bend by being kept partially flexed on one side and extended on the other. So, neurologically and muscularly, the reflex background of these basic head movements had been very simply contrived at the mammalian outset.

Head rotation, however, is unique, in being localized to the atlas's swinging the head around its own but separated off-body, or centre (now the odontoid process of the axis). This swinging of the head-carrying atlas is facilitated in mammals like ourselves by the superior and inferior oblique (extensor) muscles attached on either side to the transverse processes of the atlas. Their tips are the only bones we can palpate with our two digits just under the mastoid processes, moving as we rotate our heads. To let this happen, the two obliques on the one side contract while those of the other side relax, the muscles of the two sides alternating in this contraction and relaxation.

But these movements which occur reflexly and spontaneously in most animals could easily be interfered with by a big-headed or flop-headed creature like Man, who has striven to become erect after having passed through such a parade of adaptation-demanding habitats. Especially was this the case once he had forsaken the ancient four-footed posture with which some 500 million years of piscine, amphibian, reptilian, mammalian and primate evolution had endowed him. He has been clambering along and swinging by his hands from branches and rearing himself up on his hind legs during only the past 10 million years or less. Many of his modern successors are still incapable of, or fail to become skilled in, sustaining themselves—or the big brains of which they are so proud—in that fantastic and (evolutionarily speaking) unpremeditated, bipedal posture.*

The first, or head-nodding and rotating, cervical (*i.e.* neck) segment of the spinal cord performs this critical function of linking the brain stem with the spinal cord. The most curious characteristic of the sensory part of this crucial bridge is its being completely deprived of sensory information from the skin. It has no direct contact whatever with the outside world. The only sensory information it receives from its own body segment is internal, or *proprioceptive*. Its direct and presumptively dominant information thus comes entirely from the first cervical muscles, from the atlas vertebra, and the cranial occiput to which the muscles of its own segment are attached, and from the joints and the ligaments between these two bones alone.

Any sensory information from the skin upon which the motor cells of those important muscles of the first neck segment are dependent for nodding (*i.e.* flexing and extending) the head perfectly, whatever position your body may happen to assume, is that coming

---

* See 'The Floppy Ape' by M. Trupp in *Proc. 2nd int. Cong. Primat.* vol. 2, (Karger, New York and Basal, 1969), pp. 143–46.

Table 2.1. Cranial nerves

Nerve	Type	Function
I. Olfactory	Sensory	Smell (olfaction).
II. Optic	Sensory	Vision (reflex of focusing and constricting the pupil).
III. Oculomotor	Motor	Movements of eyelid, elevation of eyelid, constriction of pupil and focusing of lens.
IV. Trochlear	Motor	Eye movements (up and down).
V. Trigeminal		
1.	Sensory	General senses from cornea of eyeball, upper nasal cavity, front of scalp, forehead, upper eyelid and others.
2.	Sensory	General senses from cheek, upper lip, upper teeth, mucosa of nasal cavity, palate, parts of pharynx.
3.	Mixed	Sensory: general senses from tongue (not taste), lower teeth, skin of lower jaw. Motor: chewing.
VI. Abducens	Motor	Abduction of eye (lateral movement).
VII. Facial	Mixed	Sensory: taste. Motor: salivation, lacrimation, movement of facial muscles.
VIII. Vestibulocochlear		
Cochlear	Sensory	Hearing.
Vestibular	Sensory	Equilibrium.
IX. Glossopharyngeal	Mixed	Sensory: taste, other sensations of the tongue. Motor: secretation of saliva; swallowing.
X. Vagus	Mixed	Swallowing. Monitors oxygen and carbon dioxide levels in blood, senses blood pressure, other visceral activities of affected systems.
XI. Accessory (spinal accessory)	Motor	Voice production (larynx); muscle sense; movement of head, shoulders.
XII. Hypoglossal	Motor	Movements of tongue during speech, swallowing; muscle sense.

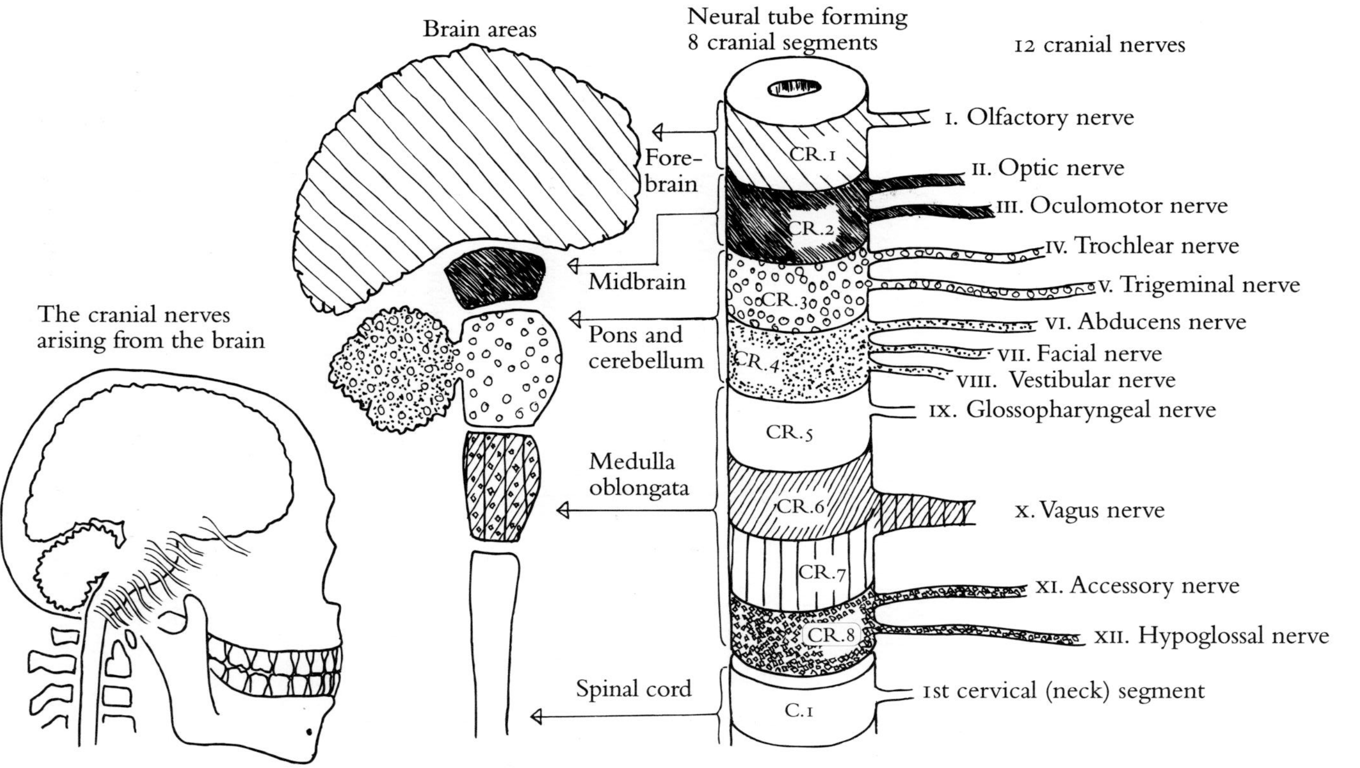

Fig. 2.1. The brain and its cranial nerves. The neural tissue of 8 cranial segments forms 12 cranial nerves and becomes areas of brain.

into the segment after filtration through the adjacent skin-supplying body segments other than its own. In the human squatting or standing (or *orthograde*) positions, the dominant segmental skin information concerned in human head balance is probably that coming from the sacral or hindmost body segments supplying the soles of the feet, especially the pads of the toes and heels. That for sitting is from even further back, around the tail morphologically.

Nearest to the first cervical segment, however, and therefore necessarily implicated in every head movement, especially the rotational ones, is the information coming in from below, from the adjacent *second cervical* segment. It comes from the skin covering the back, or occipital, half of the head and from the collar-like skin area around the junction of the head with the neck. Far more important from the ancestral, or phylogenetic, point of view is the information flooding in from above, through the trigeminal nerve—from the whole of the skin of the entire face (nose, eyelids, ears, mouth, jaws, teeth and tongue), both outside and inside the mouth and palate, from as far back as the fauces of the pharynx. So much exteroceptive, or external, sensory skin information can come in through that single trigeminal (or fifth cranial) nerve route that many acrobatic people can, and do, spend their lives suspending the whole weight of their whirling bodies from their teeth, jaws and heads. Naturally, in this sort of activity, not only is the strength of the masticatory muscles supplied by that nerve involved, but also the sensory information coming in from those jaw muscles, bones, and temporo-mandibular joints. This stupendous exteroceptive information load is carried to its huge trigeminal nucleus in the brain stem or medulla oblongata and extends down into the cervical part of the spinal cord.

So this staggeringly immense trigeminal and extensive second cervical sensory information coming in from the upper part of the neck and from the entire head (both back and front), as well as that from the mouth-closing, food-ingesting, masticating, and even swallowing, head-nodding and head-rotating musculature is, and can all be, directly involved with that from the soles of the feet and their muscles in affecting this vital head-moving-on-neck relationship in human beings. In a complete but rather less direct way, the skin and voluntary muscles of every other segment of the body can be involved therein. Amongst these other segments, too, there are, naturally, varying degrees of involvement. Those most nearly involved are the succeeding third, fourth and fifth cervical segments. They bring in information from the skin, muscles, and joints of these other neck segments and also from the diaphragm—and so, similarly, do all the other body segments, particularly those assisting in the respiratory function of our bodies.

All this ordinary sensory skin, muscle and joint information from the body is also channelled upwards through the hind-brain and pons into the cerebellum, the equilibratory mechanism of the brain, by means of two massive neural pathways (the direct and indirect, spino-cerebellar tracts). They both enter the cerebellum—the direct, or superior, tract in front of, and the indirect, or inferior, tract behind a third cerebellar pathway—the pons, or middle peduncle of the cerebellum. This pontine, or middle-cerebellar peduncle, relays posteriorly to the cerebellum those intelligent, or voluntary, impulses coming downwards directly from the cerebral cortex to the nuclei or grey matter in the pons. By means of them we are, or should be, able to cause our bodies to carry out those intentional movements requiring skill in balancing.

The motor portion of the trigeminal (or fifth cranial) nerve comes out of, and its sensory fibres enter into, the brain through the middle of the pons. This simple anatomical fact made it obvious to me before 1923—when my paper on the zeuglodont (or primitive cetacean or whale brain) was published—that the pons and the cerebellum had simply developed by an expansion of what had originally been the sensory territory, or sensorium, of this trigeminal (or fifth cranial) nerve but which had originally been the third cranial segment of the vertebrate brain. The cerebellar cortex had evolved by a succession of sensory nerve invasions of the third cranial (or ancestral trigeminal) area in a fashion comparable with the origin of the forebrain cortex by similar successive sensory invasions of the first cranial, or ancestral olfactory sensory, segment; and comparate also with the origin of the midbrain and thalamus by similar successive sensory intrusions into, or invasions by, nerves carrying other types of sensory information into the second cranial, or ancestral visual sensory, segment. The most important, if not primary, cerebellum-forming invader, was the eighth, or balancing nerve, of the adjacent or fourth cranial segment.

Each of these three anterior segments of the brain—olfactory, visual and trigeminal—had vied with one another and with the last, vestibular (or eighth cranial nerve) member of the anterior four cranial segments ancestrally for securing, in its own particular way, the dominant role or position in controlling reflexly the movements of the bodies of animals as wholes.

The success story of all vertebrate animals from the dogfish, or shark stage, to Man thus depended at the very outset upon evolving from eight simple cranial segments the special type of food-snatching head their eight-cranial-segmented, fishy ancestor had evolved some 500 million or more years ago. The static first (or smelling) and mobile second (or seeing) organs in the two front segments of both the brain and the skull were protected by the growth anteriorly over them of the skin and tissue layer supplied by the third cranial, or trigeminal (or food-catching jaw) body segment behind them. Having taken over this tactile skin function for the two cranial segments in front [*i.e.* CR. 1 and CR. 2], it ultimately did the same for the six body segments behind it [*i.e.* CR. 4, 5, 6, 7, 8 and 1st cervical], right back to the second cervical segment.

In the same way as the two most anterior or olfactory organs became fixed in the roof of the trigeminally-supplied mouth in front, so the two hindmost, equilibratory or vestibular organs in the fourth brain and skull segment (whose information about the body's position in space comes from the swirl of the fluid inside their semicircular canals) also lay embedded in the cartilaginous tissue furnished by the same third, or trigeminal, body segment. The jaw-snapping (trigeminal) and face-orifice-closing and sucking (the seventh cranial or facial nerve) muscles come from the flexor or ventral halves of the somitic musculature in these two posterior members (*i.e.* trigeminal and vestibular) of the four anterior, chiefly sensorial cranial or body segments we have been considering. The rest is ocular, being the dorsal or extensor halves of these two somites (the muscles supplied by the fourth, or trochlear, and sixth, or abducens, cranial nerves) together with all of the musculature of the anterior two (smell and sight) cranial segments, which is supplied by the third cranial nerve. In other words, two and two half somites were devoted purely to making the visual organs mobile—to enabling the eyes to move and see in every possible direction, whether left and right, up and down, or inwards and outwards, fore and aft.

I have been recalling that the fifth cranial nerve, or *trigeminus* (which is the third sensory nerve and also tripartite, having ophthalmic, maxillary and mandibular divisions structurally) took over the function of peripheral skin sensation for all of the eight cranial segments (except for the fragmentary post-auricular part of the vagus), and also for the first cervical segment—*i.e.* for nine body segments altogether.

Upon this unique skin-sensorial achievement (for there is nothing in the biological world comparable with it in the realm of tactual sensitivity, unless it be the tips of our fingers and toes) the whole further development of vertebrates depended, for this trigeminal specialization ensured their feeding and thus their growth, as well as their offensive protection. It meant that whatever came into contact with any part of the torpedo-like front end of the free-swimming, piscine body, the tactile information therefrom would be channelled with the speed of a segmental reflex to the jaw-snapping and gill-moving (later sucking) musculature for seizure of food and its ingestion or rejection, and for defence by means of the same maxillo–mandibular and hyoid muscle and nerve segments (fig. 2.2).

Meanwhile, the descending root (or tract) of the trigeminal nerve and its sensory nucleus (which extends through the posterior four cranial segments and the upper two and possibly more cervical segments) exercises a similar direct control over the muscles innervated by the motor-nuclei of all these respiratory, swallowing and head-neck-and-body-rotating muscles. Its sensory 'facial' information operates, of course, conjunctly with information from the balancing, visual, smelling and gustatory organs, simultaneously or consecutively bursting in through their sensory nerves and tracts to modify the motor reactions of these muscles, which we will now consider very briefly. In some animals, like the egg-laying Australian mammal called the platypus, the snout end is so sensitive and its trigeminus so large that some of its tract may extend throughout many more, if not all, of their spinal segments.

When the ancestral torpedo-like, food-searching piscine body moved in swimming, the swirl of the fluid in its semicircular canals sent information into its brain about gravity and its swimming po-

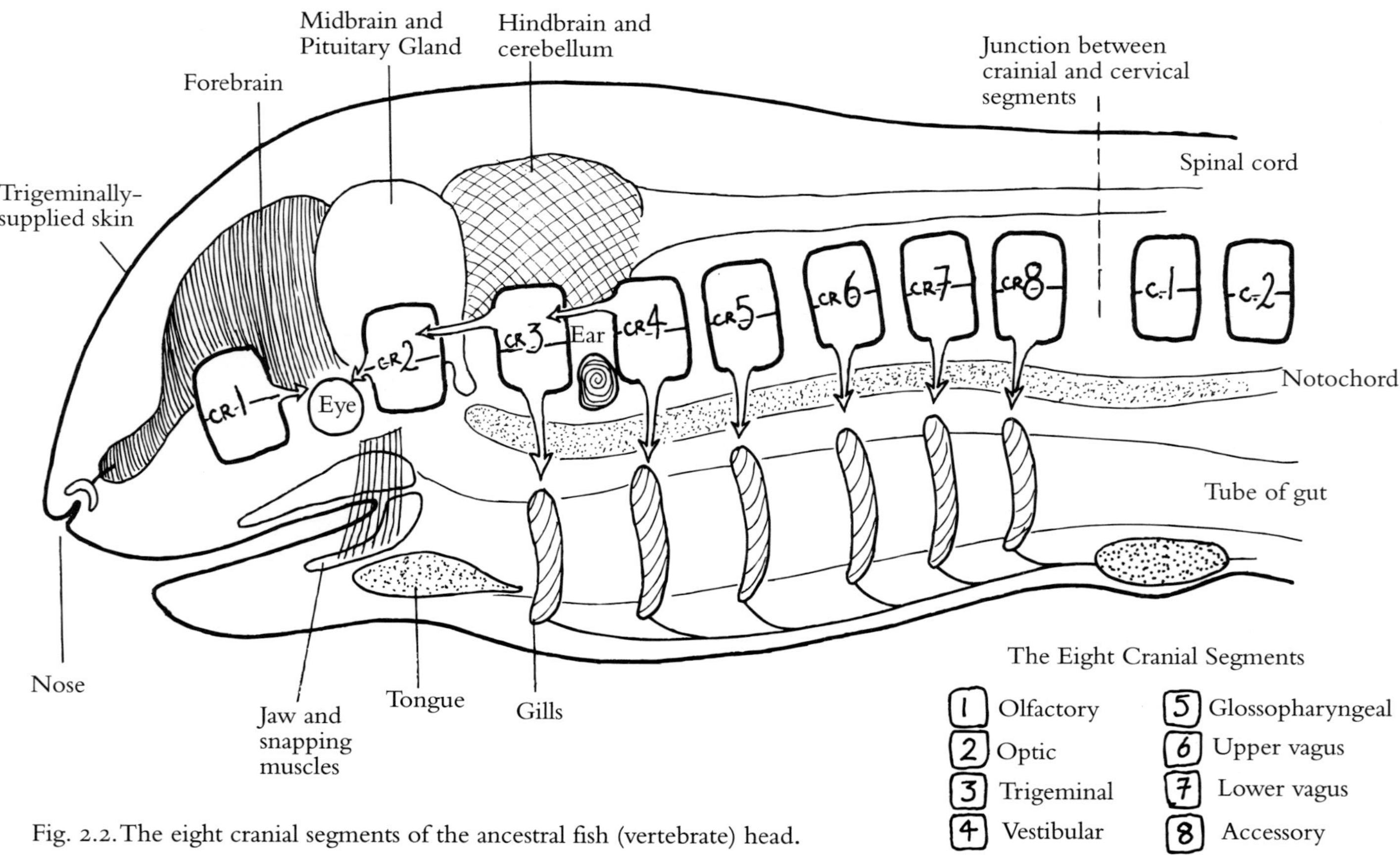

Fig. 2.2. The eight cranial segments of the ancestral fish (vertebrate) head.

sition, or orientation in watery space, through those two vestibular organs. They kept the vestibular nuclei in the medulla oblongata part of the hind-brain reflexly informed about the spatial orientation of its seeing and food-catching head, and thus, incidentally, about whether the fish-like body temporarily lost and then regained an even keel, or not. If thrown out of balance by what the jaws seized, the body spontaneously righted itself by means of vestibulo–spinal impulses that flowed directly through the tract running from the vestibular nuclei in the hind-brain to all the nuclei of the spinal cord segments controlling the body muscles and the fins, especially those of the pectoral and pelvic fins. Those two pairs of fins were the ancestors of the fore and hind limbs of the succeeding amphibian, reptilian, mammalian and primate types that gave birth finally to the hominids. They all employed those fins increasingly as front (or upper) and hind (or lower) limbs as they adapted successively to terrestrial, arboreal and, finally, bipedal existence.

Connections were also established from the outset between the vestibular nuclei and all the nuclei concerned with reflexly controlling the eye muscles by means of the very ancient but most effective association tracts called the *medial longitudinal bundles*. These bundles

---

Fig. 2.2 illustrates the phylogeny of the octomeral (8-segmented) vertebrate fish head. The first four are:

1st segment: The 'olfactory' forms the forebrain and the smelling apparatus: the nose.

2nd segment: The 'optic' forms the midbrain and the seeing apparatus: the eyes, their muscles and nerves.

3rd segment: The 'trigeminal' is the largest cranial segment, forming the pons and cerebellum, the bones of the skull and jaw, the jaw-snapping muscles and the skin from the nose to the 2nd neck segment with their accompanying nerves.

4th segment: The 'vestibular' forms the cerebellum and hearing parts of the hindbrain, the balancing apparatus and the facial muscles and nerves.

These anterior four segments are responsible for smelling, seeing, food seizing, balancing and feeling (sense of touch).

The posterior, or occipital four cranial segments are: 5th: glossopharyngeal; 6th: upper vagus; 7th lower vagus; 8th: accessory. They jointly form (from their extensor musculature) the tongue muscles, supplied by the hypoglossal nerve. These segments are responsible for food tasting, swallowing, gill moving (in fish) or respiration and vocalisation (in humans) and blood circulation. They also make the vital connection between the sensing head, the moving limbs and the supporting spine.

run upward as natural continuations of the spinal tracts connecting the anterior horn or motor cells on both sides of the spinal cord. Their fibres are the first of all to become *myelinated* in the human fœtal brain because instant correlation of the equilibrated body's position with what it happens to see and smell, so as to discover its potential nutritive or harmful significance, is supremely important for that creature's future. Only if it could respond to such information immediately and effectively was the fishy creature's further growth, development and reproduction assured.

Just as four anterior body (or cranial) segments developed into the front, food-seeking and seizing half of the head and brain, so another four posterior body (or cranial) segments produced the posterior, tasting and swallowing and breathing half of the head and brain. It is also called the medulla oblongata, and here the transition occurs between this self-regulating part of the brain (containing also its important intrinsic respiratory and circulatory or oxygenating centres) and the uppermost end of the spinal cord, or medulla spinalis. So these four—the ninth, tenth, eleventh and twelfth—posterior cranial nerves resemble the trigeminal segment and any typical spinal nerve in having both motor and sensory portions; but they have become artfully modified because of the reflex quasi-peristaltic or swallowing (and vomiting or rejecting) work they also have to do.

The twelfth (or hypoglossal) nerve supplies the muscles of the tongue to extend it or push it out, and twist it around in the mouth so as to put food where it can be swallowed reflexly (*i.e.* involuntarily). This, of course, involves intense collaboration between the tongue's musculature and that of the cheeks (seventh, sucking or facial nerve), jaws and palate (fifth or trigeminal nerve) for mastication which, like the movement of the tongue, is under voluntary control.

The ninth, tenth, and eleventh (or glosso–pharyngeal, vagus and accessory) nerves supply the elevating and constricting muscles of the pharynx, those for closing and opening the larynx, and also the sternomastoid and trapezius muscles that attach the mobile shoulder girdle (clavicle and scapula) to the nodding and rotating skull. In this delicate work of bodily adjustment of the head, these last four cranial nerves and muscles are aided by the nerves and muscles of the neck (or cervical) segments when a neck emerges and develops, in amphibia, reptiles, birds and mammals.

These last four cranial nerves coming from the four posterior or occipital segments of the head arise alongside one another: the twelfth in front of, and the others, in the sequence of their enumeration (*i.e.* 9, 10, and 11), directly behind the hypoglossal (and the olive separating them). The hypoglossal (or twelfth) nerve supplies muscles derived from the entire dorsal, or extensor, halves of all four occipital segments. The glosso–pharyngeal (or ninth cranial) nerve transmits, along with the seventh nerve, taste sensations from the tongue, and also contains pharyngeal muscle motor fibres which were derived from only one (the ventral or flexor) half of the first occipital segment. The vagus (or tenth nerve) supplies muscles derived from the ventral, or flexor, halves of both the second and the third occipital segments and has the small post-auricular sensory nerve previously mentioned as supplying the skin behind the ear.

The accessory (or eleventh) nerve is very strange. It supplies muscles derived from the fourth (or bulbar, *i.e.* medulla oblongata) ventral or flexor half of the fourth occipital segment, and from correspondingly lesser parts of the first, second, third, fourth, and even lower cervical segments behind it and within the spinal canal. These all join up to pass out of the skull together, and link up with a more direct supply from these same neck segments outside in the neck. This rather special arrangement was apparently also necessary to enable the very mobile heads of mammals to control the movements of their forelimbs (and incidentally those of their hindlimbs) while these fully extended and speedy, digitigrade limbs support the terrestrialized body in the stupendous variety of its positions and postures during rapid and skilled acrobatic bodily movement.

This occipital or posterior cranial control work, as far as human beings are concerned, is a somewhat more complicated skill to acquire because the muscles those four occipital segments supply guard reflexly the two body portals, the throat and the larynx. Through them each and every particle of food we eat, of fluid we drink, or of air we breathe must pass down as correctly and comfortably as possible, whatever position in space our bodies may temporarily be adopting, or whatever actions we may be causing our bodies to carry out, or whatever our thoughts and our emotional states may happen to be when we are in the process of expressing ourselves in words or song. We can only control them by harmonizing our wills with their automatic functioning.

The fantastic thing about the seemingly intricate occipital brain mechanism as a whole is its segmental simplicity, especially if we consider the variety and complexity of the activities for which and to which it has become modified and adapted in the various amphibian, reptilian, avian, and mammalian, or primate types of life. It has been constructed from no more than four such somites or body segments; but they, too, have had a long and extraordinary history, or prehistory.

Since we have had to refer to these four occipital segments, it is appropriate to recall that the body of each one of us consists (neurologically, myologically and osteologically speaking) of a specific number of repetitive segmental parts or somites—42 or 43 in all: eight cranial, eight cervical, twelve dorsal (or thoracic), five lumbar, five sacral (or pelvic), and four or five coccygeal (or tail) segments (fig. 2.3).

Although we enumerate the nerves in this fashion to correspond as nearly as possible to our mammalian-type vertebral columns, we should remember that, functionally, their plexuses conserve a more ancient quadrupedal segmental pattern evolved from reptilian and amphibian paddling life.

We found the eight cranial segments divided functionally into the food-seizing and air-admitting anterior four segments, and the posterior four food-swallowing and air-respiring segments. Similarly, the upper four cervical segments are head-, neck- and upper limb-adjusting and respiratory segments; the lower four cervical segments collaborate with the first thoracic segment to form the anterior or upper limb itself. Just as the accessory nerve and its segment help to connect the head with the neck, so the fourth cervical segment links the neck and upper limb, and the second thoracic nerve tightens the upper-thorax connection.

We tend to regard the thorax as something separate from the belly or abdomen. This is only partly true because the diaphragm (innervated by the second, third and fourth cervical nerves) and the heart and lungs above it are slipped-down neck structures that the twelve-segmented, thoracic rib-cage protects only in mammals. Meantime,

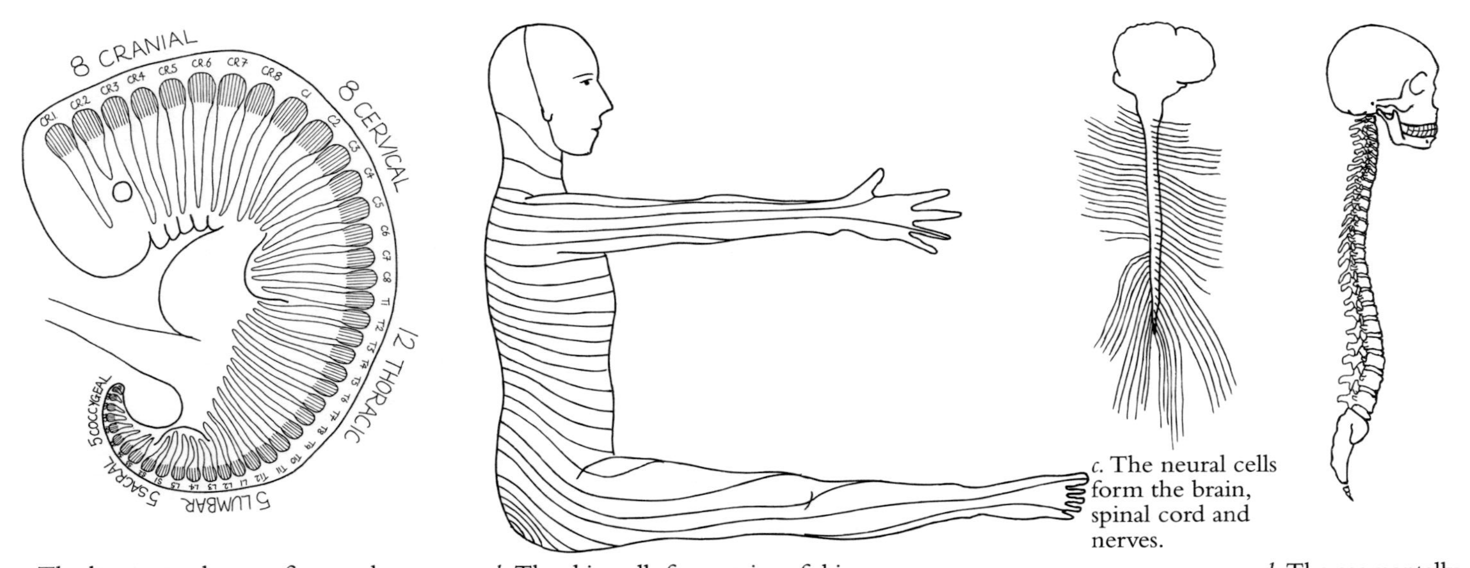

a. The human embryo at five weeks showing how the muscle cells within the 43 segments divide into flexor and extensor halves.

b. The skin cells form strips of skin that envelop the body.

c. The neural cells form the brain, spinal cord and nerves.

d. The segmentally-arranged bone cells form the skull, jaw and spinal colum, i.e. vertebrae, ribs, sacrum and coccyx.

Fig. 2.3. Derivatives of the 43 somites (segments): (*a*) muscle cells, (*b*) skin cells, (*c*) neural cells and (*d*) bone cells.

the muscles of the lower six thoracic nerves form the side walls and front of the mammalian belly, along with the bridging first lumbar segment.

There are five lumbar, five sacral, and four or five coccygeal (or tail) segments, but only five of them (the third, fourth, and fifth lumbar and the first and second sacral) were needed to form the lower or hind limbs, and the muscles of the tail segments were employed to control the uro–genital organs.

Just as a symphony is erected upon a simple, basic theme, so each body is a symphysis or growing together and functioning collaboration, usually in groups of four, five, six, seven, eight or twelve, of this series of 42 basically simple and similar body segments. They came to differ, evolutionally, merely according to the nature of the work—muscular, nervous or osseous—that they did. The overall objective or continuous purpose of each living creature is also simple: the maintenance of its life and the reproduction of that life. The value of these repetitive segments and their collaborative group mechanisms lies in their directive mobility. They enable the jaw-furnished, air-breathing vertebrate creature to move its body in perfect balance towards, to seize and swallow its food, and also to relieve itself of its waste products and its procreative elements.

When analysing thus our own elemental human structure, we are considering the latest, most recent, and so most complicated edition of this segmented apparatus for moving our body and its supra-segmental parts. To understand how it arose we have been emulating as far as it is necessary the mental work of the biologists, chemists, physicists and geologists whose labours, over the past two centuries, have provided us with the structural information we now possess.

What, then, are the basic requirements of all these similarly structured animals, including ourselves, from fishes (or even cœlenterates such as sea anemones and jellyfish) upwards? They are food, drink and oxygen from fresh air! Our food has been split up by our chemist brethren into solids known as proteins, fats, carbohydrates, vitamins and all their subdivisions; the liquid water into its hydrogen and oxygen and the substances soluble therein; and the gaseous air into its oxygen, nitrogen, ozone and other elements. Meantime, the physicists have split the nuclear material of which all elements are composed into their sub-elements.

Our pharynx and gullet can swallow food only in a mushy or semi-solid form; the larynx can admit air only in its natural or gaseous condition.

All animals, from dogfish or shark to Man, typically have jaws, furnished with teeth or beaks to *seize* their food, which is salivated and either *swallowed* whole as reptiles and birds do, or, in the case of mammals, first masticated and then swallowed.

The four cranial body segments with which we carry out these functions of eating and swallowing are part and parcel of the body, which must integrate these with the cervical, thoracic and lower body segments that enable us to carry out the functions of breathing and speaking and singing, whether we are politicians or playboys, miners or mezzo-sopranos. We all have this same quota of head and body segments, whether we totter about like children, run around the sports field, or perform programs on public platforms or in Olympic contests. The way we use them depends on the degree of neural organization or bodily and intellectual skill attained individually.

How any intelligent individual can study his or her own self

The personal issue is whether the things we are doing day by day are done in a conscious and balanced way or are part of a pain-ridden struggle. If yours be the latter method, stop! Then lie down on a carpeted floor with a big book under your head and pull your heels up as near as possible to your buttocks and study yourself first while resting in a *semi-supine* flexed position. Then read an interesting article, preferably after lunch, for at least 10 or 15 minutes; and longer if possible. Note occasionally in a diary what aches, or other sensations you felt as you rested, and where they were.

If you keep a record day by day you will be astonished before long at how many of those creaks and aches you have localized, how much your awareness of the *weight-bearing parts* of your aching body has increased, and how greatly from time to time their situation and severity has changed.

If you want to vary things a bit a few weeks later you can try lying in the fully supine position with your arms relaxed at your sides, or at right angles to your torso, and your legs as widely separated as you find feasible. The fully supine position is a splendid one from which to begin one's exploration of posture and the parts of our bodily awareness. But you must keep the record of what you did with yourself, otherwise you will lose track of the parts of yourself and where the transitory sensations of unease were, and which were the joints that creaked.

As the weeks pass and the notes increase you can try turning over into the fully *prone* position with your arms down at your sides and the back, or dorsum, of each hand and foot on the floor and, if necessary, a suitably large book under your breast-bone (sternum). Then you can let your forehead rest on the floor and thus give to the frontal (forehead) portions of your trigeminal nerves perhaps their first chance of establishing mutual understanding with your vestibular (body balancing) nerves while your relaxed, resting head feels the carpet and nods up and down or rolls gently to the right and left with your lips closed and the teeth of both jaws resting in gentle apposition with one another. Both the mouth and the eyes can stay closed but not clenched, so that you can think about what changes are happening in your joints, and the character of the muscular sensations as you alter the positions of your body and the movements of its parts. If you do these things and note the effects this novel and grovelling flat-out, or Chinese *kowtow*, position has had from day to day upon your breathing, circulation and feelings, you can record them with considerable advantage for the next week or month.

The handicap that can make any book useless and even minimizes the value of any lecture like this one, or series of instructions that require personal activity on the part of the reader, is that he can skip, in a few seconds, by reading or simple listening, over activities that may have consumed years of experience on the part of the writer. So it is just as well to remind my readers at this point that what I have been preaching here is a practice I have been following in a leisurely, explorative fashion since September 1943, so it has been in progress for more than a quarter of a century. During that time very many notes have been made about some, but not necessarily all, of the changes I have observed to occur in the parts of my body. So I am writing only for those who have some correspondingly objective view of the body they may happen to have, and of the projecting parts of its bones that come into contact with the carpet, floor or ground upon which they may move those bones.

Manage firstly to do the *kowtow* posture and then, in this posture, try out the effects on your neck and shoulders of the variant nodding and rotational head movements opened up for exploration thereby. Once these can be done whilst breathing comfortably and without the help of the thinnest books under your chest, you can proceed to the five-minute study of each, and progressively all, of the right- and left-arm movements that you will find can be carried out in this first, and safest, of all ancestral positions for a terrestrial vertebrate.

As the weeks pass and the notes accumulate you can proceed, secondly, to the various synchronous movements that one's upper and the lower limbs can execute—separately, of course, at the outset, and later on in unison, but not tiring yourself ever, nor forgetting to make notes about any improving awarenesses you may achieve in your breathing, or facility therein, and about the locations of 'painful or aching' joints that may by now loosen and creak or unlock.

Thirdly, from this basic and completely safe *prone* posture, being entirely free from fear, you can proceed to the study of what happens as soon as one begins to roll over slowly and studiously—by pressing lightly on the floor with the dorsum or back of your right hand or the dorsum of your right foot, using each hand or foot singly at the outset, and subsequently with pressure on the dorsa of the right hand and right foot together—onto the opposite, *i.e.* the left shoulder and hip. As you balance on these two weight-bearing points and the side of your left leg, your head will be in the air, unless you have put a small book under the place where it will be as you roll onto the midline of your left ear and left side of your head and body.

In that midline position, however, as your head rolls quietly on the book, you can let your two left (*i.e.* trigeminal and second cervical) 'head-skin' nerves participate sequentially, making their much-needed personal acquaintance with your internally-located vestibular organs and their potentialities for equilibrating when operating collaboratively or separately. Then you can gently allow your improved body to subside into its original prone posture and do the same sort of easy first exercises in studying how cranially inspired equilibration of the body came into existence. Then, starting with pressure from the opposite, *i.e.* left, hand or foot, roll onto your right ear and side, subsequently comparing and recording the results of your head-rolling experiences, and the new sorts of aches, pains, breathing, or other sensations you elicited from your body.

As your knowledge about safe equilibrium progresses you may become able to do it all without any book support, simply by letting your head bend laterally to make and keep contact with the carpet. Because of the increasing loosening of your neck (which must never be strained after as an objective), or because you will gradually have learned to allow your body to move up over your shoulder, or to depress the shoulder enough, you will ultimately let your head do its gentle rolling in comfort, quietly, on the carpet. I do not suffer nowadays from the stiffness or soreness of the neck with which I was accustomed to contend.

After learning how the body can roll onto its left and right sides and back from the new *prone* posture, carry the movement onwards posteriorly through the midline into the *supine* posture. Then you may gently master rolling back through the midline into the prone posture, and gradually become skilled with both sides in this leisurely, explorative sort of rolling. (Restriction of the word *crawling* to apply only to movement of the body forward on the abdomen with the aid of the limbs (*i.e. ventigrade* progression) has been advocated for over a decade and a half in order to define its application therapeutically.*)

It will have become patent gradually to the more or less persistent explorer of one's own personal capacity for body movement that the *prone* position is an ideal one from which to bring the front half of the body into the *forehead–elbow* body-supporting position by resting the forehead on the floor with the forearms folded under the breastbone and the hands (dorsa downward) overlapping, or alongside one another.

Then you can try to lift up the chest from the forehead and elbows and let it subside gently, while breathing regularly in and out through the nostrils with the lips closed and the tooth rows gently opposed. Until this novel lifting movement of the front part of the torso and the new type of breathing (that any such new posture, safe as it is,

---

* 'Children with Severe Brain Injuries: neurological organization in terms of mobility' by R. J. Doman, E. B. Spitz, E. Zuchman, C. H. Delacato, G. Doman in *Journal of the American Medical Association*, 174:257–62, 1960.

generally demands) can be carried out without any interference by holding the breath but by letting the air flow easily in and out through the nostrils, the movement cannot be considered mastered. Your notes on what happened when you first tried and when you ultimately achieved this feat should be specially useful.

When this upper-torso-lifting movement has been mastered one can add to it, first by attaining the forehead–elbow position and then flexing or drawing the knees up into their natural body-supporting position without respiratory distress of any kind. This *forehead–elbows–knees posture*, when attained, is the next sort of exploratory posture, and the first, and easiest, from which to learn in perfect safety the lessons of raising our bodies and letting them roll gently over our shoulders or our hips separated, each in turn or both at once, onto the floor without injury.

Man is the creature of fear! In other words, he is the most fearful (in every sense of that word) just as he can and has become the most fearless of all animals. This is because he has become the most nearly tip-toed of all the two-footed, or bipedal, creatures. His walking is a constant precarious process of saving himself from falling. So the primary fear to overcome is his fear of falling.

Restriction of the use of the word *creeping* to apply only to movement forward on the palms of the hands and the knees in this position has been advocated in order to define the application therapeutically of this *palmigrade-knee position.**

Perhaps the greatest tribute we could pay to the memory of F. M. Alexander a century after his birth would be to compose a textbook on anatomy and physiology, or on successful applications or modifications of his ideas for modern and future exponents of the Alexander Technique, perhaps utilizing a wider range of exploratory positions and activities for those therapeutically involved, alone or together, in bettering human ills. But this was not my purpose. It is sufficient to have indicated in the most elementary but direct way known to me something of the amplitude of the knowledge of the body and its prehistoric movements that is already becoming available to eve-

---

* 'Children with Severe Brain Injuries: Neurological organization in terms of mobility' by R. J. Doman, E. B. Spitz, E. Zuchman, C. H. Delacato, G. Doman in *Journal of the American Medical Association*, 174:257–62, 1960.

ryone today from the immense labours of zoologists and palæontologists, anatomists and physiologists, embryologists and neurologists, developmental educationalists and psychologists, as well as from psychiatry, anthropology and other fields of enquiry that have fructified during the past century and especially during the last couple of decades. These have provided the minima about human structure and movement and how they have come to be as we find them today. Those minima should now be, or will soon become, readily available to every person who becomes sufficiently educated to appreciate a personal need for a more detailed awareness of his or her own body.

A forward look—general and individual

Celebrating the centenary of Alexander's birth in the fashion of this address and such a book as I have envisaged may not be what he would have approved; but such works would, I believe, be of considerable assistance to those who are handing on the torch that he lit. The serious purpose of Maisel's *The Resurrection of the Body* has been to select for a far more vast modern audience (that is, far more conscious of and deeply concerned about their bodies, and perhaps also their minds, than their forebears had time to) an objective insight into the life and influence of one of the first, if not actually the first person, not only to declare but also to demonstrate by his living, teaching and writing the verity of that unity—the self.

If, in the pursuit of the same objectives, these manners we have chosen to celebrate his birth should prove to be an introduction to the means whereby increasing numbers of human beings learn—whether directly from this pioneer's own self-analysing process or from the hands of its teachers—how to better their own uses of themselves, we will have succeeded far beyond the expectations of our contemporaries.

Any such enlargement of our horizons is bound to reveal that not only Alexander but also a vast multitude of his contemporaries were piling up, both consciously and unconsciously, as their predecessors had also done, a hitherto relatively unexploited wealth of knowledge. This is affording now a relatively small return; but it will yield in the future an immeasurable harvest of well-being for humanity to enjoy and extend, and thus not only to garner but also to use.

The electronic technological era, into which the whole of an as yet ill-adapted humanity has suddenly been hurled, with all its ultra-rapid colour television and even infrared telephotographic gadgetry, its computerized industrial mechanisms and electronically monitored scientific experimentation, has had at least one most significant by-product. From the 1920s to the 1950s most scientists, including most of our medical colleagues and even the psychologists, avoided discussing, or positively rejected, such concepts as awareness, consciousness and attention as too vague, subjective and mentalistic for scientific study. Today, however, as mentioned at the outset, electromyography, electro-encephalography and telemetry have thrown all these subjects, in particular, wide open for present and future revelations even at the stage of their anticipation.

Perhaps science has brought us already within measurable distance of envisaging the seemingly impossible goal of a psycho-physically improved humanity, such as inspired the early manhood of Alexander in the last decade of the last century.

Having travelled thus far together, let me summarize briefly before we separate. The electronic facilities of the '60s have confirmed Alexander's insight and authenticated the technique he discovered in the 1890s of teaching both average and skilled adult individuals how to become aware of their wrong body use, to eliminate handicaps and thus achieve better, *i.e.* increasingly skilled, use of themselves both physically and mentally.

Through her insight into herself and into children, educationally and developmentally, Irene Tasker extended the application of Alexander's and Montessori's techniques both to adolescents and infants that had been seriously handicapped, as well as to average persons, with impressive success, in Johannesburg, South Africa, during the late 30s and early 40s of this century.

Stimulated particularly by Temple Fay, Glenn Doman and Carl Delacato in Philadelphia applied their physiotherapeutic and psychological understanding, along with their wives' nursing and educational knowledge, to instructing parents in how to pattern the body, head and limb movements of brain-injured children. Many of these brains thus became organized neurologically for crawling on their bellies, then for creeping on their hands and knees, and ultimately for talking and for walking erectly. This happened in the 1950s.

The crossing of their life paths with ours has enabled me to portray for you some of the incongruity between this ambitious concept of Institutes for the Achievement of Human Potential and the realities of discord and conflict that have characterized human behaviour up to the present moment of historically recorded time. It is a reasonable inference that each individual's part in the totality of human social behaviour is not confined in its effectiveness to the skill we succeed in attaining bodily and mentally in our use of ourselves, but extends far beyond our daily acts and thoughts to our becoming as skilled as possible, as Alexander himself did, in communicating our knowledge about the better usage to others by the human practices of recording, of speaking and also of writing thereupon.

3

Voluntary Musculature in the Human Body: The Double-Spiral Arrangement

Universality of spiral movement

I recall an elderly otologist named Miller, 30 years ago in New York City, demonstrating by means of examples ranging from the spiral nebulæ to the human cochlea, and from the propagation of sound to the propulsion of solid bodies, that all things move spirally and that all growth is helical.

Mathematical convention had already claimed that a straight line is a particular case of the more general term, curve; as we have since learned that space itself is curved, there was more truth in the general contention which he advanced than any of his auditors probably appreciated. To that discourse I trace my deepening interest in the cyclical aspects of human behaviour, history and structure.

On certain overt physiological periodicities in mankind I ventured to publish some general remarks (Dart, 1935). The modulating effects of climatic cycles upon human and other faunal patterns in South Africa had been engaging my attention for many years before that time (Dart, 1933). An unexpected development of this curiosity in respect of fluctuations was the discovery that cyclical phenomena of some (probably climatic) sort had been responsible during the past 7,000 years for providing (at intervals of about 2,000 years) four separate migrations of peoples from North-Western Europe across Northern Africa, Asia Minor, and Egypt (Dart, 1939).

This article was first published in *The British Journal of Physical Medicine*, vol. 13, no. 12:265-68, December 1950.

Postural fixations—living curvature

Experiences of a more personal sort impressed upon my practical attention another variety of living curvature. These spirals are structural, their interest clinical. Our first child, now almost ten years of age, suffered from night terrors. Our second child, eleven months junior to his sister, was premature (six and a half months) and spent six weeks in an incubator. Muscular co-ordination was so delayed that when upper-limb movements and walking should have occurred spontaneously, he was found to be spastic. This condition, though vastly improved, is still present, but only in a mild degree.

Superficially regarded, night terrors and spasticity have little in common with one another or with the 'round shoulders' of the sedentary student. During 1943 I had been forced, by reason of my own indifferent health, being 'run-down by overwork', to take a year's rest. Searching for assistance at that time in dealing with the infant's spastic condition, I met Miss Irene Tasker, who had been practising the Alexander Technique upon comparable cases in Johannesburg. A course of her manipulative demonstrations upon myself and others showed how the exaggerated spinal curvature—manifested in 'round shoulders', scoliosis and lordosis— was due to postural fixations (or spasticities) due to improper or unco-ordinated management of my own body in rest and movement, and that they were capable of improvement.

Subsequent experience in modifying my own scoliosis (and its concomitant postural twisting of the body framework), in assisting my son to acquire increasing control over his body movements (and the concomitant postural twisting of the body framework, which such seizures involve), gave me ample opportunity during the next seven years to observe what I have now come to regard as 'the spiral mechanism of the body' in action, and to appreciate the extent to which habitual or acute spasticity in a reflexly operating mechanism can be modified by a thoughtful individual.

'Relationing' in the human body

Mungo Douglas of Bolton (Lancashire), through his knowledge of Alexander's work, wrote an important little pamphlet entitled *Reorientation of the Viewpoint upon the Study of Anatomy* (Douglas, 1937; later reprinted in *The Universal Constant in Living*). There he claimed: (1) that the primary function of muscle is the 'relationing' of the various parts of the body to one another; (2) that their function as movers of body parts upon body parts is secondary; and (3) that, of all such 'relationing' in the body, the head–neck relation, brought about by the suboccipital group of muscles (atlas–occipital, axis–occipital, atlas–axis), is of paramount importance, and that it is worthy of the distinction of being recognized as 'the primary relation upon which all more ultimate relations depend'.

The head–neck relationship

What Mungo Douglas calls 'relationing of parts' is a neat way of describing the customary postural positions which adjacent body parts assume as the result of the groups of muscles moving them. His purpose was to demonstrate the muscular anatomical background of Alexander's 'primary control'—that is to say the head–neck relation (Alexander, 1932). A further significant anatomical fact is that this important suboccipital group of muscles controlling the head–neck relationship is supplied by a single (sub-occipital) nerve from a single (first cervical) segment of the spinal cord.

This single somite, or body-segment, doubtless for a special reason, is the only segment of the entire series of postcranial segments to have a nerve supply which is purely motor in character. In other words, this segment of the body musculature is the only one that has been deprived of a segmental skin area proper to itself, to the stimulation of which it would have been too susceptible of reflex response. If its corresponding neural segment has any indigenous sensory receptors they can only be those lying in the muscles and joints of that segment, and are therefore purely proprioceptive. In other words, reflex responses of these muscles and joints as end-organs are immune from skin-receptor interference by the segmental area of skin.

Receptors affecting the head–neck relationship

Responses of a reflex sort, evoked by touch and leading to postural contraction of the suboccipital musculature, can only be elicited in this muscle group by stimuli coming in from receptors of skin segments other than its own. The nearest tactual receptor segments are the trigeminal skin area anteriorly and the second cervical skin area posteriorly. Doubtless it was primarily to determine in as direct a segmental reflex manner as possible such tactually evoked postural head–neck relationships that the trigeminal nerve (which receives all the tactual stimuli entering the body from the entire anterior end of the vertebrate body) invaded centrally the posterior column of grey matter, or substantia gelationosa Rolandi, by a downward or spinal extension of its descending root. This root proceeds in Man as far posteriorly as the fourth cervical segment and in some sensitive-snouted animals such as *Ornithorhynclus* (duck-billed platypus) may even reach the lumbar part of the spinal cord.

There are receptors other than tactual, however, which profoundly affect this head–neck relationship. There is a brain tract of such high importance in every creature with a head articulated to the trunk (that is to say, every vertebrate), that it forms one of the largest bundles in the brain-stem of fishes, amphibians, and reptiles. This tract becomes medullated between the sixth and seventh months of intra-uterine life in Man, simultaneously with the anterior intersegmental tract of the spinal cord, of which it is the proximal extension. This tract, the medial longitudinal bundle, binds together anteriorly the three motor nuclei (oculomotor, trochlear, and abducens) supplying the eyeball muscles and, posteriorly, it connects the anterior horn cells supplying the musculature that links the head to the trunk.

The most important sensory element, however, in determining the postural adjustments evoked by this bundle is formed by the intersegmental fibres running from the vestibular nucleus to the eye muscle nuclei anteriorly, and to the anterior cervical segments and the posteriorly co-extensive spinal nucleus of the accessory nerve. The intersegmental fibres coming from the brain segment supplied by the eighth (or vestibular) nerve cause those simultaneous modifications in tension in the musculature that controls the position of the eyes relative to the head, and of the head relative to the trunk and forelimbs, which are occasioned reflexly by the ever-changing positions of a mobile head (supplied by a single pair of tactual nerves), whether in water or on land.

Evolution of the voluntary musculature

The ancestral relation of the trigeminal nerve to the cerebellum was pointed out by me in 1923. I had published a paper in the

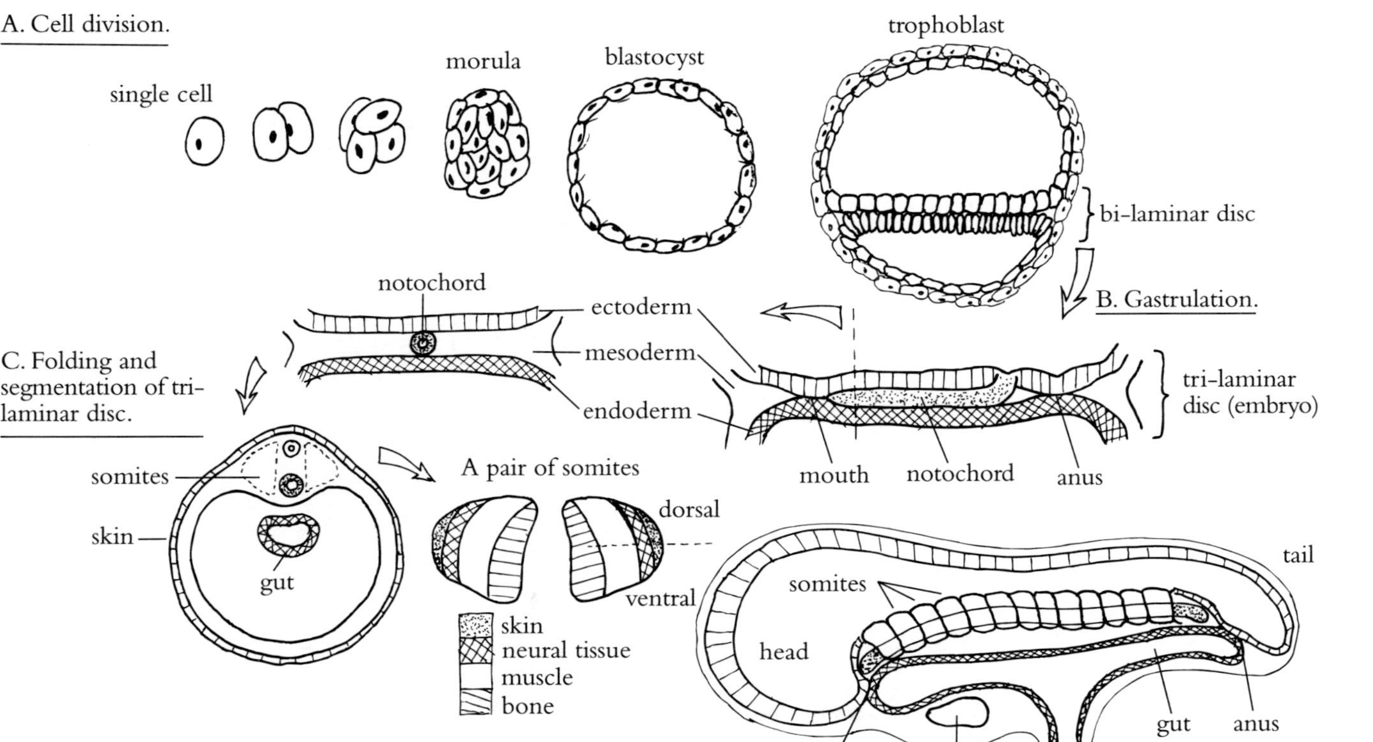

Fig. 3.1. The human developmental sequence.

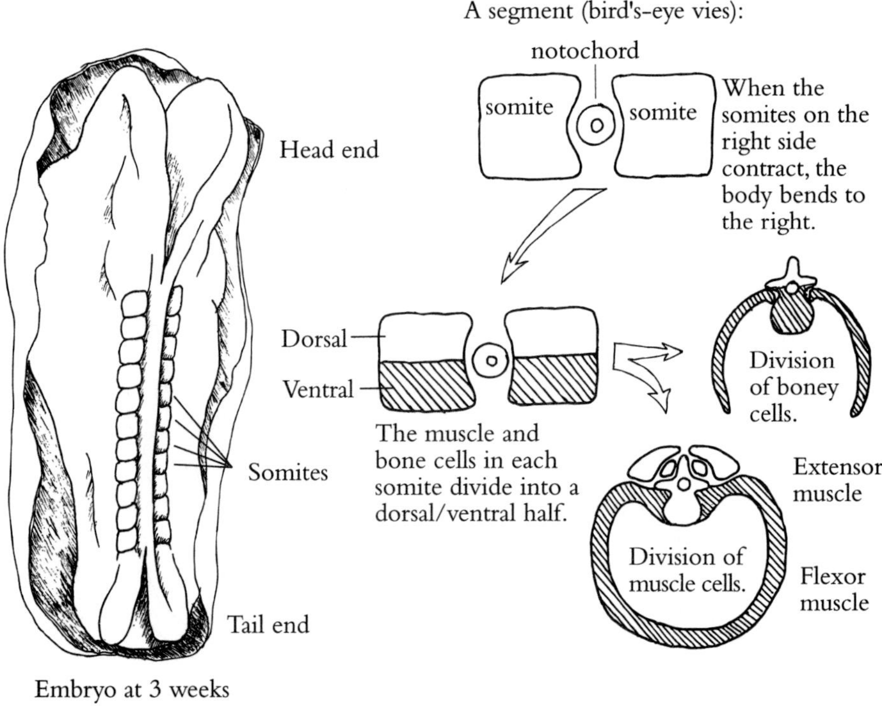

Fig. 3.2. Segments and somites.

Three weeks after conception the embryo divides into cellular blocks or segments. Each segment consists of two 'somites' which sit on either side of the notchord (primitive spine). Within each somite there are muscle cells and bone cells: when the muscle cells from the somites on one side of the body contract, the body bends laterally (to the side) and vice versa.

The muscle and bone cells then gradually divide into a ventral and dorsal half. The ventral muscle cells become flexor muscles; the dorsal muscles become extensor muscles; this enables the torso to bend forwards and backwards). The dorsal bone cells form the spinous and transverse processes of the spinal column; the ventral bone cells form the ribs and the bodies of the vertebrae.

Soon after these bi-lateral and ventral-dorsal splittings have happened, the muscle cells divide again into layers whose lines of force interweave diagonally to form a muscular and fascial double spiral that suspends the torso from the head (see figs. 3.5, 3.6, and 3.7).

preceding year in which I showed (contrary to a great deal of speculation by embryologists and neurologists caused by a historically developing misuse of the term 'visceral') that there was no support morphologically, developmentally, neurologically or histologically for regarding the muscles of the head and neck (or cranial and brachial) segments as differing in any way other than functionally from the other voluntary muscles of the body situated behind the neck (Dart, 1922). I took up the same question of voluntary muscular unity from the developmental point of view two years later because it was an essential preliminary in resolving the basic question of antero–posterior orientation in the vertebrate series. In that article (Dart, 1924) I enunciated the concept that 'the segmental apparatus is first and foremost a locomotor tissue—for directive movement of the body as a whole'.

The trinity of (1) brain and spinal cord, (2) voluntary musculature and (3) skeletal tissue emerged as a bodily unity in response to the unitary demand of providing directive (antero–posterior) movement simultaneously with the achievement of the tubular gut (by forming a new mouth and an anus). That event transformed the ancestral cœlenterate into a chordate creature. This concept has not been questioned, but it has not attracted as much attention from anatomists as so fundamental a morphological issue demands. The proposition entails recognition of its corollary that, just as the segmented or voluntary musculature became adapted posteriorly in the tail region of land animals to the bodily functions of defæcation, micturition and parturition, so, at a much earlier period in water-living creatures, the front segments of the segmented (or voluntary) musculature had become adapted anteriorly to the bodily functions of eye movement, food seizure, swallowing and respiration.

The first division—bilateral arrangement of somites

The first splitting of the muscle-producing mesoderm is its cleavage antero–posteriorly into the bilaterally arranged somites. The segmented musculature thus disposed laterally to the tubular gut was able, by alternating contractions of the entire musculature of the two sides, to produce those massive lateral bending movements of the whole body (posterior to and pivoting upon the head) which constitute the first type of movement seen in vertebrate embryos (figs. 3.1–3.5*a*). The discovery by Davenport Hooker that such lateral bending of the trunk and neck, often accompanied by pelvic rotation, is the first reflex movement to appear in the human fœtus, and that it appears shortly after the second month or eighth week of intra-uterine life only in response to stimulation (usually contra-lateral) of

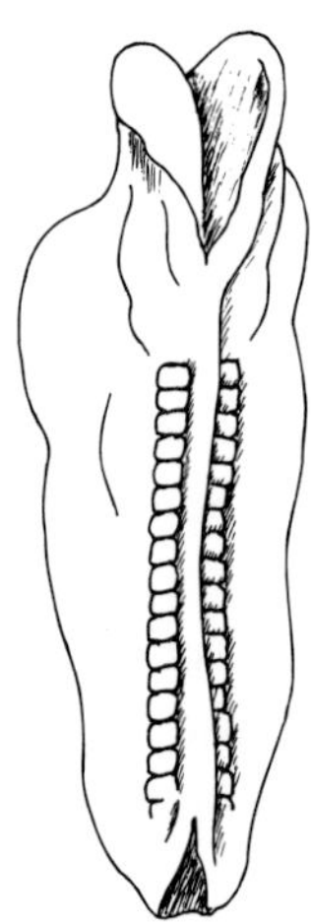

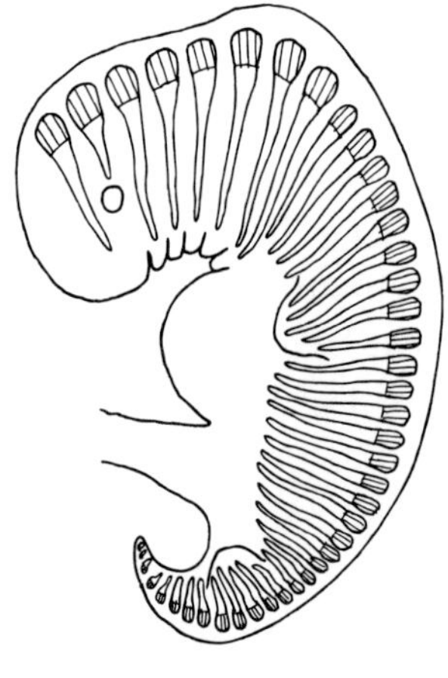

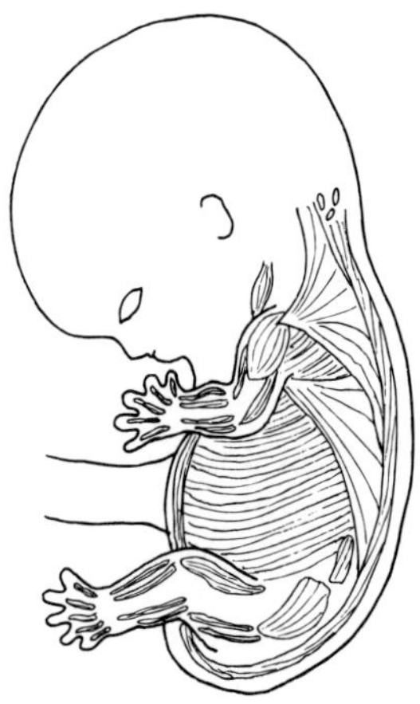

a. At the end of the 3rd week block-like groupings of cells (somites) form. These contain muscle cells.

b. The muscle cells divide into ventral and dorsal portions, forming flexor and extensor muscles.

c. By 8 weeks these muscle cells have combined to form flexor and extensor sheets that wrap around and through the body.

Fig. 3.3. Segmentation and growth of muscle cells at 3rd (*a*), 5th (*b*) and 8th (*c*) weeks after conception. See also fig. 2.3. for skin and nervous segementation.

the upper lip and the alæ of the nose (stimulation of the second division of the trigeminal nerve) is of the greatest interest in view of the anatomical arrangements and morphological facts about the trigeminal nerve and the upper cervical segments which are discussed above (Hooker, 1942). They constitute the oldest and functionally most important tactual reflex paths that involve head and body segments because they were so important for bringing the anterior end of the vertebrate creature into actual contact with its food supply.

The second division—dorsal and ventral extensors and flexors

The second fundamental division of the segmented musculature is the bilateral antero–posterior splitting of each segment into a dorsal (or extensor) and a ventral (or flexor) half on each side of the body (fig. 3.5*b*). This second cleavage was accompanied by division of the spinal nerves into their anterior and posterior divisions and corresponding cell columns and by rearrangements of their commissural and inter-segmental paths in the spinal cord. These developments enabled the ventral halves of the somites on both sides of the body

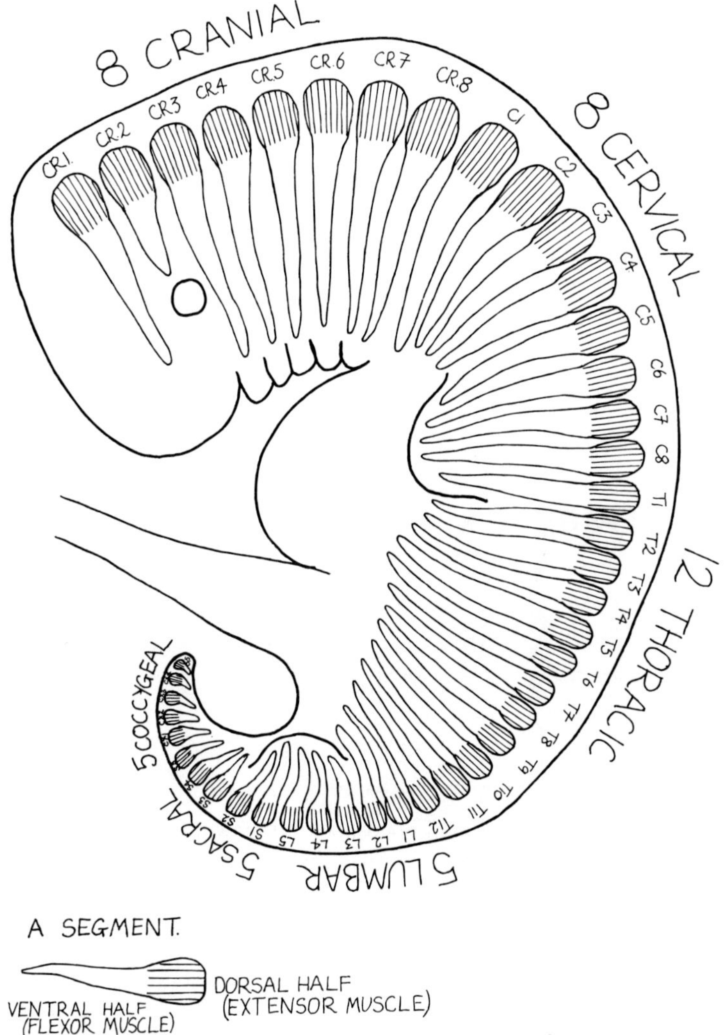

Fig. 3.4. The human embryo at 5 weeks after conception.

From the 3rd week of life onwards, the tissues of the developing embryo segment into 43 units (somites). There are 8 cranial (head) segments; 8 cervical (neck), 12 thoracic, 5 lumbar, 5 sacral and 5 coccygeal (tail) segments.

The tissues of the cranial segments will become the head; the tissues of the cervical segments will form the neck etc. This diagram shows the muscle cells within each segmental unit dividing into front and back portions that will grow either forwards to form the flexor musculature of the face, neck, torso and limbs, or backwards to form the extensor musculature of the head, neck and back.

As these segmentally arranged flexors and extensors develop, they gradually merge together, forming two interweaving spiral sheets of musculature, responsible for twisting, turning, wriggling and primitive locomoting movements.

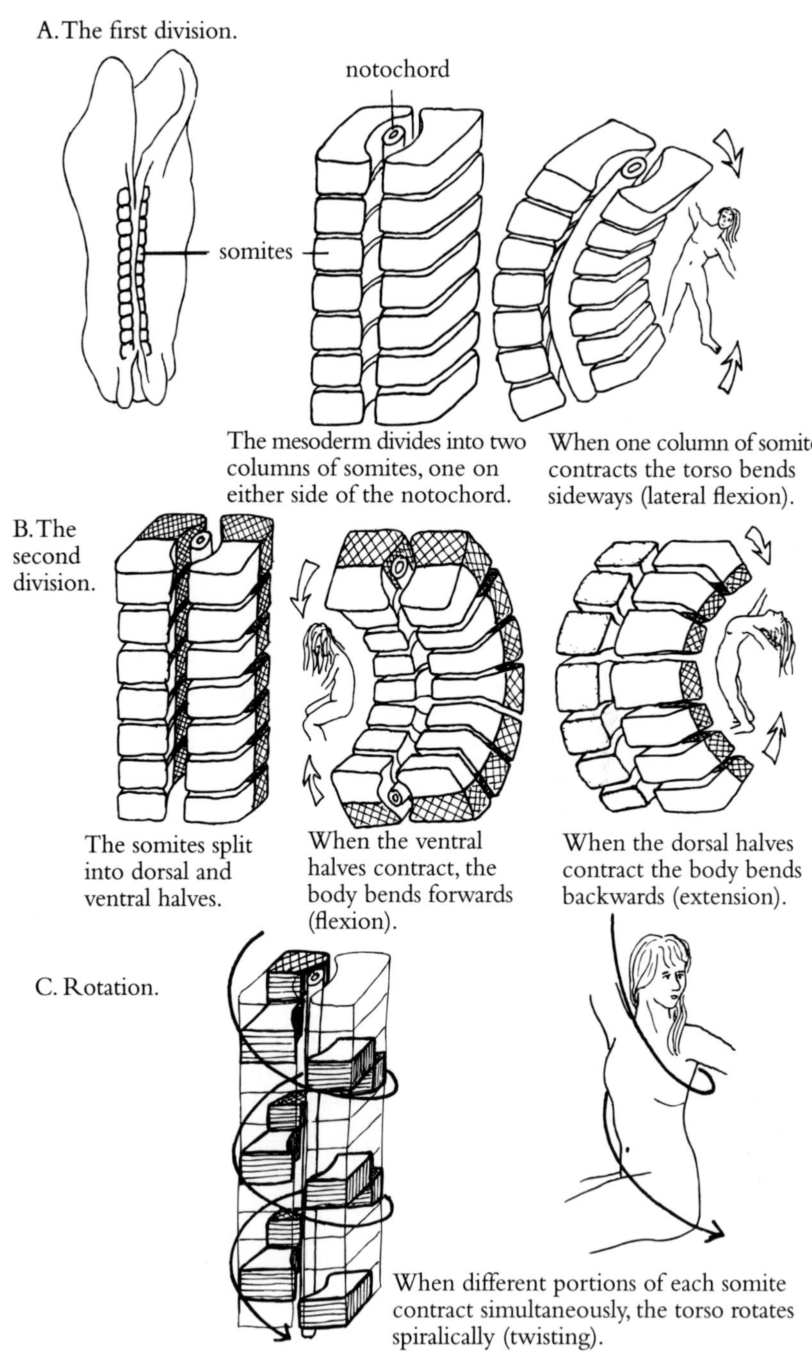

Fig. 3.5. Embryological origin of the double-spiral arrangement.

to contract or relax, separately or as a whole, independently from and antagonistically to the relaxing or contracting dorsal halves of the somites. This bilateral longitudinal splitting of the musculature gave to the laterally-bending creature the further ability to extend the body dorsally or to flex it ventrally.

As soon as it became possible, neurologically and muscularly, to maintain one end of the segmented and antero–posteriorly doubly-divided body in a state of tonic ventral or flexor contraction, while the other end was in a state of tonic extension, any deviation from the total body state of symmetrical tonic postural contraction between the two ends resulted in a postural torsion, or twist of the body, to one side or the other—that is to say, a rotation of the junctional region between the tonically flexed and tonically extended halves of the moving body (fig. 3.5*c*). This is the type of body movement with which everyone is familiar who has observed a caterpillar bending and twisting its body. Broadly considered, no other types of movement effected by voluntary musculature are possible. All muscles are either flexors or extensors; all torsions of the body as a whole or of its constituent parts—whether they be rotation of the spinal column, pronation or supination, inversion or eversion, and adduction, abduction or circumduction of the extremities—are based upon tonically maintained differential pulls between adjacent groups of flexor and extensor segments. Developmentally, therefore, there is no further splitting up of the myotomes.

Layering of muscles

Such splitting as occurs has been principally confined to the production of the three-sheeted layering (1) inner or transverse, (2) intermediate or internal oblique, and (3) outer or external oblique characteristic of the trunk flexors (thoracic and abdominal, fig. 3.6*a*). In like fashion the longitudinally-split arrangement characteristic of the double-sheeted limb flexors and extensors was produced, as were the various subdivisions of the *sacrospinalis* mass.

This splitting into sheets, however, has given origin to a simple double-spiral mechanism of great importance to bodily economy, the essential simplicity of which is frequently forgotten amidst anatomical detail. For example, let us follow the oblique direction of the

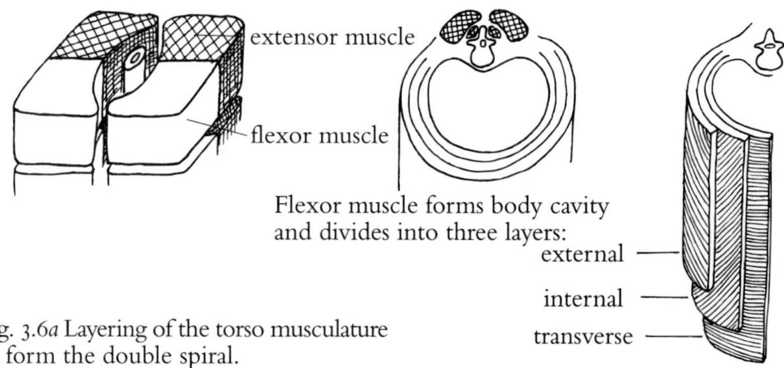

Fig. 3.6*a* Layering of the torso musculature to form the double spiral.

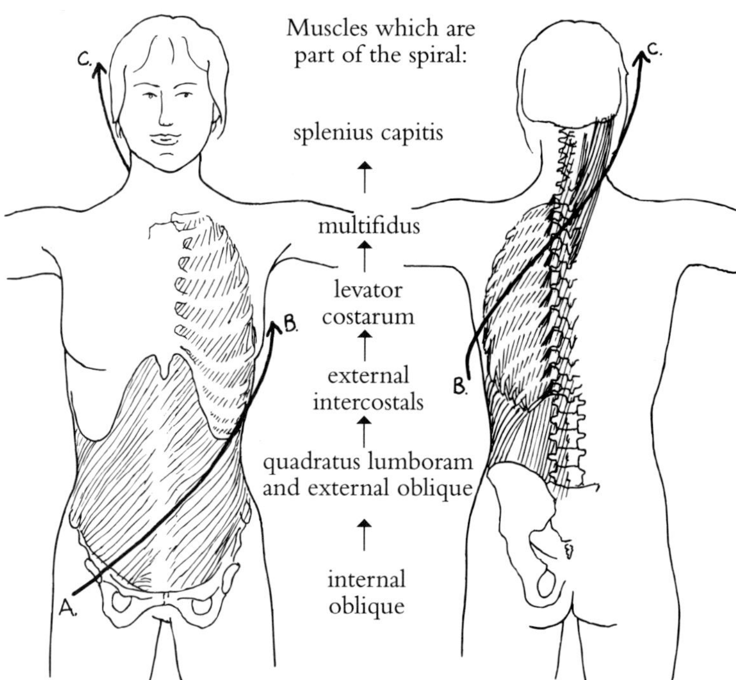

Fig. 3.6*b*. The diagonally-arranged external and internal layers jointly form a double spiral.

fibres of the external oblique muscle from the midline of the body, pubic symphysis and iliac crest, upwards through the single morphological sheet formed by the external intercostals, ribs, and scalene musculature to the transverse processes of the cervical vertebræ, and thence through the deeper-lying sheet formed by the *semispinalis*

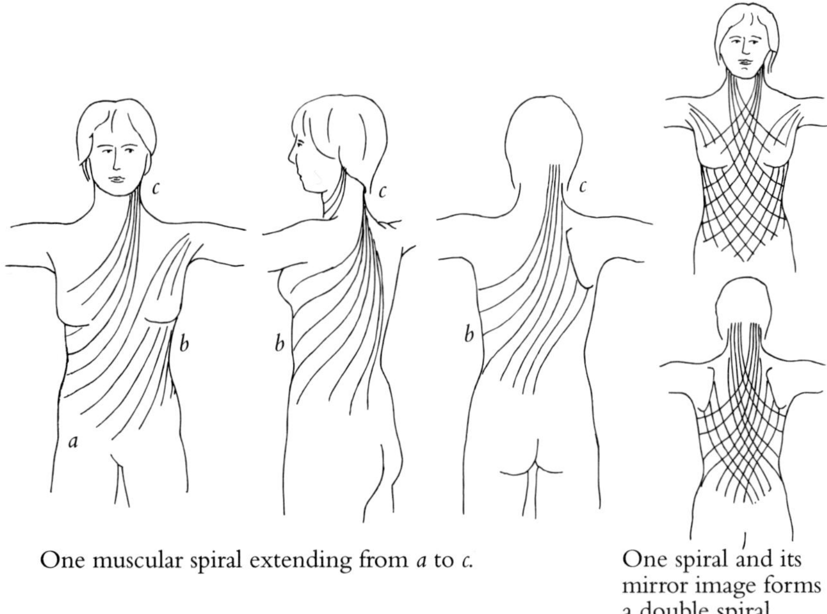

One muscular spiral extending from *a* to *c*.

One spiral and its mirror image forms a double spiral.

Fig. 3.7. The double spiral. The voluntary musculature of the human body is arranged in two spiralling sheets. This double spiral consists of one spiral and its mirror image. These muscular spirals extend from the brim of the pelvis, wrap around the torso, running between ribs and vertebrae, to insert around the base of the skull.

A single spiral line can be traced within either of these broad muscular sheets. Regardless of where the traced line begins, e.g. front of right hip or side of left hip, the spiral will cross the mid-line of both the front and the back of the torso and end up at the ear on the same side of the head as the side on which it originated. If, for example, a spiral is traced from the front of the right hip (*a*), it will end up at the back of the right ear (*c*), by the mastoid process.

It is important not to mistake the path of a single traced line for the wholeness of a broad, torso-encompassing spiral.

These spirals suspend the torso from the mobile head and enable twisting, turning, wriggling and primitive locomotion to take place.

musculature to the cervical spines and occiput. Thus we get a picture, or bird's-eye view, of the manner in which the single superficial sheet, formed by these two opposed, diagonally-running flexor muscles in front, is continued through a deeper-lying extensor sheet on each side of the spine behind to suspend the pelvis from the occiput and neck vertebræ (fig. 3.6).

Diagonal suspensional (double-spiral) arrangement

This diagonal suspensional arrangement becomes the more impressive when we recognize that the diagonal direction of pull exercised by each external oblique sheet (intercostal muscles and *levatores costarum*) is continued across the midline through the deeper-lying internal oblique sheet to the perimeter of the pelvis on the opposite side of the body. Thus, any postural twist of the body (and the customary twist in a right-handed person is a twisting of the trunk to the left) results in a postural rotation of the thorax, shoulder (right), and head, together with the vertebral column itself, towards the opposite (left) iliac crest; there is also a relative inability to rotate the opposite or heterolateral (left) shoulder towards the homolateral (right) iliac crest.

These diagonally disposed sheets, when followed in their continuity around the body, constitute two interwoven spiral layers. The pull exercised on the circumference of the pelvic basin through the deeper-lying (internal oblique) sheet from the ribs and the transverse processes of the spinal vertebræ of the contralateral side, by the superficial layer of muscles (external oblique, *quadratus lumborum*, external intercostal, *levatores costarum* and scalene), is a plane of traction that is being simultaneously exerted upon the transverse processes themselves and again along the deeper-lying plane of pull by the deep (*multifidus–semispinalis*) sheet of the *sacrospinalis* from the spines of the vertebræ and the occiput. Thus, in a very real sense, the occiput and spines of the vertebræ suspend the body by means of two spiral sheets of muscle encircling the trunk (fig. 3.7).

This arrangement of the trunk musculature, in the form of interwoven double-spiral sheets, is continued across the dorsal midline just as it is carried over the ventral midline. The superficial layer of the *sacrospinalis* sheet (*iliocostalis*, *longissimus* and *splenius*) continues on to the posterior aspect of the ribs, cervical transverse processes, and mastoid process the same oblique line of traction as is being exercised on the spines by the deep (or *multifidus*) sheet of the opposite side of the back. The whole trunk repeats, in its own fashion, the muscular story of the intestinal tract and of the heart by becoming enwrapped by spiral coils of muscle which are only prevented by the bony framework of the thorax and pelvis from completely emptying its contents when they are contracted forcibly.

Spiral torsion and its untwisting

This double-spiral arrangement, characterizing the disposition of the voluntary musculature of the trunk, can easily be pursued into the head, neck and limbs. Sufficient has been said to show that any habitually asymmetrical adjustment of the body, either during states of mental anxiety that suppress respirational rhythm or during occupations or exercise, results in postural torsion of the head, vertebral column and trunk, as a whole, towards the right or towards the left (whichever is the more commonly used side).

The spiral (or torsional) factor in the production of scoliosis and other deformations of the spinal column is dealt with by Truslow (1943), who cites A. Mackenzie Forbes' theory of the rotary mechanism in lateral curvature of the spine. Truslow has elaborated remedial exercises of a rotatory character to 'derotate' (or 'untwist') the trunk affected by such distortions, and has pointed out how some sports may distort the body. He has appreciated many of the factors involved in these rotations, but not all of them.

The majority of people—as a result of their single handiness and their fixed and frequently sedentary occupations, to say nothing of their food and clothing—suffer from mild, moderate and even serious grades of permanent postural twist, although the condition has not been recognized by themselves or by their medical advisers.

In the members of my family and in myself, the 'undoing' of previously unrecognized leftward twists, whether congenital or acquired, has been a major preoccupation of the past seven years. That employment has led me to recognize and to correlate many facts about the body and its functioning both as a whole and in parts, which had previously eluded my notice. Amongst those anatomical facts, the double-spiral arrangement of the voluntary musculature is basic. In ontogeny, as in phylogeny, Man grows and moves spirally.

*Summary**

1. A primary function of musculature is the 'relationing' of parts of the body. In bipedal man the relationship of the head to the erect body is of primary importance.
2. Relationing is accomplished by muscular groupings that arise and specialize in different ways, involving differing degrees of independence and collaboration.

---

* This summary was prepared for its reprint in *Human Potential*, vol. 1, no. 2, 1968.

3. Early in the course of embryonic development these groupings of muscles arise and carry with them a distribution of nervous components by means of which integration and co-ordinative function is achieved.
4. Noteworthy are the dorsal and ventral muscle groups that arise very early as a consequence of somite segmentation, longitudinal splitting and layering to form the extensor and flexor muscle masses whose lines of force act through fascial sheets and tendinous connections upon the head, spinal column and rib cage to execute the rotary movements of the body and thus provide the human body with that erectness and perfection in its twisting actions so characteristic of the skilled human body.
5. The cranio-cervical groups especially important from the standpoint of integrative function are:
   (*i*) the muscles that aid the first cervical segment in balancing the cranium upon the spinal column; (*ii*) the muscles of the eyes which aid the body in judging distance and relative position of objects in the environment; (*iii*) muscles of facial expression which communicate our moods and feelings, and (*iv*) the muscles of the mouth, tongue throat and larynx which not only assist in breathing and swallowing, but also in communication by verbalization.

References

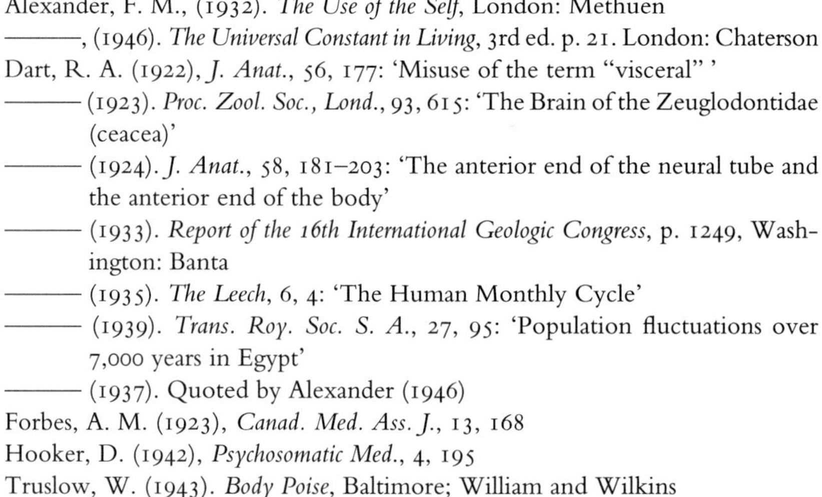

Alexander, F. M., (1932). *The Use of the Self*, London: Methuen

———, (1946). *The Universal Constant in Living*, 3rd ed. p. 21. London: Chaterson

Dart, R. A. (1922), *J. Anat.*, 56, 177: 'Misuse of the term "visceral" '

——— (1923). *Proc. Zool. Soc., Lond.*, 93, 615: 'The Brain of the Zeuglodontidae (ceacea)'

——— (1924). *J. Anat.*, 58, 181–203: 'The anterior end of the neural tube and the anterior end of the body'

——— (1933). *Report of the 16th International Geologic Congress*, p. 1249, Washington: Banta

——— (1935). *The Leech*, 6, 4: 'The Human Monthly Cycle'

——— (1939). *Trans. Roy. Soc. S. A.*, 27, 95: 'Population fluctuations over 7,000 years in Egypt'

——— (1937). Quoted by Alexander (1946)

Forbes, A. M. (1923), *Canad. Med. Ass. J.*, 13, 168

Hooker, D. (1942), *Psychosomatic Med.*, 4, 195

Truslow, W. (1943). *Body Poise*, Baltimore; William and Wilkins

4

The Postural Aspect of Malocclusion

Introduction

The diagnosis of an Angle Class II Division I malocclusion in both of our children, aged six and five respectively, has directed my attention recently to the factors regarded as responsible for malocclusion and the current techniques adopted for its correction. Independently of these personal reasons, I had found that alterations in occlusion were inextricably linked with changes occurring in my own body as the result of experiments I had been making in its muscular education during the last three years. The object of this paper is to correlate these several matters in so far as they bear upon the topic of malocclusion.

The first arresting fact was that the boy's condition was less marked than that of his sister. The elder child, the girl, had had a normal birth and an infancy free from complications; the boy, on the other hand, had been prematurely born (six-and-a-half months, 2 lb. 6 oz. weight) and had spent his first six weeks in an incubator, during which he had had so many recurrent cyanotic attacks threatening respiratory failure, that his survival was unexpected. During the first six months of post-natal life he was an emaciated, poorly-nourished child with tense, œdematous legs. His motor development was greatly delayed owing to spasticities of various kinds resulting from muscular incoordination which are not yet completely under his control. Theoretically considered, his state of malocclusion should have been the more serious.

We do not know today to what extent malocclusions are the result of heredity or of environment. Excluding the hereditary divergences that occur between brother and sister, a very distinctive environ-

This article was first published in *The Official Journal of the Dental Association of South Africa*, vol. 1, no. 1:1-21, September 1946.

mental factor has operated upon the boy (as contrasted with the girl), *viz.* the amount of daily manipulation (to inhibit wrongful or unuseful movements) to which he has been subjected at his parents' hands as a result of his postural infirmity. The study and observations upon his motor mechanism (and my own) incidental to this protracted inhibitional and educational manipulative process are principally responsible for the comments I am making here; but these are put forward with considerable confidence because recent literature on malocclusion affords corroboration of the view I have gradually formed that malocclusion in Man is primarily a postural defect. The mandible assumes a particular or characteristic posture in each human being and this mandibular posture is related to, or part of, the postural set-up of that individual.

The first corroborative evidence that a postural concept of malocclusion would be recognized more as a reasonable than as a revolutionary idea by my dental colleagues was a recent article on 'Cervico–facial orthopædia', which Arnold A. Nove has been writing in the last available (February–May) numbers of the *Dental Record* (1946) and to which Professor Shaw kindly drew my attention. Instead of approaching malocclusion narrowly from the orthodox clinical perspective of faulty dental eruption and arch formation, Nove considers malocclusion widely as embracing '*all* the structural units of the head and neck, with the alveolo–dental structures as only *part* of the clinical picture'. Malocclusion he regards as 'a cervico–facial orthopædic problem' arising from structural and functional imbalance of the musculature of the head and neck. Nove treats malocclusion, therefore, by intermittently immobilizing the mandible upon the maxilla in a position of optimum occlusion by means of a splint during sleeping hours. He relies on the resultant improved and balanced reflex actions of swallowing and respiration (and concomitantly therewith an improved posture of the head relative to the cervical column and other bony structures of the neck) to overcome the condition.

In a series of papers during the last twenty years, Milo Hellman has been recording, on the other hand, the individual histories of numerous infantile and adolescent occlusions and has thrown grave doubt upon the efficacy of various orthodontic appliances that have been elaborated to treat malocclusions and the relevance of their employment in many instances. Not more than 10% of malocclusion cases coming to him for orthodontic consultation are treated with appliances, and many dentitions that seem to display urgent need of instrumental treatment at the outset spontaneously correct themselves during the period between infancy and maturity. These self-righting malocclusions reported by Hellman are corroborative of Nove's belief that functional factors of a physiological sort are responsible for the original state of malocclusions; it is implicit in Hellman's work that, amongst these factors, growth changes play an outstanding role. But the particular importance of Nove's work lies in the ingenuity whereby, through temporarily fixing the masticatory apparatus, he makes practical use of the reflex functions of swallowing and respiration during growth in moulding the jaws and adapting their biting surfaces to one another.

During infancy the human being is attempting to integrate the spontaneous operation of these ancestral (amphibian) occipital and cervical reflexes of food seizing, swallowing and respiring with the much more recently acquired primate mammalian postural reflexes employed in standing upright (and in performing the bodily activities distinctive of human beings); simultaneously, anomalies of occlusion become patent. As these postural reflex activities often improve greatly during normal adolescence, the concurrent malocclusion may become righted anatomically; but caution demands that the process of occlusal self-righting or otherwise be kept under careful observation in the manner adopted by Hellman. That process of self-righting could scarcely fail in being enhanced by Nove's orthopædic technique.

Nove, like M. B. Cohen (*vide* Strang, 1943, pp. 157–158), has pointed out that cases of malocclusion form, along with the adenoid facies and the allergies, a common ground for joint study by the physician, rhinologist, and orthodontist. Like Stillwell (1927) and Stallard (1930), I go further and say that unless the postural syndrome of the entire body receives simultaneous attention, the observation and treatment of such conditions, being local will be, at best, partial.

The interconnection between malocclusion and body posture has not been overlooked. Brown and Losch (1939) discussed five cases of muscular dystrophy occurring in the Children's Hospital in Boston; all of them displayed 'either beginning or actual arch deformity not accounted for by other ætiological factors which we believe are related to the loss of muscular strength and to the increased size of the tongue'. This inter-relation also could scarcely have been better illustrated than by Capon's 'Notes on glossoptosis and micrognathia' (1946) and the illustration he reproduces from Robin's work on the bodily syndromes of the glossoptotic states. The protruded and retracted positions relative to the maxilla assumed by maloccluded mandibles are each associated with imperfect or improperly co-ordinated habits of breathing which themselves depend in turn upon, or are secondary to, the body posture. Capon (*op. cit.*, p. 62) takes exception (and rightly so, in my estimation) to the term 'mouth breathing' because 'true mouth breathing is never seen'; use of the term 'mouth breathing' really implies 'parted lips and sagging mouth'. This vacuous expression is taken up, he declared, because it is 'one of (postural) comfort, the relaxation of the oral tissues affording maximal freedom for combined oral and nasal breathing'.

For the last forty years, A. P. Rogers (*vide* J. A. Salzmann, 1943) has been teaching that many occlusal and dento–facial abnormalities are due to 'mal-use or imbalance of numerous groups of facial muscles' and has proposed numerous corrective exercises to develop proper muscular tonicity and to establish proper muscular function. To Rogers, muscles are 'living orthodontic appliances'; mechanical tooth movement and retention are not alone sufficient to ensure correction of malocclusion; the muscles of the face must be trained to function properly; correction of malocclusion by 'myo-functional therapy' does not require 'retention' treatment. In consequence, he has elaborated (with and without the use of orthodontic appliances) pterygoid, *masseter*–temporal, tongue, *mentalis*, *orbicularis oris*, and general facial muscle exercises to correct malocclusion. From the attention given to general muscular development and to improvement in the respiratory and speech habits of his patients, it is clear that Rogers recognizes that their facial postural habits are merely an aspect of their general postural condition, but he has confined his attention principally to the actions of the trigeminal-facial groups.

Generally, orthodontic appliances are designed to be fixed in the mouth and to exert forces on individual teeth or groups of teeth and through them on to the bone surrounding their root sockets; the resultant bony changes carry the teeth in the desired directions. The appliances in the so-called 'Norwegian system', originated by Andresen (1936), are 'activators' designed to provide a 'working bite' and are not fixed to the teeth in any way, but are removable and worn loose in the mouth and mostly at night. The purpose is not to push or pull the teeth, but to provide a passive transmitter to the teeth and alveolar processes of forces exercised by the mimetic masticatory, tongue, and swallowing musculature. The maloccluding teeth are thus influenced by the resultant pressures upon the palate to grow into their proper places rather than bringing about palatal alterations by direct pressures exercised by appliances upon the maloccluding teeth.

Other removable orthodontic appliances are the bite-planes or bite-plates of Kingsley, Rogers, and Kelsey which cover the hard palate and have an inclined or flat plane at their anterior border. This plane offers resistance to the mandibular incisors and thus causes all the mandibular teeth to change their positions relative to the maxillary teeth. The posterior teeth, being kept out of contact, are said to elongate and the incisor over-bite to become thereby decreased. Most important of all is the postural alteration in the mandible produced by adequate traction in the temporo–mandibular joint region caused by such appliances and said to have been observed by Riesner (1936), *viz.* 'a readjustment of the angle of the (mandibular) head and neck in the direction of the force' (*vide* Salzmann, *op. cit.*, p. 615).

These techniques of training the muscles of the head, tongue and throat to carry out their largely reflex functions properly, and of forcing this musculature to re-adapt its reflex functioning to a removable activator (or bite-plate, or to a removable jaw-locking splint) do not differ from one another nearly so greatly as may appear to superficial consideration. All these techniques have shifted the emphasis in orthodontia away from the teeth and the jaw-bones to the muscles moving the jaws. The advantage of Nove's outlook is that he has diverted attention still further away from the teeth, the jaw-bones and even from the muscles moving the jaws to *the posture of the head relative to the neck*; and to the nervous system which integrates all motor and postural activities. In this way he has added meaning to the work of Stillwell (1927) and Stallard (1930) who demonstrated nearly two decades ago that extra-oral forces (or pressures) due to malposture exercised torques or twists on the spinal column and simultaneously caused cranial asymmetry, facial distortion and dental defects. For, just as the head of the mandible can be twisted on its neck by muscle force when sufficiently great, so, when the mandible is gripped strongly or seized spastically by the muscles of mastication above and the flexor sheet of neck muscles (linking the mandible to the sternum and scapula through the hyoid bone) below, this adequate traction causes 'a readjustment of the angle of the (human) head and neck in the direction of the force'.

The skull pivots antero-posteriorly on its condyles. Hence, according as the 'palato-spinal' angle between the vertical cervical column and the horizontal plane formed by the palate (or the 'mandibulo-spinal' angle formed by the vertical cervical column with the help of a plane through the lower borders of the mandible, if the mouth is held securely closed) is diminished, so the 'occipito-spinal' angle between the *squama occipitalis* (or nuchal plane of the occipital bone) and the cervical column is proportionately increased. The head whose jaws are kept in occlusion becomes correspondingly tilted forwards and downwards. Then, combinatorially, to bring the skull back or to pivot it upon a more vertically-oriented spinal column, the concavity formed by the cervical spines becomes wider and shallower. These are the primary postural results of the improving bite or occlusion. Children or adults who can sit erect in a poised way with their back-muscles tonically adjustable respond instantly to the slightest pressure of one's finger-tip upon the philtrum of the upper lip in the midline below the nasal septum by an immediate anteflexion of the head, closure of the lips, diminution of the 'palato-spinal' angle, and a corresponding increment of the 'occipito-spinal' angle.

These readjustments in the angle of the human head and neck, that can be rendered habitual in childhood by orthodontic procedures, are of such crucial importance for the establishment of bodily as well as of mandibular posture that each should be considered separately.

The neuromuscular background of mandibular posture

The highly sensitive postural adjustments of the mandible in Man result primarily from its direct synovial, ligamentous, and muscular attachments to the temporal bones; these bones also happen to house the organs of equilibration. To the chordate animal, when first evolving a head, the fundamental criterion of a good food-seizing apparatus was one whose snapping movements (and the movements of the prey it has seized) would be most rapidly conveyed to its consciousness and so least affect the precarious aquatic equilibrium of its torpedo-like body. This problem was most happily solved by articulating the snapping jaw as directly as possible with the solid tissue of cartilage or bone holding the equilibrating organs and by swinging the counterpoised body from the cranial box formed by welding the pair of otic capsules together with cartilage or bone.

The muscles that preserve the posturally-maintained relationships of the head to the vertebral column in Man (and other primates) have cranial insertions that are confined for the most part to the occipital bone which links the two temporal bones together. They are the *recti capitis anteriores, laterales, posteriores* (*minores et majores*) and the *obliqui superiores et inferiores*; and these are one and all supplied by the single segmental pair of sub-occipital or first cervical nerves. In addition, anteriorly, we find this underlying sub-occipital group of muscles supported by the *longus capitis* and posteriorly by the *semispinalis capitis*, both of these muscles being chiefly innervated by the second, third, and fourth cervical nerves. There is, however, a very great disparity in number, strength and size between the anterior (or flexor) group of muscles of the head and the posterior (or extensor) groups, as Mungo Douglas (1937) has pointed out. The force of gravity compensates for the relatively few, weak, and small flexors in pronograde animals; but in an orthograde creature such as Man, this disparity between the strong head extensors and the weak head flexors is still more accentuated by further posterior muscle attachments.

The *trapezius*, although ancestrally a flexor muscle, suspends the shoulders in part from the occiput and thus can operate, but quite inappropriately, as an additional retractor (or extensor) of the head. The two spinal muscles attached to the mastoid process of the temporal bone (namely, the *splenius capitis* and *longissimus capitis*), although their real function on either side is to act as a posterior counter-stay to the anteriorly-situated sternomastoids in rotational movements of the head and neck, may subordinate these primary cranial guy-rope functions and, by assisting the over-weighted extensor group, also become retractors of the head.

The spinal accessory nerve supply of the *trapezius* further complicates this business of 'head retraction' because of the entirely reflex or automatic functions in which this eleventh cranial nerve participates. The spinal (cervical) part of the accessory nerve, which arises centrally from the spinal cord as far posteriorly as the fifth or sixth cervical segment, supplies the sternomastoid and *trapezius* after further direct peripheral linkages with the cervical nerves from the second, third, and fourth segments in the posterior triangle. Thus, the spinal (cervical) half of the accessory nucleus is intimately concerned with all movements and postural adjustments of the head; meanwhile, the cranial (medulla oblongata or nucleus ambiguous) portion of the nerve controls part, and is inextricably associated with all of the movements of the pharynx in swallowing, and of the larynx in respiration and vocalization, because it arises from the same central nucleus of grey matter as the glossopharyngeal and vagus and assists them peripherally in forming the plexuses that supply the 'voluntary' (or striated) musculature controlling these activities. Arising coterminously from the same four medulla oblongata (or occipital) neuromeres as give origin to the glossopharyngeal, vagus, and accessory nerves, the hypoglossal nucleus controls the movements of the tongue in mastication and swallowing. To carry out properly these almost automatic or reflex functions at the same time as the body is being held erect with the head nicely poised or swinging upon the vertical spinal column calls for an intimate harmony of action between the muscles of the body on the one side and those supplied by the four posterior cranial and the four anterior cervical motor nerves on the other side.

The mandible articulates directly with the temporal bone; the muscles of mastication are attached proximally in the main to the bone. But the temporo-mandibular joints differ from most other joints of the body (excepting also the costo-vertebral, cranio-vertebral, and upper-limb joints in Man) in being not weight-bearing but weight-suspending joints. The weight suspended from the temporal bones of the skull includes the mandible; the forces exerted by the muscles of the joints and floor of the mouth during mastication of the resistant food; and, in addition, during swallowing, such tractional forces as are necessary to lift the relaxing pharyngeal musculature upwards and to anchor it while it is contracting behind each bolus

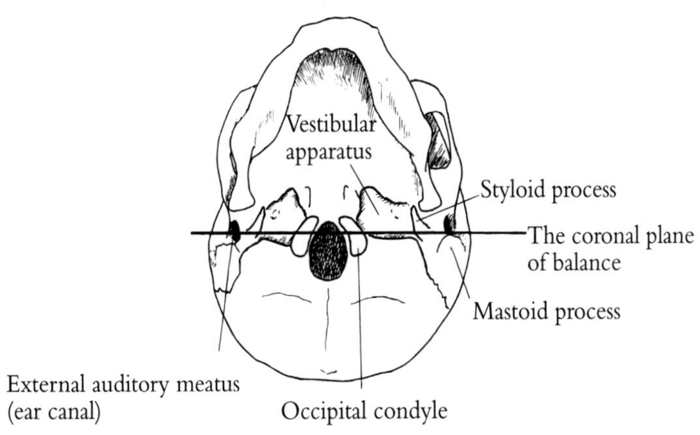

Fig. 4.1. The coronal plane of balance.

of food. The pharyngeal musculature in the midline reaches the basilar-occipital portion of the skull at the pharyngeal tubercle; but the lateral attachments (of the stylohyoid and stylomandibular ligaments and of the stylohyoid, styloglossus and stylopharyngeus muscles) concentered upon the elongated tip of the styloid process imply that every movement of the tongue, pharynx and larynx as well as each adjustment of the mandible in biting or chewing, swallowing or respiring results in symmetrical or asymmetrical direct traction upon both of the bones containing the balancing organs of the body. In brief, the mouth, pharynx and larynx are swung from the temporal bones, as the body is suspended from the occipital plate rigidly interlocking them.

The vertical or coronal plane passing through the posterior aspects of the bases of the styloid processes passes approximately through the centre of the bony external auditory meatus, through the middle of the atlanto–occipital joint, and through the vestibular organs of equilibration themselves on either side; it may be designated as *the coronal plane of balance* (fig. 4.1). All the muscles operating on the jaws, the hyoid bone, and the floor of the mouth are attached superiorly to the skull (and chiefly to the temporal bone) in situations anterior to this important coronal plane running through the balancing organs. The whole of the trigemino-facial, suprahyoid, infrahyoid and pharyngo-laryngeal sheet of muscle which we may call, for convenience, the *rectus cervicalis*, thus acts as an accessory, but immensely important, flexor of the cranium upon the thoracic cage. Without the contribution made by this *rectus cervicalis* sheet to head-positioning, the postural evolution of land animals (including Man) would have been impossible.

The only and important exceptions to the rule of *cranial flexor attachment in front of the coronal plane of body balance* are the digastric and the sternomastoid muscles. The digastric muscles, operating from their grooves on the medial aspect of the mastoid processes, can most easily, in an orthograde creature, displace the mandible posteriorly by an excessive exercise of their guy-rope, or bearing-rein, function on the jaw and thus upset the symmetrical functioning of the tongue and pharyngeal musculature which operates chiefly from the mandible and styloid processes during swallowing. In glossoptosis, micrognathia, and, indeed, in all conditions of malocclusion where the mandible and the alveolo-dental structures it carries are displaced posteriorly relative to the maxilla, the imbalance we should suspect primarily is overaction of this particular pair of muscles (supplied by the facial nerve). The only muscles that can antagonize the digastrics (and even then most disadvantageously) in their retraction and depression of the mandible are the lateral pterygoids which protract the lower jaw. When, for any cause (and in orthograde Man gravity alone is sufficient cause), the trigeminal musculature is relaxed, the lower jaw both sags and protracts.

Where, for any further reason such as bodily malposture, the occipital half of the skull is itself retracted and deflected downwards by faulty opisthotonus or over-extension (while the facial half is correspondingly tilted upwards), then the mastoid processes become displaced forward relative to the *coronal plane of body balance* and the digastric muscles are posturally shortened. The digastric muscles then drag the mandible downwards and backwards permanently, while the sternomastoid muscles (acting in retractional sympathy with the *trapezii*, supplied like them from the accessory nerves), still further retract and depress the occiput. The total effect of these overacting muscles is to pull persistently the back of the head down towards the thorax; the resultant postural maladjustment is to accentuate unduly the anterior convexity and posterior concavity of the cervical curvature in the vicinity of the central (third, fourth, and fifth) cervical vertebræ. This is why Nove's improving occlusions display a concurrent elongation of the neck; the distortional compression of the neck has ceased.

Nature has over-emphasized the extensor mechanism of Man so that he might achieve the erect posture; but she will not tolerate postural short cuts. The only mechanism wherewith the growing child can counteract, and so to some extent compensate for, any overaction of the disproportionately powerful head-extensors (or head-retractors, *i.e.* the upper part of the *sacrospinalis* system) and their dominance over the weak head-flexor mechanism (provided by the prevertebral muscles) is to call into play antagonistically and most improperly the auxiliary trigemino-facial-suprahyoid-infrahyoid flexor sheet, *i.e.* the *rectus cervicalis*. But this postural employment of the *rectus cervicalis* sheet can easily cause a condition of spasticity or imbalance in the musculature of the mouth floor, soft palate, pharynx, and even in the diaphragm itself, which is supplied from these critical central cervical (third, fourth, and fifth) segments. Consequently, any strenuous effort of exercise on the part of the erect body becomes characterized, especially in posturally-imbalanced people, by throwing this auxiliary head-flexor sheet (in part or as a whole) into improper states of antagonistic contraction and strain. The resultant play of the straining flexor musculature in the face and neck has particularly engaged the attention of the painter and sculptor when portraying incidents of human combat and violence. The truly orthograde posture is a relatively recent human acquisition. To the human infant, especially the handicapped infant, striving to attain the erect posture and to gain facility in his employment of that posture (so as to carry out the bodily activities characteristic of a human being), and simultaneously to acquire the human skills of tool-using and speech, every phase in the business of becoming orthograde is at the outset a strenuous effort leading to muscular imbalances of a transitory or permanent sort that are experienced by every human individual. Consequently many children develop, and often retain during adolescence and even carry on into adult life, traces of the battle they waged in infancy in becoming erect in the form of curious (and from the point of view of orthograde perfection, improper) chewing, swallowing, breathing and speech habits. These quaint habits or conditioned reflexes are based on customs formed during infancy of always and quite unnecessarily continuing to employ to excess, or in unbalanced fashion, one or another part (or parts) of this *rectus cervicalis* or 'neck-righting' sheet (or indeed the whole of the sheet) in bodily posture and in bodily movements which they should have learned to maintain or perform with only the minimal and nicely balanced assistance of individual elements in this very highly specialized sheet of voluntary striated musculature that Nature originally intended to be devoted principally to the alimentary and respiratory requirements of a water-life. A muscular sheet, adapted when the vertebrate head was first formed to discharge such peculiar and delicate functions as are involved in seizing and swallowing food, and modified later for respiring air and voice production, cannot but be grossly embarrassed in one, or other, or all of these functions, if that muscular sheet is forced into contraction in part or whole and spastically or intermittently, in the misguided attempt to compensate for (or actually oppose) other muscles (*e.g.* the head-extensors) that do not carry out their postural functions (*e.g.* of relaxation) properly.

Having seen why and how the *rectus cervicalis* sheet is called into action, it is instructive to consider how posture is affected by the manner of holding the head. In decerebrate animals, *attitudinal reflexes* are evoked by changing the position of the head (a) *in space* or (b) *in relation to the body*. These postural or attitudinal reflexes are tonic reflexes resulting from the stimulation both of labyrinthine receptors and of upper cervical proprioceptors. R. Magnus pointed out in his Croonian Lecture (1925) on animal posture that 'many masterpieces of painting or sculpture representing human beings are consistent with the laws of attitudinal reflexes'; that several of these attitudinal reflexes are present in the infant child; and that instantaneous or fast cinema photographs sometimes show adult postures in agreement with these laws. Thus, in golf, players 'the fixating of the head in the line of sight of the ball' while 'at the top of the swing the shoulders are turned by 180° in relation to the head, which is kept fixed in space as firmly as possible' evokes a tendency 'to extend the left arm and to twist the body to the left—movements which seem to be facilitated and strengthened by the preliminary starting posture of the head and body'.

The centres for the labyrinthine and cervical attitudinal reflexes of the body, according to Magnus, lie along with the motor nuclei of the occipital nerves (ninth, tenth, eleventh, and twelfth cranial) and of the cervical nerves (supplying the muscles we have been considering) 'behind the plane of entrance of the eighth cranial nerve in the medulla oblongata and in the two highest cervical segments of the spinal cord'. The automatic body-righting reflexes found in midbrain animals include, in addition to these labyrinthine and cervical reflexes, those resulting from stimulation of body surface exteroceptors and of the retina, and those arising from the positions assumed by the eyes. Thus, their centres extend forward from the medulla oblongata into the midbrain. By means of these further stimuli, these sub-cortical brain-stem centres in the midbrain restore muscular imbalances caused by disturbances in the relationship of the parts of the body to one another and bring the body of the midbrain animal back into the posture normally assumed by animals of that class or order when standing. Hence, the apparatus for maintaining our posture is sub-cortical or reflex in nature. The neuromuscular apparatus, being reflex, should keep our posture perfect always, whatever the position in space may be that our bodies or their parts may temporarily adopt.

The forebrain is neither an initiator nor regulator of posture; it follows immediate objectives as consciousness of them awakens, and employs the apparatus of movement momentarily at its disposal, whatever the postural development of the apparatus may be. When the postural development of the individual is such as to place at the forebrain's disposal a perfectly poised apparatus, the conscious and subconscious aspects of movement are happily integrated. Unfortunately, conscious objectives so outstrip postural evolution as to produce bodily disharmony more frequently than body poise.

The expert golf player (whose skill depends upon an intelligent employment of *attitudinal* and *body-righting* reflexes) and the sculptor's or painter's masterpiece (which imprisons some dramatic moment of bodily poise based on these subconscious manifestations of neuromuscular activity) both exhibit, in relative perfection, the integration between the conscious and subconscious aspects of movement that characterizes the smooth working of the various body parts concerned in a given operation. Similarly, what we are concerned with in malocclusion is not a simple over-action on the part of the digastrics or any other muscle pair in the occipital or cervical region, but a failure of the *rectus cervicalis*, the auxiliary flexor mechanism of the neck, to become dissociated from the attitudinal and body-righting reflexes underlying postural activities and so to execute its reflex operations smoothly. The neck mechanism is unable to work smoothly and harmoniously in the active (or even in the passive) erect body.

A great deal of the isolation or automatism necessary in the neck mechanism is effected, and Nove's series of cases proves that pronounced improvements arise, by fitting jaw splints that force the auxiliary cranial flexor sheet of muscles to operate symmetrically during sleep and thus accustom the subconscious brain to a balanced reflex use of the swallowing and respiratory musculature during its non-waking hours. But the orthodontist can enlarge his perspective with Stillwell and Stallard beyond the cervico–facial orthopædic horizon, to which it has been extended by Nove, so that it embraces the global phenomenon of body posture and body poise. The cranial and cervical muscular imbalances made manifest by the malocclusion and corrected locally by the splinting and the improved swallowing and respiring are themselves merely a single element, although an extremely important (or ancestral) element in the total problem of faulty posture and poise, *i.e.* faulty integration of attitudinal and righting reflexes in the execution of the body's work. The education of the body in mastering the employment of these postural reflexes—unless it occurs spontaneously as a result of the orthodontist's procedure—will require even more attention than the education of the body in mastering the reflexes of chewing, swallowing and respiration, if the postural defects leading to the malocclusion are themselves to be removed.

The orthodontist may not undertake this wider educational responsibility nor treat the postural defects with which malocclusions are so intimately associated, but he requires to understand the relationship between the conditions he is ameliorating and the general welfare of his patient. Neurologically, the dentist may have little concern with more than dealing effectively with pain sensations transmitted through the branches of the trigeminal nerve; as for muscles, beyond those of mastication, he may be excused if he exhibits little interest in their manner of working. The work of orthodontists, however, has demonstrated how an understanding of the neuromuscular mechanisms of deglutition and respiration, in addition to that of mastication, has been turned in the hands of the thoughtful dentist to the general advantage of growing children. If, on the other hand, malocclusion is regarded rightly as constituting *one of the signs of malposture*, then those dentists who practise orthodontics should familiarize themselves with the neuromuscular mechanism of the body upon which the head and neck under attention is poised, or, at least, with the general principles underlying bodily equilibrium and its maintenance.

The neuromuscular background of body posture

Because medical like dental practitioners tend to lose amidst our modern forest of anatomical detail the main trees of principle upon which body movement rests, I recently published (1946) an article on 'The double-spiral mechanism of the voluntary musculature of the human body'. There I pointed out that, as a result of the disposition of the striated muscular system in three layers (of which the inner is circular and the outer two are oblique or diagonal in arrangement and assume the form of two interwoven spirals), every human adult individual suffers to a greater or lesser extent as the result of having acquired a mild, a moderate, or even a serious degree of permanent postural obliquity, rotation, or twist (without the condition being recognized by themselves or by their medical advisers); and that this condition of postural twist is a fundamental factor to be taken into account in clinical conditions as widely separated as night terrors, spasticity and scoliosis appear to be when superficially considered.

Though we give many names to the results of muscle movements—flexion, extension, adduction, abduction, circumduction, pronation, supination and the like, physiologically considered, only two types of muscles, *viz*. flexors and extensors, are required to carry our movements of great directional divergence. Rotation or twisting occurs not because there is a third type of physiological result from muscle movement, but because torsion of soft, or of moveable but hard parts (joints) must occur when the flexor half of a somite (or several somites) is hypertonic in one segment (or part of the body) and in an adjacent segment (or part of the body) the extensor portion is hyptertonic. Because these torsional activities are so important in the economy of body-movement, two strata of the flexor and extensor sheets are arranged obliquely in order to do the twisting.

But we can adopt an even more basic view about movement itself (as opposed to the results of movement) and recognize that there is only one thing muscles can do, namely, contract; but their state of contraction can vary to produce anything from a minimal to a maximal amount of tone. When flexion is actively occurring, the position assumed merely expresses the difference between an excess of tone in the flexors concerned and a relative lack of tone in the extensors. Moreover, muscles (and the segments which each flexor and extensor half form) do not act independently. Rest, therefore, is purely a relative term. While the flexor half of a segment is hypertonic its corresponding extensor half is acting tonically and antagonistically thereto and *vice versa*. Thus, all movements, however restricted they seem to be, involve all the muscles of the body, because if they are not directly concerned in the local resultant of movement they are indirectly concerned therein, since they have then to be kept in a state of minimal contraction. The chief business of the nervous system is not the initiation but *the inhibition of movement*. More particularly is every muscle concerned in activities involving the upright posture so that there results a minimum of movement and a maximum of poise.

If we consult any anatomy textbook concerning the musculature of the trunk, we can trace the curiously interwoven arrangement that each spiral body-sheet has assumed and which I described in the article aforesaid. Beginning on a deep plane of traction as the deep or internal oblique (internal oblique–internal intercostal) sheet of muscle and running from each iliac crest (and lumbo-dorsal fascia and rib series) it runs diagonally upwards in a latero–medial direction around the trunk to the front midline (*i.e.* from the symphysis pubis to the root of the neck. Along the anterior median line the same diagonally ascending direction of traction (passing upwards across the midline in a medio–lateral direction) is now assumed by the superficial or external oblique (external oblique–external intercostal–scalene–*levatores costarum*) sheet, through which the slanting muscular pull of the whole sheet encircles the trunk, and on its posterior aspect is redirected latero–medially and distributed in the final analysis to the entire series of vertebral transverse processes.

The transverse processes of the spinal vertebræ, taken serially, form a most important morphological line, *i.e. the lateral line of the body*, marked superficially in fishes by a row of sense organs supplied by the vestibular nerve. This lateral line of the body separates the anterior or flexor half of each muscle segment in the body from its posterior or extensor half, each half being innervated by corresponding anterior or posterior divisions of the spinal nerves.

From the morphologically important coronal plane passing through the two lateral lines (and cleaving the neuromuscular mechanism of the body cranio-caudally into flexor and extensor halves), the tractional plane of the superficial or external oblique muscular sheet we have been considering is now continued latero–medially upwards to the posterior midline of the body. But, once again, the diagonal pull, although it maintains the same cranialward direction, has shifted to the deeper level of the internal sheet of the extensor *sacrospinalis* mass (formed by the *multifidus* and *semispinalis* musculature), to find ultimate distribution to, or attachment in, the vertebral spines, *ligamentum nuchæ* and occiput. Then, just as this spiral arrangement crossed the midline of the front, it is continued across the midline of the back of the body. Along the posterior median line the same upward diagonal direction of pull becomes transmitted, and once more medio–laterally, through the external sheet of the extensor *sacrospinalis* mass (formed by the *iliocostalis*, *longissimus*, and musculature *splenius*) ascending from the spinous processes of the vertebræ to the lateral processes of those higher up in the series, to the angles of the ribs and finally to the mastoid process of the temporal bone on that side. Thus the double spiral muscular ensheathment of the body is completed.

By taking two grease pencils of contrasting colour and marking out on the surface of a human body two broad lines spiralling latero–medially upwards from each anterior iliac spine across the front of the body and around the back of the neck to the mastoid process of the same side of the body, these facts can be more vividly represented than by any verbal description. Two such spiral lines, following the general line of traction outlined, cross the *linea alba* in the *hypogastrium*, *i.e.* about the solar plexus, or midway between the navel and the lower end of the sternum. Then, separating from one another as they pass upwards, each line crosses over the middle of the opposite clavicle to encircle the nape of the neck well above the *vertebra prominens* and there, crossing one another over the *ligamentum nuchæ* and running up the back of the neck, each line ends on the mastoid process of that side of the body from which it began.

Any number of lines parallel with these primary lines and in appropriate corresponding colours can be added to represent the two opposed spiral sheets encircling the body. It then becomes patent, if paradoxical, how Man suspends the remainder of his body from his head and spine. He swings his body from his head by means of two spirally-arranged but interwoven sheets of voluntary musculature in exactly the same manner that his fishy and amphibian forefathers swung their bodies from their heads, before their lateral fins became transformed into body-struts. Although customarily we regard the globular head as being poised upon the vertebral column, we should not forget that in swimming, in standing on their heads, or in performing feats of strength with their jaws and necks while suspended from their feet, a considerable proportion of mankind in every generation has celebrated in a direct manner the predominant part the positioning of the head in relation to the rest of the body plays in body movement. But, directly or indirectly, every sort of bodily movement and skill illustrates the same principle—if the head containing the balancing organs is not the prime mover, if it is incorrectly placed and maintained for equilibrated execution of the movements planned, the movements will be unbalanced and, in brief, caricatures of what those movements should be. For this reason smoothly executed, *i.e.* skilled, movements are only mastered after long tutelage, whether in the fields of athletics and sports, in the workshops of craftsmen, or in the studios of artists. The vast majority of people, relying more on one torsional sheet than on the other, develop a right-handed twist or asymmetry of movement.

The tutelage that results in skill is devoted, whether recognized or not by the participants, to the process of co-ordinating the existing attitudinal and righting reflexes of the body (well , badly, or indifferently integrated as they may already be) with new movements now being personally designed for the first time. But, if the new sets of movements have an asymmetrical attitudinal effect on the body, and the body, as a result of its previous neuromuscular experience, has already attained an oblique postural state (*i.e.* with a bias or slope in one direction, whether rightward or leftward) or asymmetry, the new movements can have no other effect, however seemingly accurate their performance, than of still further emphasizing and consolidating the postural asymmetry resulting ontogenetically from previous faulty integration. Faulty attitudinal integration or imperfections in the use of both spiral sheets and inability to secure the balance or body poise essential for the truly skilled execution of movements is the general characteristic of all human beings at the outset. Unfortunately, we understand so little of the reflex nature of the body poise we should be aiming at when, as infants, we are becoming erect, that we prevent the emergence of the underlying attitudinal and body-righting reflexes essential to acquiring postural poise. We acquire, despite our asymmetrical rigidity, a passable degree of skill (or one that succeeds in satisfying us) without ever knowing or experiencing the postural poise for whose endowment Nature consumed millions of years. Thus, the only people who acquire true poise of body are those fortunate few who acquire the balanced use of their postural reflexes spontaneously as reflexes or those who (under expert instruction as dancers, jugglers, sportsmen, and the like) spend most of their lifetime in achieving and maintaining their body poise by concentrating on the acquirement and retention of these reflexes.

Nor is any royal road to the acquisition of undeveloped body poise known at the present time because no technique is as yet generally applicable whereby the underlying attitudinal and body-righting reflexes can be spontaneously unmasked and allowed to do their symmetrical reflex work without interference. Remedial exercises for faulty posture are given only to the grossly deformed or injured, and few can resort to dancers, jugglers or acrobats to learn postural poise, even if they or their teachers could actually devote the time that such bodily reeducation entails. Further, unless the underlying integration between these self-operating reflexes and the purposive movements essential to bodily poise has already been established, physical exercises of a routine nature and strenuous bodily sports carried out by an asymmetrical body merely emphasize the existing asymmetry by neglecting balance. As far as I am aware, the only technique aiming at integrating the activities of the individual by developing new habits based on the conscious control of the body is that of Matthias Alexander as set forth in *The Use of the Self* (1932) and other publications. But this technique also demands the personal assistance of the individual at the hands of one or other of the few that are skilled in the application of the technique.

This sorry state of affairs cannot be readily altered, for very few people know how their bodies are constructed and carry out their functions in respect of movement. Nor can bodily education be any more easily effected than is any particular sport, craft or art without personal instruction on the spot. One cannot learn swimming by correspondence! But if the basic principles governing the movements and the poise of the body can be isolated, proportionately increasing circles of people may, by comprehending the underlying principles, undertake their own physical improvement and prevent growing infants and youths from complete enslavement to the bodily errors of their parental generation.

Knowledge of their individual muscles is still regarded as far too abstruse for average persons, even if educated, to absorb today. Fortunately, no extravagant intellectual effort is involved in picturing in the fashion portrayed the two interwoven spiral sheets of trunk musculature responsible for the postural and intentional twisting of the body, and their direct attachment above to the skull, and thus their ultimate suspension like the auxiliary cranial flexor sheet of muscle from the temporal bones containing the equilibrating organs. Those who have dissected the body will recall that the same sort of spiral twisting of the (superficial and deep strata of) flexors and extensors is continued into the upper and lower limbs, and that this twisted arrangement is responsible for their (the limb flexors and extensors) combining to produce movements of internal and external limb rotation (in addition to their ancestral purposes of simple limb flexion and extension). A permanent degree of inward (postural) rotation of man's extended lower limbs has provided him with his flat foot-surfaces; a permanent degree of inward (postural) rotation of his free upper limbs has afforded him implement-using hands that he folds across his chest. Man's powerful hip musculature has allowed him finally to twist his whole body permanently upwards and poise it in a state of postural fixation on top of his hip bones. Thus, paradoxically enough, it is Nature's most twisted, distorted creature (*i.e.* crooked Man) that is capable of the supreme achievements of poise—balancing on head, hand, heel or toe.

Man's place in Nature is thus due to his conquest (subconscious as the achievement may have been) of the problems of body-poise by means of postural twisting. We should, therefore, first recognize as a principle that star performers in the further spiralling realms of body poise, whether jugglers or acrobats, dancers or sportsmen, are merely outstanding examples of the well-balanced but gyratory bodies Nature aimed at for mankind, bodies which every person should possess. Secondly, we should realize that failure to develop a perfectly poised body represents, like any other teratomatous condition, a developmental arrest.

The developmental arrest, in this widespread or pandemic human disease of malposture, is not expressed in a lack of tissue or of body parts such as we find in digital or limb deficiencies, anencephaly or cleft palate. The bones, joints, muscles, nerves and co-ordinating brain are all present in malpostured people and, as far as we know, complete in every detail. The shortcomings in respect of body poise are purely functional; the degree of neuromuscular co-ordination is not high; the muscles do not act in such an integrated manner as produces smooth, balanced movements of bodies and limbs. This failure to behave integratedly occurs because certain channels (or tracts) in the nervous system and the muscles they mobilize, being overexcitable, work excessively while others, more sluggish, are underworked or never even awakened. As a result, there is an improper timing and confusion in the sequence of neuromuscular events of contraction and relaxation in the groups of muscles essential for carrying out complex movements smoothly. In conscious attempts to execute movements, the brain or mind, instead of clearing the ground, as it were, for that movement by inhibiting all unnecessary movement and allowing the movement to take place by the free (or uninhibited) operation of the attitudinal and body-righting reflexes involved in the twisting movements, is obsessed with the determination or will to perform the movement despite the reflexes involved therein. The forebrain and cerebellum, probably through the fronto–ponto–cerebellar fibre system, override the reflexes by resorting to postural fixation by inhibiting further movement in positions of incomplete or unconsummated twist.

It is the business of the vestibular apparatus, operating through its own reflex paths, the medial longitudinal fasciculus, and through the cerebellum, to bring such information to the neck and body musculature as will lead to a spontaneous state of poise, whatever the position of the body in space and the mutual relationships of its parts may happen to be. This business it would unquestionably discharge in such a way as to awaken no sense of alarm whatever in the mind of the creature concerned, provided it had been given during infant life the opportunity and practice essential to the discharge of those reflex duties. But, on account of the immediate and overwhelming state of alarm arising in creatures so precariously poised posturally as human beings, as soon as they sense a potential loss of their balance, they respond to stimuli of disequilibrium by going into *a state of muscular fixation* or spastic rigidity at that point and in that particular postural position. Frequent repetition of this type of reaction in that and similar positions results in stabilizing this habit of muscular fixation at that postural position of unconsummated poise, *i.e.* confining the body as a whole to a very restricted range of variation in movement, namely, the range within which it feels secure.

The result is that, instead of developing and improving their knowledge and practice of muscle–joint sensation and body poise so that their bodies are constantly in a state of equilibrium wherever they are and whatever they are doing, the bodies of most human beings are held static by unsuitable groups of muscles in undue states of strain through lack of that knowledge. They cannot even feel security while reversing in a waltz. This lack is the more regrettable in that the underlying neuromuscular knowledge is not a novel acquisition restricted to mankind but is something extremely ancient, his despised or neglected or overlooked heritage from the very remote past of phylogeny. Paradoxically enough, lower animals that have less need of such knowledge (because of their less precarious or pronograde type of posture and more restricted arenas of bodily skill) have, generally speaking, better body poise than have human beings. Within the limitations of their four-footed posture they leap and contort their bodies with abandon. Similarly, less sedentary and less civilized human beings enjoy, for the most part, better body poise than do dwellers in cities.

Another factor responsible for restricting the acquisition of body-poise by human children is the addition to their own fears of the fears of their parents and guardians. Lacking a knowledge of the degree of poise attainable by the twisting body and the gyroscopic perfection of body balance to be aimed at during development, and being themselves habituated to a poorly poised body and grossly distorted muscle–joint sense, most adults interfere by ridicule or force with the spontaneous practices of infancy and youth in poise, balancing and contortion.

Education of the body for poise

How, then, is poise to be acquired if lost or defective? How is equilibrium to be set free if held in abeyance? The shortest road towards neuromuscular education of the body is doubtless at the hands of skilled people who practise an appropriate technique. The technique designed by Alexander is appropriate because it is based on the fundamental biological fact that the relation of the head to the neck is the primary relationship to be established in all proper positioning and movement of the body. But, if we are not so fortunate as to have expert personal assistance, can the individual do anything? Alexander himself holds out little hope for the unassisted person beyond the patient process of self-correction relative to movement before a mirror which he followed out himself in improving the use of his own body and in discovering the important principles at which he arrived.

The medical or dental practitioner, however, with a detailed knowledge of anatomy and physiology should, with the aid of further general principles, be better able to assist himself and others in understanding what to do and how to do it. The orthodontists have now shown how, by inhibiting intermittently or actually immobilizing the hard moving parts concerned in the very ancient phylogenetic reflex of jaw-closure, the muscles concerned with food-seizing (and the perhaps equivalently ancient reflexes of) swallowing and respiring can be harnessed to the service of the individual and bring about 'a readjustment of the angle of the human head and neck' by being unable to work otherwise than symmetrically. This inhibition of improper, or cultivated reflex manners of using individualized body parts such as the jaws, swallowing and breathing apparatus and limbs plays a fundamental role in Alexander's technique of securing a correct 'primary relation of the head and neck', though in that technique the inhibitional control is exercised not by the pieces of apparatus but by the individual's own will. By refusing to carry out this or that observed habitual but inappropriate response (of head retraction, knee adduction and so forth) during given movements, *e.g.* sitting, standing, lying down or getting up, the individual allows these movements to occur in their natural or ancestral, and therefore most useful, mass-reflex manner, unimpeded by volition.

Whether appreciated by the orthodontist or not, his procedure of harnessing the reflexes in such a way that they must work symmetrically is *a principle of temporary fixation* that can be widely applied in postural therapy, because the immobilization of the jaws is an enforced *inhibition* of the moving parts to which the reflexly contracting muscles must posturally adapt themselves. Stutterheim (1946), by the use of a prism battery which predetermines the amount of angular twist eye muscles must overcome (in order to maintain the type of vision they have been habitually cultivating), temporarily fixes or inhibits them and so forces the eye muscles to adapt themselves posturally in such a way as to unmask their innate reflex capacity for convergence. He thus cures both asthenovergence and squint—postural conditions of the eyes.

If volitionally-unimpeded movements of these mass-reflex types are allowed to occur with sufficient frequency, they become automatic—because they are part and parcel of the phylogenetic history of the human race—and replace the previous wrongful or malcoordinated movements. But it would be misleading to assume that the inhibition of our *old* (*i.e.* infantile or childish) habits of movements and their replacement with *new* habits of movement is an easy or a rapid process. The so-called *new habits* of movement are, of course, paradoxically enough, based upon postural reflexes much older than the individual, primæval body movements, which are now inherited ancestral mass-reflexes. What is new and what takes a lot of time is therefore better described as learning to integrate conscious or purposeful movements with the inherited mass-reflexes, learning not to interfere with and distort ancestral habits by calling inappropriate muscles into unnecessary and futile play during intentional movements. We must break, for example, by inhibiting in some way, the infantile habits of holding our breath, of gritting our teeth, of pulling our heads back, and of not letting our knees separate when rising from the squatting or sitting posture into the erect posture. These common forms of interference are introduced by human beings into the muscular activities of squatting, sitting and standing, that should be discharged in a spontaneous and unimpeded fashion. Similarly, chewing movements, facial contortions, tongue rollings, throat gulps, laryngeal spasms and arrested breathing cannot be introduced into the complex phenomenon of speech if it is to occur unimpededly in the erect posture.

Man may be defined as a being who, by exerting the maximum degree of bodily twist to preserve his equilibrium, should be able simultaneously to maintain without strain the erect posture (or move about in the erect posture) and respire rhythmically through the nostrils, whilst engaged in eating and speech and actively employing his hands with tools. Individuals unable to behave in this complex and highly-skilled neuromuscular way; folks whose breathing is arrhythmical and not confined to their nostrils as soon as they eat, speak, write or work; people who cannot eat or speak, write or work unless they are supporting their bodies with their elbows, rolling their tongues, or lolling against a piece of furniture, have failed to experience the bodily capacities of equilibrated human beings. They have arrested their progress in bodily equilibrium at any one of the numerous stages at which it can be arrested by postural fixation during its ontogentic evolution.

If a person is squatting, sitting or standing in an equilibrated fashion, the tensions of the muscles on both sides are equally distributed, each weight-bearing point or area taking spontaneously its appropriate part in the support of the body; and in such equilibrated positions the upper limbs hang freely, or hold implements, or move across surfaces without being employed simultaneously as secondary body supports. Similarly, the head, somewhat forwardly inclined, pivots freely on the vertebral column and the musculature of the neck, without displaying any stiffness, pain or tension, freely suspends the jaws, tongue and laryngeal apparatus, so that unimpeded chewing, swallowing, breathing or speech can occur concurrently.

Where these conditions are not present (where the body weight is thrown on to the feet in a disproportionate manner in standing, or is not supported in an equilibrated fashion by the ischial tuberosities and feet in sitting, but is slumped asymmetrically on to the elbows or hands, and the head is drawn down posteriorly towards one or other shoulder), steps should be taken to train or to educate the respective parts to undertake their proper relative roles in body support in the posture under consideration. This training, however, is not so much a training to do good movements as a restraining of the individual from performing improper and inappropriate movements by means of manipulative and personal inhibition.

A sharp distinction should therefore be drawn between the inhibitional manipulative education of the body in respect of symmetry and poise and the procedures carried out by naturopaths, chiropractors, osteopaths, bonesetters, and others who manipulate body parts on one or more occasions for the purpose of relieving aches and pains but not for the inculcation of new habits of movement. Manipulation or support of the body and its parts by an expert assistant is of the greatest possible advantage while it is practising mental inhibition and accustoming itself to new positions (which, though based upon ancestral reflexes, are novel to the individual in whom they are being unmasked) during the carrying out of such ordinary activities as sitting, standing, walking about and lying down. In this co-ordinational neuromuscular education, as in all other bodily education, the studies of muscle and joint sensation (during inhibition and non-interference with his body) made by the pupil are of greater importance than anything done or inculcated by the tutor, more especially because in the realm of muscle movement human language, being grossly deficient in descriptive terminology, is not as helpful educationally as it is in the realms of sight and hearing. Yet even where there is a rich terminology, as of colour and of sound, practical personal instruction is most desirable for the prospective painter or pianist.

The actual equilibrational education of the body thus sketchily outlined in respect of its principles is time-consuming, humiliating and disappointing to those who expect rapid and obvious physical returns for the labour and mental effort involved. To forestall such disappointment it may be worthwhile to state that my own efforts began in September 1943 and have continued with tolerable persistence over the intervening three years. The process is still far from complete but is sufficiently advanced for me to have learned certain underlying principles and possibly to clarify them for others who desire to educate their own bodies in poise. The slowness of my progress is related to the degree of scoliotic deformity acquired in the fifty preceding years of my life and is not necessarily typical, since I preferred to advance cautiously rather than speedily where considerable body change was unavoidably involved. With greater understanding of the principles involved and happier techniques of exploiting the different phases in postural betterment as they emerge, cases of my sort might be improved more rapidly and lesser defects eliminated in relatively briefer periods.

Had I appreciated at the outset the basic and perpetual significance of the twisting process in bodily evolution, that, apart from flexion and extension, the bodily rotation (resulting from the collaborative and antagonistic operation of flexors and extensors) is the fundamental and permeating characteristic of all voluntary muscular movement in ontogeny and phylogeny, I would have been placed in a situation of greater advantage. Having recognized this fact, it was gratifying to find these views about spiral twisting anticipated to some extent by the *rotary curvature* concept of scoliosis set forth by Truslow in *Body Poise* (1943) and to discover that he had elaborated derotational or untwisting exercises to remedy that condition. In concentrating upon the twisting effects of the shoulder musculature upon the thoracic cage, Truslow did not prosecute the operation of the rotational principle throughout the whole body, but he did recognize that poise is fundamental for the human body and that many sports and occupations destroy body-poise by promoting bodily asymmetry due to fixed postural twists.

The major aims, therefore, in bettering bodily poise are, firstly, *inhibition*, or suppression of the factors promoting asymmetry; and, secondly, *derotation* of the twisted body. In practice it is difficult to separate passive inhibition from active derotation because as soon as we cease to twist we are to that extent untwisting; further, the better way of causing some people to desist from their habitual manner of twisting is to encourage them actively but cautiously to untwist themselves.

Inhibition and derotation can only occur successfully when two states of the body have been achieved—one is that the customary vegetative activities of the body (*e.g.* jaw and mouth closure, swallowing, circulation and especially respiration) are proceeding normally; the second is that all fear of falling, *i.e.* of disturbing equilibrium, should be minimal. The latter fear becomes irresistible strength if, like Antæus, we retain close contact with mother earth. Respiratory embarrassment, the first premonition of the anxiety preceding postural change, disappears with regular respiration through the right and left nostril in strict alternation with one another. This alternation appears to be essential because inspiration through one nostril facilitates the entry of air into the homolateral lung probably as the result of a mass-reflex in response to nasal (trigeminal) stimulation.

To take an actual example such as the retracted head in the right-handed person; in such an individual the neck extensors are not merely contracted but the habitual contracture has produced a fixed postural twist such that the skull is tilted not only posteriorly but also towards the left side while the shoulders in sympathy become correspondingly displaced (the left backwards and upwards, the right forwards and downwards) on the thoracic cage, whose right half is becoming increasingly twisted towards the left iliac crest. (*Cf.* illustrations in Stillwell's paper, *op. cit.*)

In such a type of asymmetry or deformity, common enough in our sedentary population, let the individual recline in static security for 15–20 minutes after luncheon in the supine position on a carpeted floor with the head resting as comfortably as possible on one or more books forming a hard bolster (two to three inches thick) and the feet brought as close to the buttocks as is possible without muscular strain (knees in the air and slightly abducted, elbows on the floor and the hands resting on the junction of thorax and abdomen, fig. 7.12). This brief midday rest induces a gradual relaxation or inhibition of the *sacrospinalis* mass and all the extensor musculature of the body, and a temporary release from their inevitable state of torsional strain. Simultaneously it trains seven distinct 'dorsal' body areas (occiput, *scapulæ*, hip bones and feet) to share gradually in an equilibrated fashion the business of sustaining the body weight *in the supine body* on a resistant base where the areas can be felt instead of on a spring mattress where exteroceptive sensual discrimination is obliterated. Thereby on each daily occasion there is added to the extensor relaxation of the supine posture partial untwisting between each pair of relatively fixed weight-bearing sites of the leftwardly-rotated body as well as between the *scapulæ* and occiput, and an education of several parts of the back in sensory discrimination that is basic for bodily movement of a poised or equilibrated sort.

This procedure, simple as it is, if persisted in over two years, can scarcely fail of itself in producing widespread effects in derotating and improving the equilibration of the body. It is the puny, *infantile supine posture* from which there emerged ontogenetically all our body movements and from which we developed our particular and individual habits of twisting the body, as we first learned to roll over using one or more of these relatively fixed weight-bearing sites as fulcra. But its reverse, namely the prone (fronto–olecrano–tibial or forehead–elbow–knee) or crawling variety of the fœtal posture has much greater, direct effects in evoking the ancestral postural mass-reflexes of the body, more especially if it is employed for 15–20 minutes subsequent to the relaxational and derotational influence exerted by the supine posture described. According to Stillwell (*op. cit.*) the supine posture is the proper posture for sleep.

The advantages of this *primary crawling posture* are more than can be expressed in a single paragraph. In addition to its being a posture devoid of fear, being a variation of the fœtal posture, it approximates the primary mammalian posture. From it we can proceed to the *initial pronograde* (fronto–palmal–plantar or forehead–palm–sole) *posture* or revert to the *ancestral ventigrade* (fronto–dorso–manual–dorsopedal or forehead–dorsum of hand–dorsum of foot) *posture*. Each of these ancestral body postures has immense significance in the education of the antagonistic groups of muscles surrounding each individual joint of the body for the acquisition of poise; indeed, the inadequate exploitation, short-circuiting, or actual elimination of these ancestral phases of posture by the human infant, in its own (or its parents') haste to become erect, seems to be chiefly responsible for the lack of poise so frequently encountered in human adults.

Close attention to infantile rolling movements shows that certain restricted bony sites (sometimes approximately punctate in character and usually well supplied with bursæ) act as fulcra (or leverage points) and that it has been their development as fulcra which has enabled the various postural mechanisms exhibited by land creatures to be evolved.

The quadrupedal mechanism has evolved because four props provide a minimal type of fulcral apparatus for land movement, because it is possible to equilibrate and support securely the body on a temporarily spastic or posturally fixed tripod while the fourth limb is relaxed and placed in a suitable position forwards or laterally to assume its sequential role in the business of tripodal postural support during progression. But when the weight-supporting body-base is restricted, as in marsupials, the tripodal hopping mechanism of hind toes and tail, so perfectly adapted for speedy movement, is replaced by a pentapodal fulcral apparatus of hind toes, hind 'heels' and tail while at rest. Man succeeds in supporting his poised body in the erect posture on only two feet because the transformation of each foot into a tripodal arch (heel, big toe and lateral ball of foot) has provided him with six weight-bearing sites on his restricted but highly modifiable body-base.

The pentapodal character of the body support (occiput, scapular spines and posterior superior iliac spines) in the supine posture and the pentapodal fulcral stability of the primary crawling (forehead, tibial tuberosities and *olecrana*) posture inculcates in ten other body-sites their appropriate roles in weight-bearing. Rolling over adds to the six actual (pedal) and ten potential weight-bearing sites numerous further fulcral points for body movement. The principal addition in the lower limbs are the trochanters upon which the fixed femur, by means of its head, can pivot the pelvis and therewith the rest of the body. But it is in the upper limbs (that have been freed from weight-bearing) that the most numerous additions can be made to the ordinary repertoire of fulcral points for body movement. These are the acromial processes of the scapular spines, the internal and external epicondyles of the *humeri*, the thenar and hypothenar eminences, and the fingertips (acting together as the third element in the manual tripod) on the volar aspect of the hand, and the three rows of knuckle bones together with the dorsal aspects of the thumb and little finger metacarpals on the dorsum of the hand.

This means that, without further subdivision, ten further fulcral areas are available in each upper limb and one in each lower limb, or twenty-two in all for the limbs. To these must be added at least three more fulcral areas on each side of the cranium, namely, postero–lateral (parietal boss), lateral (temporal) and anterolateral (frontal boss) area, and three in the midline on top of the skull, namely, anterior (bregmatic), middle (vertical) and posterior (lambdoid), or nine more sites in all for the cranium. Adding these further potential twenty-two limb sites and nine cranial sites to the previous ten, we have at least forty-one potential weight-bearing sites as well as the six usual pedal areas employed in this manner.

The possible permutations and combinations open to the individual in employing these half hundred fulcral points for so apparently simple a purpose as to turn the body over from the supine to the ancestral ventigrade posture (or any other prone posture) or, to reverse the process, in rolling over from a prone to a supine posture, is very great indeed. The plastic, well-poised body will be able to use any of the possible combinations of fulcral points and it is a matter of great exploratory interest to take note of how in such movements the numbers of fulcral points employed can vary from one to eight (or more) at different stages of the movement and of how the bodily stability varies proportionately with the number of fulcral sites in contact with fixed surfaces.

Without entering further into the evolutionary or mathematical aspects of these matters, the *primary crawling* or *forehead–elbow–knee posture* (which, apart from its grotesque absurdity to an adult person, is at the outset most uncomfortable and painful and may only be achieved in heavy individuals if the weight-bearing sites are protected by cushions or pads), by distributing the body weight principally on the five extremely sensitive 'ventral' body areas mentioned and only very slightly on the palms and toes, evokes immediate postural adjustments on the part of the extensor–flexor muscle groups attaching the limbs to the trunk and on the part of the extensor–flexor mechanism of the neck and head to distribute the body weight symmetrically while the spinal column equilibrates itself as a continuous arch supported by the limb side-struts. Jaw movements, facial movements, swallowing and rhythmical respiration can each be isolated from one another and from trunk and limb activities in this position of head, trunk and limb fixation. Equally instructive is the information maintenance of this posture (*i.e.* inhibition of all save predetermined movements, such as are possible in this posture) gives to the intelligent individual about the astonishing inequality in weight-bearing capacity of his separate upper and lower limbs. From this *primary crawling posture* the leverage capacity (employing these five sensitive fulcra) of each limb upon the trunk can be explored with the utmost deliberation, and the capacity of the shoulder joints and hip joints to carry out their rotational functions be tested and steadily improved in excursion and equilibration. From this position, too, recoil in an equilibrated manner upon the dorsiflexed toes and from this *heel–haunch posture* to the *squatting posture* upon the feet is a natural evolution. However simple this portrayal of postural ontogeny may appear to be, experience in perfecting each of its phases will demonstrate its complexity. I have been amazed at the number of medical students I meet who imagine their posture is perfect but who cannot maintain the crawl posture in comfort, squat properly on their heels, or rise without a concomitant reel from their disequilibrated squatting posture.

It is not until times of national crisis that the handicaps of pandemic malposture become exposed. Then, in the phraseology of Le Gros Clark (1946), 'fitting the machine to the man' is the only feasible solution. Thus 'hardly more than 20% of the personnel' selected for training as observers in the gun-fire directors of battleships 'could elevate (their eyes when looking through binoculars) to 60° without strain and even with great straining only 75% could reach this level of elevation'. If only 20% of the healthy young men selected as fit for active service can carry out such ordinary or modest head-movements without strain, it is probable that 90% or more of human beings are posturally defective in this important respect.

Most important of all in this *primary crawling* or *forehead–elbow–knee posture* is the carrying out, study and improvement of head movements and their correlation with eye movements. These head movements appear simple enough in their nodding and rotation, but they become very complex indeed when we correlate head-nodding and head-rotation in an equilibrated fashion with movements of the eyes, on the one hand, and with the flexion, extension, lateral bending and rotational capacity of the neck on the other hand, and when we then finally strive to learn to combine these correlations with spinal rotations in the several positions in which the *scapulæ* can be fixed from the pivoting elbows, and in those further positions the shoulders can assume in rotations of the whole column from the fixed pelvis. Such controlled and correlated movements as these instruct us in the profound postural effects of altering the position of the eyes (*i.e.* extending the visual range).

Much of the importance attaching to head movements in this *primary crawling posture* lies in its unmasking our lopsided or asymmetrical visual habits. In our anxiety to look forward most of us (whilst crawling as right-handed infants) consolidated our earlier supine postural habit of improperly tilting our heads to the left (while we pushed and rolled ourselves over with our more powerful right limbs) by adding thereto a further habitual and inappropriate tilt of the head posteriorly. This had the further distortional effect of making our crawling lopsided and of causing us to see objects more clearly when they lay within a compass lying rather to the left side of our two fields of vision, and thus to place visual reliance principally on conjugate deviational movements of the eyes to the left with the consequent failure (in my own case) to master rightward conjugational movements of the eyes. By keeping the head, elbows and knees tethered to the floor in the *primary crawling posture*, correlational movements of the head and the eyes (which of are the greatest importance for the maintenance of equilibrium in the erect posture) can be cultivated in a position of maximum bodily stability at the same time as the inverted, anteflexed head is completely freed from its customary gravitational and tilting (*i.e.* twisting) restraints. While the head is being nodded and rotated and the eyes are kept trained on objects lying to the right and left respectively of their fields of vision, the student of bodily poise gradually learns that his head really is globular and actually does pivot on his vertebral column and that, when held in some such pivoted position, the cervical portion of the spinal column, upon which it is pivoted, can be isolated from the shoulders and moved in a rotational manner relatively to the temporarily fixed arms and shoulders. By such procedures factually and mentally we isolate the movements of the parts of the body concerned and allow the medial longitudinal bundle, the most important and ancient of reflex paths, to discharge without impediment its numerous correlational functions.

Just as this forehead–elbow–knee posture evolves by limb flexion into the squatting posture, so by extension of the limbs it develops into the *completely prone* or *ventigrade posture* (but still maintaining an anteflexed position of the head). This *ventigrade posture* may not be attainable (like the squatting posture) until after a long series of trials extending over months, for, simple and secure as these positions may appear to be, they are not to be done recklessly or foolishly, especially by elderly people of fixed postural habit. In this ancestral ventigrade or amphibian position (of the creature emergent from the water to the land) the primary flexion, extension and rotation of the head and of the spinal column, and of the extended limbs upon the ball and socket joints of shoulder and hip, are the only possible movements, save for the fulcral activities of the digits and of the hands (about the wrists) and of the feet (about the ankles) in rotating the trunk. In this ventigrade position the limitations of hip and shoulder movement can be best noted and their improvement in movement gradually effected, and from this position the body can be educated (as it should have been in early babyhood) to roll over on to the back equally well whether to the left or to the right by the assistance of any chosen limb combination, after the eye and head movements have become correlated and co-ordinated.

This brief statement about the pronograde and ventigrade phases of postural evolution is not intended as a guide to bodily education for the acquisition of poise; it is merely designed to open up to competent students the field that it lays bare for the exploration of posture and poise and to indicate the general relationship between malocclusion and body posture, *i.e.* between the primæval reflexes of the head and neck and the postural reflexes of the trunk and limbs. None of these ancestral postures can be frequently practiced nor the movements concerned be fully and completely carried out in their leftward and rightward rotation without the most profound effects upon the *rectus cervicalis* and accessory flexor muscular sheet of the head and neck whose remote ancestral reflexes are of primary interest to the dentist concerned with the correction of malocclusion.

Bibliography

Alexander, F. Matthias, 1923 (seventh edition, 1938): *Constructive Conscious Control of the Individual*, Methuen and Co., London.

———, 1932 (second reprint, 1939): *The Use of the Self*, Methuen and Co., London.

Andresen, Viggo, and Karl Haupl, 1936: *Functions—Kiefer Orthopadie die Grundlagen des Norwegischen Systems*, H. Meusser, Leipzig.

Baker, H. A., 1904: 'Treatment of protruding and receding jaws by the use of intermaxillary elastics', *Int. Dent. Jour., Vol.* 25, pp. 344–356.

Brown, J. C., and Losch, P. K., 1939: 'Dental occlusion in patients with muscular dystrophy', *Amer. Jour. Orthod.*, Vol. 25, pp. 1040–1046.

Capon, P. G., 1946: 'Notes on glossoptosis and micrognathia', *The Dental Record*, Vol. LXVI, No. 3, March.

Clark, W. E. le Gros, 1946: 'The contribution of anatomy to the War', *British Medical Journal*, Vol. 1, Jan. 12, p. 39.

Dart, R. A., 1946: 'The double-spiral mechanism of the voluntary musculature of the human body', *British Journal of Physical Medicine*, Vol. 13, p. 265.

Douglas, Mungo, 1937: 'Re-orientation of the viewpoint upon the study of anatomy', pamphlet privately published.

Grude, Rolf, 1938: 'The Norwegian system of orthodontic treatment', *The Dental Record*, Vol. 58, pp. 529–551.

Ludovici, Anthony M., 1933: *Health and Education through Self-Mastery*, Watts and Co., London.

Magnus, R., 1925: 'Animal Posture', Croonian Lecture, *Proceedings of the Royal Soc.iety* Series B, Vol. XCVIII, No. 3, p. 690.

Nove, A. A., 1946: 'Cervico–facial orthopædia', *The Dental Record*, Vol. LXVI, Nos. 2, 3, and 4, February–May.

Riesner, Sidney E., 1936: 'Temporo–mandibular articulation: 'its consideration in orthodontic diagnosis', *Int. Jour. Orthod. and O. Surg.*, Vol. 27, pp. 154–156.

Rogers, Alfred P., 1922: 'Stimulating arch development by the exercises of the masseter–temporal group of muscles', *Int. Jour. Orthod. O. Surg. and Rad.*, Vol. 8, February.

———, 1935: 'The behaviour of the temporo-mandibular joint in response to the myofunctional treatment of distocclusion', *Int. Jour. Orthod. and Dent. Child.*, Vol. 21, pp. 426–436.

———, 1936: 'Place of Myofunctional Treatment in the Correction of Malocclusion', *Jour. Amer. Dent. Assoc.* 23, pp. 66–78.

———, 1939: 'Evolution, development, and application of myofunctional therapy in orthodontics', *Amer. Jour. Orthod. and O. Surg.*, Vol. 25, pp. 1–19.

———, 1940: 'Myofunctional treatment from a practical standpoint', *Amer. Jour. Orthod. and O. Surg.*, Vol. 26, pp. 1131–1137.

Salzman, J. A., 1943: *Principles of orthodontics* (second edition), Lippincott, Philadelphia, London, and Montreal.

Stallard, Harvey, 1930: 'A consideration of extra-oral pressures in the etiology of malocclusions', *Int. Jour. Orthod.*, Vol. 16, May.

Stillwell, F. S., 1927: 'The correlation of malocclusion and scoliosis to posture and its effect upon the teeth and spine', *The Dental Cosmos*, Vol. 69, pp. 154–163.

Strang, R. H. W., 1943: *A Textbook of Orthodontia* (second edition), London.

Stutterheim, In. A., 1937: *Eyestrain and Convergence*, Lewis and Co., London.

———, 1946: *Squint and Convergence*, Lewis and Co., London.

Truslow, Walter, 1943: *Body Poise*, Williams and Wilkins, London.

5

The Attainment of Poise

SIR Charles Sherrington (1946) has drawn attention to the fact that 'in urbanized and industrialized communities bad habits in our motor acts are especially common'. Concomitant with, and probably causally related to, the intensification of civilized life during the last century is *the pandemic condition of malposture* amongst urbanized mankind. The effects of malposture pervade all the tissues of the body; but it has taken a long time for physiologist and physician to collate the evidence concerning malposture and demonstrate its repercussions in terms of dysfunction throughout the human framework.

Simultaneously, therapeutic procedures have been directed towards reducing or eliminating malposture; these procedures, based on partial understanding, have had limited success. To elaborate a logical therapeusis for malposture, its real nature must be apprehended. We must agree first of all that, in using the word *poise*, we know what is under discussion. We should also be able to elaborate the essential terminology without misusing, by tautology or qualification that is misleading, words so full of meaning as *posture* and *poise*.

> To stand erect, to walk or move easily, to have the various parts of the body so perfectly adjusted that easy balance and graceful use must result is to be desired for reasons of far greater importance than the æsthetic. Such elements are of absolute importance for perfect health and the fullest economic efficiency, since the use of the body in proper poise insures the least friction with consequently the greatest amount of energy available for what may be required of the individual.

In using this quotation about 'proper poise' from the writings of J. E. Goldthwait, one of the leaders in America amongst those who have

This article was first published in the *South African Medical Journal*, 21: 74–91, 8 February 1947.

'laboured to determine to what extent and in what manner posture influences health and efficiency', F. D. Dickson (1931) says 'this statement is basic in its importance and cannot be controverted'. Nobody disputes today that body balance is essential for health and that faulty posture promotes ill-health; but the use of such a qualified term as 'proper poise' is misleading.

The human machine certainly meets more differing conditions and performs work of greater diversity than any known mechanism. These functions are efficiently discharged when the body is in a state of *poise*. Visceral functions (such as those of digestion, circulation, respiration and excretion) as well as physical activities must continue with the maximum of efficiency and the minimum interference with their rhythm whether the body is supine or prone, erect or bent, twisted or straight. Integration of these vegetative and voluntary activities of the body occurs, and their rhythm is maximal, when the body enjoys *poise*, because it is only when the voluntary (or striated) musculature is working in a balanced way that it is making minimal demands on the vegetative (or unstriated) musculature. The striated musculature which was elaborated for movement of the body as a whole (Dart, 1924) can only work in a really balanced way when it is responding without impediment to the vestibular organs of balance through the mechanisms elaborated for that purpose by the central nervous system—in other words, when the reflex neuromuscular apparatus of body balance is integrated with the neuromuscular apparatus of non-reflex, purposeful or intentional movement.

It is tautological for Goldthwait to qualify the term *poise* and to speak of 'proper poise'. Dickson, however, commits a worse offence when he defines the 'position of the body most usually assumed' indifferently as either *poise or attitude*. Attitude is a suitable word to apply to the physical posture of the body, that is, its habitual modes of standing, sitting or lying. The dictionary synonyms we find for *attitude* are *pose* or *posture*. A body may be symmetrical in structure but asymmetrical in its attitude (like the leaning tower of Pisa) and the word *attitude*, like its synonyms, conveys, like a solid cube or cylinder, the further symbolism of stability, fixity and settled habit. *Poise*, on the other hand, comes to us from the language of weighing and movement and connotes the temporarily suppressed mobility of balance, equilibrium or equipoise, and, figuratively, equanimity and rest. About *poise*, therefore, there is nothing fixed. Primarily it denotes the suspended motion of a linear object. Applied to the physical positioning of the body, the word poise can and should convey only its very important and contrasted symbolism of 'the momentary halt in which the muscular forces concerned are in a state of equilibrium; any position that indicates suspended motion'. Consequently, while there are innumerable forms of 'faulty attitudes, poses or postures' which the solid human body can assume, in which the individual 'hangs on to himself' and from which he can only move by 'gathering himself with a preliminary waste of energy preparatory to action', there fortunately never can be any such thing as the 'faulty body poise' that Dickson talks about.

Terminological failure to distinguish the static symbolism of *posture* from the dynamic plasticity of *poise* has thus been responsible for a great deal of confusion both in the nomenclature of, and medical thought concerning, movement. In the proper carrying out of a movement, *e.g.* rising from the lying to the standing position, a considerable number of *intermediate positions* are necessarily assumed momentarily by the body in proceeding from the initial posture of lying to the terminal posture of standing. But these intermediate positions should always be positions of *poise* or equilibrium. A further considerable number of alternative *intermediate positions of poise* would have been temporarily assumed and passed through by the body had the individual adopted in rising any one of the other numerous routes of rising that he (or an acrobat, or a gymnast) might have employed for the purpose. There are, however, great differences between the carryings-out of single movements by individuals entailing such numerous and variant body positions. These differences correspond with the bodily skill or versatility relative to *poise* of the performer concerned. The movements of the acrobat are performed by a body which at every phase of the movement (*i.e.* in the initial, intermediate or terminal positions) is in a state of *mobile equipoise* or balance.

The physicist defines equilibrium as the state of a body susceptible of easy displacement but so acted upon by several counteracting forces that it has no tendency to move. Equilibrium is *stable* if after a slight displacement the body returns to its former position; it is *unstable* when such displacement causes it to move still further from its position; it is *mobile*, *neutral* or *indifferent* when after such displacement it remains at rest. A solid body is easily displaced only when spherical or rounded. *Stable equilibrium* is therefore properly exemplified by a suspended sphere, *unstable equilibrium* by a sphere balanced on a needle-point, and *mobile equilibrium* by a sphere resting on a level surface. If we are to apply (I had almost said, because of the fixity of human beings, *misapply*) the term equilibrium to human posture, then the postures (or malpostures) ordinarily adopted by individuals are positions of such *stable equilibrium* that they—like Pisa's periculous structure—are not easily displaced, and when displaced they instantly return. The poised individual, on the other hand, like the sphere, with its centrally-placed centre of gravity and resting on a level surface, has a *mobile equilibrium*, being easily displaced like a balance, yet in a state of rest both before and after the displacement; and what is still more important, in a state of internal equilibrium or rest during the movement.

One of the most thoughtful and copiously illustrated papers that has recently appeared on the topic claiming our attention is by Howorth (1946) who has proceeded by another terminological route. He has attempted to give the static word posture dynamic significance by introducing the rather hybrid or paradoxical term *dynamic posture* to express ideas similar to those which I am putting forward in respect of the term *poise*. He says that posture 'should include not only the fundamental static positions in lying, sitting and standing, and the variations of these positions, but also the dynamic postures of the body in motion or in action.' And again:

> Dynamic posture is posture in motion, or in action, or in preparation for action. It includes the transitions between the *static* positions of lying, sitting and standing and also such activities as pushing, lifting, walking, running, climbing, jumping, dancing, swimming, work and play. Dynamic posture includes the uses of the upper extremities and the trunk as well as the legs and the relationships between the various parts of the body in action.
>
> Children, athletes, labourers, artists, and dancers apply to their special activities some phases of dynamic posture which they have discovered for themselves or been taught by their instructors or coaches. But the concept of dynamic posture

> as a part of posture, related to the everyday activity of each of us, is new and has received little or no attention in medical and orthopædic literature . . . .
>
> Good dynamic posture implies the use of the body or its parts in the simplest and most effective way, using muscle contraction and relaxation, balance, co-ordination, rhythm and timing as well as gravity, inertia and momentum to optimum advantage. The smooth integration of these elements of good dynamic posture results in neuro-musculo-skeletal performance which is easy, graceful, satisfying and effective.

In brief, *dynamic posture* is nothing other than *approximate poise* or *approximate mobile equilibrium* if it is to be employed and to admit of qualifications such as good, better or best. *Poise*, on the other hand, is either present or absent; towards the attainment and retention of *poise* the plastic body continually strives. Posture—being something habitual and fixed (the term posture being very appropriately used of the pronograde or orthograde habit)—must with increasing fixation become ultimately *malposture*. But the further the body is released from the static attitudes of malposture by assuming a *dynamic posture* or by approximating *mobile equilibrium*, the closer it approximates the ideal state of *poise*.

For Howorth the *basic dynamic posture* is 'a slight crouch, with the ankles, knees and hips flexed, the head and trunk inclined forward, and the trunk slightly flexed, the arms relaxed and slightly flexed.'

This basic dynamic posture is a primitive posture, approximating that of the Kalahari Bushman, which I shall later discuss as the *humanoid orthograde posture*. Howorth recognizes, however, that

> the common admonition 'Throw back your shoulders' is a poor and ineffective approach to good posture, while 'Tuck in your stomach and throw out your chest' usually results in a tense, rigid, tiring posture which may be as bad as the posture it is intended to correct.

He expects the shoulders to rest comfortably on the chest, and the spine to maintain the standing position rather than the shoulders; the head and chin should be level, not tilted back; there should be 'a feeling of tallness, with the top of the head pulling away from the feet'.

To improve poor posture Howorth inculcates 'posture consciousness' by exercises to develop tone, relaxation and co-ordination and by sports such as swimming, æsthetic dancing, tumbling, rock-climbing, wrestling, weightlifting, boxing, ball games and rowing, according to the specific needs of the individual. He also attends to all extrinsic factors, such as the bed, chair, desk, lighting, shoes and clothes, that may contribute to malposture.

Despite this serviceable and somewhat heterodox outlook upon posture and this unusually wide appreciation of the factors contributing towards malposture, Howorth has forgotten *poise*, and has consequently overlooked a great deal of information which would have expanded his treatment of the subject and probably have modified his definitions and therapeutic procedures. For, if we recognize that *poise* is the single objective of human physique, we will concentrate attention not on any substitute for, or approximation towards poise, such as *dynamic posture* appears to be, but simply upon the acquisition of *poise*. *Poise*, however, is not acquired like physical strength, as Howorth apparently believes, through the violent performance of exercises and sports, but through restful study and observation. *Poise* is a body state achieved only by steady and carefree education of the body and the maintenance of balance. *Poise* is a character of repose or rest in the good body, whether it is in the relatively static positions of lying, sitting, or standing or is actually in progressive motion during the activities of life's daily routine or of sport.

The pandemic distribution of malposture

Lack of poise, *i.e.* fixity of positioning and its terminal result, faulty posture, unfortunately is the most prevalent condition of the human body. According to Goldthwait, Brown, Swaim and Kuhns (1945), 'extensive surveys reported at the White House Conference for Child Health and Hygiene showed that 80% or more of the children of this country (United States) exhibit bad body mechanics'.

Since this represents the postural state of the comparatively well-nourished, prewar, youthful population of North America, we may well contemplate aghast the world-wide spectacle of postural imperfection that human childhood displays today as a result of our recent and present deprivation and want. During the interval between the two World Wars 'examination of 100 British schoolboys revealed that 68 had deformities, such as knock-knees, bow-legs or flat-feet' (Dickson, *op. cit.*, p. 53). W. A. Cochrane (1924) said, 'Nearly all the chronic conditions have what may be termed an orthopædic facet to their solution in the need for correcting the poor posture of the body'.

Cochrane drew attention to Swaim's declaration 'that he saw no more than twenty well-postured individuals among 3,000 patients at Clifton Springs Sanatorium', and he himself stated that 'at a training camp for youths and men held in 1921, 75% were physically inefficient'.

Just over a century ago, *i.e.* when our modern industrial civilization was beginning to reveal its baleful postural effects, E. P. Banning (1844) was directing attention to the underlying significance of posture relative to ill-health. The literature descriptive of malposture that has grown up in the intervening period (*vide* Goldthwait and others, *op. cit.*) has assumed extensive proportions. It has been sufficiently summarized by these authors and by others cited by them, not to delay our detailed attention here. Physicians have come to appreciate the part played by malposture in circulatory disturbances and in complaints which involve the abdominal viscera. Orthopædists have familiarized us with the rôle of malposture in diseases of the spinal column, pelvic joints and the bones of the lower limbs. There is less general understanding amongst medical practitioners of the part malposture plays in muscular complaints, in neurological disturbances, respiratory complaints, dental conditions (such as malocclusion) and visual defects.

These less obvious complications of malposture have not escaped attention. W. J. Kerr and J. B. Lagen (1936) have discussed the postural syndrome related to obesity leading to postural emphysema and cardio-respiratory failure. W. S. Kountz and H. L. Alexander had already in 1933 taken up the study of emphysema from this point of view. J. L. Livingstone (1928) had some years previously studied the variations in the volume of the chest with changes in posture.

One of the most remarkable recent studies in malposture and vasomotor phenomena has been that of Col. I. S. Wright (1945).

People often complain of paraesthesias, numbness or tingling after sleeping or working with their arms in the hyperabducted position. Wright cites Wingate Todd's postural experiment of deliberately sleeping with his right arm stretched out in this fashion at night under his head during a period of eight years (1913–1921) with some interruptions. There finally developed in the hand thus abducted, and within the space of three months, tingling, loss of sensation, swelling, desquamation, causalgia, and paronychia affecting especially the right thumb and index-finger. After encountering five cases of hyperabduction producing symptoms leading even to superficial gangrene in one instance, Wright examined 150 normal young adults—apparently American soldiers—to discover to what extent hyperabduction was responsible for the obliteration of the pulse found to characterize patients suffering from the 'hyperabduction syndrome'. He then discovered that

> In one hundred twenty-five of one hundred fifty 'normal' subjects (83.3%), obliteration of the right arm pulse could be produced by hyperabduction of the right arm above the head. On one hundred twenty-four of the one hundred fifty (82%) 'normal' persons, obliteration of the left pulse could be produced by hyper-abduction of the left arm above the head. Obliteration of the radial pulse paralleled that of the brachial pulse.

In 94 (62%) the right arm pulse and in 95 (63%) the left arm pulse was easily obliterated. Only in 11 (7.4%) could no obliteration be produced. Those whose pulses were not obliterated are stated to belong chiefly to the 'loose-jointed' type of person. It was also noted that turning the head to the right or to the left sometimes restored the obliterated pulse and that flexion of the head and neck reduced the incidence of obliteration. The conclusion we must draw from these experiments (although Wright does not appear to be conscious of the fact) is that nearly 90% of the 'normal' young adult American population is malpostured—like Wingate Todd was—in respect of their upper extremities and their circulation. They cannot hold up their arms for any length of time without obliterating the circulation in their upper extremities.

As for the neurological side, it is patent that the circulatory and other visceral complaints that are aggravated by malposture are responsible for much of the pain suffered by human beings. However, although E. Jones (1907) attempted forty years ago to gauge the influence of bodily positions on mental activities, there has been little attempt in the intervening period to make a direct assessment of the interrelationship between malposture and mentality.

Having had my attention forcefully directed during the last three years to several divergent clinical results of malposture, I published recently one paper [not published until 1950] dealing with the *double-spiral musculature mechanism of the voluntary musculature of the human body*, in order to demonstrate that the type of postural defect to which the body was liable was spiral in nature and had a spiral anatomical background. Another paper (1946) was devoted to the cumulative evidence which has demonstrated that malocclusion in infantile dentitions is one of these spiral postural complaints and that orthodontia is an orthopædic pursuit. Incidentally, in describing the practical measures that I had found useful in dealing with such spiral malpostural states, I described the manner in which improving posture involved the correlation of eye movement with body movement. I have therefore been interested to notice from the literature, although I have not been able to consult the works, that H. Mills (1913) wrote over thirty years ago on 'Posture and eye-strain in children' and L. Mills (1919) six years later on 'The effect of faulty cranio–spinal form and alignment upon the eyes'.

In the meantime, Dr N. A. Stutterheim of Johannesburg has been carrying out over many years his important work upon asthenovergence and squint. He has published two books (1937 and 1942) in which he demonstrated that both these conditions are postural. They are cured by unmasking the postural reflex capacity of the eyes to work as a single (bi-foveal) unit. In a typical primary school population like that of the Transvaal, Stutterheim (*op. cit.*, p. 30) estimates that 1% suffer from squint. The less profound postural ocular disturbance of asthenovergence (or asthenopia, or eyestrain, with its complications of amblyopia, field contraction and migraine) is, of course, prevalent, being the commonest of all the eye complaints in mankind.

The incapacity of the phylogenetically recent power of convergence in human eyes to meet the visual requirements of modern life was disclosed dramatically during the recent World War. Air attacks demanded artillery observers who could scan the heavens with binocular sights to pinpoint and follow rapidly-moving ærial targets. Amongst the 'normal' trainees selected to discharge this important function with the original form of sight with a fixed pivot, Le Gros Clark (1946) and his fellow-workers at Oxford 'found that hardly more than 20% of personnel could elevate to 60° without strain, and that, even with great straining, only 75% could reach this level of elevation'. Hence, even when a capacity for sustained convergence exists in human individuals, very few people have the power to integrate their convergent eye movements with neck and body movements, if the postural requirements of the situation are at all unusual for them.

Cinematography revealed that in such ocular–postural adjustments 'the centre of the movement up to about 40° elevation is in the neighbourhood of the atlanto–occipital joint, but at higher elevations it rapidly moves downwards along the spine'. The pivot of the optical apparatus was accordingly moved downwards and backwards a few inches to correspond much more closely to the track of the eyes exhibited by the majority of the trainees.

> However, although with this new position 100% personnel could elevate to 60° without strain, not more than 60% could reach 90° even with straining, and with the development of ærial attack on ships it had become an urgent requirement that operators should be able to follow their target accurately almost up to the zenith.

Corresponding alterations of the apparatus with the objective of 'fitting the machine to the man' were thereupon devised.

The urgent demands of warfare necessitate the designing of mechanical apparatus to fit its operative personnel. We are concerned here rather with the appalling fact that—as with American soldiers—even when the physically fittest British personnel selected from the community for naval service have been further ransacked ophthalmologically for trainees as observers in the binocular fire-directors of battleships, 80% of them have bodies so maladjusted relative to their eyes that they are unable to elevate their eyes 60° above the horizon without suffering severe postural strain.

The percentage of the total population incapable in this visuo–postural respect (which must naturally include all the asthenovergent) must be well over 80%. The percentage of adult British people posturally maladjusted in respect of vision is probably even greater than the 80% of the infantile population displaying bad body mechanics in the United States, or the (80% odd of the) young adult American population revealing malposture of their upper extremities and circulation.

Amongst diseases there is, therefore, no condition more entitled to the term pandemic than malposture. Perhaps it would be preferable to say that there can scarcely be a disablement which brings an individual into a hospital, a clinic, or the consulting-room of a dental or medical practitioner without presenting simultaneously (as a background to the condition that occupies temporarily the front stage) a condition of lesser or graver malposture. Most accidents causing broken limbs are due in the last resort to the faulty postures that occasion or accompany the impacts. The vast majority of mankind are unacquainted with poise, either physical or psychical. Cochrane (*op. cit.*) was therefore justified in saying, 'The great duty of the medical profession is to see that they (children) develop properly. Whatever else is taught, *insistence must always be put on poise*, with its resulting efficiency'. (My italics).

The nature and mechanism of poise

If, then, *poise* is such a rarity, the reader may well ask who is poised and how can an individual attain *poise*? The answer is that the 5% or 10% of human beings who exhibit *poise* are those few who, as dancers, jugglers, tightrope artists, skating enthusiasts, top-line sportsmen and the like, execute every bodily movement in graceful balance, in the plastic harmony of perfect neuro-musculo-skeletal integration. The manner in which *poise* is attained is by the spontaneous occurrence of the neuromuscular integration it represents, or by assiduous training at the hands of those (parents or teachers) who are expert in the 'tricks of the trade'; of experts who are able to put their pupils through intentional movements that spontaneously evoke the essential neuromuscular integrations. Some are born poised, others achieve poise; whether the remainder will have poise thrust upon them the future alone can show, but it would probably be to their great advantage.

Although defects in human posture have engaged medical attention for the past century, it is only within the last quarter of that period that we have come to understand the magnitude of the evolutionary achievement which man's upright posture connotes and the disabilities inevitably associated with the lateness or recency of human erectness. Sir Arthur Keith (1923) rendered a great service by familiarizing practitioners with this type of outlook and the medical significance of the process whereby, during the last three million years, Man's predecessors removed half of their weight of their pronograde (or four-footed) bodies from their hands, and by successive hylobatian (or gibbon-like) and troglodytian (or chimpanzee-like) stages of orthograde habit finally became, in his opinion, truly plantigrade (or two-footed). The discovery of our South African Man-apes has shown that the plantigrade habit is older than Keith imagined it to be. On the other hand, the studies of Wells (1931) on the feet of South African races have demonstrated that living peoples vary considerably in the evolution of their plantigrade mechanisms. This shows that certain of the stages in the plantigrade process are still striving after perfection.

The prime fact about human body movement is that it entails the cooperation or integration of both conscious and unconscious mechanisms, *i.e.* the 'will' and the 'reflex'. As Sir Charles Sherrington has said (1946, p. 87):

> Today's knowledge teaches us that every so-called 'voluntary' muscle with its nervous supply is a little 'reflex' system. Any act, of whatever provenance, which employs such a muscle cannot fail to enlist reflex action from it, and from muscles related to it—synergists, antagonists. These (proprioceptive) reflexes are unconscious as such, but on them depends in large part the *rightness of the muscular act.* They adjust duly the muscles' length and tension. They control duly its starting and its going out of action. This reflex factor is as important for the right performance of movement and posture as is the tuning of a string for the harmonious use of it in music. This tuning is just part of the reflex robot operation of the body. We are not conscious of these reflexly main-

tained and adjusted muscular lengths and tensions as such. They self-regulate themselves unconsciously. All we are aware of is their outcome in our act. With each movement of head or neck or limb, whether passive or active, the pattern of the unconscious proprioceptive reflex changes. We are aware only of the movement or posture which is its accompaniment. Often even this latter is not within the field of our direct attention. Our attention is directed to the 'aim' of the act, not to the 'how' of it; the 'how' often enough takes care of itself. Conscious effort would seem unable to put us in touch actually with the proprioceptive reflex itself. So elusive is this last, that for long our muscles were unrecognized as affording any sensual basis of our motor acts. When we bend a finger we can, without looking at the finger and without the finger touching anything, tell within a little how much or little we bend it; no hint, however, is vouchsafed to us that muscles doing the act lie up the forearm, or of the tensions or lengths they assume in doing it. When we turn our gaze we are not aware of the muscles of our eyeballs, nor can any mental effort or intensity of purpose make us so. None the less, the unconscious reflexes at work in them are indispensable to the due performance of our act. . . .

In evolutionary history, behaviour, such as that part of our own which Descartes relegated to 'reason' and 'free-will', seems of later development than is the robot-behaviour, operated reflexly. . . . Descended from a long stock of less mentalised creatures, as we are, and living less reflexly than did they, our more mentalised status has arrived at putting the reflex mechanism as a going concern, within the control, to a certain extent, of the reactions of the brain. This mastery of the brain over the reflex machinery does not take the form of intermeddling with reflex details; rather it dictates to a reflex mechanism 'you may act' or 'you may not act'. The detailed execution of the motor act is still in immediate charge of the reflex. . . .

It is largely the reflex element in the willed movement or posture which, by reason of its unconscious character, defeats our attempts to know the 'how' of the doing of even a willed act. Breathing, standing, walking, sitting, although innate, along with our growth, are apt, as movements, to suffer from defects in our ways of doing them. A chair unsuited to a child

> can quickly induce special and bad habits of sitting and of breathing. . . . But verbal instructions as to how to correct wrong habits of movement and posture is very difficult. The scantiness of our sensory perception of how we do them makes it so. The faults tend to escape our direct observation and recognition. Of the proprioceptive reflexes as such, whether of muscle or ear (vestibule), we are unconscious. We have no direct perception of the 'wash' of the labyrinthine fluid or, indeed, of the existence of the labyrinths at all. In their case subjective projection, instead of indicating, blinds the place of their objective source. Correcting the movements carried out by our proprioceptive reflexes is something like trying to reset a machine whose works are intangible, and the net output all we know of the running. Instruction in such an act has to fall back on other factors more accessible to sense; thus, in skating, to 'feeling' that edge of the skate-blade on which the movement bears. To watch another performer trying the movement can be helpful; or a looking-glass in which to watch ourselves trying it. The mirror can tell us often more than the most painstaking attempt to 'introspect'. Mr Alexander has done a service* to the subject by insistently treating each act as involving the whole integrated individual, the whole psychophysical man. To take a step is an affair, not of this or that limb solely, but of the total neuromuscular activity of the moment—not least of the head and the neck. [Italics added.]

It was at the hands of Miss Irene Tasker, M. A., a pupil of Mr F. Matthias Alexander, that I received a series of daily demonstrations (extending over the months of September and October 1943) of Alexander's technique. She revealed to me how my own malpostured habits of sitting, standing, walking and lying down could be bettered by her manipulating my moving body concurrently with my consciously inhibiting that wrongful 'intermeddling with reflex details' of such activities, mentioned by Sherrington, which previously had characterized their performance. Unfortunately, Miss Tasker departed to England shortly afterwards, but I have continued studying the wrongful and rightful performance of muscular acts over the

---

* *The Universal Constant in Living*, Chaterson Ltd., 1942.

intervening three years, being driven thereto (as I had been at the outset) by the necessity of doing my utmost to make it possible for my spastic infant son to enjoy the maximum of neuromuscular co-ordination, when similarly assisted manipulatively. Incidentally I discovered that my own scoliotic deformity and my daughter's 'night terrors' and our common defects of dental occlusion were merely alternative forms of manifestations of malposture, and were rightly and successfully treated as such. All of us required urgently an educational improvement in co-ordinating the conscious and reflex aspects of movement and posture, *i.e.* an ability to maintain our bodies in a state of *poise*.

The consciousness cannot play its proper part in movement unless we have an interest in our movements. Our bodies reflect our minds, just as vehicles portray their owners. The attitude of a person's mind towards the framework, by whose operation each and every action of life is performed, has a profound effect upon that framework, even as the attitude of a driver to his carriage results before long in a well-preserved trap or a woebegone truck. Some of the most curious human practices down the ages have arisen from the attitude of neglecting or despising the body, as though it were beneath contempt, or of hating and even maltreating it, as though it were vile and foreign to its indwelling spirit. We all suffer to a greater or lesser degree from this primitive social tradition.

According to Herodotus, the ancient Egyptians thrashed their bodies during the annual Isis festival. In Sparta children were whipped before the altar of Artemis Orthia till the blood flowed, and at Alea, in Arcadia, women were flogged in the temple of Dionysus. Scourging by way of discipline or penance occurs in almost all the religions of the world. Flagellation is only one of the sad rites in the discordant gamut of affronts and ordeals from fasting, chastity, nakedness and silence on the one hand, to torture, exposure and mutilation on the other hand, which human beings have inflicted upon themselves and their fellows. The pretended ultimate design of such practices was to benefit their own personalities through self-control or to render service to their deities by 'bringing under' or 'yielding up' their bodies. This archaic type of attitude towards the body and its employment is not very helpful to the individual interested in poise. He loves the body.

The mental attitude of any given human individual towards his own body and its physical attitude today is so complicated by his religious outlook, his social environment, and the variety of so-called educational forces operating upon him since infancy, that very few people take the trouble to unravel their thoughts, whatever they may be, concerning themselves, or to bring their ideas about their bodies into some sort of order. We accept our warped adult bodies, as they may happen to be after the play of these varied influences of infancy and adolescence upon them, and we subject them to all the further strains and stresses incidental to our civilized work and play, until discomfort or pain to some part or other is grievous enough to force our attention upon the existence of our bodies and the relative disposition of their parts. By means of the anatomical and physiological knowledge learned chiefly at their mother's knee and the crude repertoire of household medicine imbibed during their schooldays, and occasional reading, the average individual attempts to assuage his pain. If, finally, it yields neither to these nor to the medicaments of the local chemist, he visits the physician or dentist. There would be less need for such visits and the visits would be more valuable to them when made if they had more knowledge about their bodies and how they move.

The attitude is still almost as prevalent amongst physicians, as it was formerly amongst priests, that the less people know or even think about their bodies, the better for their peace of mind. So doctors often share unwittingly the aforementioned ascetic outlook of bodily denial. We forget or fail to remember that to every savage, however ignorant, a language of elementary anatomy and physiology was, and is, a necessity, and that physicians who have a considerable knowledge of the human body and the workings of its various parts are themselves relatively recent arrivals on this planet. Although four centuries have passed since Vesalius introduced a more exact teaching of human structure into Italian medical education and Harvey discovered the circulation of the blood, the public attitude in the western world towards human flesh has always been so antagonistic—despite the universal necessity for anatomical knowledge—that during most of this time the only bodies that found their way to the dissecting rooms of medical schools in civilized European countries were those of condemned criminals, or those feloniously robbed by 'body-snatchers' from recent burials. The sinister flavours of crime and sacrilege were not removed from the understanding of human structure until the passage, only a century ago, of the necessary legislation governing the practice of dissection. Thus, from the earliest times down to about the middle of the nineteenth century, when there occurred in Europe a notable awakening of interest in anatomy as in all branches of natural science, the average practicing physician did not require to know much more about the muscles, bones and nerves of the human body than was known by his more intelligent patients. Today the layman needs more anatomical knowledge than physicians required aforetime.

Anatomical knowledge moves on parallel lines with the development of general education; civilized human beings require more of such knowledge than does the savage. Until well into the nineteenth century there was a total absence of schools providing elementary education for the people at large. In 1845, a public inspector reported that 'of the population of England and Wales only one in six could read Scripture with ease, one-half left school unable to read at all, three-quarters left unable to write, and only two in a hundred could do any arithmetic' (Foster, 1930).

The general public, therefore, could not get a knowledge of human structure, however greatly they desired it. In these present days of universal education, however, textbooks of student nurses contain more accurate anatomical and physiological knowledge than did those of many medical students a century ago. Popular books like Huxley and Wells' *Science of Life*, Wheeler's *The Miracle of Life*, and Robert's *The Miracle of the Human Body* demonstrate the demand (in an age of machinery and atoms) by thinking citizens for detailed information about the greatest machines of all—living creatures.

The minutiæ of anatomy are relevant even today only to the specialist surgeon and the research worker interested in some particular part of the body, but the basic principles of body movement should be known to everyone. The general practitioner, general physician, general surgeon, pathologist, medical officer of health, indeed 90% of those practicing medicine, have little need of anatomical details. Amidst the forest of anatomical facts and terms they have great need, like the ordinary individual, of the simpler wood of human structure and function. In short, what is generally required for doctor and layman alike is a connecting link between the simplest sort of anatomy such as a child learns at its mother's knee and the detailed anatomy of the investigator. This sort of anatomy is already available as far as the circulatory, respiratory and genito-urinary systems are concerned. It is lacking principally (where it is most required by the average person) in respect of the apparatus of movement, that is, the muscles, the nerves that supply them, and the manner in which they move the parts of the body by pulling upon the bones. Thus, paradoxically enough, any nurse and even any person qualified in first aid will be able to identify and describe all the bones and the principal bloodvessels of the body, and even the histology of the organ of Corti, but is ignorant of the muscles and the nerves that cooperate in moving the bones. Yet the dry bones have no significance apart from the muscles and nerves that move them. The principal reason for the existence of bloodvessels is to supply sufficient oxygen to contracting muscles as they move the bones appropriately.

This failure of the anatomist to present a simple picture of the musculature and its innervation is doubtless due to the recency of our comparative anatomical knowledge about these two systems and the failure to understand the ancestral simplicity of the bodily needs and elementary material from which their seeming complexity in Man has been derived. Thus, we are only in the process of recognizing today that all the voluntary muscles together with the segmentally arranged nerves and bones in the body are merely three parts of a single purpose or unitary apparatus *a neuro–musculo–skeletal apparatus*. This neuro–musculo–skeletal machine was produced by Nature to keep the body straight while moving by undulant *lateral bending*, that is, to perform linear (or antero–posteriorly) directed movement, or, in other words, to carry out such a type of body movement as would keep the mouth end of the body continuously pointed forwards and in active contact with its food. Until a somitic mesoderm appeared capable of producing such muscles (bilaterally and symmetrically arranged relative to the digestive tube) and therewith segmental nerves and skeletal parts, no such uni-directional movement as typifies higher invertebrate and all vertebrate creatures was possible. All moving creatures were merely pulsating balls, bells, or tubes like jellyfish, squids and roundworms.

Once a living body became thus permanently maintained in a state of antero–posterior orientation and undulant *lateral bending* movement, the evolution of the front end of its lengthening body into a sensitive food-searching mouth or head, and of the back end into a wagging tail, was inevitable. Thus, all invertebrates, from the segmented worm and caterpillar to the crustacean and insect, and all vertebrates, from fish to Man, are built on the same sort of linear plan comprising segmentally repeated nervous, muscular, and skeletal parts each of which is bilaterally symmetrical; each part is the mirror image of its fellow on the opposite side of the linear body. The main differences between insect and vertebrate are, firstly, that the invertebrate skeleton is outside (or covers) the muscles while the vertebrate skeleton is inside (or covered by) the muscles or flesh; and, secondly, that the invertebrate nervous system lies along its belly, completely encased by the skeleton, while the vertebrate nervous system lies along its back and is only partly covered by the skeleton.

This *tripartite movement-apparatus* or body machine of nerve, muscle and skeleton enables the invertebrate or vertebrate creature at the outset to carry out only this one sort of body movement or achieve only one kind of result, namely, bending the body from side to side. This *lateral bending* occurs if the serially-arranged muscle blocks on one side of the body contract while those of the corresponding segments on the other side of the body lengthen or, in other words, are inhibited or prevented from contracting. But the beneficial result of alternating bendings, as they proceed in rhythmical waves from the front to the back end of the creature, is that the animal squirms forwards. Wriggling or waddling (*i.e. lateral bending* of the body) is the most ancient of all movements; it is the main means whereby the eel, tadpole, snake and whale, as well as all other creatures, move forwards. It is the first type of movement to appear in the fœtal, or baby creature, whether fish or human being. In the eighth week of intra-uterine life the human fœtus starts its first wriggling movements. If aborted at this age, these movements can be elicited from the fœtus by stroking it at the one and only sensitive spot it then possesses, and this is the area of the upper lip between the nostrils and the mouth; this is the part of the body serving as an orifice to the nasal organs and over which the air subsequently rushes in breathing (*vide* Davenport Hooker, 1942).

By dividing each block of muscle in each segment on either side of the body into two (dorsal and ventral) parts so that each half is supplied by its own (posterior or anterior) division of the motor nerve for that segment, the linear or strap-like animal becomes able to bend the body up and down, *i.e.* extend and flex its body. *Extension* (*i.e.* bending it upwards) is caused by contracting the dorsal halves or by inhibiting the ventral halves from contracting. *Flexion* (*i.e.* bending it downwards) is caused by stopping the dorsal halves from contracting.

Although there are many other types of movement in the creature than these three, *viz.* lateral, upward and downward bending, there is in point of fact only one kind which is of outstanding importance. This is *rotation*, torsion or twisting, and it is merely the result of combining simultaneously the three simple types of movement already described. *Rotation* of the body or its parts occurs when proximal (or forwardly situated) segments are flexing and segments at the other end (*i.e.* distal or backwardly situated) are extending, while those in between are bending to one side or the other. Similarly, *rotation* occurs in the reverse direction if proximal segments extend while more distal segments flex. Such twisting, torsion, or *rotation* of a segmented creature is seen in its simplest form in the silkworm (or any other kind of caterpillar) when its hind 'feet' grip in tonic flexion the leaf or stalk and its front end is held up in tonic extension while the intermediate segments bend to the left or the right.

Rotational movements have become increasingly important for maintaining the body's posture during evolution. Consequently, we find the entire voluntary musculature of animal bodies arranged in a perpetually twisted way so as to produce either *permanent postural twists* (*e.g.* the inward rotations of the upper and lower limbs in all four-footed creatures and the upward rotation of the trunk upon the thighs in Man) or to facilitate the further reflex and volitional twisting of the body and its parts. These twists are phylogenetic achievements and are symmetrical in character. The interwoven spiral muscular sheets that encircle the human trunk result from the dominant part rotation plays in every body movement. As I have discussed the arrangements in Man of these oblique torsional muscular sheets in the papers previously mentioned it would be redundant to recapitulate the facts here. It is only necessary to state the conclusion drawn there, namely, that malposture in mankind is due to a one-sided emphasis upon twisting, *i.e.* a right-handed or left-handed *torque*. Malposture is a postural obliquity or twist of an asymmetrical character developed as a result of relying habitually upon one torsional sheet of the body more than on the other. This faulty attitudinal integration or imperfection in the properly balanced use of both spiral voluntary muscular sheets frustrates the achievement of the *poise* or equilibrium essential to bodily skill.

The permanent inward (postural) rotation of Man's extended lower limbs provided flat surfaces for his feet. A permanent degree of inward (postural) rotation of his free upper limbs afforded him implement-using hands to swing about or to fold across his chest. Man's powerful hip musculature allowed him finally to twist his whole body permanently upwards and backwards so as to poise it in a state of orthograde postural fixation on top of his thigh bones. Thus, paradoxically enough, Nature's most twisted, distorted creature (*i.e.* crooked Man) becomes capable of the supreme achievements of *poise*—balancing on head, hand, heel, or toe.

Hence Man's place in Nature is due to his conquest of the problems of body poise by means of *postural twisting*. Star performers in the realms of body poise, whether jugglers or acrobats, dancers or sportsmen, are merely outstanding examples of the well balanced gyratory bodies Nature designed for all mankind; they have bodies every person should actually possess or be gradually discovering for himself. Failure to develop a perfectly poised body merely represents, like any other teratomatous condition, a developmental arrest. This arrest in development is purely functional. In creatures so precariously poised posturally as human beings, fear of falling is the outstanding characteristic of their functional ontogeny. This ever-present fear interferes with the co-ordination of the conscious and reflex aspects of *poise*. Hence most people arrive at adulthood without having enough *poise* to feel secure whilst reversing in a waltz. Adults lacking real knowledge of *poise* and the gyroscopic perfection to be aimed at during development and being habituated to the grossly distorted muscle–joint sense of their own malpostured bodies, impose their private fears on their children and interfere by ridicule or force with the spontaneous efforts of infants and youths to twist and contort their bodies symmetrically in precarious positions. These spontaneous efforts demand and stimulate the exercise of *poise*. Human beings fail for these and similar reasons to develop symmetrically, and most of their sports and civilized pursuits consolidate and emphasize the right-handed or left-handed asymmetry they bring to such performances. Consequently, practically all human beings, without being aware of their deformity, suffer from a mild, a moderate, or even a severe permanent asymmetrical attitudinal twist or *torque*. In a considerable number of people the severity of the twist leads to gross malformations and the associated clinical distresses previously discussed.

It is necessary, therefore, in order to cultivate *poise*, to know, in the first place, that the whole body and its parts should be capable of being bent without strain or pain laterally (to either side), ventrally (flexed upon the belly), or dorsally (extended backwards), and of being rotated (or twisted) to either the right or left; and in the second place, that poise has never been experienced if the various joints of the body perform the lateral bending, flexing, extending and rotating movements for which Nature designed the joints only with difficulty and soreness due to stiffness of one sort or another. In the third place, we require to recognize whether the right-handed or left-handed postural twist, which we have developed during our own lifetime and which causes our aches and pains, is simple or complex. Is it a twist of the head to the left over the neck and of the thorax to the left over the pelvis and of the pelvis to the left over the left leg? That is the commonest type of *torque* characteristic of the right-handed individual; it may be only partially developed and distort the body only slightly; or it may be strongly and obviously patent, as in the hunchback. The differences are not qualitative, but rather quantitative.

Having diagnosed the direction and degree of twist, *poise* is attained by the dual process of *inhibition*, or suppressing the factors promoting asymmetry, and of *derotation*, or untwisting the asymmetrically twisted body. But this is easier to state than to perform because the *torque* from which the individual suffers is the reflex postural resultant of a lifetime, short or long as the case may be. This torture is the product of twistings to which he has become so habituated that he is incapable of performing any movement, whether he is sitting down, standing up or reclining, without reflexly adopting this accustomed twisted posture of the body while executing the movement. The inhibition of this postural reflex twist cannot therefore be achieved simply by a decision not to twist or by a resolve to untwist, although this helpful attitude of the consciousness is essential to its ultimate achievement. In addition to the appropriate mental attitude, it is essential to have an expert person (or a technique) aiding the volition of the individual by maintaining the body (*i.e.* temporarily fixing it) in an untwisted or partially untwisted postural situation during the execution of the movement. In this manner the assistant or the technique educates the individual and his reflex apparatus in performing the movements (and experiencing the sensations accompanying them) while he remains untwisted or, more accurately expressed, somewhat less twisted. In practice, therefore, it is difficult to separate passive *inhibition* from active *derotation*, because as soon as we cease twisting we are to that extent untwisting. Further, although it is easier to have derotation performed upon us than to allow it to occur in ourselves, some people may be assisted in desisting from their habitual manner of twisting (*e.g.* to the left) by encouraging them actively but cautiously to untwist themselves (*e.g.* by twisting to the right). *Derotational* or *untwisting* exercises of this sort have been set forth by Truslow (1943) for the cure of scoliosis, which he has recognized as being a *rotary curvature*. But it is logical to inculcate in individuals inhibition of habitual asymmetrical twists rather than to encourage their attempts at active *derotation* or untwisting; because the outstanding function of the higher nervous centres is inhibition. The brain does not so much initiate movement; rather, the mentality should control movement by inhibiting those cultivated habits which interfere with the automatic execution of movements by the muscles. But, as Sherrington (*op. cit.*) has said,

> It is largely the reflex element in the willed movement or posture which, by reason of its unconscious character, defeats our attempts to know the 'how' of the doing of even a willed act. Breathing, standing, walking, sitting, although innate, along with our growth, are apt, as movements, to suffer from defects in our ways of doing them.

We have therefore to see that while carrying out movements we do not allow improper ones resulting from our bad habits to occur.

The inhibition of improper movements can be facilitated by carrying out movements, as Sherrington states (*op. cit.*) and as Alexander originally advised, before 'a looking-glass in which to watch ourselves trying it' and so checking bad habits by observation. Alternatively, a skilled instructor maintains the head in a proper, or less twisted, position relative to the neck, while the pupil consciously inhibits habitual movements (*e.g.* adducting the thighs during the acts of sitting down or getting up) which interfere with its proper performance. A further way of inhibiting the improper movements that intermeddle with the reflex details of body movements is *temporary fixation* of the improperly moving parts by pieces of apparatus. A good example of such a piece of inhibiting apparatus is the splint used by Nove (*vide* Dart, 1946) to immobilize the mandible upon the maxilla in a position of optimum occlusion during sleeping hours. By inhibiting the inessential and wrongful opening of the mouth during sleep, the muscles concerned with swallowing and breathing are forced to do their reflex work rhythmically and symmetrically every night. This unmasking of their symmetrical reflex behaviour by enforcing symmetrical functioning upon these muscles leads to such balanced activity of the *flexor cervicalis* (the flexor sheet of head and neck musculature) that malocclusion is corrected and the posture of the head relative to the neck is spontaneously improved.

Temporary fixation of a somewhat different but analogous sort is the principle underlying Stutterheim's (*op. cit.*) technique for curing asthenovergence and squint. By means of a prism battery, which predetermines the increasing amount of angular twist eye muscles must overcome from day to day during treatment (in order to maintain the type of vision to which they have become habituated), the eye muscles are forced to adapt themselves posturally in such a way as to unmask their innate capacity for convergence. Both asthenovergence and squint thus become spontaneously corrected.

The same *principle of temporary fixation* has been advocated (Dart, *op. cit.*) as underlying in somewhat divergent form the business of unmasking the postural mass-reflexes of the body for the attainment of *poise*. Since 'the rightness of the muscular act'—as Sherrington puts it—depends on robot or reflex operations of the body (operations that ordinarily elude our consciousness), this type of temporary fixation technique is required to provide our consciousness with sensory perceptions or awareness of our proprioceptive reflex mechanisms by unmasking them. Despite the admitted difficulty of correcting wrong habits of posture and movement by means of verbal instruction, any individual can effect these improvements if he is prepared to place his own body daily in postures calculated to evoke the 'feelings' necessary to its educational improvement in terms of symmetry and *poise*. He must be capable of patient waiting and of observing objectively the 'feelings' that arise from the new positions. He must also take careful note of the reflex responses that emerge from these positions. Indeed, it is no exaggeration to state that unless he carries out these procedures, or others better designed to elicit the same sort of information, the student of poise is unlikely ever to appreciate the respective limits of the *robot* and *free will* (or the reflex and the conscious) contributions to his own movement-mechanism and those of the malpostured people who may seek his aid in their own muscular education.

The theory put forward (Dart, *op. cit.*) was that lack of *poise* in human adults is the result of inadequately exploiting, of short-circuiting, or of actually eliminating the ancestral phases of posture (represented by the supine, ventigrade, and pronograde postures—to which we may add with advantage the primate, anthropoid, and humanoid stages of orthograde evolution) during ontogeny in the infant's (or its parents') haste to become erect. The temporary fixation technique proposed was that of remaining at rest in these ancestral postures (starting with the infantile supine posture and the primary crawling postures) for fixed periods of approximately 15 minutes each at least once daily to educate the corresponding weight-bearing sites of the body in their proportional fulcral responsibilities during bodily immobility and movement. In other words, unless we are prepared to become little children we do not discover and cannot unmask the basic reflex neuro–musculo–skeletal information deleted from our infantile experience.

The quadrupedal (or four-props) mechanism provided a minimal fulcral apparatus for movement on land because the solid animal body could be equilibrated on a temporarily spastic tripod while the relaxed fourth limb was suitably displaced forwards (or elsewhere) to assume its sequential role in the business of tripodal postural support during quadrupedal progression. Man supports his body on only two feet because each foot has been transformed into a tripodal arch (heel, bigtoe, and lateral ball of foot), thus providing him with six weight-bearing sites on a very restricted but highly modifiable body-base.

The *infantile supine posture* advocated is to lie on a carpeted floor with the occiput resting comfortably on several books forming a hard bolster (ordinarily two to three inches high, though some may prefer it varied to six inches or more in height) and the feet drawn as close to the buttocks as possible without muscular strain (knees in the air and slightly abducted, elbows on the floor, and the relaxed hands resting on the junction of thorax and abdomen). Fifteen to twenty minutes' midday rest in this symmetrical posture induces a gradual and progressive relaxation or inhibition of the *sacrospinalis* mass in particular, and of the extensor musculature in general, and a temporary release from their inevitable state of torsional strain in the erect posture. Being pentapodal (or heptapodal if we include the feet), the supine posture trains simultaneously five distinct dorsal body areas (overlying the occiput, scapular spines, and posterior superior iliac spines respectively) to share with the feet in an equilibrated fashion the business of sustaining the bodyweight. A resistant base where the sensations evoked by these several contacts with a hard surface can be felt and experienced (instead of on a spring mattress where sensory discrimination is obliterated) gradually elicits with daily repetition, in addition to the extensor relaxation, a progressive postural untwisting of the spinal column between each pair of the temporarily fixed, weight-bearing sites of the leftwardly (or rightwardly) rotated body, as well as an untwisting of the neck between the occiput and the scapular spines.

This procedure in postural education, simple as it is, if persisted in over a couple of years, is not merely relaxational, but produces widespread effects in derotating the spine and improving the equilibration of the body by bringing the head into this more forward and appropriate position relative to the neck and by cultivating the individual's habit of keeping it there. This forward postural relationship of the head to the neck, characteristic of the position of the head in classical Greek sculpture, is regarded by F. Matthias Alexander as the *primary relationship*. In the paper cited above, I devoted a considerable amount of attention to the various anatomical, physiological and phylogenetic facts which corroborate his concept. Consequently, it is sufficient to have quoted here Sherrington's recognition of the service rendered to the subject by Alexander's insistence of the fact that taking a step is an affair 'of the total neuromuscular activity of the moment—not least of the head and the neck'.

By rolling over from the *infantile supine posture* to the reverse or prone (fronto-olecrano-tibial, or forehead-elbow-knee) posture, we assume what I have called (*op. cit.*) the *primary crawling posture.* In so rolling we become acquainted (especially if we persistently perform the action in slow motion) with the fixed habits we developed during infancy, of using our various body parts (hands, elbows, knees, and feet) relatively to the trunk in this rolling or body-twisting type of movement. We also learn by way of contrast all the alternative ways that were at our disposal for the purpose of 'rolling over', but which we failed to exploit and employ during our infancy. With these it will now repay us to make our acquaintance gradually. We will be even more encouraged to initiate such alternative body-twisting experiments when we have increased our knowledge of the reflex responses of our body to the exercise of remaining for 15–20 minutes daily in the *primary crawling posture* and testing therefrom our sensitivity and flexibility in the various positions of imbalance the body can assume in this posture when it is bent slightly and asymmetrically towards any one or several of its five fulcral supports.

The systematic preliminary of adopting these primary postures is advocated, firstly, because they provide the occasions necessary for experience in infantile or phylogenetic forms of equilibration and, secondly, because they are postures devoid of fear in consequence of their stability, being broad-based and multi-supported from the fulcral point of view. To people of advancing age these postures are both ludicrous and uncomfortable—ludicrous because they are infantile and reminiscent of their pronograde primate ancestry; uncomfortable because the fulcral areas concerned have forgotten (or perhaps never previously received and transmitted to the central nervous system) the exteroceptive (pressure) and proprioceptive (muscle and joint sense) stimuli (*e.g.* from their foreheads, elbows and knees) which are often extremely painful but must be experienced before the mass-reflexes they evoke can be elicited from the responsive body.

The adoption of the posture inculcates in the individual, in consequence, *an objective attitude towards pain*, using the term in its widest connotation, to embrace all the curious subjective forms of unpleasant sensation, *e.g.* tingling, tickling, prickling, stabbing, throbbing, bursting, numbing, leaden, dull or wooden, which become manifest during these periods devoted to the process of attaining *poise* by postural adaptation. Any student of *poise*, such as a gymnast or ballet-dancer, knows that his training consisted principally in the assumption of certain poised attitudes and the maintenance of them in the face of whatever bodily sensations the attitudes evoked until, with the passing of the various stages of painful sensation, the attitudes were katatonically (*i.e.* with perfect adaptation of the antagonistic groups of muscles concerned in the posture) maintained for the required (or for indefinitely long) periods. As painful conditions are the preoccupation of the malpostured, prime importance attaches to postural procedures of this sort being recommended that enable the malpostured individual in positions of security to study at leisure and understand by postural experience the biological purpose of his pain symptomatology.

Fear and pain are inextricably linked together. The purpose of pain is dual—to evoke the reflex mechanism of pain-avoiding movement and to awaken the consciousness of the organism, as far as that may be necessary relative to its own body during the movement. But when the awareness of the potential pain involved in the movement (*i.e.* the fear) prevents the reflex mechanism from discharging its automatic functions, fear and pain are at cross-purposes biologically. In precariously-poised Man the ever present fear of the livelong day (and of sleeping hours also in many individuals) is that of falling.

At the point of subsiding into unconsciousness the lower limbs of such people suddenly jerk as if recovering after stumbling over a curbstone; they dream of tripping, slipping or tumbling from great heights. When abroad about their daily duties they have faint turns, or they swoon as things swim or go black before their eyes; they do not trust themselves on stepping-stones or on planks over running water, they are subject to various fears, especially those of body elevation and rotation. When fears of the falling that might happen obtrude themselves upon conscious and subconscious movements in this fashion, it is apparent that the individual has little capacity to discriminate between that moiety of 'pain' or sensation whose purpose is solely to evoke the reflexes that occur spontaneously to orient our bodies in space, and should barely, if ever, reach consciousness; and that other moiety of 'pain' whose purpose is to make us aware with the greatest possible precision of our environment while so oriented so that we may be poised and fearless. The capacity of people to exercise discrimination in respect of pain becomes enhanced when, the possibility of fear having been removed by a safe posture, they are forced by the novelty and fixity of that posture to experience self-inflicted 'pains' whose intensity is under their control and which emerge, culminate, evoke reflex responses, and then disappear if they are tolerated. Pains and aches thus become classifiable by the individual as temporary or permanent; and, as far as reflexes and consciousness are respectively concerned, as insignificant or significant. When pains become sufficiently objective as to be classifiable they are no longer foes but friends; pain and fear should never be at biological cross-purposes.

This discriminative understanding of the usefulness to the body of its diverse pains and the mass-reflexes evoked by the pains is particularly important; since the chief fears which the student of *poise* has to confront, apart from his fear of falling, are fears of the localized and widespread pains the various parts of his body experience in sustaining unusual, if safe, postures over any length of time. For the inhibition and derotation associated with sustaining an unusual posture demands for its success an unimpeded continuance of the ordinary rhythmical phenomena of movement associated with mammalian life, namely, keeping the mouth closed and the dental arcades in unstrained apposition, allowing free swallowing movement, and maintaining rhythmical inspiration and expiration through the nostrils. Some people are of such a nervous disposition that they become alarmed even by such transient circulatory phenomena as goose-flesh, redness of the skin or sweating in unusual sites; and nothing is more striking physiologically or worthy of further study than the peripheral vasomotor phenomena associated with such controlled postural alterations. But, apart from these, *the most common source and premonition of fright is respiratory embarrassment.* In fact, it is doubtful if postural change can occur without the individuals experiencing over and over again at the outset difficulties in breathing which, though temporary, can be most alarming and must be overcome. They will not trust themselves to breathe in an altered postural setting, so fixed have their respiratory habits become.

We recognize that Man is distinctive in being erect, but we forget that the requisite of being truly poised in the erect posture is an unimpeded rhythmical respiration in and out through the nostrils. People are malpostured whose breathing is arrhythmical and not confined to their nostrils as soon as they eat, speak, write or work. Individuals who cannot breathe rhythmically without leaning on their elbows, rolling their tongues or lolling against pieces of furniture, have failed to achieve equilibration. If a person is squatting, sitting or standing in an equilibrated fashion, the tensions of the muscles on both sides of the body are equally distributed, each weight-bearing point or area taking spontaneously its appropriate part in the support of the body. In such equilibrated positions the upper limbs hang freely, or hold implements, or move across surfaces without being employed simultaneously as secondary body supports. The head, somewhat forwardly inclined, pivots freely on the vertebral column and the musculature of the neck, without displaying any stiffness, pain or tension, freely suspends the jaws, tongue and laryngeal apparatus, so that unimpeded chewing, swallowing, breathing or speech can occur concurrently.

As soon as respiration becomes embarrassed in any novel postural situation, the individual will discover a remarkable and progressive ability to cope with it by insisting simply on *alternant breathing*. In this type of breathing, air is taken in through one nostril and out through the other; then the following inspiration is taken through the nostril thus opened and is breathed out through the opposite nostril (*i.e.* the one through which the first inspiration started). If the student proceeds with persistence in this strictly alternating fashion (using the fingers to aid the process by nasal compression where necessary and counting each inspiration and expiration to ensure rhythm) he will find himself gradually asserting the voluntary dominance he is able to exercise over his breathing in an appropriate and useful fashion. The value attaching to this practice of alternating respiratory rhythm is apparently due to a mass-reflex of nasal (trigeminal) origin which facilitates the entry of air into the lung of the side of the body concerned, thus causing a relaxation of all the muscles on that side.

It seems to relax the whole spiral sheet compressing the (homolateral) side of the body concerned. At any rate, with the opening up of the clogged nostril a feeling of relief supervenes. People generally say that they cannot do this because their nostrils are blocked. Unless there is actual physical obstruction the worst sorts of blockage yield to persistence.

The importance of muscular mass-reflexes of trigeminal origin have been brought to light in a dramatic way by the study of fœtal reflexes. Every student of neural anatomy is familiar with the descending tract of the trigeminal nerve and the direct path thus afforded for this nerve to evoke reflex movements of the neck and upper muscles. But, as mentioned above, it has only recently been discovered by Davenport Hooker (1942) that the very first skin area to become sensitive to touch in the human fœtus is the ala of the nose and the adjacent part of the upper lip. If a hair, bending under 10 milligrams or more of pressure, is brought into contact with this area (supplied by the maxillary division of the trigeminal nerve), it elicits a widespread mass-reflex involving rotation of the whole body because it causes:

1. lateral (usually contralateral) bending of the trunk and neck, accompanied by
2. slight rotation of the pelvis in the same direction as the trunk flexure, and
3. extension (retraction) of the brachia, the elbows and hands not moving themselves, but the hands describing arcs as a result of the bilateral arm extension.

These are the first movements that can be evoked from a human fœtus by peripheral stimulation; they occur shortly after the eighth week of fœtal life. Within another fortnight such rotation movements are spontaneous and the fœtus rolls rhythmically, first to one side, then to the other, the area of excitation gradually extending during the third month to those areas of the skin which are innervated by the other branches of this expansive cranial nerve that supplies the anterior end of the body in general and the respiratory tract in particular with cutaneous sensation. Even in adult life there are probably few localized spots in the body from which the stimulus of pressure can produce more profound reactions than can be elicited by this naso–labial skin-fold guarding the orifices of the nasal organs.

Fears having thus been allayed, it is possible for the student of poise to concentrate on individual aspects of the reflex control of body movement, such as the relative parts played in the phenomenon by the spatial positions in which the other sense organs, namely, the ears and eyes, are maintained relative to one another and to the body. The ear-bones contain the organs of balance and the work of Magnus (1925) has demonstrated that *attitudinal reflexes* are evoked by changing the position of the head (a) *in space* or (b) *in relation to the body*. It is recognized that the principal reason for the head's exercising this reflex power is the fact that it contains the balancing organs. They exert this postural influence reflexly by virtue of the vestibulospinal tract and the medial longitudinal bundle. Through the latter tract fibres from the vestibular nucleus run down to the upper cervical segments innervating the neck muscles.

I defined (Dart, 1946) the *coronal plane of balance* as a plane transecting vertically the bony external auditory meatus, the atlanto–occipital joints and the vestibular organs, and pointed out that the cranial extensors were attached principally behind this plane, and the flexors of the *flexor cervicalis* sheet in front of this plane. I strove thereby to demonstrate that the vestibular organs were dependent for the sensory information they gave to the body (and consequently for the sort of reflexes they evoked) upon whether the position of the head relative to the neck was supple and plastic (and thus the neck muscles allowed the head to be poised), or whether it was in a position of muscular fixity and consequent distortion from the outset. One of the prime objectives of postural education, therefore, is to untwist the neck and let it become supple by teaching the head to take a fair share of the bodyweight on its front, top (vertex), sides and back (occiput), and so to assume without strain any and all of the positions, (a) *in space* and (b) *in relation to the body*, which a human head is capable of assuming. This objective is attained not by fixing the head in a single position or within the orbit of one posture, but by letting it go, so that it can nod (*i.e.* flex and extend) and swing (rotate) freely in any position of the body whatsoever. The stability of the body is the outcome, paradoxically enough, of incessant wobbling of the cranial box upon the vertebral column by the cranial flexors and extensors.

Because the cranial box houses both the ears and the eyes, and because the ocular globes, like the cranial globe, depend for their stability upon the incessant antagonistic tugging of numerous muscles, the integrity in functioning of the vertebrate head depends upon the linkage of the two sets of muscles (ocular and cervical) and the two pairs of sense organs (visual and vestibular) through the medial longitudinal fasciculus. This neuromuscular integration, *i.e.* between sense organs and muscles, being perhaps the oldest, in the vertebrate body, might have been expected to escape interference even if pronograde creatures became orthograde. But, although sight and the influence of the visual organs upon muscular tone are ancient biological phenomena, binocular stereoscopic vision is a recent acquirement restricted to primates. Instead of letting his head dangle freely from the front end of the vertebral column like his quadrupedal ancestors, Man has taken the liberty and risk of transforming it into a ball and of juggling it into position on top of his disadvantageously placed spine. His offspring pay the penalty with wrynecks, visual disturbances and malposture.

While, then, we are educating the head in these two basic infantile postures to bear a fair share of the bodyweight on any part of its periphery that happens to be in contact with the floor or other resistant surface, we can and must train the eyes, singly and together, to exploit the range of their potential movement. In so doing we unmask their postural limitations in respect of visual capacity as well as mobility.

It would lead us too far from the general theme to enter into particular detail about any one group of reflex movements that occurs in response to such visual exercises, but we should note that, just as trigeminal stimulation leads in the fœtus to strong contralateral bending of the trunk and rotation of the pelvis, so in the child or adult *closure of one eye facilitates rotation of the head and the whole body towards the temporarily blind side.* This procedure of closing the eye on the side to which one wishes to rotate (that is, of looking deliberately at objects situated on one side with the contralateral or opposite eye) facilitates rotation so remarkably that, like alternant nasal respiration or pressure upon the contralateral naso–labial area, it forms an essential element in the technique of postural derotation. I suspect that it produces its unlocking effect *by inhibiting the contralaterally spiralling muscular sheet of the body* and that this ability of the eye to promote bodily rotation towards the contralateral side was primarily developed to enable creatures at the piscine stage of development to rotate the body freely and so to keep their prey under continuous visual observation, whichever eye first spotted it, and especially when the prey being followed moved rapidly towards the opposite side. The importance of such contralateral inhibitory postural adjustments to a free-swimming creature may also provide an explanation for neurologists' greatest enigma—the optic chiasma, whose decussation appears to have been the forerunner of all major neural decussations.

If we picture the eyes set on either side of a fish but unfurnished with muscles and as motionless as the vestibular organs, it is clear that the fish's range of lateral vision could be increased (as the animal swam forward) only by flexing and extending the head on the spine, or by rotating it in a rightward (or clockwise) or leftward (or anti-clockwise) direction. But, unlike the vestibular organs, whose immobility within the head renders their motions relative to one another in space a function of cranial movement upon the spine, the eyes possess an exclusive motory machine. The singularity of this machine is such that the eyes alone amongst sense organs are capable of movements independent of the head, and are even free from one another in such creatures as the chameleon. The training of the eye upon prey was effected reflexly by its own musculature, but it was essential that, when the eye was so trained, afferent impulses from the visual organ should be enabled reflexly through the optic tract and tecto–spinal tract to inhibit all muscular contractions in the body which would interfere with the pursuit. The application of these facts to the education of the visually malpostured needs no further discussion at this stage.

Having discussed sketchily some of the more outstanding concomitant reflex phenomena of postural education, I will deal briefly with another formidable group of concomitant happenings and close this communication with a general comment upon some of the developments in the human direction of the two primary postures previously discussed.

No aspect of education in *poise* excites the interest and oftentimes the alarm of the subject more than the sounds of squelching, grating, snapping, cracking and the like, that accompany the 'giving way' or releasing of posturally contracted muscles and the joints that they have been guarding. In the case of large joints like the sacro–iliac, knee, elbow and shoulder joints, the sounds are so grossly audible as to resemble knocks. Where a series of small joints like the lumbar or cervical vertebræ attain release concurrently, the sounds emitted on subsequent movement sound more like the rattling of a bag of bones. J. B. Roston and R. Wheeler Haines (1945–46) have consequently rendered a timely service by communicating to the Anatomical Society of Great Britain and Ireland at its Summer Session an abstract of their radiographic studies upon the articulating bone surfaces and joints in the process of separating and cracking when pulled apart. In favourable subjects a half-millimetre increase of the articular gap occurs at the outset; then when tension is increased (to 7 kg for metacarpo–phalangeal joints) a further separation of the articular elements occurs by about 2 mm which is accompanied by an audible crack or snap, and the appearance of a bubble (presumed to be filled with water vapour and blood masses under reduced tension) in the radiograph. Once formed, the bubble can be maintained or enlarged by a moderate tension less than that required to form it initially; it dissolves if tension is relaxed, but usually persists for about twenty minutes once it has been formed. Apparently, this capacity of the synovial fluid to form gas bubbles, and the subsequent physical modifications in the quantity and surface tension of the synovial fluid, enables joints, which for years have moved little if at all, to assume gradually, or even rapidly, the mobility they were fashioned to experience systematically.

The *infantile supine posture* and the *primary crawling posture* are naturally only the first, but the fundamental postures from which the subject will proceed in any biologically based system of education for *poise*. Gradually, as the supporting capacity of the elbows and knees improves, the distances between them can be increased until they have accustomed themselves to letting the body subside with extended limbs into the completely prone or *ventigrade posture* (but still maintaining an anteflexed position of the head relative to the neck, whether it is retained in the midline or rotated to either side). The ability so to lower the body symmetrically may not be attained by elderly people of fixed postural habits until after a long series of trials extending over many months but, when attained, as it may be in people more plastic, simply by rolling over from the extended supine position with the limbs maintained in extension during the movement, this *ventigrade* or *amphibian* posture (of the creature emergent from the water to the land) provides opportunities for exercising the most powerful sorts of leverages of the extended limbs upon the ball and socket joints of the shoulders and hips, upon the spinal column itself, and upon the digits and the joints of the ankle and wrist. In the modification of the *ventigrade posture*, which I have called the *ancestral ventigrade* (fronto–dorsomanual–dorsopedal) *posture*, the individual rolls the upper limbs over on to the backs of the hands in the abducted position at an angle of 90° to the body and recapitulates the ancestral swimming movements of the limbs.

Just as the *ventigrade posture* produces the primary *crawling posture* by limb flexion, so it produces the *heel–haunch posture* in a natural sequence by further limb flexion. From the fœtal crouch of the heel–haunch posture (with the head still anteflexed and weight-bearing) diagonal rolling (over the right and left shoulders and right and left hips alternatively), especially when essayed and ultimately performed in slow motion, gives to the bodyweight-bearing prominences of the shoulders and hips concerned in each of these *diagonal rotational movements* of the body the experience they require in body support.

Rolling back over the dorsi-flexed toes (while the knuckles support the body anteriorly) from the *heel–haunch posture* on to the soles of the feet brings the body equilibratedly into the *squatting posture* which, simple as it may seem to be, in my experience can rarely be performed accurately and maintained over any length of time even by youthful folk like medical students. But the capacity to adopt the squatting posture in comfortable equilibrium is an absolute prerequisite for the poised erect posture which, by clambering (or *primate pronograde*) and chimpanzoid (or *anthropoid pronograde*) and semi-erect (or *humanoid orthograde*) stages, evolved therefrom.

The student of *poise* who has pursued the educational path outlined will not be long in discovering that his struggles in life are chiefly provoked not by external objects and persons but by the expenditure of neuromuscular energy in combating the asymmetrical rigidity of his own body, and therewith its incapacity to breathe, sit, squat, rise, stand or lie. To myself as an anthropologist nothing has been more arresting than the study of those movements which are essential for bridging the gap between the pronograde and the orthograde posture.

The *initial pronograde posture* is the fronto–palmar–plantar (or forehead–palm–sole) posture which, when repeatedly adopted, spontaneously evokes the desire to take the bodyweight principally upon the hypothenar eminences and medial borders of the hands and the outer ball* and lateral borders of the feet, in the manner customary amongst the lower primates and even the anthropoids, and which we may therefore call the *primate pronograde posture*. In this posture the digits involuntarily assume the grasping attitude so essential to the clambering, or branch-clutching, arboreal primate. Wooden pegs, pieces of hosepipe or other suitable objects to form hand grips can be employed as useful accessories in the exploitation of this posture. Lacking these, there is a tendency—which should be encouraged—for each hand to exercise its powerful reflex grip on its fellow on the opposite side.

The *primate pronograde posture* evolved naturally, though most surprisingly and paradoxically, into the *anthropoid pronograde* (or chimpanzoid) *posture*, which is characterized by the spontaneous desire to transfer the support of the anterior half of the bodyweight from the hypothenar eminences and medial borders of the hands on to the ends of the fifth (and fourth) metacarpal knuckles and from there, for relief, to the ends of the second and third metacarpal knuckles. As practice continues in this fantastic repetition of our anthropoidal ontogeny, it becomes possible for the dorsum of the wrist, the proximal and distal rows of phalangeal knuckles, and finally the fingertips to take up in succession their weight-bearing functions, and so for the bodyweight to be transferred during human phylogeny from the hands to the feet. The *anthropoid pronograde posture*, in its early stage of weight-bearing upon the metacarpal knuckles, gives to those who never mastered the art of boxing an unexpected command over their fists by loosening up the digital extensor tendons. To those who recollect their anatomy it lends the postural significance of wrist fixation to the attachments of the radial flexor and the long and short

* I use this convenient term 'outer ball' to apply to the plantar pad covering the heads of the fourth and fifth metatarsal in contradistinction to the 'inner ball' similarly covering the head of the first metatarsal and the 'posterior ball' forming the heed pad.

radial extensor tendons of the wrist to the bases of the second and third metacarpals, and of the ulnar extensor of the wrist to the base of the fifth metacarpal, while the ulnar flexor attains the same fifth metacarpal destination through the piso–metacarpal ligament. To all who pass through this stage in their postural education it demonstrates the significance for all arts and crafts, where finger flexibility and digital skill is at a premium, of ensuring that the *anthropoid pronograde posture* is not elided from their experience.

The *humanoid orthograde posture*, or semi-erect phase as I am defining it here, is neither the anthropoid pronograde posture found in the chimpanzee and gorilla (and often referred to as *semi-erect*), nor the hylobatian brachiating posture observed in the gibbon (and often actually called erect). These terms *erect* and *semi-erect*, however useful for popular description, are inadequate to meet simultaneously the needs of scientific nomenclature of posture, because it is impossible to cover satisfactorily the variant forms of posture intermediate between the pronograde and orthograde posture with a single term, *viz. semi-erect*. If the posture assumed by the gibbon is to be classified as erect, its development of 'brachiating erectness' from the stage of 'primate clambering' was a precocious development that has little other than analogical significance for understanding how human erectness arose. Certainly it is impossible to regard, as Keith appears to regard, the hylobatian 'erect' posture as preliminary to the troglodytian 'semi-erect' posture in human evolution. The principal postural phase intermediate between the *anthropoid pronograde posture* and the *human orthograde posture*, and to which I have given here the term *humanoid orthograde posture*, finds its nearest living illustration in the 'infantile or *proptotic* type of posture' described previously (Dart, 1937) as characteristic of Kalahari Bushmen. The protuberant belly of the Bushman juts forward relative to the pelvis and the thorax develops little compensatory posterior curvature, so that the vertebral column seems to rise vertically over the anterior part of the pelvis or even slopes forward in standing upright; the buttocks are thus prominent behind and the head is carried—'ostrich-like'—well forward over the chest instead of vertically over the trunk. The Bushman, like a European child, is incompletely erect in standing; extension of the legs is usually incomplete and the body is characteristically tilted forward; the crouched posture is assumed automatically in sport and dance, hunting and work. The Bushmen favour games that cultivate quadrupedal activities; they squat over their fires, stoop and kneel over their work, and sleep curled up in the fœtal posture. From the Neanderthal features of their vertebral columns, limb bones and feet, it is apparent that the Boskop and Bush human types, which have mingled to form the modern Bushmen, share with the Neanderthal (and probably all the more primitive human and pre-human stocks) a crouched, or incompletely erect, *humanoid orthograde posture* in which the bodyweight is principally borne on the outer or lateral part of the plantar aspect of the foot. It is this posture to which orthograde Man reverts for the purpose of running, wrestling and boxing and it is adapted for cursorial and pugnacious rather than arboreal activities because, for its acquirement, emphasis has been placed on the length and strength of the lower limbs rather than the power of the upper limbs. Consequently the human child, after exploiting to a greater or lesser extent the anthropoid pronograde posture, elevates himself with the aid of any handy resistant structure into the humanoid orthograde posture, for the purpose not of tree-climbing, but of rocking and balancing himself upon his fully extended lower limbs and of extending fully his upper limbs, firstly as equilibrating organs. Subsequently, when the hands are free, they can brandish about or propel smaller objects that chance brings within their casual or exploratory range.

The *humanoid orthograde posture* can thus be broadly compared with Howorth's 'dynamic posture' (*vide supra*) with its crouch, flexure of ankles, knees and hips, forward inclination of head and trunk, flexure of the trunk and flexure of the relaxed arms. But the human being can adopt this kind of posture and still remain unequilibrated, retaining all his acquired twists. The acid test of *poise* is the ability of the human being not to adopt a particular posture but to remain poised or, in other words, not to fall, whatever movement his body may require to perform—in any posture. The most difficult of all postures in which to perform poised movements is, of course, the *human orthograde posture*, or fully erect position, which only certain races of mankind and only a small proportion of the members of those races can assume.

In the *human orthograde posture* the trunk and the limbs, both upper and lower, must be capable of complete and sustained extension;

flexion or semi-flexion will not suffice. The character of the movements of the human body that are possible in this posture is exhibited in the performances of ballet-dancers, jugglers, sportsmen and other exponents of the poised body. This posture reproduces in the vertical plane the potentialities for flexion, extension and rotation that the human body displays horizontally in the *ventigrade posture* on the floor. Just as the perfection of the *squatting posture* is an absolute prerequisite for acquiring the *humanoid orthograde posture*, so the perfection of the *sitting posture* appears to be an absolute prerequisite for acquiring the *human orthograde posture*. This is doubtless one of the reasons why this fundamentally human posture in its various modifications plays so outstanding a part in oriental philosophy and art. But the relationships of posture with religion, social ritual, drama and the plastic arts are too varied and numerous to be discussed in this communication.

If, however, any individual wishes to test the capacity of his body for symmetrical sitting, he can easily test it out by adopting the *cross-legged sitting posture* of pre-stool days which, until recent times, was used by tailors for comfort and is still widely employed in the East. Alternatively, he can sit on a low stool or other resistant surface which enables him to keep his feet planted evenly on the floor while his bodyweight is distributed proportionately upon his feet and his ischial tuberosities. Meantime, the weight of his fully extended arms can be supported by an overhead shelf or upon the table in front of him. The maintenance of such a posture where the limbs are temporarily fixed in such positions, which they should be able to maintain for long periods or indefinitely while sitting, will quickly lead to pains in the back, neck, or limbs as a result of the attempts of the distorted body to untwist itself, or, in other words, to the 'hyper-abduction syndrome' of Wright (*vide supra*).

It is in the exploitation of the various phases of the *humanoid orthograde posture* and by the development of the *sitting posture* into the *human orthograde posture* that the individual comes to appreciate the enormous potential range of movement of the human head in relation to the feet and, therewith, what the real range of the human being's vision is relative to his environment. In this penultimate stage of postural development, the head asserts its rotational freedom of movement relative to the neck; the head and neck assert their freedom relative to the thoracic cage; the head, neck and trunk assert their freedom relative to the pelvis, and so on. But these freedoms of head and trunk movement are not attainable without concurrent evolution in the movement of the 'katatonically' extended upper limbs upon the shoulders, and of the similarly extended lower limbs upon the hips. Simultaneously with these changes, corresponding flexibilities emerge in the individual joints of the limbs so that they acquire their proper range of movement; but this true range is so greatly in excess of what the general run of human beings display that people exhibiting such a range are liable to be classified as 'loose-jointed'.

The reader will probably appreciate at this stage why no obliteration of the pulse occurs in the 'loose-jointed' type of person when their arms are fully extended or 'hyper-abducted'. He will also understand why head rotation and flexion of the head and neck restores the obliterated pulse or reduces the incidence of obliteration. To the student of poise, these reflex responses of the head and neck to extension of the arms are positive evidence of the postural rigidity present in the head and neck movements of those whose pulses become obliterated when their arms are hyper-abducted. But the head moves in human beings in order to extend the range of vision; to better his vision Man became completely upright. Perhaps the richest comedy presented by the evolutionary process is that the creatures Nature designed to have perfect posture and vision should today present a picture of bespectacled decrepitude.

I have dealt with these later phases of postural education and have used the proposed nomenclature to emphasize the fact that the early human and pre-human phases of posture, if not fully erect, were none the less *humanoid* and not *anthropoid*. Their significance for our present discussion lies in the fact that it is at this latest or truly orthograde phase of postural development that arrested development most usually seems to occur and to result in the commonly observed inabilities to squat, sit, stand, lie, run and, in brief, perform the ordinary skills of human beings without impeding the circulation, respiration or other vital activities. Human beings should be able to discharge all their vital activities without their suffering from impediment of any kind whatsoever in a state of *poise*—with their heads pivoted on their spinal columns and their bodies pivoted upon their feet while their convergent eyes are so pivoted upon their objective that the entire apparatus of movement is the reflexly operating instrument of their concentrated purpose.

References

Alexander, F. Matthias (1942): *The Universal Constant in Living*, London, Chaterson Ltd.

Banning, E. P. (1844): reference missing.

Clark, Le Gros (1946): reference missing.

Cochrane, W. A. (1924): 'The importance of physique and correct posture in relation to the art of medicine', *British Medical Journal*, 1:310.

Dart, R. A. (1924): 'The anterior end of the neural tube and the anterior end of the body', *Journal of Anatomy*, 58:181–203.

———, (1937): 'Physical characters of the /?auni ≠khomani Bushmen', *Bantu Studies*, II, 3:176–295.

———, (1950): 'Voluntary musculature in the human body: the double-spiral arrangement', *British Journal of Physical Medicine*, XIII, 12:265–68.

———, (1946): 'The postural aspect of malocclusion', *Official Journal of the Dental Association of South Africa*, 1: 1–21 (September).

Dickson, F. D. (1931): *Posture, its Relation to Health*, Lippincott, Philadelphia and London.

Foster, T. S. (1930): *From Savagery to Commerce*, Jonathan Cape, London.

Goldthwait, J. E., Brown, L. T., Swaim, L. T., and Kuhns, J. G. (1945): *Essentials of Body Mechanics in Health and Disease*, Lippincott, Philadelphia (4th ed.), p. 241.

Hooker, Davenport (1942): 'Fœtal reflexes and instinctual processes'. *Psychosom. Med.*, 4:199–205.

Howorth, Beckett, A. (1946): 'Dynamic posture', *Journal of the American Medical Association*, 24 August.

Jones, E. (1907): reference missing.

Keith, Sir Arthur (1923): 'Hunterian Lectures: Man's posture: Its evolution and disorders', *British Medical Journal*, 1, 451–99.

Kerr, W. J., and Lagen, J. B. (1936): 'Postural syndrome related to obesity leading to postural emphysema and cardiorespiratory failure', *Ann. Int. Med.*, 10:569–595.

Kountz, W. S., and Alexander, H. L. (1933): 'Non-obstructive emphysema'. *Journal of the American Medical Association*, 100:551–555, 25 February 25.

Livingstone, J. L. (1928): 'Variations in volume of chest with changes of posture', *Lancet*, 1:754–755, 14 April.

Magnus, R. (1925): 'Croonian Lecture: Animal posture', *Proceedings of the Royal Society*, Series B, Vol. 98, 3:690ff.

Mills, H. (1913): 'Posture and eye-strain in children', *Boston Medical and Surgical Journal*, 168:128.

Mills, L. (1919): 'The effects of faulty cranio–spinal form and alignment upon the eyes', *Amer. J. Ophthalm.*, 2:493–99.

Nove, A. (1916): 'Cervico–facial orthopædia', *The Dental Record*, LXVI, 2, 3, 4 (February–May).

Robert, H. (1941): *The Miracle of the Human Body*.

Roston, J. B., and Haines, R. Wheeler (1945–46): 'Joint "cracks" ', Summer Meeting, Anatomical Society of Great Britain and Ireland, Abst. of Communications, p. 6.

Sherrington, C. (1946): *The Endeavour of Jean Fernel*, Cambridge University Press, p. 89.

Stutterheim, N. A. (1937): *Eye-strain and convergence*, Lewis and Co., London.

Stutterheim, N. A. (1942): reference missing, perhaps *Squint and Convergence* (1946)

Truslow, Walter (1943): *Body Poise*, Williams and Wilkins, London.

Wheeler: in H. F. Baker (ed.) *The Miracle of Life* (1938).

Wright, I. S. (1945): reference missing.

Wells, H. G., G. P. Wells, J. Huxley (1931): *Science of Life—A Summary of contemporary knowledge about life and its possibilities*.

6

Weightlessness

THIS year—1961—is another momentous one in human history. As we enter the second decade in the second half of the twentieth century some men are venturing out into space, yet return to the earth's atmosphere safe and sound. This new era, which Man has been approaching since the forces of steam, electricity and atoms have been to some extent harnessed, is one in which fears of many new kinds are being faced and overcome and in which physiotherapy, to my mind, has particular significance. So I am pleased and proud to occupy your presidential chair at this eventful moment in human progress.

In these spatial adventures, like those of scaling earth's highest mountain or plumbing her deepest sea, those few are chosen who, as far as human tests and judgments can foretell, are the fittest both physically and mentally. The production of innumerable such fit and courageous men and women is, I take it, the objective of physiotherapy, although today, as physiotherapists, we are preponderantly concerned with the re-establishment of function in those temporarily disabled by sickness or accident. This can only be a foretaste of the widespread role physiotherapists will discharge amongst future generations of mankind.

Just as the objective of medicine is the prevention rather than the cure of disease, so the objective of physiotherapy must be the prevention rather than the cure of the wounds, dysfunctions and deformities with which human beings are presently confronted and assailed.

All of us, therefore, will have been deeply impressed by the splendid mechanism Dr A. L. Lomey, the Head of the Department of

---

The lecture to physiotherapists was first published in the *South African Journal of Physiotherapy*. The lecture is drawing attention to Feldenkrais' *Body and Mature Behaviour* (1949). Dart did not know that Feldenkrais had had lessons in the Alexander Technique with Walter Carrington and had worked closely with Charles Neil, who had also trained with Alexander.

Physical Medicine in the University of Witwatersrand, has been building up in the Johannesburg General Hospital for the specific purpose of rehabilitation—for putting the hospital patient back into employment and maintaining his fitness there. Such mechanisms are a long overdue recognition of the fact that the task of medicine is not complete when the patient is cured physically. He must be restored to society—an integrated, productively functioning element in his old or a new occupation. It is the particular responsibility of physiotherapy in human society to enable its members to discharge their chosen functions with maximum physical efficiency. Otherwise they experience anxiety and fear.

I spoke of men in space! Why? Because of weightlessness, the complete removal, even if only temporarily, of the embarrassment of gravity. 'It is easy to sleep in outer space,' was the comment yesterday of Gherman Titov, as reported in *Pravda*, according to the *Rand Daily Mail* of August 23, 1961, 'There is nothing to turn over on. Limbs do not become numb. You feel as though you are on top of a sea wave'.

None of us can readily understand what possibilities this new type of situation, the state of weightlessness, opens up for physiotherapy. You will remember what remedial work early air trips in open planes did for whooping cough cases. An inkling, of course, is provided by the supportive effect of water as in swimming and skin-diving and the numberless aquatic pursuits and pleasures it has brought to mankind, along with the assistance rendered by its buoyancy to weak muscles in the process of recovery and regaining strength. Other inklings are afforded to us when we dream, or venture on swings, switchback railways, æroplanes, or other precarious adventures that at first flush thrust our hearts into our mouths, but subsequently, as we become accustomed thereto, give us all something of the thrills of speed, or of rocking up and down, or of gyrational movement as in dances, or on toboggans, skates or skis. Yet another inkling, and to my mind a vastly important one—and interestingly enough it emerged from a decompression chamber—has been provided for parturient women, and also for people, female or male, with slipped discs and other backaches, by Professor O. S. Heyn's application of reduced atmospheric pressure to their bodies.

The history of medicine, as of all other branches of knowledge, is progressive. Man's outstanding mental characteristic is his consciousness of weakness or fear because of his defenseless body, his lack of built-in defenses and weapons. In infancy he is utterly dependent on others and fears any lack of support; as soon as he is ill he becomes again subject to fear and anxiety. So, at first, human beings attributed unaccountable illnesses—as still in biblical times—to malevolent spirits who had to be appeased or liberated from the body. The external spirits of mankind's pre-scientific era Greek science replaced with the theory that the earth consisted of four essences or elements: earth, air, fire and water; and human bodies were supposed to be composed of four 'humours' or liquids—blood, phlegm, black bile (melancholy), and yellow bile (choler). Disease was then explained as being due to excess or defect of one of these liquids.

By Galen's time (AD 130–200) the internal liquids or spirits had become three—the *natural spirits* formed in the liver and carried by the veins, the *vital spirits* elaborated in the heart and transformed by the arteries, and the *animal spirits* formed in the brain and distributed by the nerves. This working concept dominated intelligent medical practice for the following 1,200 years until, with the Renaissance of Learning and the discovery of the New World and of the Cape route to the eastern half of the Old World, increasing knowledge of other people's sicknesses and healing drugs revolutionized these old Roman medical ideas.

Vesalius and his anatomical followers brought to surgeons an increasingly detailed knowledge of human structure. Harvey and his experimental followers opened up to physicians an accurate understanding of blood circulation and other bodily functions during the 16th and 17th centuries. Then the chemical discoveries of the 17th and 18th centuries and the cellular and bacteriological discoveries of the 18th and 19th centuries led to our modern knowledge of infection by germs and viruses and their control by sanitation, water purification, isolation of patients, immunization and the rest of today's preventive medicine's armamentarium.

But the 19th and 20th centuries have also brought us neurologists, psychiatrists and neurosurgeons to demonstrate that each human being consists not only of a body, the plaything of the dreaded germs in its physical environment, but also of an anxious mind, the arena of his or her ambitions and frustrations, of their objectives and passions, of their collaborations and oppositions arising from the environment in which each individual has been reared. With the candid recognition of the importance in medical analysis and treatment of the patient's resultant fearful attitude to his own life and those of his fellows in his daily environment has come what we have learned to call the psychosomatic outlook.

Pavlov and Sherrington, Freud, Jung and Adler, conditioned reflexes and integration of the nervous system, psychoanalysis and inferiority complex, extrovert and introvert—these and numerous other names of scientists and the terms to which they have given meaning are topics of current world-wide conversation as well as of medical investigation. What average well-informed person is ignorant of shell-shock? Or of the fact that anxiety and worry produce ulcers and other alimentary disorders and cause circulatory troubles as well as mental disturbances?

Medical practitioners vary in their estimates of what proportion of the ills they treat are produced by mental anxieties and fears as opposed to germs and other purely physical or chemical factors. Some say 50%; others have told me that they estimate 80% or even more. So I have been particularly interested recently in reading *Body and Mature Behaviour: A Study of Anxiety, Sex, Gravitation and Learning*, by M. Feldenkrais (1949), whose purpose has been to show that, however much may be done by doctors to improve the functioning of human minds, 'radical changes cannot be expected without reforming muscular and postural habits'. It is only through bodily movements that minds can express themselves.

This book was first published twelve years ago and no book is perfect. Nor am I advocating all that is found in this one; but it relates to my topic. Its substance was presented before the Association of Scientific Workers in a series of lectures given at Fairlie, Scotland in 1943–44 and the text was submitted for criticism to some distinguished authorities before publication. Any information desired, more detailed than it gives, can easily be found in the numerous classical works cited therein and brought up to date by any of you who care to delve into the matter further.

The chapters that interested me most for their relevance to physiotherapists in producing well-balanced people were the four consecutive ones dealing with anti-gravity mechanisms, erect posture and action, sensation and the vestibular apparatus, and the body pattern of anxiety. My interest was seized by the applicability of the author's viewpoint to the technique of avoiding fear and anxiety that I had attempted to outline for dentists in 'The Postural Aspect of Malocclusion' (1946) and for my medical colleagues in 'The Attainment of Poise' (1947).

I had outlined there a method of dealing with the postural twists of the body caused by the double-spiral arrangement of the voluntary musculature (Dart, 1950) through our unilateral habits that destroy our equilibrium. I would have found much that I desired to say then expressed more interestingly and at greater length in the lectures Feldenkrais had already given, had they been published at the time of my earlier writings.

For, as he says (*op. cit.* p. 83),

> McDougall distinguishes fourteen different instincts—parental, sex, food-seeking, fear or escape, combat, constructiveness, curiosity, repugnance, acquisitiveness, appeal (reciprocal of parental instinct), herd instinct (gregariousness), self-assertion, self-submission, and laughter. Pavlov thinks that there is an instinct for freedom, that an animal objects to being tied up or enclosed in a confined space limiting its movements. However, even if we accept for a moment the above classification, we observe a remarkable thing—*that only one of the instincts inhibits motion, namely, fear or escape* (my italics).

Then Feldenkrais comments on the remarkable similarity of physical and mental reactions between those of a newborn babe to withdrawal of support and those of fright or terror in an adult—violent contraction of all flexors with halted breath, followed in the infant by crying, accelerated pulse and vasomotor disturbance; or in the adult by the inhibited diaphragm, pounding heart and sensation of intense anxiety.

From that dramatic and exact comparison he proceeds to Freud's contention that *anxiety is the central problem of neuroses*; and to Paul Schilder's claim that '*dizziness is as important* from the psychoanalytic point of view *as anxiety*'; and his expectation that 'study of the vestibular apparatus would have great importance for understanding psychotic and neurotic states' (my italics). Man's perpetual fear, in short, is that of falling—he cannot trust his body balance everywhere. This fear of falling means that we do not trust our vestibular organs in what should be the automatic or reflex discharge of their balancing functions.

Feldenkrais then goes into these questions more fully than I can go here and rightly indicates the successive stages passed through in the development of the normal human individual's adjustment by vestibular balance to gravitation. The test of completing its potential perfection which he applies (p. 113) is: 'he must learn to balance easily and serenely on one leg, to jump, to turn himself around, and finally perform all these movements *with the eyes shut*'.

He also points out that 'with every phase of this development *the breathing mechanism is altered* as different parts of the trunk become rigid, and the parts that are left free to contract and expand are different. . . . In fact, there are as many breathing mechanisms as distinct attitudes of the body. In proper development, breathing follows a definite rhythm, unhampered by the position of the body' (my italics).

Now it would be a waste of your time to tell you about the incidence of the postural defects in humanity that result from this imbalance. If you want these figures you can find them in my papers and in those of the authors to whose works I have referred. I estimated then that barely 10% of humanity ever came to experience what *poise* of the sort Feldenkrais describes really is physically and mentally. Nor do I feel today that that low estimate was incorrect because I read that

> one out of every two young Americans trying to join up (in the rush of volunteers for the United States forces to meet the Berlin crisis) is turned down because of ill health. Heart disease, hypertension, digestion disorders, mental illness and physical disability are rife. Teenage girls are not much better. Health authorities are appalled at the widespread lack of fitness. President Kennedy's youth fitness adviser, Mr Bud Wilkinson, says, 'It is incredible, but there are a great many American girls who have not the strength to hold and swing a racket long enough to play a game of tennis'.

This is the present state of affairs in the most favoured country on earth; but I did not include in my earlier estimate of the malpostured, as Feldenkrais has, all mental cases as well as the physical. However, you yourselves know, from the part that physiotherapy, occupational therapy and physical education generally play in mental therapy, the extent to which his claim is justified. One thing of which we can rest assured is that for generations to come there will be plenty of employment for physiotherapists.

So far so good, but it is when he comes to the corrective side that we are left in the air. The alteration of habitually faulty erect carriage is, as we are all aware, a difficult enterprise, because whatever technique aiming at balance they are taught, people fall back into the one-sided postural habits contracted during infancy, childhood and adolescence.

To break this vicious circle Feldenkrais finds different suggestions have been made. One theory advocates educating the feet first because they carry the body; another, more sensible, starts with head movements; but, however one proceeds, the problem is to cause the unlearned pattern of being balanced to feel right and conscious control of it superfluous.

Now I have as little idea as any of you what the future will reveal as the best technique to adopt for enabling people to become physically balanced and to achieve equanimity—the Romans called it that—*æquanimitas*—and so to overcome their psychophysical (or psycho-somatic) fears; but I have no doubt that re-educative physical procedures are always an essential and that physiotherapists have an onerous and splendid part to play in this process of humanity's rehabilitation. I am confident, too, that the main objective is this acquisition of poise—of establishing vestibular balance in the performance of all our activities. That is why I congratulate the Johannesburg teachers on their collaboration in the work being done by Professor Heyns and in familiarizing themselves with the physiotherapeutic applications of his apparatus.

One of its basic importances is that it forces into our thinking the floating aquatic environment of the human fœtus and the shock of its transition from a warm liquid to cold air—from dependence on the maternal bloodstream to breathing in one's own oxygen from the atmosphere. But what of that buoyancy in space that Titov described, where 'a few drops of currant juice escaped from its toothpaste tube and hung before his face like berries. He scooped them up in the cap of the tube and swallowed them'. Strapped to his couch during his 435,000 mile journey for 25 hours 18 minutes round the earth, he slept, but woke three times—once to find his arms floating in the air by his side. To keep them under control he tucked them under the straps. Even he found some difficulty in orientating his movements because of the unpleasant sensations due to disturbances in his inner ear.

Our muscular mechanisms were elaborated by Nature over a thousand million years not to be the types of static painful machines into which human society and its machines have so far transformed the vast majority of them. They were built up against the forces of gravity specifically to make us capable of such perfection in balancing as to float, as it were, in space over the surface of the earth, joyfully, painlessly. We will not be able to produce that future generation of properly adjusted humanity until the factors that cause the reflex and conscious aspects of body movement to conflict, instead of to collaborate, with one another during intra- and extra-embryonic growth become more generally understood and thus capable of being reproduced correctly.

Those who wish to understand the origin of some of these conflicting factors found in adults will find Wilfred Barlow's (1959) article on 'Anxiety and muscle-tension pain', and a number of the writings to which he has referred there, relevant. Those who wish to delve more deeply into the developmental aspect and understand how vital it is that each human being should pass through every phase of his muscular growth pattern successfully will be impressed by the logical classificatory procedures based on the early movement of children that Robert. J. Doman and his team of assistants (1960) adopted to deal with children with severe brain injuries.

It is not my intention to cover, however briefly, these vast fields of physical education and rehabilitation. They are major concerns of every civilized country and thousands of people the world over. My aim has been simply to draw your attention to the primary part that balance plays in the whole process. I have stressed this vestibular aspect of all fear because I feel it should dominate our outlook; and that if it does, it will lead progressively to the removal of many fears by our daily activities; and so, through the future of your profession, equanimity will be promoted beyond measure within the Republic of South Africa.

Bibliography

Barlow, Wilfred (1959): 'Anxiety and muscle-tension pain', *British Journal of Clinical Practice* 13: No. 5, May, 339–350.

Dart, R. A. (1946): 'The postural aspect of malocclusion', *Journal of the Dental Associaiton of South Africa*, 1:1–21.

Dart, R. A. (1947): 'The attainment of poise', *South African Medical Journal*, 21: 74–91.

Dart, R. A. (1950.): 'Voluntary musculature in the human body: the double spiral arrangement', *Brititish Journal of Physical Medicine*, 13: 265–268.

Doman, R. *et al.* (1960): 'Children with severe brain injuries', *Journal of the American Medical Association*, 174: 257–262.

Feldenkrais, M. (1949): *Body and Mature Behaviour: A Study of Anxiety, Sex, Gravitation and Learning*. London: Routledge and Kegan Paul.

7

The Dart Procedures

by Alexander Murray

Introduction

These are not exercises. Though muscular work is being done in response to gravity, this is a process of self-examination. What is perceived in the way of aches and pains, disturbing or other emotional experiences, may be noted, which will enable the path of progress to be retraced in tranquillity.

The 'Procedures' as we presented them to Professor Dart in 1967 were habitually done in the following sequence:

1. *Start on the toes.* When this is done with the assistance of a skilled teacher, the primary control is activated and the whole system is tonified (fig. 7.1).
2. *Shallow monkey position*: hands on the back of the chair (fig 7.3).
3. *Knuckles on the back of the chair* (fig 7.4). This relates to what Dart calls 'anthropoid' progression in 'The Postural Aspect of Malocclusion'(p. 73).
4. *Knuckles on the seat of the chair.* The limbs are gradually folding, approximating more nearly to a creeping position (fig. 7.5).

The continuation until the final 'fœtal crouch' is a reversal of the developmental sequence (figs. 7.6–11).

Each change should be guided by the teacher, maintaining the activity of the primary control. These are all 'positions of mechanical advantage' for improving the conditions present. As Alexander says in *Man's Supreme Inheritance*:

> The position of mechanical advantage, which may or may not be a normal position, is the position which gives the teacher the opportunity to bring about, with his own hands, a co-ordinated condition in the subject.

The Procedures are informative to anyone who will do them patiently and openly. With the guidance of a skilled teacher, they are

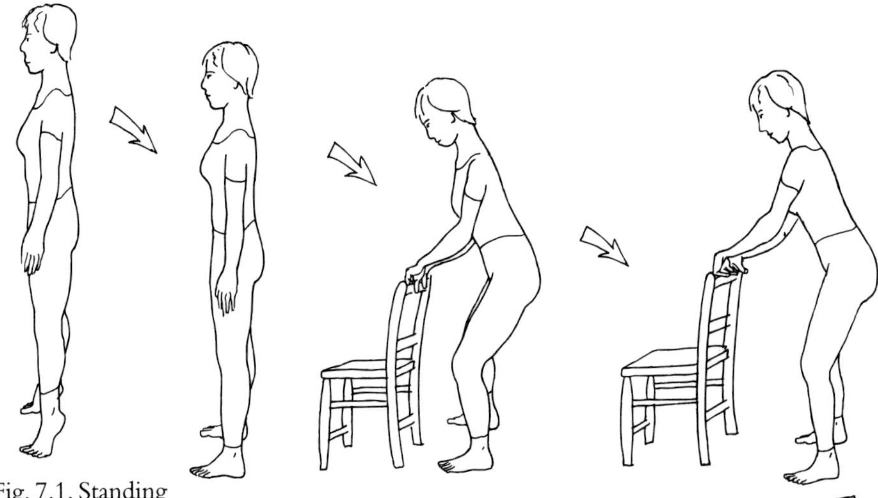

Fig. 7.1. Standing on toes.

Fig. 7.2. Standing.

Fig. 7.3. 'Monkey' with hands on back of chair.

Fig. 7.4. Antrhopoidal 'monkey' with knucles on chair.

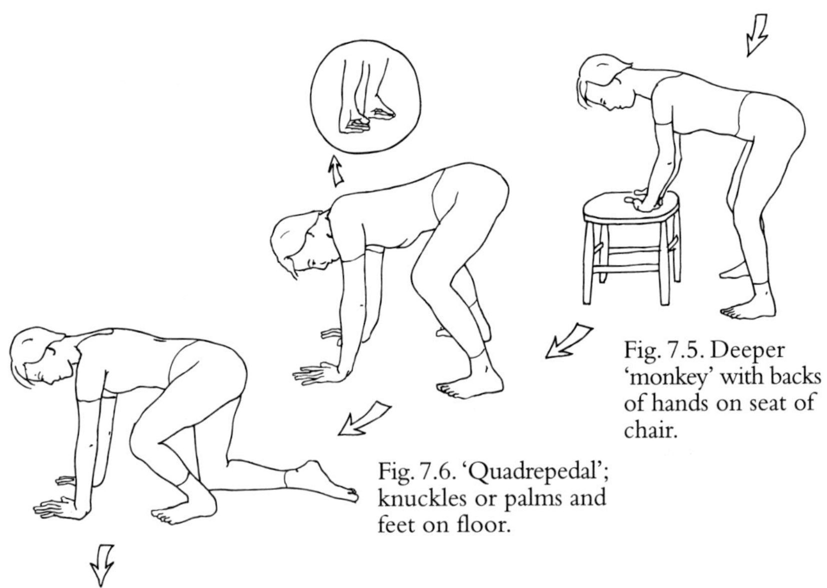

Fig. 7.5. Deeper 'monkey' with backs of hands on seat of chair.

Fig. 7.6. 'Quadrepedal'; knuckles or palms and feet on floor.

Fig. 7.7. Pre-creeeping.

Fig. 7.8. 'Creeping.'

Fig. 7.9. Pentapodal: forehead-elbows-knees on floor.

Fig. 7.10. 'Pre-fœtal.'

Fig. 7.11. 'Fœtal crouch.'

an invaluable addition to the repertoire of natural movements, the facilitation of which is part of the Alexander teacher's responsibility. Experience has shown the initial sequence from the upright to the fœtal to be the most fruitful with the assistance of a teacher.

General considerations

The conditions under which bodily mobility is explored should be as favourable as can be devised.

1. Choose a draught-free floor with a firm but soft covering (rug, carpet, or large towel).

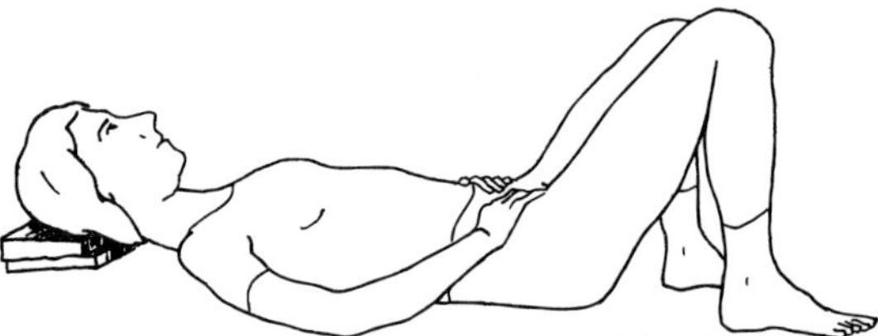

'Semi-supine': lie on the floor with the back of the head supported by a few books. Rest the hands on the lower abdomen, with elbows pointing away from each other. Bend the knees and place the feet roughly a foot from the pelvis and hip-width apart.

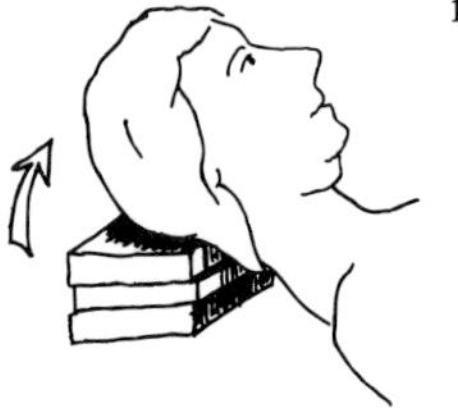

If there are too many books, the throat is restricted, the face tilts towards the chest and the neck is 'straightened.'

If there are too few books the neck arches, the chin sticks upwards and the face tilts away from the chest.

Fig. 7.12. Basic postion: the 'semi-supine'.

2. Wear comfortable clothing or none at all.
3. Experiment daily (as frequently as desired) for short periods. Moderation is the byword. It is better to stop while interested than to continue compulsively when tired or bored.
4. Do not expect instant or remarkable changes. Though they may occur, a small, regular improvement over a long period is more likely.
5. *Breathing*. If in any position you discover a tendency to hold the breath, exhale gently but audibly (in a whispered 'aaah', a hiss, or a whistle) through the mouth, or through the nostrils, then close the lips and allow the air to return through the nose.

Basic positions

In order to explore your bodily mobility, start from the basic positions—semi-supine, supine, prone, crouch. Move in step-wise

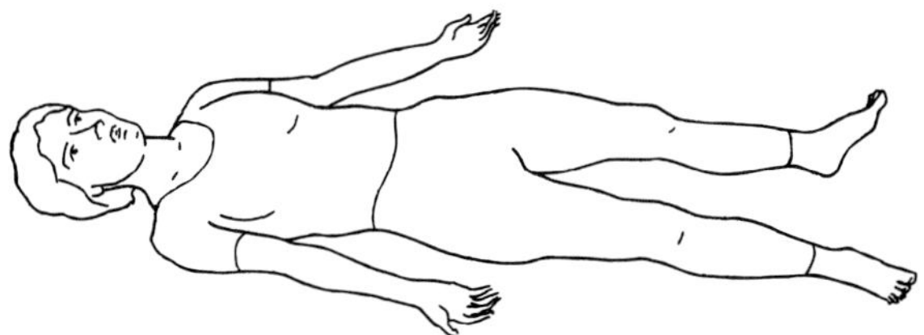

Fig. 7.13. Supine ('fully supine'). Begin in semi-supine; remove books and gently slide heels away from pelvis to straighten legs. Let the backs of the hands and arms rest on the ground.

Fig. 7.14. Prone. Let the forehead, front of torso, legs, tops of feet and backs of hands rest on the floor.

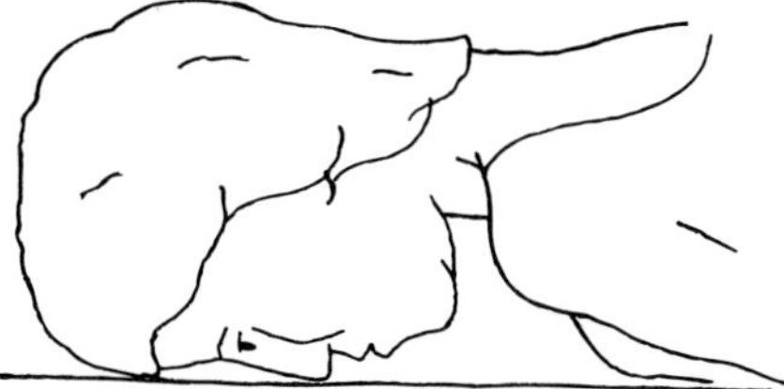

The centre of the forehead contacts the ground.

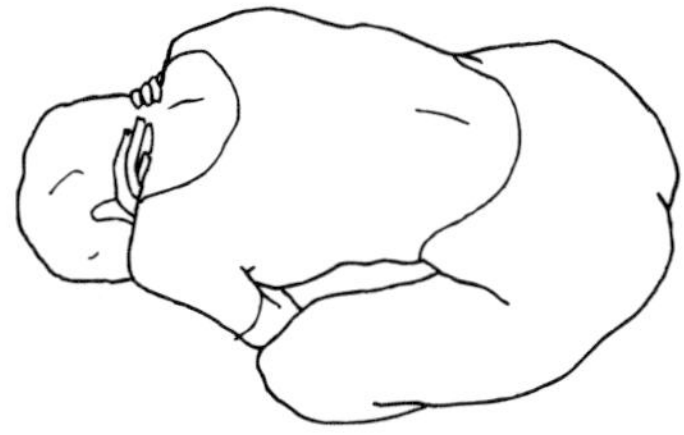

Fig. 7.15. 'Fœtal crouch.' The hair-line of the head contacts the ground. The arms fold at the elbows, crossing the chest so that the fingers can wrap around the base of the neck. The torso rests on the folded legs and the ankles cross each other under the tail.

progression from a position of absolute security and stability to one requiring some degree of skill in balancing, and in which there is an initial sense of insecurity. The basic positions, when maintained for 10 or 15 minutes without strain, bring about a gradual alteration in the balance of the musculature, whether flexed or extended. By drawing attention to the weight-bearing parts of each bone, each position familiarizes us with them in a way which is, or should be, devoid of fear. (The fear of falling is instinctive. Each of these basic

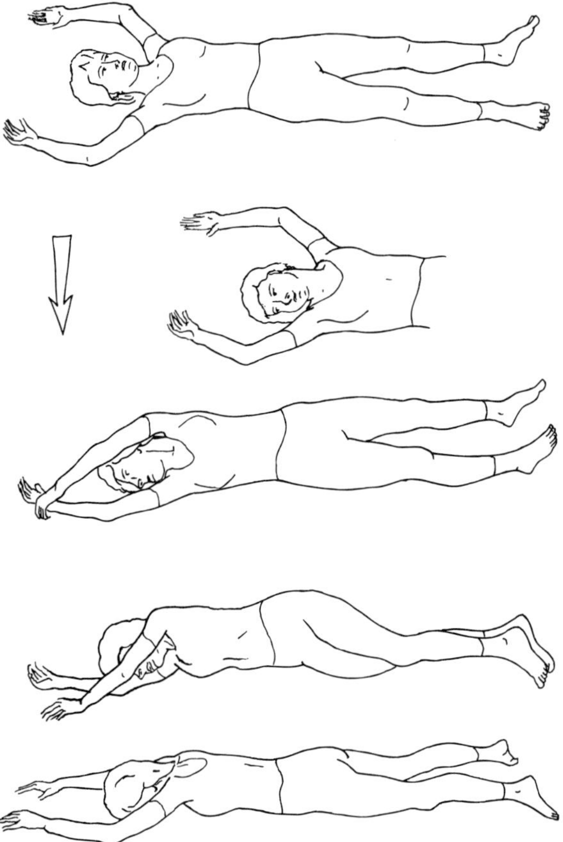

Fig. 7.16. Rotational movements: fully supine to prone.

positions is completely secure; when the body is in intimate contact with the ground there is nowhere to fall.)

Begin in the semi-supine position (fig 7.12). Read a magazine article or enjoy a record. Extend the legs, slide the book from under your head and, from fully supine, roll slowly over into the prone position. Five minutes in this posture can be followed by five in crouch, which can be smoothly attained by placing the hands close to the shoulders (in prone) and using head and hands to move the tail backwards over the knees (figs. 7.13–15).

Familiarize yourself with each of these positions separately and then consecutively. Make a daily (preferably midday) habit of spending a half-hour resting your body, using the time in intelligent self-

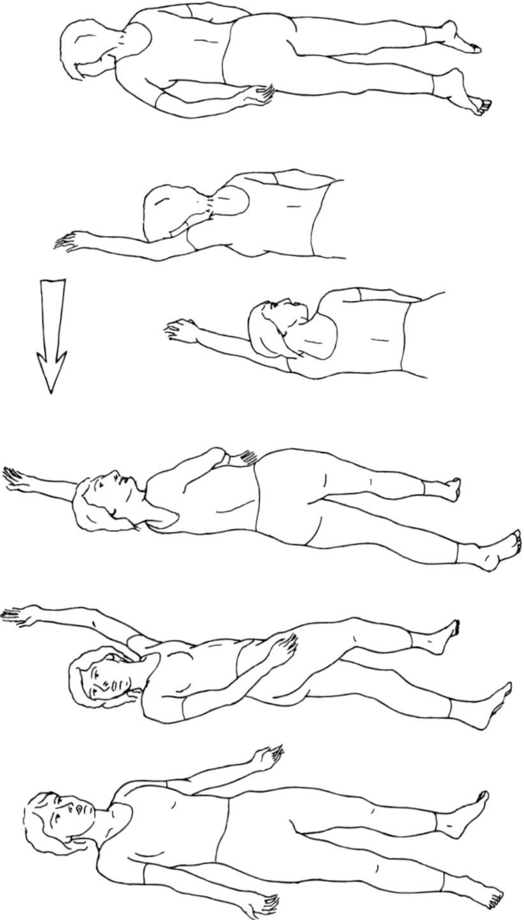

Fig. 7.17. Rotational movements: prone to fully supine.

observation, noting what happens when you move some piece or other of yourself.

Note. To stand after lying in the supine or semi-supine position, first roll over into the prone position, then slowly rise up, beginning on the hands and knees (see the anti-gravity progression).

Starting from the basic positions, make the smallest possible movements, which gradually expand until what begins as a movement of the eye becomes a movement of the whole body.

Partial movements

Explore the following according to your inclination and the time available:

1. *Eye movements.* Keep the head still but explore the field of vision, closing one eye, then the other, then with both open. Look up, down, left, and right; then rotate the eyes in one direction, then the other.

   Note. In the prone position, though the eyes may see simultaneously, each eye has its own field of vision and vision is not stereoscopic.
2. *Head movements.* Move the head on the neck in all directions, using the eyes to explore all corners of the room (vision may then be stereoscopic). Notice the effect of occluding one eye with the hand (or a shield). Movement of the head in the direction of the closed eye is then facilitated.
3. *Arm movements.* Keep the hand in contact with the floor and investigate all the possible movements of the fingers, wrist, forearm, and whole arm.
4. *Leg movements.* Keep the foot (heel, toes, or side of foot) in contact with the ground. The left foot may move along the right leg and *vice versa.* The increased tactile inflow from the skin of a passive limb assists smooth movement. Explore limb movements first singly, then in combination (both arms, both legs, left arm and left leg, left arm and right leg, and so on). The eyes and head may track the hand or foot.

Total movements

These are divided into two categories: horizontal movements (along the floor) by rotation, creeping and crawling; and vertical movements (against gravity). The importance of rotational movements cannot be over-emphasized. Crawling (on the belly) and creeping (on all fours) have been extensively dealt with in the writings of Delacato to which you should refer if these movements have not been part of your developmental experience.*

Rotational movements. Try these in both directions, to the left and then the right. In particular, experiment in turning to the side which seems the least natural to you. When rolling over, move as slowly as

* C. H. Delacato, *The Treatment and Prevention of Reading Problems.* Springfield, Thomas, 1959. *The Diagnosis and Treatment of Speech and Reading Problems.* Springfield, Thomas, 1963.

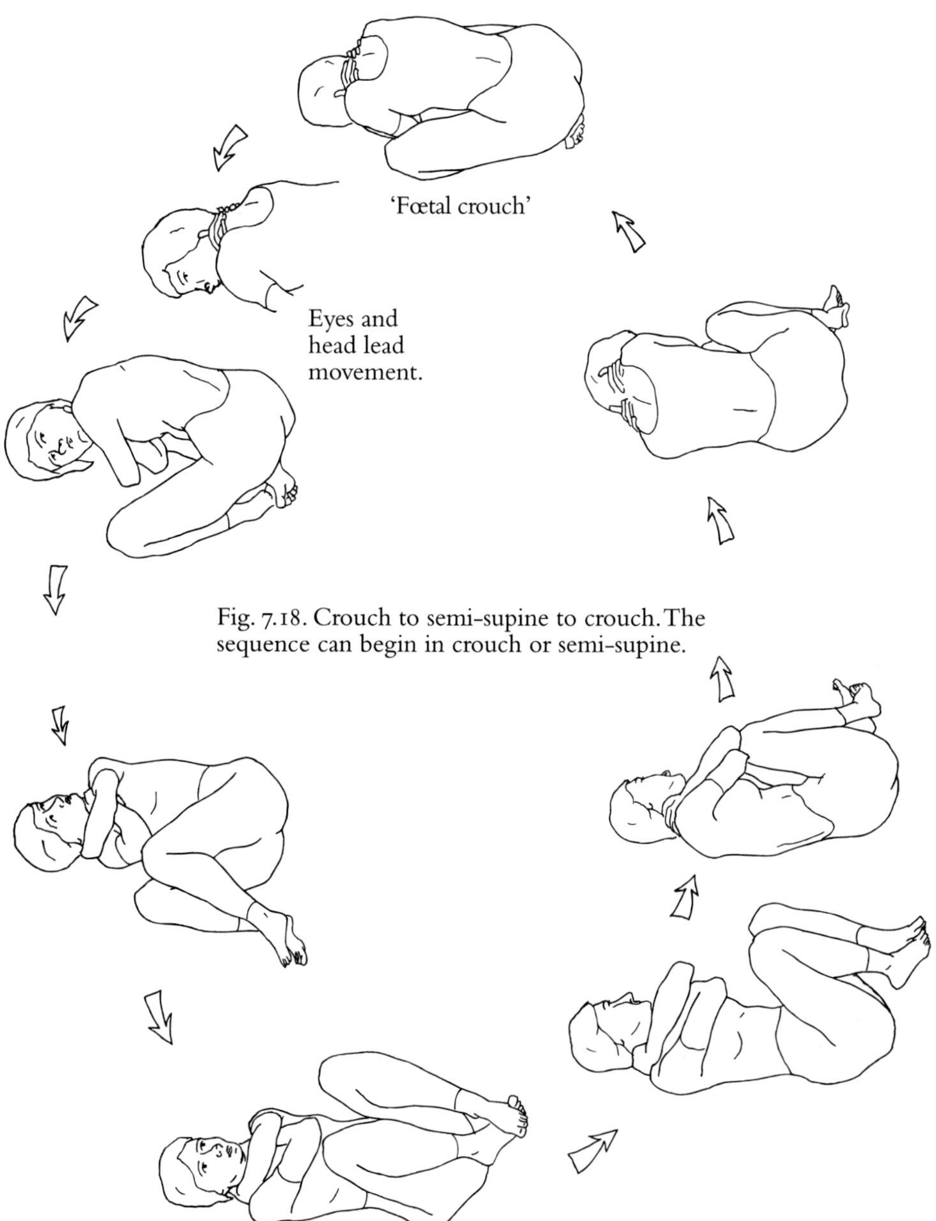

Fig. 7.18. Crouch to semi-supine to crouch. The sequence can begin in crouch or semi-supine.

Variation of semi-supine (without books).

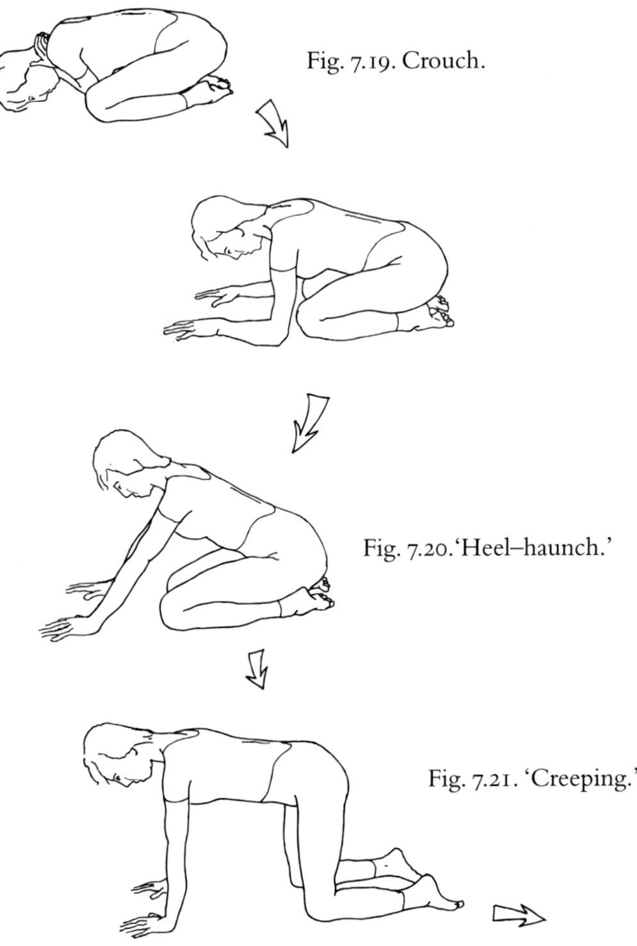

Fig. 7.19. Crouch.

Fig. 7.20.'Heel–haunch.'

Fig. 7.21. 'Creeping.'

possible; pause when the body is poised ready to fall, and note any tendency to strain or hold the breath, which should then be exhaled as suggested with whispered 'aaah'.

1. Fully supine to prone (fig. 7.16).
2. Prone to fully supine (fig. 7.17).
3. From semi-supine to crouch (fig. 7.18).
4. Crouch to semi-supine. Rolling over from this position can be done in a number of ways. Remember to do it as slowly as possible. Notice the difference between the moment of fall when the eyes are open and when they are closed (fig. 7.18).

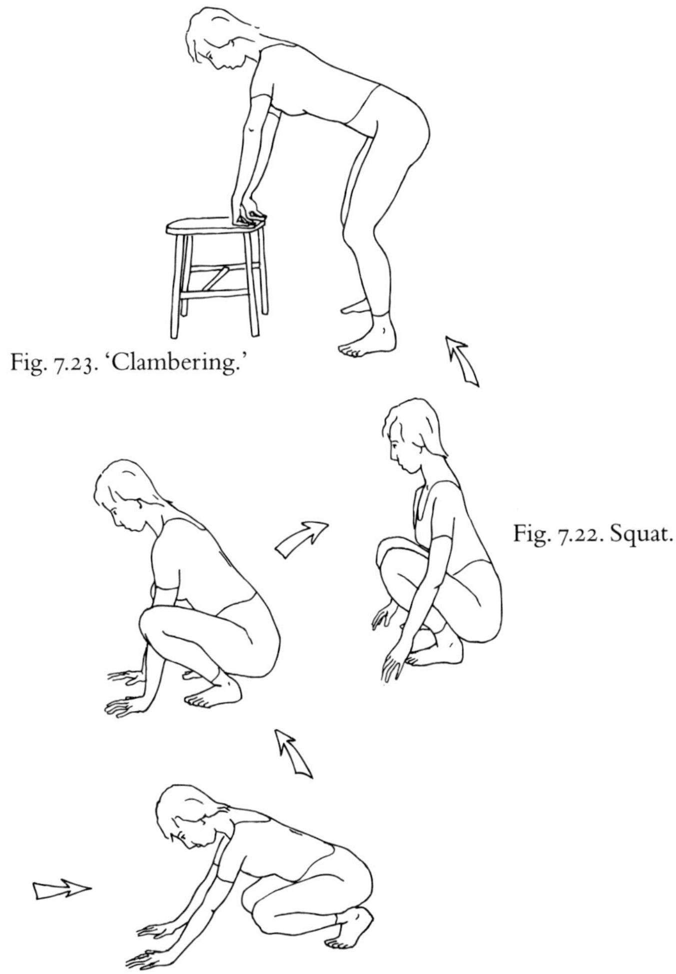

Fig. 7.23. 'Clambering.'

Fig. 7.22. Squat.

Anti-gravity movements. These movements begin on the floor and progress by degrees into the upright position (and, ultimately, into the leap, when all contact with the earth is removed):

1. Fully prone to crouch.
2. Crouch to heel–haunch or squat (fig 7.19–20).
3. Creeping position from heel–haunch (figs. 7.20–21).
4. Squat from creeping (figs. 7.21–22).
5. Clambering (squat with knuckles or palms on chair, fig. 7.23).
6. Semi-upright. Tail or head against corner of room (or door).
7. Fully upright (fig. 7.24).

8. On toes (fig. 7.24).
9. On toes on one leg (fig. 7.24).

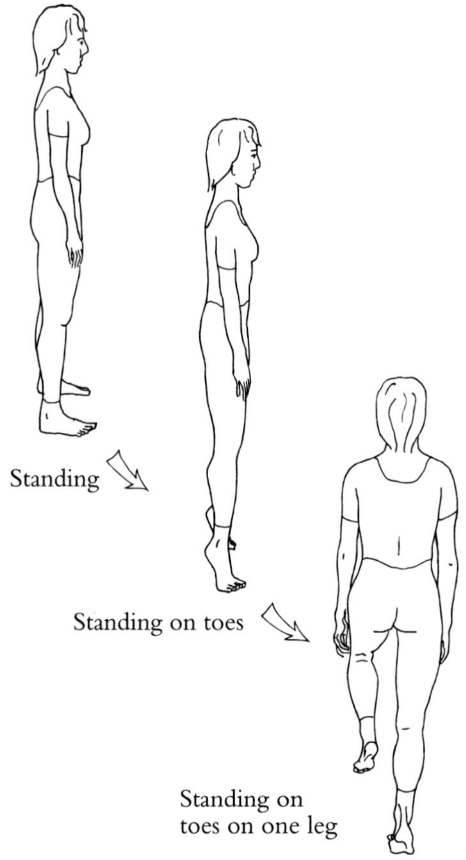

Fig. 7.24. Standing on toes.

These movements may be practised with the head in contact with the wall.

The ultimate test of poise is to achieve the one-legged stance on tiptoe, with the eyes closed, and then to hop confidently. A true leap in the dark is the step without which nothing new can be learned.

Further suggestions

Some of the rotational movements carried out on the floor may be practised with advantage in the vertical plane. For example, make contact with the head against the wall. Turn the body as far as possible until it becomes necessary to turn the head again. You will have spun full circle. When you work in contact with the wall, it represents a change of 90° in the body's relationship to the gravitational field, as compared with a similar movement made on the floor. A further change (180°) can be made as follows:

Headstand (fig. 7.25). Do not attempt this if it causes any discomfort, and do not maintain it for any length of time. The neck was not intended to bear the full weight of the body, and this posture is only beneficial when the weight is pulling away from the head at all times.

1. Crouch with head close to the wall.

Fig. 7.25. Headstand. This can be practised against a wall.

2. Uncross legs and arms; turn toes to the ground; place arms near shoulders.
3. Straighten legs to raise tail.
4. Bring feet back as close to wall as possible.
5. Flex legs and straighten to send tail against wall.
6. Flex legs in headstand position.
7. Straighten legs against wall.

If this can be accomplished without strain and holding the breath, attempt the headstand free of the wall, remembering that at no time must there be pressure on the head and neck.

These are but a few of the potential directions in which the student of poise may experiment. When each is part of a progressive sequence with a familiar beginning, you will find you can accomplish, with ease and confidence, movements which hitherto seemed impossible. What is possible is limited only by the imagination of your mind and the flexibility of your body, both of which cannot fail to benefit by repetition of the experiences outlined above.

Key to positions and the names Dart uses to describe them.

Glossary

Names of bones and muscles are not included. For information on cranial nerves see fig. 2.1 and accompanying table on pp. 36–37.

acromial processes: the outer ends of the spines of the scapulae which articulate with the clavicles.
adenoids: lymphoid tissue that normally exists in the nasopharynx (above the pharyngeal tonsil) of children; the excessive growth of this tissue.
adenoid facies: a dull facial expression, with open mouth, sometimes seen in children with adenoid growths.
œdematous: affected by œdema: swelling due to excess accumulation of watery fluid in the tissues or cavities of the body.
alveolo-dental structures: the structures of both the teeth, their sockets, roots and the ligamentous fibres which hold the roots.
amblyopia: a permanent impairment of vision without obvious defect of or change in the eye. It is due to disturbance of the visual pathway between the retina and the brain, often caused by imperfect co-ordination of the eyes in very young children (which, in turn, may be caused by a squint or congenital cataract).
amphibian position: with the body prone; horizontal. According to Dart, identical to the ventigrade position.
anencephaly: absence at birth of the brain and cranial vault (top of the skull). Most affected infants are stillborn or survive only a few hours.It is caused by a maldevelopment of the neural tube.
Angle Class II malocclusion (distoclusion): the lower jaw is smaller in relation to the upper (the lower dental arch is posterior to the upper in one or both lateral segments). **Division I:** basically meaning that the upper teeth are straight and normal.
Antæus: in Greek myth a giant, son of the god Poseidon and Gaia (Earth). Heracles wrestled with him, and whenever he was thrown he arose stronger than before from his contact with his mother Earth. Heracles, perceiving this, lifted him in the air and crushed him to death.

anthropoid: *see* pronograde.
asthenovergence (syn. asthenopia): weakness or susceptibility to fatigue of the visual organs, frequently with other symptoms like pain in the eyes, headache, dimness of vision, etc.
attitudinal reflexes: reflexes which change the positioning (attitude) of the body following a change of the position of the head relative to the body.
auditory meatus (external): the ear canal, extending from the ear membrane to the outer ear.
bioscope: South African term for cinema.
brachia (pl. of brachium): the arm, specifically from the shoulder to the elbow.
bursa (pl. bursæ)**:** a fluid-filled sack or sack-like cavity situated in places in the tissues where harmful friction would otherwise develop.
cœlenterate: any marine animal of the phylum *cœlenterata* with a simple tube-shaped or cup-shaped body, e.g. jellyfish, corals and sea anemones.
causalgia: a persistent burning pain, usually in the arm or leg. It is caused by injury to a peripheral nerve, especially the median nerve, and treatment is rarely satisfactory. The skin overlying the painful area may be red or blue, tender and/or cold.
commissura: a junction of corresponding anatomical structures, frequently across the median plane of the body, e.g. fibres crossing from one side of the spinal cord to the other; the *corpus callosum.*
Corti, (spiral) organ of: situated in the cochlea, it consists of rows of hair cells sensitive to vibrations. Sound waves temporarily displace the hairs and this displacement excites the cochlear nerve, from which signals are sent to the brain.
crawling: in Doman-Delacato usage (which Dart adopted) it refers to the moving of the body when in a prone position, similar to amphibian position; on the belly.
creeping: in Doman-Delacato usage (which Dart adopted) it it refers to the moving of the body on all fours; pronograde; on hands and knees.
crustacean: of the class *crustacea*; an invertebrate with a segmented body, jointed limbs, an external skeleton and usually aquatic, e. g. the crab, lobster or shrimp.
cyanotic attacks: a bluish discolouration of the skin due to defi-

cient oxygenation of the blood.
decerebration: elimination of cerebral function by cutting just below the midbrain (between the the inferior colliculus and the vestibular nuclei), leaving only the functions of *pons*, *medulla oblongata* and the spinal cord.
decussation: here, the intersection or crossing over of nerve tracts, e.g. the pyramidal decussation in the medulla or the optic chiasma.
deglutition: the act of swallowing.
desquamation: shedding of skin, in scales or small sheets.
digitigrade: walking on the toes and not touching the ground with the heels, like dogs, cats and rodents (opp. of plantigrade).
epicondyles: the two protuberances of the humerus just above the elbow.
eutherian: a member of the *eutheria*, the placental mammals. *Pro–* and *meta–eutheria* may refer to the monotremes and marsupials respectively. The monotremes are egg-laying animals (e.g. the platypus). Examples of marsupials are the kangaroo, possum and wombat.
fauces: the cavities at the back of the mouth, situated just above the epiglottis.
fronto-ponto-cerebellar fibre system (syn. frontopontine tract, *fibrae frontopontinae*): nerve fibres arising in the frontal lobe of the cerebral hemisphere and, through the internal capsule and peduncle, ending in the pontine nuclei.
gangrene: death and decomposition of a part of the body tissue, usually caused by obstructed circulation, e. g. as in frostbite.
glossoptosis: downward displacement or retraction of the tongue.
heptapodal: seven-footed.
homolateral: on or affecting one side of the body; same side. In homolateral walk all the limbs of one side move before the limbs of the other side (opp. bilateral).
hylobatian: a subfamily of the *pongidae* (gorilla, chimpanzee and orang-utan etc.) including the smaller genera of apes that are today found in Asia, e.g. the gibbon (*hylobates*).
hypothenar eminences: the fleshy part of the palm on the little finger side of the hand (formed by the hypothenar muscles which move the little finger).
katatonic: simultaneous toning of flexors and extensors (co-contraction) to create supportive extension of limb; see also Dart's de-

scription on p. 136. (It must not be confused with catatonic.)
medial longitudinal bundle: a bundle of nerves descending from the midbrain down into the spinal cord; it connects a number of brain stem nuclei with each other (syn. *fasciculus longitudinalis medialis*).
mesoderm: the middle layer of germ cells which, like the inner (endoderm) and outer (ectoderm) layers, differentiates early in the development of the embryo (3rd week). Most skeletal muscles develop from mesodermal tissue arranged in paired, segmented cell masses called somites.
metaeutherian: *see* eutherian
micrognathia: unusual or undue smallness of the jaw (mandible).
micturition: urination.
neuromeres: a part of the spinal cord to which a pair of dorsal roots and a pair of ventral roots are attached (syn. neural segment). Also: the transitory segmental elevations in the wall of the neural tube of the developing embryo.
olive: an olive-shaped swelling on the lateral anterior surface of each pyramidal tract of the *medulla oblongata*. It is formed by the inferior olivary nucleus, whose fibres project and convey excitatory signals through the inferior cerebellar peduncle to the cerebellum.
ontogeny: the origin and development of the individual being; the science of the development of the individual being; embryology, (opp. phylogeny).
opisthotonus: a form of spasm consisting of extreme hyperextension of the body; the head and the heels are bent backward and the body bowed forward.
optic chiasma: where the optic nerves (carrying visual information from the eyes) meet; the fibres from the nasal half of each retina cross over, but the fibres from the temporal half of each retina do not, ensuring each side of the brain receives visual messages from both eyes.
orthograde: holding the body upright; carrying the axis of the body in a vertical position. For Dart's definition of 'humanoid orthograde', *see* pp. 146–48.
panem et circenses: (Lat.) bread and circuses.
paraesthesia: an abnormal skin sensation, such as burning or prickling ('pins and needles'), often without an external stimulus.
paronychia: infection and inflammation of the skin fold at the base

or side of the nail. It is often associated with poor circulation.
parturition: the act of giving birth.
pentapodal: five-footed.
philtrum: the shallow vertical groove on the middle of the upper lip.
phylogeny: the genesis and evolution of the phylum, tribe or species; ancestral or racial evolution of an animal or plant type, or of particular organs, etc. of a plant or an animal (opp. ontogeny).
plantigrade: walking upon the soles of the feet with the heels touching the ground (opp. digitigrade); homo sapiens is a plantigrade animal as are various quarupedal carnivorous mammals such as the bear, wolverene, badger etc.
plexus: a general term for a network of lymphatic vessels, nerves or veins.
pronograde: carrying the axis of the body in a horizontal position; four-footed; frequently syn. with quadrupedal (moving on all fours). For Dart's definition of variations of pronograde, *see* pp. 145–46.
proptotic: semi-erect; slightly dropped forward position as sometimes featured in the Alexander Technique position of mechanical advantage known as 'monkey'.
protoeutherian: *see* eutherian
rhinology: the science concerned with the nose and its diseases.
substantia gelatinosa (syn. *substantia Rolandi*): one cell group in the dorsal column of the grey matter, extending through the whole length of the cord.
tecto–spinal: extending from the *tectum mesencephali* to the spinal cord. The *tectum* contains the colliculi, which are reflex centres mainly responsible for co-ordinating movements of the eyes with head movements, for adjustment of the pupils and for conveying auditory signals to the thalamus and eventually to the auditory cortex.
teratomatous condition: teratoma is a tumour, but Dart here uses the word in its original greek meaning: being an innate, often aberrant, condition.
thenar (or thenar eminence): the mound on the palm at the base of the thumb.
torque: a twisting or rotary force; also the moment a series of forces produces rotation.
tract (tractus): bundle of nerve fibres which, in having the same

origin, termination and function, connect different points of the nervous system.

troglodytes: *pan troglodytes* is the common chimpanzee, as opposed to *pan paniscus*, the pygmy chimpanzee or bonobo.

ventigrade: completely prone (syn. amphibian posture): lying with the front part downwards with palms facing downwards. In 'ancestral ventigrade' the palms face upwards.

volar: palm or sole; plantar; the flexor surface of wrist or hand.

Index

Text accompanying illustration is not indexed. Bones and muscles are listed under their individual name. Individual nerves, however, are listed under 'nerve(s)'. Page numbers in bold refer to the glossary.